A DESCRIPTIVE Grammar of Nepali AND AN ANALYZED CORPUS

Jayaraj Acharya

1789 Georgetown University Press / Washington, D.C.

Printed in the United States of America
THIS VOLUME IS PRINTED ON ACID-FREE OFFSET BOOK PAPER.

10 9 8 7 6 5 4 3 2 1

Library of Congress Cataloging-in-Publication Data

Acharya, Jayaraj.
A descriptive grammar of Nepali and an analyzed corpus / Jayaraj Acharya.
p. c.m.
Includes Bibliographical references.
1. Nepali language--Grammar--1950- I. Title.
PK2596.A334 1991 491'.49--dc20 91-10097
ISBN 0-87840-282-9

CONTENTS

Preface xi
List of abbreviations xii

Part one: Grammar

1 Introduction 1
1.1 The Nepali language 1
1.2 The name Nepali 1
1.3 Nepali as an Indo-European language 2
1.4 Nepali and other languages of Nepal 4
1.5 Geographical distribution of Nepali 4
1.6 Dialects of Nepali 6
1.7 Nepali and Hinduism 7
1.8 Previous descriptions of Nepali 7
  1.8.1 Teaching materials 7
  1.8.2 Grammars 8
  1.8.3 Dictionaries 9
1.9 The purpose and scope of this study 10
1.10 Corpus 11
1.11 Transcription 12
1.12 Motivation of this description 13

The sound system

2 Segmental Phonemes 14
2.0 Introduction 14
  2.0.1 Phones, phonemes, and allophones 14
  2.0.2 Segmental vs. suprasegmental phonemes 14
  2.0.3 Inventory of the principal consonantal and vowel sounds of Nepali 15
  2.0.4 Symbols employed in the phonetic and phonemic transcription 15
  2.0.5 Listing of the phonemes 16
2.1 Consonant sounds 16
  2.1.1 Definition and classification 16
  2.1.2 Supplementary sets of minimal pairs 19
  2.1.3 Variants of Nepali consonant phonemes 25
    2.1.3.1 Positional variants 25
    2.1.3.2 Deletion of aspiration 26
    2.1.3.3 Deletion of voicing 26
    2.1.3.4 Nasalization 26
    2.1.3.5 Minor variations 26
  2.1.4 Distribution of Nepali consonants 27
2.2 Vowel sounds 30
  2.2.1 Definition and classification 30

2.2.2 Supplementary sets of minimal pairs 31
2.2.3 Variants of Nepali vowel phonemes 31
2.3 The pronunciation of orthographic word-initial consonant clusters 32
2.4 The pronunciation of long consonants vs. geminates 33
2.4.1 Gemination as a result of assimilation 34
2.4.2 Sandhi without gemination 35

3 Suprasegmentals in Nepali 36
3.0 Introduction 36
3.1 Inventory of Nepali segmental phonemes 36
3.2 Syllable and syllable structure in Nepali 37
3.3 Light vs. heavy syllables 38
3.3.1 Light and heavy syllables in Nepali 41
3.4 Phonotactics 42
3.4.1 Consonantal phonemes in syllable-initial position 42
3.4.2 Consonantal phonemes in intervocalic position 42
3.4.3 Consonantal honemes in syllable-coda position 42
3.5 Phonetic stress: Its definition and function of stress in Nepali 42
3.5.1 Stress and stress placement in Nepali 43
3.5.2 Stress rules in Nepali 43
3.5.3 Regular phonetic stress 43
3.5.3.1 Nepali phonetic stress rule-1 (NSR-1) 43
3.5.3.2 Nepali phonetic stress rule-2 (NSR-2) 44
3.5.3.3 Compound words phonetic stress rule (CWSR) 45
3.5.3.4 Phrase phonetic stress rule (PSR) 46
3.5.3.5 Sentence phonetic stress rule (SSR) 46
3.5.4 Emphatic functional phonemic stress (ES) for extra semantic emphasis 46
3.5.4.1 Emphatic phonemic stress (ES) on free forms 47
3.5.4.2 Emphatic stress (ES) on suffixes 47
3.5.4.2.1 Emphatic stress (ES) and vowel lengthening 47
3.5.4.2.2 Emphatic stress (ES) and vowel shortening 48
3.6 Pitch 50
3.7 Juncture 50
3.7.1 Types of juncture 51
3.7.2 Minimal pairs for open juncture (+) vs. close juncture (unmarked) 51
3.8 Rhythm 53
3.9 Pause 53
3.10 Intonation 55
3.10.1 The grammatical role of intonation 55
3.10.1.1 The intonation of statement and imperative statements 55
3.10.1.2 The intonation of *ho/hoina* questions 56
3.10.1.3 The intonation of *K*-questions 56
3.10.2 The communicative role of intonation 57
3.10.2.1 The lengthening of high pitch vowel 57

3.10.2.2 The lengthening of low pitch vowel 59
3.10.2.3 The lengthening of mid-level pitch vowel 60

The writing system

4 From phoneme to grapheme and grapheme to phoneme 62
4.0 Introduction 62
4.1 From phoneme to grapheme 63
4.1.1 Vowels 64
4.1.1.1 Free forms of vowels 64
4.1.1.2 Conjunct forms of vowels 65
4.1.2 Glides 66
4.1.3 Consonants 66
4.1.3.1 Free forms of consonant symbols 66
4.1.3.2 Conjunct forms of consonant symbols 67
4.1.3.2.1 Regular conjunct forms of the consonant symbols 67
4.1.3.2.2 Irregular conjunct forms of the consonant symbols 69
4.1.4 Additional symbols: bindu, anusvār and visarga 70
4.1.4.1 Bindu 70
4.1.4.2 Anusvār 70
4.1.4.3 Visarga 70
4.2 From grapheme to phoneme 72
4.2.1 Vowels 72
4.2.2 Glides 72
4.2.3 Consonants 72
4.2.3.1 Pronunciation of consonants without the virām stroke 72
4.2.3.2 Voiced aspirates 73
4.2.3.3 Pronunciation of the symbols स,ष,श 73
4.2.3.4 The special consonant conjunct graphemes 74
4.2.3.5 The pronunciation of orthographic word-initial CC clusters 74
4.2.3.6 The symbol ह् 74
4.3 Numeral 75
4.4 Punctuation marks 75

The form classes

5 The inflected and uninflected forms 77
5.0 Introduction 77
5.1 Nouns 77
5.2 Adjectives 79
5.3 Verbs 80
5.4 Adverbs 82
5.5 Pronouns 83
5.6 Coordinating conjunctions 84

5.7 Subordinating conjunctions 84
5.8 Postpositions 85
5.9 Interjections 85
5.10 Vocatives 85
5.11 Nuance particles 86
5.12 Prefixes and suffixes 86

6 Substitute forms 87
6.0 Introduction 87
6.1 The major substitute forms 87
6.1.1 The K-form substitutes or interrogatives 87
6.1.1.1 The *K*-form classes 87
6.1.1.2 The distribution of *K*-forms 88
6.1.2 The *J*-form substitutes 89
6.1.2.1 The *J*-form classes 89
6.1.2.2 The distribution of *J*-form classes 89
6.1.3 The *D*-form substitutes or demonstratives 90
6.1.3.1 The *D*-form classes 91
6.1.3.2 The distribution of *D*-form classes 92
6.2 Numerals 93
Notes for Chapter 6 97

Nominal structures

7 The common noun phrase 98
7.0 Internal structure of the common-noun phrase 98
7.1 Common nouns as heads 98
7.2 Gender of nouns 99
7.3 Determiners in the CNP 100
7.3.1 Demonstratives 100
7.3.2 Limiters 100
7.3.3 Quantifiers (numbers) and classifiers 100
7.3.4 CNPs functioning as quantifying determiner 101
7.4 Modifiers in he CNP 101
7.4.1 Nouns or nominals as modifiers in CNP 101
7.4.2 Adjectives or adjective phrases as modifiers 102
7.4.3 Clauses as modifiers 102

8 The proper noun phrase 103
8.0 Internal structure of the proper-noun phrase (PNP) 103
8.1 Person names as heads 104
8.2 Place names as heads 105
Notes for Chapter 8 105

9 The pronoun phrase 106
9.0 Internal structure of the pronoun phrase (ProP) 106
9.1 Pronouns as heads 106

9.2 Modifiers in the pronoun phrase 109
Notes for Chapter 9 109

10 Dependent nominals functioning as modifiers in larger nominals 110
10.0 Introduction 110
10.1 Characterizing modifiers 110
10.2 Appositive modifiers: Double-headed constructions 111
10.3 Genitive modifiers 112
10.4 Delimiting modifiers 116

Adjectival structures

11 The adjective phrase 118
11.0 Internal structure of the adjective phrase (AdjP) 118
11.1 Adjectives as heads 119
11.2 Quantifiers in the AdjP 120
11.2.1 Adverbs of quantity 120
11.2.2 Comparative quantifier phrases 121
11.2.2.1 Comparatives with *bhandā* 'than' 121
11.2.2.2 Comparative adjective phrase with *jhan* 'the more' 121
11.2.3 Superlative quantifier phrases 121
11.2.4 Elative superlative quantifier 122

12 Dependent adjectivals functioning as modifiers within CNPs 123
12.0 Introduction 123
12.1 The imperfect participle *-ne* as modifier 124
12.2 The perfect participle *-eko* as modifier 125

Adverbial structures

13 The adverb phrase 127
13.0 Internal structure of the adverb phrase (AdvP) 127
13.1 Simple adverbs 127
13.1.1 Derived adverbs 127
13.1.1.1 Adverbs ending in *-ari* 'doing' 127
13.1.1.2 Adverbs ending in *-sāth* 'with' 128
13.1.1.3 Adverbs ending in *-pūrvaka* 128
13.1.2 Nonderived adverbs 128
13.1.3 Interrogatives, relaters, and demonstratives 129
13.2 Compound adverbials 130

14 The adverbial postpositional noun phrase 132
14.0 Introduction 132
14.1 Postposition and its complements (NPs) 132
14.2 Postpositions occurring with the NPs in genitive case 133

14.3 Postpositions occurring with morphologically unmarked forms of the NPs 133

15. Conjunctions: Coordinate and subordinate 135
15.0 Introduction 135
15.1 Coordinating conjunctions 135
15.2 Subordinating conjunctions 138

16 Interjection, vocatives, and nuance particles 141
16.0 Introduction 141
16.1 Interjections 141
16.2 Vocatives 141
16.3 Nuance particles 142
16.3.1 Phrasal nuance particles 143
16.3.2 Statement nuance particles 144
16.3.2.1 Imperative statement nuance particles 144
16.3.2.2 Declarative statement nuance particles 144
16.3.2.3 Question statement nuance particles 144
Notes for Chapter 16 146

Verbal structures

17 The verb phrase 147
17.0 Internal structure of the verb phrase (VP) 147
17.1 Verbs as heads 148
17.2 Auxiliary verbs in the VP 149
17.3 The negative verb forms 149
17.3.1 The negative prefix *na-* 149
17.3.2 The negative suffix *-na-* 150
17.4 Verbs which require the obligatory fronting of the dative complement 150
17.5 Modifiers in the VP 150
Notes for Chapter 17 151

Clausal structures

18 The clause: A general overview 158
18.0 Internal structure of the clause (Cl) 158
18.1 Verbals as predicates 158
18.2 Subjects in the clause 159
18.3 Complements in the clause 159
18.3.1 Transitive verbs and their complements 160
18.3.1.1 Transitive-1 verbs (tv-1) 160
18.3.1.2 Transitive-2 verbs (tv-2) 161
18.3.1.3 Transitive-3 verbs (tv-3) 161
18.3.1.4 Transitive-4 verbs (tv-4) 162
18.3.2 Equational verbs and their complements 162

18.3.2.1 The identifcational *hunu* 'be' 162
18.3.2.2 The existential *hunu* 'be' 163
18.3.2.3 The equational verbs-2 *dekhinu* and *lāgnu* 163
18.3.3 Intransitive verbs and their complements 163
18.3.3.1 Intransitive-1 verbs (iv-1) 164
18.3.3.2 Intransitive-2 verbs (iv-2) 164
18.3.3.3 Intransitive-3 verbs (iv-3) 164
18.4 Subject-predicate linking by person-number-gender-honorific level inflection 164
18.5 Optional adverbial adjuncts 164
18.6 Other optional elements 165
18.6.1 Adverbial disjuncts (AD) 166
18.6.2 Exclamations 166
18.6.3 Connectors 166
18.6.4 The subjects 167
Notes for Chapter 18 167

19 Special types of clauses 169
19.0 Introduction 169
19.1 Passive clauses 169
19.2 Imperative clauses 170
19.3 Question clauses 170
19.3.1 *K*-question clauses 170
19.3.2 *Ho/hoina*-question clauses 170
19.3.2.1 *Ho/hoina*-question with question intonation 170
19.3.2.2 *Ho/hoina* question with the tag *hagi* 170

20 Finite dependent clauses: Nominal, adjectival and adverbial 171
20.0 Introduction 171
20.1 Finite dependent noun clause 171
20.2 Finite dependent adjective clause 171
20.3 Finite dependent adverbial clause with *bhane* 'if', *kinaki* or *kinabhane* 'because' 172

21 Nonfinite dependent clauses: Infinitive, participial and conditional 173
21.0 Introduction 173
21.1 Nonfinite dependent noun clause with a verb in infinite form 173
21.2 Nonfinite dependent adverbial clause as adverbial adjunct 173
21.3 Nonfinite dependent adverbial clause with a verb phrase in conditional form 174
Note for Chapter 21 176

22 Dependent clauses in expression of comparison 177
22.0 Introduction 177
22.1 Comparisons of inequality 177

22.1.1 Symmetrical comparisons 177
22.1.2 Asymmetrical comparisons 179
22.2 Comparisons of equality 179

Sentential structures

23 The sentence 181
23.0 The internal structure of the sentence (S) 181
23.1 Clauses as segmental constituents 181

24 The sentence as speech act 182
24.0 Introduction 182
24.1 Direct speech act 182
24.2 Indirect speech acts 183
24.2.1 Indirect speech acts with *re, are* 183
24.2.2 Indirect speech with *bhanera* 183
24.2.2.1 Reporting the actual speech act 183
24.2.2.2 Reporting the intention 184
24.3 Elliptical sentences as declarative speech acts 185
24.3.1 Reduced sentence with elliptical subject and object 185
24.3.2 Reduced sentences with elliptical predicate 185
Notes for Chapter 24 186

References 187

Part two: Analyzed corpus

1. *Nāso:* Text in Devanagari script 191
2. *Nāso:* 'Ward': Literal English translation 197
3. *Nāso:* The roman transliteration of the Devanagari text 205
4. *Nāso:* Clause structure analysis 213
5. *Nāso:* Phrase structures (sorted) 309
6. *Nāso:* Lexicon in order of occurrence 316
7. *Nāso:* Lexicon in alphabetical order 357

PREFACE

This is a descriptive grammar of Nepali, the national language of Nepal. The theoretical framework for this description is provided by the tagmemic system of linguistic analysis developed by K. L. Pike, and used by the Summer Institute of Linguistics. In tagmemic analysis language is seen as comprising three levels -- phonology, lexicon, and grammar. The present study attempts to describe the structure of Nepali at all the three levels—sound system (phonology), form classes (lexicon), and the phrase, clause, and sentence structures (grammar).

Although there are a few courses in Nepali, there is no systematic descriptive grammar of the language yet available. This work is intended to fulfill the need of such a grammar. It contains a precise description of the sound system, writing system, morphology, and syntax of Nepali. Thus, it is a reference grammar which can be used as a guide by a language teacher with some linguistic training to teach Nepali. Based on this work, one can also develop scientific teaching materials. For this purpose, the description has been made more practical than theoretical. Each grammatical rule has been illustrated by examples taken from an analyzed corpus. A famous short story by Guruprasad Mainali (1900-1971), namely *Nāso* 'Ward', was selected as corpus. All the clauses, phrases and words in the story have been analyzed, and the analysis has been presented in Part two. So in this description the examples prefaced by a reference number refer to the numbered text of *Nāso* cited in Part two.

My heartfelt thanks are due to Professor Richard J. O'Brien, S. J. without whose constant guide and advice this work was not possible. My thanks are also due to Professors Shaligram Shukla and Richard Lutz who, together with Prof. O'Brien, formed the committee to read this work which was earlier submitted as a Ph. D. dissertation. I am also thankful to Dr. David L. Red, Language Training Supervisor at the Foreign Service Institute of the U. S. Department of State, for reading the manuscript and making several corrections. I want to thank also my friend Peter V. Thorne at the Energy and Environment Analysis for his computer assistance without which this work could not be done in the way it has been done.

The Fulbright scholarship (1984-1886) and a Georgetown University Graduate School Fellowship (1986-1989) made it possible for me to do this work. I am, therefore, thankful to the Fulbright scholarship program and the Graduate School of Georgetown University for their generosity. I am also thankful to the Georgetown University Press for publishing this book.

Since May, 1989 I have been completely dependent on the income of my wife Usha Acharya, who worked very hard to support my study despite the fact that she was expecting our second child (Achal) in September 1989. I cannot remain without acknowledging my profound appreciation of her patience and hard work with which she supported the whole family.

June 5, 1990 — Jayaraj Acharya

List of abbreviations

+	Obligatory
±	Optional
AA:	Adverbial Adjunct function
ab	ablative case
AbA:	Ablative adjunct function
ab cs.mkr	ablative case marker
abs.prt	absolutive participle
ac	accusative case
ac cs.mkr	accusative case marker
AD:	Adverbial disjunct function
adj	adjective
adjl	adjectival
AdjP	Adjectival phrase
adv	adverb
AdvCl	Adverbial clause
advl	adverbial
AdvP	Adverbial phrase
ag sb.mkr	agentive subject marker
AppCNP	Appositive common noun phrase
AppPNP	appositive proper noun phrase
aux	auxiliary verb
Aux:	Auxiliary function
C:	Connector function
cc	coordinate conjunction
cl	clausal
Cla:	Classifier function
cla.	classifier form
Cmpd	compound
Cmpdadj	compound adjective
Cmpdadjl	compound adjectival
Cmpdcn	compound common noun
CmpdCNP	Compound CNP
Compdev	compound equational verb
Cmpdiv	compund intransitive verb
Cmpdtv	compound transitive verb
CmpdtVP	Compound transitive verb phrase
cn	common noun
CNP	Common noun phrase
cond	conditional mode of verb
conj.prt	conjunctive participle
cs	case
DC:	Dative complement function
Dem.	Demonstrative
Det.	Determiner
DO:	Direct object function
dt	dative case
dt cs.mkr	dative case marker
emph	emphatic
ev	equational verb
eVP	equational Verb Phrase
EX	Exclamation function
ex	exclamatory
f	feminine
fut	future tense of verb
gn cs.mkr	genitive case marker
H:	Head
hon	honorific
IA:	Instrumental adjunct function
imp	imperative of verb
impf	imperfective aspect
impf.prt	imperfect participle
in	instrumental case
in cs.mkr	instrumental case marker
inf.	infinitive form
intj	interjection
iv	intransitive verb

iVP	intransitive verb phrase
LA:	Locative Adjunct function
LC:	Locative Complement function
lc	locative case
lc cs.mkr	locative case marker
lim	limiter
mkr	marker
m	masculine
mod	modified
n	noun
NCl	Noun clause
neg	negative
nl	nominal
NlP	Nominal phrase
NP	Noun phrase
nm	nominative case
nm.plzr	nominal pluralizer
NU:	Nuance semantic function
nu	nuance
num	numeral
OC:	Object complement function
onomat	onomatopoeic
P:	Predicate function
pers	person
pl	plural number
plzr	pluralizer
pn	proper noun
PNP	Proper Noun Phrase
poss	possessive
postf	postfinal
pp	postposition
PP	Postpositional Phrase
pres	present tense of verb
pres.prog	present progressive of verb
prf	perfective aspect of verb
prf.prog.prt	perfect progressive participle
prf.prt	perfect participle
pro	pronoun
pro-dem	pronoun (demonstrative)
pro-interrog	pronoun (interrogative)
prol.adj	pronominal adjective
pro-pers	pronoun (personal)
pro-reflx	pronoun (reflexive)
pro-rel	pronoun (relative)
prob.pst	probability past tense of verb
prog	progressive aspect of verb
prol	pronominal
PrtCl	Participial clause
ProP	Pronominal phrase
pst	past
pst.prf	past perfect of verb
pst.prog	past progressive of verb
Q:	Question function
Qnt	Qantifier
qw	question word
S:	Subject function
sb	subject
SC:	Subject complement function
sc	subordinate conjunction
sg	singular
specif	specifier
tv	transitive verb
tVP:	transitive Verb Phrase

PART ONE: GRAMMAR

Chapter 1
Introduction

1.0 Introduction. This chapter presents brief introductory notes on the Nepali language focussing especially on the number of native speakers of Nepali (1.1), the name Nepali (1.2), Nepali as an Indo-European language (1.3), Nepali and the other languages of Nepal (1.4), geographical distribution of Nepali (1.5), dialects of Nepali (1.6), Nepali and Hinduism (1.7), previous descriptions of Nepali (1.8), the purpose and scope of this study (1.9), corpus of this study (1.10), transcription (1.11), and motivation of this description (1.12).

1.1 The Nepali language. This study consists of a descriptive grammar of Nepali, the national language of Nepal. Nepali is spoken as a mother tongue by 58.4 per cent of Nepal's total population, which according to the 1981 census was 15,022,839. Besides the 58.4 % of the nation's population who speak Nepali as their mother tongue the rest of the people of Nepal speak Nepali as their second language. Thus, Nepali is the *lingua franca* for the nonnative speakers of Nepali in the country. Nepali is also a medium of a uniform, nationwide, educational system, public administration, and mass communication (radio, newspapers, and TV). According to the Department of Communication, there were about 900 Nepali newspapers, journals, magazines and other periodicals registered in the department.

The Nepali language has also been used by literary writers in their literary works: poetry, novels, short stories, plays, essays, and research articles. The first major poet to use Nepali in his literary writing was Bhanubhakta Acharya (1814-1868), who translated the *Ramāyaṇa* from Sanskrit, and wrote several other original works in Nepali, and thus contributed to the standardization of Nepali through his writings which are still popular in Nepal.

Today Nepali is also spoken and used in mass communication and literary works outside Nepal by about eight million people, especially in northern India (the Darjeeling district of West Bengal, the Dehra Dun area of Uttar Pradesh, Sikkim, and Assam) and in the independent country of Bhutan.

1.2 The name Nepali. The language spoken by the Khas tribes of the hills of Nepal as their mother tongue was called by various names in different periods during the approximate 700 years of its development. The oldest name of this language was probably *Khas bhāṣā* or *Khas kurā* 'the language of the Khas', a Himalayan mountain tribe whose origin is still obscure, although its language was definitely Sanskrit-derived. The name of the language 'Nepali' comes from the name of the country Nepal, not *vice versa.* The name Nepali was first used by Ayton, who wrote *A grammar of the Nepalese language* (1820). In Nepal itself the people continued calling it *Khas kurā* or *Parbartiyā* or *Parbate* 'the language of the hill people'. Likewise, it was called *Pahāri* 'the language of the mountains' by the people of the Gangetic plains of India. Clark (1969), however, used the term *Pahāri* as a cover term, not just for Nepali but for all other languages of the mountains of Nepal.

The Sanskrit scholars of Nepal, e.g. Śaktiballabh Arjyal, called this language *lokabhāṣā* 'vernacular' as opposed to Sanskrit, which for several centuries in Nepal was the language of scholars and royal edicts. Hinavyākaraṇī Vidyāpati, a poet of the early 19th century, used the name *Rājabhāṣā* 'the royal language' for the reason that it was the language of the royal court after the unification of modern Nepal since 1768.

The name *Gorkhali* 'the language of the people of Gorkha' was also used to refer to Nepali for about two centuries especially after the unification of modern Nepal by Prithvinarayan Shaha (1720-1775), king of Gorkha, a principality in the hills of central Nepal. The name *Gorkāhlī* or *Gorkhā Bhāṣā* 'the language of Gorkha' was used in Nepal until 1930 when the name of the *Gorkhā Bhāṣā Prakāśinī Samiti* 'The Gorkha language publishing committee' was changed into *Nepālī Bhāṣā Prakāśinī Samiti* . 'The titles of early Indian Nepali journals such as *Gorkhālī* (1916), *Gorkhā Mitra* (1924), *Gorkhā Samsār* (1926), *Gorkhā Sevak* (1935), and *Gorkhā* (1945), demonstrate the continuing prevalence of the name' (Hutt 1988:33).

1.3 Nepali as an Indo-European language. Nepali belongs to the Indo-European family of languages. The relation of Nepali to other Indo-European languages of South Asia is listed in Figure 1.1

Figure 1.1 Nepali and other Indo-European languages of South Asia (Based on Shukla 1981:2).

Romany	Armenian Romany, Asiatic Romany, European Romany
Sinhalese	Maldivian, Sinhalese, Vedda
Eastern zone	Assamese, Bengali, Bhojpuri, Magahi, Maithili, Oriya
Northwestern zone	Lanhanda, Sindhi
Central zone	Banjiri, Bhili, Gujrati, Khandesi, Panjabi, Rajasthani, Western Hindi
East Central zone	Eastern Hindi
Northern zone	Gahrwali, Kumauni, Nepali, Western Pahari

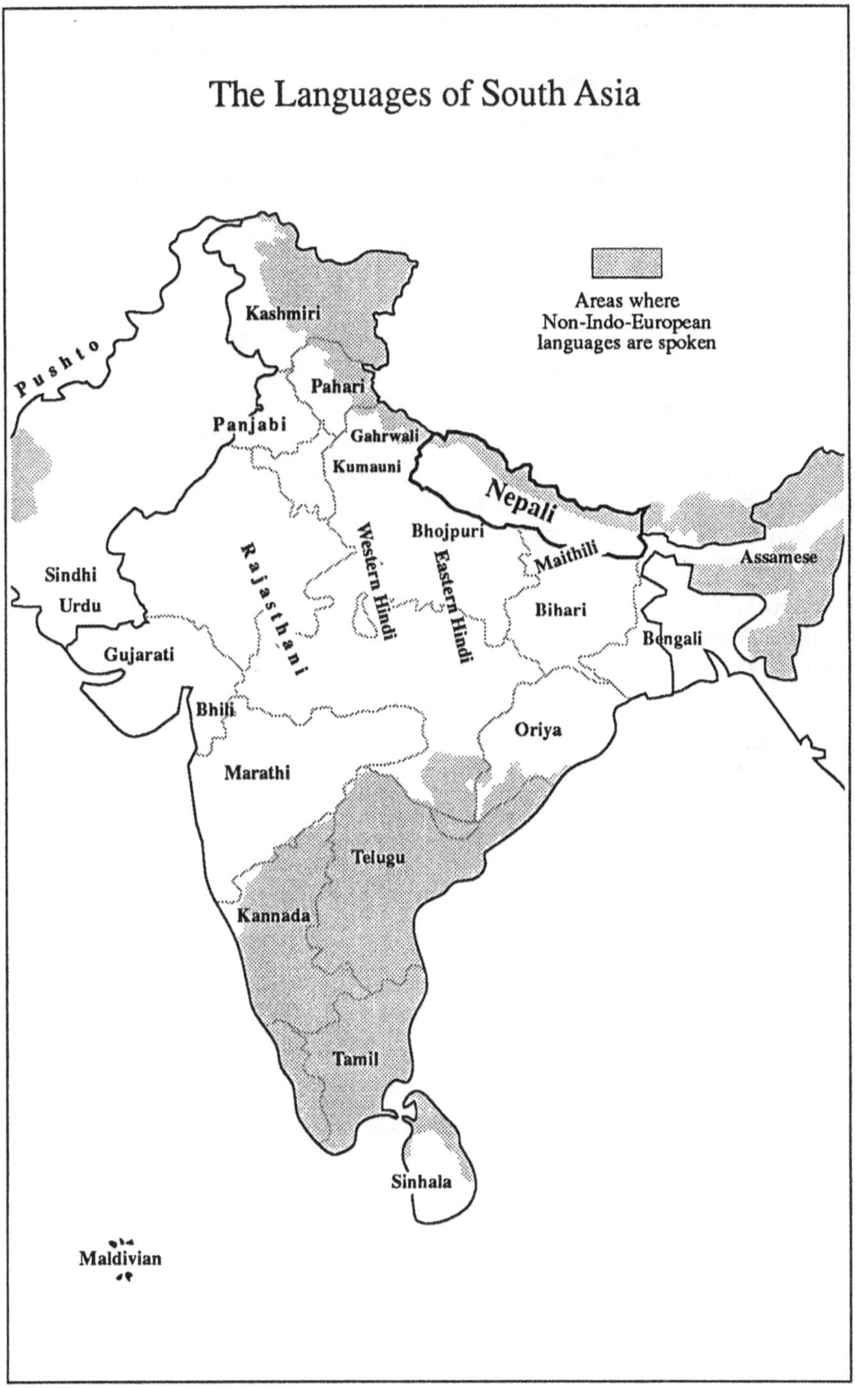
The Languages of South Asia
Areas where Non-Indo-European languages are spoken
Kashmiri
Pushto
Pahari
Panjabi
Gahrwali
Kumauni
Nepali
Bhojpuri
Maithili
Assamese
Sindhi
Urdu
Rajasthani
Western Hindi
Eastern Hindi
Bihari
Bengali
Gujarati
Bhili
Oriya
Marathi
Telugu
Kannada
Tamil
Sinhala
Maldivian

1.4 Nepali and the other languages of Nepal. Nepal is a multilingual nation. Because of its location between two major language families of the world, namely the Indo-Aryan and the Tibeto-Burman, Nepal has been a meeting point of several languages and cultures. There are as many as 36 different languages spoken in Nepal. They belong to four major language families: Indo-European (IE), Tibeto-Burman (TB), Austro-Asiatic (AA), and Dravidian (D). Some of them are spoken by less than 5000 speakers. Figure 1.2 lists the number of the native speakers of Nepali and those of the other languages spoken in Nepal.

Figure 1.2 Native speakers of Nepali and of the other languages spoken in Nepal in 1981 according to the Central Bureau of Statistics.

Language	Number of speakers	Percentage
Nepali (IE)	8,767,361	58.4
Maithili (IE)	1,668,309	11.1
Bhojpuri (IE)	1,142,805	7.6
Tharu (IE)	545,685	3.6
Tamang (TB)	522,416	3.5
Newari (TB)	448,746	3.0
Avadhi (IE)	234,343	1.5
Rai Kirati (TB)	221,353	1.5
Magar (TB)	212,681	1.4
Gurung (TB)	174,464	1.2
Limbu (TB)	129,234	0.9
Bhote Sherpa (TB)	73,589	0.5
Rajvamshi (IE)	59,383	0.3
Satar (AA)	22,403	0.4
Danuwar (IE)	13,522	0.1
Sunuwar (TB)	10,650	0.1
Santhal (AA)	5,804	0.1
Thakali (TB)	5,289	0.1
Other languages	764,802	5.1
Total	15,022,839	100.%

1.5 Geographical distribution of Nepali. Nepali, besides being the national language and the *lingua franca* of Nepal, is also widely distributed in all geographical regions of the country. Nepali is spoken in fourteen administrative zones, and the percentile distribution of the speakers of Nepali in these zones (Figure 1.3) indicates its nation-wide dominance over other languages in Nepal.

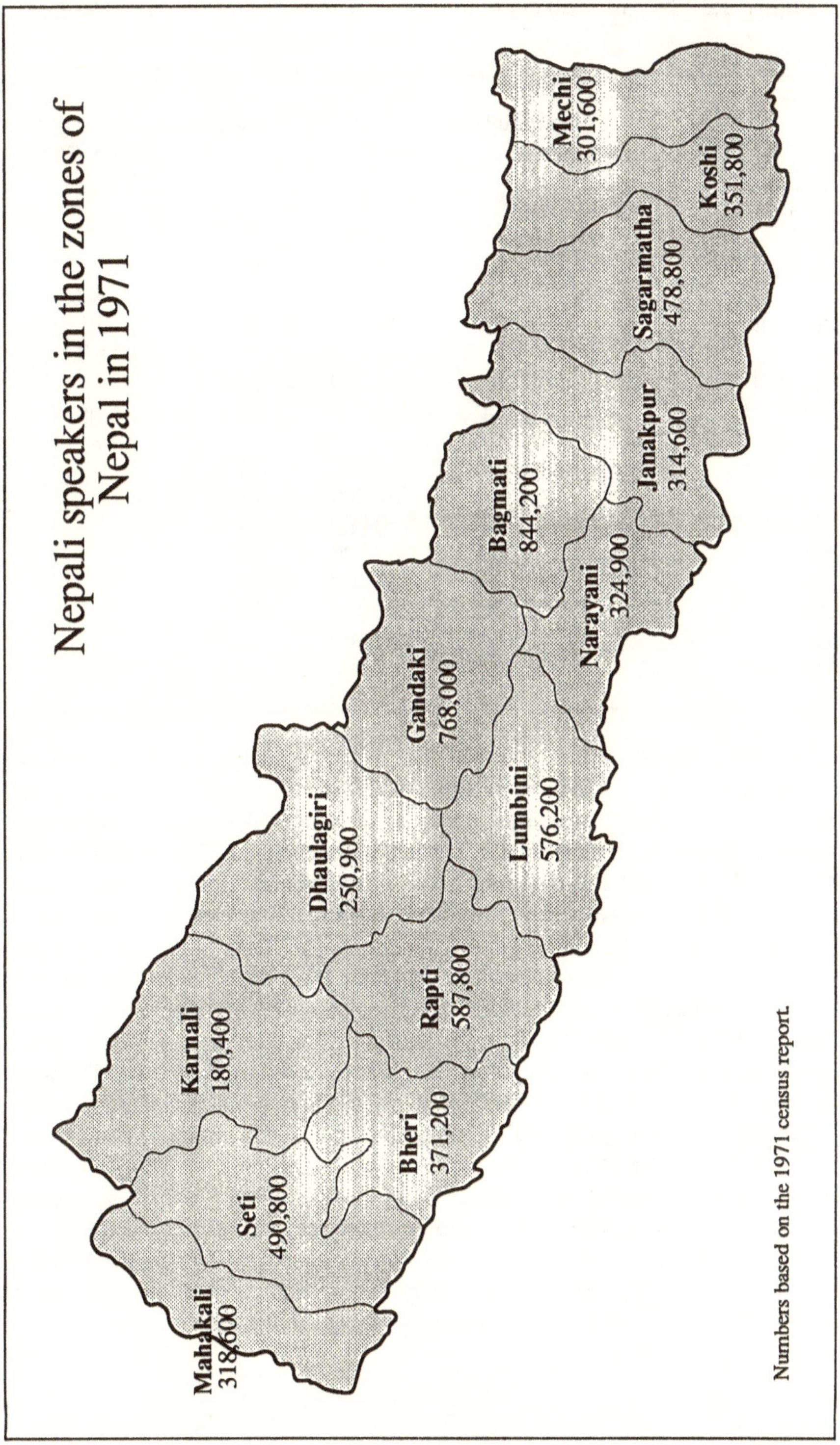

Nepali speakers in the zones of Nepal in 1971

Numbers based on the 1971 census report.

Figure 1.3 Nepali speakers in the zones of Nepal in 1971. (Hutt 1988:33).

Zones	Total population	No. of Nepali speakers	Nepali speakers as a %	Other languages (over 25%)
Mechi	617,800	301,600	48.8	
Koshi	866,300	351,900	40.6	
Sagarmatha	1,313,500	478,800	36.5	Maithili 43.8%
Janakpur	1,265,800	314,600	24.9	Maithili 49.8%
Bagmati	1,497,000	844,200	56.4	
Narayani	1,103,000	234,900	21.3	Bhojpuri 65%
Gandaki	1,023,100	768,000	75.1	
Lumbini	1,165,700	567,200	48.7	
Dhaulagiri	267,700	250,900	90.7	
Rapti	705,800	587,800	83.3	
Karnali	188,000	180,400	96.0	
Bheri	575,100	371,200	64.5	
Seti	597,100	490,800	82.2	
Mahakali	361,200	318,600	88.2	

1.6 Dialects of Nepali. Nepali, like every language, has many dialects or social variants. Although in this study it is not possible to go into the details of these social variations, it can be mentioned that such variations are found at all levels: phonological, lexical, and grammatical. The definition of a different dialect depends on how narrow or broad regional distinctions one decides to note. Within Nepal itself, there may be three broad dialectal divisions: Eastern (spoken in the hill districts of Mechi, Koshi, Sagarmatha and Janakpur zones), Central (spoken in Bagmati, Gandaki, Dhaulagiri zones, and the hill districts of Narayani, Lumbini and Rapti zones), and Western (spoken in Karnali zone, and the hill districts of Bheri, Seti and Mahakali zones). The Nepali spoken in Darjeeling district of West Bengal is regarded as yet another distinctly different dialect of Nepali. Of these dialects, the Western dialect shows greater difference (at phonological, lexical, and grammatical levels) from the rest.

A dialect may also be defined in terms of the social hierarchy of its speakers. In terms of the social hierarchy, the Central Nepali dialect is spoken as a mother tongue by the low (uneducated), middle (educated), and upper classes of the Brahmans and Ksatriya castes. The Central dialect of Nepali used in the textbooks and literary writings has been spoken by many generations of speakers who have lived in Kathmandu and the adjacent hills in the east and west.

1.7 Nepali and Hinduism. The dialectal variations of Nepali based on social hierarchy are related to some extent to the caste system of Hinduism, which is the major religion in Nepal. There are four castes *(varnas)* in a Hindu society, which divide the society into four classes. These classes, from the most prestigious to the least, are: the religious leaders *(Brāhmaṇas)*, the administrators and warriors *(Kṣatriyas)*, the traders and craft workers *(Vaiśyas)*, and the ordinary workers *(Śūdras)*. A fifth class, called the *achut* 'untouchables' (those who traditionally did the most undesirable jobs), is outside the caste system.

The Nepali language reflects the caste system in Nepal. Karn (1986:3) observed that 'when addressing someone, it is necessary to use the appropriate level of respect by employing the pertinent form of the second person pronoun.' Although there are not as many lexical forms to differentiate levels of respect for the third person pronoun as there are for the second person pronoun, it is, nevertheless, quite necessary to select the appropriate form of the third person pronoun when referring to someone not to offend the addressee or the third person.

1.8 Previous descriptions of Nepali

1.8.1 Teaching materials. There are a few English-language texts designed to teach Nepali. The first is Major M. Meerendonk's *Basic Gurkhali grammar* (1949). The title of the book is misleading as it calls Nepali 'Gurkhali', and claims to be a grammar, but it is a course book with grammatical notes. Meerendonk's 'grammar' has two parts. Part I: Elementary has forty lessons with exercises and a few vocabulary lists. Part II: Advanced has ten lessons. In addition, the volume contains seven appendices: (a) Nepalese time, weights, and measures, (b) table of family relationships, (c) list of words common to English and Gurkhali, (d) the Darjeeling dialect, (e) letter writing, (f) the Nagari script, and (g) orthography.

The second important course book along the same line is T. W. Clark's *Introduction to Nepali* (1963), divided into three sections: (1) pronunciation, (2) noun and verb paradigms, (3) and texts in the Devanagari script. Although phonology is described in modern linguistic terms, the grammar is described in traditional semantic terms.

Clark's text concentrates almost entirely on morphology. He provides grammatical notes on the syntactic structures only as clues to the translation of the dialogues or short readings.

As a supplement to Clark's *Introduction to Nepali* (1963) Ruth Laila Schmidt prepared *A Nepali conversation manual* (1968) which has two parts containing 27 chapters in total. In addition to the 27 chapters, there are two supplementary reading sections. In the words of its author, 'The purpose of this manual is to provide a collection of drills and dialogues, or narrative descriptions, as a supplement to section II of T. W. Clark 1963.'

Another English-language volume with teaching material is *Basic course in spoken Nepali* by Tika B. Karki and Chij K. Shrestha (no date). This coursebook was prepared to teach Nepali to American Peace Corps volunteers in Nepal. The text has forty lessons with vocabulary and dialogues. Grammatical notes accompany each lesson. In addition, the book contains a Nepali-English word list, a section on pronunciation, a section on the Devanagari script, and conjugation tables. The roman letters of this text represent the phonemic system of Nepali, unlike Clark's transliteration of the spelling system.

Although the pedagogical focus of Karki and Shrestha is different from that of Clark (speaking vs. reading), the theoretical basis for the two grammars is similar. Both texts emphasize the traditional system of cases. In addition, the structural analyses (e.g. the verbal structures) are, for the most part, based on traditional grammar and not formal descriptive linguistics.

Conversational Nepali (1971) by Maria Hari is a course for persons beginning to study Nepali. Nepali phonology is presented in the first 30 pages; then the lessons are presented, 120 in all. All the lessons are in the form of conversations. The first 16 lessons appear in a roman transliteration of the standard written Nepali. In lessons 16 to 30, the texts of all the early conversations are presented in the Devanagari script at the rate of two per lesson. From lesson 31 on, all new material is presented in the Devanagari script. Each lesson, consisting of eight to ten utterances, is followed by a list of vocabulary, grammatical notes, build-up drills, substitution drills, and, often, transformation drills. The conversations are grouped into different areas of experience, e.g. 1 Getting to know Nepal, 2 The market, 3 The home, 4 The school, 5 The office, 6 Conversation starters, etc. There is a grammatical index which helps the learner find particular grammatical structures incorporated in different lessons.

Recently, *A course in Nepali* by David Matthews (1984) has been available for learning Nepali. Like Clark's *Introduction to Nepali* (1963), Matthews (1984) concentrates on reading and translation. This course is different from that of Clark (1963) in that Matthews presents the lessons in Devanagari script, which may be a disadvantage to those who do not want to learn the script, but only wish to acquire a speaking knowledge. Matthews' coursebook is a better one in that the language data Matthews uses is more the language of daily life.

Nepali newspaper reader (1984) by Champa Jarmul is, as its title suggests, a coursebook in advanced reading. Excerpts are taken from Nepalese newspapers and advanced level vocabulary and idioms are glossed. At the end of the book there is a word list in Devanagari alphabetical order with English glosses.

The structure of spoken Nepali Volume I (1989) by Krishna B. Pradhan is another volume of teaching material divided in eleven chapters. Like Matthews (1984), this material is presented in Devanagari script from the very beginning. *A practical guide to the script and pronunciation of the Nepali language* (1989), also by Pradhan, is available for learning the Devanagari script.

1.8.2 Grammars. The first grammars of Nepali were written by foreign scholars who were neither equipped with the insights of modern linguistics, nor did they have a very good command of the language which they attempted to describe. J. A. Ayton wrote *A grammar of the Nepalese language* (1820) which can be best described as a very preliminary sketch by a foreigner. Rev. A. Turnbull attempted a more elaborate work, *Nepali grammar and vocabulary* (1888); but the language he described was the Darjeeling dialect of Nepali. Even if he had described the dialect of Kathmandu, it would sound archaic today since a century has lapsed since the first publication of his Grammar. Turnbull's methodology in writing his grammar was that of many traditional English grammars, which was to emulate the Latin grammatical model.

The first native Nepali grammarian who attempted to describe Nepali was Virendrakesari Arjyal (1849-1931), but his grammar was confiscated by the Rana rulers, and the manuscript remained unavailable until 1980 when a part of it was first published by J. Acharya (1980). The most well-known native grammars were Sharma (1912), Dikshitacharya (1913), Sharma (1919), Pradhan (1932), and Pandey (1947). All those native grammarians (except Arjyal) wrote prescriptive grammars, laying down rules for proper spelling and usage of words according to their concept of 'correctness'. They were inspired by the grammars of either Sanskrit or English. They borrowed the traditional definitions and classifications of the parts of speech of English and padded them with Nepali examples. In short, they produced Nepali versions of English prescriptive grammars taught in the British Indian schools. Most of the other grammars of Nepali by native grammarians followed Sharma (1919).

Recent works of foreign scholars are: Morland Hugh (1947), Meerendonk (1949), Clark (1963), Hari (1971), and Matthews (1984); but, as mentioned in (1.8.1), all these, except Morland Hugh, are courses in Nepali. So, their organization and presentation of materials is motivated by pedagogical needs.

There are also partial descriptions of the structure of Nepali by scholars associated with the Summer Institute of Linguistics (SIL). They include the following: Bandhu *et al* (1971), which describes the segmental phonology of Nepali leaving the suprasegmental phonology out of its scope. Bandhu (1973) analyses the clause patterns of Nepali on Pike's model of a four-cell tagmeme. Hari (1973) presents a 'Tentative systemic organization of Nepali sentences' focusing on the sentence level constructions.

A transformational sketch of Nepali syntax is presented in Southworth (1967). Although the book is available in some libraries and archives, it is not very useful to an ordinary reader who wants to learn about the structures of Nepali at phonological, morphological, phrase, clause, and sentence levels but is unacquainted with the formulations of modern transformational grammar.

1.8.3 Dictionaries. There is no comprehensive English-Nepali or Nepali-English dictionary. Meerendonk published a pocket dictionary *Basic Gurkhali dictionary* (1958) which has two sections: English-Nepali and Nepali-English. This dictionary, however useful, is too small containing barely 2,500 words.

A fairly comprehensive Nepali-English dictionary is Turner's *A comparative and etymological dictionary of the Nepali language* (1931). As its title suggests, the primary purpose of this dictionary is to give the etymology of Nepali words. However, the dictionary also gives English meanings of the Nepali words. Although the dictionary has been organized on the Devanagari alphabetical order, a standard roman transliteration of the Devanagari script is also provided.

There are some Nepali-Nepali dictionaries such as those published by the Nepal Rājakīya Prajñā Pratiṣṭhāna (Royal Nepal Academy): *Nepālī śabdakośa* [Nepali dictionary] (1962) and *Nepali bṛhat śabdakośa* [A comprehensive Nepali dictionary] (1984). Dikshit's *Aṅgrejī Nepālī sājhā saṅkṣipta śabdakośa* (1976, 2nd ed.1987) is an English-Nepali dictionary which can be used by learners of Nepali as it helps them to find Nepali correspondences of English words.

1.9 The purpose and scope of this study. The purpose of this study is to provide a description of present-day standard Nepali as spoken in Kathmandu by means of techniques of structural analysis and description developed by post-Bloomfieldian linguistics. The analytical model employed in this study is tagmemic analysis developed by K. L. Pike, and used by the Summer Institute of Linguistics (SIL) to describe many languages of the world. Tagmemic analysis keeps track of language by means of the strings of form-function tagmemes at word, phrase, clause, and sentence levels. In Tagmemic analysis, the unit is the tagmeme--a correlation of a functional slot with a filler class. Thus, each function is filled by a form class in the construction of language, e.g. in a clause such as *I read your article*, there are three functional slots, namely Subject, Predicate, and Object. The subject functional slot is filled by the form *I* (personal pronoun), the predicate functional slot is filled by the form *read* (transitive verb), and the object functional slot is filled by the form *your book* (common noun phrase). (For further examples see Chapter 18). This form-function model includes a transformational component of the surface sentence forms such as active-passive transformation as one way of accounting for various sentence types. The purpose of this study, therefore, is:

(1) to provide a detailed analysis and description of what is sometimes labeled 'the surface grammar' of Nepali, accounting for all the items noted in previous grammatical descriptions of the language, and to incorporate them in their proper place and level within a total grammar of Nepali (Part One), and

(2) to analyze all the items which occur in a typical, standard Nepali text *Nāso* 'Ward' (Part Two).

Attempting to achieve the stated purposes, this study provides, as far as a native speaker can, a taxitive (exhaustive) list of all the functional items which comprise the closed grammatical classes of the Nepali language.

In concrete terms, then, this description attempts (at the phonological level) to provide an accurate description of the Nepali sound system: its segmental phonemes and their principal allophones (Chapter 2), the Nepali syllable, and the suprasegmental features of Nepali stress, pitch, and intonation (Chapter 3).

This study also describes the writing and spelling system of Nepali and a description (1) of the fit between its writing system and its sound system and (2) of the fit between its sound system and its writing system (Ch. 4).

The inflected and noninflected form classes and a description of the inflectional morphology and of those open, and productive derivational formations which would not be listed in a standard dictionary are described in the study (Ch. 5 and Ch. 6);

Then this study attempts to provide a description of the phrase level structures: nominal structures (Chs. 7-10), adjectival structures (Chs. 11-12), adverbial structures (Chs. 13-16), verbal structures (Ch.17), clausal structures (Chs. 18-22), and sentential structures (Chs. 23-24).

Thus this description attempts to provide a practical grammar which may be useful to (1) anthropologists, (2) those faced with the necessity of learning the language, (3) computational linguists interested in applying computational techniques to texts written in Nepali, or (4) those interested in the structure of Nepali.

In accord with the practical purpose of the work as a reference grammar, those lexical stems are in preference chosen as basic for paradigms which most easily fit in with the existing dictionaries, e.g. Turner 1931. For the most part, only that part of derivation is treated which concerns those open derivational classes which are frequently not listed in current dictionaries, e.g participles, adverbs, comparative and superlative forms, etc. Thus the detailed study of the stem derivation is left to the philologists and historical linguists to whom it most properly and profitably belongs (cf. O'Brien 1965:3).

A comprehensive treatment of Nepali as such has not been attempted yet. However, the author is aware that no grammar of any language is completely exhaustive. It is my hope that this descriptive grammar gives an adequate, fairly detailed outline of Nepali structure since it is based on the thorough tagmemic analysis of the Nepali text in Part Two.

1.10 Corpus. The corpus selected for the purpose of the proposed description is the present-day prestige dialect of Nepali spoken as the mother tongue by the Brahman and Ksatriya castes in Kathmandu, the capital city of Nepal, and in the hills around it. This dialect is regarded as the standard Nepali used in textbooks, newspapers, radio, TV, and administration.

In order to have a definite control over the corpus, and as a test of the validity of the grammar, one of the most famous short stories, *Nāso* 'Ward' by Guruprasad Mainali has been analyzed, and this analysis has yielded the categories described in the grammar. The function of the corpus text is:

- to provide a source to illustrate the structure of the language,
- to provide a test of the validity of the grammatical analysis,
- to provide a check that the grammar can in fact account for all the items in the text,
- to find out whether there is anything in the text which by chance was omitted in the grammatical description, and
- to provide an illustrative corpus of some length where a language-learner can observe the employment of the structures presented in the grammar.

This story *Nāso* is found in the Mainali's anthology entitled *Nāso*, and in most of the school and college textbooks of Nepali language and literature. Although the English translation which is given in Part Two was done by the author, another English translation of this story was also published by Professor Theodore Riccardi, Jr. in the *Himalayan Research Bulletin* (vol. 6, No. 8, 1988). Mainali, a Supreme Court judge, was a Brahman native speaker of standard Nepali. Thus, the corpus selected for this study is a most representative specimen of standard Nepali. Instances of the syntactic structure of Nepali taken from the *Nāso* text are cited by section, sentence and clause numbers, e.g. 3.2.1. Instances that are not taken from *Nāso* are supplied by the author of this grammar, who is also a native speaker of the same prestige dialect of Nepali. Such instances are not marked with a reference number.

In order to verify the adequacy of this description, instances of the syntactic structures of Nepali in all the studies listed in the References of this description have been used as a checklist.

1.11 Transcription. In this description, the Nepali text is presented in the phonemic transcription until the writing system is described (Chapter 4). After Chapter 4 onwards it is presented in transliteration of the written forms. This is done so since this study is based on the analysis of a written text. The system of transliteration of the Devanagari text is summarized in Figure 1.6.

Figure 1. 6 Transliteration of Devanagari used in this study

Vowels:	अ a	आ ā	इ i	ई ī	उ u	ऊ ū	ऋ ṛ	ॠ ṝ
	ऌ ḷ	ए e	ऐ ai	ओ o	औ au	ं ṃ	ँ ~	: ḥ

Consonants:	Voiceless		Voiced			
	unaspirate	aspirate	unaspirate	aspirate	nasal	
	क ka	ख kha	ग ga	घ gha	ङ ṅa	Velars
	च ca	छ cha	ज ja	झ jha	ञ ña	Palatals
	ट ṭa	ठ ṭha	ड ḍa	ढ ḍha	ण ṇa	Alveopalatals
	त ta	थ tha	द da	ध dha	न na	Dentals
	प pa	फ pha	ब ba	भ bha	म ma	Bilabials
	य ya	र ra	ल la	व va	*Antasthas*	'remaining inside'
	श śa	ष ṣa	स sa	ह ha	*Uṣmas*	'warm'
	क्ष kṣa	त्र tra	ज्ञ jña	Special consonant cluster symbols		

For further explanation of the terms *antasthas* and *uṣmas* see also the notes no. 3 and 4 under Figure 4.1.

Thus, this study employs two systems: (1) transliteration of the Devanagari text, and (2) transcription of the phonemes of Nepali. The difference between the two systems is summarized in the following columns

(1) Transliteration symbols for the Devanagari text:	(2) Transcription symbols for the phonemes in Nepali:
ā , ī , ū	/a:/, /i/, /u/
ṛ	/ri/
ś, ṣ , s	/s/
v	/b/
ṇ ñ n	/n/

The illustrations (phrases, clauses, sentences) quoted from the written text of *Nā̃so* 'Ward' follow the transliteration system, especially from Chapter 5 onwards, i.e after the writing system is described in Chapter 4.

1.12 Motivation of this description. This section, reviewing what has, or has not been done so far in terms of describing Nepali from a synchronic point of view, attempts to justify that such a description is urgent and worthwhile. Although Nepali has been used as the language of administration ever since modern Nepal's history began in 1768, the use of Nepali as a literary language was first made only by Bhanubhakta Acharya (1814-1868). Even then because of socio-political reasons the growth of Nepali as a medium of education and literature was not possible during the autocratic Rana regime (1846-1950) Although the regime did not impose any other language in Nepal, no books in Nepali were allowed to be published. Even the grammar of the language written by a native grammarian Virendrakesari Arjyal (1849-1931) was suppressed (J. Acharya 1980:103). The Rana regime was simply against the enlightenment of the people.

A comprehensive synchronic description of Nepali has never been attempted by any Nepali linguist. The proposed description of Nepali, therefore, attempts to be as comprehensive as possible and present its phonological, morphological, and syntactic structure based on the study of forms and functions from a purely descriptive point of view. And, without going into the discussion of the merits of different linguistic approaches, the study attempts to describe the structure of Nepali in the clearest possible terminology so that an average educated reader trying to learn Nepali can readily see the structural map of the language and explore its data with a reliable tool in hand. Each technical term of linguistics has, therefore, been explained when it first occurs in the following chapters.

The need for such a description can be seen in view of the growing number of the learners of Nepali both in Nepal and overseas. It is hoped that the foreign learners of Nepali (Peace Corps Volunteers, development workers, and scholars of art, music, economy, anthropology, archaeology, architecture, sociology, history, religion, and culture of Nepal) will find it helpful in learning Nepali.

The Sound System

Chapter 2
The segmental phonemes

2.0 Introduction. This chapter describes the sounds which together constitute the Nepali 'stream of speech.' That stream may be viewed as constituted by a set of functional sound segments, namely the set of Nepali (1) consonant sounds (2.1) and (2) vowel sounds (2.2).

The environments in which the set of Nepali consonants and vowels occur are called syllables. This set of Nepali segmental sounds and syllables are accompanied by other sound features, 'the suprasegmentals' which cooccur with the distinctive set of Nepali consonants and vowels arranged in syllables. The structure of Nepali syllable and the accompanying suprasegmental features are described in Chapter 3.

2.0.1 Phones, phonemes, and allophones. The study of the sound system of any language is the subject matter of the subject of linguistics called phonetics which describes and classifies the sounds, or 'phones' of that language in terms of the way they are 'articulated' or produced. Not all of the sounds that human beings can articulate occur in any given language. So the phonetics for a particular language lists, classifies, and describes only the particular sounds which actually occur in that particular language, e.g. Nepali phonetics lists, describes, and classifies only the sounds which occur in Nepali.

The sounds, or 'phones' which do occur are further organized into a smaller set or system of functionally contrasting sounds for that particular language. These functionally contrastive sounds are called the 'phonemes' of that language, e.g. the set of Nepali phonemes. These are the sounds which are capable of signalling a difference of meaning for the speakers of Nepali. In English, for example, note the initial sound in the minimally contrasting pair *pit* vs. *bit*.

'Allophones' are the phonetic variants of particular phonemes; they are the particular phones which represent an individual phoneme in specific phonetic or syllabic environments. They are usually predictable according to the sound system of a given language.

In transcription, the 'phones' and 'allophones' are enclosed within square brackets ([ ]); the phonemes are enclosed within slant lines (//).

2.0.2 Segmental vs. suprasegmental phonemes. The sets of contrasting sounds which constitute the phonemes of Nepali may be grouped into two subsets: (1) the 'segmental' phonemes of Nepali and (2) the 'suprasegmental' phonemes of Nepali.

Segmental phonemes are the set of functionally contrasting sounds which are obtained by segmentation of a stretch of Nepali speech into a set of individual articulations.

The 'suprasegmental' phonemes in contrast to the segmental phonemes of Nepali are that set of contrasting sound features that may cooccur with the set of segmental sounds in order to signal a difference in meaning. They are stress, pitch, and juncture; they are discussed in Chapter 3.

The segmental phonemes are of two types: (1) consonants and (2) vowels. The description of the segmental sounds of Nepali is, therefore, a description of the particular set of consonants and vowels which occur in Nepali.

2.0.3 Inventory of the principal consonantal and vowel sounds of Nepali. Figure 2.1 presents an inventory of the principal consonantal and vowel sounds which occur in Nepali. The sounds are classified according to their type, manner, and point of articulation. Allophones of the same phonemes are enclosed within a circle. Allophones which are distant from their phonemic counterparts are connected by lines with arrowheads. The consonant sounds are described in section 2.1, and the vowel sounds are described in section 2.2.

2.0.4 Symbols employed in the phonetic and phonemic transcription. The symbols employed in Figures 2.1, 2.2, 2.3 etc. are not exclusively those employed by the International Phonetic Association (IPA). In fact, in the interest of convenience, this description of the Nepali sound system deliberately uses a set of symbols which are readily available on a standard typewriter or computer. The transcription also uses some diacritical marks which differ from the IPA recommendations. The reasons for doing this were the same: ease, availability, and convenience.

For the definition of the terms as "aspirated", "voiceless", "voiced", "stops", "palatal", "alveopalatal", "velar" etc. see (2.1.1). The symbols employed to represent them are the following:

(1) The aspirated voiceless and voiced stops are represented by /ph th ṭh ch kh/ and /bh dh ḍh jh gh/.
(2) The alveopalatal (retroflex) voiceless, voiced and nasal stops are represented by /ṭ ṭh ḍ ḍh ṇ/.
(3) The palatal stops are represented by /c ch j jh ñ /
(4) The velar nasal is represented by the digraph /ng/ (IPA [ŋ]).
(5) The mid central vowel (schwa) is represented by /a/ (IPA [ə])
(6) The low central vowel is represented by /a:/
(7) The oral vowels are represented by /i e a a: o u/ and the nasal vowels are represented by the diacritical marks on top, e.g.

/ĩ , ẽ , ã, ã: , ũ /

Thus, a dot (.) under a consonant symbol represents an alveopalatal (retroflex) stop; the tilde (~) on top of a vowel symbol represents nasalization; an *h* following a consonant represents an aspirated consonant. Note that this transcription is at the phonemic level. Note also that the transcription system of the *Nāso* text as presented in (1.11) is slightly different, and reflects the writing system of Nepali, which does not show a one-to-one correspondence with the phonemic inventory of Nepali. See also Chapter 4 The writing system.

2.0.5 Listing of the phonemes. In this work, the so-called retroflex stops are listed as alveopalatal stops. The term 'alveopalatal' is preferred for the following reasons: (1) These stops are not retroflex to the extent they are in other Indian languages (Hindi, Marathi, Gujarati, etc.); (2) Speakers of Nepali hear a clear difference between their own pronunciation of these stops and that of the speakers of other neighboring Indian languages, i.e. these Nepali alveopalatal stops (/ṭ/, /ṭh/, /ḍ/, and /ḍh/, are more fronted than those in Hindi; the amount of retroflexion is minimal. Thus, their pronunciation by the speakers of Nepali is characterized more by 'stoppage' than retroflexion.

Again, Nepali palatals (/c/, /ch/, /j/, and /jh/) are listed as stops rather than as affricates because the amount of affrication is minimal. They are articulated with the lamina of the tongue raised against the hard palate and their point of articulation is somewhat prepalatal (slightly ahead of English /c/ and /j/) and they are articulated with far less affrication than the English /c/ and /j/.

In Figure 2.1 the nasal stops (/m/, /n/, /ng/) are listed immediately after the stops, which is in conformity with the IPA Figure of consonant sounds and the Devanagari alphabet (see Ch 4) used in writing the Nepali texts. In Nepali there are no other sounds that can be inserted between the stops and nasals.

The flap [ṟ] (which is not a standard IPA symbol for a flap sound) and the trill [r] are listed separately in the Figure 2.1 because of phonetic and phonemic reasons in Nepali. Phonetically, there is only one flap in the articulation of [ṟ], but there are several flaps (or taps) of the tongue in the articulation of [r]. The phonemic reason is that in Nepali the difference between a flap and a trill sounds is a phonemic contrast, although many Indian languages do not make such a functional distinction. In other words, a flap [ṟ] in Nepali is an allophone (i.e. predictable variant) of the voiced alveopalatal stop (/ḍ/) and the voiced aspirated alveopalatal (/ḍh/) whereas the trill /r/ is an independent (i.e. contrastive) phoneme. Contrasts for the flap and trill are given in 2.1. set #12.

2.1 Consonant sounds. Consonant sounds are defined as sounds that involve stoppage, friction or turbulence of the pulmonic air stream passing through the vocal tract.

2.1.1 Definition and classification. Nepali consonant sounds can be defined and classified in three ways: (1) according to their type, (2) according to their manner and (3) according to their point of articulation.

According to their type of articulation the Nepali consonants can be classified as belonging to one of the following seven types of sounds:

(1) 'stop', a sound articulated by the complete closure for a moment of the air stream in the oral tract with a simultaneous closure of the

nasal cavity as well; the sudden release of the air stream (that builds up behind the closure) produces the 'stop' sound, e.g. English /p/;

(2) 'nasal', a sound articulated with a closure of the air stream at a specific point of the oral cavity and with a simultaneous opening of the nasal cavity in order to allow the air stream to pass through it, e.g. English /n/;

(3) 'lateral', a sound articulated with the air stream escaping through the oral cavity along the sides of the tongue; the tip of the tongue is kept in touch with the alveolar ridge and the nasal cavity is simultaneously closed, e.g English /l/

(4) 'flap', a sound articulated with a closure of the nasal cavity and as a single rapid contact between the tip of the tongue which flaps against the alveolar ridge causing momentary stoppage of the air stream through the oral cavity producing a stop-like sound, e.g. Spanish /r/ as in /pero/ 'but';

(5) 'trill', a sound articulated similarly to a 'flap' except that the articulation results in a quick succession of multiple flaps, taps or vibration of the tip of the tongue, e.g. Spanish /rr/ as in /perro/ 'dog';

(6) 'fricative ', a sound articulated by the air stream being forced through a narrow passage at a specific point in the oral cavity with simultaneous closure of the nasal cavity; e.g. English /f/;

(7) 'glide' a sound produced when the body of the tongue moves toward or away from a prominent adjacent vowel, e.g. /y/ and /w/.

According to the manner of articulation Nepali consonants may be further classified. They may be either (1) voiced or (2) voiceless.

(1) A 'voiced' sound is the one in the articulation of which the vocal cords vibrate, e.g. English /b/;

(2) A 'voiceless' sound is the one in the articulation of which the vocal cords do not vibrate, e.g. English /p/;

Both voiced and voiceless consonants may be further subclassified as (3) aspirated or (4) unaspirated

(3) An 'aspirated' sound is a sound which is articulated with an audible (and simultaneous) burst of the pulmonic air stream, e.g. the /p/ in the English word *pot;*

(4) An 'unaspirated' sound is the one which does not involve an audible burst of the air in its articulation, e.g. the /p/ in the English word *spot.*

The third basis of classifying the Nepali consonants is the point of articulation, i.e. the points at which the closure of the air or friction takes place. They are: (1) lips, (2) the back of the upper teeth, (3) a point slightly behind the alveolar ridge and ahead of the center of the palate, (4) the center of the hard palate, (5) soft palate or velum, and (6) glottis. Thus, they are correspondingly called (1) bilabial, (2) dental, (3) alveopalatal, (4) palatal, (5) velar, and (6) glottal.

(1) A 'bilabial' sound is articulated when the upper and lower lips come together to close the air stream momentarily and suddenly release the air to produce sounds, /p/ and /b/.

(2) A 'dental' sound is articulated with the blade of the tongue coming in contact with the back side of the row of the upper front teeth, e.g. /t/.

(3) An 'alveopalatal' sound is articulated by the tip and the blade of the tongue raised to come in contact with the area behind the alveolar ridge, i.e. behind the alveolar ridge and slightly ahead of the center of the hard palate, e.g. /ṭ/.

(4) A 'palatal' sound is articulated with the central part of the tongue raised to come in touch with the hard palate, e.g. English /ch/. The differences between the English palatal affricates and the Nepali palatal stops are these: (a) there is much less affrication in the Nepali palatals; (Thus, they are perhaps more properly listed as 'stops' rather than 'affricates'); (b) they are articulated at slightly front part of the hard palate; and (c) the tongue is lax; i.e. there is not so much tension in the tongue muscles in the articulation of Nepali palatal stops as in the articulation of the English palatal affricates.

(5) A 'velar' sound is articulated with the back of the tongue raised so that it comes in contact with the soft palate to form a closure of the air stream. When the air stream is released, it yields a velar sound, e.g. /k/, /g/ etc.

(6) A 'glottal' sound is articulated by the vocal cords coming toward each other to create friction, e.g. [h], or even complete stoppage of the air stream, the glottal stop [ʔ]

Figure 2.1 Inventory of the principal contoid and vocoid sounds of Nepali. Phones which are allophones of the same phoneme are enclosed in a circle, or connected by circles.

Type	Manner of articulation		Points of articulation B	D	AP	P	V	G
Stops	vl.	unasp.	p	t	ṭ	c	k	
	vl.	asp.	ph	th	ṭh	ch	kh	
	vd.	unasp.	b	d	ḍ	j	g	
	vd.	asp.	bh	dh	ḍh	jh	gh	
Nasals	vd.		m	n	ṇ	ñ	ng	
Fricatives				s	ṣ			h
Laterals	vd.			l				
Flap	vd.				ṛ			
Trill	vd.				r			
Glides					y		w	
Vowels	High oral and nasal				i ĩ		u ũ	
	Mid oral and nasal				e ẽ	a ã	o	
	Low oral and nasal					a: ã:		

AP Alveopalatal	B Bilabial	D Dental	asp. aspirate
G Glottal	P Palatal	V Velar	unasp. unaspirated
vd. voiced	vl. voiceless	~ nasal vowel	

Note 1. In a narrow phonetic transcription, which attempts to represent the features of phonetic items in greater details, retroflexed consonants might be prefixed by a [?] as a reminder of the subglottal tension which cooccurs with the articulation of these consonants. Similarly, vowels following aspirated consonants might be suffixed with a [*] as a reminder of the breathy vowel allophones which occur in these positions.

Note 2. The digraphs /ph/, /th/, /kh/, etc. represent a single aspirated phoneme. The digraph /ng/ stands for velar nasal.

Note 3. The alveopalatal consonants are also termed 'retroflex consonants'. I prefer the term 'alveopalatal' because that is where they are articulated. Moreover, retroflex is not a point of articulation, but a manner of articulation in which the tip of the tongue curls backward to touch the alveopalatal region. Retroflexion is more perceptible in other Indo-European languages of South Asia than in Nepali.

2.1.2 Supplementary sets of minimal pairs. The following are supplementary sets of minimal pairs to support the phonemic oppositions among the segmental phonemes. The purpose of the present list is not to establish the phonemic oppositions--that was already adequately done by Bandhu et al. (1971)--but to provide supplementary data which would support the validity of their findings, and provide a resource for the phonological drills for students of Nepali.

The minimal pairs are listed in 14 sets. The Figure 2.2 provides an index which shows what oppositions are illustrated in the pairs listed in each set.

Figure 2.2 Sets of minimal pairs of Nepali consonant phonemes.

Set	Contrasts illustrated	Set	Contrasts illustrated
1	(a)#p-/#ph-	6	#p-/#t-, #ṭ-/#c-/#k-, #t-/#ṭ-, #c-/#k-
	(b)#b-/bh-	7	#ph-/#th-, #th-/ṭh, #ṭh-/ch-/kh-,
2	(a) #t-/#th-		VthV/VṭhV, -th#/ -ṭh#, #ch-/#kh-
	(b)#d-/dh-	8	#b-/#d-/#ḍ-/#j-/#g-
		9	#bh-/#dh-, #dh/#ḍh, #jh-/#gh-
3	(a) #-ṭ/-ṭh, #ṭ-/ṭh-, VṭV/VṭhV	10	#m-/#n-, -n#/-ng#,
	(b) #ḍ-/#ḍh-		VmV/VngV, VnGV/VngGV
4	(a) #c-/#ch-	11	#l-/#r-
	(b) #j-/#jh-, VjV-/VjhV	12	-r̲#/-r#
5	(a) #k-/#kh-, -k#/-kh#,	13	#s-/#h-
	(b) #g-/gh-	14	#ya:-/#wa:-

Note 1. The sign # represents the word-boundary. A hyphen (-) followed by a slash (/) represents the environment in which the items occur. For instance, the set 1 (a) #p-/#ph- means that the phonemes /p/ and /ph/ are contrasted in the environment where no other phonemic item precedes them, and where unspecified items follow them.

Set 1 Bilabials.

(a) Contrasts for voiceless bilabial stops: unaspirated vs. aspirated, e.g. /p/ vs. /ph/

/pa:lnu/ 'keep' (domestic animals)	/pha:lnu/ 'throw'
/parsi/ 'day after tomorrow'	/pharsi/ 'pumpkin'
/pul/ 'bridge'	/phul/ 'flower/egg'
/pohor/ 'last year'	/phohor/ 'dirt'
/pa:ṭo/ 'side'	/pha:ṭo/ 'estrangement'
/pal/ 'moment'	/phal/ 'fruit'

(b) Contrasts for voiced bilabial stops: unaspirated vs. aspirated, e.g. /b/ vs. /bh/

/ba:ri/ 'a dry cultivated field'	/bha: ri/ 'load'
/bal/ 'strength'	/bhal/ 'flood'

/ba:ṭo/ 'path'	/bha:ṭo/ 'a long stick'
/ba:t/ 'talk'	/bha:t/ 'cooked rice'
/boṭ/ 'tree'	/bhoṭ/ 'Tibet'
/bok/ 'carry'	/bhok/ 'hunger'
/boko/ 'male goat' (uncastrated)	/bhoko/ 'hungry'
/boli/ 'speech	/bholi/ 'tomorrow'
/bira:lo/ 'cat'	/bhira:lo/ 'steep'
/bir/ 'brave'	/bhir/ 'precipice'

Set 2 Dentals.
(a) Contrasts for voiceless dental stop: unaspirated vs. aspirated, e.g.
/t/ vs. /th/

/ta:l/ 'lake'	/tha:l/ 'plate'
/ta:p/ 'heat'	/tha:p/ 'hold'
/ta:ro/ 'star'	/tha:ro/ 'barren female animal'
/ta:knu/ 'aim at'	/tha:knu/ 'be tired'
/tok/ 'decision'	/thok/ 'stock of salable goods
/tal/ 'surface'	/thal/ 'the earth'
/sa:t/ 'seven'	/sa:th/ 'company'

(b) Contrasts for voiced dental stops: unaspirated vs. aspirated, e.g.
/d/ vs. /dh/

/da:n/ 'donation'	/dha:n/ 'rice (unhusked)'
/da:i/ 'elder brother'	/dha:i/ 'nurse, midwife'
/da:m/ 'money'	/dha:m/ 'a religious shrine'

Set 3 Alveopalatals.
(a) Contrasts for voiceless alveopalatals: unaspirated vs. aspirated, e.g.
/ṭ/ vs. /ṭh/

/ka:ṭ/ 'cut (imp.)'	/ka:ṭh/ 'wood'
/ṭok/ 'bite (imp.)'	/ṭhok/ 'hit (imp.)'
/ba:ṭo/ 'path'	/ba:ṭho/ 'clever'
/la:ṭo/ 'dumb'	/la:ṭho/ 'large stick'
/ṭa:ṭo/ 'blot'	/ṭa:ṭho/ 'smart'

(b) Contrasts for voiced alveopalatal stops: unaspirated vs. aspirated, e.g.
/ḍ/ vs. /ḍh/

/ḍoka:/ 'bamboo baskets'	/ḍhoka:/ 'door'
/ḍa:knu/ 'invite'	/ḍha:knu/ 'cover (v.)'
/ḍa:li/ 'small basket, small branch'	/ḍha:li/ '(she) felled, knocked'

Set 4 Palatals.
(a) Contrasts for voiceless palatal stops: unaspirated vs. aspirated, e.g. /c/ vs. /ch/

/cori/ 'theft'	/chori/ 'daughter'
/curi/ 'bangle'	/churi/ 'dagger'
/ca:k/ 'buttock'	/cha:k/ 'meal'
/ca:la:/ 'movement'	/cha:la:/ 'leather, hide, skin'
/cola:/ 'life cycle'	/chola:/ '(he) will touch'
/cop/ 'gum, resin, paste'	/chop/ 'cover (imp.)'

(b) Contrasts for voiced palatals: unaspirated vs. aspirated, e.g. /j/ vs. /jh/

/jel/ 'jail'	/jhel/ 'foul play'
/jutta:/ 'shoes'	/jhutta:/ 'bunches'
/ja:ri/ 'alimony'	/jha:ri/ 'pitcher'
/joḍi/ 'couple'	/jhoḍi/ 'easily losing temper (adj.)'
/juṭho/ 'contaminated'	/jhuṭho/ 'false'
/ba:je/ 'grandfather'	/ba:jhe/ '(they) quarreled'

Set 5 Velars.
(a) Contrasts for voiceless velar stops: unaspirated vs. aspirated, e.g. /k/ vs. /kh/

/ka:ṭ/ 'cut (imp.)'	/kha:ṭ/ 'bed frame'
/ka:m/ 'work, job'	/kha:m/ 'envelop'
/kera:/ 'banana'	/khera:/ 'waste'
/koṭ/ 'coat'	/khoṭ/ 'blame'
/kor/ 'leprosy'	/khor/ 'trap, prison'
/ka:lo/ 'black'	/kha:lo/ 'skin' (derogatory)
/kol/ 'oil pressing instrument'	/khol/ 'cover'
/ka:uli/ 'cauliflower'	/kha:uli/ '((you) (fem.)) shall eat'
/kinna/ 'buy (infinitive)'	/khinna/ 'sad'
/kaṭa:yo/ '(he) caused to cut'	/khaṭa:yo/ '(he) appointed'
/kasyo/ '(he) tightened'	/khasyo/ '(it, he) dropped'
/kar/ 'tax'	/khar/ 'a grass used in making roof'
/ca:k/ 'buttock'	/ca:kh/ 'interest'

(b) Contrasts for voiced velar stops: unaspirated vs. aspirated, e.g. /g/ vs. /gh/

/ga:m/ 'village'	/gha:m/ 'sun'
/goḍa:/ 'legs'	/ghoḍa:/ 'horse'
/gar/ 'do (imp.)'	/ghar/ 'house'
/ga:u/ 'sing'	/gha:u/ 'wound'

Set 6. Contrasts for voiceless unaspirated stops, e.g.
/p/, /t/, /ṭ/ /c/, and /k/

/pa:t/ 'leaf'	/ta:t/ 'warm up (imp.)'
/ṭa:ṭ/ 'bankrupt'	/ca:ṭ/ 'lick (imp.)'
/ka:ṭ/ 'cut (imp.)'	

/pa:l/ 'tent'	/ta:l/ 'lake'
/ṭa:l/ 'put a patch (imp.)'	/ca:l/ 'move (n.)'
/ka:l/ 'death, time'	

Set 7. Contrasts for voiceless aspirated stops, e.g.
/ph/, /th/, /ṭh/, /ch/ and /kh/

/pha:l/ 'throw (imp.)'	/tha:l/ 'plate'
/thok/ 'stock of salable goods'	/ṭhok/ 'strike (imp.)'
/tha:n/ 'roll of cloth'	/ṭha:n/ 'take (it) in mind (imp.)'
/pha:m/ 'wooden jug'	/tha:m/ 'pillar'
/ṭha:m/ 'place, room'	/cha:m/ 'feel (imp.)'
/kha:m/ 'envelop'	

/sa:thi/ 'friend'	/sa:ṭhi/ 'sixty'
/jetha:/ 'estate'	/jeṭha:/ 'oldest'
/math/ 'churn (imp.)'	/maṭh/ 'abbey'
/pa:thi/ 'a measure (2.5 kg.)'	/pa:ṭhi/ 'young female goat'
/chal/ 'conspiracy'	/khal/ 'mortar'
/chola:/ '(it, he) will touch'	/khola:/ 'river'

Set 8. Contrasts for voiced unaspirated stops, e.g.
/b/, /d, /ḍ/, /j/ and /g/.

/bar/ 'bunyan tree'	/dar/ 'rate'
/dar/ 'rate'	/ḍar/ 'fear'
/da:m/ 'price'	/ḍa:m/ 'branded scar'
/das/ 'ten'	/ḍas/ 'sting (imp.)'
/dil/ 'heart, mind'	/ḍil/ 'edge of a terrace'
/jara:/ 'roots'	/gara:/ 'terraces'
/ja:la:/ '(he) will go'	/ga:la:/ 'cheeks'
/joḍa:/ 'pair'	/goḍa:/ 'legs'

Set 9. Contrasts for voiced aspirated stops, e.g.
/bh/, /dh/, /ḍh/, /jh/ and /gh/

/bha:g/ 'share, run away (imp.)'	/dha:g/ 'boasting'
/dhoka:/ 'deception'	/ḍhoka:/ 'door'

/dhoi/ '(she) washed'	/ḍhoi/ 'female elephant'
/dhak/ 'nervousness'	/ḍhak/ 'a measure of weight'
/dhussa:/ 'thick rough blanket'	/ḍhussa:/ 'blow of fist'
/dher/ 'many'	/ḍher/ 'pile'
/dha:p/ 'patting on the shoulder (n.)'	/ḍha:p/ 'swamp'
/jhar/ 'come down'	/ghar/ 'house/home'
/jhoḍi/ 'easily losing temper'	/ghoḍi/ 'mare'

Set 10. Contrasts for nasals, e.g.
/m/, /n/ /ng/

/mel/ 'rapport'	/nel/ 'shackles'
/pin/ 'grind (imp.)'	/ping/ 'swing'
/na:mlo/ 'rope to carry loads'	/na:nglo/ 'winnowing tray'

Set 11. Contrasts for lateral and trill, e.g.
/l/ and /r/

/luga:/ 'clothes'	/ruga:/ 'cold'
/la:m/ 'line'	/ra:m/ 'a proper name'
/loṭi/ 'tumbler'	/roṭi/ 'bread'

Set 12. Contrasts for flap and trill, e.g.
/r̲/ and /r/.

/ma:r̲/ 'rice broth'	/ma:r/ 'kill (imp.)'
/par̲/ 'read' (imp.)'	/par/ 'fall' (imp.)

Note that the flap [r̲] in Nepali is an allophone of /ḍ/. Thus, the real contrast here is between the /ḍ/ (which, in postvocalic position is realized as the flap [r̲]) and the trill /r/.

Set 13. Contrasts for fricatives, e.g.
/s/ and /h/

/sa:t/ 'seven'	/ha:t/ 'hand'
/sola:/ 'shaft'	/hola:/ 'will be'

Set 14. Contrasts for glides, e.g.
/y/ and /w/

/ya:hã:/ 'here'	/wa:hã:/ 'there'

2.1.3 Variants of Nepali consonant phonemes. The norm of the form of the Nepali consonant phoneme is established by its occurrence in the word-initial position because it shows little allophonic variation in this position. However, in the word-medial and word-final positions many Nepali consonant phonemes show systematic allophonic variants. These changes are described under the following subheadings:

2.1.3.1 Positional variants
2.1.3.2 Deletion of aspiration
2.1.3.3 Deletion of voicing
2.2.3.4 Nasalization
2.1.3.5 Minor variations

2.1.3.1 Positional variants. Figure 2.3 lists the principal positional variants of the Nepali consonant phonemes. Since all of the consonant phonemes occur in word-initial position, that variant is taken as the 'norm' or cover symbol.

Figure 2.3 Principal positional variants of the Nepali consonant phonemes.

Initial	Medial			Final
#_V	/V_V/	/V_C/	/VC_V/	/V_#/
/ph/	[ph]	[ph]	[ph]	[ph]
/b/	[b]	[b]	[b]	[b]
/d/	[d]	[d]	[d]	[d]
/ḍ/	[r̲]	[r̲]	[r̲]	[r̲]
/ch/	[h]	...	...	...
/kh/	[x]	[x]	...	...
/r/	...	[r]	...	...

Notes:
Word boundary _ environment [V] vowel
[C] consonant [r̲] flap [x] velar fricative
[h] voiceless glottal fricative
... nonoccurrence of an allophone of the phoneme

2.1.3.2 Deletion of aspiration. In a less careful and more normal speech the voiced aspirated stops of Nepali generally lose aspiration in word-medial and word-final positions. This phenomenon can be summarized in the Figure 2.3

Figure 2.4 Deletion of aspiration. (cf. Bandhu et al. (1971: 26)

Phonemes	Replacement	Environment
/h/	Ø	/V_C/
/bh/	/b/	/V_V, /V_C/, /V_#/
/dh/	/d/	/V_V, /V_C/, /V_#/
/ṭh/	/ṭ/	# _ Voiceless stops
/ḍh/	/ṛ/	/V_V/, /V_C/, /V_#/
/jh/	/j/	/V_V/, /V_C/, /V_#/
/gh/	/g/	/V_V/, /V_C/, /V_#/

2.1.3.3 Deletion of voicing. The voiced bilabial stop /b/ and the voiced velar stop /g/ tend to be devoiced at the word final position.

2.1.3.4 Nasalization. The voiced unaspirated stops /b/, /d/, /g/ are replaced by /m/, /n/, /ng/ respectively, in postvocalic position before a nasal vowel. This phenomenon is supposedly distinct from the one whereby a syllable-final nasal nasalizes the preceding vowel.

2.1.3.5 Minor variations. There are other minor phonetic variations which occur in Nepali. They are termed 'minor variations' because they are quite obvious, quite ordinary, and quite predictable. Technically they can be termed as assimilation which refers to the influence exercised by one sound segment upon the articulation of another, so that the sounds become more alike, or identical. The following six minor variations are the most notable:

(1) Vowels following aspirated stops. Vowels following aspirated consonants tend to be quite 'breathy' (articulated with a great deal of air passing through the vocal tract). This is most noticeable in instances of vowels following /kh/, e.g. /khip/ 'safety pin', /khel/ 'play', /khola:/ 'river'. The vowels which occur in such positions are given a somewhat 'breathy' articulation, as one might expect.

(2) Fronting of velar stops before /i/ and /e/. The velar stops, i.e. /k/, /kh/, /g/, /gh/ are slightly fronted before the front vowels /i/ and /e/, e.g. /killa:/ 'fort', /khil/ 'sting', /khel/ 'play', /gilo/ 'soft', /ghera/ 'circle'.

(3) Variants of /l/. Although very slightly backed variants of /l/ occur before the back vowels /u/ and /o/, the velarized or so-called "dark" /l/ does not occur. All the variants of the Nepali lateral phoneme are nonvelarized. Contrast the syllable initial /l/ in English *live* ("light") vs. syllable final /l/ in English *ball* ("dark").

(4) Backing of /s/ before alveopalatal stops. The phoneme /s/ shows alveopalatal variants in medial consonant clusters before alveopalatal stops, e.g. /kha:ṣṭo/ 'shawl', /puṣṭa/ 'plump' etc.

(5) Alveopalatal and palatal variants of /n/. Before alveopalatal and palatal consonants the dental /n/ shows alveopalatal and palatal variants, e.g.

[aṇḍa:] 'eggs'
[raṇḍa:] 'plane (carpenter's tool)'
[ṭaṇṭa:] 'unnecessary trouble'
[pañja:] 'gloves'
[sañco] 'in good health'

but, it remains the same elsewhere:

[anda:j] 'guess'
[anta] 'elsewhere'
[santa:n] 'children'.

(6) The phonemic status of /ng/. Given the assimilation described in (5), one is tempted to question the phonemic status of /ng/. The fact is that in Nepali this phoneme has a very low functional load (use in making a linguistic contrast). In the word-initial position it occurs only in some onomatopoeic words, e.g. /nga:r nga:r/ 'sound of cats quarrelling'.

However, /ng/ does show phonemic contrast with both /m/ and /n/ in the word-final positions, such as:

/m/ vs. /ng/

/dam/ 'breath, asthma'	/dang/ 'happily surprised'
/sim/ 'swamp'	/sing/ 'horn'
/ra:m/ 'Ram (personal name)'	/ra:ng/ 'solder (a metal welding substance)'

/n/ vs. /ng/

/pin/ 'grind (imp.)'	/ping/ 'ferris wheel'
/ma:n/ 'obey (imp.)'	/ma:ng/ 'ask for (imp.)'

2.1.4. Distribution of Nepali consonants. This section describes the distribution of Nepali consonants by giving examples in Sets 15-19. Figure 2.5 lists the sets.

Figure 2.5 Distribution of Nepali consonants.

Set	Environment illustrated
15	/#_V/
16	/V_#/
17	/V_V/
18	/V_CV/
19	/VC_V/

Set 15. Consonants in the environment /#_V/:

/p/	/pa:lnu/ 'keep'	/ph/	/pha:lnu/ 'throw'
/b/	/ba:t/ 'talk'	/bh/	/bha:t/ 'cooked rice'
/t/	/ta:l/ 'lake'	/th/	/tha:l/ 'plate'
/d/	/da:n/ 'donation'	/dh/	/dha:n/ 'brown rice'
/ṭ/	/ṭok/ 'bite (imp.)'	/ṭh/	/ṭhok/ 'hit (imp.)'
/ḍ/	/ḍoka:/ 'bamboo baskets'	/ḍh/	/ḍhoka:/ 'door'
/c/	/cori/ 'theft'	/ch/	/chori/ 'daughter'
/j/	/jutta:/ 'shoes'	/jh/	/jhutta:/ 'bunches'
/k/	/ka:m/ 'work,job'	/kh/	/kha:m/ 'envelop'
/g/	/ga:m/ 'village'	/gh/	/gha:m/ 'sun'
/m/	/ma:la:/ 'garland'	/n/	/na:m/ 'name'
/ng/	/nga:r nga:r/ 'imitation of cats' quarrel'		
/s/	/sa:t/ 'seven'	/h/	/halo/ 'a plow'
/l/	/la:m/ 'row, line'	/r/	/ra:to/ 'red'
/y/	/ya:m/ 'season'	/w/	/wa:ri/ 'on the speaker's side of a river, or road'

Set 16. Consonants in the environment /V_#/:

/p	/ã:p/ 'mango'	/ph/	/sa:ph/ 'clean'
/b/	/sab/ 'all'	/bh/	/lobh/ 'greed'
/t/	/pa:t/ 'leaf'	/th/	/sa:th/ 'company'
/d/	/khed/ 'chase (imp.)'	/dh/	/bã:dh/ 'barrage'
ṭ/	/ka:ṭ/ 'cut (imp.)'	/ṭh/	/a:ṭh/ 'eight'
/ḍ/	/ga:ḍ/ 'bury (imp.)'	/ḍh/	/ba:ḍh/ 'flood'
/c/	/sã:c/ 'save (imp.)'	/ch/	/kach/ 'groin'
/j/	/ka:j/ 'deputation'	/jh/	/ba:jh/ 'quarrel'
/k/	/ca:k/ 'buttock'	/kh/	/ca:kh/ 'taste'
/g/	/la:g/ 'stick'	/gh/	/ba:gh/ 'tiger'
/m/	/na:m/ 'name'	/n/	/ka:n/ 'ear'
/ng/	/sing/ 'horn'	/s/	/sa:s/ 'breath
/l/	/pha:l/ 'throw (imp.)'	/r/	/ba:r/ 'barrier'
/h/	...	/y/	...
/w/	...		

Set 17.Consonants in the environment /V_V/:

/p/	/ṭa:pi/ 'liar'	/ph/	/ma:phi/ 'amnesty'
/b/	/sabai/ 'all'	/bh/	/sobha:/ 'a proper name'
/t/	/ta:to/ 'hot'	/th/	/sa:thi/ 'friend'
/d/	/madat/ 'help'	/dh/	/ã:dhi/ 'storm'
/ṭ/	/pa:ṭi/ 'rest house'	/ṭh/	/pa:ṭhi/ 'young female goat'
/ḍ/	/ja:ḍo/ 'cold'	/ḍh/	/buḍho/ 'old'
/c/	/sã:co/ 'true, key'	/ch/	/sa:chi/ 'witness'
/j/	/a:ja/ 'today'	/jh/	/bã:jho/ 'barren'
/k/	/ka:ki/ 'aunt'	/kh/	/ka:khi/ 'armpit'
/g/	/bagar/ 'river bed'	/gh/	/lagha:r/ 'chase (imp.)'
/m/	/sama:/ 'hold (imp)'	/n/	/suna:r/ 'goldsmith'
/ng/	/sanga/ 'with'	/s/	/basa/ 'sit down'
/h/	/mohi/ 'tenant on land'	/l/	/malam/ 'ointment'
/y/	/a:yo/ '(he) came'	/w/	/kuwa:/ 'well'

Set 18. Consonants in the environment /V_CV/:

/p/	/apṭhero/ 'difficult'	/ph/	/a:phno/ 'one's own'
/b/	/sabda/ 'word, sound'	/bh/	/ka:bhre/ 'Kabhre (a district)'
/t/	/pa:tro/ 'calender'	/th/	/na:thro/ 'joining string'
/d/	/gaddi/ 'throne'	/dh/	/sodhla:/ '(he) will ask'
/ṭ/	/ka:ṭla:/ '(he) will cut'	/ṭh/	/uṭhla:/ '(he) will rise'
/ḍ/	/laḍnu/ 'fall/fight'	/ḍh/	/baḍhnu/ 'grow'
/c/	/sã:cnu/ 'save'	/ch/	/pa:chnu/ 'lacerate'
/j/	/bajnu/ 'ring (v.)'	/jh/	/ba:jhnu/ 'quarrel (v.)'
/k/	/ba:klo/ 'thick'	/kh/	/ba:khro/ 'goat'
/g/	/ga:gro/ 'pitcher'	/gh/	/tighro/ 'thigh'
/m/	/ra:mro/ 'good'	/n/	/suntala:/ 'tangerine'
/ng/	/na:nglo/ 'winnowing tray'	/s/	/basca/ '(he) lives'
/h/	... ...	/l/	/pa:lcha/ '(he) keeps'
/r/	/garcha/ '(he) does'		
/y/	... ...		
/w/	... ...		

Set 19. Occurrence of consonants in the environment /VC_V/:

/p/	/latpate/ 'clumsy'	/ph/	/chalphal/ 'discussion'
/b/	/subba:/ 'clerk'	/bh/	/garbhe/ 'posthumous (child)'
/t/	/anta/ 'elsewhere'	/th/	/hunthyo/ 'used to be'
/d/	/sabda/ 'word, sound'	/dh/	/bandhan/ 'bondage'
/ṭ/	/chaṭṭu/ 'sly'	/ṭh/	/baṭhṭha:/ 'overly clever'
/ḍ/	/jhanḍa:/ 'flag'	/ḍh/	/okhalḍhungga:/ 'a place name'

/c/	/sacca:/ 'true'	/ch/	/pucchar/ 'tail'
/j/	/darja:/ 'rank'	/jh/	/ramjham/ 'glamour'
/k/	/sarka:r/ 'government'	/kh/	/carkha:/ 'spinning wheel'
/g/	/cangga:/ 'kite'	/gh/	/nirgha:t/ 'severely'
/m/	/samma/ 'until, plain'	/n/	/sutnu/ 'sleep'
/ng/	/charlangga/ 'clearly'	/s/	/ca:ksi/ 'a citrus fruit'
/h/	...	/l/	/halla:/ 'noise'
/r/	/khasro/ 'rough'	/y/	/ma:ryo/ '(someone) killed'
/w/	...		

2.2 Vowel sounds. This section describes the Nepali vowel phonemes and their variants.

2.2.1 Definition and classification. Vowel sounds are those sounds in the articulation of which there is no stoppage, friction, or turbulence of the air stream passing through the vocal tract. Since there is no stoppage, friction, or turbulence of air in the articulation of the vowel sounds, they are defined and classified in terms of:

(1) the height to which the body of the tongue is raised in the mouth (High, Mid, Low),

(2) whether the body of the tongue is fronted or retracted in the mouth (Front, Center, Back),

(3) whether with the velum raised the air is passing through only the oral cavity (oral vowels) or whether with the velum lowered the air is simultaneously passing through the nasal cavity (nasal vowels).

Thus, the Nepali vowels can be distinguished as high, mid, or low in tongue-height and front, center, or back in terms of tongue fronting or tongue retraction. Moreover in all of these dimensions they may be divided into two sets with the further contrast of oral vowels vs. nasal vowels. Figure 2.6 displays the vowel phonemes of Nepali.

Figure 2.6 The oral and nasal vowel phonemes of Nepali.

	Front	Central	Back
High	/i/ /ĩ/		/u/ /ũ/
Mid	/e/ /ẽ/	/a/ /ã/	/o/
Low		/a:/ /ã:/	

Note 1. The central vowels are listed as they are in order to indicate that the mid-central oral and nasal vowels /a/ and /ã/ at times (when in stressed position) show lower mid back allophones and the low central vowel /a:/ and /ã:/ at times (when preceded by the palatal stops) show some low front allophones. Impressionistically,

the heaviest functional load seems to be carried by the low central nasal vowel /ã:/ and more minimal pairs are available for this oral/nasal opposition. In contrast, the high nasal vowels /ĩ/ and /ũ/ manifest the least functional load.

Note 2. Note also the fact that there is no oral vs. nasal contrast for /o/.

Note 3. Because of heavy lexical borrowing from Sanskrit, which Nepali speakers consider their 'classical language', the traditional Nepali writing system preserves the orthographic signs for both short and long vowels even though vowel length is not phonemic in Nepali. This, however, does not mean that at the phonetic level Nepali does not have phonetically long vs. short vowels. For example, stressed vowels are phonetically longer than unstressed vowels, and nasal vowels tend to be longer than oral vowels. Moreover, /e/ /a:/ and /o/ are phonetically longer than /i/ /a/ and /u/. This last point is of interest in the description of 'heavy' vs. 'light' syllables and in predicting the position of word stress; see 3.2-3.5).

2.2.2 Supplementary sets of minimal pairs. This section lists supplementary sets of minimal pairs for the Nepali vowel phonemes.

Set 20. Oral vowels: /i/, /e/, /a/, /a:/, /o/, /u/

/khip/ 'safety pin'
/khep/ 'trip'
/khap/ 'tolerate,bear the pain (imp.)'
/kha:p/ 'overlap (imp.)'
/khop/ 'vaccination'
/khup/ 'very'

Set 21. One more set of minimal pairs for the same oral vowels

/mil/ 'agree (imp.)'
/mel/ 'agreement'
/mal/ 'fertilizer, manure'
/ma:l/ 'goods'
/mol/ 'price'
/mul/ 'source, main, chief'

Set 22. Oral vs. nasal vowels: /i/ vs. /ĩ/, /e/ vs. /ẽ/, /a/ vs. /ã/, /a:/ vs. /ã:/, /u/ vs. /ũ/

/uhi/ 'same'	/uhĩ/ 'at the same place'
/pa:e/ 'they received	/pa:ẽ/ 'I received'
/ta/ 'then'	/tã/ 'you, thou'
/ka:ṭh/ 'wood'	/kã:ṭh/ 'suburbs'

2.2.3 Variants of Nepali vowel phonemes. In general it may be said that the allophonic distribution of the Nepali vowel phonemes is relatively simple. The variants which do occur can be quite easily described in a few general statements.

(1) Vowel allophones following aspirated consonants tend to be 'breathy' or more aspirated. This is especially true after /kh/.

(2) Stressed vowels tend to show slightly longer allophones than unstressed vowels.

(3) The vowels /i/ /a/ and /u/ tend to be phonetically shorter than /e/ /a:/ and /o/.

(4) Stressed /a:/ tends to show both longer and most open allophones. Moreover, this vowel also shows slightly fronted allophones before the palatal stops.

(5) The glides (nonsyllabic) /i/ and /u/ which occur as pre-peak and post-peak satellites are transcribed as /y/ and /w/. They tend to show slightly more characteristically contoid allophones in pre-peak position and more characteristically vocalic allophones in post-peak position.

2.3 The pronunciation of orthographic word initial consonant clusters. Because of the heavy borrowing of vocabulary from Sanskrit, Nepali orthography, i.e. the Devanagari alphabet, does use CC clusters in the word-initial position in writing although a CC cluster is not allowed in the syllable structure of Nepali (see 3.2-3.4) .

Educated speakers of Nepali, whose pronunciation can be called "received pronunciation" may be able to pronounce the initial CC clusters in the same way as they are spelled. However, that goes against the grain of Nepali phonology. Majority of the speakers of Nepali pronounce the orthographic initial CC clusters according to the norms of the syllable structure of their language, which leads to the phonological phenomena such as **epenthesis, metathesis, deletion**, and **replacement**.

Epenthesis (insertion of a vowel sound between two consonants)

Orthographic transcription:	Phonemic transcription:
śrāpa	/sara:p/ 'curse' (n.)
trāsa	/tara:s/ 'fear'
prāṇa	/para:n/ 'life'
kṛyā	/kiriya:/ 'post-obital rites'

Metathesis (transposition of the vowel sound between the two consonants)

Orthographic transcription:	Phonemic transcription:
pramāṇa	/parma:n/ 'evidence'
śraddhā	/sardha:/ 'respect`
mṛga	/mirga/ 'deer'

Deletion (dropping off of one of the sounds--consonant sounds in this case):

Orthographic transcription	Phonemic transcription
spasṭa	/pasṭa/ 'clear'
stotra	/totra/ 'hymn'
sthāpanā	/tha:pana:/ 'founding'
grāma	/ga:m/ 'village'

Replacement (changing the nonexistent sound cluster into one that is totally different):

Orthographic transcription:	Phonemic transcription:
deviramaṇa	/debiraman/ 'a proper name'
kṣatriya	/chetri/ 'a caste name'
kṣaṇa	/chin/ 'moment'
kṣetra	/khet/ 'field'
śrāvaṇa	/sa:un/ 'a Nepali month' (July-Aug.)
jñāna	/gya:n/ 'knowledge'

2.4 The pronunciation of long consonants vs. geminates. Like many other Indian languages, Nepali has both long consonants and geminates. Though some phoneticians have referred to these consonants by only one term (i.e. either 'long consonants' or 'geminates'), it appears to be more logical to have both the terms as we can reasonably distinguish long consonants from geminates, at least in Nepali. For instance, the fricative, lateral, trill and nasals can be called long consonants whereas the stops can be termed geminates.

Long consonants are those in whose articulation the air passes continuously through the oral or nasal cavity. In this sense, they can be called continuants, although the "distinctive feature" phoneticians such as Chomsky and Halle do not call nasals continuants because the air does not pass through the oral cavity, but through the nasal cavity. However, it cannot be denied that the air does continuously pass through the nasal cavity just as it does in case of the nonnasal continuants,-- enough reason for us to call them continuants for our purpose.

Thus, it seems that the continuants can be subclassified as oral continuants and nasal continuants. We may also term all the continuants as long consonants as their articulation can be lengthened.

Geminates comprise those stops in whose articulation the tongue is held longer at a specific point where a given consonant is articulated. However, no matter how long the tongue is held, in its position, the articulation is not complete until it is released from the point where it is held. Thus, in the case of the geminates the hearer is uncertain what sound is going to be articulated; whereas in case of the long consonants the hearer hears what consonants are being lengthened.

In the case of geminates, the passing of the air cannot be lengthened as in case of long consonants; what can be lengthened is the stoppage or the closure of the passage before the consonant is articulated. When the continuants (e.g. /s/, /f/) are lengthened, we know what is being lengthened, because their actual articulation is lengthened; but in case of the stops, since the prearticulatory stoppage is held longer, we cannot know (until the stoppage is released) what stop sound is being articulated. Thus, geminates can be defined as an intermittant sequence of identical stops, but because of the syllable division between the two segments "a geminate cannot be regarded as simply a 'long' consonant" (Crystal, 1984: 158). This distinction leads us to group the long consonants and the geminates separately in Nepali.

The following are the Nepali long consonants:
/m/, /n/, /ng/, /l/, /r/ /s/

The following are examples of their occurrence:

/m/	/samma/ 'very plain (land)'
/n/	/ranna/ 'manner of getting heated'
/ng/	/ṭhingnga/ 'manner of standing straight'
/l/	/salla/ 'manner of flowing easily'
/r/	/sarra/ 'manner of blowing easily'
/s/	/wha:ssa/ 'manner of smelling bad'

The following are the Nepali geminates:
/p/, /b/, /t/, /d/, /ṭ/, /ḍ/ /c/, /j/, /k/, /g/

The following are examples of the occurrence of geminates. As defined, the geminates are a sequence of identical adjacent segments of a sound in a single morpheme. The syllable boundary is marked between the geminates.

Examples of the occurence of geminates (syllables are divided one from the other by a period (.):

/p/	/sap.pai/ 'all'
/b/	/dhab.ba:/ 'blot'
/t/	/pat.ti/ 'blade'
/d/	/rad.di/ 'useless'
/ṭ/	/saṭ.ṭ a:/ 'exchange'
/ḍ/	/aḍ.ḍa:/ 'office'
/c/	/sac.ca:/ 'truthful'
/j/	/saj.ja:/ 'decoration'
/k/	/pak.ka:/ 'certainly'
/g/	/ag.ga:/ 'one in the front'

2.4.1 Gemination as a result of assimilation. There are frequent instances of gemination in Nepali because of the assimilatory processes that take place within a morpheme (minimal grammatical unit) and across the morpheme boundaries. In this section, for the sake of completeness, gemination across the morpheme boundaries is mentioned. It is generally believed that the gemination takes place only within "a single morpheme". However, according to Acharya (1974: 182-183), the following instances of gemination across morpheme boundaries deserve consideration. In the following examples a period (.) marks syllable boundaries; a space marks the morpheme boundaries.

/bha:b. bha.na/ 'explain the meaning'
/ã:p. pa:.kyo/ 'the mango riped'
/dud. dew/ 'give milk'
/ha:t. ta:.to cha/ 'the hand is hot'
/ḍhoḍ. ḍa.ḍyo/ 'the corn stalk burned'
/kha:ṭ. ṭe.ḍo cha/ 'the cot is crooked'
/ra:j. ja:n.cha/ 'Raj goes'
/na:c. chi.na/ 'try to recognize the dance'
/jug. ga.e/ 'ages passed by'
/ka.ti.thok. kha:.ne/ 'how many things shall we eat?'
/na:k. ka.nya:.yo/ '(he) picked (his) nose'

There are also instances of gemination after an assimilatory process takes places. Consider the following:

/lop. bha.yo/ => /lob. bha.yo/ '(it) disappeared'
/da:p. ba.na:u/ => /da:b bana:u/ 'make a sheath (imp.)'
/ha:t. dho/ => /ha:d. dho/ 'wash (your) hands'
/bhat. de/ => /bha:d. de/ 'give rice' (imp.)
/kha:ṭ. ḍha.la:.yo/ => /kha:ḍ ḍha.la:.yo/ '(he) knocked the cot'
/pec.jha.ryo/ => /pej.jha.ryo/ 'the screw fell'
/pã:c. ja.na:/ => / pã:j ja.na:/ 'five persons'
/ek. gha.ṭa:u/ => /eg. gha.ṭa:u/ 'subtract one'
/na:k. ga.yo/ => /na:g. ga.yo/ 'the honor was lost'

2.4.2 Sandhi without gemination. Sandhi is a term first used by Sanskrit grammarians to describe the phonological phenomena which occur at adjoining borders when two items are juxtaposed. Because of the assimilatory process, certain consonants lose some of their features such as voicing, as they are assimilated by the adjacent phonemes. This phenomenon may not result in gemination, but it does result in assimilation, e.g.

/buj.pa.ca:.yo/=>/buc.pa.ca:.yo/ '(he) pretended ignorance'.

After this description of the segmental phonemes of Nepali, Chapter 3 describes the suprasegmental phonemes of Nepali.

Chapter 3.
Suprasegmentals in Nepali

3.0 Introduction. This chapter describes the suprasegmental features which are those phonological features that cooccur with the phonological segments and may characterize elements larger than the segmental phonemes of a language, e.g. syllables, phonological phrases, and longer utterances. The suprasegmental features of those elements are: stress, defined as the force used in producing a syllable (3.5), pitch, defined as auditory sensation in terms of which a sound may be ordered on a scale from 'low' to 'high' (3.6), juncture, defined as phonetic boundary features which may demarcate grammatical units such as morpheme, word, or clause (3.7), rhythm, defined as perceived regularity of prominent units in speech (3.8), pause, defined as silence marking the grammatical boundaries in the stream of speech (3.9) and intonation, defined as a distinctive use of patterns of pitch, or melody (3.10).

3.1 Inventory of Nepali segmental phonemes. The suprasegmental features cooccur with the segmental phonemes of Nepali presented in Figure 3.1.

Figure 3.1 Inventory of Nepali segmental phonemes

Type	Manner of articulation		Points of articulation B	D	AP	P	V	G
Stops	vl.	unasp.	p	t	ṭ	c	k	
	vl.	asp.	ph	th	ṭh	ch	kh	
	vd.	unasp.	b	d	ḍ	j	g	
	vd.	asp.	bh	dh	ḍh	jh	gh	
Nasals	vd.		m	n			ng	
Fricatives				s				h
Laterals	vd.			l				
Trill	vd.				r			
Glides					y		w	
Vowels	High oral and nasal				i ĩ		u ũ	
	Mid oral and nasal				e ẽ	a ã	o	
	Low oral and nasal					a: ã:		

AP Alveopalatal B Bilabial D Dental G Glottal P Palatal
V Velar asp. aspirated vd. voiced ~ nasal vowel
unasp. aspirated vl. voiceless

3.2 Syllable and syllable structure in Nepali. The structure of Nepali syllables is described in this section as a background to the description of the suprasegmental features (stress, pitch, juncture, rhythm, pause, and intonation). Syllable has been defined in many ways: according to the pulse theory, or prominence theory. According to the prominence theory some sounds are intrinsically more sonorous than others, and that each peak of sonority corresponds to the center of a syllable. These peaks are best illustrated by vowels, which have the greater carrying-power (Crystal 1980:342).

Nepali syllables are of the syllabic peak type. So, Nepali syllables are defined on the basis of syllabic peak. The peak of the Nepali syllable is simple: a syllable with a simple peak consists of a single vowel (V). A syllable with a simple vowel (V) may be accompanied by a pre-peak or a post peak satellite which consists of a glide (G) either palatal /y/ or velar /w/. (Glides are "transitional sounds" in the articulation of which "the vocal organs move towards or away from an articulation" (Crystal 1980:162)). The structure of the Nepali syllable is illustrated by the display in Figure 3.2.

Figure 3.2. The structure of Nepali syllable.

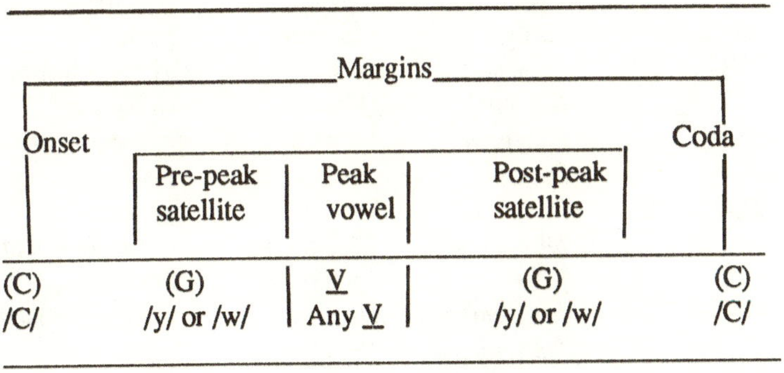
Margins
Onset
Coda
Pre-peak satellite
Peak vowel
Post-peak satellite
(C) /C/
(G) /y/ or /w/
V Any V
(G) /y/ or /w/
(C) /C/

The same information can be conveyed more simply by the following formula (the parentheses indicating which items are optional, and the vowel V with the underscore indicating the element that constitutes the peak of the syllable):

Syllable peak = (C)(G)V(G)(C)

Examples of Nepali syllable structure:

V	/u/	'that one (over there)'
VC	/oṭh/	'lip'
CV	/ko/	'who?'
CVC	/bas/	'sit down (imp.)'
CGV	/tyo/	'that one (close to you)'
CGVC	/pwa:l/	'hole'
CVGC	/cayt/	'name of a month (April-May)'

The allophones of the palatal and velar glides namely /y/ and /w/ which occur in pre-peak position are more consonantal in their phonetic characteristics than the allophones of the same glides /y/ and /w/ which occur in the post-peak position. The post-peak allophones of /y/ and /w/ are more vocalic in their phonetic characteristics. In the following list of Nepali words, the phonemic and phonetic variants are exemplified. The syllable boundaries are indicated by a period (.).

CVG.CV	/may.lo/	[mai.lo]	'dirty'
VG.CV	/aw.lo/	[au.lo]	'malaria'
CVG	/bha:y/	[bha:i]	'brother'
CVG	/kha:y/	[kha:i]	'having eaten'
CVG	/kha:w/	[kha:u]	'(please) eat'
VG	/ey/	[ei]	'this very one'
VG.CV	/ew.ṭa:/	[eu.ṭa:]	'one (item)'
CVG	/dhow/	[dhou]	'(please) wash'
VC.CVG	/um.ra:w/	[um.ra:u]	'nobleman'
CVG.CV.CV	/kha:y.ka.na/	[kha:i.ka.na]	'having eaten'
CGVG	/cya:w/	[cya:u]	'mushroom'
CV.GVG	/chi.ya:w/	[chi.ya:u]	'peep (imp.)'
CGVG	/bya:w/	[bya:u]	'give birth (imp.)'
CGVG	/bhya:w/	[bhya:u]	'finish (imp.)'
CV.GVG	/si..ya:w/	[si.ya:u]	'cause to stitch (imp.)'
CV.GV	/ma:.ya:/	[ma:ya:]	'love'
CVG.GV	/may.ya:/	[mai.ya:]	'princess'
CV.GVG	/dhu.wa:w/	[dhu.wa:u]	'cause to wash (imp.)'
CGVG	/rwa:y/	[rwa:i]	'(she) caused to weep'
CGV.GV	/swa:.yo/	[swa:.yo]	'clothing looked good'
CVC.GV	/ka:ṭ.yo/	[ka:ṭ.yo]	'cut it (imp.)'
CV.CGV	/ka:.ṭyo/	[ka:.ṭyo]	'he cut'
CVC.CGVC.CV	/pak.kwa:n.na/	[pak.kwa:n.na]	'cooked grain'
CVC.CVC	/khal.lwaṭ/	[khal.lwa:ṭ]	'bald'
CGVC.CV	/cya:p.nu/	[chya:p.nu]	'press hard'
CGV.CV	/kwã:.ṭi/	[kwã:.ṭi]	'germinated beans'
CGVC	/pwa:l/	[pwa:l]	'hole'
CGVG	/mwa:y/	[mwa:i]	'kiss (n.)'
CV.CGV.GV	/pa.tya:.yo/	[pa.tya:.yo]	'(he) believed'
CVC.CGV.GV	/hut.tya:.yo/	[hut.tya.yo]	'(he) threw'
CVC.CGVG.GV	/hut.tya:y.yo/	[hut.tya:y.yo]	'he was thrown'

3.3 Light vs. heavy syllables. Bloomfield (1933:120-121) describes sounds on the basis of sonority value. Sonority refers to the overall loudness of a sound relative to others of the same pitch, stress, and duration. The concept of sonority value has great pertinence to the description of Nepali syllables. In Nepali, the high and low sonority values are a key factor in determining the light and heavy syllables. Figure 3.3, therefore, groups Nepali vowels sounds into (1) light and (2) heavy, which constitute the peak of light and heavy syllables. This grouping is based on the phonetic (not phonemic) length of the vowel sounds. Length of vowel is not phonemic in Nepali. However, this phonetic length of vowels is useful in defining the heavy vs. light syllables.

Figure 3.3. Phonetically light and heavy vowel sounds of Nepali

Light vowels:	i	a	u
Heavy vowels:	ĩ	ã	ũ
	i: ĩ:		u: ũ:
	e ẽ		o
		a: ã:	

1. Some linguists have used the terms 'weak syllable' vs. 'strong syllable' (Shukla 1981:31-32). Others use the terms 'light syllable' vs. 'heavy syllable' (Hogg & McCully 1987:37-41). The use of the terms 'light syllable' vs. 'heavy syllable' are preferred for two reasons: (1) the weight of the syllable may be better described as 'light' and 'heavy' than 'weak' and 'strong'. (2) Moreover, the terms 'light syllable' and 'heavy syllable' have already been in use in Nepali grammar which has borrowed the terms *laghu* 'light' and *guru* 'heavy' from Pāṇini.

Pāṇini (1.4.10-12), describing the syllables of Sanskrit, defined the short vowel as 'light', the long vowel as 'heavy', and a short vowel followed by CC as heavy. Pāṇini's definition holds good in defining the weight of Nepali syllables. Although CC does not occur in a single Nepali syllable, the C.C sequence does occur, e.g. /pak.ka:/ 'mature'. In such sequences as CVC.CV the first syllable is heavy because of the C.C sequence that follows. In such sequences the primary phonetic stress occurs on the first syllable in Nepali (see 3.5.3.1)

2. Nasal vowels tend to be phonetically heavier than their nonnasal counterparts. Note also the fact that [i:, ĩ:] and [u:, ũ:] represent phonetically longer allophones in the stressed syllables. They are not phonemic, nor is stress phonemic in Nepali.

3. The mid vowels /e/ and /o/ are phonetically longer, and therefore heavier than the high short vowels /i/ and /u/ in Nepali. A possible explanation may be found in articulatory phonetics as well as the concept of sonority value of vowels. In articulatory terms, the articulation of /e/ involves greater muscular effort as the mouth opens wider and lips stretch wider than in the articulation of short /i/. The articulation of /o/ also involves wider opening of oral cavity than the articulation of /u/ as the tongue lowers further down or away from the roof of the oral cavity in the articulation of /o/ than in the articulation of /u/. The difference in muscular tension, tongue height, and the aperture in the oral cavity is the basis for assigning higher sonority values to the mid vowels than to the high vowels. For the same reason the low central vowel /a:/ is heavier, and has higher sonority value than the high vowels /i/ and /u/, and the mid vowels /e/ and /o/.

To further explain the weight of Nepali syllables, Figure 3.4 assigns several degrees of heaviness to the Nepali phonemes on the basis of sonority scale. Thus, by assigning different sonority values to the segmental phonemes of Nepali, Figure 3.4 attempts to present a clearer and more functionally useful basis on which the relative heaviness of syllables may be defined. As a result, phonetic stress assignment becomes predictable.

Assigning different values in a sonority scale is based on the concept, which Saussure (1966:44-62), Bloomfield (1933:120- 121) and many modern linguists have already used. Based on their works, particularly that of Silkirk (1984), Hogg and McCully (1986:33) define syllables in English on the basis of sonority values. The sonority value of a Nepali phoneme corresponds to the weight assigned to it in the present study: the higher the sonority value of a phoneme, the heavier it is; the lower its sonority value the lighter it is.

Figure 3.4. Sonority scale of Nepali phonemes.

Sounds	Sonority value	Examples				
Voiceless unasp. stops	.1	p	t	ṭ	c	k
Voiceless asp. stops	.2	ph	th	ṭh	ch	kh
Voiced unasp. stops	.3	b	d	ḍ	j	g
Voiced asp. stops	.4	bh	dh	ḍh	jh	gh
Nasals	.5	m	n			ng
Fricatives	.6		s			h
Laterals	.7		l			
Trills	.8			r		
Glides	.9		y			w
Phonetic short vowels	1		i		a	u
Nasal vowels	2		ĩ		ã	ũ
Phonetic long vowels	2		e ɛ		a:	o
Vowels + glides	2		iw[iu]			uy[ui]
			ey[ei]		ay[ai]	oy[oi]
			ew[eu]		aw[au]	ow[ou]
					a:y[a:i]	
					a:w[a:u]	
Vowels + nasal glides	3		iw[iũ]			uy[uĩ]
	3		ey[eĩ]			uy[uĩ]
	3		ew[eũ]			ow[oũ]
Any extra-long vowel	4		V3		V3	V3

Note 1. In vowels + glides the post-peak satellites (glides) make a syllable heavier. The pre-peak glides are more contoid and do not add to the weight of the syllabic peak.

Note 2. Any extra-long vowel is represented in standard written Nepali by the Devanagari character for three (3) immediately after the vowel. I have used the same convention so that the readers of Nepali texts will find it convenient.

As there are different ways of assigning pitch levels (Pike 1 to 4 = high to low vs. Trager-Smith 1 to 4 = low to high), similarly there are different ways of assigning sonority values. For instance, for Bloomfield (1933:120) the number 1 represents the highest sonority value, which he assigns to the vowels whereas for Hogg and McCully (1986:33) the number 1 represents the lowest sonority value, which they assign to the voiceless stops. Hogg and McCully (1987:33) also emphasize the usefulness of the concept as they write: "The usefulness of the concept of a sonority scale in the definition of a syllable lies in the fact that where sonority is greatest we have the center of a syllable, whereas where the sonority is lowest we are near the edge of the syllable."

Using the concept of sonority value for the purpose of defining the light and heavy syllables in Nepali, I have assigned sonority values to the Nepali phonemes, as Bloomfield does, with but a few slight modifications. These modifications are intended to make the description simpler and clearer. I have assigned fractions represented by decimal numbers to the consonants to indicate their 'nonsyllabicity'. Following Bloomfield, I assign sonority value 1 to high vowels (for the definition of high, mid and low vowels see 2.2.1). For the practical purpose of defining the heaviness of certain syllables I have assigned sonority value 2 to mid and low vowels, nasal vowels, and nonnasal diphthongs; value 3 to nasalized diphthongs; and value 4 to phonetically extra-long vowels.

3.3.1 Light and heavy syllables in Nepali. Any CV syllable with short V without nasalization is defined as light syllable in Nepali. In other words, the short V with a consonant (voiced or voiceless) in the syllable onset position is not heavy. As Panini (1.4.11), long ago said of Sanskrit, 'a short V followed by a consonant cluster (CC) is heavy' and makes the syllable a heavy one, similarly, in Nepali, in a sequence such as VCCV where the syllable boundary is between the two Cs, the first of the two syllables (VC.CV) is heavy. Moreover, a light vowel becomes a heavy syllable if the syllable is nasalized. Figure 3.5 summarizes the Figure 3.4, and the discussion so far.

Figure 3.5. Degrees of heaviness of Nepali syllables according to the phonological components which compose them.

Segment component	Resultant degree of heaviness of syllables
1. Consonants	.1-9
2. /i/ /u/ and /a/	1
3. /ĩ/, /ũ/, /ã/, /e/, /o/ /a:/ and all vowels + glides	2
4. Vowels + nasal glides e.g. /ay/[aĩ], /aw/ [aũ], /a:y/[aĩ], /a:u/[a:ũ]	3
5. Phonetically extra-long vowels	4

After this description of the canonical shapes of Nepali syllables (3.2) and their weight (3.3), the next question that logically follows is: What phonemes can or cannot occur in the various positions of a syllable? The answer to the question leads to the description of the phonotactics of Nepali (3.4).

3.4. Phonotactics. Phonotactics refers to the 'specific arrangements (or "tactic behavior") of sounds or phonemes which occur in a language' (Crystal 1980:270). In Nepali, all of its vowel phonemes that constitute the syllabic peak can occur alone (V), with a pre-peak or post-peak glide (GV/VG) or single consonants in the margins (CGVGC). The CC clusters do not occur in the syllable-onset and syllable-coda positions. What happens to the CC clusters in the syllable-onset position in the loan-words from Sanskrit, Hindi, English has been described in (2.3).

The single consonant phonemes (Cs), which do not occur in syllable-onset, intervocalic, and syllable-coda positions are described in (3.4.1, 3.4.2, and 3.4.3).

3.4.1 Consonantal phonemes in syllable-onset position. All the consonants except velar nasal /ng/ and alveopalatal nasal /ṇ/ occur in the syllable-onset position. Though the velar nasal /ng/ is a phoneme in Nepali, minimal pairs can be found with /ng/ in the syllable-onset position. The velar nasal /ng/ occurs in the syllable-onset position only in onomatopoeic forms, e.g. imitation of cats' cry, /ngya:r ngya:r/. The alveopalatal nasal /ṇ/ does not occur in the syllable-initial position even in onomatopoeic forms.

3.4.2 Consonantal phonemes in intervocalic position. All consonantal phonemes except the voiced aspirate stops /bh/, /dh/, /ḍh/, /jh/, /gh/ occur in intervocalic position. (The phonemes /bh/, /dh/, /ḍh/, /jh/ and /gh/ show minimal pairs only in the word-initial positions and these voiced aspirate stops (/bh/, /dh/, /ḍh/, /jh/, and /gh/) are replaced by their unaspirate allophones (/b/, /d/, /ḍ/, /j/ and /g/) in intervocalic and syllable-coda positions.

3.4.3 Consonantal phonemes in syllable-coda position. All consonantal phonemes except the glottal fricative phoneme /h/ occur in the syllable-coda position in Nepali. The glides in the syllable-coda positions tend to be more vocalic in their phonetic characteristics e.g /bha:y/ [bha:i] 'brother', /dew.ta:/ [deu.ta:] 'god' etc. However, when the glides are followed by their corresponding counterparts i.e. /y/ followed by a /y/ and /w/ followed by /w/, their post-peak allophones are more contoid. For instance, /pa:yyo/ [pa:i.yo] 'was found', /pawwa:/ [pau.wa:] 'inn'. (The period in the middle marks the syllable boundary).

3.5.0 Phonetic stress: Its definition and function in Nepali. Stress is defined as the relative loudness with which a syllable is uttered. The loudness of the stressed syllable is also accompanied by longer duration and higher pitch than that of the unstressed syllables. As Panini (1.2.29) said of Sanskrit, there is more muscular tension in the vocal cords in the articulation of a stressed syllable.

In Nepali stress is not phonemic. Nevertheless, three levels of phonetic stress may be identified: primary stress ('), secondary stress (ˋ) and the unstressed level (unmarked). The stress marks are placed before the stressed syllable in the present work.

3.5.1 Stress and stress placement in Nepali. The following sections describe the placement of stress in Nepali. The section (3.5.2) describes the rules for the placement of regular phonetic stress. All of these degrees of phonetic stress are merely predictable allophonic variants of unstressed Nepali syllables. As phonemically unstressed syllables they contrast not with each other functionally (although to achieve a 'good pronunciation', a language learner should try to produce the correct variant for each syllable when stress occurs), but with the functional phonemic 'emphatic stress' which can occur to mark any word. Sections (3.5.3.1-4) illustrate the regular stress rules with Nepali examples; section (3.5.4) describes the emphatic stress (phonemic) which can occur on any word (in a phrasal or clausal string), or even a bound morpheme. A bound morpheme (or bound form) is one which cannot occur on its own as a separate word, e.g. suffixes.

3.5.2 Stress rules in Nepali. With the exception of the unstressed clitics, the phonetic stress in Nepali words falls on the word-initial syllable, if the other syllables in the word are of equal weight, or heavier by only 1 degree. If any of the succeeding syllables is heavier than the word-initial syllable by 2 degrees, then the stress occurs on the succeeding heavy syllable. But this shift of allophonic stress takes place only if the succeeding syllable (heavier by 2 degrees) is immediately adjacent to the word-initial syllable. In other words, if there is an intervening syllable between the word-initial syllable and the heavier syllable, the phonetic stress does not occur on the succeeding heavier syllable. Some loan words from foreign languages show a different stress pattern e.g. /ki.'ta:b/ 'book' from Arabic.

What follows are examples and more detailed description of the allophones of the phonetic stress in Nepali i.e. Nepali stress rule (NSR).

3.5.3 Regular phonetic stress. The following sections (3.5.3.1-3.5.3.4) illustrate the Nepali phonetic stress rules with examples and sections (3.5.4.1-3.5.4.2) illustrate occurrences of phonemic emphatic stress in Nepali.

3.5.3.1 Nepali phonetic stress rule-1 (NSR-1). The phonetic stress in Nepali words occurs on the word-initial syllable if the syllables are of equal weight, or one is heavier than the other by just one degree of heaviness. For example, the following words, with the weight of their syllables indicated in the square brackets ([ ]), illustrate the regular phonetic stress pattern:

/'ka:.ka:/ [2-2] 'uncle'
/'ba.sa/ [1-1] 'sit down (imp.)'
/'ra:m.la:l/ [2-2] 'Ramlal (name of a person)'
/'cha:.no/ [2-2] 'roof'
/'cha:.ya:/ [2-2] 'shadow'
/'dar.ba:r/ [2-2] 'palace'

3.5.3.2 Nepali phonetic stress rule-2 (NSR-2). The NSR-2 is that a syllable which is heavier by 2 degrees than its immediately preceding syllables has the primary stress on it; the word-initial syllable does not have the primary stress. Thus the NSR-2 overrides the NSR-1. Consider the following examples in which the stress falls on the heavier syllable which is not in the word-initial position:

/pa.'ka:w̃.cha/ [1-3-1] '(he) cooks'
/ba.'na:w̃.cha/ [1-3-1] '(he) makes'
/ga.'na:w̃.cha/ [1-3-1] '(it) smells (bad)'
/ḍa.'ra:w̃.cha/ [1-3-1] '(he) fears'

The second syllable in each of the tri-syllabic words is the heaviest one since it consists of a long vowel /a:/ as the peak nucleus followed by the glide /w/ at the post-peak position, which is phonetically realized as a nasalized vowel [ũ]at the post-peak position. The syllable [a:w̃], with 3 degree of heaviness (Figure 3.5), in each example is heavier by 2 degrees than its immediately adjacent syllable which is of 1 degree. The NSR-2 also explains the stress placement in strings such as: /'bho.ka:w̃.cha/ [2-3-1] '(he) feels hungry'

In /bho'ka:w̃cha/, the peak of the word-initial syllable /bho/ has the mid vowel /o/, which is assigned 2 degree of heaviness (Figure 3.5). The third syllable [ka:w̃] which is assigned degree 3 of heaviness is heavier by only 1 degree (not 2 degrees) than its preceding neighbor /bho/. So, the stress does not occur on the second syllable. The NSR-2 also explains the stress placement in:

/'bhak.bha.ka:w̃.cha/ [2-1-3-1] '(he) stutters'
/'phat.pha.ta:w̃.cha/ [2-1-3-1] '(he) jabbers'
/'phaṭ.pha.ṭa:w̃.cha/ [2-1-3-1] '(he) flutters'
/'chaṭ.pa.ṭa:w̃.cha/ [2-1-3-1] '(he) wriggles'

in which case, the stress occurs on the word-initial syllable, having 2 degrees of heaviness (See 5.3.1). So the third syllable /ka:£/ having 3 degrees of heaviness is heavier than the word-initial syllable by only 1 degree, not 2 degrees.

3.5.3.3 Compound words phonetic stress rule (CWSR). The NSR-1 (i.e the stress falling on the word-initial syllable) is the compound words' stress rule (CWSR) as well. When two words, each having the primary stress (') on the word-initial syllable, form a compound, the compound-word-initial syllable has the primary stress ('). The word-initial syllable of the second word of the compound has the secondary stress (`). For instance:

/'ka:.ka:/ [2-2] 'uncle'
/'ba:.bu/ [2-1] 'father'
/'ka:.ka:-`ba:.bu/ [2-2-2-1] 'uncle (who is like father)'

/'ba:.bu/ [2-1] 'father'
/'cho.ra:/ [2-1] 'son'
/'ba:.bu-`cho.ra:/ [2-1-2-1] 'father and son'

/'di.di/ [1-1] 'sister'
/'bha:y/ [2] 'brother'
/'di.di-`bha:y/ [1-1-2] 'sister and brother'

/'ka:ṭh.ma:ṇ.ḍu/ [2-2-1] 'Kathmandu'
/'po.kha.ra:/ [2-1-2] 'Pokhara'
/'ka:ṭh.ma:ṇ.ḍu-po.kha.ra:/ [2-2-1-2-1-2] 'Kathmandu-Pokhara'

The vowels in the unstressed syllables, especially of compound words, tend to be reduced to either a mid central vocoid (schwa [a]) or are deleted (Ø). For instance:

/'cho.ra:/ [2-2] 'son(s)'
/'cho.ri/ [2-1] 'daughter(s)'
/'chor.`cho.ri/ [2-2-1] 'sons and daughters'

/'ṭhu.li/ [1-1] 'older (feminine)'
/'na:.ni/ [2-1] 'girl/daughter'
/'ṭhul.`na:.ni/ [2-2-1] 'older girl/daughter'

/'ṭhu.la:/ [1-2] 'big'
/'da:y/ [2] 'brother'
/'ṭhul.`da:i'/ [2-2] 'older brother'

/'je.ṭha:/ [2-2] 'older'
/'ba:.bu/ [2-1] 'father'
/'je.ṭha:-`ba:.bu/ [2-2-2-1] 'older uncle'

/'pu.ra:.no/ [1-2-2] 'old (thing)'
/'ḍi.hi/ [1-1] 'farm'

/'pu.ra:n.`ḍi.hi/ [1-2-1-1] 'old farm'

In the dialect of Nepali spoken in the rims of the Kathmandu valley, the unstressed vowels in both words of a compound are reduced. For instance:

/'ka:.ka:/ [2-2] 'uncle'
/'ba:.bu/ [2-1] 'father'
/'ka:.ka.`baw/ [2-1-2] 'uncle (who is like father)'

3.5.3.4 Phrase phonetic stress rule (PSR). In Nepali, the phrase stress rule also follows the compound stress rule. For instance:

/'ka:ṭh.ma:ṇ.ḍu ja:.ne ba:.ṭo/ [2-2-1-2-2-2-2]
kathmandu go-impf.prt. way
'The way to Kathmandu'

/'phe.wa:-ta:l ja:.ne ba:.ṭo/ [2-2-2-2-2-2-2]
phewa-lake go-inf.prt. way
'The way to Phewa lake'

/'bi.ra:.la:.ko na:k/ [1-2-2-2-2]
cat-of nose
'The cat's nose'

3.5.3.5 Sentence phonetic stress rule (SSR). The sentence phonetic stress rule in Nepali puts stress on any one of the words in a sentence for emphasis. However, the stress in a word follows the word stress rule. For instance, the emphatic stress can occur on any free form in the following sentence:

/ma a:ja ghara ja:nna/
I today home-acc. go-not-1sg.pres.
'I do not go home today'

Depending on the emphasis on a specific part of the message, the word-initial syllable of any of the four words of the sentence /ma a:ja ghara ja:nna/ 'I do not go home today' can be stressed.

3.5.4 Emphatic functional phonemic stress (ES) for extra semantic emphasis. In longer strings such as phrases and sentences, a syllable of a free or bound form may be stressed functionally and phonemically to contrast with the nonemphasized items which exhibit only the degree of phonetic stress which pertains to semantically unstressed Nepali items. This type of stress is phonemic in Nepali as it has a special semantic function.

3.5.4.1 Emphatic phonemic stress (ES) on free forms. Emphatic phonemic stress (ES) falling on the initial syllable of a word emphasizes its lexical meaning. Generally, it is the lexical word, e.g. noun, adjective, verb, adverb, or their suffixes that are stressed. Grammatical words e.g. postpositions, conjunctions etc. are not usually accorded emphatic phonemic stress. However, in certain instances, conjunctions such as /ra/ 'and' are phonemically accorded emphatic stress when they assume extra semantic load as indicated by the emphatic stress, e.g.

/ha:mi buddhu chaũ 'ra ta bir chaũ /
we dumb be-1pl.pres. and *ta* (nuance particle) brave are
'We are dumb, therefore we are brave'

In this context what the speaker means is that 'we [the Gurkhas, fighting as mercenaries, and losing lives for others] could not be brave <u>and</u> wise', i.e. 'brave without being dumb'.

As noted in (3.5.1), the regular stress occurs on the word-initial syllable. The emphatic stress (ES) can occur even on the suffixes (e.g. verbal suffixes) which do not necessarily constitute the word-initial syllable. However, it is notable that the emphatic stress still follows the pattern of regular stress as it occurs on the first syllable if it is a multisyllabic suffix.

3.5.4.2 Emphatic stress (ES) on suffixes. Unlike the regular stress (described in 3.5.3), and emphatic stress on free forms (described in 3.5.4.1), emphatic stress (ES) occurs on suffixes as well. The ES on suffixes, besides emphasizing the meaning of those suffixes, communicates the attitude of the speaker toward the addressee (understood in the social and linguistic context). Phonetically, the stress on these suffixes results either in lengthening (3.5.4.2.1) or shortening (3.5.4.2.2) of the stressed vowel.

3.5.4.2.1 Emphatic stress (ES) and vowel lengthening. The examples that follow illustrate the placement of emphatic stress in the suffixes. The emphatic stress in the suffixes is so heavy (as opposed to the regular stress) that it is accompanied by a phonetic lengthening of the stressed vowel and by a momentary glottal closure and sudden release of breath audible at the end of each stressed syllable, and is transcribed as [ḫ].

In the following examples, the suffixes to the verbs are stressed and marked with ('). Such stress, accompanied by other factors, namely, lexical meaning, context and paralinguistic features (body gestures) results in communicating different shades of the speaker's attitudes. The following examples are sentential structures although the first seven strings consist only of verbs in different persons, numbers and tenses, they still constitute sentences. Since the verbs in Nepali inflect for persons, numbers, gender and tenses, the subject is optional. (See Chapter 18 for more details).

/tar'chuḫ/ (Confidence, when one's ability is doubted)
cross-1sg.pres.
'(I can) cross (the river etc.)'

/sak'chuḫ/ (confidence)
can-1sg.pres.
'(I) can'

/a:w̃.chaḫ/ (Certainty, when possibility is questioned)
come-3sg.pres.
'(he will certainly) come'

/lai'ja:ḫ/ (Emphatic order)
take-go-imp.
'Take it away'

/bha'yoḫ/ (Disbelief even when something is true)
happen-3sg.pst.
'(It) happened (but I don't believe)'

/ho'la:ḫ/ (Disbelief)
be-3sg.fut.
'(I don't believe that) it will be'

/je garchaw ga'raḫ/ (Angry, reluctant permission)
whatever do-2sg.pres. do-imp.
'Do whatever you want'

/ke gare'koḫ?/ (Angry question)
what do-prf.prt.
'What (on earth) have you done?'

3.5.4.2.2 Emphatic stress (ES) and vowel shortening. This section describes the occurrence of emphatic stress and shortening of the stressed vowel, a particular phonological phenomenon in Nepali. The shortened vowel is indicated by (‘), an arbitrarily chosen sign in the present work. The definition of stress as 'involving a muscular tension' is applicable in such shortening of the stressed vowels as well. This phonological phenomenon in Nepali was fairly well described by the very first native grammarian Arjyal in his description of Nepali written c. 1891, who called it *ardha-hrasva* 'half short (vowel)'. However, none of the subsequent grammarians of Nepali, native or foreign, have treated this phenomenon in their works.

The stress and shortening of the stressed vowel occurring at the same time result in a kind of glottal closure. The stress and shortening takes place at the final syllables of the verbs as in the following examples, each of which indicates a particular attitude of the speaker.

/naga'ra'/ (Friendliness, softening of prohibition)
not-do-imp.
'(Please) do not do (it)'

One can contrast the utterance of friendliness in /naga'ra'/ '(Please) do not do (it)' with the utterance /naga'ra3/ 'Don't do it' in which the same vowel is stressed with added length to mean a threat. These two types of phonological phenomenon are in mutually contrastive distribution in their semantic function. In the following statement

/tyo ta garna hŭdai'na'/
that *ta* -(nu) do-inf. be-not-3sg.pres.
'That one should not be done'

because of the shortening of the stressed vowel both the speaker and hearer are aware of friendliness or softened prohibition although the statement just made is in contradiction to what is expected. Similarly,

/ga'ra'/ (Permission, softly given)
do-imp.
'Do (it); (I have no objection)'

/cor a:'yo' cor a:'yo'/ (Hurry)
thief come-3sg.pst. thief come-3sg.pst.
'The thief came, the thief came!'

/'ja:w' 'ja:w'/ (Avoiding distraction)
go-imp. go-imp.
'Go, go (Don't be distracted)'

/le'kha' le'kha'/ (Avoiding distraction)
write-imp. write-imp.
'Please write, please write (don't be distracted)'

/ciṭhi le'khyaw'?/ (Softened question)
letter write-2sg.pst
'Did (you) write the letter?'

/pa:ṭh pa'ḍhyaw'?/ (Softened question)
lesson read-2sg.pst.
'Did (you) read the lesson?'

/yo ho'la:'?/ (Softened doubt)
this be-3sg.fut.
'Can it (possibly) be?'

/tyasle gar'la:'?/ (Softened doubt)
that-agt. do-3sg.fut.
'Will he (possibly) do it?'

/usle yo ka:m garna sak'la:'?/ (Softened doubt)
he-agt. this work do-inf. can-3sg.fut.
'Will he (possibly) be able to do this work?'

/na'ja:'/ (Secretly telling a secret)
not-go-imp.
'Do not go (there is danger!)'

/'ja:'/ (Secretly telling a secret)
go-imp.
'Go (there is no danger)'

/bha'yo'?/ (Softened confirmation question)
be-1sg.pst.
'(Did you say) it happened?'

3.6 Pitch. Pitch is the relative height of the tone on which a syllable is produced. As an "attribute of auditory sensation" (Crystal 1980:272) pitch corresponds to the acoustic feature of frequency, which is based upon the number of complete cycles of vibration of vocal cords. Frequency is measured in Hertz (Hz), e.g. 440 Hz = 440 cps (cycles per second).

In the linguistic literature the levels of pitch in English, like the notation of the levels of stress, have been assigned in different ways, e.g. 1-2-3-4 (Trager-Smith) representing the levels of pitch from the low to the high, or conversely 4-3-2-1, i.e. low to high (Pike) to represent the same. In the present study three levels of pitch are distinguished in Nepali. The low level pitch is represented by 1, mid level pitch is represented by 2, and the high level pitch is represented by 3. These levels are of course relative to one another and each of these pitches varies according to the difference of stresses and junctures with which it cooccurs. A sequence of pitch levels and stress usually in a sentence or a part of sentence constitutes intonation pattern which is described and illustrated in (3.10).

3.7 Juncture. Juncture refers to the phonetic boundary features which may demarcate grammatical units such as morpheme, word or clause. The most obvious junctural feature is silence, but there may be other features which mark the beginnings and endings of grammatical units in connected speech. For instance, word division may be signalled by a complex of stress, pitch, length and other features, as in the potential contrast between *that stuff* and *that's tough,* or *Ice cream* and *I scream.*

Terminal juncture refers to how an utterance ends. Internal juncture refers to the relative closeness with which syllables follow each other within the words or phrases of an utterance.

3.7.1 Types of juncture. There are two types of terminal junctures or ways in which an utterance can end: terminal juncture (#), and abrupt juncture (|). The terminal juncture (#) is accompanied by a pitch height that falls before a silence. The abrupt juncture is accompanied by a quick cessation of sound and is usually accompanied by a sustained holding of the pitch height of the voice at the conclusion of the group of syllables.

The distinction between these two types of terminal juncture is that they are used to signal the difference between complete utterance (terminal juncture #) and an incomplete utterance (abrupt juncture |).

The two types of internal junctures are: (1) open juncture (marked by +) and (2) close juncture (unmarked). In open juncture (+) there is a slight pause (+) between the syllables. In close juncture (unmarked), the syllables follow one upon the other closely with no perceptual pause between them.

3.7.2 Minimal pairs for open (+) vs. close juncture (unmarked). The following examples illustrate the contrast between open juncture (+) and close juncture (unmarked) in Nepali words, phrases and clauses. The boundaries of syllables in close juncture are marked by a period (.).

(1) /sa:k+khay/ 'Where is the vegetable?'
/sa:k.khay/ 'Blood relation'

(2) /sun+di.na/ 'To give gold (inf.)'
/sun.di.na/ '(she) does not listen/hear'

(3) /ma:n+di.na/ 'to confer honor (inf.)'
/ma:n.di.na/ '(she) does not agree/obey'

(4) /swa:s.ni+ma:n.che/ 'wife agrees'
/swa:s.ni.ma:n.che/ 'wife'

(5) /dha:n+di.yo/ '(he) gave rice'
/dha:n.di.yo/ '(he) sustained (something)'

(6) /ha.ri+yo/ 'this (one is) Hari'
/ha.ri.yo/ 'green'

(7) /ko+pa.ryo/ 'what (relation of yours) is (he)?'
/ko.pa.ryo/ '(he) scratched'

(8) /ko+yo/ 'who (is) this?'
/ko.yo/ 'seed of the mango fruit'

(9) /ja:.ne+ko/ 'who (is it that) is going?'
/ja:.ne.ko/ 'known/understood'

(10) /la.ga:+yo/ 'put it on (imp.)'
/la.ga:.yo/ '(he) put it on'

(11) /la:+yo/ 'take it (imp.)'
/la:.yo/ 'he put it on'

(12) /ra:kh+yo/ 'put it (imp.)'
/ra:.khyo/ '(he) put it'

(13) /ka:ṭ+yo/ 'cut it (imp.)'
/ka:.ṭyo/ '(he) cut it'

(14) /ho+la:/ 'yes, take it (imp.)'
/ho.la:/ 'it may probably be'

(15) /her+la:/ 'take a look (imp.)'
/her.la:/ '(he) may look at it'

(16) /paḍh+la:/ 'take (and) read it'
/paḍh.la:/ '(he) may read'

(17) /bas+cha/ 'there is a bus (there)'
/bas.cha/ 'he sits/lives (there)'

(18) /ba:s+cha/ 'there is a shelter (there).
/ba:s.cha/ '(rooster) crows'

(19) /phul+cha/ 'there is flower (there)'
/phul.cha/ '(flower) blossoms'

(20) /ban+cha/ 'there is forest (there)'
/ban.cha/ '(it) can be made'

(21) /u+ka:.lo cha/ 'he is dark/black'
/u.ka:.lo cha/ '(it) is uphill'

(22) /ban.da+cha/ '(it) is closed'
/ban.da.cha/ 'it is made'

(23) /ka:m+cha/ '(there) is work'
/ka:m.cha/ '(he) shivers'

(24) /ga:w̃+chan/ 'there are villages'
/ga:w̃.chan/ '(they) sing'

(25) /yo+ni/ 'how about this?'
/yo.ni/ 'vagina'

(26) /na+gar/ 'do not do (it)'
/na.gar/ 'town'

(27) /pai.sa:+le/ 'give (me) money (imp.)'
/pai.sa:.le/ 'with money'

(28) /ki.ta:b+ma:.thi cha/ 'the book is upstairs'
/ki.ta:b.ma:.thi cha/ '(something) is over the book'

(29) /ʈe.bul+ma:.thi.cha/ 'the table is upstairs'
/ʈe.bul.ma:.thi.cha/ '(something) is on the table'

(30) /sya:m+ka.hã: ga.yo?/ 'Where did Shyam go?'
/sya:m.ka.hã: ga.yo?/ 'Did (someone) go to Shyam's (home)?'

3.8 Rhythm. Rhythm is defined as "perceived regularity of prominent units in speech" (Crystal 1980:307). Accordingly, "these regularities may be stated in terms of patterns of stressed vs. unstressed syllables, syllable length (long vs. short syllables), or pitch (high vs.low pitch), or some combination of these variables." English exhibits stress-timed rhythm.

Nepali, as Spanish and many other languages, exhibits a 'syllable-timed' rhythm. In other words, what determines the rhythm of an utterance is the number of syllables, whether stressed or unstressed, which occur in an utterance. Since stress is not phonemic in Nepali, the native speaker is not generally aware of the phonetically longer duration of a stressed syllable. For him each syllable is allotted approximately the same amount of time for its articulation.

3.9 Pause. Pause is a silence between the parts of utterances. Linguists (Cruttenden 1986:36, Crystal 1980:260) describe two types of pause: 'silent' or often 'filled' by certain sounds or fumble vowels (e.g. in English a mid central vowel schwa /ə/, in French a rounded lower mid front vowel /ø/ in Spanish /n/) or a continuous phonation of a the last phoneme before the next item is uttered.

Pause has several functions. One of them is to demarcate "grammatical boundaries" (Crystal 1980:260) and "intonation groups" (Cruttenden 1986:36). In a normal speech event, the speakers of Nepali tend to pause at each of the grammatical functional slots. This type of pause at the end of each phrase or clause is more perceptible when the sentence is too long to be finished at one breath. Thus, the longer the sentence the more perceptible the pauses at the grammatical functional slots; the shorter the sentences, the less perceptible the pauses.

A pause of longer than normally expected duration may be described as hesitation or 'performance error' on the part of the speaker. However, the speakers of Nepali sometimes deliberately choose to pause longer to communicate a specific message (softening of statement, or contemplation) which is not communicated otherwise. This type of pause has a communicative function. However, since these are technically 'pragmatic' matters, they are not discussed systematically here, but merely mentioned and briefly illustrated to alert language learners to such phenomenon.

For instance, consider a case of 'filled' pause softening the statement (by the longer phonation of a vowel filling the pause):

Softened statement:	Harsh (impolite) statement:
/timi3 naja:w/	/timi naja:w/
you not-go-imp.	you not-go-imp.
'You do not go please'	'Don't go'

Note that the word /timii3/ 'you' in (a) is the focus of prevention, or negative statement. The speaker knows that it will be impolite and offending to prevent the addressee from going. So, he softens the prevention by lengthening the final vowel of the word /timi/ 'you' so that the prevention sounds to be well-thought and well-meaning, and, therefore, even in the interest of the addressee. When the vowel is so lengthened as in (b), the statement is not polite.

The following are some more examples of pause, filled by the prolongation of a vowel, to indicate internal reflection on the semantic content of the statement:

Contemplated statements:	Abrupt statements:
/yo ka:3m nagara/	/yo ka:m nagara/
this work not-do-imp.	this work not-do-imp.
'Please don't do this work'	'Don't do this work'
/timi3 paḍha; ma ka:m garchu/	/timi paḍha, ma ka:m garchu/
you study-imp. I work do-1sg.pres.	you study-imp. I work do-1sg.pres.
'You study; I will do the work'	'You study; I will do the work'

/ka:si3 ja:nu parcha/	/ka:si ja:nu parcha/
Ka:si go-inf. must	Ka:si go-inf. must
'(We) must go to Kasi (Banaras)'	'(We) must go to Kasi (Banaras)'

The words /ka:m/ 'work', /timi/ 'you', and /ka:si/ 'Banaras' are the focus of contemplation.

As stated in (3.9), pause marks the boundaries of intonation phenomena. The intonation boundaries marked by pauses are called variously by various linguists, e.g. "sense groups, breath groups, tone-groups, tone-units, phonological phrases, phonological clauses, or intonational phrases" (Cruttenden, 1986:35).

3.10 Intonation. Intonation consists of a combination of particular stress and pitch patterns to form an intonation contour which extends over an utterance. Intonation contours may contrast, one with the other; indeed most languages use a small set of such contrastive intonation contours to signal various grammatical meanings.

Thus, intonation may play several roles in a language. The first and most important role of intonation is to signal a grammatical structure. In this its role is similar to that of punctuation in written texts. Intonation marks sentences, clauses, and other boundaries. Intonation can also mark contrasts between clause types, e.g. questions, statements, or commands.

The 'second role of intonation is in the communication of personal attitude: sarcasm, puzzlement, anger etc. can be signalled by contrasts in pitch, along with other prosodic and paralinguistic features' (Crystal 1980:191).

The following sections illustrate both roles of intonation, i.e (1) the grammatical role in which intonation marks contrasts between clause types (3.10.1) and (2) the communicative role in which the speaker's personal attitude is communicated by intonation (3.10.2).

3.10.1 The grammatical role of intonation. The grammatical role of intonation described in this section is the role of intonation to mark the contrasts between clause types: statements, commands, and questions. Three basic intonation patterns marking three different clause types have been identified in Nepali:

(1) The intonation of statements and imperative statements (3.10.1.1),
(2) The intonation of *ho/hoina* -questions 'yes/no-questions (3.10.1.2),
(3) The intonation of *K*-questions '*wh* -questions (3.10.1.3).

3.10.1.1 The intonation of statement, and imperative statements. The intonation of the statements and imperative statements shows 2-2-1 intonation pattern in contrast to *ho/hoina* questions 'yes/no-questions',which show a 2-1-3 intonation pattern, and *K*-questions *'wh* -question' which show a 2-2-2 intonation pattern:

Statements:	*ho/hoina* -questions:
/timi^2 ghara^2 gayaw^1/[2-2-1]	/timi^2 ghara^1 gayaw^3/ [2-1-3]
you home-ac go-2sg.pst	you home-ac go-2sg.pst
'You went home'	'Did you go home?'
/usle^2 bha:t^2 kha:yo^1/[2-2-1]	/usle^2 bha:t^1 kha:yo^3/ [2-1-3]
he-nm(agt) rice eat-3sg.pst	he-nm(agt) rice eat-3sg.pst
'He ate rice'	'Did he eat rice?'

The intonation of imperative statements shows the same pattern as that of the statements. An imperative statement is distinguished from a nonimperative statement by the inflected morphological form of the verb which is inflected for imperative vs. nonimperative statement.

Imperative statement:	Nonimperative statement:
/(timi^2) ghara^2 ja:w^1/ [2-2-1]	/timi^2 ghara^2 gayaw^1/[2-2-1]
(you) home-acc. go-imp.	you home-ac go-2sg.pst
'Go home'	'You went home'
/(timi^2) bha:t^2 kha:w^1/[2-2-1]	/usle^2 bha:t^2 kha:yo^1/[2-2-1]
(you) rice eat-imp.	he-nm(agt) rice eat-3sg.pst
'Eat rice'	'He ate rice'

3.10.1.2 Intonation of *ho/hoina*-questions 'yes/no-questions'. The intonation of *ho/hoina*-questions 'yes/no questions' in contrast to statements and imperative statements shows a 2-1-3 intonation pattern. The *ho/hoina* -questions are so called because the answer to them is either *ho* 'yes' or *hoina* 'no'. Since there is no difference in the word order or verb form between statements and intonation questions, it is the intonation pattern itself which signals whether the utterance is a statement or question.

/timi^2 ghara^1 gayaw^3/[2-1-3]
you home-acc. go-2sg.pst.
'Did you go home?'

/usle^2 bha:t^1 kha:yo^3/[2-1-3]
he-agt. rice eat-3sg.pst
'Did he eat rice?'

3.10.1.3 Intonation of *K*-questions '*wh*-questions'. *K*-questions are comparable to the '*wh*-questions' in English, where the question words begin with *wh*-. In Nepali these questions begin with the *K*-. The *K*-questions in contrast to statements, imperative statements and *ho/hoina-* questions 'yes/no'-questions show a /2-2-2/ intonation pattern in addition to the *k*-words (/ke/ 'what', /ko/ 'who', /kahã:/ 'where', /kahile/ 'when', /kasari/ 'how', and /kasto/ 'what kind'.

/timi^{2} ke^{2} garchau^{2}?/[2-2-2]
you what do-2sg.pres.
'What do you do?'

3.10.2 The communicative role of intonation. Apart from the role that intonation plays in signalling grammatical structures, it also plays the role of communicating the attitude of the speaker toward the addressee and the content of the message. This section describes the role of intonation in communicating the speaker's attitudes of warning, certainty, surprise, intensity etc., i.e. pragmatics in Nepali. To communicate those attitudes, the speakers of Nepali use the extra lengthening of vowels at high, low, or mid level pitches. The extra lengthened vowels are indicated by the Devanagari symbol for three (3) following immediately after the lengthened vowels, e.g. /i3/, /u3/, /e3/, /o3/, /a3/, /a:3/ etc. Like the emphatic stress described in (5.4), the extra lengthening of vowels at high, mid, or low level pitch takes place in the initial syllable of any (free or bound) morpheme. The following three subsections illustrate the communication of different attitudes by: (1) the lengthening of high pitch vowel indicated by 3^{3} (3.10.2.1), (2) the lengthening of low pitch vowel indicated by 3^{1} (3.10.2.2), and (3) the lengthening of mid pitch vowel indicated by 3^{2} (3.10.2.3). Again, since these are 'pragmatic roles', they are merely illustrated here, not treated systematically.

3.10.2.1 The lengthening of high pitch vowel. The speakers of Nepali communicate intensification of the message by lengthening the high pitch vowel of the initial syllable of the verbal suffixes. For instance, in an imperative statement such as:

Intensified imperative:	Simple imperative:
/juwa: nakhele3^{3}s/	/juwa: nakheles/
gambling not-play-imp.	gambling not-play-imp.
'Do not gamble (I warn you)'	'Don't gamble'

the the syllable-initial vowel of the verbal suffix /-es/ is lengthened (e.g. /-e3^{3}s/) to express the intensitiy of warning. The following are further examples of the lengthening of vowels which indicate the intensification of statements made:

Intensification:	Nonintensification:
/bhayo3^3/	/bhayo/
happen-3sg.pst.	happen-3sg.pst
'It happened (vindication)'	'It [just] happened'
/gara3^3/	/gara/
do-imp.	do-imp
'Do it (all-out permission)''Do it'	'Do it'
/a:wno3^3s/	/a:wnos/
come-imp.(honorific)	come-imp.(honorific)
'Come please'(urgency)	'Come please'
/bã:ci3^3rahe/	/bã: cirahe/
live-cont.asp.-3sg.pst.	live-cont.asp.-3sg.pst
'He lived (very long)'	'He continued living'
/gari3^3rahe/	/garirahe/
do-cont.asp.-3sg.pst	do-cont.asp.-3sg.pst
'He continued doing (intensely)'	'He continued doing'

Note that in the previous examples of intensification the vowel of the initial syllable (/-i/) of the continuative aspect-marker /-irah-/ is lengthened because it is the continuative aspect that is the focus of intensification. In case of the monosyllabic continuative aspect-marker /-tay/ or /-day/, /ay/ is lengthened, e.g.

Intensified statement:	Nonintensified statement:
/siktay3^3 ja:w/	/siktay ja:w/
learn-cont.asp go-imp.	learn-cont.asp go-imp.
'Go on learning (intensely)'	'Go on learning'
/ganday3^3 ja:w/	/ganday ja:w/
count-cont.asp. go-imp.	count-cont.asp. go-imp.
'Go on counting (intensely)'	'Go on counting'

Similarly, note that the initial syllabic vowel /-e/ of the suffix /-era/ (of the absolutive past participial suffix) is lengthened to indicate the intensity of absoluteness in the following example:

/bache3^3ra ja:w/
protect-abs.pst.prt. go-imp.
'Go protecting (yourself) very much'

Consider the intensification in the following adjectives:

/ṭhu3^{3}lo/ 'very big'	/ṭhulo/ 'big'
/sa3^{3}no/ 'very small'	/sa:no/ 'small'
/bu3^{3}ḍha:/ 'very old (man)'	/buḍha:/ 'old man'
/hãsi3^{3}lo/ 'very smiling (face)'	/hãsilo/ 'smiling (face)'
/ghãsi3^{3}lo/ 'very grassy (land)'	/ghãsilo/ 'grassy (land)'
/kalkala:w̃3^{3}di/ 'very tender (girl)'	/kalkala:w̃ di/ 'tender (girl)
/taru3^{3}ni/ 'very young (girl)'	/taruni/ 'young (girl)'

The adjectives /ṭhulo/ 'big', /sa:no/ 'small' and /buḍha:/ 'old man' show the lengthening of the vowel in the word-initial syllable. Adjectives formed by suffix /-ilo/ such as /hãsilo/ 'smiling (face)', /ghãsilo/ 'grassy (land)' and by the suffix /-a:w̃di/ e.g. /kalkala:w̃di/ 'tender (girl)' show the lengthening of the vowel of first syllables of /-ilo/, and /a:w̃di/. In the last example (/taruni/), the speaker feels (on the basis of analogy) that there is a morpheme boundary between /tar-/ and /-uni/, and lengthens the vowel /u/.

Note also that the vowel of the initial syllable of an adverb is similarly lengthened for intensification:

/timi ja3^{3}stay/ (Intensified)	/timi jastay/ (Nonintensified)
you (very) like	you like
'Exactly like you'	'Like you'

3.10.2.2 The lengthening of low pitch vowel. The speakers of Nepali communicate intensification of statements (and other connotations understood in the social and linguistic contexts) by lengthening the vowel at the low level pitch. For instance:

Intensification:	Nonintensification:
/naja:w3_1/ (Persuasion)	/naja:w/
not-go-imp.	not-go-imp.
'Do not go please'	'Do not go'
/nakuṭa3_1/	/nakuṭa/
not-beat-imp.	not-beat-imp.
'Do not beat (someone) please'	'Do not beat'
/u ja:la:3_1/	/u ja:la:/
he go-3sg.fut.	he go-3sg.fut.
'He will go (don't let him go)'	'He will go'

Note that the lengthening of low level pitch vowel in the verb from /ja:la:/ 'he will go' results not only in the intensification of the possibility of someone's going, but in the demand of extra attention and implication that the hearer is expected not to let the person go. A larger sociolinguistic context besides the phonemic intonation may help to condition them.

Note also that in the following two examples the lengthening of vowels at the low-level pitch is in phonemic contrast with the lengthening of the same at the high-level pitch. The lengthening of vowel at the low-level pitch means the intensification of softness; the lengthening of vowels at the high-level pitch means the intensification of threat/warning.

Intensification of softness:

/ra:mba:bu, ciṭhi lekhyaw3_1?/
Rambabu, letter write-2sg.pst.
'Rambabu, did you write the letter?'

/ra:mbabau, a:ja ka:m nagara3_1/
Ra:maba:bu, today work not-do-imp.
'Rambabu, do not work today'

versus intensification of warning:

/ra:mba:bu, ciṭhi lekhyaw3^3?/
Rambabu, letter write-2sg.pst.
'Rambabu, did you write the letter?'

/ra:mbabau, a:ja ka:m nagara3^3/
Ra:mba:bu today work not-do-imp.
'Rambabu, do not work today'

10.2.3 The lengthening of the mid-level pitch vowel. The speakers of Nepali communicate the intensity of warning by lengthening the mid-level pitch vowels at the initial syllable of the verbal suffix (/-es/):

/naku:ṭe3^2s/
not-hit-imp.
'Do not hit (I warn you)'

/nakha:e3^2s/
not-eat-imp.
'Do not eat (it may hurt your health)'

The speaker's intent is to warn the addressee of the negative repercussions in the instances given.

The following examples indicate that the lengthening of the vowel of the verbal suffix (/-cha, /-la:/, /-o/) is restricted to the verb of the first of the two clauses juxtaposed to each other. The lengthening of vowels indicate specific connotations besides the general intensification of the statements. In the following statement, for instance, disapproval of action is indicated by lengthening the vowel, whereas the same sentence without the lengthening of vowel is makes a simple statement of the fact.

/a:phu ghoḍa:ma: caḍcha3^2, gurula:i hĩḍa:w̃cha/
self-nm horse-lc ride-3sg.pres., teacher-ac walk-cause-3sg.pres.
'He (himself) rides the horse, (and) makes (his) teacher walk'

In the following statements persuasiveness is indicated by the lengthening of the vowels:

/yagya garawla:3^2 ani ban ja:wla:/
sacrifice do-2sg.fut. and-then forest go-2sg.fut.
'You will perform sacrifices (first); and you will go to the forest (afterwards)'

/yati paḍha3^2 ghara ja:w/
this-much read-imp. home go-imp.
'Read this much; and go home'

/timi jastai cha3^2; hos gara/
you like be-3sg.pres.; care do-imp.
'(He) is just like you; be careful'

Writing System

Chapter 4
From phoneme to grapheme and grapheme to phoneme

4.0 Introduction. This chapter describes the writing system of Nepali, which uses the Devanagari alphabet, originally devised to transcribe Sanskrit. Devanagari is written from left to right. The Devanagari alphabet has no capital and small letters. In terms of dictionary citation, the alphabet is written in separate groups, i.e. the vowels and consonants. The alphabet also sub-groups the consonants on the basis of (1) the points of articulation and (2) manners of articulation (Figure 4.1).

Figure 4.1 The Devanagari alphabet with standard roman transliteration

Vowels: अ a आ ā इ i ई ī उ u ऊ ū ऋ ṛ ॠ ṝ ए e ऐ ai ओ o औ au

Consonants:	Voiceless		Voiced			
	unasp.	asp.	unasp.	asp.	nasal	
	क ka	ख kha	ग ga	घ gha	ङ ṅa	Velars
	च ca	छ cha	ज ja	झ jha	ञ ña	Palatals
	ट ṭa	ठ ṭha	ड ḍa	ढ ḍha	ण ṇa	Alveopalatals
	त ta	थ tha	द da	ध dha	न na	Dentals
	प pa	फ pha	ब ba	भ bha	म ma	Bilabials
	य ya	र ra	ल la	व va	*Antaḥsthas* (see note 3)	
	श śa	ष ṣa	स sa	ह ha	*Uṣmas* (see note 4)	
	क्ष kṣa	त्र tra	ज्ञ jña		Special clusters (see note 5)	

Note 1. The transliterations of the Devanagari consonant symbols in Figure 4.1 indicate that a vowel phoneme /a/ (mid central vowel schwa), without any graphic representation, is present in every consonant symbol. The absence of this vowel (/a/) is indicated in two ways: (1) by writing a half or incomplete form of the consonant, as न् /n/ in the word-medial position, and (2) by using a stroke (्) called *virām*, under the consonant symbol in word-final position, e.g. भन्छन् /bhanchan/ 'they say'.

2. The Devanagrai alphabet in Figure 4.1 is presented in the same way as in any textbooks of the Nepali language. The alphabet presents the symbols for the consonant stops beginning with the phonemes articulated in the back of the oral cavity, i.e., velars, and proceeds toward the front of the oral cavity. The voiceless stops are listed first and the voiced phonemes afterwards. In the groups of both voiceless and voiced phonemes, the unaspirated phonemes are listed before the aspirated ones.

3. The phonemes /y/, /r/, /l/ and /w/, and their Devanagari symbols य, र, ल and व representing them respectively are called *antasthas* 'remaining inside'. The phonetic fact is that in the articulation of these Nepali phonemes the pulmonic airstream does not release with as much force as in the articulation of the stops or plosives. Thus, the relatively weak release of breath in the articulation of /y/, /r/, /l/, and /w/ seems to be the reason for calling them *antasthas* '(the pulmonic air-stream) remaining inside (the oral cavity) '

4. The fricatives /ś/, /ṣ/, /s/, /h/ and their Devanagari symbols श, ष, स and ह are termed *uṣmas* 'warm' for the fact that the articulation of these fricatives is characterized by the continuous outflow of warm pulmonic airstream. The warmth of the air in their articulation is more perceptible owing to the fact that they involve continuation of the outflow of air. In articulation of the stops (plosives) the outflow of the airstream is quicker, and the perception of the warm air is less prominent.

5. Although there are many more conjuncts than just the three listed in Figure 4.1, they are transparent in the sense that the reader can identify the consonants in the conjuncts. In case of the consonant conjuncts /kṣ/, /tr/ and /jñ/, the symbols representing them (क्ष, त्र, and ज्ञ respectively) are not so transparent. They are, therefore, included in the alphabet as new symbols. However, the consonant clusters represented by these symbols do not occur in Nepali words; these symbols are used only in transcribing the words borrowed from Sanskrit. Since the consonant conjuncts /kṣ/, /tr/ and /jñ/ represented by the symbols क्ष, त्र and ज्ञ do not occur in Nepali words, the speakers of Nepali pronounce them differently, e.g. क्ष /kṣa/ [chya], त्र /tra/[tara] and ज्ञ /jña/ [gyã].

4.1 From phoneme to grapheme. The stress, whether phonetic or phonemic, is not marked in Nepali. Although most of the phonemes have one-to-one correspondences in written forms, there are a number of exceptions which are explained in (4.2.1-4.2.3). One major exception is in the case of Hindi and Sanskrit loan words, which are spelled the same way as they are spelled in the source languages regardless of the nativization process in Nepali. The resultant descrepancy is due to the difference in the phonemic inventories of Nepali, Sanskrit, and Hindi.

A quick glance at Figure 4.1 and Figure 4.2 will show that the Devanagari alphabet (adopted by Nepali without necessary modifications) has more graphemes than the phonemes of Nepali.

The argument presented by the traditional grammarians in favor of borrowing the Devanagari alphabet without modification is that Nepali has also borrowed about 80 % of its literary words from Sanskrit, and that the borrowed words must be spelled in the same way as they are spelled originally in Sanskrit and

Hindi. So, although it is possible to have one-to-one correspondence in the phonemic representation of Nepali using Devanagari, a prescriptive tradition has been followed in the Nepali writing system.

Figure 4.2 Inventory of Nepali segmental phonemes and the corresponding Devanagari graphemes

Type	Manner of articulation	B	D	AP	P	V	G
Stops	vl. unasp.	p प	t त	ṭ ट	c च	k क	
	vl. asp.	ph फ	th थ	ṭh ठ	ch छ	kh ख	
	vd. unasp.	b ब	d द	ḍ ड	j ज	g ग	
	vd. asp.	bh भ	dh ध	ḍh ढ	jh झ	gh घ	
Nasals	vd.	m म	n न			ng ङ	
Fricatives			s स				h ह
Laterals	vd.			l ल			
Trill	vd.			r र			
Glides				y य		w व	
Vowels:							
	High oral and nasal			i इ ĩ इँ		u उ ũ उँ	
	Mid oral and nasal			e ए ẽ एँ	a अ ã अँ	o ओ	
	Low oral and nasal				a: आ ã: आँ		

AP Alveopalatal B Bilabial D Dental G Glottal
P Palatal V Velar asp. aspirated unasp. unaspirated
vd. voiced vl. voiceless ~ nasal vowel

4.1.1 Vowels. The Devanagari symbols of the vowels have two forms: (1) free forms which are written when the single vowels constitute the syllables, and (2) conjunct forms which are written when the vowels are preceded by consonants or glides to constitute CV or GV syllabic structures.

4.1.1.1 Free forms of vowels. The free forms of the Devanagari vowel symbols are the following:

a	ā	i	ī	u	ū	ṛ	ṝ	e	ai	o	au
अ	आ	इ	ई	उ	ऊ	ऋ	ॠ	ए	ऐ	ओ	औ

4.1.1.2 Conjunct forms of vowels. The corresponding conjunct forms of the free forms of the vowel symbols used in the CV or GV syllable structures are the following:

Vowels	a	ā	i	ī	u	ū	r̥	r̥̄	e	ai	o	au
Free forms	अ	आ	इ	ई	उ	ऊ	ऋ	ॠ	ए	ऐ	ओ	औ
Conjunct forms		ा	ि	ी	ु	ू	ृ	ॄ	े	ै	ो	ौ

Note that the vowel symbol अ /a/, has no corresponding conjunct form, which means its presence is indicated by nothing but the shape of the bare consonant symbol. The absence of the vowel phoneme /a/ is marked by the stroke (्) called *virām*. Following are illustrations of the conjunct forms of vowels with क् (/k/), forming CV syllables:

k + a = ka	क् + अ =	क
k + ā = kā	क् + आ =	का
k + i = ki	क् + इ =	कि
k + ī = kī	क् + ई =	की
k + u = ku	क् + उ =	कु
k + u = kū	क् + ऊ =	कू
k + r̥ = kr̥	क् + ऋ =	कृ
k + r̥̄ = kr̥̄	क् + ॠ =	कॄ
k + e = ke	क् + ए =	के
k + ai = kai	क् + ऐ =	कै
k + o = ko	क् + ओ =	को
k + au = kau	क् + औ =	कौ

Following is the same information in summary:

ka	kā	ki	kī	ku	k	kr̥	kr̥̄	ke	kai	ko	kau
क	का	कि	की	कु	कू	कृ	कॄ	के	कै	को	कौ

All the other consonant symbols (except र /r/) join with the conjunct vowel symbols in the same fashion. The symbol र shows an exception to this regularity when it joins with the vowel symbols उ /u/ and ऊ /ū/ as it is written as रु /ru/ and रू /rū/ respectively, not as रु and रू as expected. The symbol र also shows a number of irregular conjunct forms when it is conjoined with other consonant symbols (see 4.1.4.2).

4.1.2 Glides. The Nepali glides /y/ and /w/ are more consonantal in their phonetic characteristics in pre-peak position, and are represented by symbols य and व respectively. In post-peak position the glides are more vocalic in their phonetic characteristics, and are represented by the Devanagari vowel symbols इ and उ in the writing system of Nepali. For instance,
In pre-peak position:

GV.	/yo/ [io] यो	'this'
GV.CV	/ya.hã: /[ia.hã:] यहाँ	'here'
GV.CV	/wa.ri/[ua:ri] वारि	'on this side'
GV.CV	/wa.hã: /[ua.hã:] वहाँ	'there (remote)'
CGV.CV	/tya.hã: /[tia.hã:] त्यहाँ	'there (proximate)'
CGVC	/lwa:ng/[lua:ng] ल्वाङ्	'clove'

In post-peak position:

VG	/a:w/[a:u] आउ	'come (imp.)'
VG.CV	/a:w.la:/[a:u.la:] आउला	'he will come'
VG.CVG	/a:w̃.chaw̃ /[a:ũ.chaũ] आउँछौं	'we come'
CVG	/bha:y/[bha:i] भाइ	'brother'
CVG.CV	/la:w.la:/[la:u.la:] लाउला	'he will wear'
CVG.CV	/ma:y.lo/[ma:i.lo] माइलो	'second eldest male'

Thus, in VG structures (post-peak position), glides are transcribed by the writing symbols as vowels because of their phonetically vocoid characteristics.

The glide /y/ followed by another glide /y/ as in CVG.GV structures, e.g /pa:y.yo/ 'was found', is spelled with half of the grapheme य as पाय्यो or alternatively as पाइयो. No instance of the glide /w/ followed by similar glide /w/ being represented by the half form of व is found.

4.1.3 Consonants. Just as the vowel symbols have both free and conjunct forms, similarly the consonant symbols also have both free and conjunct forms. However, the free and conjunct symbols of the consonants do not look so radically different as the free and conjunct symbols of the vowels do. They are exemplified in section (4.1.3.2).

4.1.3.1 Free forms of the consonant symbols. Free forms of the Devanagari consonant symbols are listed in Figure 4.1. They are presented again in section (4.1.3.2) with a viram stroke (्) indicating the absence of the mid central vowel schwa /a/ which is otherwise supposed to be present in every single, free consonant symbol. In other words, Devanagari writing system does not have a separate distinct written symbol for schwa (ə) when it is conjoined with the consonant symbols.

4.1.3.2 Conjunct forms of the consonant symbols. When two consonants conjoin with each other in CC or CG clusters, they are written in regular ways (4.1.3.2.1) and irregular ways (4.1.3.2.2).

4.1.3.2.1 Regular conjunct forms of the consonant symbols. The regular conjunct forms of the consonant symbols are written in three ways:

(1) The first way of writing a conjunct consonant symbol is the one in which the first consonant's symbol is written half-shape, and the second consonant's symbol is written full-shape. This group consists of those consonant symbols in which the first consonant has a vertical stroke somewhere on it. Following are the examples in Devanagari alphabetical order:

k + kā क् + का क्का as in पक्का pak.kā 'mature'
kh + ya ख् + य = ख्य as in मुख्य mukhya 'main'
g + ya ग् + य = ग्य as in योग्य yogya 'proper' etc.
gh + yo घ् + यो = घ्यो as in नाघ्यो nāghyo 'he crossed'
c + cā च् + चा = च्चा as in बच्चा baccā 'child'
j + jā ज् + जा = ज्जा as in मज्जा majjā 'fun'
j + ya ज् + या = ज्या as in ज्याला jyālā 'wages'
jh + yā झ् + झ्या = झ्या as in झ्याल jhyāl 'window'
ñ + ca ञ् + च as in पञ्च pañca 'five, a political worker'
ṇ + ya ण् + य = य as in पुण्य puṇya 'religious merit'
t + yo त् + यो = त्यो as in त्यो tyo 'that one'
th + yo थ् + यो = थ्यो as in हुन्थ्यो hunthyo 'it used to be'
dh + yā ध् + या = ध्या as in ध्यान dhyān 'meditation'
n + yā न् + या = न्या as in न्यानो nyāno 'warm'
p +yā प् + या = प्या as in प्यारो pyāro 'dear'
ph + yā फ् + या = फ्या as in फ्याउरो phyāuro 'fox'
b + yā ब् + या = ब्या as in ब्याउनु byāunu 'to give birth'
bh + yā भ् + या = भ्या as in भ्याकुतो bhyākuto 'frog'
m + wā म् + वा = म्वा as in म्वाइ mwāi 'kiss'
y + yā य् + या = य्या as in शय्या śayyā 'bed'
l + lo ल् + लो = ल्लो as in पल्लो pallo 'next'
v[b] + yā व् + व्या = व्या as in व्यायाम vyāyāma 'exercise'
ś + yā श् + या = श्या as in श्याम śyāma 'Shyam (proper noun)'
ṣ + ṭa ष् + ट = ष्ट as in शिष्ट śiṣṭa 'cultured, educated'

(2) The second way of writing a conjunct consonant symbol is the one in which the first consonant symbol is written full-shape, and the second consonant

symbol is written half-shape, or is at least modified. These consonant symbols include the letters ङ, छ, ट, ठ, ड, ढ, which has the first consonant with य to form CG clusters. The absence of the inherent /a/ in the first consonant symbol is not symbolized by the *virām* stroke (্), but by a modification in the symbol य which is written as ्य to indicate the conjunct:

ṅ + yā ङ् + या = ङ्या as in ङ्याउ ṅyāu ' "mew" sound of cat'
ch +yā छ् + या = छ्या as in छ्याप्नु chyāpnu 'splash'
ṭ + yā ट् + या = ट्या as in ट्याम्को ṭyāmko 'a small drum'
ṭh + yā ठ् + या ठ्या as in ठ्याम्म ṭhyāmma 'manner of exactly fitting'
ḍ + yā ड् + या = ड्या as in जँड्याहा jā̃dyāhā 'drunkard'
ḍh + yā ढ् + या ढ्या = as in ढ्याम्म ḍyāmma 'sound of explosion (onomatopoeic form)'

When ङ्, छ, ट, ठ, ड, ढ, are conjoined with व, the absence of the inherent /a/ in the first symbol is indicated by the virām stroke (্) given under the first symbol because the second symbol in the conjunct remains unchanged, e.g.

ṅ + wā ङ् + वा = as in ङ्वार्र ṅwārra 'snarling of cat'
ch + wā छ् + वा = as in छ्वाली chwāli 'stalk of wheat'
ṭ + wā ट् + वा as in ट्वाक् ṭwāk 'a small drinking vessel'
ḍ + wā ड् + वा = वा as in ड्वाङ्ङ ḍwāṅṅa 'falling sound'
ḍh + wā ढ् + वा as in ढ्वाङ् ḍhwāṅ 'dustbin'

There is an exception in this second way of writing conjunct consonants. The symbol ङ conjoined with the symbols क, ख, ग and घ is written on top of those symbols:

ṅ + ka ङ् + क = ङ्क as in अङ्क aṅka 'number'
ṅ + kha ङ् + ख = ङ्ख as in शङ्ख śaṅkha 'conch'
ṅ + ga ङ् + ग = ङ्ग as in अङ्ग aṅga 'body'
ṅ + gha ङ् + घ = ङ्घ as in सङ्घ saṅgha 'union'

Likewise, ट् + ट, ठ् + ठ and ड् + ड are also written one on top of the other, e.g.

ṭ + ṭā ट् + टा = ट्टा as in लट्टा laṭṭā 'matted hair'
ṭ + ṭhā ट् + टा = ट्टा as in चिट्ठा ciṭṭhā 'lottery'
ḍ + ḍā ड् + डा as in अड्डा aḍḍā 'station, post, district headquarters'

(3) The third way of writing a consonant conjunct symbol is the one in which the second consonant symbol in the CC clusters is written half. This is

illustrated by the case in which the second item in the conjunct is the symbol र which is conjoined in various ways with other symbols in the Devanagari alphabet.

With the letters having vertical strokes:

g + ro ग् + रो = ग्रो as in गाग्रो gāgro 'pitcher'
gh + rā घ् + रा = घ्रा as in तिघ्रा tigrā 'thigh'
p + ra प् + र = प्र as in प्रश्न praśna 'question'
b + ra ब् + रा = ब्रा as in ब्राह्मण brāhmaṅa 'Brahman (a caste)'

With the symbols having rounded bottoms such as छ, ट, ड, and ढ the symbol र is conjoined in the following way:

ch + re छ् + रे = छ्रे as in माछापुछ्रे māchāpuchre 'Machapuchre (proper name of a mountain in the Himalayas)'
ṭ + ra ट् + र = ट्र as in ट्रक ṭrak 'truck'
ḍ + ra ड् + र = ड्र as in ड्रम ḍram 'drum'
ḍh + ra ढ् + र = ढ्र as in मेढ्र meḍhra 'penis (Sanskrit word)'

When the symbol र stands for the phoneme /r/ that is in the onset position of the second syllable as in CV.CGV structure, the /r/ is represented by symbol ‐ , e.g. पऱ्यो *pa.ryo* 'it fell in', गऱ्यो *ga.ryo* 'he did it'

When the symbol र stands for the phoneme /r/ that is in the coda position of the the first syllable as in CVC.CV, the /r/ is represented by the symbol ॅ e.g. गर्न *gar.na* 'to do (inf.)', मर्न *mar.na* 'to die (inf.)'.

4.1.3.2.2 Irregular conjunct forms of the consonant symbols. Following are the irregular conjunct forms of different consonant symbols; they are listed in the Devanagari alphabetical order:

k + ta क् + त = क्त as in भक्त bhakta 'devotee'
k + ṣa क् + ष = क्ष as in अक्षर akṣar 'letter'
j + jā ज् + जा as in मज्जा majjā 'pleasure'; regular form मज्जा
j + ñā ज् + ञा as in ज्ञान jñān 'knowledge'
ñ + ca ञ् + च = ञ्च as in मञ्च manca 'pavilion'
ñ + ja ञ् + ज = ञ्ज as in मञ्जरी mañjarī 'sprout'; regular form: मञ्जरी
t + to त् + तो = त्तो as in पत्तो patto 'whereabouts'
d + ga द् + ग = द्ग as in सद्गति sadgati 'Deliverance'
d + ghā द् + घा = द्घा as in उद्घाटन udghāṭana 'inauguration'; regular form उद्‌घाटन
d + dā द् + दा = द्दा as in मुद्दा muddā 'legal case' regular form मुद्‌दा
d + dha द् + ध as in शुद्ध śuddha 'correct, pure'

d + ma द् + म = द्म as in पद्म padma 'lotus' regular form: पद्म
d + ya द् + य as in पद्य padya 'verse'
d + ra द् + र = द्र as in शूद्र śūdra ' Shudra (a caste)'
d +wā द् + द्वा as in विद्वान् vidwān 'scholar'
h + na ह् + न = ह्न as in अपराह्न aparāhna 'afternoon'; regular form अपरान्ह
h + ma ह् + म = ह्म as in ब्राह्मण brāhmaṇa 'Brahman (a caste)'
h + ya ह् + य = ह्य as in गुह्य guhya 'secret'
h + ro ह् + रो as in गाह्रो gāhro 'difficult'; regular form गार्‍हो
h +lā ह् + ला = ह्ला as in प्रह्लाद prahlāda 'Prahlad (name of a man)'
h + wā ह् + वा = ह्वा as in ह्वात्त whātta 'manner of throwing'

4.1.4 Additional symbols: bindu, anusvār and visarga. The Devanagari writing system also uses additional symbols which are called *bindu, anusvār* and *visarga* (all Sanskrit names).

4.1.4.1 Bindu. *Bindu* is called *'sirbindu'* in Nepali, and is inconsistently used to represent the nasal stops that are homorganic with the adjacent stops, e.g

aṅka अङ्क is also written as अंक 'number'
añcal अञ्चल or अञ्चल is also written as अंचल 'zone'
kaṇṭaka कण्टक is also written as कंटक 'thorn'
panta पन्त is also written as पंत 'Panta (a family name)'
samma सम्म is also written as संम 'plain, flat'

The inconsistency in the use of *bindu* lies also in the fact that *bindu* is used to represent nasal stops that are not homorganic, e.g.

/kangsa/ कंस 'Kaṅsa (a proper name)'
/sya:ngja:/ स्यांजा 'Syāṅjā (name of a district in Nepal)'
/ramgha:/ रंघा 'Ramghā (name of a village)'

4.1.4.2 Anusvār. *Anusvār* is the sign (ँ) used to indicate the nasalization of vowel, e.g.

sãga सँग 'with'
gāũ गाउँ 'village'

In Nepali the *anusvār* is also used inconsistently, since *sirbindu* is often used interchangeably with the *anusvār*, e.g.

sãga सँग or संग 'with'
gāũ गाउँ or गाउं 'village'

4.1.4.3 Visarga. *Visarga* is a sign (:) which is used in the Devanagari writing system to represent a vowel followed by a glottal fricative. This sign is used only in the words borrowed from Sanskrit, e.g.

duḥkha [du*kha] दुःख 'sorrow, hardship'
antaḥkaraṇ [anta*karaṇ] अन्तःकरण 'soul, heart'

The phonemic transcription of the Nepali text is the following:

/na:so/

/gharma: cancala:sri bhaykana pani debiramanka: santa:n thienan. santa:n hos bhanna:ka: nimitta haraek upa:ya gare, cauta:ro cine, ba:ṭo khane, pasupatima: maha:dip ba:le, gae sa:l haribamsa pura:n laga:e, taypani subhadra:ko kokh saphal huna sakena. joripa:ri sãga ṭhoka:baji parda: dhan, bal, buddhi sabai kura:ma: unko jit hunthyo tara aputo bhaneko sunnebittikai unko abhima:n dhulo hunthyo, a:tmaglanile pa:ni hunthe. pura:na: bica:rka: ma:nis thie, santa:n bina: a:phno baibhabla:y tuccha samjanthe/.

The Devanagari transcription of the Nepali text is the following:

नासो

घरमा चञ्चलाश्री भइकन पनि देवीरमणका सन्तान थिएनन् । सन्तान होस् भन्नका निमित्त हरएक उपाय गरे, चौतारो चिने, बाटो खने, पशुपतिमा महादीप बाले, गए साल हरिवंश पुराण लगाए, तैपनि सुभद्राको कोख सफल हुन सकेन । जोरीपारीसंग ठोकाबाजी पर्दा धन, बल, बुद्धि सबै कुरामा उनको जित हुन्थ्यो तर 'अपुतो' भनेको सुन्ने-बित्तिकै उनको अभिमान धूलो हुन्थ्यो, आत्मग्लानिले पानी हुन्थे । पुराना विचारका मानिस थिए, सन्तान विना आफ्नो वैभवलाई तुच्छ संझन्थे ।

Standard roman transliteration of the Devanagari text is the following:

nāso

gharamā cañcalāśrī bhaikana pani devīramaṇakā santāna thienan. santāna hos bhannākā nimitta haraeka upāya gare, cautāro cine, bāṭo khane, paśupatimā mahādīpa bāle, gae sāla harivaṃśa purāṇa lagāe, taipani subhadrāko kokha saphala huna sakena. jorīpārīsaṃga ṭhokābājī pardā dhna, bala, buddhi savai kurāmā unako jita hunthyo tara 'apūto' bhaneko sunnebittikai unako abhimāna dhūlo hunthyo, ātmaglānile pāni hunthe. purānā vicārakā mānisa thie, santāna vinā āphno vaibhavalāī tuccha samjhanthe.

4.2 From grapheme to phoneme. The phonemic transliteration, the Devanagari transcription, and the standard transliteration of a Nepali text indicate that there is no one-to-one correspondence in the Devanagari transcription of Nepali. One of the reasons for such a lack of correspondence is that loan words from Sanskrit and Hindi are written in their Sanskrit and Hindi spellings. But they are pronounced according to a different phonemic system of Nepali. This phenomenon leads one to the question: How does one go from graphemes to phonemes, or how are the Devanagari graphemes pronounced phonemically in Nepali? This question is addressed in sections (4.2.1-4.2.3).

4.2.1 Vowels. In the writing system of Nepali, the Devanagari symbols for both short and long vowels are used. However, since length is not phonemic in Nepali, both the short and long vowel symbols are pronounced as short by Nepali native speakers, e.g.

i free form: इ as in इच्छा 'desire'	conjunct form ि as in किन 'why'
i: free form: ई as in ईश्वर 'god'	conjunct form: ी as in चीन 'China'
u free form: उ as in उठ 'get up'	conjunct form: ु as in कुन 'which'
u: free form: ऊ as in ऊन 'wool'	conjunct form: ू as in कूत 'rent of land'

The grapheme ऋ representing the vocalic /ṛ/ is used only in loan words from Sanskrit, and is pronounced as /ri/ (consisting of two Nepali phonemes) by the speakers of Nepali, e.g ऋषि, ऋण, कृष्ण are pronounced as: /risi/, /rin/, /kisna/ or /kirisna/. Note that the vocalic /ṛ/ does not exist in the phonemic inventory of Nepali. But it does exist in the graphemic inventory of Nepali. Hence this transition from grapheme to phoneme.

4.2.2 Glides. The Devanagari symbols य and व for glides /y/ and /w/ respectively, are pronounced more like consonants (with certain degree of friction) in the onset position. The glides /y/ and /w/ are transcribed with the vowel symbols इ and उ respectively in coda position, and are pronounced as [i] and [u].

4.2.3 Consonants. The Devanagari consonant symbols represent a one-to-one correspondence to the Nepali consonant phonemes. The exceptions are described in the sections (4.2.3.1-4.2.3.5).

4.2.3.1 Pronunciation of consonants without the virām stroke. All free forms of consonant symbols in Nepali such as क, च, ट, त, प, unless otherwise indicated, are pronounced as /ka/ /ca/ /ṭa/ /ta/ pa/. Thus, the symbols क, च, ट, त, प represent consonant phonemes /k/, /c/, /ṭ/, /t/, /p/ followed by a mid central vowel schwa /a/, which has no written symbol when conjoined with a consonant. The absence of /a/ is marked either by writing a half-form of the consonant symbol in the word-medial position, or by the *virām* stroke (्) at the word-final position. However, the virām stroke is not always used in written Nepali. So, there arises a question: where is the *virām* stroke used to mark the absence of the vowel /a/, and where is it not used? The answer is the following:

The *virām* stroke is consistently used to mark the absence of the vowel /a/ in the verbal forms, so भन, भन्, भन्छ, भन्छन्, भनिस् are pronounced exactly the way they are written. The viram stroke is not used to mark the absence of the vowel /a/ in the word-final position of nouns and other forms, so the vowel /a/ in the final position of those forms is not pronounced, e.g. राम /ra:ma/ (CV.CV) is pronounced as राम् /rām/ (CVC). In complex or compound forms the morpheme-final /a/ is omitted, e.g.

केशवदेव *keśavadeva* is pronounced as केसव्देव् /kesabdeb/
रामप्रसाद *rāmaprasāda* is pronounced as राम्प्रसाद् /rāmprasād/
जवाहरलाल *jawāharalāla* is pronounced as जवाहर्लाल् /jawāharlāl/
छिमेकका *chimekakā* is pronounced as छिमेक्का /chimekkā/
उनलाई *unalāī* is pronounced as उन्लइ् /unlāy/

However, the final /a/ in the written form रत्न *ratna* is not omitted in pronunciation because such omission of the final /a/ creates a CVCC syllable which does not exist in Nepali. So the written forms like रत्न पुस्तक भण्डार *ratna pustaka bhaṇḍāra* is pronounced as रत्न पुस्तक् भण्डार् ratna pustak bhaṇḍa:r 'Ratna Book Store'.

4.2.3.2 Voiced aspirates. The graphemes representing the voiced aspirate stops घ, झ, ढ, ध, भ are pronounced as their unaspirate counterparts ग, ज, ड, द, ब in post-vocalic positions, e.g.

बाघ is pronounced as बाग् 'tiger'
बाँझो is pronounced as बाँजो 'barren'
बाढी is pronounced as बाडि 'flood'
बाधा is pronounced as बादा 'obstacle'
उँभो is pronounced as उँबो 'upward'

4.2.3.3 Pronunciation of the symbols श, ष, स. The symbols श *śa*, ष *ṣa*, and स *sa* are pronounced as स *sa*. The symbols श and ष are used only in words borrowed from Sanskrit, e.g.

शोषण pronounced as सोसण् 'exploitation'
शिशु pronounced as सिसु 'child'
विशेष pronounced as बिसेस् 'special'
भाषा pronounced as भासा 'language'
सुशील pronounced as सुसिल 'Sushil (personal name)
विशिष्ट pronounced as बिसिस्ट 'special'

4.2.3.4 The special consonant conjunct graphemes. The special consonant conjunct graphemes क्ष ,त्र and ज्ञ are pronounced as /chya/ /tara/, and /gyã/ respectively by the Nepalese, e.g.

क्षेत्र *kṣetra* pronounced as छेत्र 'field'
कक्षा *kakṣā* pronounced as कछ्या 'class'
त्रिलोक *triloka* pronounced as तिर्लोक् 'three worlds'
त्रिभुवन *tribhuvana* pronounced as तिर्भुबन् 'three worlds'
ज्ञान *jñāna* pronounced as ग्यान् 'knowledge'
अज्ञान *ajñāna* pronounced as अग्यान् 'ignorance'

Besides the special conjunct symbols क्ष, त्र, ज्ञ, a special Devanagari conjunct symbol ॐ is also used in Nepali, and is pronounced as /om/ although in Sanskrit it stands for /aum/ which means the trinity of Hindu gods.

4.2.3.5 The pronunciation of orthographic word-initial CC clusters. The other conjuncts representing CC clusters which do not occur in the word-initial positions in Nepali are pronounced with the insertion of the phoneme /a/. See also section (2.3).

व्रत pronounced as बर्त 'vow'
प्रथम pronounced as पर्थम् 'first'
श्राद्ध pronounced as सराद्द 'annual obeisance to the deceased ancestors'
ग्रहण pronounced as गरन् 'eclipse'
मृग pronounced as मिर्ग 'deer'
क्रिया pronounced as किरिया 'post-obital rites'
प्रीति pronounced as पीर्ति 'love'
कृष्ण pronounced as किरिस्न or किस्न Krishna (personal name)'
स्कूल pronounced as इस्कुल "school'
स्थिति pronounced as इस्थिति 'situation'
स्पष्ट pronounced as इस्पष्ट 'clear'
प्रधानमन्त्री pronounced as पर्धानमन्त्री 'Prime Minister'

4.2.3.6 The symbol ह. The symbol ह for glottal fricative phoneme /h/ is not pronounced in the post-vocalic position. For instance,

अहिले pronounced as ऐले 'now'
कहिले pronounced as कैले 'when?'
पहिले pronounced as पैले 'before'
पहिरो pronounced as पैरो 'landslide'
गहिरो pronounced as गैरो 'deep'
थाहा is pronounced as थाआ or था 'knowledge'

4.3 Numerals. The Devanagari numerals are written and pronounced in the following way:

Devanagari	Arabic	Spelled in letters	Prononced as:
०	0	शून्य	sunne or sunna:
१	1	एक	ek
२	2	दुइ	dui
३	3	तीन	tin
४	4	चार	ca:r
५	5	पाँच	pã:c
६	6	छ	cha
७	7	सात	sa:t
८	8	आठ	ā:ṭh
९	9	नौ	nau
१०	10	दस	das

The Devanagari symbols for numerals, after a thousand (haja:r), are divided at every tenth position, and are spelled and pronounced as:

1	एक ek
10	दश das
100	शय sae
1000	हजार haja:r
10, 000	दश हजार das haja:r
1, 00, 000	लाख la:kh
10, 00, 000	दश laK das la:kh
1, 00, 00, 000	करोड karoḍ
10, 00, 00, 000	दश करोड das karoḍ
1, 00, 00, 00, 000	अरब/अर्ब arab/arba
10, 00, 00, 00, 000	दश अरब! दश अर्ब das arab/das arba
1, 00, 00, 00, 00, 000	खरब/खर्ब kharab/kharba
10, 00, 00, 00, 00, 000	दश खरब/दश खर्ब das kharab/das kharba

4.4 Punctuation marks. In many printed texts of Nepali one may not find consistency in the use of the punctuation marks. Most of the punctuation marks used in modern Nepali texts are borrowed from Hindi and English. The older Nepali texts used a few punctuation marks, e.g. full stop mark (।) or double full stop marks (॥) used in Sanskrit texts majority of which were in verse.

The following punctuation marks are used in modern Nepali texts:

।	Full stop to mark the end of a statement, as म नेपाली हुँ ।
,	Comma to mark the concatenation of the same functional slot, as राम, सीता र लक्ष्मण वन गए ।
-	hyphen to mark the compound forms as भलो-कुभलो, सुख-दुःख, Hyphen also is used to mark the break of a word, as देवी-रमणलाई
" ... "	Quotation to mark the reporting speech, as उसले भन्यो -- "आज म स्कूल जान्न ।"
;	Semi-colon like full stop marks the end of a complete statement followed by another complete statement closely related to the previous one, as पुराना विचारका मानिस थिए; सन्तान विना आफ्नो वैभवलई तुच्छ सम्झन्थे ।
. .	Abbreviation marks, as एम्. ए., त्रि. वि. वि.
...	To mark a part of text missing, as म ... स्कूल गइन ।
–	Dash to mark that the following statement is proposed by the current statement as, उसले भन्यो-- "आज म स्कूल जान्न ।"
( )	Parentheses to mark a remark which, without being a grammatically integral part of the statement, explains the statement made, as प्याण्टको बगलीमा देब्रे हात हालेर, दाहिनेले छडी हल्लाउँदै (तेस्रो हात भएको भए त्यसले चुरोट अवश्य लिने थियो) त्यसले कसरी हाम्रो भाव जानेछ र भन्यो-- "यो सूट गुलाम मुहम्मदले सिएको; ठट्टा होइन ।"
?	Question mark to mark a question statement: यो के हो?
!	Exclamation mark to mark an exclamatory statement: धेरै राम्रो ! गजब ! स्याबाश !

The Form Classes

Chapter 5
The inflected and uninflected forms

5.0 Introduction. This chapter describes the inflected and uninflected forms which are the open and closed form classes (traditionally called 'the parts of speech') of Nepali. The open classes are those classes whose membership is in principle indefinite or unlimited. New items are continually being added, as new ideas, inventions, etc. emerge. The open form classes are noun (5.1), adjective (5.2), verb (5.3), and adverb (5.4). The closed form classes are those whose membership is fixed or limited; new items are not regularly added. The closed classes are pronoun (5.5), coordinating conjunction (5.6), subordinating conjunction (5.7), postposition (5.8), interjection, (5.9), vocative (5.10), and nuance particle (5.11).

Cutting across these major form classes are substitute forms (described in Chapter 6) which manifest an overlaid grammatical function independent of the particular form class to which the form belongs.

The open form classes are divided and classified on the basis of the following four criteria which are more or less useful for each form class to define the members of each class. Those criteria are: (1) whether a particular form class is inflected or not, (2) what function a form class has in a grammatical structure, (3) what dependents does it take as the head of that grammatical structure, and (4) what characteristic lexical morphology does it have to isolate it from other form classes. The descriptions of each form class in the following paragraphs further clarify the four criteria used to define them. These four criteria for each form class might be discussed in different order for each class depending upon which criteria might be more useful or practical in defining a particular class. However, in this description a uniform order has been followed to avoid confusion.

5.1 Nouns.

Inflection. Nouns are defined as those forms which inflect for number (singular vs. plural) and for the set of seven cases listed and displayed in Figure 5.1 and 5.2. They do not inflect for gender (masculine vs. feminine) but belong directly to a determined or undetermined gender class.

Traditional grammars define nouns as inflected for gender as well as inflected for case and number, e.g. *choro* 'son' vs. *chori* 'daughter' but this grammar prefers to treat such forms as separate lexical items, independent of each other.

Professional titles and caste names in Nepali show a gender contrast, but this contrast is shown by derivational morphology, not by inflectional morphology (Cf. 7.2).

Nepali nouns show inflectional contrasts for singular vs. plural, e.g *mānis* 'man' *mānisharu* 'men', and show inflectional contrasts for nominative, accusative, instrumental, dative, ablative, genitive, and locative cases. These case-number suffixes are presented in Figures 5.1 and 5.2.

Nepali nouns (except those that end in *-o*) do not show contrast for a vocative case form. Although nouns ending in *-o* do show a form which is lexically a vocative, e.g. *chorā* 'O son' which contrasts with the nominative case form *choro* 'son', it would seem preferable to assign such instances to either the lexicon or derivational formation. The same might be said of similar formations such as *lāṭā* 'O dumb one' vs. *lāṭo* 'dumb'. Moreover, such contrasts are diminishing in certain dialects of Nepali, e.g. Darjeeling dialect.

Figure 5.1 The number and case suffixes of nouns

Cases	Singular	Plural
Nominative (Nm)	- Ø	-haru
Accusative (Ac)	-lāi	-haru-lāi
Instrumental (In)	-le	-haru-le
Dative (Dt)	-lāi	-haru-lāi
Ablative (Ab)	-bāṭa	-haru-bāṭa
Genitive (Gn)	-ko	-haru-ko
Locative (Lc)	-mā	-haru-mā

Figure 5.2 Number and case inflections of the noun *mānis* 'man'

Cases	Singular	Plural
Nm	mānis	mānis-haru
Ac	mānis-lāi	mānis-haru-lāi
In	mānis-le	mānis-haru-le
Dt	mānis-lāi	mānis-haru-lāi
Ab	mānis-bāṭa	mānis-haru-bāṭa
Gn	mānis-ko	mānis-haru-ko
Lc	mānis-mā	mānis-haru-mā

Function. Nouns function as the heads in noun phrase (NP) structures; such NPs function in the clauses as verb subjects for all verbs, as nominative subject complements for equational verbs, as accusative (direct) object complements of transitive verbs, dative complements of intransitive verbs, and adverbial complements and adjuncts for all classes of verbs. Moreover, they also function as dependents of postpositions (pp) in the postpositional phrases (PP).

Dependents. The dependents of noun are determiners, i.e. demonstratives (7.3.1), specifiers (7.3.2), and modifiers, i.e adjectives, numerals, (7.4) and the dependent nominals (10.1-10.4).

Lexical morphology. The most frequent noun-forming derivational suffixes are *-yāī̃, -āi*, e.g. *mūrkha* 'foolish' < *mūrkhyāī̃* 'foolishness', *hā̃:s* 'laugh' < *hā̃sāi* 'laughter', *hī̃ḍ* 'walk' < *hī̃ḍāi* 'walking'.

5.2 Adjectives.

Inflection. Adjectives end in *-o* and inflect for gender (masculine vs. feminine), and number (singular vs. plural), e.g.

Singular number: Masculine	Feminine	Plural number: Masculine / feminine
rāmro 'handsome'	rāmrī 'beautiful'	rāmrā 'handsome, beautiful'
bāṭho 'clever'	bāṭhī 'clever'	bāṭhā 'clever'
lāṭo 'dumb'	lāṭī 'dumb'	lāṭā 'dumb'
kālo 'black'	kālī 'black'	kālā 'black'
moṭo 'fat'	moṭī 'fat'	moṭā 'fat'
sāno 'small'	sānī 'small'	sānā 'small'
ṭhulo 'big'	ṭhulī 'big'	ṭhulā 'big'
buḍho 'old'	buḍhī 'old'	buḍhā 'old'
taruno 'young'	tarunī 'young'	tarunā 'young'

Nepali adjectives (adj) end in *-o* e.g. *rāmro* 'handsome' *bāṭho* 'clever', *lāṭo* 'dumb', *kālo* 'black', *moṭo* 'fat', *sāno* 'small', *ṭhulo* 'big', *buḍho* 'old' *taruno* 'young', etc. which inflect for gender and number.

Nepali also includes a set of uninflected adjectival forms borrowed from Hindi or Sanskrit, which show the same distribution and functions as adjectives, e.g.

asal keṭo 'good boy' *asal keṭī* 'good girl'
asal keṭāharu 'good boys' *asal keṭīharu* 'good girls'

Function. The adjectives function as the heads of the adjective phrase (AdjP) structures. The AdjP's function as subject complements in clauses with equational verbs, e.g. *u dherai baliyo cha* 'he is very strong'. The AdjP's also function as pre-head modifiers in the noun phrases (NP) structures, e.g. *birāmī mānis* 'a sick man'.

Dependents. The dependents of the adjectives are quantifiers which quantify the adjectives, by showing degrees of intensity including the comparative and superlative forms.

Lexical morphology. There are several derivational suffixes that mark the adjectives in Nepali. The suffix *-ilo* derives adjectives from nouns and verbs, e.g. *ras* (n.) 'juice' >*rasilo* 'juicy'; *hā̃:s* ' smile' >*hā̃silo* 'smily'; *mal* 'fertilizer' >*malilo* 'fertile'. Similarly, the suffix *-lī* derives the adjectives from place names, e.g. *gorkhā* 'Gorkha (name of a district), >*gorkhālī* 'related to Gorkha', pālpā 'Palpa (name of a district)', >*pālpālī* 'related to Palpa'; *jhāpā* 'Jhapa (name of a district)' >*jhāpālī* 'related to Jhapa'.[1]

5.3 Verbs

Inflection. Verbs in Nepali inflect to show contrasts for the first, second, and third persons, singular and plural numbers, masculine and feminine gender of a subject in third person singular and tense (present, past, and future), for person: *jā̃chu* 'I go', *jā̃chas* 'you go', *jā̃cha* 'he goes'; for number: *jā̃cha* 'he goes', *jā̃chan* 'they go'; for gender: *jā̃cha* (m) 'he goes', *jā̃che* (f) 'she goes'; and for tense: *jā̃chu* 'I go', *jā̃nechu* 'I will go', *gaē* 'I went'. The verbs also inflect to show contrasts of the grades of honorifics in second and third persons, e.g. *jā̃chas* 'you go (low grade honorific (LGH))', *jā̃chau* 'you go (mid grade honorific (MGH))', *jā nuhuncha* 'you go (high grade honorific (HGH))'.

The verbs also inflect for infinitive, e.g. *jānu* 'go' <*jāna* 'to go'; for perfective participle, e.g. *gaeko* 'gone'; for imperfective participle, e.g. *jāne* 'going'; for conjunctive participle, e.g. *jā̃dā* 'when going'; for absolutive participle, e.g. *gaera* 'having gone'.

The verbal inflections or verbal inflectional suffixes indicate that there are at least three levels of honorifics reflected in everyday spoken Nepali. Those three levels are: Low grade honorific (LGH), mid grade honorific (MGH) and high grade honorific (HGH). The difference of gender is also marked in LGH second and third person singulars. This makes the verbal inflectional system fairly complicated. So, in Figure 5.3 the LGH forms of second and third person masculine only are presented. However, in actual social interactions, mostly the HGH forms are used by the people. Among close friends the MGH is common. The LGH is used by the speaker only in referring to those persons whose social status is clearly lower than that of the speaker. The forms of address determined by social relations are presented in Chapter 9. For a foreign learner, it is better not to use the LGH since there is a risk of offending someone. Figure 5.3 represents the inflectional suffixes of Nepali verbs in 'Present tense', 'Simple past tense' and 'Definite future tense'. (For a full range of inflectional suffixes of Nepali verb in finite forms is see Figure 17.1).

Figure 5.3 The inflectional suffixes of Nepali verbs

Present tense Singular	Plural	Persons and genders (m/f)
-chu	-chaũ	First person
-chas	-chau	Second person (LGHm)
-ches	-chau	Second person (LGHf)
-chau	-chau	Second person (MGHm)
-chyau	-chau	Second person (MGHf)
-nuhuncha	-nuhuncha	Second person (HGHmf)
-cha	-chan	Third person (LGHm)
-che	-chan	Third person (LGHf)
-chan	-chan	Third person (MGHm)
-chin	-chan	Third person (MGHm)
-nuhuncha	-nuhuncha	Third person (HGHm/f)
Simple past tense Singular	**Plural**	**Persons and genders (m/f)**
-ẽ	yaũ	First person
-is	-yau	Second person (LGHm/f)
-yau	-yau	Second person (MGHm/f)
-nubhayo	-nubhayo	Second person (HGHm/f)
-yo	-e	Third person (LGHm)
-i	-e	Third person (LGHf)
-e	-e	Third person (MGHm)
-in	-e	Third person (MGHf)
-nubhayo	-nubhayo	Third person (HGHm/f)
Definite future tense Singular	**Plural**	**Persons and genders (m/f)**
-nechu	-nechaũ	First person
-nechas	-nechau	Second person (LGHm/f)
-nechau	-nechau	Second person (MGHm/f)
-nuhunecha	-nuhunecha	Second person (HGHm/f)
-necha	-nechan	Third person (LGHm/f)

-ncchan	-nechan	Third person (MGHm)
-nechin	-nechan	Third person (MGHm/f)
-nuhunecha	-nuhunecha	Third person (HGHm/f)

Function. The verbs function as the head of the clause structure. As heads of the clause structure, verbs stand either alone or in construction with various types of complements, e.g. direct object, object complement, and subject complements, adverbial complements, and optional adverbial adjuncts. (For further details see Ch. 18).

Dependents. Verbs show various dependents, called complements, which subclassify them into three main types: (transitive, equational, and intransitive). Transitive verbs take direct objects as complements; equational verbs take subject complements as dependents; and intransitive verbs are marked by the absence of either direct object or subject complements.

Verbs, as heads of the clausal structures, also cooccur with indirect dative complements (dependents) such as adverbial complements, adverbial adjuncts, and adverbial disjuncts.

Lexical morphology. The verbs have simple or compound stems, marked by the infinitive suffix *-nu* when they are cited in the dictionary, e.g. *khānu* 'eat', *lāunu* 'wear', *sutnu* 'sleep', *runu* 'cry' etc. The forms *khā-*, *lā-*, *sut-*, *ru-* are simple stems, and *-nu* marks their citation forms. In compound verb stems, the first stem is suffixed with *-i-* and then the second stem is joined, e.g. *khāidinu* 'eat at someone's request, or without someone's knowledge'. In *khāidinu* the first stem *khā-* is followed by the suffix *-i-*, and the second verb stem *di-* . Then follows the citation form marker *-nu*. Verbs derived from nouns and adjectives are marked by the derivational suffix *-āu*, e.g. *rog* (n.) 'disease' *rogāunu* (v.) 'be sick'. The derivational suffix *-āu* also marks the causative verb stems, e.g. *garnu* 'do'<*garāunu* 'cause someone to do'. Likewise, the progressive mood is marked by *-irah-* 'progressive mood marker', and the perfective aspect of verbs is marked by derivational suffixes *-eko-* 'perfective aspect marker'.

5.4 Adverbs.

Inflection. Adverbs in Nepali are uninflected forms. Adverbs show the gradation of comparative and superlative degrees by syntactic means of their dependents (quantifiers or adverbs of quantity).

Function. Adverbs occur as independent of or as the head of an adverbial phrase (AdvP) structure, and function as dependents of the verb, i.e. as complements or adjuncts, e.g. *rāmrarī khāu* 'eat well'. Adverbs also function as quantifiers (or intensifiers) of adjectives, e.g. *sāhrai rāmro* 'very good', or other adverbs, e.g. *sāhrai chiṭo* 'very fast'. The adverbs which function as quantifiers of adjectives, or quantifiers of other adverbs are "adverbs of quantity" described in (11.2.1).

The comparative and superlative formations of the adverbs are syntactic, not morphological, e.g.

Comparative: *ali bistārai* or *jhan bistārai* 'more slowly'

Superlative: *jyādai bistārai* 'extremely slowly'

Dependents. The dependents of the adverb are quantifiers that indicate the gradation of adverbs, e.g. *bistārai* 'slowly', or *jhan bistārai* 'more slowly', and *jyādai bistārai* 'extremely slowly'. Such constructions with adverbs as heads and their dependent adverbs (quantifiers) are called analytic comparative and superlative constructions. (See Chapter 13 for a detailed description of adverbs).

Lexical morphology. Adverbs are marked by the derivational suffixes *-arī*, *-sāth*, *-bittikai*, and *-pūrvak*, e.g. *rāmrari* 'well', *khuśīsāth* 'happily', *jānebittikai* 'as soon as going', and *ānandapūrvak* 'happily'. Those adverbs which are not so marked by derivational suffixes are adverbials. Adverbials function and distribute in the same way as adverbs in phrasal and clausal constructions.

5.5 Pronouns.

Inflection. Pronouns constitute a small closed class of forms that inflect for case and number in a way analogous to nouns. (See Chapter 9 for further details). Pronouns belong indirectly to the gender of nouns to which they anaphorically refer.

The gender of pronoun, like the gender of a noun, is shown syntactically in the third person by its cross reference tie to verb for which they function as subject.

Function. Pronouns occur as head of the Pronoun phrase (ProP), and function as subject, or (direct or indirect) object complements, and adjuncts of verbs.

Dependents. Pronouns, as heads of the Pronoun phrases (ProP), do not occur with dependents such as determiners since the pronouns are inherently [+definite] or [+determined]. Note in contrast that the common nouns as the heads of the common noun phrases (CNPs) do take the determiners as their dependents.

Lexical morphology. Pronouns are marked by their simple (underived) forms that distinguish them from other form classes. The traditional grammars sometimes speak about pronominal adjectives as if they were pronouns, e.g. *tyo* 'that', *yo* 'this', *kun* 'which'.

5.6 Coordinating conjunctions.

Inflection. The coordinating conjunctions are a closed class of uninflected forms. They are the following:

ani 'and then'	*athavā* [athaba:] 'or',
ki 'or'	*ki ... ki* 'either ... or',
kintu 'but'	*na ... na* 'neither ... nor',
naki 'but not'	*parantu* 'but'
ra 'and'	*taipani* or *(yadyapi)... taipani* 'even then'
tara 'but'	*tathā* 'and'
vā 'or'	*yā* 'or' and

Function. The coordinating conjunctions function as connectors of equal level constituents at all levels -- word, phrase, and clause level. The items which precede coordinating conjunctions and those that follow them need not both be of the same filler class, but both fill the same functional slot (Cf. 15.1).

Dependents. The words, phrases and clauses connected by the coordinating conjunctions are not dependents since the coordinating conjunctions are not the heads of such constructions, but connect coordinate structures. Items in a series show the connector (coordinating conjunction) only between the last two items in the series.

Lexical morphology. As uninflected and underived class, the coordinating conjunctions are marked by their simple stems, or complex stems (e.g. *atha-vā* or *tai-pani* 'but then'), and lack of lexical morphology.

5.7 Subordinating conjunctions

Inflection. Subordinating conjunctions are a closed uninflected class. The closed list is: *ki* 'that', *bhane* 'if', *pachi* 'after', *aghi* 'before', *pachi* 'if', *pani* 'although', *yadi* 'if', and the subordinating relative conjunctions, i.e the *J*-form substitutes described in (6.1.2).

Function. The function of subordinating conjunctions is to mark dependent (adverbial, or noun) clauses as subordinate to the principal clause in sentential structures.

ki 'that' (marks noun clause)	*agāḍi* 'before' (marks adverbial cl.)
pachāḍi 'after' (marks adverbial cl.)	*bhane* 'if' (marks adverbial cl.)
pachi 'after' (marks adverbial cl.)	*aghi* 'before' (marks adverbial cl.)
pachi 'if' (marks adverbial cl.)	*pani* 'although' (marks adverbial cl.)
yadi 'if' (marks adverbial cl.)	*yadyapi* 'if' (marks adverbial cl.)

Dependents. The dependent of a subordinating conjunction is a subordinate clause. The subordinate clause may be a relative adjectival clause, relative adverbial clause marked by the *J*-form substitutes, adverbial clause, or a noun clause. (For further details see 15.2).

Lexical morphology. The subordinating conjunctions are simple forms which do not show derivational or inflectional morphology.

5.8 Postpositions.

Inflection. Postpositions (comparable to prepositions in English) are called postpositions (pp) in Nepali since they occur after the nouns or noun phrases (NPs) with which they stand in construction. Postpositions are an uninflected, simple, or complex closed class of forms which function as the head of adverbial postpositional phrases (PP) which function as adverbial complements or adjuncts to the verbs in clausal structures.

Function. The postpositions (pps) function as head in the postpositional adverbial phrase (PPs) structure. The PPs are dependent on verbs since they stand in a clausal construction as adverbial adjuncts, e.g. *agāḍi* 'in front of'; *ghar agāḍi bagaĭcā cha.* 'There is a garden in front of the house.'

Dependents. The dependents of the postpositions are nouns or noun phrases (NPs) or pronoun phrases (ProPs) of which the postpositions are heads.

Lexical morphology. Postpositions are a simple, or complex closed class without inflectional morphology. Postpositions are described in greater detail in Chapter 14.

5.9 Interjections. Interjections constitute a small closed class of forms which show no inflection, dependents, or lexical morphology. They function as syntactically independent parenthetical minor sentences, semantically complete, but structurally reduced. Thus the interjections are in a way syntactically complete and syntactically independent of other elements in phrasal, or clausal structures. The most frequent interjections in Nepali are:

ā̃ 'yes, (approval)'	ā̃hā̃ 'no (disapproval)'
oho (in great surprise)	e3 (in surprise)
ābui (in fear)	ayyā (in pain)
lau (in surprise)	laukhā (in vindication)
chiḥ 'Fie!'	dhat (Indignation)
dhatterikā (Frustration)	jā (Regret)
la (Here you go)	lā (Vindication)

5.10 Vocatives. Vocatives are also uninflected forms. They differ from interjections in that the vocatives, e.g. *e, ai, he, o, oi* may stand in construction with the nouns, e.g. *e gopal* 'O Gopal!', *he īśvar* 'O God' to form independent parenthetical minor sentence types. The forms *sarkār* 'Lord (lit. government)' and *hajur* 'Sir!' are also used as vocatives. Noun stems without inflectional or derivational suffixes (i.e. nominative forms) also function as vocatives, as *gopal* 'Gopal !'

5.11 Nuance particles. Nuance particles belong to a small closed set of uninflected forms, show no characteristic lexical morphology, and occur in a syntactically independent way in phrases and statements. They are characterized by their having no dependents. Hari (1973) calls them "attitudinal particles", "undefined particles", "emphasis particles" and "specification particles", which 'nuance' the lexical and emotional import of clauses. These particles without distinct lexical meaning of their own add a special nuance to the statements which are otherwise devoid of such nuance. The nuance particles in Nepali are: *are, cāhī̃, hai, ki, kyāre, lau, na, nai, ni, po, ra,* and *ta*. These are described in greater details in (16.3).

5.12 Prefixes and suffixes. This list of the form classes of Nepali might be concluded by referring to the fact that the items discussed so far are all free forms in contrast to both the derivational prefixes and suffixes which are bound forms. The prefixes precede the forms to which they are attached, e.g. *be-, nir- an-* 'negative' as in *bekārī* 'unemployment', *nirdos* 'innocent', *anapaḍh* 'illiterate'; suffixes follow the forms to which they are attached, e.g. - *lī* as in *gorkhālī* 'related to Gorkha'. Prefixes and suffixes are not treated as separate class of forms since they are bound to one or other of the major form classes or 'parts of speech'.

Chapter 6
Substitute forms

6.0 Introduction. The substitute forms are defined as "those classes of free forms which manifest a particular overlaid grammatical function, independent of the form class to which the items belong and dependent upon the lexical content of the stem as formal marker or specifier of either a domain of reference or of a formal grammatical structure" (O'Brien 1965:131).

Thus, the total lexicon of Nepali consists of a number of form classes; but cutting across the divisions of those form classes are substitute forms which include words that have already been classified as belonging to various form classes. The various substitute forms signal and specify domains of reference and grammatical meaning, over and above the meaning of the item (lexical meaning), or of a class of items. Thus, the substitute forms have double function: (1) as members of a form class, and (2) as members of a function class.

As members of a form class they manifest the function proper to the form classes (nouns, pronouns, adjectives, and adverbs) as constituents of their own proper construction.

As members of a function class they are recognized as items which simultaneously perform an overlaid function by signalling ether a domain of reference or grammatical meaning, that is not proper to any other form class, and which operates independently of the form class to which the item belongs.

6.1 The major substitute forms. The major substitute forms in Nepali are: (1) The *K*-forms, or interrogatives which signal questions, (2) The *J*-forms, or subordinators, which signal dependent constructions (clauses), and (3) *D*-forms, or demonstratives, which signal independent constructions (nouns or noun phrases).

6.1.1 The *K*-form substitutes or interrogatives. The *K*-forms are those forms which in Nepali are all *K*-initial (forms beginning with the /k/), and signal a question, particularly a question asking for supplementary information. (However, not all forms beginning with *K* are interrogative substitutes.)

6.1.1.1 The *K*-form classes. The *K*-forms are grouped according to the classes they belong. Following are the K-form classes that occur in Nepali:

(1) *K*-form pronouns

ko 'who?' — *ke* 'what?'

kun 'which one?'

(2) *K*-form adjectives

kati 'how much?'	*kun* 'what, which one?'
kasto (m.) 'what kind/type?'	*kastī* (f.) 'what kind/type?'
kastā (pl) 'what kinds/types?'	*katro* 'what size?'

Note that the *K*-form substitute *kasto* 'what kind/type', like the other o-ending adjectives in Nepali, inflects for gender, number and case. Similarly, the *J*- form substitute *jasto* 'which kind', and *D*-form substitute *tyasto* 'that kind' inflect for gender, number and case when they distribute as adjectives (adjectivals).

(3) *K*-form adverbs

kahile 'when?'	*kahā̃* 'where?'
katā 'whither?'	*kahī̃* 'wherever?'
kasari 'how?'	*kina* 'why?'

(4) *K*-form interjection

ke (unstressed) signals yes/no type questions.

6.1.1.2 The distribution of *K*-forms. The *K*-forms are distributed according to their class, but they must be recognized as signaling items in order to understand the grammatical meaning of the utterance, e.g.

(1) *K*-form pronouns

ko	*ko ho?* 'Who is it?'
kun	*kun ho?* 'Which one is it?'
ke	6.32.3 *ke khāū* 'What shall I eat?'

(2) *K*-form adjectives

kati	*kati paisā cha tyahā̃?* 'How much money is there?'
kun	2.62.3 *kuna daulathako caina garekī chu ra?* 'What wealth have I enjoyed?'
kasto (m)	6.20 *sāno bābu kasto cha ni?* 'How is the little boy?'
kastī (f)	7.73 *kastī thi.ī?* 'How was she?'
kastā (pl)	6.21.1 *kastā hunthe?* 'How could he be?'
katro	*katro ghar cha?* 'What size house is it?'

(3) *K*-form adverbs

kahile	6.46 *kahile jānches?* 'When will you go?'
kahā̃	7.15 *kahā̃ basekī raicha?* 'Where is she staying?'
katā	*nepāl katā?* 'Whither Nepal?'
kahī̃	*usalāi kahī̃ dekhyau?* 'Did you see him anywhere?'

kasarī 1.15.1 *kasarī kṛtaghna banūn?* 'How could he be ungrateful?'

kina 2.43 *kina pallo koṭhāmā sāreko?* 'Why did you move it to the next room?'

(4) *K*-form interjection

ke 2.16.2 *ke subhadrāle sãco manale sallāha dieko ho?* 'Did Subhadra give her consent with sincere mind?'

6.1.2 The *J*-form or relative substitutes. The *J*- form substitutes are those forms which are *J* -initial and, while being a constituent of a clause, signal that the clause is a dependent (adjective or adverbial) clause. Thus the *J*-forms are similar to subordinate conjunctions as they mark the subordinate adjectival or adverbial clause (Cf.15.2), but they are different from subordinate conjunctions as they are constituents of the subordinate clause. The *J*-forms signal dependence while replacing the noun, or noun phrase in a clause.

6.1.2.1 The *J*-from classes. The *J*-forms are grouped according to the classes they belong. Following are the the *J*-form classes that occur in Nepali:

(1) *J*-form pronouns

jo 'who (+human)'	*jas* 'who (allomorph of *jo* in oblique cases)'
jaso 'whatever'	*josukai* 'whosoever (+human)'
jesukai 'whatsoever'	*junsukai* 'whosoever (allomorph of *jesukai* in oblique cases)'

(2) *J*-form adjectives

jasto (m) 'that kind'	*jasti* (f) 'that kind'
jastā (pl) 'those kind'	*jatro* 'which size'
jati 'as much'	*jun* 'which'
junsukai 'whatsoever'	

(3) *J*-form adverbs

jahile 'when'	*jahā̃* 'where'
jasarī 'in which way'	

The Hindi cognate *jaba* 'when' (of Nepali *jahile* 'when') is also commonly used in Nepali.

6.1.2.2 The distribution of *J*-form classes. The *J*-forms are distributed according to their form class, for they substitute the noun, adjective, or adverb in the clause (whether anaphoric or nonanaphoric); but they must be known as signalling items, for they have overlaid function of signalling that the relative clause in which they appear is dependent, e.g.

(1) *J*-form pronouns

jo	2.28.2 *jo aghillo dinako pāṭha birsera abelā gurukahā̃ pugdacha* 'Who, forgetting his lesson, arrives late at his guru's.'
jas	4.23.2 *jasalāi parameśvarale ṭhageko cha* 'whom the god has deceived.'
jaso	*jaso bhannuhuncha* 'Whatever you say'
je	*je cha tyahī deu* 'Give what you have'
josukai	*jesukai hos* 'Whosoever may be'
jesukai	*jesuakai gar* 'Do whatsoever (imp.)'

(2) *J*-form adjectives

jasto	*jasto bābu ustai choro* 'Like father, like son.'
jastī	*jastī āmā ustai chorī* 'Like mother, like daughter.'
jastā	*jastā guru ustai celā* 'Like teacher, like students.'
jatro	*jatro ghar bahe pani sānai huncha* 'Whatever size the house is, it is still small.'
jati	*jati paisā cha uti deu* 'Give as much money as is there.'
jun	*jun kām garna khojyo tyahi kām gāro huncha* 'Whatever job one tries to do, the same job becomes hard.'
junsukai	*junsukai kurā pani gāro cha* 'It is hard to do whatever one tries to do.'

(3) *J*-form adverbs

jahile	*jahile bhanchau uhile jānchu* 'I will go when you ask me to do so.'
jahā	*jahā̃ icchā tyahā̃ upāya* 'Where there is a will, there is a way.'
jasarī	*jasarī maile bhaneko thiẽ, tyasarī kām bhaena* 'The work was not done in the way I had asked.'

6.1.3 The *D*-form substitutes or demonstratives. The *D*-form substitutes or demonstratives, as a function class, are not as distinct as the *K*-forms and *J*-forms but are presented here because of the obvious parallelism with the other two classes. The *D* -form substitute are so called, not because they are *D*-initial as the *K*-form and *J* -form substitutes are *K*-initial and *J*- initial respectively, but because they function as demonstratives. In conjunction with the *K*-forms, the *D*-forms signal a response; in conjunction with the *J*-forms, the *D*-forms signal independence or co-relativity. So they can also be called correlative forms.

6.1.3.1 The *D*-form classes. The *D*-form classes are grouped according to the classes they belong. The following are the *D*- form classes that occur in Nepali:

(1) *Y*-form pronouns (proximate demonstrative)

yo 'this'	*yī̃* 'these'
yaso 'like this'	*yasto* 'like this'

(2) *T*-form pronouns (mediate demonstrative)

tyo 'that'	*tī̃* 'those'
tyaso 'like that'	

(3) *U*-form pronouns (remote demonstrative)

u 'he, she'

The *Y*-form, *T*-form, and *U*-form demonstrative adjectives in Nepali are homophonous to the *Y*-form, *T*-form, and *U*-form pronouns. Besides the homophonous forms, there are also other forms, e. g.

(1) *Y*-form adjectives (proximate demonstrative)

yo 'this'	*yī̃* 'these'
yasto 'like this (nonemphatic)'	*yastai* 'like this (emphatic)'
yatro 'this size'	

(2) *T*-form adjectives (mediate demonstrative)

tyo 'that'	*tī̃* 'those'
tyasto 'like that (nonemphatic)'	*tyastai* 'like that (emphatic)'
tyatro 'that size'	

(3) *U*-form adjectives (remote demonstrative)

u 'that'	*usto* 'like that (nonemphatic, archaic)'
ustai 'like that (emphatic)'	*utro* 'that size'

The *D*-form adverbs interlock with the *K*-form and *J*- form adverbs. The *D*-form adverbs, like *D*- form (demonstrative) pronouns, also have the proximate and remote demonstrative forms, e.g.

ahile 'now (nonemphatic temporal proximate)'
ahilyai 'right now (emphatic temporal proximate)'
uhile 'then (nonemphatic temporal remote)'
uhilyai 'then (emphatic temporal remote)'
yahā̃ 'here (nonemphatic spatial proximate)'
yahī̃ 'right here (emphatic spatial proximate)'

tyahā̃ 'there (nonemphatic spatial mediate)'
tyahī̃ 'right there (emphatic spatial mediate)'
uhā̃ 'there (nonemphatic spatial remote)'
uhī̃ 'right there (emphatic spatial remote)'
yasarī̃ 'this way (proximate)'
tyasarī̃ 'that way (mediate)
usarī̃ 'that way (remote)'

6.1.3.2 The distribution of D-form classes. The *D-* form classes occur in independent clauses, and need to be known as signalling items when they occur in conjunction with the *J-* forms, or the *K*-forms.

(1) *Y*-form pronouns (proximate demonstrative)

yo — *yo mero choro ho* 'This is my son'
yī̃ — *yī̃ merā chorā hun* 'These are my sons'
yaso — *yaso nagara* 'Don't do like this.'
yasto — 5.13.1 *yasto andhakāra rātrimā pani kasaile dekhcha ki ...* 'Someone may see even in such a dark night ... .'
yastai — 2.6 *eka dina yastai rīta sā̃ga unale subhadrāko pāṇigrahaṇa garethe* 'One day he had married Subhadra in the same way.'
yatro — 7.18.2 *yatro sampattikī māliknī bhaikana subhadra...* 'Subhadra, being owner of such a big property ... .'

(2) *T*-form pronouns (mediate demonstrative)

tyo — *tyo rāmro chaina* 'That is not good'
tī̃ — *ti rāmrā chainan* 'Those are not good'
tyaso — 2.58 *kina tyaso bhanis?* 'Why did you say so?'
tyatro — 6.29.2 *āphno tyatro daulatha choḍera yahā̃ eka chāka khāera yahā̃ basekī chu* 'Leaving that big property of my own, I am staying here having just one meal a day.'

(3) *U-* form pronouns (remote demonstrative)

u — *u ko ho?* 'Who is he?'

(1) *Y-* form adjectives (proximate demonstrative)

yo — 2.5 *prārabdhale yo umeramā unalāi pheri dulāhā banāyo* 'Destiny made him a bride at this age again.'
yī̃ — 4.29 *...yī̃ rukha vṛkṣa savai yinai santānahīnā ramaṇīkā sāthī thie* 'These trees were friends of this very childless lady.'

(2) *T*-form adjectives (mediate demonstrative)

tyo	4.32.3 ... *tyo kurā manovijñāna najānekā devīramaṇalāi thāhā bhaena* 'That fact was not known to Deviraman who did not know psychology'
tī	3.5 *tī mūka pakṣīharu pani bālakasãga ānanadapūrvaka kheli-rahekā thie* 'Those mute birds played happily with the child.'

(3) *U*- form adjectives (remote demonstrative)

u	1.13.1 *u avasthā samjhãdā gahabharī ãsu hunthyo* 'When he remembered that condition, his eyes would be filled with tears.'
usto	*tã usto vyakti hos?* 'Are you that kind of person?'
utro	*tã utro byakti hos?* 'Are you that great a person?'

The distribution of the *D*- form adverbs

ahile	1.15.1 *ahile ... kasarī kṛtaghna banūn* 'How could he be ungrateful now?'
ahilyai	*ahilyai jāu* 'Go right now (emphatic)'
uhile	*uhile yasto calan thiyo* 'Such was the practice then.'
uhilyai	*u uhilyai gayo* 'He went right then.'
yahā̃	*yahā̃ timi ke garchau?* 'What are you doing here?'
yahī	6.6 *yahī gaurighāṭa phupukahā̃ basekī chu* 'I am staying right here at my aunt's place at Gaurighat.'
tyahā̃	*tyahā̃ ko cha?* 'Who is there?'
tyahī	*kitāb tyahī cha* 'The book is right there.'
uhā̃	*uhā̃ kohī pani chaina* "There is nobody there'
uhī	*uhī jāu* 'Go right there.'
yasarī	*yasarī gara* 'Do it this way.'
tyasarī	*tyasarī gara* 'Do it that way.'
usarī	*usarī* (archaic) *nagara* 'Do not do it that way.'

6.2 Numerals. The numerals in Nepali may be divided into:
(1) cardinal adjectives or adjectivals, answering 'how many'
(2) ordinal adjectives answering 'which one of a series',
(3) distributive adjectives answering 'how many each', and
(4) ordinal adverbials answering 'which time of a series'

(1) Cardinal adjectives	(2) Ordinal adjectives	(3) Distributive adjectives	(4) Ordinal adverbials
1 ek	pahilo	ek-ek[1]	ek palṭ a[2]
2 dui	dosro	dui-dui	dui palṭa
3 tin	tesro	tin-tin	tin palṭa
4 cār	cautho	cār-cār	cār palṭa
5 pā̃c	pā̃caũ	pā̃c-pā̃c	pā̃c palṭa
6 cha	chaiṭaũ	cha-cha	cha palṭa
7 sāt	sātaũ	sāt-sāt	sāt palṭa
8 āṭh	āṭhaũ	āṭh-āṭh	āṭh palṭa
9 nau	navaũ	nau-nau	nau palṭa
10 das	dasaũ [3]	das-das	das palṭa
11 eghāra	eghāraũ	eghāra-eghāra	eghāra palṭa
12 bāra	bāraũ	bāra-bāra	bāra palṭa
13 tehra	tehraũ	tehra-tehra	tehra palṭa
14 caudha	caudhaũ	caudha-caudha	caudha palṭa
15 pandra	pandraũ	pandra-pandra	pandra palṭa
16 sohra	sohraũ	sohra-sohra	sohra palṭa
17 satra	satraũ	satra-satra	satra palṭa
18 aṭhāra	aṭhāraũ	aṭhāra-aṭhāra	aṭhāra palṭa
19 unnāis	unnāisaũ	unnāis-unnāis	unnāis palṭa
20 bis	bisaaũ	bis-bis	bis palṭa
22 ekkāis	ekkāisaũ	ekkāis-ekkāis	ekkāis palṭa
23 teis	teisaaũ	teis-teis	teis palṭa
24 caubīs	caubīsaũ	caubīs-caubīs	caubīs palṭa
25 paccīs	paccīsaũ	paccīs-paccīs	paccīs palṭa
26 chabbīs	chabbīsaũ	chabbīs-chabbīs	chabbīs palṭa
27 sattāis	sattāisaũ	sattāis-sattāis	sattāis palṭa
28 aṭṭhāis	aṭṭhāisaũ	aṭṭhāis-atthāis	aṭṭhāis palṭa
29 unantīs	unantīsaũ	unantīs-unantīs	unantīs palṭa
30 tīs	tīsaũ	tīs-tīs	tīs palṭa
31 ekatīs	ekatīsaũ	ekatīs-ekatīs	ekatīs palṭa
32 battīs	battīsaũ	battīs-battīs	battīs palṭa
33 tettīs	tettīsaũ	tettīs-tettīs	tettīs palṭa
34 cautīs	cautīsaũ	cautīs-cautīs	cautīs paṭta
35 paĩtīs	paĩtīsaũ	paĩtīs-paĩtīs	paĩtīs palṭa
36 chattīs	chatttīsaũ	chattīs-chattīs	chattīs palṭa
37 saĩtīs	saĩtīsaũ	saĩtīs -saĩtīs	saĩtīs palṭa
38 aṭhtīs	athtīsaũ	aṭhtīs -aṭhtīs	aṭhtīs palṭa
39 unancālis	unancālisaũ	unancālis-unāncalis.	unancālis palṭa
40 cālis	cālisaũ	cālis-cālis	cālis palṭa

41 ekcālis	ekcālisaũ	ekcālis-ekcālis	ekcālis palṭa
42 bayālis	bayālisaũ	bayālis-bayālis	bayālis palṭa
43 tricālis	tricālisaũ	tricālis-tricālis	tricālis palṭa
44 cawālis	cawālisaũ	cawālis-cawāis	cawālis palṭa
45 paĩtālis	paĩtālisaũ	paĩ tālis-paĩ tālis	paĩtālis palṭa
46 chayālis	chayālisaũ	chayālis-chayālis	chayālis palṭa
47 satcālis	satcālisaũ	satcālis-satcālis	satcālis palṭa
48 aṭhcālis	aṭhcālisaũ	aṭhcālis-aṭhcālis	aṭhcālis palṭa
49 unancās	unancāsaũ	unancās-unancās	unancās palṭa
50 pacās	pacāsaũ	pacās-pacās	pacās palṭa
51 ekāunna	ekāunnaũ	ekāunna-ekāunna	ekāunna palṭa
52 bāunna	bāunnaũ	bāunna-bāunna	bāunna palṭa
53 tripanna	tripannaũ	tripanna-tripanna	tripanna palṭa
54 caunna	caunnaũ	caunna-caunna	caunna palṭa
55 pacpanna	pacpannaũ	pacpanna-pacpanna	pacpanna palṭa
56 chapanna	chapannaũ	chapanna-chapanna	chapanna palṭa
57 santāunna	santāunnaũ	santāunna-sant.	santāunna palṭa
58 anṭhāunna	anṭhāunnaũ	anṭhāunna-anṭ.	anṭhāunna palṭa
59 unānsāṭhi	unānsāṭhiyaũ	unānsāṭhi-un.	unānsāṭhi palṭa
60 sāṭhī	sāṭhiyaũ	sāṭhi-sāṭhī	sāṭhī palṭa
61 ekasaṭṭhī	ekasaṭṭhiyaũ	ekasatthī-ekasaṭṭhī	ekasaṭṭhī palṭa
62 baysaṭṭhī	baysaṭṭhiyaũ	baysaṭṭhī-baysaṭṭhī	baysaṭṭhī palṭa
63 trisaṭṭhī	trisaṭṭhiyaũ	trisatthī-trisaṭṭhī	trisaṭṭhī palṭa
64 causaṭṭhī	causaṭṭhiyaũ	causatthī-causaṭṭhī	causaṭṭhī palṭa
65 paĩsaṭṭhī	paĩsaṭṭhiyaũ	paĩsaṭṭhī - paĩsaṭṭhī	paĩsaṭṭhī palṭa
66 chayasaṭṭhī	chayasaṭṭhiyaũ	chayasaṭṭhī-cha.	chaysaṭṭhī palṭa
67 satasaṭṭhī	satasaṭṭhiyaũ	satasaṭṭhī-sata.	satasaṭṭhī palṭa
68 aṭhsaṭṭhī	aṭhsaṭṭhiyaũ	aṭhasaṭṭhī-aṭha.	aṭhasaṭṭhī palṭa
69 unānsattarī	unānsattariyaũ	unānsattarī-unān.	unānsattarī palṭa
70 sattarī	sattariyaũ	sattari-sattari	sattarī palṭa
71 ekahattar	ekahattaraũ	ekahattar-ekahattar	ekahattar palṭa
72 bahattar	bahattaraũ	bahattar-bahattar	bahattar palṭa
73 trihattar	trihattaraũ	trihattar-trihattar	trihattar palṭa
74 cauhattar	cauhattaraũ	cauhattar-cawhattar	cauhattar palṭa
75 pacahattar	pacahattaraũ	pacahattar-pac.	pacahattar p.
76 chayahattar	chayahattaraũ	chayahattar-cha.	chayahattar p.
77 satahattar	satahattaraũ	satahattar-satah.	satahattar
78 aṭhahattar	aṭhahattaraũ	aṭhahattar-aṭh.	aṭhahattar palṭa
79 unāsi	unāsiyaũ	unāsi-unāsi	unāsi palṭa
80 asi	asiyaũ	asi-asi	asi palṭa
81 ekāsi	ekāsiyaũ	ekāsi-ekāsi	ekāsi palṭa
82 bayāsi	bayāsiyaũ	bayāsi-bayāsi	bayāsi palṭa

83 triyāsi	triyāsiyaũ	triyāsi-triyāsi	triyāsi palṭa
84 caurāsi	caurāsiyaũ	caurāsi-caurāsi	caurāsi palṭa
85 pacāsi	pacāsiyaũ	pacāsi-pacāsi	pacāsi palṭa
86 chayāsi	chayāsiyaũ	chayāsi-chayāsi	chayāsi palṭa
87 satāsi	satāsiyaũ	satāsi-satāsi	satāsi palṭa
88 aṭhāsi	aṭhāsiyaũ	aṭhāsi-athāsi	aṭhāsi palṭa
89 unānnabbe	unānnabbeaũ	unānnabbe-unān.	unānnabbe palṭa
90 nabbe	nabbeaũ	nabbe-nabbe	nabbe palṭa
91 ekānnabbe	ekānnabbeaũ	ekānnabbe-ekān.	ekānnabbe palṭa
92 bayānnabbe	ekānnabbeaũ	bayānnabbe-bayā.	bayānnabbe palṭa
93 triyānnabbe	triyānnabbeaũ	triyānnabbe-tri.	triyānnabbe palṭa
94 caurānnabbe	caurānnabeaũ	caurānnabbe-ca.	caurānnabe palṭa
95 pancānnabe	pancānnabbeaũ	pancānnabbe-pa.	pancānnabe palṭa
96 chayānnabbe	chayānnabbeaũ	chayānnabbe-cha.	chayānbbe palṭa
97 santānnabbe	santānnabbeaũ	santānnabe-sant.	santānnabe palṭa
98 anṭhānnabbe	anṭhānnabbeaũ	anṭhānnabbe-ant.	anṭhānnabe palṭa
99 unānsae	unānsayaũ	unānsae-unānsae	unānsae palṭa
100 śaya	śayaũ	śaya-śaya	śaya palṭa

The numbers multiplied by ten are written in the following way:

1	ek
10	das
100	śaya
1,000	hajār
10,000	das hajār
1,00,000	lākh
10,00,000	das lākh
1,00,00,000	karoḍ
10,00,00,000	das karoḍ
1,00,00,00,000	arab/arba
10,00,00,00,000	das arab/das arba
1,00,00,00,00,000	kharab/kharba
10,00,00,00,00,000	das kharab/das kharba

Notes for Chapter 6

1. The distributive numeral adjectives *ek-ek, dui-dui, tin-tin, cā̃r-cā̃r, pā̃c-pā̃c, cha-cha, sā̃t-sā̃t*, which show reduplication of the stem, also have dialectal variants as *ekek, du-dui, ti-tin, ca-cā̃r, pa-pā̃c, cha-cha, sa-sā̃t, ā̃-ā̃ṭh, na-nau*, and *da-das.*

2. The adverbial marker *palṭa* 'times' has several dialectal variants: *paṭak, coṭi, tā̃li*, and *bā̃r*.

3. Forms such as *dasaũ, sayaũ, hajāraũ* etc. also mean tens, hundreds, thousands, etc. in the CNP's where the head noun is in plural number, e.g. *hajārāũ mānisharu* 'thousands of people.'

Nominal Structures

Chapter 7
Common-noun phrase

7.0 Internal structure of the common-noun phrase. This chapter describes the internal structure of the common-noun phrase (CNP) in Nepali. A common-noun phrase in Nepali consists of three functional slots: (1) the optional determiner (Det:) functional slot marked by the sign ±, (2) an optional modifier (Mod:) slot marked by the sign ±, and (3) an obligatory head (H:) slot marked by the plus sign (+). The filler classes of the determiner (Det:) slot are described in (7.3). The filler classes of the modifier (Mod.) slot are described in (7.4). The filler class of the head (H:) slot is the common (cn) described in (7.1). The structure of the CNP (and the linear order in which its constituents cooccur) is represented by the following formula:

CNP = ± Det: ± Mod: +Head:

In the formula, the sign ± means that these attributes optional since they cooccur with certain heads, but do not cooccur with others. The head is, of course, obligatory. The structural formula of the CNP is illustrated by the following examples:

5.4.2 ±त्यो ±विशाल +नभस्थल
±tyo ±viśāla +nabhasthala
±Det: demonstrative prol.adj ±Mod: adjl +H: cn
±that ±vast +firmament
'that vast firmament'

7.1 Common nouns as heads. The common noun as the head (H:) slot is filled by an obligatory (+) common noun stem and with optional (±) plural marker *-haru* followed by inflectional suffixes for cases. Thus, the formula:

H: +stem ± plural suffix +inflectional suffix

means that the common noun head is either singular or plural and that the plural suffix is occurrent in the environment of some heads, nonoccurrent in that of other heads. The inflectional suffix is required if it is necessitated by the semantic purport, e.g.

mānis 'man'

mānis(haru) 'men'

mānis(haru)lāi 'to men'

The common nouns ending in *-o* like *ḍoko, boko, choro* etc. have their allomorphs ending in *-ā* such as *ḍokā, bokā, chorā* etc. when they are followed by the optional plural marker, or by a case inflection, e.g.

Singular	Plural	Inflectional forms
ḍoko 'a basket'	*ḍokā(haru)* 'baskets'	*ḍokāmā* 'in the basket'
boko 'male goat'	*bokā(haru)* 'goats'	*bokāle* 'by the male goat'
choro 'son'	*chorā(haru)* 'sons'	*chorālāi* 'to the son'

7.2 Gender of nouns. Every noun (proper or common) in Nepali belongs to either masculine or feminine gender. Although the traditional Nepali grammars talk about masculine, feminine, neuter, and common genders, there are only two genders (masculine and feminine) as reflected morphologically in the verbs. Thus, gender in Nepali is a syntactic property. In other words, the gender of nouns is indicated morphologically by the form of verbs, not by the form of nouns, e.g.

śāradā jāncha (m) 'Sharada goes'	śāradā jānche (f) 'Sharada goes'
durgā gayo (m) 'Durga went'	durga: gaī (f) 'Durga went'

Note: The above examples indicate that *Sharada* and *Durga* can be names of a man or a woman, but the difference of gender is reflected in and by the form of verbs. As an exception, a closed set of the caste names and professional titles borrowed from other languages in Nepali indicate that these forms (referring to persons belonging to a caste, or having a professional title) differentiate the male or female individuals by means of derivational suffixes; as *-ni, -ini* for females.

Male:	Female:
ghartī 'Gharti'	ghartinī 'Ghartini (caste)'
newār 'Newar'	newārnī 'Newar (caste)'
sārkī 'Sarki'	sarkinī 'Sarki (caste)'
ḍākṭar 'doctor'	ḍākṭarnī 'doctor (professional title)'
cākar 'servant'	cākarnī 'maid (professional title)'

7.3 Determiners in the CNP. The determiners in the CNP may be filled in the strict linear order by: (1) demonstratives (pronominal adjectives), (2) limiters which may be either the limiting forms: *harek* or *haraek* 'each' *pratyek* 'each', *kehi* 'some', *sabai* 'all', *alikati* 'a little', or a pronoun in genitive case, (3) quantifiers which are the numerals (cardinal or ordinal) with (4) optional [+human] or [-human] classifiers. The demonstratives, limiters, quantifiers, and classifiers can be called 1st, 2nd, 3rd, and 4th order determiners. The formula is:

±Det: ± demonstrative ± limiter ± quantifier ± classifier

In the following example, the first four items are determiners of the common noun phrase presented in parentheses. The head of the common noun phrase is the last item in the string:

±यी ±मेरा ±चार ±जना (साह्रै प्रिय मित्रहरू)
±yī ±merā ±cāra ±janā (±sāhrai ±priya +mitraharu)
±Det: dem. ±lim(pro-gn) ±qnt(num) ±cla(+hum) (±advl ±adj +cn-pl)
±these ±my ±four ±human (±very ±dear +friends)
'These four (very dear friends) of mine'

7.3.1 Demonstratives. Demonstratives (dem) form a small closed subset of determiners which are inflected for number. They are (proximate): *yo*, 'this' *yī̃* 'these'; and (remote): *tyo* 'that' *tī̃* 'those'. These demonstratives are a closed set of forms described in details in (6.1.3.1 and 1.1.3.2).

7.3.2 Limiters. Limiters are a closed set of forms which, as determiners, follow the demonstratives in the linear order of occurrence. The limiters are either definite such as: *harek* 'each', *pratyek* 'each', or indefinite such as: *kehi* 'some' *keval* 'only', *ekai* 'same', *uhi* 'same', *aru* 'other', *kunai* 'certain', *aghillo* 'first', *pachillo* 'last', *antim* 'final', *alikati* 'a little', *thorai* 'a little' *sabai* 'all'. The nouns and pronouns in possessive forms also function as limiters.

7.3.2 Quantifiers (numbers) and classifiers. The Quantifiers (qnt) are cardinal numbers such as: ek/ 'one', /dui/ 'two', /tin/ 'three', followed by one of the two classifiers (+human classifier or -human classifier). The quantifiers followed by classifiers (cla.) distribute like adjectives when they stand in construction with the head nouns in the common-noun phrase.

The classifier *janā* occurs with [+human] count nouns; the classifier *waṭā* occurs with [-human] count nouns e.g.

[+human] classifier:	[-human] classifier:
± *pā̃c* + *janā* +*mānis*	±*tin* +*waṭā* + *kalam*
±five +[+human] +men	±three +[-human] +pens
'five men'	'three pens'

Note that the form of *ek* 'one' and waṭā 'classifier.' is *euṭā*. Other forms show two free variants each, e.g.

dui waṭā 'two ones'	duiṭā 'two ones'
tin waṭā 'three ones'	tinoṭā 'three ones'
cār waṭā 'four ones'	cāroṭā 'four ones'
p̃āc waṭā 'five ones'	p̃ācoṭā 'five ones'
cha waṭā 'six ones'	chaoṭā 'six ones'
sāt waṭā 'seven ones'	sātoṭā 'seven ones'
āṭh waṭā 'eight ones'	āṭhoṭā 'eight ones'
nau waṭā 'nine ones'	nauoṭa 'nine one'
das waṭā 'ten ones'	dasoṭā 'ten ones'

Classifiers do not occur with expressions of telling time, or with nouns which denote periods of time, e.g. ek baje 'one o'clock'; *das din* 'ten days'.

7.3.3 CNP's functioning as quantifying determiner. Noun-phrases denoting units of quantity or measure occur as quantifying determiners and are embedded CNP's in higher level CNP. For instance,

±ek kilo +rāmro ālu
±Det: CNP +H: CNP
±one kilo +good potato
'a kilo of good potatoes'

Note that the common noun phrase (CNP) *ek kilo* 'one kilo' occurs as a quantifying determiner to the higher level common noun phrase (CNP) *rāmro ālu* 'good potato'.

7.4 Modifiers in the CNP. The modifiers in the CNP are expansions of the basic CNP structure. These expansions are dependent on a higher level CNP, e.g. *devīramaṇakā duḥkhako laharī* 'the wave of Deviraman's sorrow'. A common-noun phrase stands in conjunction with optional modifiers. These optional modifiers are either nouns or noun phrases subsumed as 'nominals' discussed in Chapter 10, adjectives or adjective phrases subsumed as 'adjectivals' discussed in more detail in Chapter 12, postpositional phrases described in Chapter 14, or clauses described in Chapters 20, 21, and 22.

7.4.1 Nouns or noun phrases as modifiers in CNP. Nouns (common or proper) or noun phrases function as modifiers in the CNP when they cooccur with a common noun. In such constructions also the first noun is the modifier, and the final noun is the head of the CNP, e.g.

nepālī bhāṣā	'Nepali language'
bhaktapur jillā	'Bhaktapur district'
ganḍakī añcal	'Gandaki zone'
harivaṃśa purāṇa	'Harivaṃśa purāṇa (legends)'
hindū dharma	'Hindu religion'
pis kor swayamsebak	'Peace Corps volunteer'

7.4.2 Adjectives or adjective phrases as modifiers. Adjectives as modifiers occur after the determiners and before the head of the CNP, e.g.

5.4.2 ±त्यो ±विशाल + नभ-स्थल
±tyo ±viśāla +nabha-sthala
±Det: prol.adj ±Mod: adjl +H: compound common noun
±that ±vast +firmament
'that vast firmament'

Besides the adjectives and adjective phrases, dependent adjectivals also modify nouns or noun phrases. The dependent adjectivals are described in Chapter 12.

7.4.3 Clauses as modifiers. The clauses that function as adjectives are dependent modifiers of the noun. For instance,

1.12..2 ±सुभद्रा ± (+दुलही +भएर) +आउँदा-को +बखत
±Subhadrā ± (+dualahī +bhaera) +āūdā-ko +bakhata
±S:pn-nm ±AD:Cl (+SC:cn-nm +P:ev1-abs.prt) +P:ev1-conj.prt-ko +H:cn
±subahdrā (+bride +being) +coming-of +time
'The time when Subhadra came (as a bride)'

Note. In the analysis of *1.12..2 ±Subhadrā ± (+dualahī +bhaera) +āūdā-ko +bakhata* the first item *±Subhadrā* fills the subject slot in the clause which modifies the item *+bakhata* 'time' filling the obligatory head (H) slot of the CNP. In the clause modifying the head noun 'time', there is an embedded clause filling the slot AD (adverbial disjunct). The AD being an optional item in the main clause is marked with the plus and minus (±) sign, but the items ('bride' and 'being') in this AD clause presented in parentheses are obligatory within the structure of this AD clause, so they are marked with the plus (+) sign.

2.22.1 ±सन्तान विना ±स्वर्गको बाटो +छेकिन्छ +भन्ने +हिन्दू धर्म
±santāna vinā ±svarga-ko bāṭo ±chekincha ±bhanne +hindu dharma
±AA:PP ±S:CNP-nm +P:tv1p-3sg.pres +P:tv1-impf.prt +H: CNP
±children without ±heaven-of path +blocked-is +saying +Hindu religion
'The Hindu religion which says that without children the path to heaven is blocked'

Chapter 8.
Proper-noun phrase

8.0 Internal structure of the proper-noun phrase (PNP). This chapter discusses the internal structure of the proper-noun phrase in Nepali. The proper-noun phrase consists of a proper-noun (pn) as obligatory head and of an optional modifier. The order of the functional constituents of the proper-noun phrase is shown in the formula:

PNP = ±Mod: +H:

The modifier functional slot (Mod:) is optional, and is filled by adjectives or adjectivals. The head functional slot (H:) is obligatory and is filled by the place and person names (person names are personal names given by parents).

Person and place names in Nepali do not coocccur with determiners (demonstratives, limiters, quantifiers), e.g. **tyo deviraman*, **yo subhadrā* **mero naulī*, **kati lakṣmī*, **dui sushil* etc. Proper names as such are inherently determined as definite, and thus do not cooccur with any of the determiners that the common nouns cooccur with. However, the person names do occur with the modifiers (adjectives or adjectivals). The formula for PNP is exemplified by the following instances:

1.5.1 ± बिचरी +सुभद्रा
±Mod:adj +H:pn
±bicarī +subhadrā
±poor +Subhadra
'Poor Subhadra'

1.14.1 ± कङ्गाल +देवीरमण
±kaṅgāla +devīramaṇa
±Mod:adj +H:pn
±penniless +Devīraman
'Penniless Deviraman'

3.12.1 ± सन्तानेच्छुक + देवीरमण
±santānecchuka +devīramaṇa
±Mod:adj ±H:pn
±desirous-of-offspring +Deviraman
'Deviraman, desirous of offspring'

8.1 Person names as heads. When functioning as heads, person names consist of an obligatory person name with optional modifiers but without plural number. In other words a person name does not inflect for number since the person name is inherently singular as it refers to an individual (who has been given the name) is inherently singular. When the plural number suffix *-haru* occurs with a person name, it does not stand as a plural number marker; it stands for the other (unspecified) names semantically associated with the person name with which it cooccurs. For instance,

7.41. +देवीरमण +नौलीहरु
+H: pn-nm +H:pn-nm-pl.
+devīramaṇa +naulī-haru
+Deviraman +Nauli-plural suffix
'Deviraman, Nauli and others'

Person names, like common nouns, have a syntactic property of gender which is in one-to-one correspondence with the sex of the individual that is referred to by the name. The gender of the person names is reflected in the gender concord they have with the forms of verbs, e.g.

śāradā gayo (m.) 'Sharada went' *śāradā gaī* (f.) 'Sharada went'
durgā gayo (m.) 'Durga went' *durgā gaī* (f.) 'Durga went'

When the person names of masculine gender such as *śāradāprasād* and *durgāprasād* are reduced as *śāradā* and *durgā,* their gender is ambiguous as they can refer to females of the same names. Their gender is disambiguated by the finite form of the verb in the clausal structure.

Person names are chosen by the parents based on such factors as caste, position in the family, and sex of the child. So it may be sometimes possible to guess the caste of a person from the name if the person's first name is a typical one. However, there is not much rigidity in caste adherance in Nepal. Moreover, the names given to men and women cut across caste distinctions. So one cannot always be right in one's guess.

The family names indicate the caste of the person more accurately , though not infallibly. Some typical family names are:

Brahmans:	Acharya, Adhikari, Aryal, Baral, Bhandari, Bhatta, Bhattarai, Chapagain, Devkota, Dhakal, Dhungel, Dixit, Ghimire, Joshi, Khanal, Kharel, Koirala, Marahatta, Mishra, Nepal, Pandey, Pandit, Pant, Paudel, Pokhrel, Pudasaini, Rijal, Sharma, Subedi, Tiwari, Tripathi, Wagley.
Kṣatriyas:	Adhikari, Basnet, Bhat, Bista, Chand, Karki, Kathayat, Khadayat, Khadka, Khatri, Kuwar, Malla, Pandey, Prasai,

	Rana, Shaha, Singh, Swar, Thapa
Vaiśyas:	Baniya, Joshi, Shrestha, Sthapit,
Śūdras:	Mali, Malakar, Manandhar,

The Nepalese give their children two names, a first name, e.g. Bishwanath, Toyanath, Ramprasad (cf. Figure 8.1) and a family name. Figure 8.1 illustrates some common Nepali first names.

Figure 8.1 Common Nepali first names by caste and sex.

Male:	Female:
Caste: Brahman First names end in: *-rāj, -nidhi, -nāth, -prasād* etc. Examples: Toyaraj, Lilanidhi, Naranath, Ramprasad	Some common names are: Anita, Rita, Kamala, Sunita, Shobha
Caste: Kṣatriya First names end in: *-bahādur* Examples: Rambahadur, Shyambahadur, Haribahadur, Krishnabahadur	Same as Brahman women's names
Caste: Vaiśya Same as for Kṣatriya (men and women's first names)	
Caste: Śūdra	
Jeṭhā 'first boy'	Jeṭhī 'first girl'
Māilā 'second boy'	Māilī 'second girl'
Kānchā 'third boy'	Kānchī 'third girl'

Note: The first names Kānchā 'youngest boy' and Kānchī 'youngest girl' are usual forms of address for a member of a higher caste to any child, regardless of position in the family, in the Śudra caste.

8.2 Place names as heads. Place names when functioning as heads consist of an obligatory place name. As with the person names, place names do not inflect for number as they refer to one geographical place name, as *Kathmandu, Gaurighat, Nepal, Pokhara, Lamjung, Okhaldhunga.*[1]

Notes for Chapter 8

1. In poetry the certain place names may be found to be used with more than one modifier, e.g. *mero pyāro okhalḍhungā* 'My sweet Okhaldhunga' by a famous Nepali poet Siddhicaran Shrestha.

Chapter 9
The pronoun phrase

9.0 Internal structure of the pronoun phrase (ProP). The pronoun phrase (ProP) consists of an optional modifier slot and the obligatory head slot. In certain instances the optional modifier slot occurs after the head slot. The linear order of the functional constituents of the ProP is presented in the following formula:

ProP = ±Mod: +H: ±Mod:

In the formula the sign ± means that the element that follows this sign occurs optionally with certain personal pronouns and does not occur with other personal pronouns. For instance the plural number suffix *-haru* occurs with *timī̃* 'you', *tinī̃* 'he,she (peer level)', and *wahā̃* 'he (honorific)' as; *timi* 'you (sg.)' vs. *timī̃haru* 'you (pl)'; *tinī̃* 'he,she' vs. *tinī̃haru* 'they' and *wahā̃* 'he, she' vs. *wahā̃haru* 'they'. The plural number suffix *-haru* occurs optionally with the pronoun *hāmī̃* 'we', which shows an alternative form *hāmī̃haru* 'we'.

As indicated in the formula, certain modifiers precede the head pronoun, while others follow it. Examples of each are presented in (9.2).

9.1 Pronouns as heads. The pronouns (pro) constitute a small closed class and belong indirectly to the gender (masculine vs. feminine) of the nouns which they substitute, but are not inflected for gender. The gender of the pronouns is expressed morphologically by the verbs with which they stand in syntactic construction. Compared to nouns, pronouns inflect more irregularly for case and number. Following are the personal pronouns and their honorific forms:

Person	Singular	Plural
First	*ma*	*hāmī̃-(haru)*
Second		
Level of respect		
Low Grade Honorific (LGH)	*tā̃*	*timī̃-haru*
Mid Grade Honorific (MGH)	*timī̃*	*timī̃-haru*
High Grade Honorific (HGH)	*tapāī̃*	*tapāī̃-haru*
Third		
Low Grade Honorific (LGH)	*u, tyo*	*unī̃-haru, tinī̃-haru*
Mid Grade Honorific (MGH)	*tinī̃*	*tinī̃haru*
High Grade Honorific (HGH)	*wahā̃*	*wahā̃haru*

In formal conversations *tapāī̃* and *tapāī̃-haru* (second person HGH) show variants *yahā̃* and *yahā̃-haru.* The form *yahā̃* and *wahā̃* are also used in formal conversations as third person honorifics: *yahā̃* (lit. 'here') for proximate third person, *wahā̃* (lit. 'there') for nonproximate one.

Figure 9.1 Inflections of the personal pronouns in singular number

Cases	1st p.	2nd p. (LGH)	2nd p. (MGH)	2nd p. (HGH)	3rd p (LGH)	3rd p. (MGH)	3rd p. (HGH)
Nm	ma	tã	timī	tapāī̃	u, tyo	unī	wahā̃
Ac	malāi	tãlāī	timīlāi	tapāīlāī	uslāī	unalāi	wahā̃lāi
In	maile	taīle	timīle	tapāīle	usle	unale	wahā̃le
Dt	malāi	tãlāi	timīlāi	tapāīlāi	uslāi	unalāi	wahā̃lāi
Ab	mabāṭa	tãbāṭa	timībāṭa	tapāībāṭa	usbāṭa	unabāṭa	wahā̃bāṭa
Gn	mero	tero	timro	tapāīko	usko	unako	wahā̃ko
Lc	mamā	tãmā	timīmā	tapāīmā	usmā	unamā	wahā̃mā

Figure 9.2 Inflections of the personal pronouns in plural number

Cases	1st p.	2nd p. (LGH,MGH)	2nd p. (HGH)	3rdp. (LGH,MGH)	3rd p. (HGH)
Nm	hāmī-(haru)	timī-haru	tapāīharu	tinīharu	wahā̃haru
Ac	hāmī-(haru)lāi	timī-harulāi	tapāīharulāi	tinīharulāi	wahā̃harulāi
In	hāmī-(haru)le	timī-harule	tapāīharule	tinīharule	wahā̃harule
Dt	hāmī-(haru)lāi	timī-harulāī	tapāīharulāi	tinīharulāi	wahā̃harulāi
Ab	hāmī-(haru)bāṭa	timī-harubāṭa	tapāīharubāṭa	tinīharubāṭa	wahā̃harubāṭa
Gn	hāmro, hāmī-haruko	timī-haruko	tapāīharuko	tinīharuko	wahā̃haruko
Lc	hāmī-(haru)mā	timī-harumā	tapāīharumā	tinīharumā	wahā̃harumā

Inflections of the second person *tapāī̃* (HGH) follow the pattern presented in Figure 9.3. The formal variants of *tapāī̃* are *yahā̃* and *hajur,* both inflecting on the pattern presented in Figure 9.3. The Royal honorific used to refer to the king and his family *sarkār* (lit. 'government') is used as both second person and third person pronoun, and follows the regular pattern presented in Figure 9.3.

Inflection of the third person pronoun *wahā̃* 'he, she' (HGH) follows the pattern presented in Figure 9.3.

Figure 9.3 presents the list of personal pronouns displaying the pronouns based on all the possible combinations of person, number and honorific level. Figure 9.4 is a table of second person pronoun usage by caste and age.

Figure 9.3 Personal pronouns[1].

	Singular:	Plural
First Person:	ma	hāmī-haru
Second Person:		
Level of respect		
Low	tã	timī-haru
Equal	timī	timī-haru
High (informal)	tapāī	tapāī-haru
High (formal)	yahā̃	yahā̃-haru
Honorific	hajūr[2]	hajūr-haru
Royal honorific	sarkār	sarkār-haru
Third person		
Level of respect		
Low	tyo	tinī-haru
Equal	tinī	tinī-haru
High	wahā̃	wahā̃-haru
Royal honorific	sarkār	sarkār-haru, mausūph-haru

Figure 9.4 Second person pronoun usage by caste and age.

Speaker's caste	Addressee's caste	Addressee's age (relative to speaker)	Pronoun
1 Brahman	Brahman	Peer	tapāī
		Senior	yahā̃
		Junior	timī
2 Brahman	Kṣatriyas	Same as Brahman	
3 Brahman	Vaiśyas	Peer	timī
		Senior	tapāī
		Junior	timī
4 Brahman	Śūdras	Peer	timī
		Senior	timī
		Junior	tã
5 Brahman	Royal family	All ages	sarkār
6 Vaiśyas	Brahmin	All ages	hajūr
7 Śūdras	Brahman	All ages	hajur

9.2 Modifiers in the pronoun phrase. Pronouns do not occur with the determiners (demonstratives, numerals, and classifiers), but they do cooccur with certain modifiers.

The following modifiers precede the pronouns they stand in construction with:

keval 'only' *khāli* 'only'

The following modifiers follow the pronouns they modify:

eklai 'alone' *mātrai* 'only, alone',
dubai 'both' *sabai* 'all'
āphai 'oneself'

Notes for Chapter 9

1. Note that in Nepali, personal pronouns do not show morphological gender. The gender of the pronouns is related to, and determined by the gender of the noun of which they are anaphoric substitutes. The gender of those pronouns, which function as subjects is manifested by the morphological form of the verb with which they stand in a 'subject-predicator' relationship. The gender of the 'non-subject' grammatical complements is not manifested by the verb.

2. The pronoun *hajūr* 'you (honorific)' indicates higher honorific. Thus, there are a total of five levels of respect for the second person pronoun and four levels of respect for the third person pronoun.

Chapter 10
Dependent nominals functioning as modifiers in larger nominals

10.0 Introduction. This chapter describes the structure of the dependent nominals and their functioning as modifiers in larger CNPs. These dependent nominals are divided into four subgroups: (1) characterizing modifiers (10.1), (2) appositive modifiers (10.2), (3) genitive modifiers (10.3), and (4) delimiting modifiers (10.4). The order of the functional constituents of the larger nominals with dependent nominals as modifiers is presented in the following formula:

Larger CNP = +Mod: +H:

Although all the 'modifiers' (characteristic modifiers, appositive modifiers, genitive modifiers, and delimiting modifiers) show the identical functional slots, they are distinguished by the items which occur as fillers.

(1) The fillers of the characteristic modifier slots are adjectives, adjectival phrases, or adjectival clauses.

(2) The fillers of the appositive modifier slots are nouns filling both head slots in the double-headed constructions; the nouns filling both head slots are in the same cases.

(3) The fillers of the genitive modifier slots are marked by the genitive case forms of nouns and pronouns.

(4) The fillers of the delimiting modifier slots are pronominal adjectives. When they occur independently in a syntactic structure, they occur like pronouns (with anaphoric reference), inflecting for cases, and distribute as complements or adjuncts of the verbs. But when they occur in the CNP structures they function as modifiers as they stand in construction with the nouns (heads).

10.1 Characterizing modifiers. Characterizing modifiers, that is modifiers describing the head (noun), are formally different from other modifiers. The characterizing modifiers are adjectivals, or participial forms of verbs with their complements. The following examples drawn from Part Two (the analyzed corpus of the *Nāso* text) illustrate the structure of the characterizing modifiers:

2.25 ±गाउँले +छिमेकीहरु

±gāũle +chimekīharu

±Mod: adj. +H: cn

±villager +neighbors

'village neighbors'

2.59.1 +नरमाइलो लाग्नुपर्ने +कुरा

+naramāilo lāgnuparne +kurā

±Mod: Cl. +H: cn

+unpleasant striking +matter

'the matter to be unhappy about'

2.67.8 ± सव भन्दा ठुलो +सन्तोष

± sava bhandā ṭhulo +santoṣa

±Mod: AdjP. +H: cn

± all than great +satisfaction

'the greatest satisfaction'

3.32 ± आँगनमा चरिरहेका +परेवा

±ā̃ganamā cariraheka̅ +parevā

±Mod: Cl. +H: cn

± courtyard-in wandering +pigeons

'the pigeons wandering in the courtyard'

4.3.1 ±तीर्थ गर्ने +इच्छा

± tīrtha garne +icchā

±Mod: Cl. +H: cn

± pilgrimage doing +desire

'a desire to go on a pilgrimage'

10.2 Appositive modifiers: Double headed constructions. Appositive modifiers occur in noun phrases which are double-headed constructions consisting of two or more head slots, all obligatory, filled by two or more juxtaposed noun phrases which show the same case. This may be represented as follows:

case tie

NApp = +H: NP +H: NP

Apposition is the juxtaposition of two forms or sets of forms lexically designating the same entity. The fact that the two forms designate the same entity can only be known from the lexicon extralinguistically. Without this extralinguistic information it is impossible to distinguish apposition from the construction of connection when the second member is not marked by a connector. In addition it would otherwise be difficult to distinguish the syntactic construction of a 'compound noun'.

Although structurally apposition consists of no more than the simple juxtaposition of two noun phrases each filling a head slot, the noun phrase in the second head slot serves to identify more completely the noun phrase filling the first slot, e.g.

1.2.7 ± हरिवंश +पुराण
± harivaṃśa + purāṇa
±Mod: pn +H: cn
±harivaṃśa +legend
'Harivaṃśa the legend'

2.1 ±फागुन +महीना
± phāguna +mahīnā
±Mod: pn +H: cn
± Phagun +month
'the month of Phagun (February-March)'

2.49 ±नौली +घर्तिनी
± naulī +ghartinī
±Mod: pn +H: cn
± Nauli +slave
'Nauli the slave'

4.1 ± माघ +महीना
± māhga +mahinā
±Mod: pn +H: cn
+Magh +month
'The month of Magh (January-February)'

± काले +कामी
± kāle +kāmī
±Mod: pn +H: cn
± Kale +blacksmith
'Kale the blacksmith'

10.3 Genitive modifiers. Genitive modifiers are marked by the genitive case suffix *-ko* of nouns, or genitive cases of pronouns; as *mero* 'my, 'mine', *hāmro* 'our, ours' *timro* 'your, yours', and *āphno* 'one's own'. Thus the genitive case of nouns and pronouns represents the adjectival use of nouns and pronouns, e.g.

1.2.8 ±सुभद्राको +कोख
±subhadrāko +kokha
±Mod: pn-gn +H: cn
±Subhadra-of +womb
'the womb of Subhadra'

1.3.1 ±देवीरमणको +जित

±devīramaṇa ko +jita

±Mod: pn-gn +H: cn
±Deviraman-of +victory
'Deviraman's victory'

1.3.3 ±उनको +अभिमान

± unako +abhimāna

±Mod: pro-gn +H: cn
+he-of +pride
'his pride'

1.4.2 ±आफ्नो +वैभव

± āphno +vaibhava

±Mod: pro-gn +H: cn
± one's-own +wealth
'ones own wealth'

1.6.3 ±छिमेकका +आइमाइ

± chimekakā +āimāi

±Mod: cn-gn +H: cn
±neighborhood-of +women
'women of neighborhood'

1.6.4 ±धामी झाँक्रीको +बूटी-जन्तर

± dhāmī jhā̃:krīko +būṭī- jantara

±Mod: cmpdcn-gn +H: cmpdcn
±Shaman-sorcerer-of +herb-amulets
'the amulets of the shamans'

1.6.5 ±देवीदेवताको +भाकल

±devīdevatāko +bhākala

±Mod: cmpdcn-gn +H: cn
±goddess-gods-of +promise
'promise to the gods and goddesses'

1.14.2 ±सुख दुःखकी +साथी

±sukha duḥkhakī +sāthī

±Mod: cmpdcn-gn +H: cn
±happiness-unhappiness +friend
'a friend in weal and woes'

2.1.1 ±फागुन महीनाको +विहानी पखको +सिरेटो
±phāguna mahīnāko ± bihānīpakhako +sireṭo
±Mod: modified-cn-gn ±Mod: cn-gn +H: cn
±Phagun month-of +morning-hour-of +cold-wind
'the cold wind of the morning in the month of Phagun (Feb.-March)'

2.6 ± सुभद्राको +पाणिग्रहण
± subhadrāko +pāṇigrahaṇa
±Mod: pn-gn +H:cn
± Subhadra-of +wedding
'the wedding of Subhadra.'

2.9.2 ±बाह्र वर्षकी ±अबोध बालिका
±bāhra barṣakī ±abodha bālikā
±Mod: CNP-gn +H:CNP-nm
±twelve year-of ±innocent girl
'a twelve-year old innocent girl'

2.23.2 ±भोगको +लालसा
± bhogako + lālasā
±Mod: cn-gn +H:cn-nm
±enjoyment-of ±desire
'the desire for sense gratification'

2.29 ±आफ्नो +तीव्र इच्छा
±āphno +tīvra icchā
±Mod: pro-gn +H:CNP-nm
±one's-own +intense desire
'one's own great desire'

2.31 ±आफ्नो +काम
±āphno + kāma
±Mod: pro-gn +H:cn-nm
± one's-own +work
'one's own work'

2.41.2 ±तिम्रो +ओच्छ्यान
±timro +ochyāna
±Mod: pro-gn +H:cn-nm
±your +bed
'your bed'

2.48.2 ± आफ्नो +दोलाइँ

±āphno +dolāĩ

±Mod: pro-gn +H:cn-nm

±one's-own +quilt

'one's own quilt'

2.53.2 ±घरकी +पुरानी चाकर्नी

± gharakī +purānī cākarnī

±Mod: cn-gn +H:CNP-nm

±house-of +old maid

'the old maid in the house'

The genitive case markers *-ko*, *-ro*, and *-no* show their allomorphs (variants of minimal grammatical units) *-kā, -rā* and *-nā* when the genitive modifiers modify the nouns in plural number, or nouns in oblique cases, e.g.

1.6.4 ±सन्तानका +आशाले

± santānakā +āśāle

±Mod: cn-gn +H:cn-nm

±offspring-of +hope-by

'in the hope of [having] an offspring'

1.12.2 ±देवीरमणका +आँखा

±devīramaṇakā +ā̃khā

±Mod: pn-gn +H:cn-nm

±Deviraman-of +eyes

'Deviraman's eyes'

Since the genitive modifiers function as adjectives, they show inflections not just for number but also for gender. For instance, the genitive case markers *-ko*, *-ro* and *-no* show their allomorphs *-kī, -rī* and *-nī* when they stand in construction with the nouns of feminine gender; as:

2.50 ±घरकी +पुरानी चाकर्नी

± gharakī + purānī cākarnī

±Mod: cn-gn +H:CNP-nm

±home-of +old maid

'the old maid at home'

2.54 ±सुभद्राकी ± ... सुखदु:खकी +साथी

± subhadrākī ±... sukhaduḥkhakī ± sāthī

±Mod: pro-gn ... ±Mod: cmpdcn-gn +H:cn-nm

±Subhadra-of ... ±happiness-unhappiness-of +friend

'Subhadra's (female) friend in weal and woes'

7.21.1 ±मेरी +गृहलक्ष्मी

±merī +gṛhalakṣmī

±Mod: pro-gn +H:cn-nm

±my +gṛhalakṣmī

'My gṛhalakṣmī (symbol of prosperity)'

±तिम्री +छोरी

±timrī +chorī

±Mod: pro-gn +H:cn-nm

±your +daughter

'your daughter'

±आफ्नी +पत्नी

±āphnī + patnī

±Mod: pro-gn +H:cn-nm

± one's-own +wife

'one's own wife'

10.4 Delimiting modifiers. The difference between the characterizing modifiers and the delimiting modifiers is that the characterizing modifiers are adjectives, adjective phrases, clauses. The delimiting modifiers are only pronominal adjectives in nominal case, e.g.

1.2.1 ±हरएक +उपाय

±haraeka +upāya

±Mod: pro-nm +H:cn-nm

±every +effort

'every effort'

1.8.2 ±अर्को +विवाह

±arko +vivāha

±Mod: pro-nm +H:cn-nm

± another +marriage

'another marriage'

2.42 ±पल्लो +कोठा

±pallo +koṭhā

±Mod: pro-nm +H:cn-nm

±next +room

'the next room'

2.65.5 ±कुनै +दिन

±kunai +dina

±Mod: pro-nm +H:cn-nm
±certain +day
'certain day'

2.66 ±अलि +दिन
± ali +dina
±Mod: pro-nm +H:cn-nm
± few +day
'a few days'

7.10.1 ±सवै +कुरा
±savai +kurā
±Mod: pro-nm +H:cn-nm
± all +matters
'all things'

Adjectival Structures

Chapter 11
The adjective phrase

11.0 Internal structure of the adjective phrase (AdjP). This chapter describes the internal structure of the adjective phrase (AdjP). The internal structure of the adjective phrase (AdjP) consists of the obligatory head slot filled by an adjective, and an optional modifier slot filled by a qualifier (qul) or quantifier (qnt) adverb. The linear order in which the functional constituents of AdjP's occur is shown in the following formula:

AdjP = ±Mod: +H:

The following examples drawn from Part Two (the analyzed corpus of the *Nāso*) text illustrate the structure of the AdjP in which the quantifiers precede the head:

1.10.1 ± बहुत + पतिपरायणा
±bahuta +patiparāyaṇā
±Mod: adv (qnt) +H: adj.
± very +loyal-to-husband
'very loyal (to husband)'

5.1.1 ± झन् +भयङ्कर
± jhan +bhayaṅkara
±Mod: adv (qnt) +H: adj.
± more +dreadful
'more dreadful'

6.17.5 ± साह्रै +नराम्रो
± sāhrai +narāmro
±Mod: adv (qnt) +H: adj.
±very +bad
'very bad'

7.7.1 ± केही +शान्त

± kehī +sānta

±Mod: adv (qnt) +H: adj.

± somewhat +pacified

'somewhat pacified, quiet'

7.31.1 ± एकदम +साफ

± ekadama + sā:pha

±Mod: adv (qnt) +H: adj.

± very +clean

'Very clean'

In the following instances the place of quantifiers is filled by the interrogative adverbial substitute forms. In terms of their meanings, or as substitute forms with overlaid grammatical function (cf. Ch. 6), the interrogative adverbs pose questions, and the forms that answer those questions are quantifiers. Thus, the interrogative adverbial substitute forms fill the same slot in the AdjP as the quantifiers do, e.g.

4.24 ± कति +मतलबी ?

± kati +matalabī ?

±Mod: interrog.adv (qnt) +H: adj.

± how +selfish

'How selfish?'

6.3.4 ± कति +दुब्ली ?

± kati +dublī ?

±Mod: interrog.adv (qnt) +H: adj.

± how +thin

'How thin?'

11.1 Adjectives as heads. Within the internal structure of the adjective phrase, an obligatory adjective occurs as the head, e.g.

rāmro 'handsome'
aglo 'tall'
hoco 'short'
kangāl 'penniless'
birāmī 'sick'
asal 'good'

Adjectives ending in *-o* which occur in the head slot reflect the gender and number of the noun with which they stand in construction. In other words, they simply manifest those morphological changes to mark the syntactic relationship to the gender of nouns with which they stand in construction with, e.g.

rāmro keṭo 'handsome boy' | *rāmrī keṭī* 'beautiful girl'
rāmrā keṭāharu 'handsome boys' | *rāmrā keṭīharu* 'good girls'

The Nepali adjectives which end in *-o* show inflected 'evaluative' forms ending in *-ai* which show an evaluative degree of quality. [These 'evaluative' forms are not allomorphs but are similar to the syntactic comparative and superlative forms.] Then an evaluative connotation 'fairly' or 'more or less' is added to the meaning of such adjectives, e.g.

thulo 'big' | *thulai* 'fairly big'
sāno 'small' | *sānai* 'fairly small'
hoco 'short' | *hocai* 'fairly short'
aglo 'tall' | *aglai* 'fairly tall'
moṭo 'fat' | *moṭai* 'fairly fat'

The adjectival *sab* 'all', though not ending in *-o*, also shows an inflection for its evaluative form ending in *-ai* which adds to its meaning the connotation 'fairly' or 'more or less'. For instance, *sab* 'all' vs. *sabai* 'more or less all'

11.2 Quantifiers in the AdjP. Quantifiers in the AdjP are divided into four categories: (1) adverbs of quantity (11.2.1), (2) comparative quantifier phrases (11.2.2), and (3) superlative quantifier phrases (11.2.3), and (4) elative superlative quantifier (11.2.4).

11.2.1 Adverbs of quantity. The adverbs of quantity are the following:

ajha 'more' | *alik* 'somewhat'
alikati 'a little' | *bahut* 'very'
dherai 'many' | *jyādai* 'very'
kehi 'some, somewhat' | *sārhai* 'extremely'

These adverbs of quantity function as quantifying determiners in the CNP, e.g.

ajha gāro kām 'more difficult task'
alik pharak kāgaj 'somewhat different paper'
alikati lāmo bāṭo 'a little long way'
bahut patiparāyaṇā ramaṇī 'a very loyal wife'
dherai narāmro khabar 'very bad news'

jyādai dherai paisā 'very much money'

kehī rāmro pariṇām 'a somewhat better result'

sāhrai narāmro rog 'an extremely bad disease'

11.2.2 Comparative quantifier phrases. Comparative quantifier phrases are divided into two groups: (1) comparatives with ***bhandā*** 'than' (11.2.2.1) and (2) comparatives with *jhan* 'further' and *ajha* 'more' (11.2.2.2).

11.2.2.1 Comparative with *bhandā* 'than'. Comparative quantifier phrases with *bhandā* 'than' consist of two obligatory nominals, i.e. common noun, proper noun, pronoun, plus a comparative degree quantifier ***bhandā*** ' 'than' and a head filled by an adjective. The order of these obligatory constituents is shown in the formula:

CompP-*bhandā* = +nominal +comparative *bhandā* +nominal +head(adj)

+भाग्य +भन्दा +पुरुषार्थ +ठुलो [+हो]
+bhāgya +bhandā +puruṣārtha +ṭhulo [+ho]
+nominal +comparative +nominal +adj.head [+predicate]
+luck +than +hard-work +great [+is]
'Hard work is greater than luck.'

11.2.2.2 Comparative adjective phrase with *jhan* 'the more'. Comparative quantifier adjective phrases with *jhan* 'the more' consist of an obligatory nominal, the comparative *jhan* 'the more', and an obligatory head slot filled by an adjective. Unlike comparatives with ***bhandā*** 'than', comparatives with *jhan* 'the more' do not consist of more than one nominal in the clause. Thus, *jhan* 'the more' is anaphoric to the nominal of the proceeding clause. The order of the constituents is shown in the following formula:

Comp-*jhan* = + nominal + comparative (*jhan*) +head

5.1.1 +रात्री +झन् +भयङ्कर [+प्रतीत +हुन्थ्यो]
+rātrī +jhan +bhayaṅkara [+pratīta +hunthyo]
+nominal +comparative +complement [predicate phrase]
+night +more +terrifying [+appeared +was]
'The night appeared more terrifying.'

11.2.3 Superlative quantifier phrases. Superlative quantifier phrases with *sabbhandā* 'most-of-all' consist of an obligatory subject, the superlative *sabbhandā* 'most-of-all' and an adjective head. The order of the constituents is shown in the formula:

SupP-*sabbhandā* = +subject + superlative (sabbhandā) + complement

+सगरमाथा +सबभन्दा अग्लो [+पहाड +हो]
+sagaramāthā +sabbhandā +aglo [pahāḍa +ho]
+subject +super. (sabbhandā) +head [+subject complement +pred.]
Sagarmāthā +most-of-all +high +mountain +is
'Sagarmatha (Mt. Everest) is the highest mountain.'

The order of the constituents of the superlative quantifier phrases indicates a statistical order (the most frequent order). However, the position of the subject is changeable. This is illustrated by the following example:

2.67.8 +सबभन्दा +ठुलो [+सन्तोष +यही +हो]
+sababhandā +ṭhulo [+santoṣa +yahī +ho]
+superlative qnt. +head [+subject +subject complement +pred]
+most-of-all +great [+satisfaction +this +is]
'This the greatest satisfaction'

11.2.4 Elative superlative quantifier. The elative superlative quantifier *sabaibhandā* is used in expressions with more emphatic connotations than the superlative quantifiers express, e.g.

4.27 ± यो घर +सुभद्रालाई +संसारमा +सबैभन्दा +प्यारो [+वस्तु +थियो]
±yo ghara +subhadrālāi ±saṁsāramā +sabaibahndā +pyāro vastu +thiyo
±S: CNP-nm +DC: pn-dt +LC: cn-lc +elative superlative qnt +H: adj [subj.compl. +pred]
± this house +Subhadra-to +world-in +most-of-all +dear thing +was
'This house was the very dearest thing in the world for Subhadra.'

Chapter 12
Dependent adjectivals functioning as modifiers within CNPs

12.0 Introduction. This chapter describes the structure of the dependent adjectivals functioning as modifiers. The dependent adjectivals modify the CNPs. So it makes an easier and clearer presentation if the dependent adjectivals are described with reference to the CNPs they modify. The CNP structures with dependent adjectivals have an optional modifier slot filled by one of the two types of the dependent adjectivals described in (12.1) and (12.2), and an obligatory head slot filled by a noun. The linear order of the functional slots in the CNP structures with the dependent adjectivals as modifiers is presented in the following formula:

CNP (with DepAdjls) = +Mod: +H:

Dependent adjectivals are derived verbal adjectives (participles). The participles are divided into two subclasses: (1) imperfect participle marked by the suffix *-ne*, and (2) perfect participle marked by the suffix *-eko*. The imperfect participle marked by the derivational suffix *-ne*, functioning as a dependent adjectival, is not inflected for tense, person, number, gender, and aspect. The perfect participle marked by the derivational suffix *-eko* is not inflected for tense and person, but it is inflected for number, and gender, e.g.

Singular		Plural
Masculine	Feminine	Masculine, Feminine
-eko	*-ekī̃*	*-ekā̃*

In the cases where the mode (nonprogressive vs. progressive) is marked, the imperfect participial suffixes *-ne* , and perfect participial suffix *-eko* follow the progressive mode marker *-irah-*. The nonprogressive mode is unmarked, e.g.

Nonprogressive mode		Progressive mode	
Imperfect participle	Perfect participle	Imprf.prt.	Prf.prt
-ne	*-eko* m. sg	*-iraha-ne*	*-irah-eko* m. sg.
-ne	*-ekī̃* f. sg.	*-iraha-ne*	*-irah-ekī̃* f. sg.
-ne	*-ekā̃* pl.	*-iraha-ne*	*-irah-ekā̃* pl.

The internal structure of all participles consists of the stem of the verb, and with the addition of one of the participial suffixes, i.e. *-ne* (12.1), or *-eko* (12.2).

12.1 The imperfect participle *-ne* as modifier. The dependent adjectivals characterizing the head (noun) with the imperfect participle-*ne* consist of an obligatory derived verbal adjective, that is a verb with imperfect participle *-ne*, and an obligatory head (noun).

CNP (with DepAdjl)-*ne* = +Mod: v-impf.prt*(-ne)* +H: cn

Figure 12.1 Adjectivals formed from the imperfect participle *-ne*, modifying nouns in the CNP structures

Verb stems	Imperfect participle *(-ne)*	Head (noun)	
khā	*khāne*	*kurā*	*khāne kurā* 'eating things (food)'
jānu	*jāne*	*mānche*	*jāne mānche* 'the going man'
lekhnu	*lekhne*	*kalam*	*lekhne kalam* 'writing pen (pen for writing)'
paḍhnu	*paḍhne*	*kitāb*	*paḍhne kitāb* 'reading book'

Dependent adjectivals with the imperfect participle *-ne* may cooccur with the obligatory direct object (+DO), if the verb (in the imperfect participial form) is a transitive verb, and the head slot filled by a noun. The order of the functional constituents of the CNP with dependent adjectivals is shown in the formula:

CNP (with DepAdjl-*ne*) = (+DO:) +P: tv-impf.prt*(-ne)* +H: cn

The formula is illustrated by the following example,

2.12.1 +दुलही +अन्माउने [+वेला]
+dualhī +anmāune +velā

+DO: cn-ac +P: tv1-impf.prt*(-ne)* +H: cn-nm
+bride +giving-away +time
'The time to give away the bride'

Adjectivals formed from the perfect participle *-ne* frequently occur in Nepali. Figure 12.2 presents some examples of adjectival phrases with a direct object and the participle *-ne*.

Figure 12.2 Adjectival phrases with a nominal and the participle *-ne*.

Direct Object	Verbs in imperfect participle *-ne*	Head noun modified by the DepAdjl
2.12.1 dulahī̃	*anmāune*	*velā* 'the time to send away the bride'
2.55.1 duḥkha	*pokhne*	*bhā̃ḍo* '(lit.) the pot to pour one's sorrow' (a friend to share pain)
3.3.2 parevālāi	*pakrane*	*kośis* 'the effort to catch the pigeon'
4.3.1 tīrtha	*garne*	*icchā* 'a wish to go on a pilgrimage'
kām	*garne*	*mānche* 'a work doing man (a worker)'

12.2 The perfect participle *-eko* as modifier. Dependent adjectivals marked with *-eko* which characterize the head noun consist of an obligatory past participle *-eko* and an obligatory head. Figure 12.3 presents some examples of perfect participle *-eko* as dependent adjectivals modifying the head noun.

Figure 12.3 Perfect participle *-eko* marking the dependent adjectivals modifying the head noun.

Verb stems	Perfect participle *-eko*	Head noun
2.37.1 sut-	*sutiraheko*	*koṭhā* 'the room one slept in'
sodh-	*sodheko*	*praśna* 'the asked question'
dekh-	*dekheko*	*kurā* 'something seen'

Dependent adjectivals with the perfect participle *-eko* may cooccur with an optional complement slot (±C:), the predicate slot (+P:) filled by a verb (marked by the perfect participial suffix *-eko*), and the head slot (+H:) filled by a noun. The order of the functional constituents of the CNP with dependent adjectivals is shown in the following formula:

CNP (with DepAdjl-*eko*) = +Mod: (±C: any compl.) +P: v-*eko* +H: cn

The complement, an optional element, can be a noun in instrumental case, dative case, ablative case, locative case, or any noun phrase or postpositional phrase filling the same functional slot, i.e. complement. For instance,

Instrumental complement:

± तपाईंले +भनेको +खबर
±tapāı̃le +bhaneko + khabar
± C: pro-in +P: tv1-prf.prt (*-eko*) +H:
±you-by +told +news
'the news told by you'

Dative complement:

±उसलाइ +दिएको +पैसा
±usalāı̃ +dieko + paisā
±DC: pro-dt +P: tv2-.prf. prt +H: cn-nm
± him-to +given +money
'The money given to him'

Ablative complement:

±अमेरिकाबाट +आएको +चिठी
±amerikābaṭa +āeko +ciṭhī
±AbC: pn-ab +P: iv1-prf..prt +H: cn-nm
America-from +come +letter
'A letter from America'

Locative complement:

±लण्डनमा +भेटेको +मान्छे
± laṇḍanamā +bheṭeko +mānche
±LC: pn-lc +P: tv1-prf.prt +H: cn-nm
London-in +met +man
'A man met in London'

Adverbial Structures

Chapter 13
The adverb phrase

13.0 Internal structure of the adverb phrase (AdvP). This chapter describes the internal structure of the adverb phrase. The internal structure of the adverb phrase (AdvP) consists of an optional complement slot (±C:) filled by an instrumental, dative, ablative or locative complement, an optional modifier slot (±Mod:) filled by a quantifying adverb, and an obligatory head (+H:) filled by simple adverbs, or adverbials (13.1), or compound adverbials (13.2). The order of the functional constituents of the adverb phrase is presented in the following formula:

AdvP = (±C:) ± Mod: +H:

In the formula (±C:) means that the optional complement (±C:) is realized in certain instances, but not in others. For instance, the following adverbial phrase shows that the optional complement is realized in it:

±घरबाट ±धेरै +टाढा
±gharabāṭa ± dherai +ṭāḍhā
±C: cn-ab ±Mod: adv (qnt) +H: advl
±home-from ±very +far
'very far from home'

13.1 Simple adverbs. Simple adverbs act as the head in an adverb phrase and are divided into two categories: (1) derived adverbs (13.1.1), and (2) nonderived adverbs.

13.1.1 Derived adverbs. The derived adverbs are grouped into three subclasses: (1) adverbs ending in *-arī* (13.1.1.1), (2) adverbs ending in *-sāth* (13.1.1.2), and (3) adverbs ending in *-pūrvaka* (13.1.1.3). The derived adverbs consist of a stem (adjective, adverb, or noun) and one of the following suffixes: *-arī*, *-sāth*, and *-pūrvaka*. The suffix *-arī* occurs with the Nepali stems; the suffix *-sāth* occurs with stems borrowed from Hindi; and the suffix *-pūrvaka* occurs with stems borrowed from Sanskrit.

13.1.1.1 Adverbs ending in *-arī* 'doing'. Adverbs ending in *-arī* 'in a manner' are derived from Nepali adjectives, and Nepali adverbs. The underlying linear order consists of an adjective stem, or an adverb stem plus the adverb suffix *-arī* 'in a certain way or manner ', i.e.

Nepali Adjective stem:	Derived adverbs in *-arī*
rāmro 'good, handsome'	*rāmrarī* 'in a good manner, well'
bes 'good'	*besarī* 'very well, very much'
susta 'slow'	*sustarī* 'slowly'

Nepali Adverb stem:	Derived adverbs in *-arī*
kaso 'how (interrog.)'	*kasarī* 'in what way'
jaso 'how (relative)'	*jasarī* 'in which way'
tyaso 'that way (demonst.)'	*tyasarī* 'in that way'

13.1.1.2 Adverbs ending in *-sāth* 'with'. Adverbs ending in *-sāth* 'with' are derived from Hindi adjectives or nouns. The underlying linear order consists of a Hindi adjective or noun stem plus the adverb suffix *-sāth*, e.g.

Hindi noun, adj-stems:	Derived adverbs in *-sāth*
khuśī (adj.) 'happy'	*khuśīsāth* 'with happiness (happily)'
dikdārī (n.) 'sadness'	*dikdārīsāth* 'with sadness (sadly)'
phūrti (n.) 'vigor'	*phūrtisāth* 'with vigor (vigorously)'

13.1.1.3 Adverbs ending in *-pūrvaka*. Adverbs ending in *-pūrvaka* are derived from nouns. Adverbs ending in *-pūrvaka* are of Sanskrit origin. The underlying linear order consists of a Sanskrit noun stem plus the adverb suffix *-pūrvaka*, e.g.

Sanskrit noun stems:	Derived adverbs in *-pūrvaka*
utsāha 'enthusiasm'	*utsāhapūrvaka* 'enthusiastically'
ānanda 'happiness'	*ānandapūrvaka* 'happily'
dhairya 'patience'	*dhairyapūrvaka* 'patiently'

13.1.2 Nonderived adverbs. Nonderived adverbs are 'adverbials' since they do not show the derivational suffixes that characterize the adverbs. The adverbials are distinguished from the adverbs only on the basis of their forms (morphology). In terms of distribution, the adverbials fill the same functional slots as the adverbs do.

The Figure 13.1 presents a list of adverbials of most frequent occurrence.

Figure 13.1 Adverbials of most frequent occurrence

aba 'from now on'	abelā 'late'
ahile 'now, at this time'	āja 'today'
aghi 'before, previously'	āphukhusi 'voluntarily'
ahile 'now'	akasmāt 'suddenly'
ākhira 'finally'	ali 'a little'
atyanta 'extremely'	ahilyai 'right now'
barābar 'frequently'	bholi 'tomorrow'
bhaepani 'although'	bahut 'very'
bharkhar 'recently'	bāhira 'outside'
bittikai 'as soon as'	cā̃ḍai 'soon, quickly'
eklai 'alone'	caṭakka 'completely'
ekdam 'completely'	jahā̃ 'where'
jahile 'when'	jhanḍai 'almost'
jasari 'in which way'	jatā 'which way'
kahā̃ 'where?'	kahile 'when?'
kasari 'in which way?'	katā 'which way, whither?'
kahilekā̃hī̃ 'sometimes'	kahilyai 'ever'
kehi 'somewhat'	kina 'why?'
paraspara 'mutually'	mātra 'only'
najikai 'near'	pachi 'afterwards'
pachiltira 'behind'	pheri 'again'
pani 'also'	pilpil 'atwinkle'
saberai 'early'	sāhrai 'very'
sadaiva 'always'	samma 'only'
talatira 'downward'	tyahā̃ 'there'
tyasari 'in that way'	tyatā 'there, on that side'
uhile 'then'	utā 'on that side'
vyarthai 'unnecessarily'	yahā̃ 'here'
yastarī̃ 'in such a way'	yatā 'here, on this side'

13.1.3 Interrogatives, relators and demonstratives. Among the nonderived adverbs presented in Figure 13.1, some of them are substitute forms (cf. Chapter 6). These substitute forms are grouped into three subclasses: interrogatives, relators, and demonstratives which are correlative forms. In other words, the demonstrative adverbials answer the questions posed by the interrogatives. For instance, the question *kahā̃* 'where?', is answered by *tyahā̃* 'there', or *yahā̃* 'here'; *kahile* 'when?' is answered by *uhile* 'then' or *ahile* 'now';

kasarī 'how' is answered by *tyasarī* 'that way' or *yasarī*' 'this way'. Although these forms have already been treated in Chapter 6, Figure 13.2 presents these correlative forms for a quick reference here.

Figure 13.2 Interrogatives, relator, and demonstratives

K-Interrogatives	J-Relatives	D-(t-y-u-a)-Demonstratives
kahā̃ 'where'	jahā̃ 'where'	tyahā̃ 'there'
		yahā̃ 'here'
kahile 'when'	jahile 'when'	uhile 'then',
		ahile 'now'
kasarī 'how'	jasarī 'which way'	tyasarī 'that way'
		yasarī 'this way'
katā 'which way'	jatā 'which way	tyatā 'that way'
		yatā 'this way'

13.2 Compound adverbials. Compound adverbials are combinations of two adverbials. The fact that they are compound adverbials is indicated by the hyphen (-) in their transcribed form although there is no hyphen in their Devanagari orthography, e.g.

agāḍi-paṭṭi 'in front'
āmane-sāmne 'face to face'
mās-tira 'upward'
mun-tira 'downward'
pāri-paṭṭi 'on the other side'
aghil-tira 'in front'
bīcabīca-mā 'intermittently'
māthi-tira 'upward'
pachil-tira 'behind'
tala-tira 'beneath'

The traditional Nepali grammars call the second element in such compound adverbial 'postpositions' (comparable to 'prepositions' in the English language). Of course, they are treated as postpositions (cf. Chapter 14) when they fill the head slot in the postpositional phrase (PP) structures with complements. When they occur alone, they are called compound adverbials, and they distribute in the same way as the simple adverbs, adverbials, or adverb phrases (AdvP), i.e. as fillers of the optional adverbial adjunct (AA:) slot in clausal structures, e.g.

±उ ±अगाडिपट्टि +सऱ्यो
±u ±agāḍipaṭti +saryo
±S:pro-nm ± AA: advl +P: iv1-3sg.pst
±he ±in front +moved
'He moved in front.'

±अघिल्तिर +नबस
±aghiltira +nabasa
±AA: advl +P: iv1-neg.imp.
±in-front +not-sit
'Do not sit in front'

±उनीहरु ± आमने-सामने +उभिए
±unihru ± āmane-sāmane +ubhie
±S: pro-nm ±AA: advl +P: iv1-3pl..pst
±they ± face-to-face +stood
'They stood face-to-face'

Chapter 14
The adverbial postpositional noun phrase

14.0 Introduction. This chapter describes the structure of the adverbial postpositional noun phrase (PP) in Nepali. (Postpositions are equivalent to prepositions in English). The postpositional phrase consists of a noun or a noun phrase (NP) filling the functional slot of obligatory complement (+C:), and a postposition (pp) filling the obligatory head (+H:) slot. The linear order in which the functional constituents of the postpositional phrase (PP) occur is presented in the following formula:

PP= +C: +H:

The formula is illustrated in the following instance,

+घर +अगाडि
+ghara +agāḍi
+C: cn +H: pp
+house + in front
'In front of the house'

14.1 Postposition and its complements (NPs). A postposition filling the obligatory head slot (+H:) of the postpositional phrase (PP) stands in construction with the noun phrases (NPs) filling the optional complement slot (±C:). Some of the postpositions, e.g. *aghi* 'before' or *pachi* 'after', which may occur alone filling an optional adverbial complement or adjunct slot (±AA:) in a clausal structure may also occur as nonderived adverbials (cf. 13.2).

The forms *aghi* 'before', and *pachi* 'after' which may occur with clausal constructions are classified as subordinating conjunctions (cf. 15.2). They are homophonous forms which belong to different classes (subordinating conjunctions, postpositions, or adverbials).

The following is a list of Nepali postpositions:

agāḍi 'in front'
aghi 'before'
anusār 'according to'
bābajūd 'in spite of'
badala instead'
bāhek 'except'
bāhira 'outside'
bamojim 'according to'
bhar (bhara) 'throughout
'bhari 'all over, in full'

bhitra 'inside, in, into'	dekhi 'since'
jastai 'like'	jasto 'like'
jhaĩ 'like'	dvārā 'by'
kahā̃ 'in, at (location)'	madhye 'among'
mani 'under'	māthi 'on, above, over'
muni 'under'	nagic/najik 'near'
nagicai/najikai 'very near'	nera 'near'
nimitta 'for for the sake of'	nimti 'for, for the sake of'
nira 'near'	pachā̃ḍi 'behind'
pachi 'after'	pakha 'toward ceratain time'
pāri 'across (a river or road)'	paṭṭi 'on the side of'
sā̃ga/saṁga 'with'	samma 'up to'
sāmunne 'right in front'	sāmu 'in front of'
sita 'with'	tala 'below, under'
tira 'toward'	vāre [ba:re] 'about'
vinā [bina:] 'without'	viruddha 'against'
wāri 'on the closer of two sides'	waripari 'around'

14.2 Postpositions occurring with the NPs in genitive case. A small group of postpositions which belong to this group occur with the complements (NPs) in genitive case. These postpositions occur with the NPs in genitive case only if the NPs refer to [+human] beings. They do not occur with NPs in genitive case if the NPs refer to [-human] beings.

The following are examples of these postpositions cooccurring with complements (NPs) only in the genitive case:

agā̃ḍi 'in front of '	*mero agā̃ḍi nabasa* 'Do not sit in front of me'
bābajud 'in spite of'	*tyaskā bābajūd* 'In spite of that'
badalā	5.17.2 *ā̃śāko badalā* 'instead of hope'
nimitta 'for the sake of'	1.2.2 *santānakā nimitta* 'for the sake of offspring'
nimti 'for '	*mero nimti yo gara* 'Do it for me please'
pachā̃ḍi 'behind'	*gharako pachā̃ḍi rukh cha* 'There is a tree behind the house'
sāmunne 'right in front'	*gharako sāmunne pokhari cha* 'There is a pond right in front of the house.'
sāmu 'in front of'	1.12.2 *devīramaṇakā ā̃khākā sāmu* 'In front of the eyes of Deviraman'
viruddha 'against'	*tyo mero viruddha bolcha* 'He talks against me'

14.3 Postpositions occurring with morphologically unmarked forms of the NPs. Of the postpositions listed in (14.1) the following is a list of postpositions occurring with the morphologically unmarked forms of nouns or noun phrases (NPs):

aghi 'before'	anusār 'according to'
bāhek 'except'	bāhira 'outside'
bamojim 'according to'	bhar 'throughout'
bhari 'all over, in full'	bhitra 'inside, in, into'
dekhi 'since'	jasto 'like'
jhaĩ 'like'	dvārā 'by'
kahā̃ 'in, at (location)'	madhye 'among'
mani 'under'	māthi 'on, above, over'
muni 'under'	nagic 'near'
nagicai 'very near'	nera 'near'
nira 'near'	pāri 'across (a river or road)'
pachi 'after'	paṭṭi 'on the side of'
sãga 'with'	samma 'up to'
sita 'with'	tala 'below, under'
tira 'toward'	vāre [ba:re] 'about'
vinā [bina:] 'without'	wāri 'on the closer of two sides'
waripari 'around'	

Figure 14.1 Schematic diagram illustrating the points and directions of Nepali postpositions.

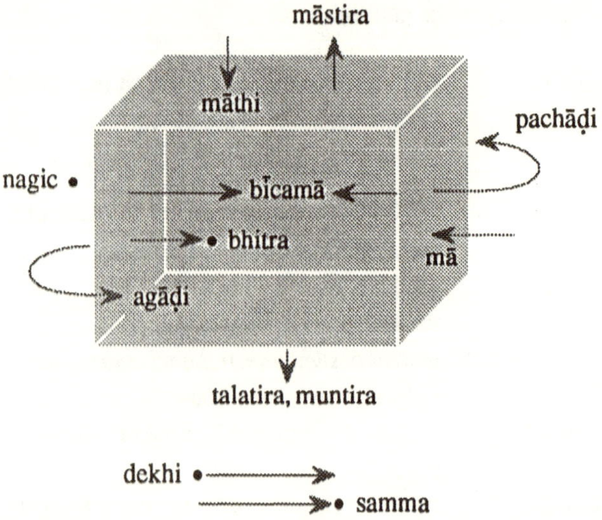

Chapter 15
Conjunctions: Coordinate and subordinate

15.0 Introduction. This chapter describes the conjunctions, which belong to a small set of uninflected particles. Conjunctions fill the connector function slot (+C:), and conjoin two or more structures (words, phrases, or clauses). Conjunctions are of two types: coordinating conjunctions conjoining any two equal structures (15.1), and subordinating conjunctions conjoining unequal structures, e.g. a clause dependent on a word, phrase, or clause (15.2). The structures conjoined by conjunctions are called conjunctive structures (CX). The linear order of the functional constituents of coordinating conjunctive structures (CoCX) is presented in the following formula:

CoCX = $\pm$H: $\pm$H: $\pm$H: ... +H: +C: +H:

The items which fill the head slots (+H:) preceding and following the connecting slot (+C:) may be words, phrases, clauses, or sentences. The preceding and following items need not both be of the same filler class but both always fill the same functional slots. This is illustrated in (15.2).

15.1 Coordinating conjunctions. The coordinating conjunctions conjoin any two equal structures: words, phrases, clauses, or sentences. Nepali coordinating conjunctions are presented alphabetically in Figure 15.1.

Figure 15.1 Coordinating conjunctions and the elements they conjoin.

Coordinating conjunctions	Words	Phrases	Clauses
ani 'and then'	-	-	+
athavā 'or'	+	+	+
ki 'or'	+	+	+
ki ... ki 'either ... or'	+	+	+
kintu 'but'	-	-	+
na ... na 'neither ... nor'	+	+	+
naki 'but not'	-	-	+
parantu 'but'	-	-	+
ra 'and'	+	+	+
taipani or *(yadyapi)... taipani* 'even then'	-	-	+
tara 'but'	-	-	+
tathā ' and'	+	+	-
vā 'or'	+	+	-
yā 'or'	+	+	-

The Figure 15.1 indicates what elements are conjoined by which coordinating conjunctions. The coordinating conjunctions *ani* 'and then', *naki* 'but not', *parantu* 'but', *taipani* 'even then', and *tara* 'but' conjoin only clauses and sentences. The coordinating conjunctions *athavā* 'or', *ki* 'or', and *ra* 'and' conjoin words, phrases, and clauses. Following are examples of coordinating conjunctions in use:

ani 'and then'
±अनि ±के +भयो ?
±ani ± ke +bhayo?
±C:cc ±S:pro-interrog +P:iv1-3sg.pst
±And then ±what +happened
'And then, what happened? '

athavā 'or'
2.28.4 ± अथवा +त्यस अपराधीको जस्तो +थियो
± athavā +tyasa aparādhīko jasto +thiyo
±C: cc +SC: AdjlP +P: ev1-3sg.pst
±or +that criminal-of like +was
'Or, it was like that of that criminal ... '

ki 'or'
4.31.1 +जान्थिन् +कि +जाँदैनथिन्
+jānthin + ki +jā̃dainathin
+P: iv1-3sg..pst. +C: cc +P:iv1-3sg..pst.neg
+she-would-go +or + she-would-not-go
'Whether she would go or not'

ki ... *ki* 'either ... or'
+कि ±त्यो +जान्छ, +कि ±म +जान्छु
+ki ± tyo +jāncha , + ki ± ma +jānchu
+C: cc ±S: pro-nm +P: iv1-3sg.pres +C: cc ±S: pro-nm +P: iv1-3sg.pres
+either ± he ±goes +or ±I +go
'Either he goes, or I will go.'

kintu 'but'
5.5.1 +किन्तु ... ±बीचैमा +लुप्त +भयो
+ kintu ... ± bīcaimā + lupta +bhayo
+C: cc ±AA: cn-lc +SC: adj-nm +P: ev1-3sg.pst.
+But ... ± middle-in +lost +was
'But it disappeared in the middle .... '

na ... na 'neither ... nor'
+न ±उ आँफु +आयो +न +कसैलाई +पठायो
+na ± u ā̃phu + āyo + na + kasailāī + paṭhāyo
+C: cc ±S: pro-nm pro-reflex +P: iv1-3sg.pst. +C: cc +DO: pro-ac +P: tv1-3sg.pst
+neither ± he himself +came +nor +anyone +he-sent
'Neither he came himself, nor did he send anyone.'

naki 'but not'
4.42.1-4.42.3 ±मानिसको पाण्डित्य ± अरूलाई उपदेश गर्नमा +काम +लाग्दछ +नकि +आफुलाई +परिआउँदा
±mānisako pāṇḍitya ± arulāī upadeśa garnamā +kāma +lāgdacha +naki +āphulāī +pariāũdā
±S: CNP-nm ±LA: CNP-lc +SC: cn-nm +P: ev1-3sg.pres +C: cc +DC:pro-dt +P: iv2-impf.prt
±man's wisdom ±other-to advice doing-in +use +strikes +but not +onself-to +when-it-comes
'A man's wisdom is useful in advising others, but not himself.'

parantu 'but'
2.15.4 +परन्तु +देवीरमणका कपालमा +अर्कै विचारको द्वन्द्व +हुन लागेको थियो
+parantu ± devīramaṇakā kapālamā ±arkai vicārako dvandva +huna lāgeko thiyo
±C: cc ±LA: CNP-lc ±S: CNP-nm +P: iVP1-pst.prf-aux-3sg.pst
+But ± Deviraman-of head-in +another thought-of conflict +being started was
'But in Deviraman's mind, another troubling thought arose.'

ra 'and'
4.14 ±आखिर + लक्ष्मी +र +सुशीललाई ±पनि ± साथमा +लिए
± ā:khira +lakṣmī +ra +suśīlalāī ± pani ± sāthamā +lie
± AA: advl +DO: pn-ac +C: cc +DO: pn-ac ±AA: advl ±AA: cn-lc +P: tv1-3sg.pst
± Lastly +Laksmi +and +Sushil ± also ±company-in +he-took
'In the end, he took Laksmi and Sushil as well.'

taipani 'even then'
1.2.8 + तैपनि ± सुभद्राको कोख +सफल +हुन सकेन
+taipani ± subhadrā:ko kokha +saphala +huna sakena
±C: cc ±S: CNP-nm +SC: adj-nm +P: eVP1-inf.aux-3sg.pst-neg
+Even-then ±Subhadra-of womb +fruitful +to-be could-not
'Even then Suubhadra's womb could not be fruitful.'

A clause, occurring with the coordinating conjunction *taipani* 'even then', stands in construction with the preceding clause which is redundantly and optionally marked by *yadyapi* which is glossed as 'although' and wrongly treated as subordinating conjunction by traditional grammars of Nepali. However, the following illustration proves that *yadyapi* is not a subordinating conjunction and that it only redundantly marks the first of the two coordinate clauses connected by the coordinating conjunction *taipani* 'even then'.

yadyapi ... *taipani* 'although ... even then'
±यद्यपि ±कुरा +सत्य +हो ±तैपनि +मलाई +राम्रो +लागेन

±yadyapi ±kurā +satya +ho ±taipani +malāī +rāmro +lāgena

±C: sc ±S: cn-nm +SC: adj-nm +P: ev1-3sg,pres ±C: cc +DC: pro-dt +SC: adj-nm +P: ev2-3sg.pst.

±although ±matter +true +is ±even-then +me-to +good +did-not-strike
'Although it is a true fact, even then I do not like it.'

tara 'but'
1.3.3 +तर +'अपूतो' +भनेको +सुन्ने ±बित्तिकै,

+tara +'apūto' +bhaneko +sunne ±bittikai,

+C: cc +DO:cn-ac +P:tv1-prf.prt +P:tv1-impf.prt ±AA: advl
+But +'childless' +called +hearing ±as-soon-as
'But as soon as he heard someone calling (him) 'childless','

tathā 'and'
4.39.3 +धर्म +तथा +विवेकको +हत्या
+dharma +tathā +vivekako +hatyā
CNP = +Mod: adjl (cn-gn) ±C: cc Mod: adjl (cn-gn) +H: cn-nm
+religious duty +and +conscience-of +murder
'The violation of religious duty and conscience.'

vā 'or
2.7.2.-2.7.4 +सुभद्राको आदेश +पाई +हो +वा +नपाई +हो ...
+subhadrā:ko ādeśa +pāī +ho +vā +napāī +ho ...
+DO: CNP-ac +P: tv1-abs.prt +P: iv1-3sg.pres +C: cc +P: tv1-neg.abs.prt +P: iv1-3sg.pres
+Subhadra-of order +having-received +was +or +not-having-received +was
'It was with the permission from Subhadra or not ...'

yā 'or'
2.10 +आशापाश +या +मृगतृष्णा
+āśā:pāśa +yā +mṛgatṛṣṇā
H: cn ±C: cc +H: cn
+snare of hope +or +mirage
'The snare of hope or mirage'

15.2 Subordinating conjunctions. The subordinating conjunctions *aghi* 'before', *agāḍi* 'before', *bhane* 'if', *pachi* 'after', and *pani* 'although' occur at the end of the subordinate clause. The subordinate clauses marked by these subordinating conjunctions occur before the principal clause.

Subordinating conjunctions *ki* 'that' and *kinaki* 'because' occur at the beginning of the subordinate clause. The subordinate clause marked by these subordinating conjunctions occur after the principal clause. (See examples of the subordinating conjunctions presented in alphabetical order in this section).

The subordinating conjunctions mark the subordinate clauses which are analyzed as axis-relater structures, consisting of two functional slots: (1) a clause as an axis, and (2) a relater or connector slot (C:) filled by a subordinating conjunction. Such a clause marked by the subordinating conjunction fulfills nominal, adjectival, or adverbial function. Because in Nepali the subordinate clauses are marked by subordinating conjunctions in two ways the formula for subordinate clauses is written in the following two ways:

SubCl = +Axis: clause +Relater: *aghi, agāḍi, bhane, pachi*, and *pani*
SubCl = +Relater: *ki* and *kinaki* +Axis: clause

In addition, the *J*-form substitutes described in (6.1.2.1-6.1.2.2) also function as subordinating conjunctions marking the adjective and adverbial clauses (Cf. 6.1.2).

The following are illustrations of the subordinating conjunctions in context:

aghi 'before'
±डाक्टर +आउनु +अघि ±बिरामी +मरिसकेको थियो
±ḍākṭara +āunu +aghi ±birāmī +marisakeko thiyo
±S: cn-nm +P:iv1-inf +C: sc ±S: cn +P: CmpdiVP1-prf.prt.+Aux-3sg.pst
±Doctor +to-come +before ± patient +died had
'The patient had died before the doctor came.'

The subordinating conjunction *agāḍi* 'before' also distributes the same way as *aghi* 'before'.

bhane 'if'
4.39.4 +सुभद्रालाई +ताडना +गरुन् +भने
+subhadrālāī̃ +tāḍanā +garun +bhane
+DC: pn-dt +DO: cn-ac +P: tv2-imp +C: sc
+Subhadra-to +rebuke +he-may-do +if
'If he rebuked Subhadra'

ki 'that'
±उसले +भन्यो ±कि ±खबर +झूटो +हो
±usale +bhanyo ± ki ± khabara + jhūṭo +ho
±S: pro-nm +P: tv1-3sg.pst ±C: sc ±S: cn-nm +SC: adj-nm
+P: ev1-3sg.pres
± He +said ±that ± news + incorrect +is
'He said that the news was incorrect'

kinaki 'because'
3.20.2-3 + आफ्नी आमालाई +दुलही +भन्थ्यो , +किनकि +लक्ष्मीलाई ±घरमा ±सवैजना +दुलही बज्यै +भन्थे
3.20. 2-3 +āphnī āmālāī +dulahī +bhanthyo, +kinaki +lakṣmīlāī ±gharamā ±savaijanā +'dulahī bajyai' +bhanthe
+DO: CNP-ac +OC: cn-ac +P:tv3-3sg.pst. +C: sc +DO: pn-ac ±LC: cn-lc ±S: Pro-nm +OC: +P: tv3-3pl.pst
+His own mother +dulahi +he-called, +because +Laksmi ± at home ± everyone +'Dulahi Bajyai' +they-called
'He called his own mother 'dulahi' because everyone at home called Laksmi 'Dulahi Bajyai.'

pachi 'after , when'
±तिमीले +कथा +भने +पछि ±मैले +बुझें
±timile +kathā +bhane +pachi ±maile +bujhé
±S: pro-nm +DO: cn-nm +P:tv1-cond. +C: sc ±S: pro-nm +P: iv1-1sf.pst
±you +story +tell +after ± I +understood
'When you told the story, I understood (it).'

pani 'although'
1.1.1 ± घरमा ± चञ्चलाश्री +भइकन + पनि ± देवीरमणका सन्तान +थिएनन्
1.1.1 ± gharamā ± cañcalāśrī +bhaikana +pani ± devīramaṇakā santāna +thienan
±LA: cn-lc ±S: cn-nm +P: iv1-abs.prt. +C: sc ±S: CNP-nm +P:iv1-3pl. pst.neg
±house-in +plenty-of-wealth +being +although +Deviraman-of children +were-not
'Although there was plenty of wealth at home, Deviraman had no children.'

As an exception to the formula for the subordinate clause in Nepali, the subordinating conjunction *yadi* 'if' (borrowed from Sanskrit) occurs at the beginning of the subordinate clause, and such a clause also occurs before the principal clause. However, such a clause is also marked according to the normal structure of the Nepali subordinate clause by *bhane* 'if' thus making *yadi* optional and redundant, e.g.

yadi 'if'
±यदि ± तिमी + आउँछौ +भने ± म ± पनि +आउँछु
± yadi ± timi +ā̃uchau +bhane ± ma ± pani +ā̃uchu
±C: sc ±S: pro-nm +P:iv1-2sg.pres +C: sc ±S: pro-nm ±AA: advl +P:iv1-1sg.pres
± If ± you ± come +then, ± I ±also +come
'If you come, I will also come '

This sentence without *yadi* is perfectly normal in Nepali.

Chapter 16
Interjections, vocatives, and nuance particles

16.0 Introduction. This chapter describes Nepali interjections, vocatives and nuance particles. These are uninflected, small, closed sets of forms which show no inflections, dependents, or lexical morphology. Interjections (16.1) are syntactically free, and function as minor sentences, semantically complete but structurally reduced.

Vocatives (16.2), like interjections, are syntactically free, and can be treated as interjections, representing minor sentences. Vocatives are, however, treated as different from interjections only on the basis that they can also occur in vocative phrasal constructions.

Nuance particles (16.3) are also uninflected, and a small, closed set of forms. They are characterized by their having no dependents, show no characteristic lexical morphology, and occur in a syntactically independent way in phrases or sentences as optional elements (16.3), and add to the meaning of a phrase or statement with which they cooccur.

16.1 Interjections. Interjections constitute a small closed class of independent particles. They function as minor sentences, semantically complete, but structurally reduced. Thus, interjections are syntactically complete, and independent of any other element in phrasal, or clausal structures. The most frequent interjections in Nepali are:

ā̃ (approval)
ā̃hā̃ (disapproval)'
oho (great surprise)
ābui (fear)
dhatteri (frustration)
dhat (indignation)
jā (regret for forgetfulness)
lāḥ (vindication)
lau khā (greater vindication)
āce (surprise)
āhā (pleasure)
e (surprise)
ayyā (pain)
chiḥ (disapproval/ disgust)
dhatterikā (frustration)
laḥ (Here you go)
lau (surprise, vindication)

16.2 Vocatives. Vocatives, like interjections, are marked by the absence of inflection, dependents, and lexical morphology. The vocatives are attention drawers. The Nepali vocatives are: *e, ai, he, o, oi.* The vocatives are similar to interjections as they occur alone and are syntactically free. The vocatives are slightly different from interjections as they may also cooccur with nouns in unmarked (nominative) case, and may be constituents of a vocative phrase as: *e gopāl* 'Hey Gopal!', *he bhagavān* 'O God'. However, even in such instances it can still be argued that vocatives are not different from the interjections they still function like interjections (as minor sentences).

16.3 Nuance particles. Nuance particles belong to a small closed set of uninflected forms, show no characteristic lexical morphology, and occur as syntactically dependent upon phrases or statements, but are characterized by their having no dependents of their own. The nuance particles in Nepali are:

are 'they say so (in reporting speech)'	*cāhĩ* 'this, that particular one'
hai '(okey)'	*ki* (expression of doubt)'
kyāre 'probably, I guess (noncommittal)'	*lau* (granted that ...)
na 'simply (?)'	*nai* really (emaphatic particle)'
ni 'and how about (question)'	*po* '(emphatic)'
ra '(in confirmation questions)'	*ta* (rather)

Certain nuance particles occur only in phrases, others occur in certain types of statements. So in terms of their distribution, the nuance particles are grouped as phrasal nuance particles (16.3.1) and statement nuance particles (15.3.2). Figure 16.1 presents the nuance particles (in alphabetical order).

Figure 16.1 Nuance particles and the structures they occur in

Nuance particles	Phrase	Statements	Types
are, *re*	-	+	Declarative
cāhĩ	+	-	
hai	-	+	Decl.,Imp.,Quest.
ki	-	+	Question
kyāre	-	+	Declarative
lau	-	+	Declarative
na	+	+	Imperative
nai	+	-	
ni	-	+	Question
po	+	-	
ra	-	+	Question
ta	+	+	Imp., Question

The plus sign (+) indicates occurrenc; the minus sign (-) indicates nonoccurrence.

16.3.1. Phrasal nuance particles. As the Figure 16.1 indicates, certain nuance particles occur with only in phrases, while others occur in only different types of statements (declarative, interrogative, and imperative). Those nuance particles which occur only with the phrases are phrasal nuance particles. The phrasal nuance paticles are: *cāhī̃*, *nai*, and *po*. The examples follow:

cāhī̃

4.12.1 +सुशील ± चाहिँ

+suśīla ±cāhī̃

+H: pn-nm ±NU: nu

+Sushil ±in-particular

'Sushil, in particular'

nai

7.9.1 +अघि ± नै

+aghi ± nai

+H: advl ±NU: nu

+before ± nai (emphatic)

'Long before ... '

po

4.17.2 +मलाई ± पो

+malāī̃ ± po

+H: cn-ac +P:tv1-inf ± NU: nu (tā)

+me ±po (rather)

'Rather me'

The nuance particle *ta* occurs in a phrase as well as question and imperative statements, e.g.

In a phrase:

+मलाई ±त

+malāī̃ ±ta

+H: pro-dt ±Nu: nu (ta)

+me-to ± particularly

'For me in particular'

In a question statement:

+तपाईँलाई ±गोर्खा +कस्तो + लाग्यो ±त?

+tapāī̃lāī̃ ± gorkhā + kasto +lāgyo ±ta?

+DC: pro-dt ±S:cn-nm +SC: adj(interrog) +P: ev2-3sg-pst ±Nu: nu (ta)

+you-to ±Gorkha +how +struck ± ta
How did you like Gorkha?

In an imperative statement:

+त्यो किताब +लेउ ± त
+tyo kitāb + leu ±ta
+DO: CNP-ac +P: tv1-2sg.imp ±NU: nu (ta)
+that book +bring ±please
'Please pass on that book'

16.3.2 Statement nuance particles. Those nuance particles that occur only with statements are statement nuance particles. They are: *are, hai, ki, kyāre, na, ni,* and *ra.* These statement nuance particles are subdivided as imperative statement nuance particles (16.3.2.1), declarative statement nuance particles (16.3.2.2), and question statement nuance particles (16.3.3.3).

16.3.2.1 Imperative statement nuance particles. The only nuance particle occurring in an imperative statement is *na.*[2] The following example illustrates its use:

malāī alikati ciyā dinos na
'Give me some tea please.'

16.3.2.2 Declarative statement nuance particles. The declarative statement nuance particle is *kyāre*. The following example illustrates its use:

2.10 ± शायद ब्रह्मवादीहरु +यसैलाई +आशापाश +या +मृगतृष्णा +भन्छन् +क्यारे
±śāyada ± brahmavādīharu +yasailāī +āśāpāśa +yā +mṛgatṛṣṇā +bhanchan +kyāre
±AA: advl ± S: cn-nm +DO: pro-ac +OC: CNP-ac +P: tv3-3pl. ±NU: nu
±Perhaps ±Philosophers +it +hope-snare +or +mirage +call +I-guess
'The Vedanta school philosophers call it a snare of hope or mirage, I guess.'

16.3.2.3 Question statement nuance particles. The question statement nuance particles are: *ki, ni,* and *ra.* They are exemplified in the following instances:

Question statements:

4.16.3 +जान्छ्यौ ±कि ?
+jānchyau ± ki?
+P: iv1-2sg.pres-f. ±NU: nu

+you-go ± ki
'Will you also go?'

6.20 ±सानो बाबु +कस्तो +छ ±नि?
±sāno bābu + kasto +cha ±ni?
±S: CNP-nm +SC: adj (interrog) +Pev1-3sg.pres ±NU: nu
±small boy +how +is +*ni* (and how about?)
'And how about the little boy?'

2.62.3 +कुन दौलथको चैन +गरेकी छु ± र?
+kuna daulathako caina +garekī chu ±ra?
+DO: CNP-ac +P: tVP1-prf.prt.aux-1sg.pres.f ± NU: nu (ra)
+Which wealth-of enjoyment +done +I-have ±ra
'Am I enjoying any wealth? '

The nuance particle *hai* cooccurs with all the three types of statements: declarative, imperative, and question statements, e.g.

In a declarative statement *hai* adds the nuance of warning:

±त्यो +तिमी जस्तै +छ ± है
±tyo +timī j astai +cha ± hai
±S: pro-nm +SC: AdjP +P: ev1-3sg,pres ±NU: nu (hai)
±he you like +is ±hai
'He is just like you, (be careful).'

In an imperative statement *hai* adds the nuance of emphasis:

+होश +गर ±है; ±कैदी +भाग्ला
+DO: cn-ac +P: tv1-imp ±NU: nu (hai); ±S: cn-nm +P:iv1=3sg.fut
+hośa +gara ± hai; ± kaidī +bhāglā
+care +do *hai;* prisoner will-run-away
'Be careful, the prisoner may run away.'

In an imperative statement with first person singular, *hai* changes the statement into a question:

±जाउँ ±है ?
+jāū ±hai?
+P: imp-1sg +NU: nu (hai)
I-go +please
'May I go, please?'

Notes for Chapter 16

1. Figure 16.1 indicates that the nuance particle *na* occurs in the phrases as well as in statements, e.g.

±बलेकै +आगो ± न
±balekai āgo +na
±Mod: advl +H: cn-nm ±Nu: nu (na)
±burning +fire ± indeed
'Indeed a burning fire.'

When the nuance particle *na* cooccurs with a statement, it cooccurs only with an imperative statement,.e.g.

+मलाई +एक किलो चिनी +दिनोस् ±न
+malāī +ek kilo cini +dinos +na
+DC: pro-dt +DO: CNP-ac +P: tv2-imp. ±Nu: nu (na)
+me-to +one kilo sugar +give ±please
'Please give me a kilo of sugar.'

Verbal Structures

Chapter 17
The verb phrase

17.0 Internal structure of the verb phrase (VP). This chapter describes the internal structure of the verb phrase (VP). The following is the structural description of the verb phrase:

V-nonfinite = ±negative*(na- ... ī kana)* +stem ±causative +voice +aspect
VP-finite = ±Prefix (±negative *na-)* +stem ±causative +voice +mode +aspect
+Aux: suffixes (+person +number +gender +tense (±negative-*na*-)

The nonfinite forms are: (1) infinitives marked by the infinitive suffix -*na* or -*nu*, (2) participles marked by the suffixes -*eko*, -*ne*, -*dai*, -*tai*, -*era* -*ī*, -*ī kana*, and (3) conditionals marked by the suffix -*e*.

(1) Infinitive forms:
jā-na or jā-nu 'to go'
khā-na or khā-nu 'to eat'
gar-na or khā-nu 'to do'

(2) Participial forms:
gar-eko '(perfect participle) done'
gar-ne '(imperfect participle) doing'
gar-dai '(conjunctive participle) doing'
gar-era '(absolutive participle) having done'
gar-ī '(absolutive participle) having done'
gar-ī kana '(absolutive participle) having done'

(3) Conditional forms:
ga-e 'if go'
khā-e 'if eat'
gar-e 'if do'

The verb stems in Nepali are grouped, into three types: 1st Conjugation, 2nd Conjugation, and 3rd Conjugation types:

1st Conjugation type: Verbs with bases which end in consonants. The bases of these verbs have only one form. For instance: *gar-* 'do', *bas-* 'sit', *dagur-* 'run'.

2nd Conjugation type: Verbs with bases which end in the following vowels: *-i-* and *-ā-*, with a single exception of *jā-* 'go'. The bases of these verbs have only one form. For instance, *di-* 'give', *li-* 'take', *khā-* 'eat', *birsi-* 'forget'.

3rd Conjugation type: Verbs with bases which end in the following vowels: *āu-*, *-ā-*, *-u-* and *-ā-* in the single case of *jā-* 'go'. These bases have two variant forms which are known as primary and secondary (Cf. Clark 1963:75).

The conjugation table of Nepali verbs:

1st Conjugation	2nd Conjugation	3rd Conjugation	
		Primary	Secondary
gar- 'do'	*khā-* 'eat'	*āu-* 'come'	*ā-*
bas- 'sit'	*lā-* 'take away'	*pāu-* 'get'	*pā-*
dekh- 'see'	*di-* 'give'	*paṭhāu-* 'send'	*paṭhā-*
sun- 'hear'	*li-* 'take'	*dhu-* 'wash'	*dho-*
bhan- 'say'	*ubhi-* 'stand'	*ru-* 'weep'	*ro-*
dagur- 'run'	*birsi-* 'forget'	*duhu-* 'milk'	*duh*
khas- 'drop (iv)'	*umli-* 'boil'	*jā* 'go'	*ga-*

17.1 Verbs as heads. The simple finite verb forms are the heads of verb phrases. Thus, the surface formula for the verb as a grammatical word is:

Verb = ±Prefix +Stem ±Causative +Voice +Mode +Aspect +Suffix

The finite forms of the verb are inflected for the following categories: causative, voice, mode, aspect, tense, person, gender, and number. The verb shows whether it is a noncausative form (unmarked) or causative (marked by the suffix *-āu*). The verb also shows one of the two voices, active (unmarked) vs. passive (marked by the suffix *-i-*), e.g. *gar-* 'do' vs. *gari-* 'be done'. If the non-causative stem is considered as a normal consonantal C stem, the causative form can be called the *A* stem. Likewise, if the active (unmarked) stem can be considered normal consonantal C stem, the passive form can be called the *I* stem because the *i* is suffixed to the normal stem to make it a passive stem (cf. Clark 1963:76). Thus, the causative and passive forms can be regarded as parts of the stem, and they can be grouped as *A* stems and *I* stems respectively, e.g.

C stems	*A stems*		*I stem*
	Primary	Secondary	
gar-	garāu-	garā-	gari-
bas-	basāu-	basā-	basi-
dekh-	dekhāu-	dekhā-	dekhi-

The verb shows one of the two modes: nonprogressive (unmarked) vs. progressive (marked by *-irah-*) and one of two aspects: nonperfect (unmarked) vs. perfect (marked by *-eko*). The verb also shows person, number, tense and gender (at least in third person singular) by a portmanteau suffix (one morpheme which simultaneously represents many categories, e.g. person, number, tense and gender).

The verb shows one of three persons (first, second, or third), one of the two numbers (singular vs. plural), one of the two genders (masculine vs. feminine), in the third person singular, and one of the three tenses (past, present or future). The past tense is further divided into simple past, habitual past, and unknown past. The unknown past refers to an activity once unknown to the speaker. The future tense is further divided into future definite and future nondefinite. The future definite indicates stronger probability than the future indefinite.[1]

17.2 Auxiliary verbs in the VP. The auxiliary verbs in Nepali are: *parnu* 'should, must', *hunu* 'be', and *saknu* 'can, may.[2] Auxiliary verb *parnu* 'should, must' is inflected for tense, but uninflected for aspect, person, number or gender, e.g.

parcha (present) 'should, must'
paryo (simple past) 'had to'
parthyo (habitual past) 'had to'
parecha (unknown past) 'had to'
parlā (future) 'will have to'

The auxiliary verbs *hunu* 'be' and *saknu* 'can, may' are inflected for aspect, person, number and gender.

With the auxiliary *hunu* 'be' the head of the VP carries the perfect participial suffix *-eko*, which inflects like an adjective for gender, and number, e.g. *-eko* (masculine singular), *-ekī* (feminine singular), and *-ekā* (plural).

With the auxiliary *saknu* 'can, may' and *parnu* 'should, must' the head of the VP is in the infinitive form.

17.3 The negative verb forms. Negative verb forms are formed at the morphological level (cf. 17.3.1-2), and the morpheme *na-* is prefixed (to the imperative, infinitive, conditional, and participial forms), or is suffixed (to the verb stems elsewhere).

17.3.1 The negative prefix *na-*. The negator *na-* 'not' is prefixed to imperative, infinitive and participial forms, e.g.

Imperative:

khānos 'Please eat.'	*nakhānos* 'Please don't eat.'
jānos 'Please go'	*najānos* 'Please do not go'
garnos 'Please do it'	*nagarnos* 'Please do not do it'

Infinitive:

jāna 'to go'	*najāna* 'not to go.'
khāna 'to eat'	*nakhāna* 'not to eat'
garna 'to do'	*nagarna* 'not to do'

Conditional forms:

khāe 'if eat'	*nakhāe* 'if not eat'
gare 'if do'	*nagare* 'if not do'

Participial forms:
nagareko '(perfect participle) not done'
nagarne '(imperfect participle) not doing'
nagardai '(conjunctive participle) not doing'
nagarera '(absolutive participle) having not done without doing'
nagarī̃ '(absolutive participle) having not done, without doing'
nagarikana '(absolutive participle) having not done, without doing'

17.3.2 The negative suffix -*na*-. The negative -*na*- is suffixed to the verb stem elsewhere, e.g.

gardaina 'He does not do it'	*gardainan* 'They do not do it
khā̃daina 'He does not eat it'	*khā̃dainan* 'They do not eat it'
jā̃daina 'He does not go'	*jā̃dainan* 'They do not go'

In the third person plural forms the negative -*na*- is followed by the third person plural suffixes. The full range of the negative verb forms is exemplified by the conjugation of the verb garnu 'do'.

17.4 Verbs which require the obligatory fronting of the dative complement. Verbs which require the fronting of the dative complements (nouns, noun phrases, pronouns, or pronoun phrases in dative case) belong to the class of iv-2 verbs. The following is a list of the most frequently occurring iv-2 verbs which require the obligatory fronting of the dative complement:

bhok lāgnu 'feel hungry'	*ḍar lāgnu* 'be afraid'
dikka lāgnu 'feel sad'	*disā lāgnu* 'have diarrhea'
gāhro lāgnu 'find difficult'	*man parnu* 'like (lit. mind fall)'
niko hunu 'be well, cured'	*raksī̃ lāgnu* 'get drunk'
thakāi lāgnu 'feel tired'	*tirkhā lāgnu* 'feel thirsty'

17.5 Modifiers in the VP. Modifiers in the verb phrase are either adverbs (adv), adverbial phrases (AdvP), or postpositional phrases (PP), e.g.

Adverb:

7.31.1 ±सुस्तरी ... +भनिन्
±sustarī ... +bhanin
±AA: adv ... +P: tv1-3sg.pst.f
±faintly ... +she-said
'She said faintly'

Adverbial Phrase:

2.26.1 ±एक-एक गरी +हेरे
±eka-eka garī +here
±AA: AdvP +P: iv1-3sg.pst
±one-one doing +he-looked
'He examined one by one'

1.2.7 ±गए साल +हरिवंश पुराण +लगाए
±gae sāla +harivaṃśa purāṇa +lagāe
±AA: AdvP +DO: PNP-ac +P:tv1-3sg.pst
±past year +Harivaṃśa-the-legend +he-organized (listened)
'He listened to the Harivaṃśa purāṇa last year'

Postpositional phrases (PP):

3.15 ±सुशील ±तुलसीका मठनेर +खेलिरहेको थियो
±suśila ±tulasīkā maṭhanera +kheliraheko thiyo
±S: pn-nm ±LA: PP +P: iVP-prf.prt +aux-3sg.pst.
±Sushil ±Tulasi-of-mound-near +playing was
'Sushil was playing near a mound of earth in which the sacred Tulsi plant was growing.'

Notes for Chapter 17

Nepali has relatively few modal verbs as compared to English. The English modals *will* and *shall* are expressed through the Nepali future tense. The English modal *would* is expressed through the Nepali habitual past tense. The English modal *might* is expressed through the Nepali nondefinite future tense.

Figure 17.1 represents the regular conjugation of the Nepali finite verbs. Figure 17.2 represents the inflections of the verb *garnu* 'do'. Figure 17.3 Inflections of the verb *hunu* 'be (existential)'. Figure 17.4 Inflections of the verb *hunu* 'be (identificational). Figure 17.5 Inflections of the verb *hunu* 'become'.

Figure 17.1 Regular inflectional suffixes of Nepali finite verbs

	Past			Present	Future	
	Known		Unknown		Definite	Nondefinite
	Simple	Habitual				
Nonprogressive mode, nonperfective aspect: Stem +						
1sg	-ẽ	-thẽ	-echu	-chu	-nechu	-aũlā̃/ũlā̃
2sg	-yau	-thyau	-echau	-chau	-nechau	-aulā̃
3sg	-yo	-thyo	-echa	-cha	-necha	-lā̃
1pl	-yaũ	-thyaũ	-echaũ	-chaũ	-nechaũ	-aũlā̃
2pl	-yau	-thyau	-echau	-chau	-nechau	-aulā̃
3pl	-e	-the	-echan	-chan	-nechan	-lā̃n
(Definite) progressive mode, nonperfective aspect						
Stem+	-irah+	-irahan+	-irahā̃do/dā̃+	-irahan+	-irahan+	irah+
1sg	-ẽ	-thẽ	-echu	-chu	-echu	-aũlā̃/ũlā̃
2sg	-yau	-thyau	-echau	-chau	-echau	-aulā̃
3sg	-yo	-thyo	-echa	-cha	-echa	-lā̃
1pl	-yaũ	-thyaũ	-echaũ	-chaũ	-echaũ	-aũlā̃
2pl	-yau	-thyau	-echau	-chau	-echau	-aulā̃
3pl	-e	-the	-echan	-chan	-echan	-lā̃n
(Indefinite) progressive mode, nonperfective aspect: Stem+dai+						
1sg	-thiẽ	-hunthẽ	-rahechu	-chu	-hunechu	-haũlā̃/hũlā̃
2sg	-thiyau	-hunthyau	-rahechau	-chau	-hunechau	-haulā̃
3sg	-thiyo	-hunthyo	-rahecha	-cha	-hunecha	-holā̃
1pl	-thiyaũ	-hunthyaũ	-rahechaũ	-chaũ	-hunechaũ	-haũlā̃
2pl	-thiyau	-hunthyau	-rahechau	-chau	-hunechau	-haulā̃
3pl	-thie	-hunthe	-rahechan	-chan	-hunechan	-holā̃n
Nonprogressive mode, perfective aspect: Stem+ -eko/-eka+						
1sg	-thiẽ	-hunthẽ	-rahechu	-chu	-hunechu	-haũlā̃/hũlā̃
2sg	-thiyau	-hunthyau	-rahechau	-chau	-hunechau	-haulā̃
3sg	-thiyo	-hunthyo	-rahecha	-cha	-hunecha	-holā̃
1pl	-thiyaũ	-hunthyaũ	-rahechaũ	-chaũ	-hunechaũ	-haũlā̃
2pl	-thiyau	-hunthyau	-rahechau	-chau	-hunechau	-haulā̃
3pl	-thie	-hunthe	-rahechan	-chan	-hunechan	-holā̃n
Progressive mode, perfective aspect: Stem+ -irah+ -eko/eka+						
1sg	-thiẽ	-hunthẽ	-rahechu	-chu	-hunechu	-haũlā̃/hũlā̃
2sg	-thiyau	-hunthyau	-rahechau	-chau	-hunechau	-haulā̃
3sg	-thiyo	-hunthyo	-rahecha	-cha	-hunecha	-holā̃
1pl	-thiyaũ	-hunthyaũ	-rahechaũ	-chaũ	-hunechaũ	-haũlā̃
2pl	-thiyau	-hunthyau	-rahechau	-chau	-hunechau	-haulā̃
3pl	-thie	-hunthe	-rahechan	-chan	-hunechan	-holā̃n

Figure 17.2 Inflections of the verb *garnu* 'do'

Past				Present	Future	
Known			Unknown		Definite	Nondefinite
	Simple	Habitual				
Nonprogressive mode, nonperfective aspect						
1sg	garẽ	garthẽ	garechu	garchu	garnechu	garaũlā/garulā
2sg	garyau	garthyau	garechau	garchau	garnechau	garaulā
3sg	garyo	garthyo	garecha	garcha	garnecha	garlā
1pl	garyaũ	garthayaũ	garechaũ	garchaũ	garnechaũ	garaũlā
2pl	garyau	garthyau	garechau	garchau	garnechau	garaulā
3pl	gare	garthe	garechan	garchan	garnechan	garlān
(Definite) Progressive mode, nonperfective aspect						
1sg	garirahẽ	garirahanthẽ	gardorahechu	garirahanchu	garirahanechu	garirahũlā
2sg	gariahyau	garirahanthyau	gardārahechau	garirahanchau	garirahanechau	garirahaulā
3sg	garirahyo	garirahanthyo	gardorahecha	garirahancha	garirahanecha	garirahalā
1pl	garirahyaũ	garirahanthyaũ	gardārahechaũ	garirahanchaũ	garirahanechaũ	garirahaũlā
2pl	garirahyau	garirhanthyau	gardārahechau	garirahanchau	garirahanechau	garirahaulā
3pl	garirahe	garirahanthe	gardārahechan	garirahanchan	garirahanechan	garirahalān
(Indefinite) Progressive mode, nonperfective aspect						
1sg	gardaithiẽ	gardaihunthẽ	gardairahechu	gardaichu	gardaihunechu	gardaihaũlā/hũlā
2sg	gardaithiyau	gardaihunthyau	gardairahechau	gardaichau	gardaihunechau	gardaihaulā
3sg	gardaithiyo	gardaihunthyo	gardairahecha	gardaicha	gardaihunecha	gardaiholā
1pl	gardaithiyaũ	gardaihunthyaũ	gardairahechaũ	gardaichaũ	gardaihunechaũ	gardaihaũlā
2pl	gardaithiyau	gardaihunthyau	gardairahechau	gardaichau	gardaihunechau	gardaihaulā
3pl	gardaithie	gardaihunthe	gardairahechan	gardaichan	gardaihunechan	gardaiholān
Nonprogressive mode, perfective aspect						
1sg	garekothiẽ	garekohunthẽ	garekorahechu	garekochu	garekohunechu	garekohũlā
2sg	garekāthiyau	garekāhunthyau	garekārahechau	garekāchau	garekāhunechau	garekāhaulā
3sg	garekothiyo	garekohunthyo	garekorahecha	garekocha	garekohunecha	garekoholā
1pl	garekāthiyaũ	garekāhunthayaũ	garekārahechaũ	garekāchaũ	garekāhunechaũ	garekāhaũlā
2pl	garekāthiyau	garekāhunthyau	garekārahechau	garekāchau	garekāhunechau	garekāhaulā
3pl	garekāthie	garekāhunthe	garekārahechan	garekāchan	garekāhunechan	garekāholān
Progressive mode, perfective aspect						
1sg	garirahekothiẽ	garirahekohunthẽ	garirahekorahechu	garirahekochu	garirahekohunechu	garirahekohaũlā
2sg	garirahekāthiyau	garirahekāhunthyau	garirahekārahechau	garirahkāchau	garirahekāhunechau	garirahekāhaulā
3sg	garirahekothiyo	garirahekohunthyo	garirahekorahecha	garirahekocha	garirahekohunecha	garirahekoholā
1pl	garirahekāthiyaũ	garirahekāhunthyaũ	garirahekārahechaũ	garirahekāchaũ	garirahekāhunechaũ	garirahekāhaũlā
2pl	garirahekāthiyau	garirahekāhunthyau	garirahekārahechau	garirahekāchau	garirahekāhunechau	garirahekāhaula
3pl	garirahekāthie	garirahekāhunthe	garirahekārahechan	garirahekāchan	garirahekāhunechan	garirahekāholān

Figure 17.3 Inflections of the verb *hunu* 'be (existential)'

Past			Present	Future	
Known		Unknown		Definite	Nondefinite
Simple	Habitual				
Nonprogressive mode, nonperfective aspect					
1sg thiẽ	hunthẽ	bhaechu	chu	hunechu	hoũlā/hũlā
2sg thiyau	hunthyau	bhaechau	chau	hunechau	houlā
3sg thiyo	hunthyo	bhaecha	cha	hunecha	holā
1pl thiyaũ	hunthayaũ	bhaechaũ	chaũ	hunechaũ	hoũlā
2pl thiyau	hunthyau	bhaechau	chau	hunechau	houlā
3pl thie	hunthe	bhaechan	chan	hunechan	holān
(Definite) Progressive mode, nonperfective aspect					
1sg bhairahẽ	bhairahanthẽ	hũdorahechu	bhairahanchu	bhairahanechu	bhairahũlā
2sg bhairahyau	bhairahanthyau	hũdārahechau	bhairahanchau	bhairahanechau	bhairahaulā
3sg bhairahyo	bhairahanthyo	hũdorahecha	bhairahancha	bhairahanecha	bhairahalā
1pl bhairahyaũ	bhairahanthyaũ	hũdārahechaũ	bhairahanchaũ	bhairahanechaũ	bhairahaũlā
2pl bhairahyau	bhairhanthyau	hũdārahechau	bhairahanchau	bhairahanechau	bhairahaulā
3pl bhairahe	bhairahanthe	hũdārahechan	bhairahanchan	bhairahanechan	bhairahalān
(Indefinite) progressive mode, nonperfective aspect					
1sg hũdaithiẽ	hũdaihunthẽ	hũdairahechu	hũdaichu	hũdaihunechu	hũdaihaũlā/hũlā
2sg hũdaithiyau	hũdaihunthyau	hũdairahechau	hũdaichau	hũdaihunechau	hũdaihaulā
3sg hũdaithiyo	hũdaihunthyo	hũdairahecha	hũdaicha	hũdaihunecha	hũdaiholā
1pl hũdaithiyaũ	hũdaihunthyaũ	hũdairahechaũ	hũdaichaũ	hũdaihunechaũ	hũdaihaũlā
2pl hũdaithiyau	hũdaihunthyau	hũdairahechau	hũdaichau	hũdaihunechau	hũdaihaulā
3pl hũdaithie	hũdaihunthe	hũdairahechan	hũdaichan	hũdaihunechan	hũdaiholān
Nonprogressive mode, perfective aspect					
1sg bhaekothiẽ	bhaekohunthẽ	bhaekorahechu	bhaekochu	bhaekohunechu	bhaekohũlā
2sg bhaekāthiyau	bhaekāhunthyau	bhaekārahechau	bhaekāchau	bhaekāhunechau	bhaekāhaulā
3sg bhaekothiyo	bhaekohunthyo	bhaekorahecha	bhaekocha	bhaekohunecha	bhaekoholā
1pl bhaekāthiyaũ	bhaekāhunthayaũ	bhaekārahechaũ	bhaekāchaũ	bhaekāhunechaũ	bhaekāhaũlā
2pl bhaekāthiyau	bhaekāhunthyau	bhaekārahechau	bhaekāchau	bhaekāhunechau	bhaekāhaulā
3pl bhaekāthie	bhaekāhunthe	bhaekārahechan	bhaekāchan	bhaekāhunechan	bhaekāholān
Progressive mode, perfective aspect					
1sg bhairahekothiẽ	bhairahekohunthẽ	bhairahekorahechu	bhairahekochu	bhairahekohunechu	bhairahekohũlā
2sg bhairahekāthiyau	bhairahekāhunthyau	bhairahekārahechau	bhairahekāchau	bhairahekāhunechau	bhairahekāhaulā
3sg bhairahekothiyo	bhairahekohunthyo	bhairahekorahecha	bhairahekocha	bhairahekohunecha	bhairahekoholā
1pl bhairahekāthiyaũ	bhairahekāhunthyaũ	bhairahekārahechaũ	bhairahekāchaũ	bhairahekāhunechũ	bhairahekāhaũlā
2pl bhairahekāthiyau	bhairahekāhunthyau	bhairahekārahechau	bhairahekāchau	bhairahekāhunechau	bhairahekāhaulā
3pl bhairahekāthie	bhairahekāhunthe	bhairahekārahechan	bhairahekāchan	bhairahekāhunechan	bhairahekāholān

Figure 17.4 Inflections of the verb *hunu* 'be (identificational)

Past			Present	Future	
Known		Unknown		Definite	Nondefinite
Simple	Habitual				
Nonprogressive mode, nonperfective aspect					
1sg thiẽ	hunthẽ	bhaechu	hũ	hunechu	hoũlā/hũlā
2sg thiyau	hunthyau	bhaechau	hau	hunechau	houlā
3sg thiyo	hunthyo	bhaecha	ho	hunecha	holā
1pl thiyaũ	hunthayaũ	bhaechaũ	haũ	hunechaũ	hoũlā
2pl thiyau	hunthyau	bhaechau	hau	hunechau	houlā
3pl thie	hunthe	bhaechan	hun	hunechan	holān
(Definite) Progressive mode, nonperfective aspect					
1sg bhairahẽ	bhairahanthẽ	hũdorahechu	bhairahanchu	bhairahanechu	bhairahũlā
2sg bhaiahyau	bhairahanthyau	hũdarahechau	bhairahanchau	bhairahanechau	bhairahaulā
3sg bhairahyo	bhairahanthyo	hũdorahecha	bhairahancha	bhairahanecha	bhairahalā
1pl bhairahyaũ	bhairahanthyaũ	hũdarahechaũ	bhairahanchaũ	bhairahanechaũ	bhairahaũlā
2pl bhairahyau	bhairhanthyau	hũdarahechau	bhairahanchau	bhairahanechau	bhairahaulā
3pl bhairahe	bhairahanthe	hũdarahechan	bhairahanchan	bhairahanechan	bhairahalān
(Indefinite) progressive mode, nonperfective aspect					
1sg hũdaithiẽ	hũdaihunthẽ	hũdairahechu	hũdaichu	hũdaihunechu	hũdaihaũlā/hũlā
2sg hũdaithiyau	hũdaihunthyau	hũdairahechau	hũdaichau	hũdaihunechau	hũdaihaulā
3sg hũdaithiyo	hũdaihunthyo	hũdairahecha	hũdaicha	hũdaihunecha	hũdaiholā
1pl hũdaithiyaũ	hũdaihunthyaũ	hũdairahechaũ	hũdaichaũ	hũdaihunechaũ	hũdaihaũlā
2pl hũdaithiyau	hũdaihunthyau	hũdairahechau	hũdaichau	hũdaihunechau	hũdaihaulā
3pl hũdaithie	hũdaihunthe	hũdairahechan	hũdaichan	hũdaihunechan	hũdaiholān
Nonprogressive mode, perfective aspect					
1sg bhaekothiẽ	bhaekohunthẽ	bhaekorahechu	bhaekochu	bhaekohunechu	bhaekohũlā
2sg bhaekāthiyau	bhaekāhunthyau	bhaekārahechau	bhaekāchau	bhaekāhunechau	bhaekāhaulā
3sg bhaekothiyo	bhaekohunthyo	bhaekorahecha	bhaekocha	bhaekohunecha	bhaekoholā
1pl bhaekāthiyaũ	bhaekāhunthyaũ	bhaekārahechaũ	bhaekāchaũ	bhaekāhunechaũ	bhaekāhaũlā
2pl bhaekāthiyau	bhaekāhunthyau	bhaekārahechau	bhaekāchau	bhaekāhunechau	bhaekāhaulā
3pl bhaekāthie	bhaekāhunthe	bhaekārahechan	bhaekāchan	bhaekāhunechan	bhaekāholān
Progressive mode, perfective aspect					
1sg bhairahekothiẽ	bhairahekohunthẽ	bhairahekorahechu	bhairahekochu	bhairahekohunechu	bhairahekohũlā
2sg bhairahekāthiyau	bhairahekāhunthyau	bhairahekārahechau	bhairahkāchau	bhairahekāhunechau	bhairahekāhaulā
3sg bhairahekothiyo	bhairahekohunthyo	bhairahekorahecha	bhairahekocha	bhairahekohunecha	bhairahekoholā
1pl bhairahekāthiyaũ	bhairahekāhunthyaũ	bhairahekārahechaũ	bhairahekāchaũ	bhairahekāhunechaũ	bhairahekāhaũlā
2pl bhairahekāthiyau	bhairahekāhunthyau	bhairahekārahechau	bhairahekāchau	bhairahekāhunechau	bhairahekāhaulā
3pl bhairahekāthie	bhairahekāhunthe	bhairahekārahechan	bhairahekāchan	bhairahekāhunechan	bhairahekāholān

Figure 17.5 Inflections of the verb *hunu* 'become'

Past			Present	Future	
Known		Unknown		Definite	Nondefinite
Simple	Habitual				
Nonprogressive mode, nonperfective aspect					
1sg bhaẽ	hunthẽ	bhaechu	hunchu	hunechu	hoũlā/hũlā
2sg bhayau	hunthyau	bhaechau	hunchau	hunechau	houlā
3sg bhayo	hunthyo	bhaecha	huncha	hunecha	holā
1pl bhayaũ	hunthayaũ	bhaechaũ	hunchaũ	hunechaũ	hoũlā
2pl bhayau	hunthyau	bhaechau	hunchau	hunechau	houlā
3pl bhae	hunthe	bhaechan	hunchan	hunechan	holān
(Definite) Progressive mode, nonperfective aspect					
1sg bhairahẽ	bhairahanthẽ	hũdorahechu	bhairahanchu	bhairahanechu	bhairahũlā
2sg bhaiahyau	bhairahanthyau	hũdarahechau	bhairahanchau	bhairahanechau	bhairahaulā
3sg bhairahyo	bhairahanthyo	hũdorahecha	bhairahancha	bhairahanecha	bhairahalā
1pl bhairahyaũ	bhairahanthyaũ	hũdarahechaũ	bhairahanchaũ	bhairahanechaũ	bhairahaũlā
2pl bhairahyau	bhairhanthyau	hũdarahechau	bhairahanchau	bhairahanechau	bhairahaulā
3pl bhairahe	bhairahanthe	hũdarahechan	bhairahanchan	bhairahanechan	bhairahalān
(Indefinite) Progressive mode, nonperfective aspect					
1sg hũdaithiẽ	hũdaihunthẽ	hũdairahechu	hũdaichu	hũdaihunechu	hũdaihaũlā/hũlā
2sg hũdaithiyau	hũdaihunthyau	hũdairahechau	hũdaichau	hũdaihunechau	hũdaihaulā
3sg hũdaithiyo	hũdaihunthyo	hũdairahecha	hũdaicha	hũdaihunecha	hũdaiholā
1pl hũdaithiyaũ	hũdaihunthyaũ	hũdairahechaũ	hũdaichaũ	hũdaihunechaũ	hũdaihaũlā
2pl hũdaithiyau	hũdaihunthyau	hũdairahechau	hũdaichau	hũdaihunechau	hũdaihaulā
3pl hũdaithie	hũdaihunthe	hũdairahechan	hũdaichan	hũdaihunechan	hũdaiholān
Nonprogressive mode, perfective aspect					
1sg bhaekothiẽ	bhaekohunthẽ	bhaekorahechu	bhaekochu	bhaekohunechu	bhaekohũlā
2sg bhaekāthiyau	bhaekāhunthyau	bhaekārahechau	bhaekāchau	bhaekāhunechau	bhaekāhaulā
3sg bhaekothiyo	bhaekohunthyo	bhaekorahecha	bhaekocha	bhaekohunecha	bhaekoholā
1pl bhaekāthiyaũ	bhaekāhunthyaũ	bhaekārahechaũ	bhaekāchaũ	bhaekāhunechaũ	bhaekāhaũlā
2pl bhaekāthiyau	bhaekāhunthyau	bhaekārahechau	bhaekāchau	bhaekāhunechau	bhaekāhaulā
3pl bhaekāthie	bhaekāhunthe	bhaekārahechan	bhaekāchan	bhackāhunechan	bhaekāholān
Progressive mode, perfective aspect					
1sg bhairahekothiẽ	bhairahekohunthẽ	bhairahekorahechu	bhairahekochu	bhairahekohunechu	bhairahekohũlā
2sg bhairahekāthiyau	bhairahekāhunthyau	bhairahekārahechau	bhairahkāchau	bhairahekāhunechau	bhairahekāhaulā
3sg bhairahekothiyo	bhairahekohunthyo	bhairahekorahecha	bhairahekocha	bhairahekohunecha	bhairahekoholā
1pl bhairahekāthiyaũ	bhairahekāhunthyaũ	bhairahekārahechaũ	bhairahekāchaũ	bhairahekāhunechaũ	bhairahekāhaũlā
2pl bhairahekāthiyau	bhairahekāhunthyau	bhairahekārahechau	bhairahekāchau	bhairahekāhunechau	bhairahekāhaulā
3pl bhairahekāthie	bhairahekāhunthe	bhairahekārahechan	bhairahekāchan	bhairahekāhunechan	bhairahekāholān

Figure 17.6 Conjugation of the verb *garnu* 'do' with negative suffix *-na* or prefix *na-*

Past			Present	Future	
Known		Unknown		Definite	Nondefinite
Simple	Habitual				
Nonprogressive mode, Nonperfective aspect					
1s garina	gardainathẽ	garenachu	gardina	garnechaina	garoina
2s garenau	gardainathyaũ	garenachaũ	gardainau	garnechainau	garoinau
3s garena	gardainathyo	garenacha	gardaina	garnechaina	garoina
1p garenau	gardainathyaũ	garenachaũ	gardainaũ	garnechainaũ	garoinaũ
2p garenaũ	gardainathyaũ	garenachaũ	gardainau	garnechainau	garoinau
3p garenan	gardainathe	garenachan	gardainan	garnechainan	garoinan
(Definite) Progressive mode, Nonperfective aspect					
1s garirahina	garirahãdainathẽ	gardorahenachu	garirahanna	garirahanechaina	nagarirahaũlā
2s garirahenau	garirahãdainathyau	gardorahenachau	garirahannau	garirahanechainau	nagarirahaulā
3s garirahena	garirahãdainathyo	gardorahenacha	garirahanna	garirahanechaina	nagarirahalā
1p garirahenaũ	garirahadainathyaũ	gardorahenachaũ	garirahannaũ	garirahanechainaũ	nagarirahaũlā
2p garirahenau	garirahãdainathyau	gardārahenachau	garirahannau	garirahanechainau	nagarirahaulā
3p garirahenan	garirahãdainathe	gardārahenachan	garirahannan	garirahanechainan	nagarirahalān
(Indefinite) Progressive mode, Nonperfective aspect					
1sg gardaithiina	gardaihunthina	gardairahenachu	gardaichaina	gardaihunechaina	gardainahaũlā/hũlā
2sg gardaithienau	gardaihũdainathyau	gardairahenachau	gardaichainau	gardaihunechainau	gardainahaulā
3sg gardaithiena	gardaihunnathyo	gardairahenacha	gardaichaina	gardaihunechaina	gardainaholā
1pl gardainathiyaũ	gardaihunnathyaũ	gardairahenachaũ	gardaichainaũ	gardaihunechainaũ	gardainahaũlā
2pl gardainathiyau	gardainahunthyau	gardairahenachau	gardaichainau	gardaihunechainau	gardainahaulā
3pl gardaithienan	gardaihunnathe	gardairahenachan	gardaichainan	gardaihunechainan	gardainaholān
Nonprogressive mode, Perfective aspect					
1s garekothiina	garekohudainathẽ	garekorahenachu	garekochaina	garekohunechaina	garekohowaina
2s garekāthienau	garekāhũdainathyau	garekārahenachau	garekāchainau	garekāhunechainau	garekāhowainau
3s garekothiena	garekohudainathyo	garekorahenacha	garekochaina	garekohunechaina	garekohowaina
1p garekāthienaũ	garekāhudainathyaũ	garekārahenachaũ	garekāchainaũ	garekāhunechainaũ	garekāhowainaũ
2p garekāthienau	garekāhũdainathyau	garekārahenachau	garekāchainau	garekāhunechainau	garekāhowainau
3p garekāthienan	garekāhudainathe	garekārahenachan	garekāchainan	garekāhunechainan	garekāhowainau
Progressive mode, Perfective aspect					
1s garirahekothiina	garirahekohudainathẽ	garirahekorahenachu	garirahekochaina	garirahekohunechaina	garirahekohowaina
2s garirahekāthienau	garirahekāhudainathyau	garirahekārahenachau	garirahekāchainau	garirahekāhunechainau	garirahekāhowainau
3s garirahekothiena	garirahekohudainathyo	garirahekorahenacha	garirahekochaina	garirehekohunechaina	garirahekohowaina
1p garirahekāthienaũ	garerahekāhudainathyaũ	garirahekārahenachau	garirahekāchainaũ	garirahekāhunechainaũ	garirahekāhowainaũ
2p garirahekāthienau	garirahekāhudainathyau	garirahekārahenachau	garirahekāchainau	garirahekāhunechainau	garirahekāhowainau
3p garirahekāthienan	garirahekāhũdainathe	garirahekārahenachan	garirahekāchainan	garirahekāhunechainan	garirahekāhowainan

Clausal Structures

Chapter 18
The clause: A general overview

18.0 Internal structure of the clause (Cl). This chapter describes the internal structure of the clause in Nepali. The underlying structure of the clause consists of optional and obligatory functional slots. The optional slots are: an adverbial disjunct (±AD:), exclamation (±EX:), connector (±C:), subject (±S:), adverbial adjuncts, namely instrumental adjunct (±IA:), locative adjunct (±LA), ablative adjunct (±AbA:), and adverbial adjunct (±AA:). The obligatory slots include the complements, namely a locative complement (+LC:), dative complement (+DC:), direct object (+DO:), subject complement (+SC:), object complement (+OC:), and an obligatory predicate (+P:) followed by an optional nuance particle (±NU:). The linear order of the functional constituents of a clause is shown in the following formula:

Cl = ±AD: ±EX: ±C: ±S: ±IA: ±LA: ±AbA: ±AA: +LC: +DC: +DO: +SC: +OC: +P: ±NU:

The fillers of these functional slots are listed in Figure 18.1 under each of these functional slots.

The clauses in which these verb phrases occur may be categorized as 'transitive', 'equational', or 'intransitive' clauses according to the type of syntactic string which occurs with particular verb. Thus a clause and its verb may be characterized as 'transitive' if the verb cooccurs with 'direct object'. A clause and its verb may be characterized as 'equational' if the verb cooccurs with a 'subject complement'. A clause and its verb may be characterized as 'intransitive' if the verb occurs without a 'direct object' and without a 'subject complement'. Each of these three types of clauses and verbs may be further subcategorized according to the other obligatory complements which cooccur in the clause.

The constituents which are obligatory to the clause are (1) predicate and (2) the obligatory complements of the predicate, e.g. the transitive verb-1 clause (tv-1Cl) obligatorily cooccurs with a direct object; the transitive verb-2 clause (tv-2Cl) obligatorily cooccurs with a direct object and a dative complement; the transitive verb-3 clause (tv-3Cl) obligatorily cooccurs with a direct object and an object complement; transitive verb-4 clause (tv-4Cl) obligatorily cooccurs with a direct object and a locative complement (Cf. Figure 18.1).

18.1 Verbals as predicates. The nucleus of a clause is a verb phrase which is either a finite or nonfinite form (infinitive, participle, conditional). The verb phrase is either a simple verb phrase or a complex verb phrase (main verb plus auxiliary).

18.2 Subjects in the clause. In Nepali the verb which fills the nuclear Predicate slot of a finite clause is marked for the person and number of the Subject. Further specification of the subject by the occurrence of a nominal in the nominative case is optional. If the subject is further specified, the form or forms which fill the optional Subject slot are nominal forms in nominative case, e.g. nouns, pronouns, nominalized adjectives, noun clauses, etc. which show a cross reference tie to the verb in person, number, and gender. In nonfinite (participial, infinitive, and conditional) clauses the subjects do not show the cross reference tie to the verb in person, number, and gender.

18.3 Complements in the clause. The complement functions in a clause are: direct object (DO), object complement (OC), subject complement (SC), dative complement (DC) and locative complement (LC). These functions are filled by nouns and pronouns in different cases, adjectives in nominative and accusative cases, and phrases (AdjPs, NPs, and PPs). Figure 18.1 presents the feature summary of subcategories of verbs and their complements.

Figure 18.1 Clause types subcategorized according to verb types and complements

	±Optional								+Obligatory_						± Optnl
				±Subject	± Adverbial adjuncts				+Predicate Complements					P:	
					Instru-ment Means	Time Loca-tion	Cause Source	Manner Purpose							
Functions:	AD:	EX:	C:	S:	IA:	LA:	AbA:	AA:	LC:	DC:	DO:	SC:	OC:	P:	NU:
Fillers:	cl	intj n-nm voc	cc sc	n-nm pro-nm NP-nm cl	n-in pro-in NP-in PP	n-lc pro-lc NP-lc PP	n-ab pro-ab NP-ab PP	adv advl AdvlP PP	n-lc pro-lc NP-lc PP	cn-dt pro-dt NP-dt	n-ac pro-ac NP-ac	n-nm adj-nm NP-nm AdjP-nm	n-ac adj-ac NP-ac AdjP-ac	tv tVP ev eVP iv iVP	nu
tv1 Cl											+	*	*	tv1	
tv2 Cl										+	+	*	*	tv2	
tv3 Cl											+	*	+	tv3	
tv4 Cl									+	*	+	*	*	tv4	
ev1 Cl											*	+	*	ev1	
ev2 Cl										+	*	+	*	ev2	
iv1 Cl											*	*	*	iv1	
iv2 Cl										+	*	*	*	iv2	
iv3 Cl									+		*	*	*	iv3	

*	nonoccurring elements	dt	dative case form	nm	nominative case form
+	Obligatory	ev1	equational verb type 1	NP	noun phrase
±	Optional	ev	equational verb form	NU:	Nuance semantic function
AA:	Adverbial adjunct function	ev2	equational verb type 2	OC:	Object complement function
ab	ablative case form	eVP	equational verb phrase	P:	Predicate function
AbA:	Ablative adjunct function	EX:	Exclamation function	PP	postpositional phrase
ac	accusative case form	IA:	Instrumental adjunct function	pro	pronoun form
AD:	Adverbial disjunct function	in	instrumental case form	Q:	Question function
adj	adjective form	intj	interjection form	qw	question word
adjl	adjectival form	iv	intransitive verb from	S:	Subject function
AdjP	adjective phrase	iv1	intransitive verb type 1	SC:	Subject complement function
adv	adverb form	iv2	intransitive verb type 2	sc	subordinate conjunction form
advl	adverbial form	iv3	intransitive verb type 3	tv	transitive verb form
AdvP	Adverbial phrase	iVP	intransitive verb phrase	tv1	transitive verb type 1
C:	Connector function	LA:	Locative adjunct function	tv2	transitive verb type 2
cc	coordinate conjunction form	LC:	Locative complement function	tv3	transitive verb type 3
cl	clausal form	lc	locative case form	tv4	transitive verb type 4
DC:	Dative complement function	n	noun form	tVP	transitive verb phrase
DO:	Direct object function	nl	nominal form	voc	vocative form

18.3.1 Transitive verbs and their complements. All transitive verbs (tv) occur with an obligatory direct object (+DO). The transitive verbs are subcategorized as transitive verb-1 (18.3.1.1), transitive verb-2 (18.3.1.2), transitive verb-3 (18.3.1.3), and transitive verb-4 (18.3.1.4) on the basis of other obligatory complements they take besides the direct object.

18.3.1.1 Transitive-1 verbs (tv-1). Transitive-1 verbs (tv-1) are verbs which occur with an obligatory direct object (+DO:). Direct objects which are [+animate] are marked by the accusative case marker *-lāi.* Objects which are [-animate] are not marked by the accusative case marker *-lāi,* i.e. the nominative and accusative cases of nonanimate nominals are identical in both the singular and plural. The constituents of the clause with the tv-1 are:

±S: +DO:-ac +P:tv-1

+म +आफ्नो छोरालाई +पढाउँछु
±ma +āphno chorālāĩ +paḍhāũchu
±S: pro-nm +DO: CNP-ac +P: tv1-1sg.pres
±I +own son +teach
'I teach my own son.'

±म +भात +खान्छु
±ma +bhāt +khānchu [-animate]
±S: pro-nm +DO: cn-ac +P: tv1-1sg.pres
±I +cooked-rice +eat
'I eat rice'

18.3.1.2 Transitive-2 verbs (tv-2). Transitive-2 verbs (tv-2) are verbs which occur with an obligatory dative complement (+DC:) besides an obligatory direct object complement (+DO:). The DC of a tv-2 verb is marked by the dative case-marker *-lāī̃* while the DO of the tv-2 is not so marked. The constituents of the clause with the tv-2 are:

±S: +DC:-dt +DO:-ac +P:tv-2

±सुभद्रा +दमाईं-डोलेहरूलाई +ज्याला +बाँड्देथिइन्
±subhadrā +damāī̃-ḍoleharulāī̃ + jyālā + bā̃ḍdaithiin
±S: pn-nm +DC: cmpdcn-dt +DO: cn-ac +P:tVP2-3sg.pst-prog.f
±Subhadra +band-litter-bearers +wage +was-distributing
Subhadra was giving away wages to the musicians and litter-bearers

±सुभद्रा +छोरालाई +भात +खुवाइरहेकी थिइन्
±subhadrā +chorālāī̃ +bhāta + khuwāiraheki̇̃ thiin
±Subhadra +son-to +rice +feeding +was
±S: pn-nm +DC: cn-dt +DO: cn-ac +P:tVP2-3sg.pst-prog.f
Subhadra was feeding rice to her son'

18.3.1.3 Transitive-3 verbs (tv-3).[1] Transitive-3 verbs (tv-3) are verbs which occur with an obligatory direct object in accusative case and an obligatory object complement in the accusative case. The constituents of the clause with the tv-3 are:

±S: +DO:-ac +OC:-ac +P:tv-3.

1.4.2 ±देवीरमण +आफ्नो वैभवलाई +तुच्छ +सम्झन्थे
±devīramaṇa +ā:phno +vaibhavalāī̃ +tuccha +samjhanthe
±S: pn-nm +DO: CNP-ac +OC: adjl-ac +P:tv3-3sg.pst.
±Deviraman +his wealth +he-considered
'Deviraman considered his wealth as worthless.'

2.5 ±प्रारब्धले ±यो उमेरमा +उनलाई ±फेरि +दुलाहा +बनायो
±prārabdhale ±yo umeramā +unalāī̃ ±pheri +dulāhā +banāyo
±S: cn-nm ±LA: CNP-lc +DO: pro-ac ±AA: advl +OC: cn-ac +P: tv3-3sg.pst
±destiny ±this age-in +him ±again +bridegroom +made
'Destiny made Deviraman a bridegroom again at this age.

3.20.2 +सुशील +आफ्नी आमालाई +दुलही +भन्थ्यो
±suśīla +ā:phnī̃ āmālāī̃ +dulahī̃ +bhanthyo
±S: pn-nm +DO: CNP-ac +OC: cn-ac +P: tv3-3sg.pst.
±Sushil +his-own mother +dulahi +called
'Sushil called his own mother 'dulahi'.'

18.3.1.4 Transitive-4 verbs (tv-4). Transitive-4 verbs (tv-4) are verbs which occur with an obligatory direct object and an obligatory locative complement. The constituents of the clause with the tv-4 are:

±S: +DO: +LC:-lc +P:tv-4

2.12.1 ±कन्यापक्षका मानिसले +दुलहीलाई +डोलीमा +हालिदिए
±kannyā:pakṣakā mānisale +dulahīlāī +ḍolīmā +hālidie
±S: CNP-nm +DO: cn-ac +LC: cn-lc +P:tv4-3pl.pst
±bride-side people +bride +litter-in +they-put
'The people of the bride put her in the litter.'

3.4.4 ±सुभद्रा +गास +मुखमा +हालिदिन्थिन्
±subhadrā +gāsa +mukhamā +hālidinthin
±S: pn-nm +DO: cn-ac +LC: cn-lc +P:tv4-3sg.pst
+Subhadra +mouthful-of-food +mouth-in +she-put
'Subhadra put the mouthfuls of food in the mouth.'

18.3.2. The equational verbs. The equational verbs (i.e verbs which cooccur with 'subject complement' (SC) in Nepali are *hunu* 'be', *dekhinu* 'appear, seem', and *lāgnu* 'feel'. The equational verb-1 *hunu* 'be' has two forms: (1) the identificational *hunu* (18.3.2.1) vs. (2) the existential *hunu* (18.3.2.2). The equational verb-2 has two members: *dekhinu* and *lāgnu* (18.3.2.3).

18.3.2.1 Identificational *hunu* 'be'. The form of *hunu* 'be' which identifies its subject shows the following inflection:

Pronouns	Present	Future	
		Definite	Indefinite
1s ma	hũ	hunechu	hũlā
2s tã	hos	hunechas	holās
3s u	ho	hunecha	holā
1p hāmī (haru)	haũ	hunechaũ	hoũlā
2p timīharu	hau	hunechau	houlā
3p unīharu	hun	hunechan	holān

The past tense forms of the identificational and existential hunu are the same (cf Figure 17.3 and Figure 17.4). The function of the identificational *hunu* is to identify the subject. The clause formula for identificational *hunu* is:

± S:n-nm +SC:adj/n-nm +P:ev-1. e.g.

±उ +नेपाली +हो
±u +nepāli +ho
±S: pro-nm +SC: cn-nm +P: ev1-3sg.pst
±he +Nepali +is
'He is a Nepali'

18.3.2.2 The existential *hunu* 'be'. The form of *hunu* 'be' which indicates the mere existence of its subject shows the following inflection:

Pronouns	Present	Future	
		Definite	Indefinite
ma	chu	hunechu	hoũlā
tã	chas	hunechas	holās
u	cha	hunecha	holā
hāmī(haru)	chaũ	hunechaũ	hoũlā
timīharu	chau	hunechau	houlā
unīharu	chan	hunechan	holān

The function of the existential *hunu* is to indicate the existence of the subject or locate it. The clause formula for existential hunu is the same as that for the identificational *hunu*, e.g. ± S:n-nm +SC:adj/n-nm +P:ev-1.

+उ +बाठो +छ
+u +bāṭho +cha
+S: pro-nm +SC: adj-nm +P: ev1-3sg.pres
+he +clever +is
'He is clever'

18.3.2.3 The equational verbs-2 *dekhinu* and *lāgnu* 'appear'. The equational verbs *dekhinu* and *lāgnu* occur with an obligatory SC plus an obligatory DC. The clause formula for the ev-2 is:

±S:n-nm +SC:adj-nm +DC:n-dt +P:ev-2.

2.37.1 +देवीरमणलाई ±कोठा +नौलो +लाग्यो
+dev īramaṇalāī ±koṭhā +naulo +lāgyo
+DC:pn-dt ±S:cn-nm +SC:adj-nm +P:ev-2-3sg.pst
+Deviraman-to ±room +strange +appeared
'The room appeared strange to Deviraman.'

18.3.3 Intransitive verbs and their complements. Intransitive verbs are verbs which do not stand in construction with a DO or a SC. Nepali has three types of intransitive verbs: iv-1 described in (18.3.3.1), iv-2) described in (18.3.3.2), and iv-3 described in (18.3.3.3).

18.3.3.1 Intransitive-1 verbs (iv-1). Intransitive-1 verbs (iv-1) are verbs which occur with no complements. The constituents of the clause with an iv-1 are:

± S:n-nm + P: iv-1.

4.25.1 ±सुभद्रा +रोइन्

±subhadrā +roin

±S:pn +P:iv1-3sg.spt.f
±Subhadra +cried
'Subhadra cried'

18.3.3.2 Intransitive-2 verbs (iv-2). Intransitive-2 verbs (iv-2) are verbs which occur with an obligatory dative complement (+DC:), e.g.

+DC: cn,pn,pro-dt ± S:n-nm + P: iv-1.

2.47.1+देवीरमणलाई ±चाँडै ±निद्रा +पऱ्यो

+devīramaṇalāi ±cā̃ḍai ± nidrā +paryo

+DC: pn-dt ±AA: advl ±S:cn-nm +P:iv-2-3sg.pst
+deviraman-to ±soon +sleep +fell
'Deviraman fell asleep soon.'

18.3.3.3 Intransitive-3 verbs (iv-3). Intransitive-3 verbs (iv-3) are verbs which occur with an obligatory locative complement (+LC:), e.g.

± S:n-nm +LC: cn-lc + P: iv-1

2.47.2 ±देवीरमण +खाटमा +पल्टे

±devīramaṇa +khāṭamā +palṭe

±S:pn-nm +LC:cn-lc +P:iv3-3sg.pst
+Deviraman +bed-in +lay
'Deviraman lay in the bed'

18.4 Subject-predicate linking by person-number-gender-honorific level inflection. The subject and the predicate of a clause are linked by person, number, gender, and honorific level inflection of the verb in the third person singular. The categories person, number, gender, tense, and honorific level at are shown only in finite forms of the verbs. In nonfinite clauses these categories are not reflected.

18.5 Optional adverbial adjuncts. As summarized in Figure 18.1, a clausal structure (transitive, equational, or intransitive) may also cooccur with one or more optional adverbial adjuncts, namely instrumental adjunct (IA:), locative adjuncts (LA:), ablative adjuncts (AbA:) or adverbial adjunct (AA:). These optional adverbial adjuncts are retrieved by question words, e.g. *kele* 'by means of what' retrieves instrumental adjunct; *kahā̃* 'where' and *kahile* 'when' retrieve locative adjunct; *kahā̃bāṭa* 'from where' retrieves ablative adjuncts; and *kasarī* 'how' and *kina* 'why' retrieve adverbial adjuncts of manner and purpose. Following are examples of each of these optional adverbial adjuncts:

Instrumental adjuncts:

1.3.6 **±आत्मग्लानिले** + पानी +हुन्थे
+ātmaglānile +pānī/ +hunthe
±IA:cn-in +SC:cn-nm +P:ev1-3sg.pst.m
±self-sorrow-by +water +he-used-to-be
'He used to be inflicted by sorrow.'

Locative adjuncts:

2.5 ±प्रारब्धले **±यो उमेरमा** +उनलाई ±फेरि +दुलाहा +बनायो
±prārabdhale **±yo umeramā** +unalāī ±pheri +dulāhā +banāyo
±S: cn-nm **±LA: CNP-lc** +DO: pro-ac ±AA: advl +OC: cn-ac +P: tv3-3sg.pst
±destiny **±this age-in** +him ±again +bridegroom +made
'Destiny made him (Deviraman) a bridegroom again at this age.'

Ablative adjuncts:

2.8.2 **±यसबाट** ±उनको भलो कुभलो के +हुने हो
±yasabāṭa ±unako bhalo kubhalo ke +hune ho
±AbA: pro-dem-ab ±S: CNP-nm +P: iVP-impf..prt +aux-3sg..pres
±this-from +his good bad what +happening is
'Whether good or evil would result from this.'

Adverbial adjuncts:

2.5 ±प्रारब्धले ±यो उमेरमा +उनलाई **±फेरि** +दुलाहा +बनायो
±prārabdhale ±yo umeramā +unalāī **±pheri** +dulāhā +banāyo
±S: cn-nm ±LA: CNP-lc +DO: pro-ac **±AA: advl** +OC: cn-ac +P: tv3-3sg.pst
±destiny ±this age-in +him **±again** +bridegroom +made
'Destiny made Deviraman a bridegroom again at this age.

18.6 Other optional elements. As summarized in Figure 18.1, the other optional elements in clausal structure are: adverbial disjuncts (18.6.1), exclamations (18.6.2), connectors (18.6.3), and the subjects (18.6.4).

18.6.1 Adverbial disjuncts (AD:). The adverbial disjunct consists of an adverbial clause which is marked by the verb with absolutive participial suffixes *-i*, *-era*, *-ikana*, imperfect participial suffix-*dā* or the conditional form suffix *-e* followed by subordinate conjunctions *pachi* 'if' and *pani* 'although'. For example,

1.1.2 ±घरमा ±चञ्चलाश्री ±भइकन ±पनि
±gharamā ±cañcalāśrī +bhaikana +pani
±LA:cn-lc ±S:cn-nm +P:iv1-abs.prt ±C:sc
± house-in ±wealth +being ±although
'Although there was wealth in his house'

1.3.2 ± जोरीपारीसँग ± ठोकाबाजी +पर्दा
±jorīpārī-saṃga ±ṭhokābājī +pardā
±AA:PP ±S:cn-nm +P:iv1-impf.prt.
±neighbors-with ±competition +while-happening
'While in competition with the (jealous) neighbors',

1.7.2 ± दैवले +नसुनिदिए ± पछि
±daivale +nasunidie ±pachi
±S: cn-nm +P:iv1-neg.cond. ±C: sc
±Fate +not-listen ±if
'If the Fate does not listen'

1.12.3 + दुलही +भएर
+dulahī +bhaera
+SC:cn-nm +P:ev1-abs.prt.
+bride +having-been
'being (as) a bride.'

18.6.2 Exclamations. The optional function of the exclamation is filled by the interjections described in (16.1), and the vocatives described in (16.2). Following is an example of the use of an interjection in context:

2.20 ± छिः! ±सुभद्राको आजीवन सेवाको पुरस्कार +यही +हो ?
±chiḥ! ±subhadrāko ājīvana sevāko puraskāra +yahī +ho ?
±EX:ex (*chih!*) ±S:CNP-nm +SC:pro-nm +P:ev1-3sg.pst.
±Fie! ±Subhadrā-of life-long service-of reward +this +is ?
'Fie! Is this the reward for Subhadrā's life-long service?'

18.6.3 Connectors. The optional connector function is filled by either coordinate conjunctions described in (15.1) or subordinate conjunctions described in (15.2). The following an example of subordinate conjunction *pani* 'although':

1.1.2 ± घरमा ±चञ्चलाश्री ±भइकन ±पनि
±gharamā ±cañcalāśrī +bhaikana +pani
±LA:cn-lc ±S:cn-nm +P:iv1-abs.prt ±C:sc

± house-in ±wealth +being ±although
'Although there was wealth in his house'

To see how the subordinate clause fits with the principal clause in the sentence see the same clause numbered (1.1.1) in Part Two: clause analysis.

18.6.4 The subjects. The functional slot of the subject filled by nouns, noun phrases, pronouns, or noun clauses is optional. The subject is optional because it is marked in the finite forms of verbs. For instance, the subject function slot is not realized in the following clause:

1.3.6 +आत्मग्लानिले + पानी +हुन्थे
+ātmaglānile +pānī +hunthe
+IA:cn-in +SC:cn-nm +P:ev1-3sg.pst.m
±self-sorrow-by +water +he-used-to-be
'He used to be inflicted by sorrow.'

The form *hunthe* in mid level honorific indicates that the subject referred to by it is a third person, singular, masculine gender. Hence the redundancy of the subject.

Notes for Chapter 18

1. In the present description, this subcategory of verbs (tv-3) includes the 'causative' or 'ergative' verbs which the traditional grammars treat as a separate group. The causative or ergative verb forms are morphologically derived from the base verb forms of tv-1, ev-1, and iv-1 by a derivational morpheme *-āu-* :

Base verb forms:	Causative or ergative verb forms:
paḍhnu (tv-1) 'read'	*paḍhāunu* (tv-3) 'make (someone) read (teach)'
khānu (tv-1) 'eat'	*khuwāunu* (tv-3) make (someone) eat (feed)'
bannu (iv-1) 'be made'	*banāunu* (tv3) 'cause (something, someone) to be made'

However, syntactically the causative verbs do not behave differently from the tv-3 types. The subject of the base verb form becomes the object complement of the derived causative or ergative verb form, e.g.

paḍhnu (tv-1) 'read'

+म +राजाको भाषण +पढ्छु
+ma +rājāko bhāṣaṇa +paḍhchu
±S:pro-nm +DO: CNP-ac +P:tv-1-1sg.pres.
±I +king's speech +read
I read the king's speech'

paḍhāunu (tv-3) 'make (someone) read (teach)'

+गुरु +मलाई +राजाको भाषण +पढाउनुहुन्छ
+guru +malāī +rājāko bhāṣaṇa +paḍhāunuhuncha
+S:cn-nm +OC:pro-ac +DO: CNP-ac +P:tv-3-3sg.pres
+teacher +me +king's speech +makes-read (teaches)
'The teacher makes me read the king's speech.'

khānu (tv-1) 'eat'

±सुशील +भात +खान्छ
±suśīla +bhāta +khāncha
±S: pn-nm +DO: cn-ac +P:tv1-3sg.pres.m
±Sushil +rice +eats
'Susil eats rice.'

khuwāunu (tv-3) make (someone) eat (feed)'

±सुभद्रा +सुशीललाई +भात +खुवाउँछिन्
±subhadrā +susīlalā+bhāta +khuwāũchin
±S: pn-nm OC:pn-ac +DO:cn-nm +P:tv-3-3sg.pres.f
±Subhadra +Susil-to +rice +makes-eat (feed)
'Subhadra feeds rice to Susil.'

bannu (ev-1) 'become'

± यहाँ +बाटो +बन्यो
±yahā̃ +bāṭo +banyo
±LC: advl ±S: pro-nm +P:iv1-3sg.pst
±here +road +became
'A road is made here.'

banāunu (tv3) 'cause (someone, something) to become (make)'

±सरकारले +यहाँ +बाटो +बनायो
±sarakārale +yahā̃ +bāṭo +banāyo
±S:cn-nm +DO:pro-ac +OC:cn-ac +P:tv-3
±government +here +road +made
'The government made a road here.'

Such examples as presented above amply prove that so-called causative or ergative verbs have no different syntactic features than the the tv-3's. So, there is no necessity to create a separate subcategory of verbs called 'ergative verbs' in Nepali.

Chapter 19
Special types of clauses

19.0 Introduction. This chapter describes the internal structure of special types of clauses: (1) passive clauses (19.1), imperative clauses (19.2) and question clauses (19.3 and 19.4). Chapter 18, describing the simple, active, declarative statement clause, prepared the background for this chapter.

19.1 Passive clauses. In Nepali the passive clause has a passive form of a verb which is marked by the derivational suffix *-i-* (Cf. 17.1). For instance,

Active stem:	Active form:	Passive stem:	Passive form
chek- 'block'	*chekcha* 'he blocks'	*cheki-*	*chekincha* 'is blocked'
pā- 'get'	*pāũcha* 'he gets'	*pāi-*	*pāincha* 'is gotten'
puch- 'wipe'	*puccha* 'he wipes'	*puchi-*	*puchincha* 'is wiped'

When the passive form of a verb is used in a passive clause, the object of the verb in active clause occurs as subject; and the number, gender, person of the noun or pronoun filling the subject function slot are shown syntactically in the third person by their reference tie to the verbs, e.g.

Passive clause:	Active clause:
±स्वर्गको बाटो +छेकिन्छ	±स्वर्गको बाटो +छेक्छ
±svargako bāṭo +chekincha	+svargako bāṭo +chekcha
±S: CNP-nm +P: tv1p-3sg.pres	+DO: CNP-nm +P: tv1-3sg.pres
±heaven-of path +blocked-is	+heaven-of path +blocks
'The path of heaven is blocked.'	'One blocks the path of heaven'
+फलेफुलेको +देख्न +पाईयोस्	+फलेफुलेको +देख्न +पाओस्
+phalephuleko +dekhna +pāiyos	+phalephuleko +dekhna +pāos
+OC:nladjl +P:tv1-inf +P:tv1p-3sg.imp	+OC:nl +P:tv1-inf +P:tv1-3sg.imp
+prosperous +see-to +may-we-see	+prosperous +see-to +may-one-see
'May we get to see prosperity.'	'May one get to see prosperity.'
±उनको आँसु +पुछिने थियो	+उनको आँसु +पुछ्ने थियो
±una ko ā̃su + puchine thiyo	+una ko ā̃su + puchne thiyo
±S: CNP-nm +P: tv1p-3sg.pst	+S: CNP-nm +P: tv1-3sg.pst
±her tears + being-wiped would-be	+her tears + wipe +someone-would
'Her tears would be wiped.'	'One would wipe her tears'

19.2 Imperative clauses. The imperative clauses are marked by the imperative form of the verb with its complements. The imperative form of the verb inflects for the following four levels of honorifics. For instance,

gar, gares 'do (LGH)'
gara 'please do (MGH)'
garnos 'please do (HGH)'
garibaksyos 'please do (Royal Honorific)'

Imperative: *gharako sambhāra rākhes* 'Take a good care of the house.'
Declarative: *gharako sambhāra rākhcha* 'He takes good care of the house.'

19.3 Question clauses. The question clauses in Nepali are of two types: (1) *K*-question clauses (19.3.1) and (2) *ho-hoina* question clauses (19.3.2).

19.3.1 *K*-question clauses. A *K*-question clause has a word which begins with a 'k' and asks an information question. The following is a list of common information questions.

ko 'who?'	*ke* 'what?'
kahā̃: 'where'	*kahile* 'when?'
kina 'why?'	*kati* 'how much, how many?'
kasarī̃ 'how?'	*kasto* 'what kind?'

19.3.2 *Ho/hoina*- question clauses. *Ho/hoina*-questions are so called because the answer to these questions is either *ho* 'yes' or *hoina* 'no'. The *ho/hoina*-question clauses are divided into two categories: *ho/hoina*-questions with question intonation (19.3.2.1), and *ho/hoina*-questions with *hagi* (19.3.2.2).

19.3.2.1 *Ho/hoina*-question with question intonation. The *ho/hoina*-question has the same grammatical or syntactic structure as the declarative sentence, but is differentiated by the shift in intonation, e.g.

Declarative: *nepāl^{2} hindu^{2} deś^{2} ho^{1}* 'Nepal is a Hindu country.'
Question: *nepāl^{2} hindu^{1} deś^{1} ho^{3}?* 'Is Nepal a Hindu country?'

19.3.2.2 *Ho/hoina*-question with the tag *hagi*. The *ho/hoina* question with the tag *hagi* has the same structural description as the declarative clause. The tag *hagi*, 'wouldn't it, isn't it, aren't you, etc.' occurs in the final position in the sentence, and makes the clause a question clause, e.g.

Declarative: *nepāl^{2} hindu^{2} deś^{2} ho^{1}* 'Nepal is a Hindu country.'
Question: *nepāl^{2} hindu^{2} deś^{2} ho^{1}· hagi^{3}?* 'Nepal is a Hindu country, isn't it?

Chapter 20
Finite Dependent clauses: Nominal, adjectival, and adverbial

20.0 Introduction. This chapter describes the structure of the finite dependent clauses functioning as nominals, adjectivals, and adverbials. A finite clause has a finite form of verb filling the predicate slot. A finite dependent clause that fills the object slot or subject slot in the principal clause is a finite dependent noun clause (20.1); a finite dependent clause that fills the modifier slot in the principal clause is a finite dependent adjective clause (20.2); and a finite dependent clause that fills the adverbial adjunct slot in the principal clause is a finite dependent adverbial clause (20.3).

20.1 Finite dependent noun clause. The dependent noun clause functions either as an object or subject to the verb in the principal clause like a noun or noun phrase except that this is a clausal structure.

Dependent noun clause functioning as object to the verb in the principal clause has a finite verb in it. The verb in the principal clause is a transitive verb. The dependent noun clause functioning as object to the transitive verb in the principal clause is connected to the principal clause by *ki bhanera*, or quotation marks in written Nepali, e.g.

2.16.1 ±मनमनले +भने, +" के सुभद्राले साँचो मनले सल्लाह् दिएको हो ?"

±manamanle +bhane, +" ke subhadrāle sā̃co manle sallāha dieko ho?"

±IA:cmpdcn-in +P:tv1-3sg.pst +DO: cl

±mind-mind-with he-said, +"Did Subhadra give her consent with sincere mind?"

'He said to himself, "Did Subhadra give her consent sincerely?"

In Nepali a dependent noun clause functioning as subject to the verb in principal clause has a verb only in nonfinite (infinitive) form, and is, therefore, a nonfinite clause described in (21.1).

20.2 Finite dependent adjective clause. The finite dependent clause functioning as an adjective clause fills the modifier slot in the sentence and modifies the noun or noun phrase in the principal clause; such a dependent adjectival clause has a finite verb or verb phrase at its nucleus. The dependent clause is marked by the *J*-class substitute forms, e.g. *jo* 'who', *jasalāī̃* ' whom', *jasale* 'who', *jasbāṭa* 'from whom', *jasko* 'whose', *jun* 'which', *jahā̃* 'where', and *jahile* 'when'. These *J*-class substitute forms described in (6.1.21-6.1.2.2) refer to the antecedent in the principal clause, e.g.

2.28.1 +आज +देवीरमणको गति +त्यस बालक छात्रको जस्तो थियो ±(जो पहिलो दिनको पाठ बिर्सेर अबेला गुरुकहाँ पुग्दछ)

±āja ±devīramaṇako gati +tyasa bālaka chātrako jasto +thiyo ±(jo pahilo dinako pāṭha birsera avelā gurukahā̃ pugdacha)

±AA:advl ±S:CNP-nm +SC:AdjP +P:ev1-3sg.pst. ±Mod: Cl (±S: pro-rel-nm +DO: CNP-ac +P:tv1-abs.prt +AA: advl +LC: avl ±P: iv1-3sg.pres.)

±today ±Deviraman's situation +that little boy's like +was ±(who +previous day's lesson +having-forgotten ±late +guru's-at +arrives)

'Today, Deviraman's situation was like that of a little boy who, forgetting his previous lesson, arrives late at his guru's place.'

20.3 Finite dependent adverbial clause with *bhane* 'if, *kinaki* or *kinabhane* 'because'. Finite dependent adverbial clauses with *bhane* 'if' *kinaki* or *kinabhane* 'because' fill the slot of adverbial adjunct in the principal clause, e.g.

4.39.2 +लक्ष्मीलाई +ताडना +गरुन् +भने ±पुत्रवती पत्नी +थिइन्

+lakṣmīlāī +tāḍanā +garun +bhane +putrvatī patnī +thiin

+DC: pn-dt +DO: cn-ac +P: tv2-imp-3sg. +C: sc ±S: CNP-nm +P:ev1-sg.pst

+Laksmi-to +rebuke +he-may-do +if ±son-having wife +she was

'If he rebuked Laksmi, she was his wife with a son '

3.20.2 +आफ्नी आमालाई +"दुलही" +भन्थ्यो, +किनकि +लक्ष्मीलाई ±घरमा ±सवैजना +"दुलही बज्यै" +भन्थे

+āphni āmālāī +"dulahi" +bhanthyo, +kinaki +lakṣmīlāī ±gharamā ±savaijanā +"dulahī bajyai" +bhanthe

+DO: CNP-ac +OC: cn-ac +P: tv3-3sg.pst. +C: sc +DO: pn-ac ±LA: cn-lc ±S: prol-nm +OC: CNP-ac +P: tv3-3pl.pst

+his-own mother +Dulahi +he-called +because +Laksmi ±home-at ±everyone "Dulahi Bajyai" +they-called

'He called his own mother "Dulahi" because everyone in the family called Laksmi "Dulahi Bajyai".'

±यो योजना +नेपालमा +संभव +छैन +किनभने ±त्यहाँ +पूँजीको कमी +छ

±yo yojanā +nepālamā +sambhava +chaina +kinabhane ±tyahā̃ +pū̃jīko kamī +cha

±S: CNP-nm +LA: cn-lc +SC: adj-nm +P: ev1-3sg.pres.neg +C: sc ±AA: advl +S: CNP-nm +P: iv1-3sg.pres

+this plan +Nepal-in +possible +is-not +because +there +capital-of shortage +is

'This plan is not feasible in Nepal because there is a shortage of capital there.'

Chapter 21
Nonfinite dependent clauses: Infinitive, participial, and conditional

21.0 Introduction. This chapter describes the structure of the nonfinite dependent clauses. These nonfinite dependent clauses are of three types: (1) nonfinite dependent noun clause, (21.1); (2) nonfinite dependent adverbial clause with a verb in either infinitive form *-nu, nā* plus *le,* or perfect participial form-*eko* plus *le,* or imperfective participial form *-ne* plus *le* functioning as adverbial adjuncts, (21.2), and (3) nonfinite dependent adverbial clause with a verb in conditional form functioning as adverbial adjuncts (21.3).

21.1 Nonfinite dependent noun clause with a verb in infinitive form. As stated in (20.1) a dependent noun clause that fills the subject slot in the principal clause in Nepali has a verb only in nonfinite (infinitive) form. Such a noun clause functioning as subject is connected to the principal clause by *bhannu* or *bhaneko*, e.g.

6.31.1 +सौताको रीसले पोइको नाक काट्नु भनेको +यही +हो

+sautāko rīsale poiko nā:ka kāṭnu bhaneko +yahī +ho

±S: Cl +SC:pro(dem)-nm +P:ev1-3sg.pres

±co-wife's jealousy-by husband's nose cut-to +calling +this +is

'This is like cutting the nose of one's husband because of anger at one's co-wife'

±बिहानमा +घुम्नु +राम्रो +हो

±bihānamā +ghumnu +rāmro +ho

±S: cl (±LA: cn-lc +P:iv1-inf) +SC: adj-nm +P: ev1-3sg.pres

±(±morning-in +walk-to) +good +is

'To walk in the morning is good.'

20.2 Nonfinite dependent adverbial clause as adverbial adjunct. The clauses described in this section are adverbial clauses filling the functional slot of adverbial adjunct to the principal clause. Such dependent adverbial clauses are marked with the perfective participial form *-eko* plus *le,* or imperfective participial form-*ne,* plus *le,* or infinitive forms *-nu, -nā* of a verb plus *-le* 'because', e.g.

± (+बिरामी +भएकोले) +हिजो +म +स्कूल +आइन

± (+birāmī +bha-eko-le) +hijo +ma +skul +āina

±AA: cl (+ SC: adj-nm +P: ev1-prf.prt-*le*) ±AA: advl ±S: pro-nm ±AA: cn-lc +P: iv1-1sg.pst

(+sick ±being-because) ±yesterday ±I ±school +did-not-come

'(Because I was sick), I did not come to school yesterday.'

5.7.4 ± (± पुण्य +सिद्धिनाले) ± स्वर्गबाट +पतन +भएका

±(+punya +siddhināle) ±svargabāṭa + patana +bhaekā

± AA: cl (±S: cn-nm +P: iv1-inf-*le)* ±AbA: cn-ab +SC: cn +P: ev1-prf.prt

± (±merit +exhaust-because) ±heaven-from +fallen +been

'Because the merit of their good deeds is used up, they have fallen down.'

The verb phrase consisting of a participial *-eko* and auxiliary *hunu* in its infinitive *hunā* with the suffix *-le* also marks a dependent adverbial clause, functioning as an adverbial adjunct, e.g.

± (± सरकारले +रोकेको +हुनाले) ±आज ±जुलुस +भएन

± (sarakārale + rokeko + hunāle) ±āja ± julusa +bhaena

± AA: Cl (± S: cn-nm +P: iVP1-prf.prt +Aux: hu-nā-le) ±AA: advl ±S: cn-nm +P:iv1-3sg.pst.neg

±(government-by prevented-because) ±today ±demonstration +was-not

'Because the government had prevented it, there was no demonstration today.'

21.3 Nonfinite dependent adverbial clause with a verb phrase in conditional form. The dependent clause with conditional form occurs in a simple verb, or verb phrase form marked either by the conditional suffix *-e* to a simple verb stem or complex verb stem, or by a verb phrase with the main verb in perfective form marked by the perfective aspect suffix *-eko*, imperfective form suffix *-ne*, or infinitive form marked by *-nu*, or *nā* and the auxiliary verbs in conditional form in the dependent clause (21.1).[1]

Verb phrase with the main verb in perfective participial form marked by *-eko* and auxiliary verbs in conditional form:

4.31.5 +एक वचन +सोधेको +सम्म +भए ±उनको आँसु +पुछिने थियो

+eka vacana +sodheko +samma +bhae +unako ā̃su +puchine thiyo

+DO: CNP-ac +P: tVP1-prf.prt +AA: advl +Aux: be-cond. ±S: CNP--nm +P: tVP1passive-impf-Aux:3sg.pst
+one word +asked +only +if-be, her tears +wiped would-be
'If she was asked a word, her tears would be wiped '

Verb phrase with the main verb in imperfective aspect marked by *-ne* and auxiliary verbs in conditional form:

+उनीहरु +जाने +भए +जाउन्
+uniharu +jāne +bhae +jāun
+S: pro-nm +P:iv1-impf.prt. +P: iv1-imp.pl
+they +going +if-be +let-them-go
'If they are going, let them go'

Verb phrase with the main verb in infinitive form marked by *-nu* and auxiliary verbs in conditional form:

2.62.2 +छोड्नु +परे +छोडिदिउँला
+choḍnu +pare +choḍidiũlā
+P: iv1-inf +Aux: must-cond. +P: iv1-3sg.fut
to-leave if-must, I-will-quit
'If I must leave, I will leave '

Nonfinite dependent clauses with negative conditional form is connected to the principal clause by subordinate conjunction *pani*[1] or *pachi* which follows the verb (in conditional form, or absolutive participial form) in the dependent clause.

1.1.1 ±घरमा ±चञ्चलाश्री +भइकन +पनि ±देवीरमणका सन्तान +थिएनन्
±gharamā ± cañcalāśrī +bhaikna +pani ±devīramaṇakā santāna +thienan
±LA: cn-lc ±S: cn-nm +P: iv1-abs.prt +C: sc ±S: CNP-nm +P: iv1-3pl.pst.neg
±home-at ± great-wealth +being +although, ±Deviraman-of children +were-not
'Although there was plenty of wealth at home, Deviraman had no children.'

2.53.3 ±आफुखुशी +भए +पनि ±नौलीले +घर +छाडिन
±āphukhuśī +bhae + pani, ± naulīle +ghara +chāḍina
±AA: advl +P: iv1-cond +C: sc ±S: pn-nm +DO: ac +P: tv1-3sg.pst.f
±voluntary +if-be +also, +Nauli +house+ did-not-leave'
'Although it was voluntary, Nauli did not leave the house'

1.7.2 +तर +दैवले +नसुनिदिए ±पछि +कसको के +लाग्दो रहेछ ± र ?
±tara ±daivale +nasunidie pachi kasako ke lāgdo rahecha ra?
±C: cc ±S: cn-nm +P: iv1-cond. ±C: sc +S: ProP-nm +P:iVP1-impf. -Aux-pres ±Q: qw
±But ±god +if-not-listen, whose what +striking is ± ra?
'But if God does not listen, who can do anything? '

Note for Chapter 21

1. In Nepali the dependent clause may not precede the principal clause as it does in English, e.g.

+उनीहरु +गए +भने, +म +पनि +जान्छु
+uniharu +gae +bhane, +ma +pani +jānchu
+they +went +if, +I +also +go
'If they go I'll also go'

*'+म +पनि +जान्छु, +उनीहरु +गए +भने
* +ma +pani +jānchu,+ uniharu +gae +bhane
+I +also +go, +they +went +if
'I'll also go, if they go'

2. The subordinate conjunction *pani* 'although' should not be confused with the homophonous *pani* 'also' which is an adverbial.

Chapter 22
Dependent clauses in expression of comparison

22.0 Introduction. This chapter describes the structure of the dependent clauses in expression of comparison. These structures represent basically two degrees of comparison: comparative degree (comparison between two equal or unequal items), and superlative degree (comparison among more than two equal or unequal items). Thus, the expressions of comparison are subdivided into two types: Comparisons of inequality (22.1) and Comparisons of equality (22.2).

22.1 Comparisons of inequality. Comparisons of inequality are structurally divided into two types: Symmetrical comparison (22.1.1) and Asymmetrical comparison (22.1.2). Both types of comparisons consist of the comparative quantifiers *ajha, bhandā,* and *jhan* in comparisons of two items.

The quantifier *sabbhandā,* or its variant *sabai bhandā* 'more than all' occurs in the superlative degree of comparison (comparing one item against many other items in symmetrical comparisons).

22.1.1 Symmetrical comparisons. In symmetrical comparisons one item is described as exceeding, or falling short of, another item with respect to some specified property or behavior. In such comparisons there are two clauses (one is reduced to the form of a phrase). The first is the principal clause, the second is a reduced dependent clause. The constituents of the two clauses perform identical functions within their respective clauses. The constituents being compared with each other may be subjects, objects, complements, or predicates.

The order of the constituents of a sentence with dependent clause in expressions of comparisons is:

+Constituent of the reduced clause +*bhandā* +constituents of the principal clause.

(1) Comparison of subjects:

+नेपाल +भन्दा +अमेरिका +ठुलो +छ
+nepāla + bhandā +amerikā +ṭhulo +cha
+S: pn-nm +bhandā +S: pn +SC: adj +P: ev1-3sg.pres
Nepal than America large is
'America is larger than Nepal.'

In the sentence *nepāla bhandā amerikā ṭhulo cha* 'America is larger than Nepal' *amerikā ṭhulo cha* 'America is large' is the principal clause. Embedded in the principal clause is the dependent clause *nepāla ṭhulo cha* 'Nepal is large' (which is reduced to *nepāla*), and is marked as a dependent clause by *bhandā* 'than'. Note in each example that the comparative marker *bhandā* 'than' follows the dependent clause, and that the principal clause follows the dependent clause.

Comparison of objects:

±म + भात +भन्दा +तर्कारी ±धेरै +खान्छु
±ma +bhāta +bhandā +tarkārī ±dherai +khānchu
±S: por-nm +DO: cn-ac +bhandā +DO: cn-nm ± AA: adv +P: tv1-1sg.pres
±I +rice +than +vegetables ± much +eat
'I eat more vegetables than rice.'

Comparison of subject complements:

±उ +धनी +भन्दा +पनि +सुखी +छ
±u +dhanī +bhandā +pani +sukhī +cha
±S: pro-nm +SC: adjl +than ±AA: advl +SC: adjl +P: ev1-3sg.pres
±he +rich +than ±even +happy +is
'He is more happy than he is rich.'

Comparison of predicates:

+लेख्न +भन्दा +बढी +पढ
+lekhna +bhandā +baḍhī paḍha
+P: iv1-inf than +AA: adv +P: iv1-imp
+writing +than +more +read
'Read more than you do writing.'

Superlative degree comparison has the same structural pattern as the comparative degree comparison in Nepali. The superlative degree comparison is marked by *savabhandā* or *savai bhandā* 'than all'.

±सगरमाथा +सवभन्दा +अग्लो पहाड +हो
±sagarmāthā +savabhandā +aglo pahāḍa +ho
±S: pn-nm +savabhandā +SC: CNP-nm +P: ev1-3sg.pres.
±Sagarmatha (Mt. Everest) +all-than +high mountain +is
'Sagarmatha (Mt. Everest) is higher than all (the highest) mountains.'

+सबभन्दा ठुलो सन्तोष +यही +हो +नौली
savabhandā ṭhulo santoṣa yahī ho, naulī
+SC: CNP-nm ±S: pro-nm +P:ev1-3sg.pres ±EX: cn-nm
+all-than great satisfaction ±this +is, Nauli
'This is the satisfaction greater than all (the greatest satisfaction).'

22.1.2 Asymmetrical comparisons. In the asymmetrical comparisons the compared item in the principal clause does not have anything overt to compare with. The compared item is said just to exceed the extent expected, apparent, understood. Such asymmetrical comparisons are marked by *ajha* and *jhan* 'further'.

±यो किताब +अझ +राम्रो +छ
±yo kitāba +ajha +rāmro +cha
±S: CNP-nm +ajha +SC: adj-nm +P: ev1-3sg.pres.
±this book +further +good +is
'This book is even better (than one expected).'

±रात्री +झन् +भयङ्कर +प्रतीत +हुन्थ्यो
±rātrī +jhan +bhayangkara + pratīta +hunthyo
±S: cn-nm +jhan +SC: adjl-nm +SC: adjl-nm +P: ev1-3sg.pst
+night +even-more +terrifying +appeared +would-be'
'The night appeared even more terrifying.'

22.2 Comparisons of equality. The quantifiers *jati* 'as much', *uti* 'as much as that (remote)', *tyati* 'as much as that (proximate)' occur in the comparisons of equality. In such comparisons of equality, the compared item is said to be equal to another item with respect to a specified property or behavior. The relative quantifier *jati* 'as much' interlocks with demonstrative quantifiers *uti* 'as much as that (remote)' and *tyati* 'as much as that (proximate).'

Comparisons of subject:
±म +राम जति +काम +गर्न +सक्छु
±ma ±rāma jati + kāma +garna sakchu
±S: pro-nm ±AA: AdvP +DO: cn-nm +P:tv1-inf Aux: 1sg.pres
±I +Ram as-much-as +work +to-do I-can
'I can do the work as much as Ram can.'

Comparisons of subject complement:
±म +राम +जति धनी +छु
±ma +rāma +jati dhani +chu
±S: pro-nm +SC: AdjP +P: ev1-1sg
±I +Ram +as-much-as rich +am
'I am as rich as Ram'

Comparison of object:

±म +राम +जति +काम +गर्न +सक्छु

±ma ±rāma +jati + kāma +garna sakchu

±S: pro-nm ±AA: Advl +DO: cn-nm +P:tv1-inf Aux: 1sg.pres

±I +Ram ±as-much-as +work +to-do I-can

'I can do the work as much as Ram can.'

Comparison of dative complement:

±म +रामलाई +त्यति +नै +चिठी +लेख्छु +जति +गोविन्दलाई +लेख्छु

±ma +rāmalā̃ī +tyati +nai +ciṭhi +lekhchu +jati +govindalā̃ī +lekhchu

±S: pro-nm +DC:pm-dt ±AA: advl ±NU: nu +P: tv2-1sg.pres. ±AA: advl +DC: pn-dt +P: tv2-1sg.pres

±I +Ram-to +as-many ±emphatic +letter +write +as +Govinda-to +I-write

'I write as many letters to Ram as I write to Govinda.'

Comparison of locative complements:

± म ± जति +यहाँ +वस्छु ±उति + त्यहाँ +वस्दिन

±ma ±jati +yahā̃ +baschu ±uti +tyahā̃ +basdina

±S: pro-nm +LC: advl +P: iv3-1sg.pres ±LC: advl +P: iv3-1sg.pres

±I ±as-much +here +stay ±that-much +there +I-do-not-stay

'I do not stay there as much as I stay here.'

Comparison of predicates:

+म ±त्यति ±नै +लेख्छु +जति +पढ्छु

±ma ±tyati ±nai +lekhchu ±jati +paḍhchu

±S: pro-nm ±AA: advl ±NU: nu (nai) +P: iv1-1sg.pres ±AA: advl +P: iv1-1sg.pres

I that-much (emphatic) write as-much study

'I write as much as I study.'

Sentential Structures

Chapter 23
The sentence

23.0 The internal structure of the sentence (S). Sentence is the highest grammatical unit, and as such it is not a constituent of any higher level grammatical structure.[1] The internal structure of the sentence consists of a segmental constituent and a prosodic constituent, i.e.

S = + segmental constituent
+ prosodic constituent

The segmental constituent in a sentence is filled primarily by a clause or clauses. In real life situations (conversational contexts), however, the responses to a speaker's questions are pragmatically reduced to a mere word, or phrase which carries the new information. The old and redundant information is dropped by means of deletion. The remainder of the clause in the form of a word or phrase is called a reduced clause.

The prosodic constituent consists of one of three intonation patterns described in Chapter 3. The intonation pattern of a statement and imperative statement is falling (3.10.1.1). The intonation pattern of a ho/hoina question 'yes/no-question' is rising (3.10.1.2). The intonation pattern of a K-question 'wh-question' is sustained (3.10.1.3).

23.1 Clauses as segmental constituents. Full clauses as segmental constituents are described in (18.0). Reduced clauses as segmental constituents are described in (24.3). A clause with a finite verb, or a number of clauses with finite or nonfinite verbs embedded in the principal clause constitute a sentence. For instance,

1.1.1 ± घरमा ± चञ्चलाश्री +भइकन + पनि ± देवीरमणका सन्तान +थिएनन्
± gharamā ± cañcalāśrī +bhaikana +pani ± devīramaṇakā santāna +thienan
±LA: cn-lc ±S: cn-nm +P: iv1-abs.prt. +C: sc ±S: CNP-nm +P:iv1-3pl.pst.neg
±house-in +plenty-of-wealth +being +although +Deviraman-of children +were-not
'Although there was plenty of wealth at home, Deviraman had no children.'

Chapter 24
The sentence as speech act

24.0 Introduction. This chapter describes the sentence as speech act. Traditional grammars distinguish four types of sentences (1) declarative, (2) interrogative, (3) imperative, (4) exclamatory. However, a sentence such as 'Can you open the door?' traditionally described as interrogative, is an imperative statement in terms of its function. So the assignment of sentences to the various categories in question depends on the function of the sentence at a higher level--discourse level where utterances are simply considered as 'speech acts'. And it is the speech act, as a unit of discourse, that either (1) makes a statement requiring no speech act in response, (2) asks a question requesting another speech act in response, or (3) issues a request or order expecting compliance in a word (speech act) or deed (other act). It is in correlation with these various pragmatic functions that the sentence as speech act possesses certain formal properties (Agard 1984, vol.I: 177).

Nepali sentences as speech acts can be divided into two main categories on formal basis: (1) direct speech acts (24.1), which are unmarked and (2) indirect speech acts (24.2), marked by lexical items: *re, are,* and *bhanera;* in such indirect speech acts the speaker reports the speech of another speaker. Sentence as speech acts also have structures pragmatically reduced to a mere word or phrase, called elliptical sentences (24.3).

24.1 Direct speech act. The direct speech acts are speech acts in which the speaker makes his own statement as opposed to reporting the speech act of someone else. include mainly four types of sentences: (1) declarative speech acts (2) interrogative speech acts, (3) imperative speech acts (Commands), and (4) exclamatory speech acts. For instance,

(1) Declarative speech acts (Statements):

±बिचरी सुभद्रा ±पनि +खिन्न +थिइन्

±bicarī subhadrā ± pani + khinna +thiin

±S: CNP +AA:advl ±SC:adjl +P:ev1-3sg.pst

±Poor +Subhadra ±also +sad +was

'Poor Subhadra also was sad.'

(2) Interrogative speech acts (Questions):

±किन ±नौली, ±किन +त्यसो +भनिस् ?

± kina ±naulī, ±kina +tyaso +bhanis?

± AA: advl ±EX: cn-nm ±AA: advl ±AA: advl +P: iv1-2sg.pst

±Why ±Nauli, ±why ±so +you-said?

'Why Nauli, why did you say so?'

(3) Imperative speech acts (Commands):

+घरको सम्भार +राखेस्

+gharako sambhāra + rākhes

+DO: CNP-ac +P:tv1-imp.

+House-of maintenance +keep

'Take good care of the house.'

(4) Exclamatory speech acts (Exclamation)

± ओहो ± बजै, +हेर +कति दुब्ली !

± oho ± bajai! + hera +kati dublī !

±EX: intj. ±EX: cn-nm +P: iv1-imp ± EX: CNP-nm

±Oh ± Bajai +Look ±How thin

'O Bajai! Look, how thin you have become! '

24.2 Indirect speech acts. Indirect speech act is the act of reporting what a third person has said. There are two ways of reporting speech in Nepali: (1) using the particle, *re* or *are* 'is said, they say' (24.1.1) and (2) using the absolutive participle *bhanera* 'having said' (24.1.2).[1]

24.2.1 Indirect speech acts with *re* or *are*. The nuance particle *are* or *re* occurs at the end of a statement to signify information that is received indirectly about a subject.[2] It carries the meaning of 'I hear that ...' or 'they say ...', e.g.

±उनीहरु ± हिजो +गए +रे

±uniharu ±hijo +gae +re

±S: pro-nm ±AA: advl +P: iv1-3pl.pst ±NU: nu *(re)*

±they ±yesterday +went ±they say

'They went yesterday, they say.'

±सारै नराम्रो रोग +हो ±अरे

±sārai narāmro roga +ho +are

±S: CNP-nm +P: iv1-3sg.pres ±NU: nu: *(are)*

±extremely bad disease +is ±they-say

It is a very bad disease, they say.'

24.2.2 Indirect speech act with *bhanera*. The most frequent way to report a speech in Nepali is to use the absolutive participle *bhanera* (lit.'having said'). The use of *bhanera* is divided into two ways: (1) Reporting the actual speech, and (2) Reporting the intention.

24.2.2.1 Reporting the actual speech act. The absolutive participle form *bhanera* of the verb *bhannu* 'say' is employed to report the words actually uttered by the speaker. The reporter does not change the words of the speaker. So the written Nepali texts present the reported speech in quotation marks, e.g.

+"मेरो राजा" +भनेर +म्वाइ +खाइन्
+"mero rājā" +bhanera +mwāi + khāin
+DO:cl+P: tv1-abs.prt +DO: cn-ac P:tv1-3sg.pst f
+"my king" +having-said +kiss +she-ate
'She kissed the boy saying "My Raja".

±लक्ष्मी ±पनि +"जान्छु" +भनेर +जिद्दी +गर्न लागिन्
±lakṣmī ± pani +"jānchu" +bhanera + jiddī + garna lāgin
±S: pn-nm ±AA: advl +DO: cl +P: tv1-abs.prt +DO: cn-nm +P: tv1-inf.aux-3sg.pst.f
±Laksmi ±also +"I'll-go" +saying +insistence +do-began
Laksmi began to insist saying "I will also go."

+सुभद्रालाई +"जान्छ्यौ कि" +भनेर ±कसैले +एक वचन ±सम्म ±पनि +सोधेन
+subhadrālāī +"jānchyau ki" +bhanera ±kasaile +eka vacana +samma +pani +sodhena
+DC: pn-dt +DO: cl +P: tv1-abs.prt. ±S: prol-nm +DO: CNP ±AA: ±AA: advl +P:tv2-3sg.pst.neg
+Subhadra-to +"Will-you-go" +saying ±anyone +one word ±even ±also +did-not-ask
'Nobody asked Subhadra even a word saying, "will you also go?"

+ "आमा कहिले आउनुहुन्छ" +भनेर +तपाईंलाई ±वरावर +संझिरहन्छन्
+"āmā kahile āunuhuncha" +bhanera +tapāīlāī ±varāvara +samjhirahanchan
+DO: cl +P:tv1-abs.prt +DO: pro-ac ±AA: advl +P: tv1-3sg.pres
+"mother when comes" +having-said +you +often +he-remembers
'He often remembers you saying, "When is mother coming?

±"दिदी, तपाईंको नासो" +भनेर ±लक्ष्मीले +सुशीलको हात +सुभद्राका काखमा +राखिदिइन्
±"didī, tapāīko nāso" +bhanera ±lakṣmīle +suśīlako hāta +subhadrākā kākhamā +rākhidi.in
±DO: cl +P: tv1-abs.prt ±S: pn-nm +DO: CNP-ac +LC: CNP-lc +P:tv4-3sg.pst.f
±"Sister, +"your ward"+having-said ±Laksmi +Susil's hand +Subhadra's lap-on +she-put
'Laksmi put Susil's hand in Subhadra's lap saying, "Sister, this is your ward."

24.2.2.2 Reporting the intention. The absolutive participle *bhanera* is also employed in the speech act to report the intention of the speaker. The words reported by means of *bhanera* in such sentences are not the actual speech acts of the person being reported about, but the speech acts of the reporter who translates in his own words the intention of the person. The fact that only the intention is reported is also reflected in written Nepali where the reported intention is not put within the quotation marks, e.g.

> +खस्नुपर्ला +भनेर ±बीचैमा +अलप +हुन्छन्
> +khasnuparlā +bhanera ±bīcaimā +alapa +hunchan
> +DO: cl +P:tv1-abs.prt ±LC: cn-lc +SC:adjl +P: ev1-3pl.pres
> +may-have-to-fall +saying ±in-the-middle +lost +are
> 'Thinking that they may have to fall, they disappear between the sky and the earth.'

> +कसैले देख्छ कि +भनेर ±ओढ्नेले +छोपेकी थिइन्
> +kasaile dekhcha ki +bhanera ±oḍhhnele +chopekī thiin
> +DO: cl +P: tv1-abs.prt ±IA: cn-in +P: tVP-prf.prt-aux-3sg.pst.f
> +someone may see" +saying +shawl-with +covered she-had
> 'Thinking that someone may see it, she covered it (the bundle) with her shawl.'

24.3 Elliptical sentences as declarative speech acts. Reduced sentential structures are elliptical sentences which lack either the subject and objects (24.2.1), or the predicate (24.2.2). Such sentences as declarative speech acts are complete semantically because the redundant element in them is deleted since these elements are anaphoric to a prior utterance.

24.3.1 Reduced sentences with elliptical subject and object. Reduced sentences with elliptical subject and object consist of a verb phrase which is a repetition of the verb form of the question, e.g.

Full sentence:

> ±तिमी +काम +गर्ने?
> ±timi kāma garne?
> ±S: pro-nm +DO: cn-nm +P: tv1-impf.prt.
> ±you +job +doing?
> 'Would you like to do the job?'

Reduced sentence with elliptical subject and object:

> +गर्ने
> +garne
> +P:tv1-impf.prt.
> +doing
> 'Yes, I would like to do the job.'

24.3.2 Reduced sentences with elliptical predicate. In speech acts of declarative statements made as short answers to the questions asked to the speaker the predicate may be elliptical in Nepali. When the predicate becomes elliptical, the optional element is obligatory. Consider the following conversation for instance,

Interrogative speech act (Question):	Declarative speech act (Answer)
±को सँग +आइस् ?	+रातमाटे भण्डारीका जहानसँग
±ko sãga +āis	+rātamāṭe bhaṇḍārīkā jahānasãga
±AA: pp +P: iv1-3sg.pst	+AA: pp
+who-with +did-you-come	+Ratmate Bhandari Pandit's family-with
'Who did you come with?'	'With Ratmate Bhandari Pandit's family.'

Interrogative speech act (Question):	Declarative speech act (Answer)
+कैले +जान्छेस्	+भोलि बिहानै
+kaile + jānches?	+bholi bihānai
±AA: advl(interrog)	+AA: adlP
±when +will-you-go?	tomorrow morning
'When will you go?'	'Tomorrow morning.'

Notes for Chapter 24

1. In Nepali there a reported speech also is marked by the nuance particle *kyāre* which does not necessarily report the speech of a third person; *kyāre* simply means that the full validity of the statement marked by *kyāre* is disowned by the speaker, e.g.

±शायद +ब्रह्मवादीहरु + त्यसैलाई +आशापाश या मृगतृष्णा +भन्छन् +क्यारे
±śāyada ±brahmavādīharu +tyasailāī +āśāpāśa yā mṛgatṛṣṇā +bhanchan ±kyāre
±AA: advl ±S: cn-nm +OC: pro-ac +DO: CNP-ac +P: tv2-3pl +NU: nu
±Perhaps +philosophers +that +hope-snare or mirage +call +I-guess
'Perhaps the philosophers call it the snare of hope or mirage, I guess.'

References

Acharya, Jayaraj. 1980. *Traditional grammars: English and Nepali: A study.* Kathmandu: Navin Press.

_______. 1986. *The sound system of Nepali: An interim report.* A Master's research paper, Georgetown University, Washington, D.C.

Acharya, Shivaraj. 1974. *Nepālī varṇoccāraṇa śikṣa: [Nepali phonetics]* (in Nepali). Kathmandu: Sajha Prakashan.

Agard, Frederick B. 1984. *A Course in Romance linguistics.* 2 vols. Washington, D.C.: Georgetown University Press.

Bandhu, Churamani. 1973. Clause patterns in Nepali. In: *Clause, sentences and discourse patterns in selected languages of Nepal,* Part II Clause, edited by Austin Hale and David Watters. Norman: Oklahoma. Summer Institute of Linguistics, University of Oklahoma. pp. 1-97

Bandhu, Churamani, B. M. Dahal, A. Holzhausen and Austin Hale. 1971. *Nepali segmental phonology.* An unpublished paper.

Bloomfield, Leonard. 1933. *Language.* New York: Holt Rinehart and Winston.

Clark, T.W. 1963. *Introduction to Nepali: A first year course.* Cambridge, London: W. Heffer and Sons.

_______. 1969. Nepali and Pahari. In: *Current trends in linguistics, vol. 5: Linguistics in South Asia,* edited by Thomas A. Sebeok. The Hague: Mouton.

Cruttenden, Allen. 1986. *Intonation.* London: Cambridge University Press.

Crystal, David. 1980. *A first dictionary of linguistics and phonetics.* Boulder, Colorado: Westview Press.

Hari, Maria. 1971. *Conversational Nepali.* Kathmandu, Nepal: Summer Institute of Linguistics and Tribhuvan University.

_______. 1973. Tentative systemic organization of Nepali sentences. In: *Clause, sentences, and discourse patterns in selected languages of Nepal, Part I General approach,* edited by Austin Hale. Norman,

Oklahoma: Summer Institute of Linguistics, University of Oklahoma. pp. 3-52

Hogg, Richard and C.B. McCully. 1987. *Metrical phonology*. London: Cambridge University Press.

Hutt, M. J. 1988. *Nepali: A national language and its literature*. New Delhi: Sterling Publishers.

Karki, Tika B. and Chij K. Shrestha. n.d. *A basic course in spoken Nepali*. Kathmandu: Jore Ganesh Press.

Karn, Helen. 1986. *A descriptive sketch of Nepali syntax*. Master's research paper. Graduate school of Georgetown University Washington, D.C.

Lyons, John. 1968. *Introduction to theoretical linguistics*. London: Cambridge University Press.

Matthews, David. 1984. *A course in Nepali*. London: School of Oriental and African Studies, University of London.

Meerendonk, M. 1949. *Basic Gurkhali grammar*. Singapore: Sen Wah Press and Co.

Nepāla Rājakīya Prajñā Pratiṣṭhāna (Royal Nepal Academy). 1984. *Nepāli Bṛhat Śabdakośa (Nepali comprehensive dictionary)*. Kathmandu: Nepāla Rājakīya Prajñā Pratiṣṭhāna (Royal Nepal Academy).

Nepāla Rājakīya Prajñā Pratiṣṭhāna (Royal Nepal Academy). 1984. *Bṛhad Nepāli vyākaraṇa (Comprehensive Nepali grammar)*. Kathmandu: Nepāla Rājakīya Prajñā Pratiṣṭhāna (Royal Nepal Academy).

O'Brien, Richard J. 1965. *A descriptive grammar of ecclesiastical Latin based on modern structural analysis*. Georgetown University Latin series. Chicago: Loyola University Press.

Pāṇini. *Aṣṭādhyāyī* (trans. S. C. Vasu, 1891). Delhi: Motilal Benarasidass.

Pike, Kenneth L. 1945. *The intonation of American English*. Ann Arbor: University of Michigan Press.

Pradhan, Krishna Bhai. 1989. *The structure of spoken Nepali*. vol 1. Madison, Wisconsin: Department of South Asian Studies.

Pradhan, Kumar. 1984. *A history of Nepali literature.* New Delhi: Sahitya Akademi.

Saussure, Ferdinand de. 1966. *Course in general linguistics* (trans. W. Baskin). New York: McGraw-Hill.

Shukla, Shaligram. 1981. *Bhojpuri grammar.* Washington, D.C.: Georgetown University Press.

Silkirk, E. O. 1984. On the major class features and syllable theory. In: Aronoff and Oehrle (eds.). *Language sounds structures: Studies in phonology,* presented to Morris Halle by his teacher and students. Cambridge, Mass.: MIT Press.

Turnbull, A. 1888. *Nepali grammar and vocabulary.* Delhi: Asian Educational Services (Reprinted in 1982).

Southworth, Franklin. 1967. Nepali transformational structure: A sketch. Poona, India: Spicer Memorial College Press.

Sprigg, R. K. 1989. The Nepali language with reference to its relationship with the Rai, Limbu, and Lepcha languages. In: *Indian linguistics.* Fall, 1989.

Turner, R. L. 1931. *A comparative and etymological dictionary of the Nepali language.* London: Routledge and Kegan Paul.

Vasu, S. C. 1891. *Aṣṭādhyāyī of Pāṇini.* 2 vols. Delhi: Motilal Benarasidass.

PART TWO: ANALYZED CORPUS

1. *Nāso:* Text in Devanāgarī script

नासो

लेखक गुरुप्रसाद मैनाली

१

घरमा चञ्चलाश्री भइकन पनि देवीरमणका सन्तान थिएनन् । सन्तान होस् भन्नाका निमित्त हरएक उपाय गरे, चौतारो चिने, बाटो खने, पशुपतिमा महादीप बाले, गए साल हरिवंश पुराण लगाए, तैपनि सुभद्राको कोख सफल हुन सकेन । जोरीपारी सँग ठोकाबाजी पर्दा धन, बल, बुद्धि, सबै कुरामा देवीरमणको जित हुन्थ्यो तर 'अपूतो' भनेको सुन्ने बित्तिकै उनको अभिमान धूलो हुन्थ्यो, आत्मग्लानिले पानी हुन्थे । पुराना विचारका मानिस थिए, सन्तान विना आफ्नो वैभवलाई तुच्छ सम्झन्थे ।

विचरी सुभद्रा पनि खिन्न थिइन् । छिमेकका आइमाईले छोरा-छोरी खेलाएको देखेर उनलाई रहर लाग्थ्यो, सन्तानका अशाले सरल नारीस्वभाववश धामी-झाँक्रीको बूटी-जन्तर बाँधिन् , देवी-देवताको भाकल गरिन् , तीर्थ, व्रत, पूजा, पाठ पनि गरिन् । तर दैवले नसुनिदिए पछि कसको के लाग्दो रहेछ र ?

ज्योतिषीहरु देवीरमणलाई अर्को विवाह गर्न सल्लाह दिन्थे । परन्तु सुभद्राको आदेश विना उनी अर्को विवाह गर्न सक्तैनथे । सुभद्रा बहुत पतिपरायणा रमणी थिइन् । आजसम्म कहिल्यै उनले देवीरमणको चित्त दुखाइनन् , मनको कुरा जानेर सेवा गर्थिन् । सुभद्रा दुलही भएर आउँदाको बखतको भयङ्कर दुःख अहिले सम्म पनि देवीरमणका आँखाका सामु नाचिरहेको थियो । उ अवस्था सम्झँदा गहभरी आँसु हुन्थ्यो । सुख-दुःखकी साथी भएर कङ्गाल देवीरमणलाई सुभद्राले धनवान बनाइन् । अहिले सन्तानका निम्ति सौता हालिदिएर कसरी कृतघ्न बनून् ?

२

फागुन महीनाको विहानपखको सिरेटो मुटु छेड्ला भने जस्तो गर्थ्यो । देवीरमण मण्डपमा वसेका थिए । नयाँ दुलही पनि एकै आसनमा बसेकी थिइन् । ब्राह्मणहरु ऋचा पढेर अग्निमा आहुति दिइरहेका थिए । प्रारब्धले यो उमेरमा उनलाई फेरि दुलाहा बनायो । एक दिन यस्तै रीत संग उनले सुभद्राको पाणिग्रहण गरेथे । सुभद्राको आदेश पाई हो वा नपाई हो आज उनले अधिकै कृत्यलाई दोहोऱ्याए । यसबाट उनको भलो-कुभलो के हुने हो यस कुराको उनैलाई पनि केही ज्ञान थिएन । बान्ह वर्षकी अबोध बालिकालाई ल्याएर उनी शून्य आकाशमा कल्पनातीत मनोमन्दिर निर्माण गर्न खोज्दथे । शायद त्यसैलाई आशा-पाश या मृगतृष्णा भन्छन् क्यारे ।

अस्तु करले होस् वा आन्तरिक प्रेरणाले होस्, उनले विवाह-विधि समाप्त गरे । दुलही अन्माउने वेलामा कन्यापक्षका मानिसले रुँदै दुलहीलाई डोलीमा हालिदिए । दुलही पनि डोली भित्र रुन लागिन् । देवीरमणलाई त्यतिखेर साह्रै नरमाइलो लाग्यो । बाटामा बरियातहरु परस्पर ग्रामीण ठट्टा गरेर खित्का छोडी हाँस्थे, पतन्तु देवीरमणका कपालमा अर्कै विचारको द्वन्द हुन लागेको थियो । मनमनले भने, "के सुभद्राले साँचो मनले सल्लाह दिएको हो ? सम्मति दिंदा किन अर्को पट्टि फर्केर 'हुन्छ' भनेकी त ? मेरो ज्यादा आग्रह देखेर 'हुन्छ' भनेकी त होइन ? अहो ! मानिसहरु आफ्नो तीव्र इच्छामा अरुको सम्मतिलाई

कसरी जबरजस्ती तान्छन् । छिः । सुभद्राको आजीवन सेवाको पुरस्कार यही हो ? म के गरूँ , मलाई के दोष ? सन्तान विना स्वर्गको बाटो छेकिन्छ भन्ने हिन्दू धर्म जानोस् । भोगको लालसाले होइन धर्मका आज्ञाले विवाह गरेको हुँ ।

बरियात देवीरमणका घर नेर पुग्यो । गाउँले छिमेकीहरु चौतारामा रमिता हेरिरहेका रहेछन् । देवीरमणले एक-एक गरी नियालेर हेरे । त्यो हुलमा सुभद्रालाई देखेनन् । बल्ल उनको छातीबाट ढुङ्गो पन्छियो । आज देवीरमणको गति त्यस बालक छात्रको जस्तो थियो जो पहिलो दिनको पाठ बिर्सेर अबेला गुरुकहाँ पुग्दछ, अथवा त्यस अपराधीको जस्तो थियो जो परिचित मानिसलाई देखेर लुक्न खोज्दछ ।

छिमेकी संग कुरा गर्नाको बहानाले उनी केही पछि भए; जाँदा दुलही भित्र्याइसकी सुभद्रा दमाईं-डोलेहरुलाई ज्याला बाँड्न लागेकी रहिछन् । देवीरमणको हृदय गद्‌गद् भयो, मनमनले भने "सुभद्रा स्वर्गकी देवी हो व्यर्थै किन शंका गरें ? छिः । मानिसहरु आफ्नो कामले कसरी आफै तर्सन्छन् ।"

पाहुना-पासा संग कुराकानी गरेर देवीरमण अबेला कोठामा सुत्न गए । पानसमा कडुवा तेलको बत्ती बलिरहेको थियो । नयाँ दुलही खाट मनि ओच्छ्यानमा सुतकी थिइन् । देवीरमण खाटमा पल्टे, उस ठाउँमा सुभद्राको ओच्छ्यान देखेनन् । अघि सुभद्राको ओच्छ्यान देवीरमणका खाट मनि हुन्थ्यो । आज उस ठाउँमा नदेख्दा बीसौं वर्ष देखि सुतिरहेको कोठा पनि देवीरमणलाई अनौठो जस्तो लाग्यो । एक छिन पछि गृहकृत्य समाप्त गरेर सुभद्रा कोठामा पसिन् , देवीरमणको गोडा मिच्न लागिन् । यो उनको दैनिक काम थियो । सुभद्रा यसमा कहिल्यै त्रुटि हुन दिन्नथिन् । देवीरमणले भने -- "सानु , तिम्रो ओच्छ्यान खोई नि ?"

"पल्लो कोठामा छ ।"

"किन पल्लो कोठामा सारेको ?"

"भोलि एकादशी हो, सवेरै गण्डकी नुहाउन जान्छु ।"

"म पनि उहीं सुत्छु ।"

"उस्, यहीं सुत्नुभए पनि हुन्छ ।"

थाकेर आएका देवीरमणलाई चाँडै निद्रा पऱ्यो । आफ्नो दोलाइँ सौतालाई खापेर सुभद्रा पल्लो कोठामा गइन् । मधुरो बत्तीको धमिलो उज्यालोमा नौली घर्तिनी पात गाँसिरहेकी थिई । नौली देवीरमणको पुरानो चाकर्नी हो । नौलीको उमेर झण्डै झण्डै सुभद्रा सँग मिल्थ्यो । ८२ सालमा स्वर्गवासी महाराज चन्द्रशमशेर जङ्गबहादूरका करुणाले दास-जीवनबाट मुक्त भएकी थिई । घरकी पुरानी चाकर्नी हुनाले देवीरमणले नौलीको मोल लिएनन् , आफुखुशी भए पनि नौलीले घर छाडिन । नौली सुभद्राको बालककाल देखिको सुख-दुःखकी साथी थिई । विधाताले सुभद्राको निमित्त नौलीरूपी एउटा दुःख पोख्ने भाँडो दिएका थिए । दुबैमा घनिष्ठ प्रेम थियो । नौलीले पात गाँस्दै भनी: "बजै, आज ता सान्है नरमाइलो लाग्यो होला ?"

"किन नौली, किन त्यसो भनिस् ? नरमाइलो लाग्नुपर्ने कुरा के छ र ?"

"तैपनि सौता भनेको मुटुको बह हो, आजै ओच्छ्यान छोड्नु पऱ्यो । भोलि घरै छाड्नुपर्छ कि, के जानिसक्नु छ ।"

"छोड्नु परे छोडिदिउँला, कुन दौलथको चैन गरेकी छु र, एक पेट खस्रो-मसिनु खाएर, दिन-रात बुहार्तन सहेकी छु । जुठो-चुल्हो गरिदिए जसले पनि एक गास खान दिन्छ । तर सोझी जस्ती छ, पस्ने बित्तिकै ढोगिदिई ।"

"सिकाएको हुँदो हो, बजै ! कुनै दिन नौलीले भनिथी भन्नुहोला । सोझो बाङ्गिन बेर लाग्दैन, अलि दिन पछि बाजेको टुपी समाउनेछिन् ।"

"जेसुकै होस् , ईश्वरले वीसासय आयु गरिदिउन् , फलेफुलेको देख्न पाइयोस् , सन्तान भए करले पनि एक अँजुलि पानी देला; यिनका हात-काखमा सास जाओस् , सब भन्दा ठूलो सन्तोष यही हो, नौली !"

३

तीन-चार वर्ष पछिको कुरा हो। एक दिन घाममा बसेर सुभद्रा छोरालाई भात खुवाइरहेकी थिइन्। सुशील चाहिं आँगनमा चरिरहेका परेवालाई पक्रने कोशिशमा थियो, सुभद्रा हातमा भातको गाँस लिएर "को खाई, को खाई" भन्थिन्। सुशील मुख बाँउदै दौडेर आउँथ्यो, सुभद्रा गाँस मुखमा हालिदिन्थिन्, बालक फेरि दौडेर परेवातिर जान्थ्यो। ती मूक पक्षीहरु पनि बालक संग आनन्दपूर्वक खेलिरहेका थिए। सुशील गई समाउन खोज्थ्यो। परेवा अलि पर गई बस्थे, सुशील फेरि उहीं पुग्थ्यो, परेवा फेरि उडेर अलि पर गई चर्न लाग्थे। सुभद्राको "को खाई" को आवाज सुनेर सुशील बीचबीचमा एक-दुई गाँस भात पनि खाएर जान्थ्यो।

देवीरमण फलैचामा बसेर यो अनुपम आनन्दप्रद बालक्रीडा हेरिरहेका थिए। उनलाई स्वर्गका डीलबाट पितृहरु पनि यस कुलावलम्बको बाललीला हेरिरहेका होलान् भन्ने भान हुन्थ्यो। उनी यो शिशु-सन्तानका आडमा एक माहान् बलिष्ठ शक्ति लुकिरहेको देख्दथे। सन्तानेच्छुक देवीरमणले आज यो दिन देख्न पाए। परिवर्तनशील संसारको गति विचित्र छ। परमेश्वर हाँस्नेलाई रुवाउँछन्, रुनेलाई हसाउँछन्।

एक दिन सुशील तुलसीका मठ नेर खेलिरहेको थियो। पिंडीबाट एक तिर लक्ष्मी, एक तिर सुभद्राले हात थापेर "नानी कता, कता, कता" भने। सुशील एक क्षण पछि दगुर्दै गै सुभद्राको छातीमा टाँसियो; सुभद्राको हृदय पवित्र पुत्र-वात्सल्यले परिपूर्ण भयो; "मेरो राजा" भनेर म्वाई खाइन्।

सुशीलालाई लक्ष्मीले जन्म मात्र दिइन्। केवल सुभद्राले हुर्काइन्। सुभद्रालाई एक छिन छोड्दैनथ्यो। सुभद्रालाई 'आमा' भन्थ्यो, आफ्नी आमालाई 'दुलही' भन्थ्यो, किनकि घरमा लक्ष्मीलाई घरमा सबै जना 'दुलही बज्यै' भन्थे।

४

माघ महीना थियो। किसानहरु बालीनाली थन्क्याई तीर्थ जाने फिक्रीमा थिए। देवीरमणलाई पनि तीर्थ जाने इच्छा भयो; मनमनले भने -- "पग चल्दै तीर्थ-वर्त नगरे कहिले गरूँला ? मानिसहरु सम्पत्ति कमाएर अन्धा बन्छन्, विवेक बुद्धिलाई खोपामा राखेर दिन-रात पैसाका निमित्त हाहाकार मच्चाइरहन्छन्। ती गोठालाहरुको सम्पत्ति एक दिन चोर या अग्निका निमित्त हुन्छ। अघि गरेको हुँदो हुँ, अहिले एक मानाको सन्तोष छ। अहिले फेरि गर्न सके सन्तानका जरामा मल पर्ला; परत्र बन्ला।" इत्यादि विचार गरेर देवीरमण तीर्थ जान तयार भए। उनको एक्लै जाने विचार थियो; परन्तु गाउँका बूढा-बूढी, विधवा स्वास्नीमानिसहरु पनि तयार भए। देख्दादेख्दै देवीरमणको विशाल आँगन तीर्थयात्रीका कुम्ले फौजले भरियो। गाउँका धेरै आइमाईहरु जान लागेको देखी लक्ष्मी पनि जान्छु भनेर जिद्दी गर्न लागिन्। सुशील चाहिं देवीरमणको दौरा समातेर रुन लाग्यो। यो बलिष्ठ बालहठलाई देवीरमणले उपेक्षा गर्न सकेनन्। आखिर लक्ष्मी र सुशीललाई पनि साथमा लिए। एक क्षण पछि त्यो तीर्थयात्रीको समूह, रानुको पछि माहुरी झैं, देवीरमणको पछि लाग्यो। किन्तु सुभद्रालाई 'जान्छ्यौ कि ?' भनेर कसैले एक वचन सम्म पनि सोधेन।

सुभद्राले मनमनले भनिन्, 'तीर्थवर्त गर्न ता मलाई पो लैजानुपर्थ्यो। मेरो को छ र, छोरा न छोरी ! उसको उमेर थियो, जाँदै गर्दा हो। उ छोरो पाएको स्वास्नी भई, वचन हार्न सक्नुभएन। म टेक्ने-समाउने केही नभएकी अनाथ, मेरो केको खोजी थियो ! मानिस बलेकै आगो ताप्छन्। जसलाई परमेश्वरले ठगेको छ, उसलाई मानिस पनि हेला गर्छन्। ओहो ! संसार कति मतलबी छ !' यस्तै तर्क गर्दै सुभद्रा धेरै बेर सम्म एक्लै रोइरहिन्।

सुभद्राले बाह्र वर्षको उमेर देखि देवीरमणको दैलो पोत्न लागिथिन्। यो घर सुभद्रालाई संसारमा सबै भन्दा प्यारो वस्तु थियो। यी वस्तभाउ, यी रुख-वृक्ष सबै यिनै सन्तानहीना रमणीका साथी थिए। यिनीहरु सँगको वियोग सुभद्रा एक छिन पनि सहन सक्तैनथिन्। जान ता जान्थिन् कि जाँदैनथिन्, एक वचन सोधेको सम्म भए उनको आँसु पुछिने थियो। एक वचन सोधि सम्म दिनाले वखतमा कत्रो काम

हुन्छ त्यो कुरा मनोविज्ञान नजानेका देवीरमणलाई थाहा भएन।

मनोमालिन्यको एउटा सानो बीज चाहिन्छ जो समयमा बढेर आफसेआफ भयङ्कर रूप धारण गर्दछ। त्यस्तै लक्ष्मी तथा सुभद्राका जीवनमा पनि यो तीर्थयात्रा मनोमालिन्यको एउटा बीज हुन गयो।

तीर्थबाट फर्केदेखि दुवैमा बहुधा झगडा हुन लाग्यो। सुभद्राले कुनै प्रश्न गर्दा लक्ष्मी छेड हानेर उत्तर दिन्थिन्। बस्, कुरैकराका हानथापबाट ठूलो कलह खडा हुन्थ्यो। देवीरमण चूपचाप भएर सुनिरहन्थे। लक्ष्मीलाई ताडना गरून् भने पुत्रवती पत्नी, सुभद्रालाई ताडना गरून् भने धर्म तथा विवेकको हत्या! के गरून्, सांसारिक सुखलिप्साको टर्रो आनन्दको अनुभव गरिरहेका थिए। त्यस बखतमा उनको त्यो प्रबल वाक्शक्ति हावा हुन्थ्यो। मानिसको पाण्डित्य अरूलाई उपदेश गर्नमा काम लाग्दछ, नकि आफुलाई परिआउँदा।

यो प्रतिदिनको गृह-कलहले सुभद्राको कोनल हृदय-कुसुम एकदम ओइलायो। उनी कारागारकी दुःखी बन्दी झैं भाग्ने मौका खोज्न लागिन्।

५

कालो अन्धकारमाथि पर्खी पर्खी कराउने हुचील पक्षीको विरसिलो हुकहुक शब्द थपिंदा रात्री झन् भयङ्कर प्रतीत हुन्थ्यो। पल्लो गाउँमा कुकुर भुकिरहेको थियो। पृथ्वीमा मानव जातिको दुःखमय अवस्था देखेर अनन्त आकाशमा तारागण पिलपिल रोइरहेका थिए। सुभद्राले आँगनमा आएर हेरिन्, एक छिन पछि त्यो विशाल नभस्थलबाट एउटा लामो ज्योति सल्ल बगेर तलतिर खस्यो। किन्तु यो कालो पृथ्वीमा झर्न नपाउँदै बीचैमा लुप्त भयो। अघि शैशवकालमा एक पटक यस्तै दृश्य देखेकी थिइन्। उस बखत आमासँग सोद्धा -- "आकाशका देवगण हुन्, पुण्य सिद्धिनाले स्वर्गबाट पतन भएका" भन्ने जवाफ मिलेथ्यो। आज उही कुरा सम्झिन्, मनमनले भनिन्, "हो, यो आकाशमा बसेर केही दिन पुण्यभोग गर्ने देवताका झैं म पनि आज सल्ल बगें। यिनीहरु पुण्य समाप्त भएपछि स्वर्गबाट चिप्लेर खस्छन्, हामी भोक, प्यास, दुःख-पीरले निस्तेज तथा ढलमल भएर पृथ्वीको पृथ्वीमै खस्छौं। हामी खसिसकेपछिको बीभत्स रूप अरु शेष भोका, प्यासा, दुःखीहरूले देख्छन्। देवताहरु चाहिं पुण्यभोगी हुनाले यो पापपूर्ण पृथ्वीमा खस्नुपर्ला भनेर बीचैमा अलप हुन्छन्। मानिसहरुमा र देवतामा केवल यत्ति अन्तर न छ!"

सुभद्राले काखीमनि एउटा पोको च्यापेकी थिइन्। यस्तो अन्धकार रात्रीमा पनि कसैले देख्छ कि भनेर ओढ्नेले छोपेकी थिइन्। यस बखत उनको जीवनाधार त्यही सानो पोको हुन आयो। कुनै बखत यो विशाल आशालता कसरी एउटा सानो ठाउँमा सीमित भएर बस्तछ! परमेश्वर, मनुष्यलाई किन आशामा झुण्ड्यायौ? प्रभु, आशाको बदला सन्तोष दिएको भए यी अनाथ प्राणीहरु सुखका कति नजीकै पुगिसक्थे।

केही बेर पछि अश्रुपूर्ण नयनले प्यारो गृहलाई सदैवका निमित्त नमस्कार गरेर अनाथिनी सुभद्रा त्यो कालो अन्धकारमा विलीन भइन्। यो करुणाजनक दृश्य सधैं जागा भइरहने विश्वको चतुर चौकीदार बाहेक अरु कसैले देखेन।

६

पशुपतिनाथका मन्दिर वरिपरि तिल राख्ने ठाउँ थिएन। सद्‌बीउ छर्ने जात्रूहरुको छिचोलीनासक्नु घुँइचो थियो। यस्तैमा पश्चिम ढोकानेर अकस्मात् सुभद्रालाई देखेर नौलीले गहभरी आँसु पारेर भनी, "ओहो बज्यै! हेर कति दुब्ली, चिन्नै नसक्ने हुनुभएछ। अलि बेर सम्म त ठम्याउनै सकिन। कहाँ बस्नुभएको छ हैं?"

"यहीं गौरीघाट फुपू कहाँ बसेकी छु।"

"खर्च-बर्च नलिइकन आधा रातमा हिंड्नुभएछ। थाहा पनि पाइन। यतिका दिन सम्म के खाएर गुजरान गर्नुभो?"

"फुपूलाई सरकारबाट एउटा हुण्डी बक्सेको रहेछ, त्यसबाट दुई जनाले गुजारा चलाएका छौं। घरको

हाल कस्तो छ, नौली ?"

"बजै, घरको हाल के भनूँ, सम्झँदा पनि आँसु आउँछ । छ महीना भो, दुलही बजै बेरामी हुनुहुन्छ ।"

"के हुन्छ ?" सुभद्राले बडो उत्सुकतासाथ सोधिन् ।

"तपनी जोरो छ, 'छाती दुख्छ' भन्नुहुन्छ । रातभर खोकिरहनुहुन्छ । गोरखा मूलका डाग्डर सुबेदारलाई देखाउँदा 'थाइसी' भने कि 'खाक्सी' भने अहिले सम्झन सकिन; साह्रै नराम्रो रोह हो अरे । सुकेर हाडछाला मात्र छ । बोकेर बाहिर-भित्र गराउनुपर्छ ।"

"सानो बाबु कस्तो छ नि ?"

"कस्ता हुन्थे, जीउभरी खटिरा छन् ! तेल लाउन हुँदैन, 'आमा कहिले आउनुहुन्छ' भनेर बराबर तपाईंलाई सम्झिरहन्छन् ।"

"भात को पकाउँछ नि ?"

"कहिले बाजे आफै पकाउनुहुन्छ, कहिले चमेना खाएर सुत्नुहुन्छ । एक दिन बार्दलीमा बसेर एक्लै रोइरहनुभएको रहेछ । 'आफूले चिनेको चौतारो पापिनीले आफै भत्काएर गई' भन्नुहुन्थ्यो । के के भनूँ बजै ! वस्तुभाउका हाडछाला मात्र छन् । खेतबारी अधियाँमा दिएको छ । असामी-पात एक पैसा उठ्दैन, नोकर-चाकर चार दिन टिक्दैनन् । सबै भताभुङ्ग छ ।"

नौलीका कुरा सुनेर सुभद्राको हृदय काटियो । मनमनै भनिन्, "छिः । 'सौताको रिसले पोइको नाक काट्नु' भनेको यही हो । उमेरदार थिई, के खाउँ के लाउँ भन्ने वेला थियो । मीठो खाई, राम्रो लाई भनेर मैले चित्त दुखाउन नहुने । उसलाई लिएर तीर्थ जानुभयो त त्यसले के भयो र ? फर्कनुभएपछि अर्को साथी लिएर म जाँदी हुँ । कहिलेकाहीं अलि झर्केर बोल्दथी लौ, अलि झडङ्गे स्वभावकी थिई; स्वभावै त्यस्तो; एक ठाउँमा भएपछि आमा-छोरीमा पनि त ठाकठुक हुन्छ । एकै घरमा बस्न नसके कटेरो बारेर बस्ती हुँ । मैले सारै बेबुझको काम गरें । जोरीपारीले के भन्दा हुन् , आफ्नो त्यत्रो दौलथ छोडेर यहाँ एक छाक खाएर बसेकी छु । त्यसका जीउमा केही भइदियो भने त्यो चिचिलो बालकको के गति होला, पितृले के भन्लान् ? चित्त दुखाए पनि आमाले दुखाई, त्यो बालकले के बिरायो ? अघि कहिलेकाहीं भात पकाउनुपर्दा दिक्क मान्नुहुन्थ्यो । आजकाल दिनहुँ कसरी पकाउनुहुदो हो ?" इत्यादि मनोवेदनाले सुभद्राको हृदय छियाछिया भयो । आँसु झार्दै भनिन्, "नौली, त्यस्ता वेलामा तैंले पनि छोडेर आइछेस् !"

"बजै, जन्म भर अर्काकी दासी भएर बस्नुपर्‍यो, चारोटा अक्षता भए पनि छरेर आउँ भनेर बीसै दिनको विदा मागेर आएकी ।"

"कोसँग आइस् ?"

"रातमाटे भँडारी पण्डितका जहानसँग ।"

"कैले जान्छेस् ?"

"भोलि बिहानै; बजै, बिन्ती छ, घर जाऔं । तपाईं नभए बाजेको जहाजै डुब्छ ।"

७

मैलो बिछ्याउनामा सुतेकी लक्ष्मी जीवनको शेष घडी गनिरहेकी थिइन् । देवीरमण रोगीका सिरानमा बसेर बखत-बखतमा चम्चाले पानी ख्वाउँथे । बालक पुत्र सुशील आमानेर बसेर यो चिर मातृवियोग हेरिरहेको थियो । लक्ष्मी कहिलेकाँहीं सुशीलको मुखपट्टि हेरेर बरर आँसु झार्थिन् । मधुरो बत्तीको प्रकाशमा रोगीको कोठा श्मशान जस्तो देखिन्थ्यो । त्यस्तैमा दैलो उघारेर नौलीले देवीरमणलाई ढोगिदिई । नौलीलाई देखेर देवीरमणका दुःखको लहरी केही शान्त भयो । भने -- "नेपालबाट कहिले आइस्, नौली ?"

"बाजे, आउँदैछु; दुलही बजैलाई कस्तो छ ?"

"तेल त अघि नै सिद्धिसकेको थियो, अब बत्ती निभ्न मात्र बाँकी छ ।"

"बाजे, यस बखतमा ठुली बजै भए सबै कुराको सम्भार हुनेथियो, के गरौं, जाऔं भनेको मान्नुभएन ।"

"के तैंले भेटिस् र ?"

"पशुपतिको मन्दिरनेर भेटेथें।"

"कस्ती थिई ?"

"एकदम दुब्ली, मैला लुगा लगाएकी, मायालाग्दी।"

"कहाँ बसेकी रैछ ?"

"गौरीघाट फुपूकहाँ बसेकी छु, फुपूलाई सरकारबाट एक हुण्डी बक्सेको छ, त्यसबाट दुई जनाले गुजारा चलाएका छौं भन्नुहुन्थ्यो।"

देवीरमणका आँखाबाट आँसुका धारा बगे। मनमनले भने, "यत्रो सम्पत्तिकी मालिक्नी भइकन सुभद्रा नेपालमा एक छाक खाएर बसेकी छ। उसमा पनि दुब्ली, मैला लुगा लगाएकी, मायालाग्दी ! हरे, परमेश्वर! म पापी हुँ, मेरो जीवनलाई हजार बार धिक्कार छ। सुभद्रा मेरी गृहलक्ष्मी हो; उ गएदेखि विपत्तिको बादलले घेरिरहेछ। हामीलाई नभए पनि यो बालक पुत्रलाई सम्झनुपर्ने, सबैलाई चटक्क बिर्सी" इत्यादि दुःखमनाउ गरेर आँसु झार्दै भने "नौली, तँ आइछेस्, घरको सम्भार राखेस्, म भोलि विहानै नेपाल जान्छु।"

त्यस्तैमा सुभद्रा घरभित्र पसिन्। अत्यन्त दुब्ली, निदाउरी, मलिन, झुत्रा लुगा लगाएकी, मुखमण्डलमा असीम करुणा तथा संयम झल्किरहेको थियो। सुभद्राको शारीरिक अवस्था देखेर देवीरमणको हृदय टुक्रा-टुक्रा भयो। दुबै हातले मुख छोपेर रुन लागे।

पतिलाई दण्डवत् गरेर सुभद्रा लक्ष्मीको सिरानमा बसिन्।

नौलीले भनी -- "ओहो! बजै, आइपुग्नुभयो ?"

"नौलीको स्वर सुनेर लक्ष्मीले आँखा उघारिन्। सुभद्रालाई आफ्ना सिरानमा बसेको देखेर, सुस्तरी लर्बरिएको स्वरले भनिन्, "दिदी, तपाईंको दर्शनलाई एक मुठी सास मुस्किलले झुण्डिइरहेको छ।"

लक्ष्मीको वचन सुनेर सुभद्राको हृदयको मैलो एकदम साफ भयो। भनिन् -- "बाबु, मैले आफ्नो कर्तव्य बिर्सिछु।"

लक्ष्मीले सुभद्राको छातीतिर देखाएर भनिन् -- "त्यहाँ साह्रै कडा चोट लागेको छ।"

सुभद्राले आँसु झार्दै भनिन् -- "निको भो बा, अस्ति नै निको भइसक्यो, सानो तिलको दाना जति पनि छैन।"

त्यस पछि "दिदी, तपाईंको नासो !" भनेर लक्ष्मीले सुशीलको हात सुभद्राका काखमा राखिदिइन्। छोरालाई काखमा लिएर सुभद्रा रुन लागिन्। यी सबै सुभद्राका निमित्त जिन्दगी भर सम्झदै रुँदै गर्ने खुड्काहरु थिए। निभ्ने वेलाको बत्ती झैं लक्ष्मीको मुख एक क्षणका निमित्त तेजोमय भयो। अनि पछि अन्धकार। लक्ष्मी यो दुःखमय असार संसारलाई छोडेर अनन्तमा पुगिन्। देवीरमण नौलीहरु पनि रुन लागे।

2. *Nāso* 'Ward'
Literal English translation

1

Although there was wealth in his house, Deviraman had no children. He made every effort for the purpose that a child be born. He built a *cautaro* (a resting platform under a tree), built a path, lit the great lamp at Pashupati; Last year, he organized [the reading of] the *Harivmasha purana* Even then Subhadra's womb could not be fruitful. While in competition with the [jealous] neighbors, Deviraman would win on all counts -- wealth, strength, and wisdom-- but his pride turned into dust as soon as he heard [someone] calling [him] 'childless'; he used to be inflicted by sorrow. He was a man of old-fashioned thinking; without a child, he considered his own wealth as trivial.

Poor Subhadra was also sad. Seeing the women of neighborhood playing with their children, she used to be excited. Because of the simple nature of a woman, she wore herbs and amulets from shamans in the hope of (having) a child . She made promises to gods and goddesses. She also went on pilgrimage, made vows, worshipped, (and) recited (the hymns). But, if the Fate does not listen, what can one do?

Astrologers offered advice to Deviraman to have a second marriage, but without the permission of Subhadra, he could not have a second marriage. Subhadra was a lady very loyal to her husband. Until today, she never hurt the feelings of Deviraman. She used to perform the services, knowing the thoughts of [her husband's] mind. The dreadful hardship of the time of Subhadrā's coming as a bride was dancing before the eyes of Deviraman even now. Remembering that condition, tears would be filled in [his] eyes. Being a friend through joy and sorrow, Subhadra made poor Deviraman wealthy. Now, how could he be ungrateful, by imposing a co-wife [on her] for having a child ?

2

The cold wind of the morning in the month of Phagun (February-March) blew as if it will pierce the heart. Devīramaṇa was seated at the (marriage) pavilion. The new bride was also seated at the same seat. The Brahmans, reading the Vedic hymns, were pouring offerings into fire. Destiny made him a bridegroom again at this age. One day, he had married Subhadra in the same manner. Today he repeated the very previous act whether it was receiving the consent of Subhadra or not. He did not have any knowledge of this matter-- Whether good or evil would result from this. Having brought a girl of twelve years, he wanted to build an imaginary castle of his mind. Perhaps, the Brahmavadi (vedanta) philosophers call it the snare of hope or mirage, I guess.

Anyway, he completed the wedding ritual, whether it was by compulsion, or by (his own) internal inspiration. At the time of giving away the bride the people on the side of the bride cried, and put the bride in the litter. The bride inside the litter also began to cry. At that time, Deviraman felt very bad. On the way the people in the wedding procession told rustic jokes to each other and laughed tittering laughter, but, in the mind of Deviraman a battle of another thought had begun to happen. He said to himself, 'was [it true] that Subhadra had given her advice with sincere mind? Why did she say 'alright', turning to the other side, when she gave her consent? Is it not true that she said alright seeing my great insistence? Oh, how people forcibly pull the consent of others to their own wishes! Fie! Is this the reward for Subhadrā's life-long service? What can I do? What [is] my fault? May the Hindu religion, which says that the way to heaven is barred to one if he does not have children, know it. I have performed the marriage by the order of religion, not by the desire for sense gratification.

The wedding procession arrived near the house of Deviraman. The rural neighbors had been watching the fun at the *chautaro* (a public gathering place under a tree). Deviraman looked into the crowd scrutinizing one by one. He did not see Subhadra in that crowd. Finally, the rock was removed from his heart. Today, Deviraman's condition was like that of a little boy who arrives late at the teacher's class forgetting the lesson of the previous day; or, it was like that of that criminal who wants to hide, seeing an acquainted person.

He remained somewhat behind by the excuse of having a conversation with a neighbor; when he arrived, Subhadrā had received the bride in, and begun to distribute the wage to the band and litter-carriers. Deviraman's heart became very delighted; he said to himself, 'Subhadra is a goddess of heaven; Why did I doubt in vain? How people are frightened by of their own work!'

Having a conversation with the guests and invited ones, Deviraman went late in his room to sleep. A mustard-seed-oil lamp was burning in a brass lamp-stand. The new bride had slept in a bed below the cot. Deviraman lay on the cot-bed. He did not see Subhadra's bed at that place. Before, Subhadra's bed used to be below the cot of Deviraman. Today when he did not see the bed in that place, the room where he slept for scores of years seemed strange to Deviraman. After a moment, having finished the chores, Subhadra entered in the room; and she began to massage the feet of Deviraman. This was her daily work. Subhadra would not let a mistake ever happen in this. Deviraman said-- "Sanu, where is your bed?"

"It is in the next room."

"Why have you moved it to the next room?"

"Tomorrow is the eleventh (day of lunar calender), I will go early to bathe in the Gandaki river."

"I will also sleep there."

"Oh, it is alright if you sleep right here."

Deviraman, who had been tired and come fell asleep soon. Having overlaid her own quilt onto her co-wife, Subhadra went into the next room. Nauli, the salve, was joining the leaves in the dim light of a faint lamp. Nauli was an old maid of Deviraman. Nauli's age agreed almost with that of Subhadra. She had been freed from a slave's life by the compassion of the Late Prime Minister Chandrashamsher Jangabahadur in the year 1982 (1925). Deviraman did not take the price of Nauli because she was an old slave at home. Nauli did not leave home, even though it was voluntary. Nauli was Subhadra's friend of weal and woes since her childhood. For Subhadra God had given in the form of Nauli a vessel for pouring (her) distress. Both had deep love for each other. Nauli, joining the leaves, said --"Bajai, today (it) must have been very unpleasant (for you)."

"Why Nauli, why did you say so? What is the matter to be unpleasant (for me)?'

"Even then, someone called a co-wife is the pain of the heart. Today (you) had to leave the bed; you may have to leave the house itself. Who knows?"

"I will leave, if I must leave. What enjoyment of wealth have I done? I have been suffering the hardship of a daughter-in-law day and night, eating a stomachful of rough food. If I do (clean) the dirty kitchen, anyone gives a mouthful (of food) to eat. But she is apparently simple; she greeted me as soon as she entered into the house. It had probably been taught to do so. Bajai, you will say some day, 'Nauli had said this.' It does not take long for something straight to be crooked. In a few days, she will be leading the old man around by his *ṭupī* (a tuft of hair the Hindus keep when they shave their head)."

"Whatever may it be; may God give a long life to her; may we get to see her flourish; if there will be a child, he will give a double-handful of water even by compulsion; may I pass away in their hands and laps. This is the greatest satisfaction of all, Nauli."

3

It was a matter after three or four years. One day, sitting in the sun, Subhadra was feeding rice to the son. Sushil, on his part, was in effort to catch the pigeons wandering in the courtyard. Subhadra, taking a mouthful of rice in hand, would say: "Who will eat? Who will eat". Sushil would come running and opening his mouth. Subhadra would put the mouthful (of rice) in his mouth. The child would go running toward the pigeons again. Those mute birds were also playing happily with the child. Sushil would go and try to catch the pigeons. Then they would go a little further and stop. Sushil would arrive there again. The pigeons would fly and go a little further and begin to feed themselves. Hearing the voice "Who will eat?" from Subhadra, Sushil would go back every now and then and and eat one or two mouthfuls of rice.

Deviraman watched this matchless pleasant child's play sitting at the porch. It seemed to him that even his ancestors were probably watching from the edge of the Heaven the play of this child, the hope of the family's future. He saw a great strong power hidden on the support of this child progeny. Deviraman, desirous of offspring, today, got to see this day. The way of the ever-changing world is peculiar. The Supreme Lord makes those who laugh weep and those who weep smile.

One day, Sushil was playing near the mound of the Tulsi plant. From the porch, Laksmi, on one side, and Subhadra, on the other, stretched their hands, shouted "Baby, which way, which way, which way.Sushil, after a moment, ran and went to stick on the chest of Subhadra.Subhadra's heart became filled with a pure love of the son. She kissed him saying "My Raja (king)". Laksmi gave only birth to Sushil. Only Subhadra raised [him]. He would not leave Subhadra even for a moment. He called Subhadra 'mother.' He called his own mother 'Dulahi' because everybody in the house called Laksmi 'Dulahi Bajai.'

4

It was the month of Magh (Jan-Feb). The farmers, having stored their crops, were concerned to go on a pilgrimage. Deviraman had also desire to go on a pilgrimage. He said to himself, "When shall I make it if I do not make the pilgrimage while I still can walk?" People become blind, gaining wealth. Putting their wisdom and good sense into a dark niche, they keep making an outcry for the sake of money day and night. The property of those boors will be for the fire or thieves. I had probably done something right before, so I have a satisfaction of a meal. The roots of my family tree will be nourished if I can do so again; my next life will be good. Having such thoughts in mind, Deviraman became ready to go on a pilgrimage. He had thought to go alone. But many old people and widows of the village were also ready to go. While one was looking on, Deviraman's courtyard was filled with an army of pilgrims loaded with their baggages. Seeing many women of the village beginning to go, Laksmi also began to insist on going, saying "I will also go". Sushil, on his part, began to cry holding on Deviraman's shirt. Deviraman could not disregard this persistence of his child. In the end, he took Laksmi and Sushil also in company. After a moment, the swarm of pilgrims, like bees following their queen, started off behind Deviraman. But no one asked Subhadra even a single word saying "Do you also want to go?"'

Subhadra said to herself, "He should have taken rather me on the pilgrimage. Who do I have? -- no son or daughter! She (Laksmi) still has [young] age; she could have gone later. She is a wife, who had borne a son. He could not reject her words. I am helpless not having anything to stand on or hold onto. Who thinks of me? (Not one thought of me). People warm themselves only at a burning fire. People have contempt for him whom God has deceived. Oh! how selfish the world is!"

Thinking as such, Subhadra kept crying alone for a long time. Subhadra had begun cleaning Deviraman's doorway (for good luck) since the age of twelve.

This house was dearest of all things in the world to Subhadra. These animals had grown to youth in the care and nourishment of this (lady). This house, these animals and these trees were all the companions of the childless woman. Subhadra could not endure the separation from them even for a moment.

As for actually going, Subhadra might have gone or, might not have gone. But her tears would have been wiped if just a word were asked. What a great work is done by asking just a word (at the right moment). That matter was not known to Deviraman who did not know psychology.

There needs to be but a small seed of ill-feeling, which assumes a terrible form of its own, growing in time. Likewise, this pilgrimage happened to be a seed of ill-feeling in the life of Laksmi and Subhadra. Since the return from the pilgrimage, quarrels began to happen frequently between the two. When Subhadra asked any question, Laksmi gave an answer with sarcasm. This went on to the point that spats developed into quarrels (when they spoke to each other). Deviraman kept listening, being silent. If he rebuked Laksmi, she was a wife with a son. If he rebuked Subhadra it would be a violation of religious duty and conscience. What could he do? He was experiencing the bitterness of one's desire for worldly pleasure. At that time, his strong power of persuasion was gone with the wind. A man's wisdom is useful in advising others, but not when it comes to oneself. Because of this daily household quarrel, Subhadra's tender heart completely withered. She began, like a suffering prisoner, to look for an opportunity to escape.

5

The night appeared more dreadful when the melancholic and intermittent hooting cry of the owl was added to it. A dog was barking in the next village. In the wide sky, stars were (seemingly) crying, seeing the miserable lot of mankind on earth. Subhadra looked up coming out into the courtyard. After a moment, a shooting star, gliding swiftly, dropped downward, but not being able to fall onto the earth, it was lost in the middle. She had seen such a sight once before in her childhood. At that time when she asked her mother, she had received an answer saying: "They are gods of the sky; because their merit has been used up, they have fallen from the heaven. Today, she remembered the same thing. She said to herself, "Yes, today I also glided swiftly like the gods after living in the sky, and enjoying the merits for some days. They fall after the merit has been used up slipping from heaven. We hungry and thirsty people, being pale and weak because of pain and suffering, fall from the earth onto the earth itself. The others, remaining hungry, thirsty, and suffering, see our terrible form after we have already fallen. Gods, because they enjoy their merits, disappear in the middle thinking that they may fall on this sinful earth. This is the only difference between gods and men. Subhadra held a bundle under her arm. She had covered it with the shawl even in such dark night so that no one may see it. At this time, that very little bundle came to be the support of her life.

Oh, how such grandiose hopes ever remain confined in a small place! O Lord, why did you suspend the people on to hope (like this)? O Lord, (5.17.2) how close to happiness these humans would be if you had given them satisfaction instead of hope! Poor Subhadra disappeared into the pitch black darkness. After some time, offering with tearful eyes a final Namaskar (goodbye) to her dear house. No one save the world's wise guardians, being ever vigilant, saw this pathetic scene.

6

Around the temple of Pashupatinath there was not room enough even to put a sesame seed. There was an impassable (thick) crowd of pilgrims scattering the *sadbiu* (lit. 'one hundred kinds of seeds'). Meanwhile, suddenly seeing Subhadra near the western gate, Nauli said with her eyes filed with tears, "Oh Bajai! Look, how thin you have become, incapable of being recognized. For a moment, I could not recognize you. Where are you staying now ?"

"I am staying here at my aunt's at Gaurighat.

"You left in the middle of the night without taking any money or food."

"I did not even know."

"How did you sustain (yourself) for so many days?"

'The King has given a pension to my aunt." The two of us have sustained ourselves from that. What is the news back home, Nauli ?"

"Bajai, what shall I say about the news from home?"

"Tears come to my eyes even when I remember it. It has been six months, Dulahi Bajai has been ill."

"What happens", Subhadra asked with a great curiosity

"She has a mild fever. She says her chest hurts. She coughs all night. When we summoned the military doctor from Gorkha, he said it was something like "phthisis" or "thesis", I could not remember exactly. It is a very bad disease, they say. She has only skin and bone. She has become so thin that she has to be carried in and out."

"And, how is the little boy ?"

"How could he be ? He has boils all over his body. We should not rub oil (on him). He says, "When will mother come?" and remembers you frequently.

"And who cooks rice?"

"Sometimes Baje (Deviraman) cooks it himself. Sometimes he goes to bed eating a few snacks. One day, he was crying alone sitting at the balcony. He said: "The sinner herself destroyed the cautaro (home) of her own making, and went away." What should I say, Bajai !' The animals have become only skin and bone. The fields and gardens are let out on half a share (to others). The debt does not return even one paisa (penny). The servants do not stay even for four days. Everything is in disarray.

Hearing the words of Nauli, Subhadra's heart was grieved. She said to herself, "Fie! This is what is said to be like cutting the nose of one's husband because of anger at the co-wife. She (Laksmi) was young. It was time for her to say what (good food) shall I eat; what (nice clothes) shall I wear?' It was not (proper) that I was upset, thinking that she ate good (food) 'she wore nice (clothes)'. He went on the pilgrimage, taking her along with him. But what did it do? I could have gone taking another friend after he returned. Sometimes, she spoke slightly angrily. She had a somewhat irritable nature. Her nature itself was like that. Sometimes a quarrel can happen even between a mother and daughter if they live at one place. I could live putting up a hut for myself. If I could not live in the same house, I did a very foolish thing. What could the neighbors possibly be saying? I am living here, leaving the great wealth of my own, and having one just one meal a day. If anything happened to her body, what will become of the little boy? What may the deceased ancestors be saying? Even if [my] mind was hurt, the mother hurt it. What wrong did the little boy do? Before, he (Deviraman) felt vexed when he had to cook one or two meals, These days, how could he cook everyday?" Subhadra's heart ached with pain as such. Shedding tears, she said, "Nauli, leaving them you too came at such a time."

"Bajai, I had to live being a slave to someone else all my life.

"Asking Baje for only twenty days' leave, I came so that I may go back scattering only a few sacred grains."

"With whom did you come?"

"I came with the family of the Ratamate Bhandari."

"When will you go?"

"I will go tomorrow morning. Bajai, I pray. Let us go home. Baje's ship will sink (he will lose everything), if you are not there."

7

Laksmi, laying on a filthy bed, marked off her life's remaining hours. Deviraman, sitting at the head of the bed, fed her water from time to time. The little boy Sushil, sitting near his mother, was watching his mother dying. Laksmi sometimes shed pouring tears, looking toward Sushil's face. In the weak light of the dim lamp the sick room looked like a crematorium. Just then, Nauli opened the door and bowed before (greeted) Deviraman. Seeing Nauli, the wave of Deviraman's sorrow abated somewhat. He said, "When did you arrive from Nepal, Naulī ?"

"Baje, I have just come; How is Dulahi Bajai ?"

'The oil had finished long before; now it only remains for the lamp to die."

"Baje, everything would be taken care of if Thuli Bajai (Subhadra) were here now; What can I do? I said, "Let us go," but she would not come."

"Did you really meet her? "

"I had met her near the temple of Pashupatinath."

"How was she?"

"Very thin, wearing dirty clothes, and pitiful."

"Where is she staying ?"

"She said, 'I am staying at Gaurighat at my aunt's. The government has given a pension to my aunt. Both of us have managed on that. Flows of tears flowed from both eyes of Deviraman. He said to himself, "Being an owner of such a big wealth, Subhadra lives eating (only) one meal. On top of that, [she is] emaciated, wearing dirty clothes, and pitiful! O Lord, I am a sinner. A thousand curses on my life. Subhadra is the goddess of my house. Since she went away, misfortune has been surrounding me. Even if (she) has no feeling for us, she ought to remember the boy. She forgot everyone completely. Making such complains, and shedding tears, he said "Nauli, you have come; Look after the house; I will go to Nepal tomorrow morning."

At that moment, Subhadra entered into in the house. She was very thin, and fatigued, wearing dirty, and torn clothes. Unlimited compassion and tranquility was shining on her face. Seeing Subhadra's physical state, Deviraman's heart was crushed. He began to cry covering his face with his hands.

Greeting her husband (by prostrating in front of him), Subhadra sat at the head of the bed of Laksmi. Nauli said, "Oh! Bajai, you have arrived?" Hearing Nauli's voice, Laksmi opened her eyes.

Seeing Subhadra seated at the head of her bed, she said in a faint and unsteady voice, "Sister, I have been hanging on to life just to have a glimpse of you."

Hearing the words of Laksmi, Subhadra forgot all her grievances. She said-- "My little one, I have forgotten my duty."

Laksmi said, pointing to the breast of Subhadra, "There is a great wound there"

'Subhadra said, shedding tears,"It has healed up, my dear baby. Indeed, it had healed up long before; There is not (even a mark) as big as a sesame seed."

Then Laksmi put Susil's hand in Subhadra's lap, saying "Sister, this is your ward (minor)."

Taking the boy in her lap, Subhadra began to cry. For Subhadra, these were the sore points (of her mind) to weep over, remembering them for the rest of her life.

Like the flame of dying lamp, Laksmi's face became bright for a moment. And then, it was dark! Leaving this sorrowful, hollow world, Laksmi arrived at the infinite. Deviraman, Nauli and others began to cry.

3. *Nāso:* The roman transliteration of the Devanāgarī text

1

1.1 gharamā cañcalāśrī bha.ikana pani devīramaṇakā santāna thienan. 1.2 santāna hos bhannākā nimitta haraeka upāya gare, cautāro cine, bāṭo khane, paśupatimā mahādīpa bāle, gae sāla harivaṃśa purāṇa lagāe, taipani subhadrāko kokha saphala huna sakena. 1.3 jorīpārīsaṃga ṭhokābājī pardā dhana, bala, buddhi sabai kurāmā devīramaṇako jita hunthyo, tara 'apūto' bhaneko sunnebittikai unako abhimāna dhūlo hunthyo, ātmaglānile pānī hunthe. 1.4 purānā vicārakā mānisa thie, santāna vinā āphno vaibhavalāī tuccha samjhanthe.

1.5 bicarī subhadrā pani khinna thi.in. 1.6 chimekakā āimāīle chorā-chorī khelāeko dekhera unalāī rahara lāgthyo, santānakā āśāle sarala nārīsvabhāvavaśa dhāmī-jhā̃krīko būṭī-jantara bā̃dhin, devī-devatāko bhākala garin, tīrtha, vrata, pūjā, pāṭha pani garin. 1.7 tara daivale nasunidiepachi kasako ke lāgdo rahecha ra?

1.8 jyotiṣīharu devīramaṇalāī arko vivāha garna sallāha dinthe. 1.9 parantu subhadrāko ādeśavinā unī arko vivāha garna saktainathe. 1.10 subhadrā bahuta patiparāyaṇā ramaṇī thi.in. 1.11 ājasamma kahilyai unale devīramaṇako citta dukhāinan, manako kurā jānera sevā garthin. 1.12 subhadrā dulahī bhaera āudāko bakhatako bhayangkara dukha ahile samma pani devīramaakā ā̃khākā sāmu nāciraheko thiyo. 1.13 u avasthā samjhā̃dā gahabharī ā̃su hunthyo. 1.14 sukha-duḥkhakī sāthī bhaera kaṅgāla devīramaṇalāī subhadrāle dhanavāna banāin. 1.15 ahile santānakā nimti sautā hālidiera kasarī kṛtaghna banūn?

2

2.1 phāguna mahīnāko bihānapakhako sireṭo muṭu cheḍlā bhane jasto garthyo. 2.2 devīramaṇa maṇḍapamā basekā thie. 2.3 nayā̃ dulahī pani ekai āsanamā basekī thi.in. 2.4 brāhmaṇaharu ṛcā paḍhera agnimā āhuti di.irahekā thie. 2.5 prārabdhale yo umeramā unalāī pherī dulāhā banāyo. 2.6 eka dina yastai rīta saṃga unale subhadrāko pāṇigrahaṇa garethe. 2.7 subhadrāko ādeśa pāī ho vā napāī ho, āja unale aghikai kṛtyalāī pheri dohoryāe. 2.8 yasabāṭa unako bhalo-kubhalo ke hune ho, yasa kurāko unalāī pani kehī jñāna thiena. 2.9 bāhra barṣakī abodha bālikālāī lyāera unī śūnya ākāśamā kalpanātīta manomandira nirmāṇa garna khojdathe. 2.10 śāyada brahmavādīharu tyasailāī āśā-pāśa yā mṛgatṛṣṇā bhanchan kyā re.

2.11 astu, karale hos vā āntarika preraṇāle hos, unale vivāha-vidhi samāpta gare. 2.12 dulahī anmāune velāmā kanyāpakṣakā mānisale rūdai dulahīlāī ḍolīmā hālidie. 2.13 dulahī pani ḍolībhitra runa lāgin. 2.14 tyasa bakhata devīramaṇalāī sāhrai naramāilo lāgyo. 2.15 bāṭāmā bariyātaharu paraspara grāmīṇa ṭhaṭṭā garera khitkā choḍī hā̃sthe, parantu devīramaṇakā kapālamā arkai vicārako dvanda huna lāgeko thiyo. 2.16 manamanale bhane, "ke subhadrāle sā̃co manale sallāha dieko ho? 2.17 sammati diṃdā kina arkopaṭṭi pharkera 'huncha' bhanekī ta? 2.18 mero jyādā āgraha dekhera 'huncha' bhanekī ta hoina? 2.19 aho! mānisaharu āphno tībra icchāmā aruko sammatilāī kasarī jabarajastī tānchan. 2.20 chiḥ! subhadrāko ājīvana sevāko puraskāra yahī ho? 2.21 ma ke garū, malāī ke doṣa? 2.22 santāna vinā svargako bāṭo chekincha bhanne hindū dharma jānos. 2.23 bhogako lālasāle hoina, dharmakā ajñāle vivāha gareko hū.

2.24 bariyāta devīramaṇakā gharanera pugyo. 2.25 gāūle chimekīharu cautārāmā ramitā heriraheka rahechan. 2.26 devīramaṇale eka-eka garī niyālera here, tyo hulamā subhadrālāī dekhenan. 2.27 balla unako chātībāṭa ḍhunggo panchiyo. 2.28 āja devīramaṇako gati tyasa bālaka chātrako jasto thiyo jo pahilo dinako pāṭha birsera abelā gurukahā̃ pugdacha, athavā tyasa aparādhīko jasto thiyo jo paricita mānisalāī dekhera lukna khojdacha.

2.29 chimekīsaṃga kurā garnāko bahānāle unī kehī pachī bhae; jā̃dā dulahī bhitryāisakī subhadrā damāī-ḍoleharulāī jyālā bā̃ḍna lāgekī rahichan. 2.30 devīramaṇako hṛdaya gadgad bhayo, manamanale bhane "subhadrā svargakī devī ho, vyarthai kina śaṅkā garē? 2.31 mānisaharu āphno kāmale kasarī āphai tarsanchan!"

2.32 pāhunā-pāsāsaṃga kurākānī garera devīramaṇa abelā koṭhāmā sutna gae. 2.33 pānasamā kaḍuvā telako battī baliraheko thiyo. 2.34 nayā̃ dulahī khāṭamani ochyānamā sutekī thi.in. 2.35 devīramaṇa khāṭamā palṭe, usa ṭhāumā subhadrāko ochyāna dekhenan. 2.36 aghi subhadrāko ochyāna devīramaṇakā khāṭamani hunthyo. 2.37 āja usa ṭhāumā nadekhdā bīsau barṣadekhi sutiraheko koṭhā pani devīramaṇalāī naulo jasto lāgyo. 2.38 eka chinapachi gṛhakṛtya samāpta garera subhadrā koṭhāmā pasin, devīramaṇako goḍā micna lāgin. 2.39 yo unako dainika kāma thiyo. 2.40 subhadrā yasamā kahilyai truṭi huna dinnathin. 2.41 devīramaṇale bhane--"sānu, timro ochyāna khoī ni?"

2.42 "pallo koṭhāmā cha."

2.43 "kina pallo koṭhāmā sāreko?"

2.44 "bholi ekādaśī ho, saberai gaṇḍakī nuhāuna jānchu."

2.45 "ma pani uhī sutchu."

2.46 "us, yahī sutnu bhae pani huncha."

2.47 thākera āekā devīramaṇalāī cā̃ḍai nidrā paryo. 2.48 āphno dolāī sautālāī khāpera subhadrā pallo koThāmā ga.in. 2.49 madhuro battīko dhamilo ujyālomā naulī ghartinī pāta gā̃sirahekī thi.i. 2.50 naulī devīramaṇako purāno chākarnī ho. 2.51 naulīko umera jhaṇḍai jhaṇḍai subhadrāsaṃga milthyo. 2.52 82 sālamā svargavāsī mahārāja candra śamaśera janggabahādurakā karuṇāle dāsa-jīvanabāṭa mukta bhaekī thi.i. 2.53 gharakī purānī cākarnī hunāle devīramaṇale naulīko mola lienan, āphukhuśī bhaepani naulīle ghara choḍina. 2.54 naulī subhadrāko bālaka-kāladekhiko sukha-duḥkhakī sāthī thi.i. 2.55

vidhātāle subhadrāko nimitta naulīrūpī euṭā du_kha pokhne bhhāḍo diekā thie. 2.56 dubaimā ghaniṣṭha prema thiyo. 2.57 naulīle pāta gāsdai bhanī--"bajai, āja tā sāhrai naramā.ilo lāgyo holā?"

2.58 "kina naulī, kina tyaso bhanis? 2.59 naramāilo lāgnuparne kurā ke cha ra?

2.60 "taipani sautā bhaneko muṭuko baha ho, ājai ochyāna choḍnu paryo. 2.61 bholi gharai chāḍnu parcha ki, ke jānisaknu cha."

2.62 "choḍnu pare choḍidiūlā, kuna daulathako caina garekī chu ra, eka peṭa khasro-masinu khāera, dina-rāta buhārtana sahekī chu. 2.63 juṭho-cūlho garidie jasale pani eka gāsa khāna dincha. 2.64 tara sojhī jastī cha, pasnebittikai ḍhogidi.ī.

2.65 "sikāeko hūdo ho; bajai! kunai dina naulīle bhanithī bhannuholā. 2.66 "sojho bāṅgina bera lāgdaina, ali dinapachi bājeko ṭupī samā.unechin."

2.67 "jesukai hos, īśvarale vīsāsaya āyu garidiun, phalephuleko dekhna pā.iyos, santāna bhae karale pani eka ājulī pānī delā; yinakā hāta-kākhamā sāsa jāos; sababhandā ṭhūlo santoṣa yahī ho, naulī!"

3

3.1 tina-cāra barṣapachiko kurā ho. 3.2 eka dina ghāmamā basera subhadrā chorālā.ī bhāta khuwā.iraheki thi.in. 3.2 suśīlacāhī āganamā cariraheka parevālāī pakrane kośiśamā thiyo, subhadrā hātamā bhātako gāsa liera "ko khā.ī, ko khā.ī" bhanthin. 3.3 suśīla mukha bāūdai dauḍera āūthyo, subhadrā gāsa mukhamā hālidinthin, bālaka pheri dauḍera parevā tira jānthyo. 3.4 tī mūka pakṣīharu pani bālakasaṃga ānandapūrvaka kheliraheka thie. 3.5 suśīla ga.ī samā.una khojthyo. 3.6 parevā ali para ga.ī basthe, suśīla pheri uhī pugthyo, parevā uḍera ali para ga.ī carna lāgthe. 3.7 subhadrāko "ko khā.ī" ko āvāja sunera suśīla bīcabīcamā eka-du.ī gāsa bhāta pani khāera jānthyo.

3.8 devīramaṇa phalaīcāmā basera yo anupama ānandaprada bālakrīḍā heriraheka thie. 3.8 unalā.ī svargakā ḍīlabāṭa pitṛharu pani yasa kulābalambako bālalīlā heriraheka holān bhanne bhāna hunthyo. 3.10 unī yo śiśu-santānakā āḍamā eka mahān baliṣṭha śakti lukiraheko dekhdathe. 3.11 santānecchuka devīramaṇale āja yo dina dekhna pāe. 3.12 parivartanaśīla saṃsārako gati vicitra cha. 3.13 parameśvara hāsnelā.ī ruvāūchan, runelā.ī hāsāūchan.

3.14 eka dina suśīla tulasīkā maṭhanera kheliraheko thiyo. 3.15 piṃḍībāṭa ekatira lakṣmī ekatira subhadrāle hāta thāpera "nānī, katā, katā, katā" bhane. 3.16 suśīla eka kṣaṇapachi dagurdai gai subhadrāko chātīmā ṭāsiyo; subhadrāko hṛdaya pavitra putra-vātsalyale paripūrṇa bhayo; "mero rājā" bhanera mvā.ī khā.in.

3.17 suśīlalā.ī lakṣmīle janma mātra di.in, kevala subhadrāle hurkā.in. 3.18 subhadrālāī eka china choḍdainathyo. 3.19 subhadrālāī 'āmā' bhanthyo, āphnī āmālāī 'dulahī' bhanthyo, kinaki lakṣmīlāī gharamā savaijanā 'dulahī bajyai' bhanthe.

4

4.1 māgha mahīnā thiyo. 4.2 kisānaharu bālīnālī thankyāī tīrtha jāne phikrīmā thie. 4.3 devīramaṇalā.ī pani tīrtha garne icchā bhayo; manamanale bhane "paga caldai tīrtha-varta nagare kahile garūlā? 4.4 mānisaharu sampatti pāera andhā banchan, viveka buddhilā.ī khopāmā rākhera dina-rāta paisākā nimitta hāhākāra maccā.irahanchan. 4.5 tī goṭhālāharuko sampatti eka dina agni yā corakā nimitta huncha. 4.6 aghi gareko hūdo hū, ahile eka mānāko santoṣa cha. 4.7 ahile pheri garna sake santānakā jarāmā mala parlā; paratra banlā." 4.8 ityādi vicāra garera devīramaṇa tīrtha jāna tayāra bhae. 4.9 unako eklai jāne vicāra thiyo; parantu gāūkā kaiyana būḍhābūḍhī, vidhavā svāsnīmānisaharu pani tayāra bhae. 4.10 dekhdādekhdai devīramaṇako āgana tīrthayātrākā kumle phaujale bhariyo. 4.11 gāūkā dherai āimāīharu jāna lāgeko dekhī lakṣmī pani jānchu bhanera jiddī garna lāgin. 4.12 suśīlacāhiṃ devīramaṇako daurā samātera runa lāgyo. 4.13 yo baliṣṭha bālahaṭhalā.ī devīramaṇale upekṣā garna sakenan. 4.14 ākhira lakṣmī ra suśīlalā.ī pani sāthamā lie. 4.15 eka kṣaṇapachi tyo tīrthayātrīko samūha, rānuko pachi māhurī jhaī, devīramaṇako pachi lāgyo. 4.14 kintu subhadrālā.ī 'jānchyau ki?' bhanera kasaile eka vacana samma pani sodhena.

4.15 subhadrāle manamanale bhanin, 'tīrtha-varta garna tā malā.ī po laijānuparthyo. 4.16 mero ko cha ra, chorā na chorī! 4.17 usako umera thiyo, jādai gardī ho. 4.18 u choro pāekī svāsnī bha.ī, vacana hārna saknubhaena. 4.19 ma ṭekne-samāune kehī nabhaekī anātha, mero keko khojī thiyo! 4.20 mānisa balekai āgo tāpchan. 4.21 jasalā.ī parameśvarale ṭhageko cha, usalā.ī mānisa pani helā garchan. 4.22 aho! saṃsāra kati matalabī cha!' 4.23 yastai tarka gardai subhadrā dherai berasamma eklai roirahin.

4.24 subhadrāle bāhra varṣako umeradekhi devīramaṇako dailo potna lāgithin. 4.25 yo ghara subhadrālā.ī saṃsāramā sabai bhandā pyāro vastu thiyo. 4.26 yī vastubhāu yinaiko lālana-pālanamā baḍhera taruṇa bhaekā thie. 4.27 yo ghara, yī bastubhāu, yī rukha-vṛkṣa sabai yinai santānahīnā ramaṇīkā sāthī thie. 4.28 yinīharusaṃgako viyoga subhadrā eka china pani sahana saktinathin. 4.29 jāna tā subhadrā jānthin ki jādainathin, eka vacana sodheko samma bhae unako āsu puchine thiyo. 4.30 eka vacana sodhisamma dināle bakhatamā katro kāma huncha tyo kurā manovijñāna najānekā devīramaṇalā.ī thāhā bhaena.

4.31 manomālinyako euṭā sāno bīja cāhincha jo samayamā baḍhera āphaseāpha bhayangkara rūpa dhāraṇa gardacha. 4.32 tyasatai lakṣmī tathā subhadrākā jīvanamā pani yo tīrthayātrā manomālinyako euṭā bīja huna gayo.

4.33 tīrthabāṭa pharkedekhi duvaimā bahudhā jhagaḍā huna lāgyo. 4.34 subhadrāle kunai praśna gardā lakṣmī cheḍa hānera uttara dinthin. 4.35 basa, kuraikurākā hānathāpabāṭa ṭhulo kalaha khaḍā hunthyo. 4.36 devīramaṇa cūpacāpa bhaera sunirahanthe. 4.37 lakṣmīlā.ī tāḍanā garūn bhane putravatī patnī, subhadrālā.ī tāḍanā garūn bhane dharma tathā vivekako hatyā! 4.38 ke garūn, sāṃsārika sukhalipsāko ṭarro ānandako anubhava garirahekā thie. 4.39 tyasa bakhatamā unako tyo prabala vākśakti hāvā hunthyo. 4.40 mānisako pāṇḍitya arulā.ī upadeśa garnamā kāma lāgdacha, na ki āphūlā.ī pariāūdā.

4.41 yo pratidinako gṛhakalahale subhadrāko komala hṛdaya-kusuma ekadama oilāyo. 4.42 unī kārāgārakī duḥkhī bandī jhaĩ bhāgne maukā khojna lāgin.

5

5.1 kālo andhakāramāthi parkhī parkhī karā.une hucīla pakṣīko virasilo hukahuka śabda thapiṃdā rātrī jhan bhayangkara pratīta hunthyo. 5.2 pallo gāũmā kukura bhukiraheko thiyo. 5.3 pṛthvīmā mānavajātiko duḥkhamaya avasthā dekhera ananta ākāśamā tārāgaṇa pilapila roiraheka thie. 5.4 subhadrāle āganamā āera herin, eka chinapachi tyo viśāla nabhasthalabāṭa euṭā lāmo jyoti salla bagera talatira khasyo. 5.5 kintu yo kālo pṛthvīmā jharna napāũdai bīcaimā lupta bhayo. 5.6 aghi śaiśavakālamā yastai dṛṣya dekhekī thi.in. 5.7 usa bakhata āmāsṃga sodhdā--"ākāśakā devagaṇa hun, puṇya siddhināle svargabāṭa patana bhaekā" bhanne javāpha milethyo. 5.8 āja uhī kurā samjhin, manamanale bhanin, "ho! yo ākāśamā basera kehi dina puṇyabhoga garne devatākā jhaĩ ma pani āja salla bagẽ. 5.9 yinīharu puṇya samāpta bhaepachi svargabāṭa ciplera khaschan, hāmī bhoka, pyāsa, duḥkha-pīrale nisteja tatha ḍhalamala bhaera pṛthvīko pṛthvīmai khaschaũ. 5.9 hāmī khasisakepachiko bībhatsa rūpa aru śeṣa bhokā, pyāsā, duḥkhīharule dekhchan! 5.10 devatāharu cāhĩ puṇyabhogī hunāle yo pāpapūrṇa jagatamā khasnuparlā bhanera bicaimā alapa hunchan, mānisaharumā ra devatāmā kevala yatti antara na cha!"

5.11 subhadrāle kākhīmani euṭā poko cyāpekī thi.in. 5.12 yasto andhakāra rātrīmā pani kasaile dekhcha ki bhanera oḍhnele chopekī thi.in. 5.13 yasa bakhata unako jīvanādhāra tyahī sāno poko huna āyo. 5.14 aho! kunai bakhata yo viśāla āśālatā kasarī euṭā sāno ṭhāũmā sīmita bhaera bastacha! 5.15 parameśvara ! manuṣyalā.ī kina āśāmā jhuṇḍyāyau? 5.16 prabhu! āśāko badalā santoṣa dieko bhae yī anātha prāṇīharu sukhakā kati najīkai pugisakthe.

5.17 kehī berapachi aśrupūrṇa nayanale pyāro gṛhalā.ī sadaivakā nimitta namaskāra garera anāthinī subhadrā tyo kālo andhakāramā vilīna bha.in. 5.18 yo karuṇājanaka dṛṣya sadhaiṃ jāgā bhairahane viśvako catura caukīdāra bāheka aru kasaile dekhena.

6

6.1 paśupatināthakā mandira waripari tila rākhne ṭhāũ thiena. 6.2 "sadbīu" charne jātrūharuko chicolī nasaknu ghuīco thiyo. 6.3 yastaimā paścima ḍhokānera akasmāt subhadrālā.ī dekhera naulīle gahabharī āsu pārera bhanī, "oho bajai! hera kati dublī, cinnai nasakne hunubhaecha. 6.4 aliberasamma ta ṭhamyāunai sakina. 6.5 kahā̃ basnubhaeko cha hā̃?"

6.6 "yahī gaurīghāṭa phupūkahā̃ basekī chu."

6.7 "kharca-barca nali.ikana ādhā rātamā hīḍnu bhaecha. 6.8 thāhā pani pāina.

6.9 yatikā dinasamma ke khāera gujarāna garnubhayo?"

6.10 phupūlā.ī sarakārabāṭa euṭā haṇḍī bakseko rahecha, tyasabāṭa duī janāle gujārā calāekā chaū. 6.11 gharako hāla kasto cha, naulī?"

6.12 "bajai, gharako hāla ke bhanū, samjhadā pani ā̃su āūcha. 6.13 cha mahīnā bho, dulahī bajai berāmī hunuhuncha."

6.14 "ke huncha?" subhadrāle sā̃hrai utsukatāsātha sodhin.

6.15 "tapanī jaro cha, 'chātī dukhcha' bhannuhuncha. 6.16 rātabhara khokirahanuhuncha. 6.17 gorakhā mulakā ḍāgḍara subidāralā.ī dekhāūdā 'thāisī' bhane ki 'khāksī' bhane ahile samjhana sakina, sā̃hrai narāmro roga ho are. 6.18 sukera hāḍachālā mātra cha. 6.19 bokera bāhira-bhitra garā.unu parcha."

6.20 "sāno bābu kasto cha ni?"

6.21 "kastā hunthe, jīubharī khaṭirā chan! tela lāuna hūdaina, 'āmā kahile ā.unuhuncha' bhanera barābara tapāīlā.ī samjhirahanchan."

6.22 "bhāta ko pakāūcha ni?"

6.23 "kahile bāje āphai pakā.unuhuncha, kahile camenā khāera sutnuhuncha. 6.24 eka dina bārdalīmā basera eklai roīrahanubhaeko rahecha. 6.25 'āphūle cineko cautāro pāpinīle āphai bhatkāera ga.ī' bhannuhunthyo. 6.26 keke bhanū bajai! bastubhāukā hāḍachālā mātra chan. 6.27 kheta-bārī adhiyā̃mā dieko cha. 6.28 asāmīpāta eka paisā uṭhdaina, nokara-cākara cāra dina ṭikdainan, sabai bhatābhuṅga cha."

6.29 naulīkā kurā sunera subhadrāko hṛdaya kāṭiyo. 6.30 manamanai bhanin, "chiḥ. 6.31 'sautāko rīsale poiko nāka kāṭnu' bhaneko yahī ho. 6.32 umeradāra thi.i, ke khāū ke lāū bhanne velā thiyo. 6.33 mīṭho khā.ī rāmro lā.ī bhanera maile citta dukhāuna nahune. 6.34 usalā.ī liera tīrtha jānubhayo ta tyasale ke bhayo ra? 6.35 pharkanubhaepachi arko sāthī liera ma jā̃dī hū. 6.36 kahilekāhī ali jharkera boldathī lau; ali jhaḍaṅge svabhāvakī thi.i. svabhāvai tyasto; eka ṭhāūmā basepachi kahilekāhī āmā-chorīmā pani ta ṭhāka-ṭhuka huncha. 6.37 ekai gharamā basna nasake kaṭero bārera bastī hū. 6.38 maile sā̃hrai bebujhako kāma garẽ. 6.39 jorīpārīle ke bhandā hun, āphno tyatro daulatha choḍera yahā̃ eka chāka khāera basekī chu, tyasakā jīumā kehī bhaidiyo bhane tyo cicilo bālakhako ke gati holā, pitṛle ke bhanlān? 6.40 chitta dukhāe pani āmāle dukhāī, tyo bālakale ke birāyo? 6.41 aghi eka-duī chāka bhāta pakāunu pardā dikka mānnu hunthyo. 6.42 ājakāla dinahū kasarī pakāunuhūdo ho? ityādi manovedanāle subhadrāko hṛdaya chiyāchiyā bhayo; ā̃su jhārdai bhanin, "naulī! tyastā belāmā taiṃle pani choḍera ā.iches!"

6.43 "bajai, janmabhara arkākī dāsī bhaera basnuparyo, cāroṭā akṣatā bhae pani charera āū bhanera bājesā̃ga bīsai dinako bidā māgera āekī."

6.44 "ko sā̃ga āīs?"

6.45 "rātamāṭe bhāḍārīkā jahānasā̃ga."

6.46 "kaile jānches?"

6.47 "bholi bihānai, bajai, bintī cha, ghara jā.aū 6.48 tapāī nabhae bājeko jahājai ḍubcha.

7

7.1 mailo bichyā.unāmā sutekī lakṣmī jīvanako śeṣa ghaḍī ganīrahekī thi.in. 7.2 devīramaṇa rogīkā sirānamā basera bakhata-bakhatamā camcāle pānī khvāūthe. 7.3 bālaka putra suśīla āmānera basera yo cira mātṛviyoga heriraheko thiyo. 7.4 lakṣmī kahilekāhī suśīlako mukhapaṭṭi herera barara āsu jhārthin. 7.5 malino battīko dhamilo prakāśamā rogīko koṭhā śmaśāna jasto dekhinthyo. 7.6 tyastaimā dailo ughārera naulīle devīramaṇalā.ī ḍhogidi.i. 7.7 naulīlā.ī dekhera devīramaṇakā duḥkhako laharī kehī śānta bhayo; bhane-- "nepālabāṭa kahile āīpugis, naulī?"

7.8 "bāje, āuṃdaichu; dulahī bajailā.ī kasto cha?

7.9 "tela ta aghi nai siddhisakeko thiyo, aba battī nibhna bākī cha."

7.10 "bāje, yasa bakhatamā ṭhulī bajai bhae sabai kurāko sambhāra hune thiyo, ke garū, jā.aū bhaneko mānnubhaena."

7.11 "ke taīle bheṭis ra?"

7.12 "paśupatināthako mandiranera bheṭethē."

7.13 "kastī thi.ī?"

7.14 "ekadama dublī, mailā lugā lagāekī, māyālāgdī."

7.15 "kahā basekī raicha?"

7.16 "'gaurīghāṭa phupūkahā basekī chu, phupūlāī sarakārabāṭa eka haṇḍī bakseko cha, tyasaibāṭa duī janāle gujārā calāekā chaū bhannuhunthyo."

7.18 devīramaṇakā dubai ākhābāṭa āsukā dhārā bage. 7.19 manamanale bhane -- 'yatro sampattikī mālikni bhaikana subhadrā eka chāka khāera basekī cha. 7.20 usamā pani dublī, mailā lugā lagāekī, māyālāgdī! 7.21 hare, parameśvara! ma pāpī hū, mero jīvanalāī hajāra vāra dhikkāra cha. 7.22 subhadrā merī gṛhalakṣmī ho; u gaedekhi vipattiko bādalale gherirahecha. 7.23 hāmīlā.ī nabhae pani yo bālaka santānalā.ī samjhanuparne, sabailā.ī caṭakka birsī' ityādi duḥkhamanāu garera āsu jhārdai bhane, "naulī! tā āiches, gharako sambhāra rākhes, ma bholi bihānai nepāla jānchu."

7.24 tyastaimā subhadrā gharabhitra pasin. 7.25 atyanta dublī, nidā.urī, malina, jhutrā lugā lāekī, mukhamaṇḍalamā asīma karuṇā tathā saṃyama jhalkiraheko thiyo. 7.26 subhadrāko śārīrika avasthā dekhera devīramaṇako hṛdaya ṭukrā-ṭukrā bhayo. 7.27 dubai hātale mukha chopera runa lāge.

7.28 patilā.ī daṇḍavat garera subhadrā lakṣmīko sirānamā basin.

7.29 naulīle bhanī--"oho! bajai āīpugnubho?"

7.30 naulīko svara sunera lakṣmīle ākhā ughārin. 7.31 subhadrālā.ī āphnā sirānamā baseko dekhera, sustarī larbarieko svarale bhanin--"didī, tapāīko darśanalā.ī eka muṭhī sāsa muskilale jhuṇḍiraheko cha."

7.32 lakṣmīko vacana sunera subhadrāko hṛdayako mailo ekadama sāpha bhayo. 7.33 bhanin-- "bābu! maile āphno kartavya birsichu."

7.34 lakṣmīle subhadrāko chātītira dekhāera bhanin--"tyahā̃ sāhrai kaḍā coṭa lāgeko cha."

7.35 subhadrāle ā̃su jhārdai bhanin-- "niko bho bā, asti nai niko bha.isakyo, sāno tilako dānā jati pani chaina."

7.36 tyasa pachi "didi, tapā̃īko nāso!" bhanera lakṣmīle suśīlako hāta subhadrākā kākhamā rākhidi.in. 7.37 chorālā.ī kākhamā liera subhadrā runa lāgin. 7.38 yī sabai subhadrākā nimitta jindagībhara samjhā̃dai rūdai garne khuḍkāharu thie.

7.39 nibhne belāko battī jhaī̃ lakṣmīko mukha eka kṣaṇakā nimitta tejomaya bhayo! 7.40 ani pachi andhakāra! 7.41 lakṣmī yo duḥkhamaya asāra saṃsāralā.ī choḍera anantamā pugin. 7.42 devīramaṇa, naulīharu pani runa lāge.

4. *Nāso:* Clause analysis

1.1.1 ±(1.1.2) ± देवीरमणका सन्तान +थिएनन्
± (1.1.2) ±devīramaṇakā santāna +thienan
±AD:Cl(1.1.2) ±S:CNP-nm +P:iv1-3pl.pst.neg
± (1.1.2) ±Devīramaṇa-of children +they-were-not
'Deviraman had no children.'

1.1.2 ±घरमा ±चञ्चलाश्री +भइकन ±पनि
±gharamā ±cañcalāśrī +bha.ikana ±pani
±LA:cn-lc ±S:cn-nm +P:iv1-abs.prt ±C:sc
±house-in ±wealth +being ±although
'Although there was wealth in his house,'

1.2.1 ±(1.2.2) +हरएक उपाय +गरे
± (1.2.2) +haraeka upāya +gare
±AA:Cl(1.2.2) +DO:CNP-ac +P:tv1-3sg.pst.m
± (1.2.2) +every means +he-did,
'(1.2.2) (He) made every effort'

1.2.2 +(1.2.3) ±भन्नाका निमित्त
+(1.2.3) ± bhannākā nimitta
+DO:Cl (1.2.3) ±AA: PP
+(1.2.3) ± saying-of purpose
'for the purpose (1.2.3)'

1.2.3 ± सन्तान +होस्
±santāna +hos
±S:cn-nm +P:iv1-3sg-imp
child+ may-be
'that a child be [born];'

1.2.4 +चौतारो +चिने,
+cautāro+ cine,
+DO:cn-ac +P:tv1-3sg.pst.m
+*cautāro* + he-built
'He built a *cautāro* [a resting platform under a tree],'

1.2.5 +बाटो +खने,
+bāṭo +khane,
+DO:cn-ac +P:tv1-3sg.pst.m
+path +he-dug
'he built a path,'

1.2.6 ± पशुपतिमा +महादीप +बाले,
± paśupatimā+ mahādīpa +bāle,
±LA:pn-lc +DO:cn-ac +P:tv1-3sg.pst.m
±Paśupati-at +great-lamp +he-lit
'he lit the great lamp at Paśupati,'

1.2.7 ± गए साल +हरिवंश पुराण +लगाए
±gae sāla +harivaṃśa purāṇa +lagāe,
±AA:AdvP +DO:PNP-ac +P:tv1-3sg.pst.m
±gone year +*Harivaṃśa Purāṇa* +he-organized
'Last year, he organized (the reading of) the *Harivaṃśa Purāṇa*.'

1.2.8 ± तैपनि +सुभद्राको कोख +सफल +हुन सकेन
±taipani +subhadrāko kokha +saphala +huna sakena
±C:cc+ ±S:CNP-nm +SC:adj-nm +P:eVP1-3sg.pst.neg
±then-even +Subhadrā-of womb +fruitful +to-be could-not
'Even then Subhadrā's womb could be fruitful.'

1.3.1 ± (1.3.2) ±धन, बल, बुद्धि सवै कुरामा ± देवीरमणको जित +हुन्थ्यो
±(1.3.2) ±dhana, bala, buddhi savai kurāmā ±devīramaṇako jita +hunthyo,
±AD:Cl (1.3.2) ±LA:modCNP-lc ±S:CNP-nm +P:iv1-3sg.pst.m
±(1.3.2) ±wealth, strength, wisdom all matters-in ±Devīramaṇ's victory +used-to-be,
'Deviraman would win on all counts -- wealth, strength and wisdom.'

1.3.2 ± जोरीपारीसंग ± ठोकाबाजी +पर्दा
±jorīpārī-saṃga ±ṭhokābājī +pardā
±AA:PP ±S:cn-nm +P:iv1-impf.prt.
±neihghbors-with ±competition +while-happening
While in competition with the (jealous) neighbors',

1.3.3 ± तर ± (1.3.4) ±उनको अभिमान +धूलो +हुन्थ्यो
±tara ±(1.3.4) ±unako abhimāna +dhūlo +hunthyo,
±C:cc ±AD:Cl(1.3.4) ±S:CNP-nm +SC:cn-nm +P:ev1-3sg.pst.m
±but ±(1.3.5) ±his pride +dust +used-to-be
'but his pride turned into dust (1.3.4-5)'

1.3.4 +(1.3.5) +सुन्ने ±बित्तिकै
+(1.3.5) +sunne ±bittikai
+DO:Cl (1.3.5) +P:tv1-impf.prt ±AA:advl
+(1.3.5) +hearing ±as-soon-as
'as soon as he heard'

1.3.5 +'अपूतो' +भनेको
+'apūto' +bhaneko
+DO:adj-nm +P:tv1-prf.prt.
+childless +called
'calling 'childless''

1.3.6 ± आत्मग्लानिले +पानी +हुन्थे
±ātmaglānile +pānī +hunthe
±IA:cn-in +SC:cn-nm +P:ev1-3sg.pst.m
±self-sorrow-by +water +he-used-to-be
'He used to be inflicted by sorrow'

1.4.1 +पुराना विचारका मानिस +थिए
+purānā vicārakā mānisa +thie,
+SC:CNP-nm +P:ev1-3sg.pst.m
+old thought-of man +he-was
'He was a man of old-fashioned thinking'

1.4.2 ± सन्तान विना +आफ्नो वैभवलाई +तुच्छ +संझन्थे
±santāna-vinā +āphno vaibhavalā.ī +tuccha +samjhanthe
±AA:PP +DO:CNP-ac +OC:adj-ac +P:tv3-3sg.pst.m
±child-without +one's-own wealth-to +trivial +he-used-to-consider
'Without a child, he used to consider his own wealth as trivial.'

1.5.1 ±बिचरी सुभद्रा ±पनि +खिन्न +थिइन्
±bicarī subhadrā +pani +khinna +thi.in
±S:CNP-nm +SC:adj-nm +P:ev1-3sg.pst.f
±Poor Subhadrā also +sad +she-was
'Poor Subhadrā was also sad.'

1.6.1 ±(1.6.2) +उनलाई ±रहर +लाग्थ्यो
±(1.6.2) +unalā.ī ±rahara +lāgthyo,
±AD:Cl(1.6.2) +DC:pro-dt ±S:cn-nm +P:iv2-3sg.pst.m
±(1.6.2) +her-to ±interest +he-used-to-strike
'She used to be interested (excited)'

1.6.2 +(1.6.3) +देखेर
+(1.6.3) +dekhera
+DO:Cl(1.6.1) +P:tv1-abs.prt.
+(1.6.1) +having-seen
'Seeing (1.6.1)'

1.6.3 ±छिमेकका आइमाईले +छोरा-छोरी +खेलाएको
±chimekakā ā.imā.īle +chorā-chorī +khelāeko
±S:CNP-nm +DO:Cmpdcn-ac +P:tv1-prf.prt
±Neighborhood-of women-by +sons-daughters +playing-with
'The women of neighborhood playing with their children;'

1.6.4 ±सन्तानका आशाले ±सरल नारीस्वभाववश +धामी झाँक्रीको बूटी-जन्तर +बाँधिन्
±santānakā āśāle ±sarala nārīsvabhāvavaśa +dhāmī-jhā̃krīko būṭī-jantara +bā̃dhin,
±AA:CNP-in ±AA:AdvP +DO:modCNP-ac +P:tv1-3sg.pst.f
±chid-of hope-by +simple woman-nature-cause +shaman's herb-amulet +she-tied
'In the hope of (having) a child, because of simple nature of woman, she wore herbs and amulets from shamans'

1.6.5 +देवीदेवताको भाकल +गरिन्
+devī-devatāko bhākala +garin ,
+DO:CNP-ac +P:tv1-3sg.pst.f
+goddess-god-of promise +she-did
'She made promises to gods and goddesses'

1.6.6 +तीर्थ व्रत, पूजा पाठ ±पनि +गरिन्
+tīrtha, vrata, pūjā, pāṭha ±pani +garin
+DO:cn-nm ±AA: advl +P:tv1-3sg.pst.f
+pilgrimage, vow, worshipping, recitation ±also +she-did
'She also went on pilgrimage, made vows, worshipping, (and) the recitation (of hymns)'

1.7.1 ± तर ±(1.7.2) ±कसको के +लाग्दो रहेछ ±र?
±tara ±(1.7.2) ±kasako ke +lāgdo rahecha ±ra?
±C:c+ ±AD:Cl (1.7.2) ±S:ProP-nm +P:iVP-3sg.pres.m ±NU:nu (*ra*)
±But ±(1.7.2) +whose what +striking he-is +*ra* (question word)
'But, (1.7.2) what could one do?'

1.7.2 ± दैवले +नसुनिदिए ±पछि
±daivale +nasunidie ±pachi
±S:cn-nm +P:iVP1-neg.cond ±C: sc (*pachi*)

±Fate +not-listen ±if
'if the Fate does not listen'

1.8.1 ±ज्योतिषीहरु +देवीरमणलाई +(1.8.2) सल्लाह् +दिन्थे ।
±jyotiṣīharu +devīramaṇalāī +(1.8.2) +sallāha +dinthe.
±S:cn-nm +DC:pn-dt +DO: ModCNP-ac +P:tv2-3pl.pst.m
±astrologers +Devīramaṇa-to +(1.8.2) advice +they-used-to-offer
'Astrologers offered advice to Devīramaṇa'

1.8.2 + अर्को विवाह् +गर्न
+arko vivāha +garna
+DO:CNP-ac +P:tv1-inf
+another marriage +to-do
'to have a second marriage'

1.9.1 ±परन्तु ±सुभद्राको आदेशविना ±उनी +(1.9.2) +सक्दैनथे
±parantu ±subhadrāko ādeśa-vinā ±unī +(1.9.2) +saktainathe
±C:cc ±AA:PP ±S:pro-nm +DO:Cl(1.9.2) +P:tv1-3sg.pst.m
±but ±Subhadrā-of permission-without +he +(1.9.2)
+he-habitually-could-not
'but, without the permission of Subhadrā, he could not (9.1.2)'

1.9.2 +अर्को विवाह् +गर्न
+arko vivāha +garna
+DO:CNP-ac +P:tv1-inf
+another marriage +to-do
'have a second marriage'

1.10.1 ±सुभद्रा +बहुत पतिपरायणा रमणी +थिइन्
+subhadrā +bahuta patiparāyaṇā ramaṇī +thi.in
±S:pn +SC:modCNP-nm +P:ev1-3sg.f
±Subhadrā +very husband-devoted lady +she-was
'Subhadrā was a lady highly devoted to (her) husband.'

1.11.1 ±आजसम्म ±उनले ±कहिल्यै +देवीरमणको चित्त +दुखाइनन्
+āja-samma +kahilyai +unale +devīramaṇako citta +dukhā.inan
±AA:PP ±AA:advl ±S:pro-nm +DO:CNP-ac +P:tv1-3sg-neg.pst.f
±today-until ±ever ±she +Devīramaṇa-of mind +she-did-not-hurt
'Until today, she never hurt the mind of Devīramaṇa.'

1.11.2 ±(1.11.3) +सेवा +गर्थिन्
+(1.11.3) +sevā +garthin
±AD:Cl (1.11.3) +DO:cn-ac +P:tv1-3sg.pst.f

±(1.11.3) +service +she-used-to-do
'She used to do the work (1.11.3)'

1.11.3 +मनको कुरा +जानेर
+manako kurā +jānera
+DO:CNP-ac +P:tv1-abs.prt.
+mind-of things +having-known
'knowing the thoughts of (her husband's) mind'

1.12.2 ±(1.12.2) बखतको भयङ्कर दुःख ±अहिले सम्म पनि ±देवीरमणका आँखाका सामु +नाचिरहेको थियो
±(1.12.2) bakhatako bhayaṅkara duḥkha ±ahile samma pani ±devīramaṇakā ā̃khākā sāmu +nāciraheko thiyo.
±S:Mod(1.12.2)CNP-nm ±AA:AdvlP ±LA:PP +P:iVP1-3sg.pst.prt
±time-of dreadful hardship ±now until also ±Devīramaṇa-of eyes-of before +dancing was
'The dreadful hardship of the time (1.12.2) was dancing before the eyes of Devīramaṇa even until now'

1.12.2 ±सुभद्रा +(1.12.3) +आउँदाको
+subhadrā +(1.12.3) +āũdāko
±S:pn-nm ±AD:Cl(1.12.3)+ +P:iv1-impf.prt.+pp
+Subhadrā (1.12.3) +coming-of
'of Subhadrā's coming (1.12.3)'

1.12.3 +दुलही +भएर
+dulahī +bhaera
+SC:cn-nm +P:ev1-abs.prt.
+bride +having-been
'being (as) a bride.'

1.13.1 +(1.13.2) +गह्भरी +आँसु +हुन्थ्यो
+(1.13.2) +gaha-bharī +ā~su +hunthyo
±AD:Cl(1.13.2)+ ±LC:PP+ ±S:cn-nm+ +P:iv3-3sg.pst.m
±(1.13.2)+ eyes-full +tears +he-used-to be'
'Tears would be filled in (his) eyes'

1.13.2 + उ अवस्था +सम्झदा
+u avasthā +samjhadā
+DO:modCNP-ac +P-tv1-imp.prt.
+that condition +while-remembering
'Remembering that condition,'

1.14.1 ±(1.14.2) +कङ्गाल देवीरमणलाई ±सुभद्राले +धनवान +बनाइन्
±(1.14.2) +kaṅgāla devīramaṇalāī ±subhadrāle +dhanavāna +banāin
±AD:PrtCl(1.14.2) +DO:PNP-ac ±S:pn-n +OC:adj-ac +P:tv3-3sg.pst.f
±(1.14.2) +poor Devīraman ±Subhadrā +wealthy +she-made
'(1.14.2) Subhadrā made poor Devīramaṇa wealthy'

1.14.2 +सुख-दुःखकी साथी +भएर
+sukha-duḥkhakī sāthī +bhaera
+SC:CNP-nm +P:ev1-abs.prt.
+joy-sorrow-of friend +having-been
'Being a friend through joy and sorrow,'

1.15.1 ±अहिले ±(1.15.2) ±कसरी +कृतघ्न +बनून् ?
±ahile ±(1.15.2) ±kasarī +kṛtaghna +banūn?
±AA:advl ±AD:Cl ±AA:adv +SC:adj-nm +P:ev1-3sg.opt.
±now +(1.15.2) ±how +ungrateful +may-he-become?
'Now, how could he be ungrateful (1.15.2)?

1.15.2 ±सन्तानका निम्ति +सौता +हालिदिएर
±santānakā nimti +sautā +hālidiera
±AA:PP +DO:cn-ac +P:tv1-abs.prt.
±child-of for +co-wife +having-put
'by imposing a co-wife (on her) for having a child'

2.1.1 ±फागुन महीनाको बिहानपखको सिरेटो +(2.1.2) +गर्थ्यो
±phāguna mahīnāko bihānapakhako sireṭo +(2.1.2) +garthyo
±S:CNP-nm +DO:Cl(2.1.2) +P:tv1-3sg.pst.m
±Phāguna month-of morning-time-of cold-wind +(2.1.2) +used-to-act
'The cold wind of the morning in the month of Phāguna (Feb.-Mar.) blew'

2.1.2 +(2.1.3) +भने +जस्तो
+(2.1.3) +bhane +jasto
+DO:Cl(2.1.3) +P:tv1-imprf.prt ±AA:advl
+saying ±as
'as if'

2.1.3 +मुटु +छेड्ला
+muṭu +cheḍlā
+DO:cn-ac +P:tv1-3sg.fut.m
+heart +pierce-he-will
'It will pierce the heart.'

2.2 ±देवीरमण +मण्डपमा +बसेका थिए
±devīramaṇa +maṇḍapamā +basekā thie
± S:pn-nm +LC:cn-lc +P:iVP3-3sg.pst.prf.m
±Devīramaṇa +pavilion-at +seated was
'Devīramaṇa was seated at the (marriage) pavilion.'

2.3 ±नयाँ दुलही ±पनि +एकै आसनमा +बसेकी थिइन्
±nayā̃ dulahī +pani +ekai āsanamā +basekī thi.in
±S:CNP-nm ±AA:advl +LC:CNP-lc +P:iVP3-3sg.pst.prf.f
±new bride +also +one-(emphatic) seat-at +seated was
'The new bride was also seated at the same seat.'

2.4.1 ±ब्राह्मणहरु ±(2.4.2) ±अग्निमा +आहुति +दिइरहेका थिए
±brāhmaṇaharu ±(2.4.2) ±agnimā +āhuti +di.iraheka thie
±S:cn-nm ±AD:Cl(2.4.2) ±LA:cn-lc +DO:cn-n +P:tVP1-3pl.pst.prf.prog.
±Brahmans ±(2.4.2) ±fire-in +offerings +giving they-were
'The Brahmans were pouring offerings into fire.'

2.4.2 +ऋचा +पढेर
+ṛcā +paḍhera
+DO:cn-ac +P:tv1-abs.prt.

+Vedic-hymns +having-read
'having read the Vedic hymns'

2.5 ±प्रारब्धले ±यो उमेरमा +उनलाई ±फेरि +दुलाहा +बनायो
±prārabdhale ±yo umeramā +unalā.ī ±pheri +dulāhā +banāyo.
±S:cn-nm ±LA:CNP-lc +DO:pro-ac ±AA:advl +OC:cn-ac
+P:tv3-3sg.pst.m
±destiny ±this age-at +him ±again +bridegroom +made
'Destiny made him a bridegroom again at this age.'

2.6 ± एक दिन ±यस्तै रीत सँग ±उनले +सुभद्राको पाणिग्रहण +गरेथे
±eka dina ±yastai rīta saṃga ±unale +subhadrāko pāṇigrahaṇa +garethe
±AA:AdvlP ±AA:PP ±S:pro-pers-nm ±DO:CNP-ac
+P:tv1-3sg.pst.prf.m
±one day ±very-such manner with ±he +Subhadrā-of hand-holding
+had-done
'One day, he had married Subhadrā in the same manner.'

2.7.1 ± (2.7.2-5) ± आज ±उनले +अघिकै कृत्यलाई ±फेरि +दोहोऱ्याए
±(2.7.2-5) ±āja ±unale +aghikai kṛtyalā.ī ±pheri +dohoryāe
±AD:Cl(2.7.2-5) ±S:pro-pers-nm +DO:CNP-ac ±AA:advl
+P:tv1-3sg.pst.m
±(2.7.2-5) ±today ±he +previous-(emphatic) +act ±again +repeated
'Today he repeated the very previous act (2.7.2-5).'

2.7.2 +सुभद्राको आदेश +पाई
+subhadrāko ādeśa +pā.ī
+DO:CNP-ac +P:tv1-abs.prt.
+Subhadrā-of order +having-received
'having received the order of Subhadrā'

2.7.3 +हो
+ho
+P:iv1-3sg.pres.
+is
'(Whether) it was'

2.7.4 ±वा +नपाई
±vā +napāī
±C:cc +P:tv1-abs.prt.neg

±or +not-having-received
'or without receiving (it),'

2.7.5 +हो
+ho
+P:iv1-3sg.pres.
+is
'was'

2.8.1 ±(2.8.2) यस कुराको +उनलाई ±पनि +केही ज्ञान +थिएन
±(2.8.2) yasa kurāko +unailāī ±pani +kehī jñāna +thiena
±AD:Cl(2.8.2) ±S:CNP-nm... +DC:Pro-dt ±AA:advl ...±S: CNP-nm +P:iv2-3sg.pst.m
±(2.8.2) this matter-of +him-to ±also +any knowledge +was-not
'He did not have any knowledge of this matter--(2.8.2)'

2.8.2 ±यसबाट ±उनको भलो-कुभलो के +हुने हो
±yasabāṭa +unako bhalo-kubhalo ke +hune ho
±AA:prol-ab ±S:CNP-nm +P:iv1-impf.prt.m
±this-from ±his good-bad what +being-is
'Whether good or evil would result from this.

2.9.1 ±(2.9.2) ±उनी +(2.9.3) +खोज्दथे
±(2.9.2) ±unī +(2.9.3) +khojdathe
±AD:Cl (2.9.2) ±S:pro-nm +DO:Cl(2.9.3) +P:tv1-3sg.pst.m
±(2.9.2) ±he +(2.9.3) +used-to-want
'(2.9.2), he wanted (2.9.3)'

2.9.2 +बाह्र बर्षकी अबोध बालिकालाइ +ल्याएर
+bāhra barṣakī abodha bālikālāī/ +lyāera
+DO:CNP-ac +P:tv1-abs.prt
+twelve year-of innocent child-girl +having-brought
'Having brought a girl of twelve years,'

2.9.3 ±शून्य आकाशमा +कल्पनातीत मनोमन्दिर निर्माण +गर्न
±śūnya ākāshamā kalpanātīta manomandira nirmāṇa +garna
±LA:CNP-lc +DO:CNP-ac +P:tv1-inf
±empty sky-in/ imaginary mental-castle construction/ do/
'to build an imaginary castle of his mind.'

2.10 ±शायद +ब्रह्मवादीहरु +त्यसैलाई +आशा-पाश या मृगतृष्णा +भन्छन् ±क्यारे
±shāyada +brahmavādīharu +tyasailāī āśā-pāśa yā mṛgatṛṣṇā +bhanchan ±kyāre.

±AA:advl ±S: cn-nm +DO:pro-ac +OC:CNP-ac +P:tv3-pl.pres ±NU: nu
(*kyāre*)
±perhaps ±philosophers +that-to +hope-snare or mirage +they-call ±I guess
'Perhaps, the Brahmavādi philosophers call it the snare of hope or mirage, I guess.'

2.11.1 ±अस्तु ±(2.11.2-3) ±उनले विवाह-विधि +समाप्त +गरे

±astu, ±(2.11.2-3) ±unale/ vivāha-vidhi +samāpta +gare.
±AD:advl ±AD:Cl(2.11.2-3) ±S:pro-nm +DO:CNP-ac +OC:adj-ac +P:tv3-3sg.pst.m
±anyway, ±(2.11.2-3) ±he +wedding-ritual +complete +made
'Anyway, he made the wedding ritual complete'

2.11.2 ±करले +होस्

±karale +hos
±IA:cn-in +P:iv1-opt.3sg.m
±compulsion-by +may-he-be
(Whether it) was by compulsion,'

2.11.3 ±वा ±आन्तरिक प्रेरणाले +होस्

±vā ±āntarika preraṇāle +hos,
±C:cc ±IA:CNP-in +P:iv1-opt.3sg.m
±or ±internal inspiration-by +may-be
'or by (his own) internal inspiration.'

2.12.1 ±(2.12.2) वेलामा ±कन्यापक्षका मानिसले ±(2.12.3) +दुलहीलाई +डोलीमा +हालिदिए

±(2.12.2) velāmā ±kanyāpakṣakā mānisale ±(2.12.3) +dulahīlā.ī +ḍolīmā +hālidie
±LA:Mod(2.12.2)CNP-lc ±S:CNP ±AA:Cl(2.12.3) +DO:cn-ac +LC:cn-lc +P:tv4-3pl.pst.
±(2.12.2) ±bride-side-of people ±(2.12.3) +bride +litter-in +they-put
'At the time of (2.12.2), the people on the side of the bride, (2.12.3), put the bride in the litter'

2.12.2 +दुलही +अन्माउने

+dulahī +anmā.une
+DO:cn-a +P:tv1-impf.prt
+bride +giving-away
'giving away the bride,'

2.12.3 +रुँदै

+rũdai
+P:iv1-conj.prt.
crying
'crying'

2.13.1 ±दुलही ±पनि ±डोलीमा +(2.13.2) +लागिन्

±dulahī/ ±pani ±ḍolībhitra +(2.13.2) +lāgin
±S:cn-nm ±AA:advl ±LA:cn-lc +DO:Cl(2.13.2) +P:tv1-3sg.pst.f
±bride ±also ±litter-inside +(2.13.2) +began
'The bride inside the litter also began (2.13.2)

2.13.2 +रुन

+runa
+P:iv1-inf.
+to-cry
'to cry'

2.14 ± त्यस बखत +देवीरमणलाई +साह्रै नरमाइलो + लाग्यो

±tyasa bakhata +devīramaṇalā.ī +sāhrai naramā.ilo +lāgyo
±AA:AdvP +DC:pn-dt ±SC:AdjP +P:ev2-3sg.pst.m
±that time +Devīramaṇa-to +very unpleasant +he-struck
'At that time, Deviraman felt very bad.'

2.15.1 ±बाटामा ±बरियातहरु ±(2.15.2-3) +हाँस्थे

±bāṭāmā ±bariyātaharu ±(2.15.2-3) +hā̃sthe
±LA:cn-lc ±S:cn-nm ±AA:C 1(2.15.2-3) +P:iv1-3pl.pst.
±way-on ±wedding-processionists ±(2.15.2-3) +used-to-laugh
'On the way the people in the wedding procession laughed (2.15.2-3)'

2.15.2 ±परस्पर +ग्रामीण ठट्टा +गरेर

±paraspara +grāmīṇa ṭhaṭṭā +garera
±AA:advl +DO:CNP-ac +P:tv1-abs.prt.
±mutually +rustic jokes +having-done
'telling rustic jokes to each other.'

2.15.3 +खित्का +छाडी

+khitkā +choḍī
+DO:cn-ac +P:tv1-abs.prt.
+titter +having-released
'releasing titter (or tittering),'

2.15.4 +परन्तु ±देवीरमणका कपालमा +(2.15.5) +लागेको थियो

+parantu ±devīramaṇakā kapālamā +(2.15.5) +lāgeko thiyo.
±C:cc ±AA:CNP-lc ±S:ncl(2.15.5) +P:iVP1-aux-pst.prf.m
±but ±Devīramaṇa-of head-in +(2.15.5) +begun had
'but, in the mind of Deviraman had begun (2.15.5)'

2.15.5 + अर्कै विचारको द्वन्द्व +हुन

+arkai vicārako dvanda +huna
±S:CNP-n +P:iv1-inf.
±another thought-of battle +to-happen
'the battle of another thought to happen.'

2.16.1 ±मनमनले +भने, +(2.16.2)

±manamanale +bhane, +(2.16.2)/
±IC:cn-in +P:tv1-3sg.pst +DO:Cl(2.16.2)
±mind-mind-by +he-said +(2.16.2)
'He said to himself (2.16.2),'

2.16.2 ±(2.16.3) +हो?

±(2.16.3) +ho?
±S:ncl(2.16.3) +P:iv1-3sg.pres.m
±(2.16.3) +is?
'Was [it true]?'

2.16.3 ±"के ±सुभद्राले ±साँचो मनले +सल्लाह +दिएको

±"ke ±subhadrāle ±sāco manale +sallāha +dieko
±Q:qw ±S:pn-nm ±IC:CNP-in +DO:cn-ac +P:tVP1-pst.prf.m
±Subhadrā ±sincere mind-by +advice +given
[that] Subhadrā had given her advice with sincere mind?'

2.17.1 ±(2.17.2) ±किन ±(2.17.2) +'हुन्छ' +भनेकी ±त?

±(2.17.2) ± kina ±(2.17.2) +'huncha' +bhanekī ±ta ?
±AD:Cl(2.17.2) ±AA:advl +AD:CL(2.17.3) +DO:Cl +P:tv1-3sg.pst.f
±NU:nu (*ta*)
±(2.17.2) ±why ±(2.17.3) +is-alright she-said *±ta*
'Why did she say 'it is alright' (2.17.2-3)?'

2.17.2 +सम्मति +दिंदा

+sammati +diṃdā
+DO:cn-ac +P:tv1-imp.prt.
+consent +while-giving

'When she gave [her] consent'

2.17.3 ±अर्को पट्टि +फर्केर
±arko-paṭṭi +pharkera
±LA:PP +P:iv4-abs.prt.
±on-another-side +having-turned
'turning to the other side'

2.18.1 ±(2.18.2) ±(2.18.3) ±त +होइन?
±(2.18.2) ±(2.18.3) ±ta +hoina ?
±AD:Cl(1.18.2) +SC:Cl(2.183) ±NU:nu *ta* +P:ev1-3sg.neg.pres.
±(2.18.2) ±(2.18.3) ±*ta* +is-not
'Is it not [true that](2.18.2) (2.18.3)'

2.18.2 +मेरो ज्यादा आग्रह +देखेर
+mero jyādā āgraha +dekhera
+DO:CNP-ac +P:tv1-abs.prt
+my much insistence +having-seen
'Seeing my much insistence'

2.18.3 +हुन्छ +भनेकी
+huncha +bhanekī/
+DO:cl +P:tv1-prf.prt.f
+it-is-alright +she-said
'she said it is alright'

2.19 ± अहो! ±मानिसहरु ±आफ्नो तीव्र इच्छामा +अरुको संमतिलाई ±कसरी ±जबर्जस्ती +तान्छन्
±aho! ±mānisaharu ±āphno tīvra icchāmā +aruko sammatilāī +kasarī ±jabarajastī +tānchan
±Ex: intj (*aho!*) ±S:cn-nm ±LC:CNP-lc +DO:CNP-ac ±AA:adv ±AA:advl +P:tv1-3pl.pres
±Oh! +men ±own excessive wish-in +others-of consent ±how ±forcibly +pull
'Oh, how people forcibly pull the consent of others to their own wishes!'

2.20 ±छि: ! ±सुभद्राको आजीवन सेवाको पुरस्कार +यही +हो ?
±chiḥ! ±subhadrāko ājīvana sevāko puraskāra +yahī +ho ?
±EX:ex (*chih!*) ±S:CNP-nm +SC:prol-nm +P:ev1-3sg.pst.
±Fie! ±Subhadrā-of life-long service-of reward +this +is?
'Fie! Is this the reward for Subhadrā's life-long service?'

2.21.1 ±म +के +गरूँ

±ma +ke +garū

±S:pro +DO:pro-interrog +P:tv1-1sg.imp

±I +what +may-I-do

'What can I do?'

2.21.2 +मलाई +के दोष?

+malā.ī +ke doṣa ?

+DC:pro-dt ±S:CNP-nm [±P:iv2-3sg.pres]

+I-to +what fault [is]?

'What [is] my fault?'

2.22.1 ±(2.22.2) हिन्दू धर्म +जानोस्

±(2.22.2) hindū dharma +jānos

±S:modCNP-nc +P:iv1-3sg.imp

±(2.22.2-3) Hindu religion +may-he-know

'May the Hindu religion (2.22.2-3) know (it)'

2.22.2 +(2.22.3) +भन्ने

+(2.22.3) +bhanne

+DO:Cl(2.22.3) +P:tv1-impf.prt

+(2.22.3) +saying

+'saying [that] +(2.22.3)'

2.22.3 ± सन्तान विना ±स्वर्गको बाटो +छेकिन्छ

±santāna-vinā ±svargako bāṭo +chekincha

±AA:PP ±S:CNP-nm +P:tv1p-3sg.pres

±children-without +heaven-of way +is-barred

'the way to heaven is barred to one if he does not have children.'

2.23.1 ±(2.23.2) ± धर्मका आज्ञाले +विवाह +गरेको हूँ

±(2.23.2) ±dharmakā ājñāle +vivāha +gareko hū.

±AD:Cl(2.23.2) ±IA:CNP-in +DO:cn-ac +P:tVP1-1sg.pres.prf

±(2.23.2) ±religion-of order-by +marriage +done I-am

'I have performed the marriage by the order of religion, (2.23.3).'

2.23.2 ±भोगको लालसाले +होइन

±bhogako lālasāle +hoina,

±IC:CNP-in +P:iv1-3sg.pres.neg.m

±enjoyment-of desire-by ±is-not

'not by the desire of enjoyment.'

2.24 ±बरियात ±देवीरणका घर-नेर +पुग्यो
±bariyāta ±devīramaṇakā ghara-nera +pugyo
±S:cn-nm ±LC:PP +P:iv3-3sg.pst.m
±wedding-procession +Devīiramaṇa-of house-near +he-reached
'The wedding procession arrived near the house of Devīramaṇa.'

2.25 ±गाउँले छिमेकीहरु ±चौतारामा ±रमिता +हेरिरहेका रहेछन्
±gāuṃle chimekīharu ±cautārāmā +ramitā +heriraheka rahechan
±S:CNP-nm ±LA:cn-lc +DO:cn-ac +P:tv1P-3pl.prf.prog.prt
±rural neighbors ±*cautārā* -at + fun +watching-had-been
'The rural neighbors had been watching the fun at the *cautārā* .

2.26.1 ±देवीरमणले ±(2.26.2) +हेरे
±devīramaṇale ±(2.26.2) +here
±S:pn-nm ±AD:Cl(2.26.2) +P:iv1-3sg.pst.m
±Devīramaṇa ±(2.26.2) +he-looked
'Deviraman looked (2.26.2)'

2.26.2 ± एक-एक गरी +नियालेर
±eka-eka garī +niyālera
±AA:AdvP +P:iv1-abs.prt.
±one-one-doing +having-scrutinized
'scrutinizing one by one.'

2.26.3 ±त्यो हुलमा +सुभद्रालाई +देखेनन्
±tyo hulamā +subhadrālā.ī +dekhenan
±LA:CNP-lc +DO:pn-ac +P:tv1-3sg.pres.neg.f
±that crowd-in +Subhadrā +he-did-not-see
'He did not see Subhadrā in that crowd.'

2.27 ±बल्ल ±उनको छातीबाट +ढुङ्गो +पन्छियो
±balla ±unako chātībāṭa ±ḍhuṅgo +panchiyo
±AA:advl ±AbA:CNP-ab ±S:cn-nm +P:iv1p-3sg.pst.m
±finally his heart-from rock was-removed
'Finally, the rock was removed from his heart.'

2.28.1 ±आज ±देवीरमणको गति +त्यस बालक छात्रको जस्तो +थियो
2.28.1 ±āja ±devīramaṇako gati +tyasa bālaka chātrako jasto +thiyo
±LA:advl ±S:CNP-nm +SC:AdvP +P:ev1-3sg.pst.m
±today ±devīraṇa-of condition +that child student-of like +he-was
'Today, Deviraman's condition was like that of a little boy'

2.28.2 ±जो ±(2.28.3) ±अबेला ±गुरुकहाँ +पुग्दछ

±jo ±(2.28.3) ±abelā ±guru-kahā̃ +pugdacha,
±S:pro-rel ±AD:Cl(2.28.3) ±LA:PP ±LA:PP +P:iv3-3sg.pres.m
±who ±(2.28.3) ±late ±teacher-at +he-arrives
'who arrives late at the teacher's (class), (2.28.3).'

2.28.3 +पहिलो दिनको पाठ +बिर्सेर

+pahilo dinako pāṭha +birsera
+DO:CNP-ac +P:tv1-abs.prt.
+first day-of lesson +having-forgotten
'forgetting the lesson of the previous day;'

2.28.4 ± अथवा +त्यस अपराधीको जस्तो +थियो

±athavā +tyasa aparādhīko jasto +thiyo
±C:cc +SC:AdjP +P:ev1-3sg.pst.m
±or +that criminal-of like +he-was
'or, it was like that of that criminal'

2.28.5 ±जो ±(2.28.6) +खोज्दछ

±jo ±(2.28.6) +khojdacha.
±S:pro-rel +DO:Cl(2.28.6) +P:tv1-3sg.pres.m
±who +(2.28.6) +wants'
'who wants (2.28.6)'

2.28.6 ±(2.28.7) +लुक्न

±(2.28.7) +lukna
±AD:Cl (2.28.7) +P:iv1-inf
±(2.28.7) +to-hide
'to hide (2.28.7).'

2.28.7 + परिचित मानिसलाई +देखेर

+paricita mānisalā.ī +dekhera
+DO:CNP-ac +P:tv1-abs.prt
+acquainted person +having-seen
'seeing an acquainted person.'

2.29.1 ±(2.29.2) बहानाले ±उनी +केही पछि +भए

±(2.29.2) bahānāle ±unī ±kehī pachi +bhae,
±IA:modCNP-in ±S:pro-nm ±AA:AdvP +P:iv1-3sg.pst.m
±(2.29.2) excuse-by ±he ±somewhat behind +became
'He remained somewhat behind by the excuse'

2.29.2 ±छिमेकीसंग +कुरा +गर्नको

±chimekī-saṃga +kurā +garnāko
±AA:cn-pp +DO:cn-ac +P:tv1-inf+pp
±neighbor-with +talk +doing-of
'of having a conversation with a neighbor;'

2.29.3 +जाँदा

jā̃dā
+P:iv1-conj.prt.
+while-going
'when he arrived,'

2.29.4 ±(2.29.5) ±सुभद्रा (2.29.6) +लागेकी रहिछन्

±(2.29.5) ±subhadrā +(2.29.6) +lāgekī rahichan.
±AD: advcl(2.29.5) ±S:cn-nm +DO:ncl(2.29.6) +P:tVP1-pst.perf.f
±(2.29.5) ±Subhadrā +(2.29.6) +she-begun had
'(2.29.5), Subhadrā had begun (2.29.6)'

2.29.5 +दुलही +भित्र्याइसकी

+dulahī +bhitryā.isakī
+DO:cn-ac +P:CmpdtV1-abs.prt
+bride +having-received-in
'having received in the bride,'

2.29.6 +दमाईं-डोलेहरुलाई +ज्याला +बाँड्न

+damā.i-ḍoleharulā.ī +jyālā +bā̃ḍna
+DC:CmpdCNP-dt +DO:cn-ac +P:tv2-inf
+band-litter-carriers-to +wage +distribute
'to distribute the wage to the band and litter-carriers.'

2.30.1 ±देवीरमणको हृदय +गद्‌गद् +भयो

±devīramaṇako hṛdaya +gadgad +bhayo,
±S:CNP-nm +SC:adj-nm +P:ev1-3sg.pst.m
±Devīramaṇa-of heart +delighted +he-became
'Devīramaṇa's heart became very delighted;'

2.30.2 ±मनमनले +भने: +(2.30.3)

±manamanale +bhane: +(2.30.3)
±IA:cn-in +P:tv1-3sg.pst +DO:(2.30.3)
±mind-mind-by +he-said: (2.30.3)
'He said to himself: (2.30.3)'

2.30.3 ±"सुभद्रा +स्वर्गकी देवी +हो

±"subhadrā +svargakī devī +ho,
±S:pn-nm +SC:CNP-nm +P:ev1-3sg.pres.f
"Subhadrā +heaven-of goddess +she-is
"Subhadrā is a goddess of heaven;"

2.30.4 ±व्यर्थै ±किन +शङ्का +गरें?

±vyarthai ±kina +śaṃkā +gareṃ ?
±AA:advl ±AA:advl +DO:cn-ac +P:tv1-1sg.pst
±in-vain ±why +doubt +I-did
'Why did I doubt in vain?'

2.31 ±मानिसहरु ±आफ्नो कामले ±कसरी ±आँफै +तर्सन्छन्!

±mānisaharu ±āphno kāmale ±kasarī ±āphai +tarsanchan !
±S:cn-nm ±IC:CNP-in ±AA:adv ±AA:advl +P:iv1-3pl.pres.
±men ±own work-by ±how ±oneself +they-are-frightened
'How people are frightened by of their own work!'

2.32.1 ± (2.32.2) ±देवीरमण ± अबेला ±कोठामा +(2.32.3) +गए

±(2.32.2) ±devīramaṇa ±abelā ±koṭhāmā +(2.32.3) +gae
±AD:Cl(2.32.2) ±S:pn-nm ±AA:advl ±LA:cn-lc ±AA:Cl(2.32.3)
+P:iv1-3sg.pst.m
±(2.32.2) ±Devīramaṇa ±late ±room-in +(2.32.3) +went
'(2.32.2)/ Devīramaṇa went (2.32.3) late in his room.'

2.32.2±पाहुना-पासासंग +कुराकानी +गरेर

±pāhunā-pāsā-saṃga +kurākānī +garera
±AA:PP +DO:cn-ac +P:tv1-abs-prt.
±guests-invitees-with +conversation +having-done
'Having a conversation with the guests and invited ones,'

2.32.3 +सुत्न

+sutna
+P:iv1-inf.
to-sleep
'to sleep'

2.33 ±पानसमा ±कडुवा तेलको बत्ती +बलिरहेको थियो

±pānasamā ±kaḍuwā telako battī +baliraheko thiyo.
±LA:cn-lc ±S:CNP-nm +P:iv1-3sg.pst.prog.
±lamp-stand-in ±mustard-seed oil-of lamp +burning was
'A mustard-seed-oil lamp was burning in a brass lamp-stand.'

2.34 ±नयाँ दुलही ± खाटमनि ±ओच्छ्यानमा +सुतेकी थिइन्
±nayā̃ dulahī ±khāṭamani ±ochyānamā +sutekī thi.in
±S:CNP-nm ±LA:PP ±LA:cn-lc +P:iv1-3sg.pst.prf.f
±new bride ±cot-below ±bed-in +slept he-had
'The new bride had slept in a bed below the cot.'

2.35.1 ±देवीरमण +खाटमा +पल्टे
±devīramaṇa +khāṭamā +palṭe
±S:cn-nm +LC:cn-lc +P:iv1-3sg.pst.m
±Devīramaṇa +cot-on +lay
'Devīramaṇa lay on the cot-bed'

2.35.2 ±उस ठाँउमा +सुभद्राको ओछ्यान +देखेनन्
±usa ṭhāũmā +subhadrāko ochyāna +dekhenan.
±LA:CNP-lc +DO:CNP-ac +P:tv1-3sg.pst.m
±that place-in +Subhadrā-of bed +he-did-not-see
'He did not see Subhadrā's bed at that place.'

2.36 ±अघि ± सुभद्राको ओछ्यान +देवीरमणका खाटमनि +हुन्थ्यो
±aghi ±subhadrāko ochyāna +devīramaṇakā khāṭamani +hunthyo.
±AA:advl +S:CNP-nm +LC:PP +P:iv3-3sg.pst.m
±before +Subhadrā-of bed +Devīramaṇa-of cot-below +he-used-to-be
'Before, Subhadra's bed used to be below the cot of Deviraman'

2.37.1 ±(2.37.2) ±(2.37.3) कोठा ±पनि +देवीरमणलाई +नौलो जस्तो +लाग्यो
±(2.37.2) ±(2.37.3) koṭhā ±pani +devīramaṇalā.ī +naulo jasto +lāgyo
±AD:Cl(2.37.2) ±S:ModCNP-nm ±AA:advl +DC:pn-ac +SC:AdjP
+P:ev2-3sg.pst.m
±(2.37.2) ±room ±also (2.37.3) +Devīramaṇa-to +strange +seemed
'(2.37.2), the room (2.37.3) seemed strange to Deviraman.'

2.37.2 ±आज ±उस ठाउँमा +नदेख्दा
±āja ±usa ṭhāũmā +nadekhdā
±AA:advl ±LA:CNP-lc +P:iv1-impf.prt
±today ±that place-in +not-seeing
'Today, when he did not see (the bed) in that place,'

2.37.3 ±बीसौं वर्षदेखि +सुतिरहेको
±bīsauṃ barṣadekhi +sutiraheko
±AbA:CNP-ab +P:tv1p-pst.prt
±scores years-from +being-slept

'being slept for scores of years'

2.38.1 ±(2.38.2) ±सुभद्रा +कोठामा +पसिन्
±(2.38.2) ±subhadrā +koṭhāmā +pasin,
±AD:advcl (2.28.2) ±S:pn-nm +LC:cn-lc +P:iv3-3sg.pst.f
±(2.38.2) ±Subhadrā/ room-in/ entered
(2.38.2) Subhadrā entered in the room;'

2.38.2 ±एक छिन पछि +गृहकृत्य +समाप्त +गरेर
±eka china-pachi +gṛhakṛtya +samāpta +garera
±AA:PP +DO:cn-ac +OC:adj-ac +P:tv1-tv3-abs.prt
±one moment-after +chores + finished +having-made
'After a moment, having finished the chores'

2.38.3 +(2.38.4) +लागिन्
+(2.38.4) +lāgin
+DO:Cl(2.384) +P:tv1-3sg.pst.f
+(2.38.4) +she-began
'(She) began (2.38.4)'

2.38.4 +देवीरमणको गोडा +मिच्न
+devīramaṇako goḍā +micna
+DO:CNP-ac +P:tv1-inf.
+Devīramaṇa-of feet/ to-massage
'to massage the feet of Devīramaṇa'

2.39 ±यो +उनको दैनिक काम +थियो
±yo +unako dainika kāma +thiyo
±S:prol-nm +SC:CNP-nm +P:ev1-3sg.pst.m
±this +her daily work +was
'This was her daily work.'

2.40.1 ± सुभद्रा +(2.40.2) +दिन्नथिन्
±subhadrā +(2.40.2) +dinnathin
±S:cn-nm +DO:Cl(2.40.2) +P:tv1-3sg.pst.neg.f
±Subhadra +(2.40.2) +she-would-not-let
'Subhadra would not let (2.40.2)'

2.40.2 ±यसमा ±कहिल्यै ± त्रुटि +हुन
±yasamā ±kahilyai ±truṭi +huna
±LA:pro-lc ±AA:advl ±S:cn-nm +P:tv1-inf
±this-in ±ever ±mistake +to-happen

'a mistake ever to happen in this.

2.41.1 ±देवीरमणले भने --
±deviramaṇale/ bhane--
±S:pn-nm +P:tv1-3sg.pst.m
±Deviramaṇa +said
'Deviramaṇa said--'

2.41.2 ±"सानु, ±तिम्रो ओछ्यान ±खोइ ±नि?"
±"sānu, ±timro ochyāna ±kho.ī ±ni?"
±EX:cn-nm ±S:CNP-nm ±NU:nu (*khoi* = +P:iv1-3sg) ±NU:nu *ni*
±"Sānu, ±your bed ±where-is ±*ni*
'"Sānu, where is your bed?"'

2.42 +"पल्लो कोठामा +छ"
±"pallo koṭhāmā +cha."
+LC:CNP-lc +P:iv3-3sg.pst
+next room-in +is
"It is in the next room."

2.43 ±"किन +पल्लो कोठामा +सारेको?"
±"kina +pallo koṭhāmā +sāreko ?"
±AA:advl +LC:CNP-lc +P:iv1-prf.prt
±why +next room-in +(you) moved
'"Why have you moved it to the next room?"'

2.44.1 ±"भोलि ±एकादशी हो,
±"bholi ±ekādaśī +ho,
±AA:advl ±S:cn-nm +P:iv1-3sg.pres
±tomorrow ±eleventh +is,
'Tomorrow is the eleventh (day of lunar calender),'

2.44.2 ±"सबेरै +(2.44.3) +जान्छु"
±"saberai +(2.44.3) +jānchu"
±AA:advl ±AA:Cl(2.44.3) +P:iv1-1sg.pres
±early +(2.44.3) +I-go
'"I will go (2.44.3) early."'

2.44.3 ±गण्डकी +नुहाउन
±gaṇḍakī +nuhāuna
±LC:cn-(lc) +P:iv1-inf
±Gaṇḍakī-(in) +to-bathe

'to bathe in the Gaṇḍaki [river]'

2.45 ±"म ±पनि ±उहीं +सुत्छु "
±"ma ±pani ±uhiṃ +sutchu."
±S:pro ±AA:advl ±LA:advl +P:iv1-1sg.pres
±I also ±there +I-sleep
'"I will also sleep there."'

2.46.1 ± (2.46.2) +हुन्छ
± (2.46.2) +huncha"
±S: cl (2.46.2) +P: iv1-3sg.pres.
± (2.46.2) +is (alright)
'It is alright (2.46.2).'

2.46.2 ±उस् ! ±यहीं +सुत्नुभए ±पनि
±"us!, ±yahīṃ +sutnubhae +pani
±Ex: intj (*us*) , ±LA:advl +P:iv1-cond ±C:sc
±Oh no ±right-here +if-sleep ±also
'Oh no, if you also sleep right here,'

2.47.1 +(2.47.2) देवीरमणलाई ±चाँडै ±निद्रा +पऱ्यो
+(2.47.2) devīramaṇalāī ±cā̃ḍai ±nidrā +paryo
+DC:ModPNP-dt ±AA:advl ±S:cn-nm +P:iv2-3sg-pst.m
+(2.47.2) Devīramaṇa-to ±soon ±sleep +he-fell
'Devīramaṇa (2.47.2) soon fell asleep.'

2.47.2 ±(2.47.3) +आएका
±(2.47.3) +āekā
±AD:Cl (2.47.3) +P:iv1-prf.prt
+had-come (2.47.3)
'who had come (2.47.3)'

2.47.3 +थाकेर
+thākera
+P:iv1-abs.prt.
+having-been-tired
'being tired'

2.48.1 ±(2.48.2) ±सुभद्रा ±पल्लो कोठामा +गइन्
±(2.48.2) ±subhadrā ±pallo koṭhāmā +ga.in.
±AD:AdvCl (2.48.2) ±S:pn-nm ±LA: CNP-lc +P:iv3-3sg.pst f

±(2.48.2) ±Subhadrā next room-in +went
'(2.48.2) Subhadrā went into the next room.'

2.48.2 +आफ्नो दोलाइँ +सौतालाई +खापेर

+āphno dolāĩ +sautālā.ī +khāpera
+DO:CNP-ac +DC:cn-dt +P:tv2-abs.prt.
+own quilt +co-wife-to +having-overlaid
'Having overlaid her own quilt onto her co-wife,'

2.49 ±मधुरो बत्तीको धमिलो उज्यालोमा ±नौली घर्तिनी +पात +गाँसिरहेकी थिई
2.49 ±madhuro battīko dhamilo ujyālomā ±naulī ghartinī +pāta +gãsirahekī thi.i
±LA:CNP-lc ±S:Mod (app) PNP-nm +DO:cn-ac +P:tv1-3sg.pst.prog f
±faint lamp-of dim light-in ±Naulī Ghartinī +leaf +joining she-was
'Naulī Ghartinī was joining the leaves in the dim light of a faint lamp.'

2.50 ±नौली +देवीरमणको पुरानो चाकर्नी +हो

±naulī +devīramaṇako purāno chākarnī +ho
±S:pn-nm +SC:CNP-nm +P:ev1-3sg.pst f
±Nauli +Devīramaṇa-of old maid +is
'Naulī was an old maid of Deviraman.'

2.51 ±नौलीको उमेर ±झण्डै झण्डै ± सुभद्रासंग +मिल्थ्यो

±naulīko umera ±jhaṇḍai jhaṇḍai ±subhadrāsaṃga +milthyo
±S:CNP-nm ±AA:advl ±AA:PP +P:iv1-3sg-pst m
±Naulī-of age ±almost almost ±Subhadrā-with +used-to-agree
'Naulī's age agreed almost with (that of) Subhadrā.'

2.52 ±८२ सालमा ±स्वर्गवासी महाराज चन्द्रशमशेर जङ्गबहादुरका करुणाले ± दास-जीवनबाट +मुक्त +भएकी थिई

±82 sālamā ±svargavāsī mahārāja candraśamaśera jaṅgabahāduraka karuṇāle ±dāsa-jīvanabāṭa +mukta +bhaekī thi.i.
±LA:CNP-lc ±IC:CNP-in ±AbA:CNP-ab +SC:adj-nm +P:eVP1-pst.prf.
±In the year '82 ±late mahārājā candrashamashera jaṅgabahādura-of compassion-by ±slave life-from +free +she-had-been was
'(She) had been freed from a slave's life by the compassion of the Late Prime Minister Chandrashamshera Jaṅgabahadur in the year 1982 (1925).'

2.53.1 ±(2.53.2) ±देवीरमणले नौलीको मोल +लिएनन्

±(2.53.2) ±devīramaṇale +naulīko mola +lienan

±AD:Cl ±S:pn-nm +DO:CNP-ac +P:tv1-3sg.pst.m
±(2.53.2) ±Devīramaṇa +Naulī-of price +did-not-take
'Deviraman did not take the price of Nauli (2.53.2)'

2.53.2 +घरकी पुरानी चाकर्नी +हुनाले
+gharakī purānī cākarnī +hunāle
+SC:CNP-nm +P:ev1-inf+in(*le*)
+home-of old slave +being-by
'(because of her) being an old slave at home'

2.53.3 ±(2.53.4) ±नौलीले +घर +छोडिन
±(2.43.4) ±naulīle +ghara +choḍina.
±AD:AdvCl(2.53.4) ±S:pn-nm +DO:cn-ac +P:tv1-3sg.pst.f
(2.53.4) / Naulī/ home/ did-not-leave
'(2.53.4), Naulī did not leave home.'

2.53.4 ±आफुखुशी +भए ±पनि
±āphukhushī +bhae ±pani
±AA: advl +P:iv1-cond ±C:sc
±voluntarily +if-be +although
'Even though it was voluntarily'

2.54 ±नौली +सुभद्राको बालक-कालदेखिको सुख-दु:खकी साथी +थिई
±naulī +subhadrāko bālaka-kāladekhiko sukha-duḥkhakī sāthī +thi.i.
±S:pn-nm +SC:CNP-nm +P:ev1-3sg.pst.
±Nauli +Subhadrā's child-time-from-of happiness-unhappiness-of friend +she-was
'Naulī was Subhadrā's friend of weal and woes since her childhood.'

2.55.1 ±विधाताले ±सुभद्राको निमित्त +नौलीरूपी एउटा (2.55.2) भाँडो +दिएका थिए
±vidhātāle ±subhadrāko nimitta +naulīrūpī euṭā (2.55.2) bhhā̃ḍo diekā thie.
±S:cn-nm ±AA:PP +DO:modCNP-ac +P:tv1-3sg.pst.prf.m
±God ±Subhadrā-of for +Naulī-formed one vessel +had-given he-was
'For Subhadrā God had given in the form of Naulī a vessel (2.55.2)'

2.55.2 +दु:ख +पोख्ने
+duḥkha +pokhne
+DO:cn-a +P:tv1-impf.prf.prt
+distress +pouring
'for pouring (her) distress.'

2.56 ±दुवैमा +घनिष्ठ प्रेम +थियो
±duvaimā +ghaniṣṭha prema +thiyo.
±LA:pro-lc ±S:CNP-nm +P:iv1-3sg.pst.m
±both-in ±fast love +was
'Both had deep love for each other.'

2.57.1 ±नौलीले ±(2.57.2) +भनी-- +(2.57.3)
±naulīle ±(2.57.2) +bhanī-- +(2.57.3)
±S:pn-nm ±AD:Cl(2.57.2) +P:tv1-3sg.pst +DO:Cl(2.57.3)
±Nauli ±(2.57.2) +she-said +(2.57.3)
'Naulī, (2.57.2), said -- (2.57.3)

2.57.2 +पात +गाँस्दै
+pāta +gā̃sdai
+DO:cn-ac +P:tv1-conj.prt
+leaves +joining
'joining the leaves'

2.57.3 ±बजै, ± आज ± ता +साह्रै नरमाइलो +लाग्यो होला ?
±"bajai, ±āja ±tā +sāhrai naramā.ilo +lāgyo holā?"
±Ex: nm ±S:nl ±NU:nu *ta* +SC:AdjP-nm +P:ev2-3sg.prob.pst.m
±Bajai, ±today ±*ta* +very unpleasant +struck will-be
"'Bajai, today (it) must have been very unpleasant (for you).'"

2.58 ±"किन ±नौली, किन +त्यसो +भनिस्?
±"kina ±naulī, ±kina ±tyaso +bhanis?
±AA:advl ±Ex:pn-nm ±AA:advl +DO:nl +P:tv1-2sg.pres
±why ±Nauli, ±why +so +you-said
"'Why Naulī, why did you say so?'"

2.59.1 ±(2.59.2) कुरा +के +छ र?
±(2.59.2) kurā +ke +cha ra ?
±S:modCNP-nm +SC:nl +P:ev1-3sg.pres m ±NU:nu *(ra)*
±matter +what +is ±*ra*
'What is the matter (2.59.2)'

2.59.2 +नरमाइलो +लाग्नुपर्ने
+naramā.ilo +lāgnuparne
+SC:adj-nm +P:eVP2-impf.prf.prt
+unpleasant +striking-must
'striking unpleasant (for me)?'

2.60.1 ±तैपनि ±(2.60.2) +मुटुको बह +हो

±taipani ±(2.60.2) +muṭuko baha +ho,
±C:cc ±S:Cl +SC:CNP-nm +P:ev1-3sg.pres
±then-even ±(2.60.2) +heart-of pain +is
'Even then, (2.60.2) is the pain of the heart.'

2.60.2 +सौता +भनेको

+sautā +bhaneko
+DO:cn-ac +P:tv1-prf.prt
+co-wife +called
'someone called a co-wife'

2.60.3 ±आजै +ओछ्यान +छोड्नुपर्‍यो

±ājai +ochyāna +choḍnu paryo.
±AA:advl +DO:cn-ac +P:tVP1-3sg.pst.m
±today +bed +to-leave had
'Today (you) had to leave the bed'

2.61.1 ±भोलि +घरै +छोड्नु पर्छ +कि

±bholi +gharai +chāḍnu parcha ±ki,
±AA:advl +DO:cn-ac +P:tVP1+Aux-3sg.pres.m ±NU:qw *(ki)*
±tomorrow +house-emph +leave must +whether(?)
'(you) may have to leave the house itself tomorrow'

2.61.2 +के +जानिसक्नु छ

+ke +jānisaknu cha."
±DO:pro-ac +P:tVP1-3sg.pres
+what +knowing-possible is
'Who knows?'

2.62.1 ±(2.62.2) +छोडिदिउँला

±(2.62.2) +choḍidiūlā
±AD:Cl +P:Cmpdiv1-1sg.fut
±(2.62.2)/ I-will-leave
'I will leave (2.62.2)'

2.62.2 +छोड्नु परे

+choḍnu pare
+P:iVP-cond.
+leave if-must
'If I must leave'

2.62.3 +कुन दौलथको चैन +गरेकी छु ±र ?
+kuna daulathako caina +gareki̇̄ chu ±ra ?,
+DO:CNP-ac +P:tVP1-1sg.pst.prf ±NU: nu *(ra)*
+what wealth-of enjoyment +done I-have +*ra*
'What enjoyment of wealth have I done?'

2.62.4 ±(2.62.5) ±दिन-रात +बुहार्तन +सहेकी छु
±(2.62.5) ±dina-rāta +buhārtana +saheki̇̄ chu
±AD:Cl(2.62.5) ±AA:advl +DO:cn-ac +P:tVP1-1sg.pres.prf
±(2.62.5) ±day-night +hardship-of-daughter-in-law +suffered I-have
'I have suffered the hardship of a daughter-in-law day and night (2.62.4)'

2.62.5 ±एक पेट +खस्रो-मसिनु +खाएर
±eka peṭa +khasro-masinu +khāera,
±AA:advl +DO:cmpdCNP-ac +P:tv1-abs.prt.
one stomach-full +rough-fine-food +having-eaten
'eating a stomachful of rough food,'

2.63.1 ±(2.63.3) ±जसले ±पनि +(2.63.2) +दिन्छ
±(2.63.3)/ jasale ±pani (2.63.2) +dincha
±AD:Cl(2.63.3) ±S:pro-nm ±AA:advl +DO:Cl(2.63.2)
    +P:tv1-3sg.pres.m
±(2.63.3) ±anyone ±also +(2.63.2) +gives
'(2.63.3) Anyone gives (2.63.2)'

2.63.2 +एक गास +खान
+eka gāsa +khāna
+DO:CNP-ac +P:tv1-inf
+one mouthful +to-eat
'to eat a mouthful (of food)'

2.63.3 +जुठो चुल्हो +गरिदिए
+juṭho-cūlho +garidie
+DO:cn-ac +P:CmpdtVP1-cond
+dirty kitchen +if-do
'if I do (clean) the dirty kitchen'

2.64.1 ± तर +सोझी जस्ती +छ
±tara +sojhi̇̄ jasti̇̄ +cha,
±C:cc +SC:adjP +P:ev1-3sg.pres.f
±but +simple like +she-is,
'But she is apparently simple.'

2.64.2 ±(2.64.3) +ढोगिदिई

±(2.64.3)/ ḍhogidi.ī
±AD:Cl(2.64.3) +P:CmpdiVP1-3sg.pst.f
±(2.64.3) +she-greeted
'She greeted (2.64.3).'

2.64.3 +पस्ने ±बित्तिकै

+pasne ±bittikai/
+P: iv1-imfp.prt ±AA:advl
+entering ±as-soon-as
'as soon as she entered (into the house)'

2.65.1 +"सिकाएको हुँदो हो

+"sikāeko hũdo ho;
+P:iVP1-3sg.prob.pst.m
+taught been might-be
'It had probably been taught'

2.65.5 ±बजै, ±कुनै दिन +(2.65.3) +भन्नुहोला

±bajai! ±kunai dina +(2.65.3) +bhannuholā
±Ex:cn-nm ±AA:AdvP +DO:cl(2.65.3) +P:tv2-2sg-fut
±bajai +anyone day +(2.65.3) +you-will-say
'Bajai, you will say (2.65.3) some day.'

2.65.3 ±नौलीले +भनिथी

±naulīle +bhanithī
±S:pn-nm +P:iVP1-3sg.pst.prf.f
±Naulī +she-had-said
'Naulī had said'

2.66.1 ± सोझो ±(2.66.2) +बेर +लाग्दैन

±"sojho ±(2.66.2) +bera +lāgdaina
±S:nl ±AA:Cl (2.66.2) +DO:cn-nm +P:tv1-3sg.pres.neg.m
±straight (2.66.2) +long-time +does-not-take
'It does not take long for something straight (2.66.2)'

2.66.2 +बाङ्गिन

+bāṅgina
+P:iv1-inf
+to-be-crooked
'to be crooked'

2.66.3 ±अलि दिनपछि +बाजेको टुपी +समाउनेछिन्
±ali dina-pachi +bājeko ṭupī +samā.unechin ."
±AA:PP +DO:CNP-ac +P:tv1-3sg.fut.f
±some days-after +Bāje-of ṭupī +she-will-hold
'In a few days, she will be leading the old man around by his *ṭupī* (a tuft of hair the Hindus keep when they shave their head)'

2.67.1 ±"जेसुकै +होस्
±"jesukai +hos,
±S:pron-nonpers +P:iv-3sg.opt
±whatever +he-may-be
'Whatever may it be'

2.67.2 ±ईश्वरले +बीसासय आयु +गरिदिउन्
±īśvarale +vīsāsaya āyu +garidi.un
±S:cn-nm +DO:CNP-ac +P:tv1-3sg-opt
±God +twenty-hundred life +may-he-make
'May God give a long life (to her),'

2.67.3 +(2.67.4) +पाइयोस्
+(2.67.4) +pā.iyos,
+DO:ncl(2.67.4) +P:tv1p-imp
+(2.67.4) +may-we-get (pass.)
'May we get (2.67.4)'

2.67.4 +फले-फुलेको +देख्न
+phale-phuleko +dekhna
+DO:nl +P:tv1-inf
+fruitioned-flowered +to-see
'to see (her) prosperous'

2.67.5 ±(2.67.6) ±करले ±पनि +एक अञ्जुलि पानी +देला
±(2.67.6) ±karale ±pani +eka añjuli pānī +delā
±AD:Cl(2.67.6) ±IA:cn-in ±AA: advl +DO:CNP-ac +P:tv1-3sg.fut
±(2.68.6) +compulsion-by ±even +one handful water +he-will-give
'He will give a double-handful of water even by compulsion;'

2.67.6 ±सन्तान +भए
±santāna +bhae
±S:cn-nm +P:iv1-cond.
±child +if-be
'If there will be a child,'

2.67.7 ± यिनका हात-काखमा ± सास +जाओस्
±yinakā hāta-kākhamā ±sāsa +jāos
±LA:CNP-lc ±S:cn-nm +P:iv1-3sg.imp
±these-of hand-lap-in ±breath +may-go
'May I pass away in their hands and laps;'

2.67.8 ±सबभन्दा ठुलो सन्तोष +यही +हो ±नौली
±saba-bhandā ṭhūlo santoṣa +yahī/ +ho, +naulī
±S:CNP-nm +SC:nl +P:ev1-3sg.pres ±EX:pn-nm
±all-than great satisfaction +this-very +is ±Naulī
'This is the greatest satisfaction of all, Nauli'

3.1 ±तीन-चार वर्षपछिको कुरा +हो
   ±tina-cāra barṣa-pachiko kurā +ho.
   ±S:modCNP-nm +P:iv1-3sg.pres.m
   ±three-four year-after-of matter +is
   'It was a matter after three or four years.'

3.2.1 ±एक दिन ±(3.2.2)± सुभद्रा +छोरालाई +भात +खुवाइरहेकी थिइन्
   ±eka dina ±(3.2.2) ±subhadrā +chorālā.ī +bhāta +khuvā.irahekī thi.in.
   ±AA:AdvP ±AD:CL(3.2.2) ±S:pn-nm +DC:cn-dt +DO:cn-ac
      +P:tv2-3sg.pres.porg.f
   ±one day ±(3.2.2) ±Subhadrā +son-to +rice +feeding was
   One day, (3.2.2) Subhadrā was feeding rice to the son.'

3.2.2 +घाममा +बसेर
   +ghāmamā +basera
   +LC:cn-lc +P:iv3-abs.prt
   +sun-in +having-seated
   'sitting in the sun'

3.3.1 ±सुशील ±चाहिं (3.3.2) +कोशिशमा +थियो
   ±suśīla ±cāhiṃ (3.3.2) +kośiśamā +thiyo,
   ±S:cn-nm ±NU: nu (ca:hi~) +LC:modCNP-lc +P:iv3-3sg.pst.m
   ±Suśīla ±for his part +(3.3.2) effort-in +was
   'Suśīla, for his part, was in effort (3.3.2)

3.3.2 +(3.3.3) +परेवालाई +पक्रने
   +(3.3.3) parevālā.ī +pakrane
   +DO:modCNP-ac +P:tv1-impf.prt
   +(3.3.3) pigeons +catching
   'to catch the pigeons (3.3.3)'

3.3.3 +आँगनमा +चरिरहेका
   +ā̃ganamā +carirahekā
   +LC:cn-lc +P:iv3-prf.prt
   +courtyard-in +wandering
   'wandering in the courtyard'

3.3.4 ±सुभद्रा ±(3.3.5) +(3.3.6-7) +भन्थिन्
   ±subhadrā ±(3.3.5) +(3.3.6-7) +bhanthin
   ±S:pn-nm ±AD:Cl(3.3.5) +DO:Cl(3.3.6-7) +P:tv1-3sg.pst.f
   ±Subhadrā ±(3.3.5) +(3.3.6-7) +used-to-say
   'Subhadrā, (3.3.5), would say (3.3.6-7)'

3.3.5 ±हातमा +भातको गास +लिएर

±hātamā +bhātako gāsa +liera
±LA:cn-lc +DO:CNP-ac +P:tv1-prf.prt
±hand-in +rice-of mouthful +having-taken
taking a mouthful of rice in hand

3.3.6 ±"को +खाई

±"ko +khā.ī,
±S:nl-mn +P:iv1-prf.prt
±who +eating
'Who will eat'

3.3.7 ±"को +खाई

±"ko +khā.ī,
±S:nl-mn +P:iv1-prf.prt
±who +eating
'Who will eat'

3.4.1 ± सुशील ±(3.4.2-3) +आउँथ्यो

±suśīla ±(3.4.2-3) ±āũthyo,
±S:pn-nm ±AD:Cl (3.42) +P:iv1-3sg.pst.m
±Suśīla ±(3.4.2-3) +used-to-come
'Suśīla would come (3.4.2-3)'

3.4.2 +मुख +बाउँदै

+mukha +bāũdai
+DO:cn-ac +P:tv1-conj.prt
+mouth +opening
'opening his mouth'

3.4.3 +दौडेर

+dauḍera
+P:iv1-prf.prt
+having-run
'running'

3.4.4 ± सुभद्रा +गास +मुखमा +हालिदिन्थिन्

±subhadrā +gāsa +mukhamā +hālidinthin,
±S:pn-nm +DO:cn-ac +LC:cn-lc +P:tv4-3sg.pst.f
±Subhadrā +mouthful +mouth-in +used-to-put
Subhadrā would put the mouthful (of rice) in his mouth'

3.4.5 ± बालक ± फेरि ±(3.4.6) ±परेवातिर +जान्थ्यो
±bālaka ±pheri ±(3.4.6) ±parevā-tira +jānthyo
±S:cn-nm +AA:advl ±AD:Cl(3.4.6) ±AA:PP +P:iv1-3sg.pst.m
±child ±again ±(3.4.6) ±pigeon-toward ±used-to-go
'The child would go (3.4.6) toward the pigeons again.'

3.4.6 +दौडेर
+dauḍera
+P:iv-abs.prt
+having-run
'running'

3.5 ±ती मूक पक्षीहरू ± पनि ± बालकसंग ±आनन्दपूर्वक +खेलिरहेका थिए
±tī mūka pakṣīharu ±pani ±bālaka-saṃga ±ānandapūrvaka +khelirahekā thie
±S:CNP-nm ±AA:advl ±AA:PP ±AA:adv +P:iv-3pl.pst.prog
±those mute birds ±also ±child-with ±happily +playing were
Those mute pigeons were also playing happily with the child.'

3.6.1 ± सुशील ±(3.6.2 +(3.5.3) +खोज्दथ्यो
±suśīla ±(3.6.2) +(3.6.3) +khojthyo
±S:pn-mn ±AD:Cl(3.6.2) +DO:Cl(3.6.3) +P:tv1-3sg.pst.m
±Suśīla ±(3.6.2) +(3.6.3) +used-to-try
'Suśīla, (3.6.2), would try (3.6.3)'

3.6.2 +गई
+ga.ī
+P:iv1-abs.prt
having-gone
'going'

3.6.3 +समाउन
+samā.una
+P:iv1-inf
to-catch
'to catch'

3.7.1 ±परेवा ±(3.7.2) +बस्थे
+parevā ±(3.7.2) +basthe,
±S:cn-nm ±AD:Cl(3.7.2) +P:iv1-3pl.pst
±pigeons ±(3.7.2) +used-to-stop
'the pigeons would stop (3.7.2)'

3.7.2 ± अलि पर +गई

±ali para +ga.ī
±AA:AdvP +P:iv1-abs.prt
±a-little further +having-gone
'going a litle further'

3.7.3 ± सुशील ±फेरि ±उहीं +पुग्थ्यो

±suśīla ±pheri ±uhī̃ +pugthyo
±S:cn-nm ±AA:advl ±AA:advl +P:iv1-3sg.pst.m
±Susila ±again ±there +used-to-arrive
'Suśīla would atrrive there again'

3.7.4 ± परेवा ±(3.7.5) ±(3.7.6) +(3.7.7) +लाग्थे

±parevā ±(3.7.5) ±(3.7.6) +(3.7.7) +lāgthe.
±S:cn-nm ±AD:Cl(3.7.5) ±AD:Cl(3.7.6) +DO:Cl(3.7.7) +P:tv1-3pl.pst
±pigeons ±(3.7.5) ±(3.7.6) +(3.7.7) +used-to-began
'the pigeons, (3.7.5), (3.7.6), would begin (3.7.7)'

3.7.5 +उडेर

+uḍera
+P:iv1-abs.prt
+having-flown
'flying'

3.7.6 ± अलि पर +गई

±ali para +ga.ī
±AA:AdvP +P:iv-abs.prt
±a-little further +having-gone
'going a liittle further'

3.7.7 +चर्न

+carna
+P:iv-inf
to-feed
'to feed'

3.8.1 ±(3.8.2) ±सुशील ±(3.8.3) +जान्थ्यो

±(3.8.2) ±suśīla ±(3.8.3) +jānthyo.
±AD:Cl(3.8.2) ±S:cn-nm ±AD:Cl(3.8.3) +P:iv-3sg.pst.m
±(3.8.2) ±Suśīla ±(3.8.3) +used-to-go
'(3.8.2), Suśīla, (3.8.3), would go (back).'

3.8.2 +सुभद्राको (3.8.3) को आवाज +सुनेर

+ubhadrāko (3.8.3) ko āvāja +sunera
+DO:modCNP-ac +P:tv1-abs.prt
+Subhadra-of (3.8.3) of sound +having-heard
'Hearing the sound (3.8.3) from Subhadra',

3.8.3 +को +खाई

+ko +khāī
+S:pro-interrog +P:iv1-3sg-fut (baby talk)
+who +will-eat
'Who will eat'

3.8.4 ±बीच-बीचमा +एक-दुई गास भात ±पनि +खाएर

±bīcabīcamā +eka-du.ī gāsa bhāta ±pani +khāera
±LA:cn-lc +DO:CNP ±AA:advl +P:tv1-abs.prt
±interval-intervarl-in +one-two mouthful rice ±also +having-eaten
'eating every now and then one or two mouthfuls of rice'

3.9.1 ± देवीरमण ±(3.9.2) +यो अनुपम आनन्दप्रद बालक्रीडा +हेरिरहेका थिए

±devīramaṇa ±(3.9.2) +yo anupama ānandaprada bālakrīḍā +herirahekā thie
±S:pn-nm ±AD:Cl(3.9.2) +DO:CNP-ac +P:tv1-3sg.pst.prog
±Devīramaṇa ±(3.9.2) + this matchless pleasant child-play +watching was
'Devīramaṇa watched this matchless pleasant child's play'

3.9.2 ± फलैंचामा +बसेर

±phalaĩcāmā +basera
±LA:cn-lc +P:iv3-abs.prt
±porch-at +having-seated
'sitting at the porch,'

3.10.1 +उनलाई +(3.10.2) भान +हुन्थ्यो

+unalā.ī +(3.10.2) bhāna +hunthyo.
+DC:pro-dt +S:modCNP-nm +P:iv2-3sg.pst.m
+him-to +(3.10.2) appearance +used-to-be
'It would appear to him (3.10.2)'

3.10.2 ± स्वर्गका डीलबाट ±पितृहरु पनि +यस कुलावलम्बको बाललीला
+हेरिरहेका होलान् +भन्ने

±svargakā ḍīlabāṭa ±pitṛharu ±pani +yasa kulāvalambako bālalīlā
herirahekā holān ±bhanne
±AbA:CNP-ab ±S:cn-nm ±AA:advl +DO:CNP-ac
+P:tVP1-3pl.perf.prog.pst ±C:sc
±heaven-of edge-from ±ancestors ±also +this family-support-of child-play

watching may be ±that

'that even his ancestors were probably watching from the edge of the Heaven the play of this child, the hope of the family's future.'

3.11.1 ±उनी +(3.11.2) +देख्दथे

±unī +(3.11.2) +dekhdathe

±S:pro-nm +DO:Cl(3.11.2) +P:tv1-3sg.pst.m

±he +(3.11.2) +used-to-see

'He saw'

3.11.2 ± यो शिशु-सन्तानका आडमा ±एक महान् बलिष्ठ शक्ति +लुकिरहेको

±yo śiśu-santānakā āḍamā +eka mahān baliṣṭha śakti +lukiraheko

±LA:CNP-lc ±S:CNP-nm +P:Cmpd.iVP1-3sg.prf.prog.prt.m

±this child-progeny-of support-on +one great strong power +hidden

'a great strong power hidden on the suppport of this child progeny.'

3.12.1 ±सन्तानेच्छुक देवीरमणले ± आज +(3.12.2) +पाए

±santānecchuka devīramaṇale ±āja +(3.12.2) +pāe

±S:PNP-nm ±AA:advl +DO:Cl(3.12.2) +P:tv1-3sg.pst.m

±desirous-of-offspring Deviramana ±today +(3.12.2) +got

'DevIramana, desirous of offspring, today, got (3.12.2)'

3.12.2 +यो दिन +देख्न

+yo dina +dekhna

+DO:CNP-ac +P:tv1-inf

this day +to-see

'to see this day.'

3.13 ± परिवर्तनशील संसारको गति विचित्र +छ

±parivartanaśīla saṃsārako gati +vicitra +cha

±S:modCNP +SC:adj-ac +P:ev1-3sg.pres.m

±changing world-of way +peculiar +is

'The way of the ever-changing world is peculiar.'

3.14.1 ±परमेश्वर +हाँस्नेलाई +रुवाउँछन्

±parameśvara +hā̃snelā.ī +ruvāũchan

±S:cn-nm +DO:nl-ac +P:tv1-3sg.pres.m

±Supreme Lord +laughing-ones +causes-to-weep

The Supreme Lord makes those who laugh weep'

3.14.2 +रुनेलाई +हँसाउँछन्

+runelā.ī +hasāũchan

+DO:nl-ac +P:tv1-3sg.pres.m

+weepers +causes-to-laugh
(and he) makes those who weep smile.'

3.15 ±एक दिन ± सुशील ± तुलसीका मठनेर +खेलिरहेको थियो
±eka dina ±suśīla ±tulasīkā maṭhanera +kheliraheko thiyo.
±AA:AdvP +S:pn-nm ±LA:PP +P:iv1-3sg.pst.prog.m
±one day ±Suśīla ±Tulasi-of mound-near +playing was
'One day, Suśīla was playing near the mound of the Tulsi plant.'

3.16.1 ±पिंडीबाट ±एक-तिर ±लक्ष्मी ± एक-तिर ± सुभद्राले ± (2.16.2) +"नानी, कता, कता, कता +भने
±piṃḍībāṭa ±eka-tira ±lakṣmī ±eka-tira ±subhadrāle ±(3.16.2) +"nānī, katā, katā, katā" +bhane
±AbA:cn-ab ±LA:PP ±S:pn-nm ±LA:PP ±S:pn-nm ±AD:Cl(3.16.2) +DO:NlP +P:tv1-3pl.pst
±porch-from ±oneside-on ±Lakṣmī +oneside-on ±Subhadrā ±(3.16.2) +baby, which-way, which-way which-way +they-said
'From the portch, Lakṣmī, on one side, and Subhadrā, on the other, (3.16.2), shouted "Baby, which way, which way, which way."'

3.16.2 +हात +थापेर
+hāta +thāpera
+DO:cn-ac +P:tv1-abs.prt
+hand +having-stretched
'stretching their hands'

3.17.1 ± सुशील ± एक क्षण पछि ±(3.17.2-3) +सुभद्राको छातीमा +टाँसियो
±suśīla ±eka kṣaṇapachi ±(3.17.2-3) +subhadrāko chātīmā +ṭā̃siyo
±S:pn-nm ±AA:PP +LC:CNP-lc +P:iv3-3sg.pst.m
±Suśīla ±one moment-after +(3.17.2-3) +Subhadrā-of chest-on +stuck
Suśīla, after a moment, (3.17.2-3), stuck on the chest of Subhadrā.'

3.17.2 +दगुर्दै
+dagurdai
+P:iv1-conj.prt
+running
'running'

3.17.3 +गै
+gai
+P:iv-3abs.prt
+having-gone
'(and) going'

3.17.4 ±सुभद्राको हृदय ±पवित्र पुत्र-वात्सल्यले परिपूर्ण +भयो
±subhadrāko hṛdaya +pavitra putra-vātsalyale paripūrṇa +bhayo;
±S:CNP-nm +SC:ModAdjP +P:iv1-3sg.pst.m
±Subhadra-of heart +pure son-love-by filled +became
Subhadra's heart became filled with a pure love of the son.'

3.17.5 ±(3.17.6) +म्वाई +खाइन्
±(3.17.6) +mvā.ī +khā.in
±AD:Cl(3.17.6) +DO:cn-ac +P:tv1-3sg.pst.f
±(3.17.6) +kiss +she-ate
'She kissed (him)'

3.17.6 +"मेरो राजा" +भनेर
+"mero rājā" +bhanera
+DO:CNP-ac +P:tv1-abs.prt
+"my rājā (king)" +having-said
'saying "My Rājā"'

3.18.1 +सुशीललाई ±लक्ष्मीले + जन्म ±मात्र +दिइन्
+suśīlalā.ī ±lakṣmīle +janma ±mātra +di.in,
+DC:pn-dt ±S:pn-nm +DO:cn-ac ±AA:advl +P:tv2-3sg.pst.f
+Suśīla-to ±Lakṣmī +birth ±only +gave
'Lakṣmī gave only birth to Suśīla,'

3.18.2 ± केवल ±सुभद्राले +[उसलाई] +हुर्काइन्
±kevala ±subhadrāle +[usalā.ī] +hurkā.in
±AA:advl +S:cn-nm [+DO:pro-ac] +P:tv1-tv1-3sg.pst.f
±only ±Subhadrā +raised +[him]
'only Subhadrā raised [him].'

3.19 +सुभद्रालाई ±एक छिन +छोड्दैनथ्यो
+subhadrālā.ī ±eka china +choḍdainathyo
+DO:pn-ac ±AA:AdvP +P:tv1-3sg.neg.pst.m
+Subhadrā ±one moment +he-used-not-leave
'He did not leave Subhadra even for a moment.'

3.20.1 +सुभद्रालाई +आमा +भन्थ्यो
+subhadrālā.ī +'āmā' +bhanthyo,
+DO:pn-ac +OC:cn-ac +P:tv3-3sg.pst.m
+Subhadrā +'mother' +he-used-to-call
'He called Subhadrā 'mother.'

3.20.2 +आफ्नी आमालाई +'दुलही' +भन्थ्यो

+āphnī āmālā.ī + 'dulahī' +bhanthyo,
+DO:CNP-ac +OC:cn-ac +P:tv3-3sg.pst.m
+one's-own mother +'dulahī' +he-used to-call
'He called his own mother 'dulahī.'

3.20.3 ± किनकि +लक्ष्मीलाई ±घरमा सवैजना +'दुलही बजै' भन्थे

±kinaki +lakṣmīlā.ī ±gharamā savaijanā +'dulahī bajyai' +bhanthe
±C:sc +DO:pn-ac ±LA:cn-lc ±S:pro+specif-nm +OC:CNP-ac
+P:tv3-3pl.pst
±because +Laksmi ±house-in ±everyone +dulahī-bajai +used-to-call
'because everybody in the house called Laksmi 'Dulahī Bajai.'

4.1 ±माघ महीना +थियो
±māgha mahinā +thiyo
±S:AppCNP-nm +P:iv1-3sg-pst.m
Māgha month +was
'It was the month of Māgha'

4.2.1 ±किसानहरु ±(4.2.2) +(4.2.3) फिक्रीमा +थिए
±kisānaharu ± (4.2.2) +(4.2.3) phikrimā +thie
±S:cn-nm ±AD:Cl (4.2.2) +LC:modCNP-lc +P:iv3-3pl.pst
±farmers ±(4.2.2) +(4.2.3) concern-in +they-were
'The farmers, (4.2.2), were concerned (4.2.3)'

4.2.2 +बालीनाली +थन्क्याई
+bālināli +thankyā.i
+DO:cn-ac +P:tv1-abs.prt
+crops +having-stored
'after storing the crops'

4.2.3 ± तीर्थ +जाने
±tīrtha +jāne
±LA:cn-(lc) +P:iv1-impf.prt
±pirgrimage +going
'to go on a pilgrimage'

4.3.1 +देवीरमणलाई ±पनि +(4.3.2) इच्छा +भयो
+devīramaṇalā.ī ±pani +(4.3.2) icchā +bhayo
+DC:pn-dt ±AA:advl ±S:modCNP +P:iv2-3sg.pst.m
+Devīramaṇa-to ±also +(4.3.2) desire +became
'Deiraman had also desire to go (4.3.2)'

4.3.2 +तीर्थ +गर्ने
+tīrtha +garne
+DO:cn-ac +P:tv1-impf.prt
+pilgrimage +doing
'to go on a pilgrimage'

4.3.3 ±मनमनले भने + (4.3.4)
±manamanale +bhane +(4.3.4)
±IA:cn-in +P:tv1-3sg.pst.m +DO:Cl(4.3.4)
±mind-mind-by +he-said +(4.3.4)
'He said to himself (4.3.4)'

4.3.4 ±(4.3.5) ±कहिले +गरुला ?

±(4.3.5) ±kahile +garulā ?
±AD:Cl (4.3.5) ±AA:advl +P:iv1-1sg-fut
±(4.3.5) ±when +shall-I-do ?
'When shall I do it (4.3.5)?'

4.3.5 ±(4.3.6) +तीर्थ-वर्त +नगरे

±(4.3.6) +tīrtha-varta +nagare
±AD:Cl (4.3.6) +DO:CmpdCNP-ac +P:tv1-neg.cond
±(4.3.6) +pilgrimage +if-not-make
'If I do not make the pilgrimage (4.3.6)'

4.3.6 ±पग +चल्दै

±paga +caldai
±S:cn-nm +P:iv1-conj.prt
±steps +while-moving
'while I still can walk'

4.4.1 ±मानिसहरु ±(4.4.2) +अन्धा +बन्छन्

±mānisaharu ±(4.4.2) +andhā +banchan,
±S:cn-nm ±AD:Cl(4.4.2) +SC:adj-nm +P:ev1-3pl
±people ±(4.4.2) +blind +become
'People become blind (4.4.2)'

4.4.2 +सम्पत्ति +पाएर

+sampatti +pāera
+DO:cn-ac +P:tv1-abs.prt
+wealth +having-gained
'gaining wealth'

4.4.3 ±(4.4.4) ± दिन-रात ± पैसाका निमित्त +हाहाकार +मच्चाइरहन्छन्

±(4.4.4) ±dina-rāta ±paisākā nimitta +hāhākāra +maccā.irahanchan.
±AD:Cl(4.4.4) ±AA:Cmpd.advl +AA:PP +DO:cn-ac
+P:tv1-3pl.pres.prog
±(4.4.4) ±day-night ±money-of for +outcry +they-keep-making
'(4.4.4), they keep making an outcry for the sake of money day and night'

4.4.4 +विवेक बुद्धिलाई +खोपामा +राखेर

+viveka buddhilā.ī +khopāmā +rākhera
+DO:CmpdCNP-ac +LC:cn-lc +P:tv4-abs.prt
+good-sense wisdom +nitche-in +having-put
'putting their wisdom and good sense into a niche,'

4.5 ±ती गोठालाहरु को सम्पत्ति ± एक दिन ± अग्नि या चोरका निमित्त +हुन्छ
+tī goṭhālāharuko sampatti ±eka dina ±agni yā corakā nimitta +huncha
±S:modCNP-nm ±AA:AdvP ±AA:PP +P:iv1-3sg.pres.m
±those boors-of property ±one day ±fire or thief-of for +is
'The property of those boors will be for the fire or thieves.'

4.6.1 ±अघि +गरेको हुँदो हुँ
±aghi +gareko hūdo hū
±AA:advl +P:iVP-1sg.prob.pst
±before +perfromed I-probably-had
'I had probably performed,'

4.6.2 ±अहिले ±एक मानाको सन्तोष +छ
±ahile ±eka mānāko santoṣa +cha.
±AA:advl ±S:modCNP-nm +P:iv1-3sg.pres
±now ±one mana-of satisfaction +is
'Now I have a satisfaction of a meal.'

4.7.1 ±(4.7.2) +सन्तानका जरामा ± मल +पर्ला
±(4.7.2) +santānakā jarāmā ±mala +parlā
±AD:Cl (4.7.2) +LC:modCNP-lc ±S:cn-nm +P:iv3-3sg.fut.m
±(4.7.2) +desendants-of roots ±nourishment +will-fall
'The roots of my family tree will be nourished;'

4.7.2 ±अहिले ±फेरि +गर्न सके
±ahile ±pheri ±garna sake
±AA:advl ±AA:advl +P:iVP1-cond
±now ±again +to-do if-can
'If I can do it again'

4.7.3 ±परत्र +बन्ला
±paratra +banlā
±S:cn-ac P:iv1-3sf.fut
±next-life +will-be[good]
'My next life will be good.'

4.8.1 ±(4.8.2) ±देवीरमण +(4.8.3) तयार +भए
±(4.8.2) ±devīramaṇa +(4.8.3) tayāra +bhae
±AD:Cl(4.8.2) ±S:pn-nm +SC:modAdjP-nm +P:iv1-3sg.pst.m
±(4.8.2) ±Devīramaṇa +ready (4.8.3) +became
'(4.8.2), Deviraman became ready (4.8.3)'

4.8.2 + इत्यादि विचार +गरेर
+ityādi vicāra +garera
+DO:CNP-ac +P:tv1-abs.prt
+such thought +having-done
'Having such thoughts in mind,'

4.8.3 ±तीर्थ +जान
±tīrtha +jāna
±LA:cn-(lc) +P:iv1-inf
±pilgrimage +to-go
'to go on a pilgrimage.'

4.9.1 ±उनको (4.9.2) विचार +थियो
±unako (4.9.2) vicāra +thiyo
±S:modCNP-nm +P:iv1-3sg.pst
±his (4.9.2) thought +was
'He had thought (4.9.2)'

4.9.2 ± एक्लै +जाने
±eklai +jāne
±AA:advl +P:iv1-impf.prt
±alone +going
'to go alone.'

4.9.3 ±परन्तु ±गाउँका कैयन बूढाबूढी विधवा स्वास्नीमानिसहरु ±पनि +तयार +भए
±parantu ±gāũkā kaiyana būḍhābūḍhī, vidhavā svāsnīmānisaharu ±pani ±tayāra +bhae
±C:cc ±S:ModCNP-nm ±AA:advl +SC:adj-nm +P:ev1-3sg.pst
±But ±village-of many old-people, widow women ±also +ready +were
'But many old people and widows of the village were also ready [to go].'

4.10.1 ±(4.10.2) ±देवीरमणको आँगन ±तीर्थयात्रीका कुम्ले फौजले +भरियो
±(4.10.2) ±devīramaṇako ā̃gana ±tīrthayātrīkā kumle phaujale +bhariyo
±AD:Cl(4.10.2) ±S:ModCNP-nm ±IA:ModCNP-in +P:iv1p-3sg.pst
±(4.10.2) ±Devīramaṇa-of courtyard ±pilgrims-of baggage-loaded army-by +was-filled
'(4.10.2) Deviraman's courtyard was filled with an army of pilgrims loaded with their baggages.'

4.10.2 +देख्दादेख्दै
+dekhdādekhdai
+P:CmpdiVP-conj-prt.
looking-looking-on
'While one was looking on,'

4.11.1 ±(4.11.2) ± लक्ष्मी ±पनि ±(4.11.3) +लागिन्

±(4.11.2) ±lakşmī ±pani ±(4.11.5) +lāgin.
±AD:Cl(4.11.2) ±S:pn-nm ±AA:advl +DO:Cl(4.11.5) +P:tv1-3sg.pst.f
±(4.11.2) Lakşmī ±also +(4.11.5) +began
'(4.11.2), Lakşmī also began (4.11.5)'

4.11.2 +(4.11.3) +देखी

+(4.11.3) +dekhī
+DO:Cl (4.11.4) +P:tv1-abs.prt
+(4.11.3) +having-seen
'Seeing (4.11.3),'

4.11.3 ±गाउँका धेरै आइमाईहरु +(4.11.4) +लागेको

±gāũkā dherai ā.imā.īharu +(4.11.4) +lāgeko
±S:modCNP-nm +DO:Cl (4.11.4) +P:tv1-prf.prt
±village-of many women +(4.11.4) +begun
'many women of the village beginnig (4.11.4),'

4.11.4 +जान

+jāna
+P:iv1-inf
to-go
'to go'

4.11.5 ± (4.11.6) +जिद्दी +गर्न

±(4.11.6) +jiddī +garna
±AD:Cl (4.11.7) +DO:cn-nm +P:tv1-inf
±(4.11.7) +insistence +to-do
'to insist'

4.11.6 +(4.11.7) +भनेर

+(4.11.7) +bhanera
+DO:Cl (4.11.7) +P:tv1-abs.prt.
+(4.11.7) +saying
'saying (4.11.7)'

4.11.7 +जान्छु

+jānchu
+P:iv1-1sg.pres
+I-go
'I will [also]go'

4.12.1 ± सुशील ± चाहिं +(4.12.2) +लाग्यो

±suśīla ±cāhiṃ +(4.12.2) +lāgyo

±S:pn ±NU: nu +DO:Cl(4.12.1) +P:tv1-3sg.pst.m

±Suśīla ±on his part +(4.12.2) +began

'Suśīla, on his part, began (4.12.2)

4.12.2 ± (4.12.3) +रून

±(4.12.3) +runa

±AD:Cl(4.12.3) +P:iv1-inf

±(4.12.3) +to-cry

'to cry (4.12.3)'

4.12.3 +देवीरमणको दौरा +समातेर

+devīramaṇako daurā +samātera

+DO:modCNP-ac +P:tv1-abs.prt

+Devīramaṇa-of shirt +having-held

'holding on Deviraan's shirt.'

4.13.1 ± देवीरमणले +(4.13.2) +सकेनन्

±devīramaṇale +(4.13.2) +sakenan

±S:pn-nm +DO:Cl(4.13.2) +P:tv1-3sg.pst.m

±Devīramaṇa +(4.13.2) +could-not

'Deviraman could not (4.13.2)'

4.13.2 +यो बलिष्ठ बालहठलाई +उपेक्षा +गर्न

±yo baliṣṭha bālahaṭhalā.ī +upekṣā +garna

+DO:CNP-ac +OC:cn-ac +P:tv3-inf

+this sttrong child-persistence +disregard +to-do

'disregard this persistence of his child.'

4.14 ±आखिर +लक्ष्मी र सुशीललाई ±पनि ±साथमा +लिए

±ākhira +lakṣmī ra suśīlalā.ī ±pani ±sāthamā +lie

±AA:advl +DO:CmpdCNP-ac ±AA:advl ±LA:cn-lc +P:tv1-3sg.pst

±in-the-end +Lakṣmī and Suśīla ±also ±company-in +he-took

'In the end, he took Lakṣmī and Suśīla also in company.'

4.15 ±एक क्षण पछि ±त्यो तीर्थयात्रीको समूह ±रानुको पछि ± माहुरी झैं ±देवीरमणको पछि +लाग्यो

±eka kṣaṇa pachi ±tyo tīrthayātrīko samūha ±rānuko pachi ±māhurī jhaĩ ±devīramaṇako pachi +lāgyo

±AA:advl ±S:modCNP-nm ±AA:PP ±AA:AdvP ±AA:PP +P:iv1-3sg.pst.m

±one moment-after ±that pilgrims-of group ±queen-of after ±bees like ±Deviramana-of after +started off

'After a moment, the swarm of pilgrims, like bees following their queen, started off behind Devīramaṇa.'

4.16.1 ± किन्तु +सुभद्रालाई ±(4.16.2) ±कसैले +एक वचन ± सम्म ± पनि +सोधेन
±kintu +subhadrālā.ī ±(4.16.2) ±kasaile +eka vacana ±samma ±pani +sodhena.
±C:cc +DC:pn-dt ±AD:Cl (4.16.2) ±S:pro-nm +DO:CNP-ac ±AA:advl ±AA:advl +P:tv2-3sg.neg.pst.m
±But +Subhadrā-to ±(4.16.2) ±anyone +one word +even +also +did-not-ask
'But no one asked Subhadrā even a single word (4.16.2)'

4.16.2 +(4.16.3) +भनेर
+(4.16.3) +bhanera
+DO:Cl(4.16.3) +P:tv1-abs.prt
+(4.16.3) +having-said
'saying (4.14.3)'

4.16.3 +जान्छ्यौ ±कि?
+'jānchyau ±ki?'
+P:iv2-sg.pres.f ±NU:nu *(ki)* ?
+you-go ±*ki*
'"Do you want to go?"'

4.17.1 ± सुभद्राले ±मनमनले +भनिन् + (4.17.2)
±subhadrāle ±manamanale +bhanin +(4.17.2),
±S:pn-nm ±IA:cn-in +P:tv1-3sg.pst.f +DO:Cl(4.17.2)
±Subhadra ±mind-mind-by +said +(4.17.2)
'Subhadra said to herself (4.17.2)'

4.17.2 ± (4.17.3) +मलाई ±पो +लैजानुपर्थ्यो
±(4.17.3) +malā.ī ±po +laijānu-parthyo
±AA:Cl (3.17.3) +DO:pro-ac ±NU:nu *(po*) +P:tVP1-3sg.pst.m
±(4.17.3) +me ± rather +should-have-taken
'He should have taken rather me (4.17.3)'

4.17.3 +तीर्थ-वर्त +गर्न ± ता
+tīrtha-varta +garna ±tā
+DO:Cmpd.CNP +P:tv1-inf ±NU:nu *(ta*)
+pilgrimage +to-perform ±*tā*
'to go on a pilgrimage.'

4.18 ±मेरो को छ र ,-- ±छोरा न छोरी
±mero ko +cha ±ra, -- chorā na chorī
±S:CNP-nm +P:iv1-3sg.pres.m ±NU: nu ±AD:AdvP
±my who +is ±ra ±no son or daughter
'Who do I have? -- no son or daughter!'

4.19.1 ±उसको उमेर +थियो
±usako umera +thiyo
±S:CNP-cn +P:iv1-3sg.pst.m
±her age +was
She still has [young] age,'

4.19.2 +जाँदै गर्दी हो
+jā~dai gardī ho
+P:CmodiVP1-prob.pst.f
+going-she-could do
'She could have gone (later).'

4.20.1 ±उ +छोरो पाएकी स्वास्नी +भई
±u +choro pāekī svāsnī +bha.ī
±S:pro-nm +SC:modCNP-nm +P:ev1-3sg.pst.f
±she +son borne wife +was
'She is a wife, who had borne a son'

4.20.2 +वचन +हार्न सक्नुभएन
+vacana +hārna saknubhaena
+DO:cn-ac +P:tVP1-3sg.pst.neg.m
+word +to-lose he-could-not
'He could not reject her words.'

4.21.1 ±म +(4.21.2) अनाथ +[छु]
±ma +(4.21.2)anātha +[chu]
±S:pro-nm +SC:modAdjP-nm [+P:ev1-1sg.pst]
±I (4.21.2) +helpless +[am]
'I am helpless (4.21.2)'

4.21.2 +टेक्ने-समाउने केही +नभएकी
+ṭekne-samāune kehī +nabhaekī
+DO:modProlP-ac +P:tv1-prf.prt.f
+standing-holding anything +not-having
'not having anything to stand on or hold onto'

4.21.3 ±मेरो केको खोजी +थियो

±mero keko khojī +thiyo
±S:modCNP-nm +P:iv1-3sg.pst.m
±my what-of search +was
'Who thinks of me? (Not one thought of me).'

4.22 ±मानिस +बलेकै आगो +ताप्छन्

±mānisa +balekai āgo +tāpchan
±S:cn-nm +DO:CNP-ac +P:tv1-3pl.pres
±men burning fire +use (for warming themselves)
'People warm themselves only at a burning fire.'

4.23.1 +(4.23.2) उसलाई ± मानिस ± पनि +हेला +गर्छन्

+(4.23.2) usalā.ī ±mānisa ±pani ±helā +garchan
+DC:modProP-dt ±S:cn-nm ±AA:advl +DO:cn-ac +P:tv2-3sg.pres
+him-to ±men ±also +contempt +do
'People have contempt for him (4.23.2)'

4.23.2 +जसलाई ±परमेश्वरले +ठगेको छ

+jasalā.ī ±parameśvarale +ṭhageko cha
+DO:pro-ac ±S:cn-nm +P:tVP1-3sg.pres
+whom ±God +deceived has
'whom God has deceived.'

4.24 ±अहो! ±संसार+ कति मतलबी +छ !

±aho! ±saṃsāra +kati matalabī cha !'
±EX: intj (*aho*) ±S:cn-nm +SC:CNP-nm +P:ev1-3sg.pres.m
±Oh! ±world +how selfish +is !
'Oh! how selfish the world is!'

4.25.1 ±(4.25.2) ± सुभद्रा ± धेरै बेर सम्म ± एक्लै +रोइरहिन्

±(4.25.2) ±subhadrā ±dherai bera samma ±eklai +roirahin
±AD:Cl(4.25.2) ±S:cn-nm ±AA:PP ±AA:advl +P:iv1-3sg.pres.prog.f
±(4.25.2) ±Subhadrā ±many moment-for ±alone +kept-crying
'(4.25.2), Subhadrā kept crying alone for a long time.'

4.25.2 +यस्तै तर्क +गर्दै

+yastai tarka +gardai
+DO:CNP-ac +P:tv1-3sg.conj.prt
+such thought +doing
'Thinking as such,'

4.26.1 ±सुभद्राले ±बाह्र वर्षको उमेरदेखि +(4.26.2) + लागिथिन्
±subhadrāle ±bāhra varṣako umeradekhi +(4.26.2) +lāgithin
±S:pn-nm ±AA:PP +DO:Cl(2.26.2) +P:tv1-3sg.pst.prf.f
±Subhadrā +twelve years-of age-since +(2.26.2) +had-begun
'Subhadrā had begun (2.26.2) since the age of twelve.'

4.26.2 +देवीरमणको दैलो +पोत्न
+devīramaṇako dailo +potna
+DO:modCNP-ac +P:tv1-inf
+Deviramana-of doorway +to-clean
'to clean Devīramaṇa's doorway (for good luck).'

4.27 ± यो घर +सुभद्रालाई +संसारमा सबै भन्दा प्यारो वस्तु +थियो
±yo ghara +subhadrālā.ī +saṃsāramā sabai bhandā pyāro vastu +thiyo
±S:CNP-nm +DC:pn-dt +SC:modCNP-nm +P:ev2-3sg.pst.m
±this house +Subhadra-to +world-in all than dear thing +was
'This house was dearest of all things in the world to Subhadra.'

4.28.1 ±यी वस्तुभाउ ±(4.28.2) +तरुण +भएका +थिए
±yī vastubhāu ± (4.28.2) +taruṇa +bhaekā +thie.
±S:CNP-nm ±AD:Cl (4.28.2) +SC:adj-nm +P:eVP-3pl.prf.pst
±these animals ±(4.28.2) +young +become had
'These animals had become young, (4.28.2)'

4.28.2 ±यिनको लालन-पालनमा +बढेर
±yinaiko lālana-pālanamā +baḍhera
±LA:CNP-lc +P:iv1-abs.prt.
±this-one-of care-nourishment-in +having-grown
'growing in the care and nourishment of this (lady)'

4.29 ± यो घर, यी वस्तुभाउ, यी रुख-वृक्ष सबै +यिनै सन्तानहीना रमणीका साथी +थिए
±yo ghara, yī vastubhāu, yī rukha-vṛkṣa sabai +yinai santānahīnā ramaṇīkā sāthī + thie
±S:CmpdCNP-nm +SC:modCNP-nm +P:ev1-3pl.pst
this house, these animals, these trees-plants all +this childless lady's friends +were
'This house, these animals and these trees were all the companions of the childless woman.'

4.30 +यिनीहरूसंगको वियोग ± सुभद्रा ± एक छिन पनि +सहन सक्तैनथिन्
+yinīharusaṃgako viyoga ±subhadrā ±eka china pani +sahana saktinathin
+DO:modCNP-ac ±S:pn-nm ±AA:AdvP +P:tVP1-3sg.pst.f
+these-with-of separation ±Subhadrā ±one momentalso +to-endure could-not

'Subhadrā could not endure the separation from them even for a moment.'

4.31.1 ± (4.31.1) ± सुभद्रा +जान्थिन्
± (4.31.1) ±subhadrā +jānthin
±AD:Cl(4.31.2) ±S:cn-nm +P:iv1-3sg.prob.pst
± (4.31.2) ±Subhadrā +might-have-gone
'(4.31.1) Subhadrā might have gone'

4.31.2 +जान ± ता
+jāna ±tā
+P:iv1-inf ±NU:nu (*tā*)
+to-go ±as for (?)
'As for actually going,'

4.31.3 ±कि +जाँदैनथिन्
±ki +jā̃dainathin
±C:cc +P:iv1-3sg.neg.pst.f
±or +might-not-have-gone
'or, might not have gone,'

4.31.4 ±(4.31.5) ±उनको आँसु +पुछिने थियो
±(4.31.5) ±unako ā̃su +puchine thiyo
±AD:Cl (4.31.5) ±S:CNP-nm +P:iVP1.impf.prt+aux-3sg.pst.m
±(4.31.5) ±her rears been-wiped-was
'her tears would have been wiped (4.31.5)'

4.31.5 +एक वचन +सोधेको ± सम्म ± भए
+eka vacana +sodheko +samma +bhae
+DO:CNP-ac +P:tv-prf-prt ±AA:advl ±C:sc
+one word +asked ±just +if
'if just a word were asked,'

4.32.1 ±(4.32.2) ±बखतमा ±कत्रो काम +हुन्छ
±(4.32.2) ±bakhatamā ±katro kāma +huncha
±AA:Cl(4.32.2) ±LA:cn-lc ±S:CNP-nm +P:iv1-3sg.pres.m
±(4.32.2) ±time-in ±how-big work +happens
'what a great work is done'

4.32.2 +एक वचन +सोधिसम्मदिनाले
+eka vacana +sodhisammadināle
+DO:CNP-ac +P:tVP-inf+*le*
+one word +ask-just by
'by askng just a word (at the right moment)'

4.32.3 ±त्यो कुरा +(4.32.4) देवीरमणलाई +थाहा +भएन

±tyo kurā (4.32.4) devīramaṇalā.ī +thāhā +bhaena
±S:CNP-nm +DC:modCNP-dt +SC:cn-nm +P:ev2-3sg.neg.pst
±that mattter +(4.32.4) Devīramaṇa-to +knowledge +was-not
'That matter was not known to Devīramaṇa (4.32.4)'

4.32.4 +मनोविज्ञान +नजानेका

+manovijñāna +najānekā
+DO:cn-nm +P:tv1-neg.prf.prt
+psychology +not-knowing
'who did not know psychology'

4.33.1 ±मनोमालिन्यको एउटा सानो बीज +चाहिन्छ

±manomālinyako euṭā sāno bīja +cāhincha
±S:modCNP-nm +P:iv1-3sg.pres.m
±ill-feeling-of one small seed +is-needed
'There needs to be but a small seed of ill-feeling'

4.33.2 ± जो (4.31.3) ±आफसेआफ +भयङ्कर रूप धारण +गर्दछ

±jo ±(4.31.3) ±āphaseāpha +bhayaṅkara rūpa dhāraṇa +gardacha
±S:pro-nm ±AD:Cl(4.33.3) ±AA:advl +DO:CNP-ac
+P:tv1-3sg.pres.m
±which (4.31.3) ±by-itself +terrible form assumption +does
'which assumes a terrible form of its own (4.33.3)'

4.33.3 ±समयमा +बढेर

±samayamā +baḍhera
±LA:cn-lc +P:iv1-abs.prt
±time-in +having-grown
'growing in time.'

4.34 ±त्यस्तै ±लक्ष्मी तथा सुभद्राका जीवनमा ±पनि ±यो तीर्थयात्रा
+मनोमालिन्यको एउटा बीज +हुन गयो

±tyasatai ±lakṣmī tathā subhadrākā jīvanamā ±pani ±yo tīrthayātrā
+manomālinyako euṭā bīja +huna gayo
±AA:advl ±LA:CNP-lc ±AA:advl ±S:CNP-nm +DO:CNP-ac
+P:ev1-3sg.pst.m
±likewise ±Lakṣmī and Subhadrā-of life-in ±also ±this pilgrimage
+ill-feeling-of one seed +to-be went
Likewise, this pilgrimage happened to be a seed of ill-feeling in the life
of Lakṣmī and Subhadrā.'

4.35.1 ±(4.35.2) ±दुवैमा ±बहुधा ± झगडा +हुन लाग्यो
±(4.35.2) ±duvaimā ±bahudhā ±jhagaḍā +huna lāgyo
±AA:Cl (4.35.2) ±LA:nl-lc ±AA:advl ±S:cn-nm +P:iVP1-3sg.pst.m
±(4.35.2) ±both-in ±frfequently ±quarrel ±to-be began
'(4.35.2) quarrels began to happen frequently between the two.'

4.32.2 ±तीर्थबाट +फर्केदेखि
±tīrthabāṭa +pharke-dekhi
±AbA:cn-ab +P:iv1-prf.prt
±pilgimage-from +return-since
'Since the return from the pilgrimage,'

4.36.1 ±(4.36.2) ± लक्ष्मी ±(4.36.3) +उत्तर +दिन्थिन्
±(4.36.2) ±lakṣmī ±(4.36.3) +uttara +dinthin.
±AD:Cl(4.36.2) ±S:pn-nm ±AD:Cl (4.36.3) +DO:cn-ac
+P:tv1-3sg.pst.f
±(4.36.2) ±Laksmi ±(4.36.3) +answer +used-to-give
'(4.36.2), Laksmi gave an answer (4.36.3)'

4.36.2 ±सुभद्राले +कुनै प्रश्न +गर्दा
±subhadrāle +kunai praśna +gardā
±S:pn-nm +DO:CNP-ac +P:tv1-impf.prt
±'Subhadra +any question +when-doing
'When Subhadra asked any question,'

4.36.3 +छेड +हानेर
+cheḍa +hānera
+DO:cn-ac +P:tv1-abs.prt
+sarcasm +having-struck
'with sarcasm.'

4.37 ±बस्, ±कुरैकुराका हानथापबाट ±ठुलो कलह +खडा +हुन्थ्यो
±bas, ±kuraikurākā hānathāpabāṭa ±ṭhulo kalaha +khaḍā +hunthyo
±EX: intj (*bas*) ±AbA:modCNP-ab ±S:CNP-nm +SC:adj.nm
+P:ev1-3sg.m
±So, talk-talk-of competition-from ±great quarrel +established
used-to-be
'This went on to the point that spats developed into quarrels (when they
spoke to each other).'

4.38.1 ±देवीरमण ±(4.38.2) +सुनिरहन्थे
±devīramaṇa ±(4.38.2) +sunirahanthe.
±S:pn-nm ±AD:Cl(4.38.2) +P:iv1-3sg.pst.m
±Devīramaṇa ±(4.38.2) +kept-listening

'Devīramaṇa kept listening (4.36.2).'

4.38.2 +चूपचाप +भएर
+cūpacāpa +bhaera
+SC:adj.nm +P:ev1-abs.prt
+silent +having-been
'being silent'

4.39.1 ± (4.39.2) +पुत्रवती पत्नी +[थिइन्]
±(4.39.2) +putravatī patnī +[thi.in]
±AD:Cl (4.39.2) +SC:CNP-nm +[P:ev1-3sg.pst.f]
±(4.39.2) having-son wife +[she-was]
'(4.39.2) she was a wife with a son,'

4.39.2 +लक्ष्मीलाई +ताडना +गरून् +भने
+lakṣmīlā.ī +tāḍanā +garūn +bhane
+DC:pn-dt +DO:cn-ac +P:tv1-3sg.imp ±C:sc
+Lakṣmī-to +rebuke +he-may-do ±if
'If he rebuked Lakṣmī,'

4.39.3 ± (4.39.4) +धर्म तथा विवेकको हत्या +[हुन्थ्यो]
±(4.39.4) +dharma tathā vivekako hatyā +[hunthyo]
±AD:(4.39.4) +SC:mod-CNP-nm +[P:ev1-3sg.pst.f]
±(4.39.4) +religion and conscience-of murder +[would-be]
'It would be a violation of religious duty and conscience,'

4.39.4 +सुभद्रालाई +ताडना+गरून् ±भने
+subhadrālā.ī tāḍanā garūn ±bhane
+DC:pn-dt +DO:cn-ac +P:tv1-3sg.opt ±C:sc
+Subhadra-to +rebuke +he-may-do +if
'if he rebuked Subhadrā,'

4.40.1 +के +गरुन्
+ke +garūn
+DO:pro-ac +P:tv1-3sg.imp
+what +he may do
'What could he do?'

4.40.2 +सांसारिक सुखलिप्साको टर्रो आनन्दको अनुभव +गरिरहेका थिए
+sāṃsārika sukhalipsāko ṭarro ānandako anubhava +garirahekā thie.
+DO:modCNP +P:tVP-3sg.pst.m
+worldy hapiness-desire-of bitter pleasure-of experience +doing he-was
'He was experiencing the bitterness of one's desire for worldly pleasure.'

4.41 +त्यस बखतमा ±उनको त्यो प्रबल वाक्शक्ति +हावा +हुन्थ्यो
±tyasa bakhatamā ±unako tyo prabala vākśakti +hāvā +hunthyo
±LA:CNP-lc ±S:ModCNP-nm +SC:cn-nm +P:ev1-3sg.pst.
±that time-at ±his that strong word-power +air +used-to-be
'At that time, his strong power of persuasion was gone with the wind.'

4.42.1 ±मानिसको पाण्डित्य ±(4.42.2) + काम +लाग्दछ
±mānisako pāṇḍitya ±(4.42.2) +kāma +lāgdacha
±S:CNP-nm ±LA:Cl(4.42.2) +SC:cn-nm +P:ev1-3sg.pres.m
±man-of wisdom ±(4.42.2) +use +strikes
'A man's wisdom is useful (4.42.2)'

4.42.2 +अरुलाई +उपदेश +गर्नमा
+arulā.ī +upadeśa +garnamā
+DC:prol-dt +DO:cn-ac +P:tv2-inf+*mā*
+others-to +advice +doing-in
'in advising others,'

4.42.3 ±नकि +आफूलाई +परिआउँदा
±naki +āphūlā.ī +pariāũdā
±C:cc +DC:pro-dt +P:iv2-impf.prt
± but not +oneself-to +when-it-comes
'but not when it comes to oneself.'

4.43 ±यो प्रतिदिनको गृहकलहले ± सुभद्राको कोमल हृदय-कुसुम ±एकदम +ओइलायो
±yo pratidinako gṛhakalahale ±subhadrāko komala hṛdaya-kusuma ±ekadama +oilāyo
±IA:mocCNP-in +S:CNP-nm ±AA:advl +P:iv1-3sg.pst.m
±this everyday's household-quarrel-by ±Subhadrā-of soft heart-flower ±completely +withered
'Becasue of this daily household quarrel, Subhadrā's tender heart completley withered.'

4.44.1 ±उनी + (4.44.2) +लागिन्
±unī +(4.44.2) +lāgin
±S:pro-nm +DO:Cl(4.44.2) +P:tv1-3sg.pst.f
±she +(4.44.2) +began
'She began (4.42.2),'

4.44.2 ±कारागारकी दु:खी बन्दी झैं +भाग्ने मौका +खोज्न

±kārāgārakī duḥkhī bandī jhaĩ +bhāgne maukā +khojna
±AA: AdvP +DO:CNP-ac +P:tv1-inf
±prison-of suffering prisoner like +escaping opportunity +to-look-for
'like a suffering prisoner, to look for an opportunity to escape.

5.1.1 ±(5.1.2) ±रात्री +झन् भयङ्कर प्रतीत +हुन्थ्यो

±(5.1.2) ±rātrī +jhan bhayangkara pratīta +hunthyo
± AD:Cl(5.1.2) ±S:cn-nm +SC:AdjP +P:eVP2-3sg.pst.m
±(5.1.2) ±night more dreadfful appeared +was
'The night appeared more dreadful (5.1.2)'

5.1.2 ±कालो अन्धकारमाथि ±(5.1.3) हुचील पक्षीको विरसिलो हुकहुक शब्द +थपिंदा

±kālo andhakāramāthi ±(5.1.3) hucīla pakṣīko virasilo hukahuka śabda +thapiṃdā
±LA:PP ±S:ModCNP-nm +P:iv1-conj.prt
±black darkness-over ±(5.1.2) owl bird-of melancholic "huk-huk" sound when-added
'When the melancholic hooting of the owl (5.1.2) was added'

5.1.3 ± (5.1.4) +कराउने

±(5.1.4) +karā.une
±AA:AdvCl (5.1.4) +P:iv1-imprf.prt
±(5.1.4) +crying
'crying (5.1.4)'

5.1.4 +पर्खी पर्खी

+parkhī parkhī
+P:iv1-abs.prt (repeated)
+waiting waiting
'intermittantly'

5.2 ± पल्लो गाउँमा ±कुकुर +भुकिरहेको थियो

±pallo gāũmā +kukura +bhukiraheko thiyo
±LA: CNP-lc ±S:cn-mn +P:iv1-3sg.pst.prog
±next village-in ±dog +barking was
'A dog was barking in the next village.'

5.3.1 ±(5.3.1) ±अनन्त आकाशमा ± तारागण ±पिलपिल +रोईरहेका थिए

±(5.3.1) ±ananta ākāśamā ±tārāgaṇa ±pilapila +roiraheka thie.
±AD: Cl (5.3.2) ±LA:CNP-lc ±S:cn-nm ±AA:advl +P:iv1-3pl.pst.prog
±(5.3.1) ±wide sky-in ±stars ±atwinkle +crying were
'In the wide sky, stars were (seemingly) crying (5.3.1)'

5.3.2 ±पृथ्वीमा +मानवजातिको दु:खमय अवस्था +देखेर
±pṛthvīmā +mānavajātiko duḥkhamaya avasthā +dekhera
±LA:cn-lc +DO:CNP-ac +P:tv1-abs.prt
±earth-on +mankind-of miserable lot +having-seen
'seeing the miserable lot of mankind on earth.'

5.4.1 ±सुभद्राले ± (5.4.2) +हेरिन्
±subhadrāle ±(5.4.2) +herin
±S:pn-nm ±AD:Cl(5.4.2) +P:iv1-3sg.pst.f
±Subhadrā ±(5.4.2) +looked
'Subhadrā, (5.4.2), looked up'

5.4.2 ±आँगनमा +आएर
±ā̃ganamā +āera
±LC:cn-lc +P:iv3-abs.prt.
±courtyard-on +having-come
'coming out into the courtyard'

5.4.2 ±एक छिनपछि ±त्यो विशाल नभस्थलबाट ±एउटा लामो ज्योति ±(5.4.2) ±तलतिर +खस्यो
±eka chinapachi ±tyo viśāla nabhasthalabāṭa ±euṭā lāmo jyoti ±(5.4.3) ±talatira +khasyo
±AA:PP ±AbA:CNP-ab ±S:CNP-nm ±AA:PP +P:iv1-3sg.pst.m
±one moment-after ±that immense firmament-from ±one long light ±(5.4.3) ±downward +glided
'After amoment, a shooting star, (5.4.3), dropped downward'

5.4.3 ±सल्ल +बगेर
±salla +bagera
±AA:advl +P:iv1-abs.prt.
±swiftly +having-glided
'Gliding swiftly'

5.5.1 ±किन्तु ±(5.5.1) ±बीचैमा +लुप्त +भयो
±kintu ±(5.5.2) ±bīcaimā +lupta +bhayo.
±C:cc +AD:Cl(5.5.2) ±LA:cn-lc +SC:adj-nm +P:ev1-3sg.pst.m
±but (5.5.2) ±middle-in +lost +was
'but, (5.5.3), it was lost in the middle'

5.5.2 +(5.5.3) +नपाउँदै
+(5.5.3) +napāũdai
+DO:Cl (5.5.3) +P:tv1-conj.prt
+(5.5.3) not-being-able-to
'not being able to (5.5.3)'

5.5.3 ±यो कालो पृथ्वीमा +झर्न
±yo kālo pṛthvīmā +jharna
±LA:CNP-lc +DO:nl +P:tv1-conl.prt
±this dark earth-on +to-fall
'fall onto the dark earth.'

5.6 ±अघि ±शैशवकालमा +यस्तै दृश्य +देखेकी थिइन्
±aghi ±śaiśavakālamā +yastai dṛśya +dekhekī thi.in
±AA:advl ±LA:Cmpdcn-lc +DO:CNP-ac +P:tv1-3sg.pst.prf.f
±before ±childhood-in +such sight +seen she-had
'She had seen such a sight once before in her childhood.'

5.7.1 ±(5.7.2) +(5.7.3-5) जवाफ +मिलेथ्यो
±(5.7.2) +(5.7.3-4) javāpha +milethyo
±AD:Cl(5.7.2) +S:ModCNP-nm +P:iv2-3sg.pst.m
±(5.7.2) +answer (5.7.3-4) +received-had
'She had received answer (5.7.3-4)'

5.7.2 ±उस बखत ±आमासँग +सोद्धा--
±usa bakhata ±āmā saṃga +sodhdā--
±AA: advl +AA:PP +P:iv1-conj.prt
±that time +mother-with +when-asked
'At that time when she asked her mother'

5.7.3 +आकाशका देवगण +हुन्
+ākāśakā devagaṇa +hun
+SC:CNP-nm +P:ev1-3pl.pres
+sky-of gods +they-are
'they are gods of the sky'

5.7.4 ±(5.7.5) ±स्वर्गबाट पतन +भएका ±भन्ने
±(5.7.5) ±svargabāṭa patana +bhaekā ±bhanne
±AA:Cl(5.7.5) ±AbA:cn-ab +SC:CNP-nm +P:ev1-prf.prt ±C:sc
± (5.7.5) ±heaven-from +fallen +they-are +saying
'saying that they have fallen from the heaven.'

5.7.5 ±पुण्य +सिद्धिनाले
±puṇya siddināle
±S: cn-nm +P:iv-inf+*le*
±merit +be-finished-by
'because their merit has been used up'

5.8.1 ±आज +उही कुरा +संझिन्
±āja +uhī kurā +samjhin
±AA:advl +DO:CNP-ac +P:tv1-3sg.pst.f
±today +same thing +she-remembered
'Today, she remembered the same thing.'

5.8.2 ±मनमनले +भनिन् +(5.8.3)
±manamanale +bhanin +(5.8.3)
±AA:advl +P:tv1-3sg.pst.f +DO:Cl(5.8.3)
±mind-mind-by +she-said +(5.8.3)
'She said to herself (5.8.3)'

5.8.3 ± हो ± (5.8.4) ± (5.8.5) देवताका झैं ± म ± पनि ± आज ± सल्ल +बगें
±ho ±(5.8.4) ±(5.8.5) devatākā jhaiṃ ±ma ±pani ±āja ±salla ±bagẽ
±EX:ex ±AD:Cl(5.8.4) ±AA:ModAdvP ±S:pro-nm ±AA:advl ±AA:advl
±AA:advl +P:iv1-1sg.pst
±Yes ±(5.8.4) ±(5.8.5) gods-of like ±I ±also ±today ±swiftly +glided
'Yes, today I also glided swiftly like the gods (5.8.3)'

5.8.4 ±यो आकाशमा +बसेर
±yo ākāśamā +basera
±LA:CNP-lc +P:iv-abs.prt
±this sky-in +having-lived
'after living in the sky'

5.8.5 ±केही दिन +पुण्यभोग +गर्ने
±kehi dina +puṇyabhoga +garne
±AA:advl +DO:CmpdCN-ac +P:tv1-impf.prt
±some days +enjoyment-of-merit +doing
'and enjoying his merits for some days.'

5.9.1 ±यिनीहरु ±(5.9.2) ±(5.9.4) +खस्छन्
±yinīharu ±(5.9.2) ±(5.9.4) +khaschan,
±S:pro-nm ±AD:C l(5.9.2) ±AD:Cl(5.9.3) +P:iv1-3pl.pres
±these ±(5.9.2) ±(5.9.4) +fall
'They fall (5.9.2) (5.9.3)'

5.9.2 ±पुण्य +समाप्त +भए ±पछि
±puṇya +samāpta +bhae ±pachi
±S:cn-nm +SC:adj-nm +P:ev1-cond ±C: sc
±merit +exhausted +having-been +after
'after the merit has been used up'

5.9.3 ±स्वर्गबाट +चिप्लेर
±svargabāṭa +ciplera
±AbA:cn-ab +P:iv1-abs.prt
±heaven-from +being-slipped
'slipping from heaven'

5.9.4 ±हामी भोका, प्यासा, ± (5.9.5) ±पृथ्वीको पृथ्वीमैं +खस्छौं
±hāmī bhoka, pyāsa, (5.9.5) pṛthvīko pṛthvīmai khaschauṃ.
±S:ProP ±(5.9.5) ±LA:CNP-lc +P:iv1-1pl
±we hungry, thristy, ±(5.9.5), ±earth-of earth-on +we-fall
'We hungry and thirsty people (5.9.5) fall from the earth onto the earth itself.'

5.9.5 ± दु:ख-पीरले +निस्तेज तथा ढलमल +भएर
±duḥkha-pīrale +nisteja tatha ḍhalamala +bhaera
±IA:CmpdN-in +SC:CNP +P:ev-abs.prt
±pain-suffering-by +pale and weak +having-been
'being pale and weak because of pain and sufffering.'

5.10 +(5.10.1) बीभत्स रूप ±अरु शेष भोका, प्यासा, दु:खीहरूले +देख्छन्!
+(5.10.1) bībhatsa rūpa ±aru śeṣa bhokā, pyāsā, duḥkhīharule +dekhchan!
+DO:ModCNP ±S:CNP-nm +P:tv1-3pl.pres
+(5.10.1) terrible form ± other remaining hungry, thirsty, miserable-ones +see
'The others, remaining hungry, thirsty, and suffering, see the terrible form (5.10.1)'

5.10.2 ±हामी +खसिसकेपछिको
±hāmī +khasisakepachiko
±S:pro-pl +P:Cmpdiv-abs.prt+pachi+ko
±we +falling-after-of
'after we have already fallen.'

5.11.1 ± देवताहरु ±चाँहिं ±(5.11.2) ±(5.11.3) ±बीचैमा +अलप +हुन्छन्
±devatāharu ±cāhiṃ ±(5.11.2) ±(5.11.3) ±bīcaimā +alapa +hunchan
±S:cn-nm ±NU:nu(cāhi~) ±AA:Cl(5.11.2) ±AD:Cl(5.11.3) ±LA:cn-lc +SC:adj-nm +P:ev1-3pl.pres
±gods ±in-turn ±(5.11.2) ±(5.11.3) ±middle-in +lost +become
'Gods, in their turn, (5.11.2) (5.11.3) disappear in the middle.'

5.11.2 +पुण्यभोगी +हुनाले
+puṇyabhogī +hunāle
+SC:adj-nm +P:ev-inf+le
+merit-ejoyer +being-by
'because they enjoy merit,'

5.11.3 +(5.11.4) + भनेर
+ (5.11.4) +bhanera
+DO:Cl(5.11.4) +P:tv1-abs.prt
+(5.11.4) +saying
'thinking that (5.11.4)'

5.11.4 ±यो पापपूर्ण जगतमा +खस्नु पर्ला
±yo pāpapūrṇa jagatamā +khasnu parlā
±LA:CNP-lc +P:iVP1-3sg.fut
±this sinful world-on +fall may
'they may fall on this sinful earth.'

5.11.5 ±मानिसहरुमा र देवतामा ± केवल ± यत्ति अन्तर ±न +छ !
±mānisaharumā ra devatāmā ±kevala ±yatti antara ±na +cha!
±LA:CNP-lc ±AA:advl ±S:CNP-nm ±NU:nu +P:iv1-3sg.pres
±men-in and god-in ±only ±this-much difference ±na +is
'This is the only difference between gods and men.'

5.12 ±सुभद्राले ±काखीमनि +एउटा पोको +च्यापेकी थिइन्
±subhadrāle ±kākhīmani +euṭā poko +cyāpekī thi.in.
±S:pn-nm ±LA:PP +DO-CNP +P:tVP-3sg.pst.prf.f
±Subhadra ±arm-pit-under +one bundle +held she-had
'Subhadrā held a bundle under her arm.'

5.13.1 ±यस्तो अन्धकार रात्रीमा ± पनि ± (5.13.2) ± ओढ्नेले ± छोपेकी थिइन्
±yasto andhakāra rātrīmā ±pani ±(5.13.2) ±oḍhnele ±chopekī thi.in
±LA:CNP-lc +AA:advl ±AA:Cl(5.13.2) ±IC:cn-in +P:iVP-3sg.pst.prf.f
±such dark night-in ±even ±(5.13.2) ±shawl-by +covered she-had
'She had covered it with the shawl even in such dark night (5.13.2)'

5.13.2 +(5.13.3) +भनेर
+(5.13.3) +bhanera
+DO:Cl(5.13.3) +P:tv1-abs.prt
+(5.13.3) +having-said
'so that'

5.13.3 ±कसैले +देख्छ ±कि
±kasaile +dekhcha +ki
±S:pro-nm +P:iv1-3sg.pres ±NU: nu *(ki)*
±anyone +sees (whether?)
'no one may see it.'

5.14 ±यस बखत +उनको जीवनाधार ± त्यही सानो पोको +हुन आयो
±yasa bakhata +unako jīvanādhāra ±tyahī sāno poko +huna āyo.
±AA:AdvP +SC:CNP-nm ±S:CNP-nm +P:CmpdeVP-3sg.pst
±this time +her life-support ±that small bundle +to-be came

'At this time, that very little bundle came to be the support of her life.'

5.15.1 ±अहो! ±कुनै बखत ±यो विशाल आशालता ±कसरी ±(5.15.2) ±बस्तछ !
±aho! ±kunai bakhata ±yo viśāla āśālatā ±kasarī ±(5.15.2) +bastacha!
±EX:ex ±AA: AdvP ±S:CNP-nm ±AA:adv ±AD:Cl(5.15.2) +P:iv1-3sg.pres
±Oh! ±some time ±this grandiose hope ±how ±(5.15.2) +remain'
'Oh, how such grandiose hopes ever remain (5.15.2) !'

5.15.2 ±एउटा सानो ठाउँमा +सीमित +भएर
±euṭā sāno ṭhāũmā +sīmita +bhaera
±LA:CNP-lc +SC:adj-nm +P:ev1-abs.prt
±one small place-in +confined +having-been
'confined in a small place.'

5.16 ±परमेश्वर! +मनुष्यलाई ±किन ±आशामा +झुण्ड्यायौ?
±parameśvara! +manuṣyalā.ī +kina ± āśāmā +jhuṇḍyāyau ?
±EX:cn-nm +DO:cn-ac ±AA:advl ±LA:cn-lc +P:tv1-2sg.pres
±Lord! +man-to ±why ±hope-in +you-suspended
'O Lord, why did you suspend the people on to hope (like this)?'

5.17.1 ±प्रभु ±(5.17.2) ± यी अनाथ प्राणीहरु ±सुखका कति नजीक +पुगिसक्थे
±prabhu ±(5.17.2) ±yī anātha prāṇīharu ±sukhakā kati najīkai +pugisakthe
±EX:cn-nm ±AD:Cl(5.17.2) ±S:CNP-nm ±AA:PP +P:CmpdiV-3pl.pst
O Lord! ±(5.17.2) ±these poor humans ±happiness-of how close +would-arrive
'O Lord, (5.17.2) how close to happiness these humans would be!'

5.17.2 ±आशाको बदला +सन्तोष +दिएको ±भए
±āśāko badalā +santoṣa +dieko ±bhae
±AA:PP +DO:cn-ac +P:tv1-prf. ±C:sc
±hope-of instead +satisfaction +had-given ±if
'if you had given them satisfaction instead of hope'

5.18.1 ±(5.18.2) ±अनाथिनी सुभद्रा ±त्यो कालो अन्धकारमा +विलीन +भइन्
±(5.18.2) ±anāthinī subhadrā ±tyo kālo andhakāramā +vilīna +bha.in.
±AD:Cl(5.18.2) ±S:PNP-nm ±LA:CNP-lc +SC:adj-nm +P:ev1-3sg.pst.f
±(5.18.2) ±poor Subhadrā ±that black darkness-in +dissapeared +she-was
'(5.18.2) poor Subhadrā disappeared into the pitch black darkess.'

5.18.2 ±केही बेरपछि ± अश्रुपूर्ण नयनले +प्यारो गृहलाई ± सदैवका निमित्त +नमस्कार +गरेर
±kehī berapachi ±aśrupūrṇa nayanale +pyāro gṛhalā.ī ±sadaivakā nimitta +namaskāra +garera

±AA:PP ±IA:CNP-in +DC:CNP-dt ±AA:PP +DO:cn-ac +P:tv2-abs.prt
±some time-after ±tearful eyes-with +dear house-to ±ever-of for +Namaskār (geeting) +having-done
'After some time, offering with tearful eyes a final Namaskār (greeting) to her dear house,'

5.19.1 +यो करुणाजनक दृश्य ±(5.19.1) विश्वको चतुर चौकीदार बाहेक ± अरु कसैले +देखेन

+yo karuṇājanaka dṛśya (5.19.1) ±viśvako catura caukīdāra bāheka ±aru kasaile +dekhena.
+DO:CNP-ac ±AA:ModPP ±S:ProP +P:tv1-3sg.pst.neg
±this pathetic scene ±(5.19.1) world's wise guardians except ±any other +did-not see
'No one save the world's wise guardians (5.19.2) saw this pathetic scene.'

5.19.2 ± सँधै +जागा +भइरहने

±sadhaiṃ +jāgā +bha.irahane
±AA:advl +SC:adj-nm +P:ev1-impf.prt
±ever +vigilant +being
'being ever vigilant'

6.1.1 ±पशुपतिनाथका मन्दिर वरिपरि ±(6.1.2) ठाउँ +थिएन
±paśupatināthakā mandira waripari ±(6.1.2) ṭhāū +thiena
±LA:PP ±S:ModCNP-nm +P:iv1-3sg.pst.neg
±Paśupatinātha-of temple around ±room (6.1.2) +was-not
'Around the temple of Pashupatinath there wasn't room (6.1.2).'

6.1.2 +तिल +राख्ने
+tila +rākhne
+DO:cn-ac +P:tv1-impf.prt
+sesame-seed +putting
'enough even to put a sesame seed.'

6.2.1 ±(6.2.2) जात्रुहरुको छिचोलीनसक्नु घुईँचो +थियो
±(6.2.2) jātrūharuko chicolīnasaknu ghuĩco +thiyo
±S:ModCNP-nm +P:iv1-3sg.pst
±(6.2.2) pilgrims-of impassable crowd +was
'There was an impassable (thick) crowd of pilgrims (6.2.2).'

6.2.2 +सद्बीउ +छर्ने
+sadbīu +charne
+DO:cn-mn +P:tv1-impf.prt
+sadbīu +scattering
'scattering the *sadbīu* (lit. 'one hundred kinds of seeds')'

6.3.1 ±(6.3.2) ±नौलीले ±(6.3.3) भनी, +(6.3.4-5)
±(6.3.2) naulīle (6.3.3) bhanī, (6.3.4-5)
±AD:Cl(6.3.2) ±S:cn-nm ±AD:Cl(6.3.3) +P:tv1-3sg.pst.f
+DO:Cl(6.3.4-5)
±(6.3.2) ±Naulī ±(6.3.3) +said, +(6.3.4-5)
'(6.3.2), Naulī, (6.3.3) said (6.3.4-5)'

6.3.2 ±यस्तैमा ±पश्चिम ढोकानेर ±अकस्मात् +सुभद्रालाई +देखेर
±yastaimā paścima ḍhokānera akasmāt subhadrālā.ī dekhera
±AA:adj-lc ±AA:PP ±AA:advl +DO:pn.ac +P:tv1-abs.prt
such-in, western gate-near suddently Subhadrā having-seen
'Meanwhile, suddenly seeing Subhadrā near the western gate,'

6.3.3 ±गहभरी +आँसु +पारेर
±gaha bharī +ā̃su +pārera
±AA:PP +DO:cn-ac +P:tv1-abs.prt
±eyes-full +tears +making
'making eyes full of tears' (he eyes filling with tears)'

6.3.4 ±ओहो बजै +हेर ± कति दुब्ली,
±"oho bajai! +hera ±kati dublī ,
±EX:intj ±EX:cn-nm +P:iv1-2sg.imp ±EX:AdjP-nm
±Oh Bajai! look how thin
'Oh Bajai ! Look, how thin (you have become)!'

6.3.5 +(6.3.6) +हुनुभएछ
+(6.3.6) +hunubhaecha
+SC:Cl (6.3.6) +P:ev1-2sg.pst
+(6.3.6) +you-have-become
'You have become (6.3.6)'

6.3.6 +चिन्नै +नसक्ने
+cinnai +nasakne
+DO:nl(inf.) +P:tv1-impf.prt
+to-recognize +incapable
'incapable of being recognized.'

6.4.1 ±अलि बेर सम्म ±ता +ठम्याउनै सकिन
±ali bera samma ±ta +ṭhamyāunai sakina.
±AA:PP ±NU:nu (*ta*) +P:iVP1-1sg.pst.neg
±some moment for ±*ta* +I-could-not-recognize
'For a moment, I could not recognize (you).'

6.5 ±कहाँ +बस्नुभएको छ ±हँ
±kahā̃ +basnubhaeko cha ±hã?"
±AA:advl +P:iv1-2sg.pres.prf ±NU:nu *(hã)*
±where lodged you-are ±hã
'Where are you living now ?'

6.6 ±"यहीं ±गौरीघाट ±फुपू कहाँ +बसेकी छु"
±"yahī̃ ±gaurīghāṭa ±phupū kahā̃ +basekī chu"
±LA:advl ±LA:pn-lc ±LC:PP +P:iv3-1sg.pres.prf.f
±here ±Gaurighat-at ±aunt's-at +lodged am
'I am living here at my aunt's at Gaurighat. '

6.7.1 ±(6.7.2) ±आधा रातमा +हिंड्नुभएछ
±(6.7.2) ±ādhā rātamā +hĩḍnubhaecha
±AD:Cl(6.7.2) ±LA:CNP-lc +P:iv1-2sg.pres.prf
±(6.7.2) half night-at walked .
'You left in the middle of the night (6.7.2)'

6.7.2 +खर्च-बर्च +नलिइकन
+"kharca-barca +nali.ikana
+DO:cn-ac +P:tv1-abs.prt.neg
+money-food +not-taking
'without taking any money or food.'

6.8 +थाहा ±पनि +पाइन
+thāhā ±pani +pā.ina
+DO:cn-ac ±AA:advl +P:tv1-1sg.pst.neg
+kowledge ±even +I-did-not-get
'I did not even know.'

6.9.1 ±यतिका दिनसम्म ±(6.9.2) +गुजारा +गर्नुभयो?"
±yatikā dina samma ±(6.9.2) +gujarāna +garnubhayo ?"
±AA:PP ±AD:Cl(6.9.2) +DO:cn-ac +P:iv1-2sg.pst
±so-many days for (6.9.2) +sustenance +you-did
'(6.9.2), did you sustain (yourself) for so many days?'

6.9.2 +के +खाएर
+ke +khāera
+DO:pro(interrog)-ac +P:tv1-abs.prt
+what +eating
'Eating what,'

6.10.1 +फुपूलाई ±सरकारबाट +एउटा हण्डी +बक्सेको रहेछ
+phupūlā.ī ±sarakārabāṭa +euṭā haṇḍī +bakseko rahecha,
+DC:cn-dt ±S:cn-nm +DO:CNP-ac +P:tv1-3sg.pres.prf
+aunt-to ± king +one pension +given has
'The King has given a pension to my aunt.'

6.10.2 ± त्यसबाट ±दुई जनाले +गुजारा +चलाएका छौं
±tyasabāṭa ±duī janāle +gujārā +calāekā chauṃ
±AbA:pro-ab ±S:NlP-nm +DO:cn-ac +P:tv1-1pl.pres.prf
±that-from two-people sustenance maintained have
'The two of us have sustained ourselves.'

6.11 ±घरको हाल +कस्तो +छ ±नौली?
±gharako hāla +kasto +cha, ±naulī ?
±S:CNP-nm ±SC:adj-nm +P:ev1-3sg.pres ±EX:pn-nm
±house-of news how is Naulī
'What is the news back home, Nauli ?'

6.12.1 ±"बजै, +घरको हाल के +भनूँ
±"bajai, +gharako hāla ke +bhanū̃
±EX:cn-nm +DO:pro(interrog)-ac +P:tv1-1sg.imp

±Bajai, +house-of news what +may-I-say
'Bajai, what shall I say about the news from home?'

6.12.2 ±(6.12.3) आँसु +आउँछ
±(6.12.3) ±ā̃su +āũcha
±AD:Cl(6.12.3) ±S:cn-nm +P:iv1-3sg.pres
±(6.12.3) ±tear +comes
'Tears come (6.12.3)'

6.12.3 +सम्झदा ± पनि
+samjhadā ±pani
+P:iv1-abs.prt ±AA:advl
+while-remembering even
'even when I remember it.'

6.13.1 ±छ महीना +भो
±cha mahīnā +bho ,
±S: CNP-nm +P:iv1-3sg.pst
±six months was
'It is six months,'

6.13.2 ±दुलही बजै +बेरामी +हुनुहुन्छ "
±dulahī bajai +berāmī +hunuhuncha."
±S:CNP-nm +SC:adj-nm +P:ev1-3sg.pres
±Dulahi Bajai +ill +is
'Dulahi Bajai has been ill.'

6.14.1 (6.14.1) ±सुभद्राले ±साह्रै उत्सुकतासाथ +सोधिन्
+(6.14.1) ±subhadrāle ±sāhrai utsukatā sātha +sodhin .
+DO:Cl(6.14.2) ±S:pn-nm ±AA:PP +P:tv1-3sg.pst.f
+(6.14.1) ±Subhadrā ±very curiousity with +asked
'Subhadrā asked with a great curiousity, (6.14.2)'

6.14.2 ±के +हुन्छ?"
±"ke +huncha ?"
±S:pro(interrog)-nm +P:iv1-3sg.pres
±what +happens
'What happens?'

6.15.1 ±"तपनी जरो +छ"
±"tapanī jaro +cha"
±S:CNP-nm +P:iv1-3sg.pres
+mild fever +is
'She has a mild fever.'

6.15.2 ±छाती +दुख्छ
±'chātī +dukhcha'
±S:cn-nm +P:iv1-3sg.pres
±chest +hurts
"The chest hurts"

6.15.3 +(6.15.2) +भन्नुहुन्छ
+(6.15.2) +bhannuhuncha .
+DO:Cl(6.15.2) +P:tv1-3sg.pres
+(6.15.3) +she-says
'She says (6.15.2).'

6.16 ±रात भर +खोकिरहनुहुन्छ
±rāta bhara +khokirahanuhuncha.
±AA:PP +P:iv1-3sg.pres.prog
±night full +she-keeps-coughing
'She coughs all night.'

6.17.1 ± (6.17.3) +थाइसी +भने
±(6.17.3) +'thāisī' bhane
±AD:Cl(6.17.3) +DO:cn-ac +P:tv1-3sg.pst.m
+thāisī +he-said
'He said, "thāisī" (phthisis).'

6.17.2 ± कि 'खाक्सी' +भने
± ki +'khāksī' +bhane
±C:cc +DO:cn-ac +P:tv1-3sg.pst.m
±or +khāksī +he-said
'or, "khāksī" (it was).'

6.17.3 +गोर्खामूलका डाग्डर सुबेदारलाई +देखाउँदा
+gorakhā mulakā ḍāgḍara subidārālā.ī +dekhāũdā
+DC:CNP-dt +P:tv2-conj.prt
+Gorakhā orgin-of doctor Subidar-to +when-showed
'When we summoned the military doctor from Gorkha,'

6.17.4 ±अहिले संझन +सकिन
±ahile samjhana +sakina ,
±AA: advl +DO:nl +P:tv1-1sg.pst
±now +remember +I-could-not
'I could not remember (exactly)'

6.17.5 ±साह्रै नराम्रो रोग +हो ±अरे
±sāhrai narāmro roga +ho ±are .
±S:CNP-nm +P:iv1-3sg.pres ±NU:nu *(are)*

±very bad disease +is +they-say
'It is a very bad disease, they say.'

6.18.1 ±(6.18.2) ±हाड-छाला ±मात्र +छ
±(6.18.2) ±hāḍachālā ±mātra +cha .
±AD:Cl(6.18.2) ±S:CmpdN-nm ±AA:Advl +P:iv1-3sg.pres
±(6.18.2) bone-skin only is
'she has only skin and bone.'

6.18.2 +सुकेर
+sukera
+P:iv1-abs.prt
+being-thin
'She has become so thin (that)'

6.19.1 ±(6.19.2) ±बाहिर-भित्र +गराउनु पर्छ
±(6.19.2) bāhira-bhitra +garā.unu parcha."
±AD:Cl(6.19.2) ±AA:Cmpdadvl +P:iVP1-3sg.pres
±(6.19.2) ±outside-inside +made must-be
'She has to be (6.19.2) in and out.'

6.19.2 +बोकेर
+bokera
+P:iv1-abs.prt
+having-been-carried
'carried'

6.20 ±"सानो बाबु +कस्तो+ छ ±नि ?"
±"sāno bābu +kasto +cha ±ni ?"
±S:CNP-nm +SC:adj-nm +P:ev1-3sg.pres ±NU:nu (*ni*)
±little boy +how +is ±*ni*
'And, how is the little boy ?'

6.21.1 +"कस्ता +हुन्थे
+"kastā hunthe,
+SC:adj-nm +P:ev1-3sg.pst
+how +he-could-be
'How could he be ?'

621.2 ±जीउभरी ±खटिरा +छन्!
±jīubharī ±khaṭirā +chan!
±AA:PP ±S:cn-nm +P:iv1-3pl.pres
±body-full ±boils +are
He has boils all over his body.'

6.21.3 +तेल +लाउन हुँदैन

+tela +lā.una hūdaina,

+DO:cn-ac +P:tVP1-3sg+aux-pres.neg

+oil +one-shuld-not rub

'We should not rub oil (on him).'

6.214 ±'आमा ±कहिले +आउनुहुन्छ'

± 'āmā ±kahile +ā.unuhuncha'

±S:cn-nm ±AA:advl +P:iv1-3sg.pres

±mother ±when +she-comes

'When will mother come,'

6.21.5 +(6.21.4) +भनेर

+(6.21.4) +bhanera

±DO:Cl(6.21.4) +P:tv1-abs.prt

+'(6.21.4) +saying'

'saying (6.21.4)'

6.21.6 ±बराबर +तपाइँलाई +संझिरहन्छन्

±barābara +tapāĩlā.ī +samjhirahanchan."

±AA:advl +DO:pro-ac +P:tv1-3sg.pres.prog

±frequently +you +keeps-remembering

'He thinks of you frequently.'

6.22 +भात ±को +पकाउँछ ±नि ?

+"bhāta ±ko +pakāũcha ±ni ?"

+DO:cn-ac ±S:pro(interrog) +P:tv1-3sg.pres ±NU:nu (ni)

+rice ±who +cooks ±*ni*

'And who cooks rice ?'

6.23.1 ±कहिले ±बाजे आफै +पकाउनुहुन्छ

±"kahile ±bāje āphai +pakā.unuhuncha ,

±AA:advl ±S:CNP-nm +P:tv1-3sg.pres

±sometimes ±Baje himself +cooks

'Sometimes Bāje (Deviraman) cooks it himself.'

6.23.2 ±कहिले ±(6.23.3) +सुत्नुहुन्छ

±kahile ±(6.23.3) +sutnuhuncha .

±AA:advl ±AD:Cl(6.23.3) +P:iv1-3sg.pres

±sometimes ±(6.23.3) +he-sleeps

'Sometimes he goes to bed (6.23.3).'

6.23.3 +चमेना +खाएर

+camenā +khāera

+DO:cn-ac +P:tv1-abs.prt
+snacks +having-eaten
'eating a few snacks.'

6.24.1 ±एक दिन ±(6.24.2) ±एक्लै +रोइरहनुभएको रहेछ
±eka dina ± (6.24.2) ±eklai +roīrahanubhaeko rahecha .
±AA:AdvP ±AD:Cl (6.24.2) ±AA:advl +P:iVP-3sg.pres.prf
±one day ±(6.24.2) ± alone +crying he-was
'One day, he was crying alone (6.24.2)'

6.24.2 ±बार्दलीमा +बसेर
±bārdalīmā +basera
±LA:cn-lc +P:iv1-abs.prt
±balconey-at +having-sat
'sitting at the balconey.'

6.24.1 +(6.25.2) +भन्नुहुन्थ्यो
+(6.25.2) +bhannuhunthyo.
+DO:Cl(6.25.2) +P:tv1-3sg.pst.m
+(6.25.2) +he-said
'He said (6.25.2)'

6.25.2 ±पापिनीले (6.25.3) +गई
±pāpinīle (6.25.3) ga.ī
±S: n-nm ±AD:Cl (6.25.2) +P:iv1-3sg.pst.f
± sinner ±(6.25.3) +went
'The sinner went (6.25.3)'

6.25.3 +(6.25.4) ±आफै +भत्काएर
+(6.25.4) ±āphai +bhatkāera
±DO:Cl(6.25.4) ±S:pro-nm +P:tv1-abs.prt
±(6.25.4) +she-herself +having-destroyed
'destroying (6.25.4) herself,'

6.25.4 ±आफुले +चिनेको +चौतारो
±āphūle +cineko +cautāro
±S:pro-nm +P:tv1-prf.prt +DO:cn-ac
±self-by +built +*cautāro*
'the cautāro (home) built by herslf.'

6.24.1 +के के +भनूँ ±बजै!
+ke ke +bhanū̃ ±bajai!
+DO:pro-interrog-ac +P:tv1-1sg.imp ±EX:cn-nm
+what +should-I-say ±Bajai
'What should I say, Bajai !'

6.26.2 ±बस्तुभाउका हाडछाला ±मात्र +छन्
±bastubhāukā hāḍa-chālā ±mātra +chan .
±S:CNP-nm ±AA:advl +P:iv1-3pl.pres
±animals-of bone-skins ±only +are
'The animals have become only skin and bone.'

6.27 +खेतबारी ±अँधियामा +दिएको छ
+kheta-bārī ±adhiyā̃mā +dieko cha .
+DO: cmpdcn-nm +LC:cn-lc +P:iv3p-pres.prf
+field-garden +half-share-on +let is
'The fields and gardens are let out on half a share (to others).'

6.28.1 ±असामीपात +एक पैसा +उठ्दैन
±asāmīpāta +eka paisā +uṭhdaina ,
±S:cn-nm +SC: CNP-nm +P:ev1-3sg.pres.neg
±The debt +one paisā +does-not-return
'The debt does not return even one paisā (penny)'

6.28.2 ±नोकर-चाकर ±चार दिन +टिक्दैनन्
±nokara-cākara ±cāra dina +ṭikdainan ,
±S:cn-nm ±AA:AdvP +P:iv1-3pl.pres.neg
±servant-serfs +four days +do-not-stay
'The servants do not stay even for four days.'

6.28.3 ±सबै +भताभुङ्ग छ
±sabai +bhatābhuṅga cha."
±S:nl +SC:adj-nm +P:ev1-3sg.pres
±everything +disarray +is
'Everything is in disarray.'

6.29.1 ±(6.29.2) ±सुभद्राको हृदय +काटियो
±(6.29.2) ±subhadrāko hṛdaya +kāṭiyo .
±AD:Cl(6.29.2) +S:CNP-nm +P:iv1p-3sg.pst
±(6.29.2) ±Subhadrā-of heart +was-cut
'(6.29.2) Subhadra's heart was grieved.'

6.29.2 +नौलीका कुरा +सुनेर
+naulīkā kurā +sunera
+DO:CNP-ac +P:tv1-abs.prt
+Naulī-of talks +having-heard
'Hearing the words of Naulī,'

6.30.1 ±मनमनै +भनिन् +"छि:"
±manamanai +bhanin, +"chiḥ .
±AA:advl +P:tv1-3sg.pres.f +DO:intj

±mind-mind +she-said +"Fie !
'She said to herself, "Fie!"

6.31.1 ±(6.31.2) +यही +हो
±(6.31.2) +yahī +ho
±S: Cl (6.31.2) +SC:pro-nm +P:ev1-3sg.pres
±(6.32.2) +this +is
'This is (6.31.2)'

6.31.2 ±सौताको रीसले +पोइको नाक +काट्नु ±भनेको
±'sautāko rīsale +poiko nāka +kāṭnu' ±bhaneko
±IA:CNP-in +DO:CNP-ac +P:tv1-inf ±C:sc
±co-wife-of anger-by +husband's nose +cut ±called
'said to be like cutting the nose of one's husband because of anger at the co-wife.'

6.32.1 +उमेरदार +थिई
+umeradāra +thi.i
+SC:adj-nm +P:ev1-3sg.pst.f
+young +she-was
'She was young.'

6.32.2 ±(6.32.3-4) भन्ने बेला +थियो
±(6.32.3-4) bhanne belā +thiyo.
±S:ModCNP-nm +P:iv1-3sg.pst
±(6.32.3-4) saying time +was
'It was time [for her] to say (6.32-3-4)'

6.32.3 +के +खाउँ
+ke +khāũ
+DO:pro(interog)-ac +P:tv1-opt
+what +should-I-eat
'what (good food) shall I eat'

6.32.4 +के +लाउँ
+ke +lāũ
+DO:pro(interog)-ac +P:tv1-opt
+what +should-I-wear
'what (nice clothes) shall I wear?'

6.33.1 ±(6.33.3) +(6.33.2) +नहुने [थियो]
±(6.33.3) +(6.33.2) +nahune [thiyo]
±AD:Cl(6.33.3) +DO:Cl(6.33.2) +P:tVP1-impf.prt[+Aux- 3sg.pst]
±(6.33.3) +(6.33.2) not-being
'It was not (proper)

6.33.2 ±मैले +चित्त +दुखाउन
±maile +citta +dukhāuna
±S:pro-nm +DO:cn-ac +P:tv1-inf
±I +mind +to-hurt
'that I was upset'

6.33.3 +(6.33.4-5) +भनेर
+(6.33.4-5) +bhanera
+DO:cl(6.33.3-4) +P:tv1-abs.prt
+(6.33.4-5) +having-said
'thinking that (6.33.4-5)'

6.33.4 +मीठो +खाई
+mīṭho +khā.ī
+DO:nl +P:tv1-3sg.pst.f
+good +she-ate
'She ate good (food)' [and]

6.33.5 +राम्रो +लाई
+rāmro +lā.ī
+DO:nl +P:tv1-3sg.pst.f
+nice +she-wore
'she wore nice (clothes)'

6.34.1 ±(6.34.2) ± तीर्थ +जानुभयो
±(6.34.2) ±tīrtha +jānubhayo
±AD:Cl(6.34.2) ±AA:cn-ac +P:iv1-3sg.pst
±(6.34.2) ±pilgrimage +he-went
'He went on the pilgrimage (6.34.2).'

6.34.2 +उसलाई +लिएर
+usalā.ī +liera
+DO:pro-ac +P:tv1-abs.prt
+her +having-taken
'taking her (along with hm).'

6.34.3 ±त ±त्यसले ±के +भयो ±र?
±ta ±tyasale ±ke +bhayo ±ra ?
±C:cc ±IA:pro(dem)-in ±S:pro(interrog) +P:iv1-3sg.pst ±NU: nu
±so ±that ±what +happaened ±*ra*
'So what did it do?'

6.35.1 ±(6.35.2-3) ±म +जाँदी हुँ
±(6.35.2-3) ±ma +jā̃dī hū̃
±AD:(6.35.2-3) ±S:pro(pers) +P:iv1-1sg.prob.pst

±(6.35.2-3) ±I +could-have-gone
"I could have gone '

6.35.2 +फर्कनुभए ±पछि
+pharkanubhae ±pachi
+P:iv1-cond. ±C:sc
+return +after
'after he returned,'

6.35.3 +अर्को साथी +लिएर
+arko sāthī +liera
+DO:CNP-ac +P:tv1-abs.prt
+another friend +having-taken
'taking another friend'

6.36.1 ±कहिलेकाहिं ±(6.36.2) +बोल्दथी ±लौ
±kahilekāhiṃ ±(6.36.2) +boldathī ±lau ;
±AA:advl ±AD:Cl(6.36.2) +P:iv1-3sg.pst.f ±EX:intj
±sometimes ±(6.36.2) +she-spoke ±lau
'Sometimes, she spoke (6.36.2)'

6.36.2 ±अलि +झर्केर
±ali +jharkera
±AA:advl +P:iv1-abs.prt
±slightly +being-angry
'slightly angrily'

6.36.3 +अलि झडङ्गे स्वभावकी +थिइ
+ali jhaḍaṅge svabhāvakī +thi.i
+SC:AdvP +P:ev1-3sg.pst.f
+somewhat irritable nature-of +she-was
'She had a somewhat irritable nature.'

6.36.4 ±स्वभावै +त्यस्तो +[थियो];
±svabhāvai +tyasto +[thiyo];
±S:cn.nm +SC:adj-nm [+P:ev1-3sg.pst]
±nature +like-that +[was]
'Her nature itself was like that.'

6.36.5 ±(6.36.6) ±कहिलेकाहीं ±आमा-छोरीमा ±पनि ±त ±ठाकठुक +हुन्छ
±(6.36.6) ±kahilekāhīṃ ±āmā-chorīmā ±pani ±ta ±ṭhāka-ṭhuka +huncha.
±AD:Cl(6.36.6) ±AA:advl +LA:CmpdN-lc ±AA:advl ±NU:nu
+P:iv1-3sg.pres
±(6.36.6) ±sometimes ±mother-daughter-between ±even ±quarrel
+happens

'Sometimes a quarrel can happen even between a mother and daughter (6.36.6).'

6.36.6 ±एक ठाउँमा +बसे ±पछि
±eka ṭhāũmā +base ±pachi
±LA:CNP-lc +P:iv1-cond. ±C:sc
±one place-at +lived if
'if they lived at one place.'

6.37.1 ±(6.37.2) +बस्ती हुँ
±(6.37.2) +bastī hũ
±AD:Cl(6.37.2) +P:iv1-3sg.pst
±(6.37.2) +living I-could -be
'I could live (6.37.2)'

6.37.2 ±(6.37.3) +कटेरो +बारेर
±(6.37.3) +kaṭero +bārera
±AD:Cl(6.37.3) +DO:cn-nm +P:tv1-abs.prt
±(6.37.2) +hut +having-put-up
'putting up a hut [for myself]'

6.37.3 +(6.37.4) +नसके
+(6.37.4) +nasake
+DO:Cl(6.37.4) +P:tv1-cond
+(6.37.4) +if-I-could-not
'If I could not (6.37.4)'

6.37.4 ±एकै घरमा +बस्न
+ekai gharamā +basna
±AA:advl ±LA:cn-lc +P:iv1-inf
±same ±house-in +to-live
'live in the same house,'

6.38 ±मैले +साह्रै बेबुझको काम +गरें
±maile +sāhrai bebujhako kāma +gareṃ
±S:pro(pers)-nm +DO:CNP-ac +P:tv1-1sg.pst
±I +very foolish work +I-did
'I did a very foolish thing.'

6.39.1 ±जोरिपारीले +के +भन्दाहुन्
±joripārīle +ke +bhandā hun,
±S:cn-nm +DO:pro(interrog)-ac +P:tv1-3pl.prob.fut
±neighbors +what +saying may-be
'What could the neighbors possibly be saying ?'

6.39.2 ±(6.39.3) ±यहाँ ±(6.39.4) +बसेकी छु
±(6.39.3) ±yahā̃ ±(6.39.4) +basekī chu ,
±AD:Cl(6.39.3) ±LA:advl ±AD:Cl(6.39.4) +P:iv1-1sg.pst.prf.f
±(6.39.3) ±here ±(6.39.4) +living I-am
"I am living here (6.39.3) (6.39.4)'

6.39.3 +आफ्नो त्यत्रो दौलथ +छोडेर
+āphno tyatro daulatha +choḍera
+DO:CNP-ac +P:tv1-abs.prt
+my-own that-big wealth +having-left
'Leaving the great wealth of my own,'

6.39.4 +एक छाक +खाएर
+eka chāka +khāera
+DO:CNP-ac +P:tv1-abs.prt
+one meal +eating
[and] 'having one meal a day'

6.39.5 ±(6.39.6) ± त्यो चिचिलो बालकको के गति +होला
±(6.39.6) ±tyo cicilo bālakhako ke gati +holā ,
±AD:Cl (6.39.6) ±S:CNP:nm +P:iv1-3sg.fut
±(6.39.6) ±that little boy-of what plight +will-become
'What will become of the little boy,'

6.36.6 ±त्यसका जीउमा ±केही +भइदियो ±भने
±tyasakā jīumā ±kehī +bhaidiyo ±bhane
±LA:CNP-lc ±S:nl +P:iv1-3sg.pst ±C:sc
±her body-on ±anything +happened ±if
'If anything happened to her body,'

6.37.7 ±पितृले +के +भन्लान्
±pitṛle +ke +bhanlān?
±S:cn-nm +DO:pro(interrog)-ac +P:tv1-3pl.fut
±Ancestors +what +may-say
'What may the ancestors be saying ?'

6.40.1 ±(6.40.2) ±आमाले +दुखाई
±(6.40.2) ±āmāle +dukhāī,
±AD:Cl(6.40.2) ±S:cn-nm +P:iv1-3sg.pst.f
±(6.40.2) ±mother +hurt
'(6.40.2) the mother hurt it '

6.40.2 +चित्त +दुखाए ±पनि
+chitta +dukhāe ±pani
+DO:cn-ac +P:tv1-cond ±C:sc

+mind +if- hurt +even-if
'Even if [my] mind was hurt,'

6.40.3 ±त्यो बालकले +के +बिरायो
±tyo bālakale +ke +birāyo?
±S:CNP-nm +DO:pro-interrog-ac +P:tv1-3sg.pst.m
±that boy +what +did-wrong
'What did the little boy do wrong ?'

6.41 ±(6.41.2) +दिक्क +मान्नुहुन्थ्यो
±(6.41.2) +dikka +mānnuhunthyo.
±AD:Cl(6.41.2) +DO:nl +P:tv1-3sg.pst
±(6.41.2) +vexation +he-felt
'He felt vexed (6.41.2).'

6.41.2 ±अघि +एक-दुइछाक भात +पकाउनुपर्दा
±aghi +eka-duī chāka bhāta +pakāunu pardā
±AA:advl +DO:CNP-ac P:tVP-conj.prt
±before +one-two meal rice +to-cook when-having
'Before, when he had to cook one or two meals,'

6.42.1 ±आजकाल ±दिनहुँ ±कसरी +पकाउनुहुँदो हो?
±ājakāla ±dinahū̃ ±kasarī +pakāunuhū̃do ho?
±AA:advl ±AA:advl ±AA:advl +P:iVP-3sg.pst
±these-days ±everyday ±how +could-he-cook
'These days, how could he cook everyday ?'

6.42.2 ±इत्यादि मनोवेदनाले ±सुभद्राको हृदय +छिया-छिया +भयो
±ityādi manovedanāle ±subhadrāko hṛdaya +chiyāchiyā +bhayo;
±IA:CNP-in ±S:CNP-nm +SC:adj-nm +P:ev1-3sg.pst
±such pain-with +Subhadra-of heart +shattered was
'Subhadra's heart ached with pain as such.'

6.42.3 (6.42.4) +भनिन् +(6.42.5),
±(6.42.4) +bhanin (6.42.5) ,
±AD:Cl (6.42.4) +P:tv1-3sg.pst.f +DO:Cl(6.42.5)
±(6.42.4), +she-said +(6.42.5)'
'(6.42.4), she said (6.42.5)'

6.42.4 +आँसु +झार्दै
+ā̃su +jhārdai
+DO:cn-nm +P:tv1-conj.prt
+tears +shedding
'Shedding tears,'

6.42.5 ±"नौली! ±त्यस्ता बेलामा (6.42.6) +आइछेस्
±"naulī! ±tyastā belāmā (6.42.6) +ā.iches! "
±EX:pn-nm ±LA:CNP-lc ±AD:Cl(6.42.6) +P:iv1-2sg.pres.f
±Nauli ±such time-at ±(6.42.6) +you-came
'Nauli, you came at such a time, (6.42.6),'

6.42.6 ±तैले ±पनि +छोडेर
±taiṃle ±pani +choḍera
±S:pro(per)-nm ±AA:advl +P:iv1-abs.prt
±you ±also +having-left
'You too leaving [them]'

6.43.1 ±"बजै, ±(6.43.2) +बस्नुपऱ्यो
± "bajai, ±(6.43.2) +basnu paryo ,
±EX:cn-nm ±AD:Cl(6.43.2) +P:iVP-3sg.pst
±Bajai , ±(6.43.2) +to-live had
"Bajai, I had to live (6.43.2)'

6.43.2 ±जन्म भर +अर्काकी दासी +भएर
±janma bhara +arkākī dāsī bhaera
±AA:PP +SC:CNP-nm +P:ev1-abs.prt
±life full +others-of slave +havig-been
'being a slave to someone else all my life.'

6.43.3 ±(6.43.4) +आएकी
±(6.43.4) +āekī ."
±AD:Cl (6.43.4) +P:iv1-prf.prt.f
±(6.43.4) +I-have-come
'I came (6.43.4)'

6.43.4 ±(6.43.5) ±बाजे संग +बीसै दिनको बिदा +मागेर
±(6.43.5) ±bāje sṃga +bīsai dinako bidā +māgera
±AD:Cl (6.43.5) ±AA:PP +DO:CNP-ac +P:tv1-abs.prt
±(4.43.5) +Baje-with +only-twenty days-of leave +having-asked-for
'Asking Baje for onlt twenty days' absence,'

6.43.5 +(6.43.6) +भनेर
+(6.43.6) +bhanera
+DO:Cl (6.43.6) +P:tv1-abs.prt
+saying +(6.43.6)
'so that (6.43.6)'

6.43.6 ±(6.43.7) +आउँ
±(6.43.7) +āū
±AD:Cl(6.43.7) +P:iv1-1sg.imp

±(6.43.7) +I-may-come
'I may come back (6.43.7)'

6.43.7 +चारोटा अक्षता ±भएपनि +छरेर
+cāroṭā akṣatā ±bhaepani +charera
+DO:CNP-ac ±AA:advl +P:tv1-abs.prt
+four sacred-grains +only +having-scattered
'scattering only a few sacred grains.'

6.44 ±"को संग +आइस्?"
±"ko saṃga ā.ĩs ?"
±AA:PP +P:iv1-2sg.pst
±who with +did-you-come
'With whom did you come ?'

6.45 ±"रातमाटे भण्डारीका जहानसंग +[आएँ]
±"rātamāṭe bhṇḍārĩkā jahāna saṃga +[āẽ]."
±AA:PP +[P:iv1-1sg.pst]
±Rātamāte Bhandāri-of family-with +[I-came]
'I came with the family of the Ratanmate Bhandari.'

6.46 ±"कहिले +जान्छेस्?"
±"kaile +jānches ?"
±AA:advl +P:iv1-2sg.pres
±when +you-go
'When will you go ?'

6.47.1 ±भोलि बिहानै +[जान्छु]
±"bholi bihānai +[jānchu],
±AA:advl ±AA:advl [+P:iv1-1sg.pres]
±tomorrow morning +[I-go]
"I will go tomorrow morning.'

6.47.2 ±बजै ±बिन्ती +छ
±bajai, bintĩ +cha ,
±EX:cn-nm +S:cn-nm +P:iv1-3sg.pres
±Bajai, ±prayer +is
'Bajai, I pray.'

6.47.3 ±घर +जाउँ
±ghara +jā.aũ
±LA:cn-lc +P:iv1-1pl.imp
±home +let-us-go
'Let us go home.'

6.48.1 (6.48.1) ±बाजेको जहाजै +डुब्छ
±(6.48.1) ±bājeko jahājai +ḍubcha .
±AD:Cl(6.48.1) ±S:CNP-nm +P:iv1-3sg.pres
±(6.48.1) ±Baje-of ship +sinks
'Baje's ship will sink (he will lose everything)'

6.48.2 ±तपाईं +नभए
±tapā.iṃ +nabhae
±S:pro(pers) +P:iv1-neg.cond.
±you +if-not-be
'If are not there,'

7.1.1 ±(7.1.2) लक्ष्मी +जीवनको शेष घडी +गनिरहेकी थिइन्
±(7.1.2) lakṣmī jīvanako śeṣa ghaḍī +ganīrahekī thi.in.
±S:ModPNP-nm +DO:CNP-ac +P:tVP1-prog.prf.prt+Aux-3sg.pstf
±(7.1.2) Lakṣmī +life-of remanining hours +counting was
'Laksmi, (7.1.2), marked off her life's remaining hours.'

7.1.2 ±मैलो बिछ्यौनामा +सुतेकी
±mailo bichyā.unāmā +sutekī
±LA:CNP-lc +P:iv1-prf.prt
±filthy bedd-on +laying
'laying on a filthy bed.'

7.2.1 ±देवीरमण (7.2.2)±बखत-बखतमा ±चम्चाले +पानी +खुवाउँथे
±devīramaṇa (7.2.2) ±bakhata-bakhatamā ±camcāle +pānī +khvāũthe .
±S:cn-nm +AD:Cl(7.2.2) +LA:cn-nm ±IA:cn-in +DO:cn-ac
+P:tv1-3sg.pst
±devīramaṇ (7.2.2) ±time-time-at ±spoon-with +water +he fed
'Devīramaṇ, (7.2.2), fed her water from time to time.'

7.2.2 ±रोगीका सिरानमा +बसेर
±rogīkā sirānamā +basera
±LA:CNP-lc +P:iv1-abs.prt
±patient-of pillow-at +having-sat
'sitting at the head of the bed,'

7.3.1 ±बालक पुत्र सुशील ±(7.3.2) +यो चिर मातृवियोग +हेरिरहेको थियो
±bālaka putra suśīla ±(7.3.2) +yo cira mātṛviyoga +heriraheko thiyo
±S:PNP-nm ±AD:Cl(7.3.2) +DO:CNP-ac +P:tv1-3sg.pst.prog
±child son Suśīl ±(7.3.2) +this long mother-bereavement +watching was
'The little boy Susīl, (7.3.2), was watching his mother dying.'

7.3.2 ±आमा नेर +बसेर
±āmā nera basera
±LA:PP +P:iv1-abs.prt
±mother-near +having-sat
'sitting near his mother,'

7.4.1 ±लक्ष्मी ±कहिलेकाहीं ±(7.4.2) ±बरर +आँसु +झार्थिन्
±lakṣmī kahilekāhī̃ ±(7.4.2) ±barara +ā̃su +jhārthin
±S:pn-nm ±AA:advl ±AD:Cl(7.4.2) ±AA:advl +DO:cn-ac
+P:tv1-3sg.pst.f
±Lakṣmī ±sometimes ±(7.4.2) +pouringly +tears +shed
'Lakṣmī sometimes shed pouring tears (7.4.2).'

7.4.2 ±सुशीलको मुखपट्टि +हेरेर
±suśīlako mukhapaṭṭi +herera
±AA:PP +P:iv1-abs.prt
±susil-of face-toward +having-looked
'looking toward Suśīl's face,'

7.5 ±मलिनो बत्तीको धमिलो प्रकाशमा ±रोगीको कोठा +श्मशान जस्तो +देखिन्थ्यो
±malino battīko dhamilo prakāśamā ±rogīko koṭhā +śmaśāna jasto +dekhinthyo
±LA+CNP-lc ±S:CNP-nm +SC:AdjP +P:ev1-3sg.pst
±dim lamp-of weak light-in ±patient-of room +crematorium like +apeeared
'In the weak light of the dim lamp the sick room looked like a crematorium.'

7.6.1 ±त्यस्तैमा ±(7.6.2) ±नौलीले +देवीरमणलाई +ढोगिदिई
±tyastaimā ±(7.6.2) ±naulīle +devīramaṇalā.ī +ḍhogidi.ī
±LA:nl-lc ±AD:Cl(7.6.2) ±S:pn-nm +DO:pn-ac +P:tv1-3sg.pst.f
±like-that-at ±(7.6.2) ±Naulī +Devīramaṇ-to +bowed-down
'Just then, (7.6.2), Naulī bowed before (greeted) Devīramaṇ.'

7.6.2 +दैलो +उघारेर
+dailo +ughārera
+DO:cn-ac +P:tv1-abs.prt
+door having-opened
'opening the door,'

7.7.1 ±(7.7.2) ±देवीरमणका दुःखको लहरी ±केही शान्त +भयो
±(7.7.2) ±devīramaṇakā duḥkhako laharī +kehī śānta +bhayo;
±AD:Cl(7.7.2) ±S:CNP-nm +SC:CNP-nm +P:ev1-3sg.pst
±(7.7.2) ±Deviraman-of sorrow-of wave +somewhat abated +was
'(7.7.2), the wave of Devīramaṇ's sorrow abated somewhat.'

7.7.2 +नौलीलाई +देखेर
+naulīlā.ī +dekhera
+DO:pn-ac +P:tv1-abs.prt
+Nauli-to +having-seen
'Seeing Naulī,'

7.7.3 +भने-- + (7.7.4)
+bhane-- +(7.7.4)
+P:tv1-3sg.pst.m +DO:Cl(7.7.4)
+he-said -- + (7.7.4)
'He said: (7.7.4)

7.7.4 ±"नेपालबाट ±कहिले +आइपुगिस्, ±नौली?"
±"nepālabāṭa ±kahile +ā.īpugis, ±naulī ?"
±AbA:pn-ab ±AA:advl +P:iv1-2sg.pst ±EX:pn-nm
±Nepal-from ±when +arrived, ±Naulī ?"
"'When did you arrive from Nepal, Naulī ?"'

7.8.1 ±"बाजे, +आउँदैछु;
±"bāje, +āũdaichu;
±EX:cn-nm +P:iv1-3sg.pst.prog
±Baje +I-am-coming
'Baje, I have just come;'

7.8.2 +दुलही बजैलाई +कस्तो +छ?
+dulahī bajailā.ī + kasto +cha ?
+DC:CNP-dt +S:nl +P:iv2-3sg.pres
+Dulahī Bajai-to +how +is-it ?
"How is Dulahi Bajai ?"

7.9.1 ±"तेल ±त ±अघि ±नै +सिद्धिसकेको थियो
±"tela ±ta ±aghi ±nai +siddhisakeko thiyo,
±S:cn-nm ±NU:nu *(ta)* ±AA:advl +NU:nu (*nai*) +P:iVP1+aux-3sg.pst
±oil ±*ta* ±before ±*nai* +exhausted was,
'The oil had finished long before,'

7.9.2 ±अब (7.9.3) बाँकी छ"
±aba (7.9.3) bā̃kī cha."
±AA:advl ±S:Cl(7.9.3) +SC:adj-nm +P:ev1-3sg.pres
±now (7.9.3) ramaning is ."
'now it only remains (7.9.3)'

7.9.3 ±बत्ती +निभ्न
±battī +nibhna
±S:cn-nm +P:iv1-inf
±lamp to-die
'for the lamp to die.'

7.10.1 ±"बाजे, ±(7.10.2) ±सबै कुराको संभार +हुने थियो
±"bāje, (7.10.2) sabai kurāko sambhāra hune thiyo ,
±EX:cn-nm ±AD:Cl(7.10.2) ±S:CNP-nm
+P:iVP1impf.prt+aux-3sg.pst
±Baje, ±(7.10.2) ±all things-of care +being was
'Baje, everything would be taken care of,'

7.10.2 ±यस बखतमा +ठुली बजै +भए
±yasa bakhatamā +ṭhulī bajai +bhae
±LA:CNP-lc ±S:CNP-nm +P:iv1-cond.
±this time-at ±ṭhulī Bajai +if-be
'If Thuli Bajai (Subhadra) were here now,'

7.10.3 +के +गरूँ
+ke +garū̃,
+DO:pro(interrog)-ac +P:tv1-1sg.imp
+what +should-I-do
'What can I do ?'

7.10.4 +(7.10.5) +भनेको
+(7.10.5) +bhaneko
+DO:Cl(7.10.5) +P:tv1-prf.prt
+(7.10.5) +said
'I said (7.10.5)'

7.10.5 +जाउँ
+jāū̃
+P:iv1-1pl.imp
+Let-us-go
'Let us go,'

7.10.6 +मान्नुभएन
+mānnubhaena."
+P:iv1-3sg.pst
+she-did-not-agree [to come]
'but she would not come.'

7.11 ±के ±तैंले +भेटिस् ±र?"
±"ke ±taiṃle +bheṭis ±ra?"
±EX: (*ke*) ±S:pro(pers)-nm +P:iv1-2sg.pst ±NU:nu (*ra*)
±what +you +met ±*ra* ?
'"Did you really meet her? "'

7.12 ±"पशुपतिनाथको मन्दिर नेर +भेटेथें"
±"paśupatināthako mandira nera +bheṭethẽ"
±LA:PP +P:iv1-1sg.pst
±paśupatinātha-of temple near +I-had-met
'I had met her near the temple of Pashupatinath.'

7.13 +"कस्ती +थिई"
+"kastī +thi.ī ?"
+SC:adj +P:ev1-3sg.pst.f
+how +she-was ?
'"How was she?"'

7.14.1 +"एकदम दुब्ली, [+हुनुहुन्थ्यो]
+"ekadama dublī [+hunuhunthyo]
+SC:AdjP-nm [+P: ev1-3sg.pst.]
+"very thin [+she-was]"
'"She was very thin"'

7.14.2 +मैला लुगा +लगाएकी
+mailā lugā +lagāekī,
+SC:Cl +P:tv1-prf.prt
+dirty closthes +wearing,
'wearing dirty clothes,'

7.14.3 +मायालाग्दी [+हुनुहुनथ्यो]"
+māyālāgdī [+hunuhunthyo]"
+SC:adj-nm [+P: ev1-3sg.pst]
+pitiable [+she was]
'and she was pitiable'

7.15 ±"कहाँ +बसेकी रैछ?"
±"kahā̃ basekī raicha?"
±LA:advl +P:iVPprf.prt.+aux-3sg.pst
±where +staying is
'Where is she staying ?"'

7.16.1 ±गौरीघाट ±फुपू कहाँ +बसेकी छु
±gaurīghāṭa ±phupūkahā̃ basekī chu,
±LA:pn-lc ±LA:PP +P:iVP-1sg.pres.prf
±Gaurīghāt-at ±aunt's-at +staying am,
'"I am staying at Gaurighat at my aunt's,'

7.16.2 +फुपूलाई ±सरकारबाट +एक हण्डी +बक्सेको छ
+phupūlā.ī ±sarakārabāṭa +eka haṇḍī +bakseko cha,
+DC:cn-dt ±S:cn-nm +DO:CNP-ac +P:tVP2-3sg.pres.prf
+aunt-to ±government +one pension +given is
'The government has given a pension to my aunt,'

7.16.3 ±त्यसैबाट ±दुई जनाले +गुजारा +चलाएका छौं"
±tyasaibāṭa ±duī janāle +gujārā +calā̃ekā chauṃ "
±AbA:prol-ab ±S:NlP-nm +DO:cn-ac +P:tVP1-1pl.pres.prf
±that-from ±both persons +sustenance +managed we-have
'Both of us have managed on that.'

7.16.4 +(7.161-3) +भन्नुहुन्थ्यो
+(7.16.1-3) +bhannuhunthyo"
+DO:Cl(7.16.1-3) +P:tv1-3sg.pst
+(7.16.1-3) +she-said
'she said (7.16.1-3)'

7.17 ±देवीरमणका दुबै आँखाबाट +आँसुका धारा +बगे
±devīramaṇakā dubai ā̃khābāṭa ā̃sukā dhārā bage .
±AbA:CNP-ab ±S:CNP-nm +P:iv1-3pl.pst
±Devīramaṇ-of both eyes-from ±terars-of flows +flowed
'Flows of tears flowed from both eyes of Devīramaṇ.'

7.18.1 ±मनमनले +भने— (7.18.2-4)
±manamanale +bhane -- (7.18.2-4)
±IA:cn-in +P:tv1-3sg.pst +DO:Cl(7.18.2-4)
±mind-mind-by +he-said -- (7.18.2-4)
'He said to himself (7.18.2-4)'

7.18.2 +यत्रो संपत्तिकी मालिक्नी +भइकन
+yatro sampattikī māliknī +bhaikana
+SC:CNP-nm +P:ev1-abs.prt
+this-big wealth-of mistress +having-been
'Being a mistress of such a big wealth,'

7.18.3 ±सुभद्रा ±(7.18.4) +बसेकी छ
±subhadrā ±(7.18.4) +basekī cha
±S:pn-nm ±AD:Cl(7.18.4) +P:iVP-prf.prt
±Subhadrā ±(7.18.4) +living is
'Subhadrā lives (7.18.4)'

7.18.4 +एक छाक +खाएर
+eka chāka +khā̃era
+DO:CNP-ac +P:tv1-abs.prt
+one meal +having-eaten
'eating (only) one meal.'

7.19.1 ±उसमा ±पनि +दुब्ली +[छ]
±usamā ±pani +dublī +[cha]
±LA: pro-lc ±AA:Advl +SC:adj.nm +[P:ev1-3sg.]
±that-on also emaciated
'On top of that, [she is] emaciated.'

7.19.2 +मैला लुगा +लगाएकी
+mailā lugā +lagāekī ,
+DO:CNP-ac +P:tv1-prf.prt
+dirty clothes +wearing
'wearing dirty clothes.'

7.19.3 +मायालाग्दी +[छ]!
+māyālāgdī +[cha]!
+SC:adj-nm +P-ev1-3sg.pres
+'pitiful +[is]!'
'Pitiful.'

7.20.1 ±हरे परमेश्वर! ±म +पापी +हुँ
±hare parameśvara! ±ma +pāpī +hũ
±EX:cn-nm ±S:pro-(pers) +SC:adj-nm +P:ev1-1sg.pres
'Oh Lord ! ±I +sinner +am
'O Lord, I am a sinner.'

7.20.2 +मेरो जीवनलाई ±हजार वार ±धिक्कार +छ
+mero jīvanalāī ±hajāra vāra ±dhikkāra cha
+DC:CNP-dt ±AA:AdvP ±S:cn-nm +P:iv2-3sg.pres
+my life-to ±thousand-times ±curse +is
'A thousand curses on my life.'

7.21.1 ±सुभद्रा +मेरी गृहलक्ष्मी +हो;
±subhadrā +merī gṛhalakṣmī +ho;
±S:pn-nm +SC:CNP-nm +P:ev1-3sg.pres
±Subhadrā +my gṛhalakṣmī +is
'Subhadrā is the goddess of my house.'

7.21.2 ±उ +गए ±देखि
±u +gae +dekhi
±S:pro-nm +P:iv1-cond ±C: sc
±she +go-if ±since
'Since she went away,'

7.21.3 ±विपत्तिको बादलले +घेरिरहेछ
±vipattiko bādalale +gherirahecha
±S:CNP-nm +P:iv1-3sg.pres.prog
±misfortune-of clouds has-been-surrounding
'misfortune has been surroundeding.'

7.22.1 ±यो बालक सन्तानलाई +सम्झनुपर्ने
±yo bālaka santānalā.ī +samjhanuparne,
±AD:Cl(7.22.2) +DO:CNP-ac +P:tVP1+Aux:*parnu*-impf.prt
±(7.22.2) +this young child +ought-to-remember
'(7.22.2), she ought to remember the boy.'

7.22.2 +हामीलाई +नभए ±पनि
+hāmīlā.ī +nabhae ±pani
+DO:pro(pers)-ac +P:tv1-impf.prt ±C:sc
+us +not-being ±even
'Even if (she) has no feeling for us,'

7.22.3 +सबैलाई ±चटक्क +बिर्सी
+sabailā.ī ±caṭakka +birsī
+DO:pro-ac ±AA:advl +P:tv1-3sg.pst.f
+everyone ±completely +she-forgot
'She forgot everyone completely.'

7.22.3 +इत्यादि दुःखमनाउ +गरेर
+ityādi duḥkhamanāu +garera
+DO:CNP-ac +P:tv1-abs.prt
+such complains +having-made
'making such complains,'

7.22.4 +आँसु +झार्दै
+ā̃su +jhārdai
+DO:cn-ac +P:tv1-conj.prt
+tears +shedding
'shedding tears,'

7.22.5 +भने -- +(7.22.6)
+bhane -- +(7.22.6)
+P:tv1-3sg.pst +DO:Cl(7.22.5)
+he-said +(7.22.6)
'He said (7.22.6)'

7.22.6 ±नौली! ±तँ +आइछेस्
±naulī! ±tã +ā.iches ,
±EX:pn.nm ±S:pro(pers)-nm +P:iv1-2sg.pst
±Naulī ! ±you +have-come
'Naulī, you have come.'

7.27.7 +घरको संभार +राखेस्
+gharako sambhāra +rākhes ,
+DO:CNP-ac +P:tv1-2sg.imp
+house-of care +you-keep
'Look after the house.'

7.22.8 ±म ±भोलि ±बिहानै ±नेपाल +जान्छु
±ma ±bholi ±bihānai ±nepāla +jānchu."
±S:pro-nm ±AA:AdvP ±AA:pn-ac ±AA: cn-ac +P:iv1-1sg.pres.
±I ±tomorrow ±morning +Nepal I-go
'I will go to Nepal tomorrow morning.'

7.23 ±त्यस्तैमा ±सुभद्रा ±घर भित्र +पसिन्
±tyastaimā ±subhadrā ±ghara bhitra +pasin
±AA:nl-lc ±S:pn-nm ±AA:PP +P:iv1-3sg.pst.f
±such-at ±Subhadrā ±house-into +entered
At that moment, Subhadrā entered into in the house.'

7.24.1 +अत्यन्त दुब्ली, +निदाउरी, +[थिइन्]
+atyanta dublī, +nidā.urī , +[thi.in]
+SC:AdjP-nm +SC:adj-nm [+P:ev1-3sg.pst.f]
+very thin +fatigued +[she-was]
'She was very thin, and fatigued.'

7.24.2 +मलिन, झुत्रा लुगा +लगाएकी
+malina, jhutrā lugā +lāekī ,
+DO:CNP-ac +P:tv1-prf.prt
+dirty, torn clothes +wearing ,
'wearing dirty and torn clothes.'

7.24.3 ±मुखमण्डलमा ±असीम करुणा तथा संयम +झल्किरहेको थियो
±mukhamaṇḍalamā ±asīma karuṇā tathā saṃyama +jhalkiraheko thiyo
±LA:CmpN-lc ±S:CNP-nm +P:iVP1-prog.prf.prt+aux-3sg.pst
±face-on +unlmited compassion and tranquility +shining was
'Unlimited compassion and tranqulitiy was shining on her face.'

7.25.1 ±(7.25.2) देवीरमणको हृदय +टुक्रा-टुक्रा +भयो
±(7.25.2) devīramaṇako hṛdaya +ṭukrā-ṭukrā +bhayo.
±AD:Cl(6.25.2) +S:CNP-nm +SC:CmpdN-nm +P:ev1-3sg.pst
±(7.25.2) Devīramaṇ-of heart +piece-piece +became
'(7.25.2), Deviraman's heart was crushed.'

7.25.2 +सुभद्राको शारीरिक अवस्था +देखेर
+subhadrāko śārīrika avasthā +dekhera
+DO:CNP-ac +P:tv1-abs.prt
+Subhadra-of physical state +having-seen
'Seeing Subhadra's physical state,'

7.26.1 +(7.26.2) +लागे
+(7.26.2) +lāge
+DO:Cl(7.26.2) +P:tv1-3sg.pst.m
+He-began +(7.26.2)
'He began +(7.26.2)'

7.26.2 ±(7.26.3) +रुन
±(7.26.3) +runa
±AD:Cl(7.26.3) +P:iv1-inf
±(7.26.3) +to-cry
'to cry (7.26.3)'

7.26.3 +दुबै हातले +मुख +छोपेर
+dubai hātale +mukha +chopera
±IA:CNP-in +DO:cn-ac +P:tv1-abs.prt
±both hands-with +face +having-covered
'covering his face with his hands.'

7.27.1 ±(7.27.2) सुभद्रा ±लक्ष्मीको सिरानमा +बसिन्
±(7.27.2) subhadrā ±lakṣmīko sirānamā +basin
±AD:Cl(7.27.2) ±LA:CNP-lc +Piv1-3sg.pst.f
±(7.27.2) Subhadrā ±Lakṣmī-of head-of-the-bed-at +she-sat
'(7.27.2), Subhadrā sat at the head of the bed of Laksmi.'

7.27.2 +पतिलाई +दण्डवत् +गरेर
+patilā.ī +daṇḍavat +garera
+DC:cn-dt +DO:cn-ac +P:tv2-abs.prt
+husband-to +prostrate +having-done
'Having greeted her husband (by prostrating in front of him),

7.21.1 +नौलीले +भनी-- +(7.28.2)
+naulīle +bhanī-- +(7.28.2)
±S:pb-nm +P:tv1-3sg.pst.f
±Naulī +said -- +(7.28.2)
'Nauli said (7.28.2)'

7.28.2 ±"ओहो! ±बजै +आइपुग्नुभो?"
±"oho! ±bajai +ā.īpugnubho ?"
±EX:intj ±S:cn-nm +P:iVP1-3sg.pst
±Oh ! ±Bajai +arrived ?
'"Oh! Bajai has arrived ?"'

7.29.1 ±(7.29.2) ±लक्ष्मीले +आँखा +उघारिन्
±(7.29.2) ±lakşmīle +ā̃khā +ughārin
±AD:Cl (7.29.2) ±S:pn-nm +DO:cn-ac +P:tv1-3sg.pst.f
±(7.29.2) ±Lakşmī +eyes +opened
'(7.29.2), Lakşmī opened her eyes.'

7.29.2 +नौलीको स्वर +सुनेर
+naulīko svara +sunera
+DO:CNP-ac +P:tv1-abs.prt
+Naulī-of voice +having-heard
'Hearing Naulī's voice,'

7.31.1 ±(7.30.2) ±सुस्तरी ±लर्बरिएको स्वरले +भनिन्-- +(7.304)
±(7.30.2) ±sustarī ±larbarieko svarale +bhanin-- +(7.30.4)
±AD:Cl(7.30.2) ±AA:adv ±IA:CNP-in +P:tv1-3sg.pst.f
+DO:Cl(7.30.4)
±(7.30.2) ±faintly ±unsteady voice-with she-said -- (7.30.4)
'(7.30.2), she said in a faint and unsteady voice (7.30.4)'

7.30.2 +सुभद्रालाई (7.30.3) +देखेर
+subhadrālā.ī (7.30.3) +dekhera ,
+DO:pn-ac +OC:Cl(7.303) +P:tv3-abs.prt
+Subhadra (7.30.3) +having-seen
'Seeing Subhadra (7.30.3)'

7.30.3 ±आफ्ना सिरानमा +बसेको
±āphnā sirānamā +baseko
±LA:CNP-lc +P:iv1-prf.prt
±one's-own head-of-the-bed-at +seated
'seated at the head of her bed'

7.30.4 ±"दिदी, ±तपाईंको दर्शनलाई ±एक मुठी सास ± मुश्किलले +झुण्डिरहेको छ"
±"didī , ±tapāiko darśanalāi ±eka muṭhī sāsa ±muskilale +jhuṇḍiraheko cha"
±EX:cn-nm +DC:CNP-dt ±S:CNP-nm ±AA:adj-in +P:iv2-3sg.pres.prf
±Sister, ±your glimpse-for ±one handful breath ±hardly +hanging is
'"Sister, I have been hanging on to life just to have a glimpse of you."'

7.31.1 ±(7.31.2) ±सुभद्राको हृदयको मैलो +एकदम साफ +भयो
±(7.31.2) ±subhadrāko hṛdayako mailo +ekadama sāpha +bhayo .
±AD:Cl(7.31.3) ±S:CNP-nm +SC:AdjP +P:ev1-3sg.pst
±(7.31.2) ±Subhadrā-of heart-of dirt ±very clean +became
'(7.31.2), the dirt of Subhadra's heart was cleansed.'
(Subhadra forgot all her grievances)

7.31.2 +लक्ष्मीको वचन +सुनेर
+lakṣmīko vacana +sunera
+DO:CNP-ac +P:tv1-abs.prt
+Lakṣmī-of words having-heard
'Hearing the words of Lakṣmī,'

7.32.3 +भनिन्-- +(7.32.4)
+bhanin-- +(7.32.4)
+P:tv1-3sg.pst +DO:Cl(3.32.4)
+She-said-- +(7.32.4)
'She said-- +(7.32.4)'

7.32.4 ±"बाबु! ±मैले +आफ्नो कर्तव्य +बिर्सिछु "
±"bābu! maile +āphno kartavya +birsichu"
±EX:cn-nm ±S:pro-nm +DO:CNP-ac +P:tv1-3sg.pres.prf.f
±Little-one! ±I +one's-own duty +have-forgotten
'My little one, I have forgotten my duty.'

7.33.1 ±लक्ष्मीले ±(7.33.2) +भनिन्-- +(7.33.3)
±lakṣmīle ±(7.33.2) +bhanin-- +(7.33.3)
±S:pn-nm ±AD:Cl(7.33.2) +P:tv1-3sg.pst.f +DO:Cl(7.33.3)
±Lakṣmī ±(7.33.2) +said -- +(7.33.3)
'Lakṣmī, ±(7.33.2), +said (7.33.3)'

7.33.2 ±सुभद्राको छातीतिर +देखाएर
±subhadrāko chātītira +dekhāera
±AA:PP +P:iv1-abs.prt
±Subhadrā-of breast-toward +having-pointed
'pointing to Subhadra's breast.'

7.33.3 ±"त्यहाँ +साह्रै कडा चोट +लागेको छ"
±"tyahā̃ +sāhrai kaḍā coṭa +lāgeko cha."
+LA:advl ±S:CNP-nm +P:iVP1-prf.prt+aux-3sg.pres
±there +very hard wound +struck is
"There is a great wound there,"

7.34.1 ±सुभद्राले ±(7.34.2) +भनिन्-- +(7.34.3-5)
±subhadrāle ±(7.34.2) +bhanin-- +(7.34.3-5)
±S:pn-nm ±AD:Cl(7.34.2) +P:tv1-3sg.pst +DO:Cl(7.34.3-5)
±Subhadrā ±(7.34.2) +said-- +(7.34.3-5)
'Subhadra ±(7.34.2) +said-- +(7.34.3-5)'

7.34.2 +आँसु +झार्दै
+ā̃su +jhārdai
+DO:cn-nm +P:tv1-conj.prt
+tears +shedding
'shedding tears,'

7.34.3 +"निको +भो ±बा,
+"niko +bho ±bā,
+SC:adj-nm +P:ev1-3sg.pst ±EX:cn-nm
+healed +became +dear-baby
'"It has healed up, my dear baby.'

7.34.4 ±अस्ति ±नै +निको +भइसक्यो,
±asti ±nai niko bha.isakyo,
±AA:advl +NU:nu (*nai*) +SC:adj-nm +P:cmpdev1-3sg.pst
±long-before ±indeed +healed +had-become
'Indeed, it had healed up long before,'

7.34.5 ±सानो तिलको दाना जति ±पनि +छैन "
±sāno tilako dānā jati ±pani +chaina "
±S: CNP ±AA: advl +P:ev1-3sg.pres.neg
±small sesame-of seed as-big +even +is-not
'"There is not (even a mark) as big as a sesame seed."

7.35.1 ±त्यस पछि ±(7.35.2) ±लक्ष्मीले +सुशीलको हात +सुभद्राका काखमा +राखिदिइन्
±tyasa pachi ±(7.35.2) ±lakṣmīle +suśīlako hāta +subhadrākā kākhamā +rākhidi.in
±AA:PP ±AD:Cl (7.35.2) ±S:pn-nm +DO:CNP-ac +LC:CNP-lc +P:Cmpdtv4-3sg.pst.f
±that after ±(7.35.2) ±Lakṣmī +Suśīl-of hand +Subhadrā-of lap-in +put
'Then Laksmi put Susil's hand in Subhadra's lap,'

7.35.2 ±"दिदी, +तपाईँको नासो!" +भनेर
±"didī, +tapāi~ko nāso!" bhanera
±EX:cn-nm +DO:CNP-ac +P:tv1-3sg.pst
Sister, +your ward (minor)" +having-said
'saying "Sister, this is your ward (minor)."'

7.36.1 ±(7.36.2) +सुभद्रा +(7.36.3) +लागिन्
±(7.36.2) +subhadrā +(7.36.3) +lāgin .
±AD:Cl(7.36.2) ±S:pn-nm +DO:Cl(7.36.3) +P:tv1-3sg.pst.f
±(7.36.2) ±Subhadra +(7.36.3) +began
'(7.36.2), Subhadra began (7.36.3)'

7.36.2 +छोरालाई ±काखमा +लिएर
+chorālā.ī ±kākhamā +liera
+DO:cn-ac ±LA:cn-lc +P:tv1-abs.prt
+son lap-in having-taken
'taking the boy in her lap,'

7.36.3 +रुन
+runa
+P:iv1-inf
+to-cry
'to cry'

7.37.1 ±यी सबै ± सुभद्राका निमित्त +(7.37.2) खुड्काहरू +थिए
±yī sabai subhadrākā nimitta (7.37.2) khuḍkāharu thie .
±S:NlP-nm ±AA:PP +SC:CNP-nm +P:ev1-3pl.pst
±these all ±Subhadra-of for +(7.37.2) sore-points +were
'For Subhadra, these were the sore points (of her mind).'

7.37.2 +(7.37.3) +रूँदै गर्ने
+(7.37.3) +rūdai garne
±AD:Cl (7.37.3) +P:iVP1-impf.prt
±(7.37.3) +weeping doing
'to weep over, (7.37.3)'

7.37.3 ±जिन्दगी भर +संझदै
±jindagī bhara +samjhãdai
±AA:PP +P:iv1-conj.prt
±life full +remembering
'remembering them in the rest of her life.'

7.38 ±निभ्ने बेलाको बत्ती झैं ±लक्ष्मीको मुख ±एक क्षणका निमित्त +तेजोमय +भयो
±nibhne belāko battī jhaĩ ±lakşmīko mukha ±eka kşaṇakā nimitta +tejomaya +bhayo
±AA:AdvP ±S:CNP-nm ±AA:PP +SC:adj-nm +P:ev1-3sg.pst
±dying time-of lamp like ±Laksmi's face ±one moment-of for +bright +became
'Like the flame of dying time, Laksmi's face became bright for a moment.'

7.39 ±अनि पछि +अन्धकार +[भयो]
±ani pachi +andhakāra! +[bhayo].
±C:cc ±S:cn-nm +[P:iv1-3sg-pst]
±and then ±darkness! +[was]
'And then, it was dark !'

7.40.1 ±लक्ष्मी ±(7.40.2) ±अनन्तमा +पुगिन्
±lakşmī ±(7.40.2) ±anantamā +pugin .
±S:pn-nm ±AD:Cl (7.402) ±LA: cn-lc +P:iv3-3sg.pst.f
±Lakşmī (7.40.2) infinite-at arrived
'Laksmi arrived at the infinite.'

7.402 +यो दु:खमय असार संसारलाई +छोडेर
+yo duḥkhamaya, asāra saṃsāralā.ī +choḍera
+DO:CNP-ac +P:tv1-abs.prt
+this sorrowful, hollow world +having-left
'Leaving this sorrowful, hollow world,'

7.41 ±देवीरमण, नौलीहरु ±पनि +(7.41.2) +लागे
±devīramaṇa, naulīharu ±pani +(7.41.2) +lāge .
±S:CNP-nm +AA:advl +P:tv1-3pl.pst
±Devīramaṇ, Naulī-and-others ±also +(7.41.2) +began
'Devīramaṇ, Naulī and others began (7.41.2)'

7.41.2 +रुन
+runa
+P:iv1-inf
+to-cry
'to cry'

5. *Nāso:* Phrases (sorted)

AdjP	ali jhaḍaṅge svabhāvakī
AdjP	atyanta dublī
AdjP	ekadama sāpha
AdjP	jhan bhayaṅkara
AdjP	kati dublī
AdjP	kati matalabī
AdjP	kehī śānta
AdjP	naulo jasto
AdjP	sojhī jastī
AdjP	sāno tilako dānā jati
AdjP	tyasa aparādhīko jasto
AdjP	tyasa bālaka chātrako jasto
AdjP	āphnā sirānamā baseko
AdvP	ali para
AdvP	ali para
AdvP	ani pachi
AdvP	eka-eka garī
AdvP	hajāra vāra
AdvP	kārāgārakī duḥkhī bandī jhaī
AdvP	māhurī jhaī
AdvP	kunai bakhata
AdvP	nibhne belāko battī jhaī
AdvP	pasne-bittikai
AdvP	pharkanubhae pachi
AdvP	sarala nārīsvabhāvavaśa
AdvP	sāhrai utsukatāsātha
AdvP	yasa bakhata
AdvP	śmaśāna jasto
CNP	aghikai kṛtyal
CNP	ananta ākāśa
CNP	arko sāthī
CNP	arko vivāha
CNP	aru śeṣa bhokā, pyāsā, duḥkhīharu
CNP	aruko sammatil
CNP	asīma karuṇā tathā saṁyama
CNP	bīsai dinako bidā
CNP	bahuta patiparāyaṇā ramaṇī
CNP	balekai āgo
CNP	bastubhāukā hāḍachālā
CNP	bhayangkara rūpa
CNP	bhogako lālasā
CNP	bholi bihānai
CNP	bhāgne maukā
CNP	bhātako gāsa
CNP	bāhra barṣakī abodha bālikā
CNP	bāje āphaī
CNP	bājeko jahāja
CNP	bājeko ṭupī
CNP	cha mahīnā
CNP	chimekakā ā.imā.īle
CNP	cinnai nasakne
CNP	cāra dina
CNP	cāroṭā akṣatā
CNP	devī-devatāko bhākala
CNP	devīramaṇako citta
CNP	devīramaṇako dailo
CNP	devīramaṇako daurā
CNP	devīramaṇako gati
CNP	devīramaṇako goḍā
CNP	devīramaṇako hṛdaya
CNP	devīramaṇako jita
CNP	devīramaṇako purāno chākarnī
CNP	devīramaṇako ā̃gana
CNP	devīramaṇakā dubai ā̃khā
CNP	devīramaṇakā duḥkhako laharī
CNP	devīramaṇakā kapāla
CNP	devīramaṇakā santāna
CNP	dhana, bala, buddhi sabai kurā
CNP	dharma tathā vivekako hatyā

CNP	dharmakā ājñā
CNP	dhāmī-jhā̃krīko būṭī-jantara
CNP	dubai hāta
CNP	eka añjulī pānī
CNP	eka china
CNP	eka chāka
CNP	eka dina
CNP	eka dina
CNP	eka gāsa
CNP	eka haṇḍī
CNP	eka mahān baliṣṭha śakti
CNP	eka muṭhī sāsa
CNP	eka mānāko santoṣa
CNP	eka paisā
CNP	eka peṭa
CNP	eka vacana
CNP	eka ṭhāũ
CNP	eka-du.ī gā̃sa bhāta
CNP	eka-duī chāka bhāta
CNP	ekai ghara
CNP	ekai āsanamā
CNP	euṭā haṇḍī
CNP	euṭā lāmo jyoti
CNP	euṭā poko
CNP	euṭā sāno ṭhāũ
CNP	gae sāla
CNP	ghaniṣṭha prema
CNP	gharakī purānī cākarnī
CNP	gharako hāla
CNP	gharako sambhāra
CNP	grāmīṇa ṭhaṭṭā
CNP	gāũkā dherai ā.imā.īharu
CNP	gāũkā kaiyana būḍhābūḍhī, vidhavā svāsnīmānisaharu
CNP	gāũle chimekīharu
CNP	haraeka upāya
CNP	ityādi duḥkhamanāu
CNP	ityādi manovedanā
CNP	ityādi vicāra
CNP	jīvanako śeṣa ghaḍī
CNP	kalpanātīta manomandira
CNP	kanyāpakṣakā mānisa
CNP	katro kāma
CNP	kaḍuvā telako battī
CNP	kuna daulathako caina
CNP	kunai dina
CNP	kunai praśna
CNP	kuraikurākā hānathāpa
CNP	kurā garnāko bahānā
CNP	lakṣmī tathā subhadrākā jīvana
CNP	lakṣmīko mukha
CNP	lakṣmīko sirāna
CNP	lakṣmīko vacana
CNP	larbarieko svarale
CNP	madhuro battīko dhamilo ujyālo
CNP	malino battīko dhamilo prakāśa
CNP	manako kurā
CNP	manomālinyako euṭā bīja
CNP	manomālinyako euṭā sāno bīja
CNP	merī gṛhalakṣmī
CNP	mero jīvana
CNP	mero jyādā āgraha
CNP	mero ke doṣa
CNP	mero keko khojī
CNP	mero rājā
CNP	muṭuko baha
CNP	mānavajātiko duḥkhamaya avasthā
CNP	mānisako pāṇḍitya
CNP	mūka pakṣīharu
CNP	naulīko mola
CNP	naulīko svara
CNP	naulīko umera
CNP	naulīkā kurā

CNP	nayā̃ dulahī
CNP	nayā̃ dulahī
CNP	pahilo dinako pāṭha
CNP	pallo gāũ
CNP	pallo koṭhā
CNP	pallo koṭhāmā
CNP	paricita mānisa
CNP	parivartanaśīla saṁsārako gati
CNP	phāguna mahīnāko bihānapakhako sireṭo
CNP	poiko nāka
CNP	purānā vicārakā mānisa
CNP	putravatī patnī
CNP	pyāro gṛha
CNP	pṛthvīko pṛthvī
CNP	rogīko koṭhā
CNP	rogīkā sirāna
CNP	saba bhandā ṭhūlo santoṣa
CNP	sabai kurāko sambhāra
CNP	santānakā jarā
CNP	santānakā āśā
CNP	sautāko rīsa
CNP	saṁsāramā sabai bhandā pyāro vastu
CNP	subhadrāko bālaka-kāladekhiko sukha-duḥkhakī sāthī
CNP	subhadrāko chātī
CNP	subhadrāko hṛdaya
CNP	subhadrāko hṛdaya
CNP	subhadrāko hṛdayako mailo
CNP	subhadrāko komala hṛdaya-kusuma
CNP	subhadrāko ochyāna
CNP	subhadrāko pāṇigrahaṇa
CNP	subhadrāko ādeśa
CNP	subhadrāko ājīvana sevāko puraskāra
CNP	subhadrāko śārīrika avasthā
CNP	subhadrākā kākha
CNP	sukha-duḥkhakī sāthī
CNP	suśīlako hāta
CNP	svargako bāṭo chekincha bhanne hindū dharma
CNP	svargakā ḍīla
CNP	svargavāsī mahārāja candra śamaśera jaṅgabahādurakā karuṇā
CNP	sāhrai bebujhako kāma
CNP	sāhrai kaḍā coṭa
CNP	sāhrai narāmro roga
CNP	sāṁsārika sukhalipsāko ṭarro ānandako anubhava
CNP	sā̃co mana
CNP	tī goṭhālāharuko sampatti
CNP	tīrtha jāne phikrī
CNP	tīrthayātrākā kumle phauja
CNP	tapanī jaro
CNP	tapāīko darśana
CNP	tapāīko nāso
CNP	tina-cāra barṣapachiko kurā
CNP	tyahī sāno poko
CNP	tyasakā jīu
CNP	tyastā belā
CNP	tyo bālaka
CNP	tyo hula
CNP	tyo kurā
CNP	tyo kālo andhakāra
CNP	tyo tīrthayātrīko samūha,
CNP	tyo viśāla nabhasthala
CNP	u avasthā
CNP	uhī kurā
CNP	unako abhimāna
CNP	unako bhalo-kubhalo
CNP	unako chātī
CNP	unako dainika kāma
CNP	unako jīvanādhāra
CNP	unako tyo prabala vākśakti
CNP	unako ā̃su
CNP	usa ṭhāũ

CNP	usa ṭhāũ
CNP	usako umera
CNP	vīsāsaya āyu
CNP	vipattiko bādala
CNP	yī anātha prāṇīharu
CNP	yī vastubhāu
CNP	yasa kulābalambako bālalīlā
CNP	yasa kurāko kehī jñāna
CNP	yastai dṛśya
CNP	yastai tarka
CNP	yasto andhakāra rātrī
CNP	yatro sampattikī mālikni
CNP	yatti antara
CNP	yinīharusaṁgako viyoga
CNP	yinai santānahīnā ramaṇīkā sāthī
CNP	yinaiko lālana-pālana
CNP	yinakā hāta-kākha
CNP	yo anupama ānandaprada bālakrīḍā
CNP	yo baliṣṭha bālahaṭha
CNP	yo bālaka santāna
CNP	yo cicilo bālakhako ke gati
CNP	yo cira mātṛviyoga
CNP	yo dina
CNP	yo duḥkhamaya asāra saṁsāra
CNP	yo ghara
CNP	yo karuṇājanaka dṛśya
CNP	yo kālo pṛthvī
CNP	yo pratidinako gṛhakalaha
CNP	yo pāpapūrṇa jagata
CNP	yo tīrthayātrā
CNP	yo umera
CNP	yo viśāla āśālatā
CNP	yo śiśu-santānakā āḍa
CNP	ādhā rāta
CNP	ākāśakā devagṇa
CNP	āntarika preraṇā
CNP	āphnī āmā
CNP	āphno dolāī
CNP	āphno kartavya
CNP	āphno kāma
CNP	āphno tībra icchā
CNP	āphno tyatro daulatha
CNP	āphno vaibhava
CNP	ṭhulo kalaha
CNP	śūnya ākāśa
CNP	ā̃ganamā carirahekā parevā
CNP	ā̃sukā dhārā
CmpdAdvP	bāhira-bhitra
CmpdCNP	bakhata-bakhata
CmpdCNP	damā.ī-ḍoleharu
CmpdCNP	dina-rāta
CmpdCNP	duḥkha-pīra
CmpdCNP	hāḍa-chālā
CmpdCNP	kharca-barca
CmpdCNP	kheta-bārī
CmpdCNP	nokara-cākara
CmpdCNP	tīrtha-varta
CmpdCNP	viveka-buddhi
CmpdCNP	āmā-chorī
CmpdCNP	ṭukrā-ṭukrā
CmpdVP	choḍi-diũlā,
CmpdVP	dekhdā-dekhdai
CmpdVP	gari-die
CmpdVP	hũdo ho
CmpdVP	pratīta hunthyo
CmpdVP	ḍhogi-di.ī
eVP	bhaekā thie
eVP	huna gayo
eVP	huna sakena
eVP	huna āyo
eVP	hune thiyo
iVP	baliraheko thiyo
iVP	basekī cha
iVP	basekī chu

iVP	basekī chu
iVP	basekī raicha
iVP	basekī thi.in.
iVP	basekā thie.
iVP	basnu paryo
iVP	basnubhaeko cha
iVP	bhukiraheko thiyo
iVP	hune ho
iVP	hīḍnu bhaecha
iVP	jhalkiraheko thiyo
iVP	jhuṇḍiraheko cha
iVP	jā̃dī hū
iVP	jā̃dai gardī ho
iVP	kheliraheko thiyo
iVP	khelirahekā thie
iVP	lāgdo rahecha
iVP	lāgeko cha
iVP	lāgeko thiyo
iVP	lāgyo holā
iVP	nāciraheko thiyo
iVP	puchine thiyo
iVP	roīrahanubhaeko rahecha
iVP	roirahekā thie
iVP	rūdai garne
iVP	siddhisakeko thiyo
iVP	sutekī thi.in
modAdjP	dāsa-jīvanabāṭa mukta
modAdjP	pavitra putra-vātsalyale paripūrṇa
modAdjP	ṭekne-samāune kehī nabhaekī
modAdvP	kehi dina puṇyabhoga garne
modCNP	arkai vicārako dvanda
modCNP	arkākī dāsī
modCNP	bīsaū barṣadekhi sutiraheko koṭhā
modCNP	choro pāekī svāsnī
modCNP	herirahekā holān bhanne bhāna
modCNP	hāmī khasisakepachiko bībhatsa rūpa
modCNP	ke khāū ke lāū bhanne belā
modCNP	naramā.ilo lāgnuparne kurā
modCNP	naulīrūpī euṭā duḥkha pokhne bhhā̃ḍo
modCNP	pakrane kośiśa
modCNP	parkhī parkhī karā.une hucīla pakṣīko virasilo hukahuka śabda
modCNP	poiko nāka
modCNP	sadbīu charne jātrūharuko chicolī nasaknu ghuīco
modCNP	subhadrā dulahī bhaera āūdāko bakhatako bhayangkara dukha
modCNP	subhadrāko "ko khā.ī" ko āvāja
modCNP	subhadrāko kokha
modCNP	tīrtha garne icchā
modCNP	tila rākhne ṭhāū
modCNP	timro ochyāna
modCNP	unako eklai jāne vicāra
modCNP	āphūle cineko cautāro
modPNP	mailo bichyā.unāmā sutekī lakṣmī
modPNP	thākera āekā devīramaṇa
modPNP	manovījāna najānekā devīramaṇa
NIP	dui janā
NIP	yī sabai
PNP	anāthinī subhadrā
PNP	bālaka putra suśīla
PNP	dulahī bajai
PNP	dulahī bajai
PNP	dulahī bajyai'
PNP	gorakhā mulakā ḍāgḍara subedāra
PNP	harivaṁśa purāṇa
PNP	kaṇgāla devīramaṇa
PNP	māgha mahīnā
PNP	naulī ghartinī

PNP	santānecchuka devīramaṇa
PNP	sāno bābu
PNP	ṭhulī bajai
PNP	bicarī subhadrā
PP	agni yā corakā nimitta
PP	ahile samma
PP	ali bera samma
PP	ali dina pachi
PP	bāhra varṣako umera dekhi
PP	bāje saṁga
PP	bālaka saṁga
PP	chimekī saṁga
PP	devīramaṇakā ā̃khākā sāmu
PP	devīramaṇako pachi
PP	devīramaṇakā ghara nera
PP	devīramaṇakā khāṭa mani
PP	dherai berasamma
PP	eka china pachi
PP	eka china pachi
PP	eka kṣaṇa pachi
PP	eka kṣaṇakā nimitta
PP	eka tira
PP	gaha bharī
PP	janma bhara
PP	jindagī bhara
PP	jiu bhari
PP	kehī bera pachi
PP	ko saṁga
PP	kālo andhakāra māthi
PP	paisākā nimitta
PP	parevā tira
PP	paścima ḍhokā nera
PP	paśupatināthako mandira nera
PP	paśupatināthakā mandira waripari
PP	pāhunā-pāsā saṁga
PP	rānuko pachi

PP	rāta bhara
PP	rātamāṭe bhaṅḍārīkā jahāna saṁga
PP	sadaivakā nimitta
PP	sadhaiṁ jāgā bhairahane viśvako catura caukīdāra bāheka
PP	santāna vinā
PP	santāna vinā
PP	santānakā nimti
PP	subhadrā saṁga
PP	subhadrāko chātī tira
PP	subhadrāko nimitta
PP	subhadrāko ādeśa vinā
PP	subhadrākā nimitta
PP	sukhakā kati najīkai
PP	suśīlako mukha paṭṭi
PP	tīrthabāṭa pharke dekhi
PP	tulasīkā maṭha nera
PP	tyasa pachi
PP	yastai rīta saṁga
PP	yatikā dina samma
PP	āmā nera
PP	āśāko badalā
ProP	hāmī bhoka, pyāsa,
ProP	kasako ke
ProP	ke ke
ProP	mero ko
ProP	savai janā
ProP	yo ghara, yī bastubhāu, yī rukha-vṛkṣa sabai
ProP	aru kasai-
tVP	bakseko cha
tVP	bakseko rahecha
tVP	bhandā hun
tVP	calāekā chaū
tVP	calāekā chaū
tVP	chopekī thi.in
tVP	choḍnu pare

tVP	chāḍnu parcha
tVP	cyāpekī thi.in
tVP	dekhekī thi.in
tVP	di.irahekā thie.
tVP	dieko cha
tVP	diekā thie
tVP	ganīrahekī thi.in
tVP	garekī chu
tVP	gareko hū
tVP	gareko hūdo hū,
tVP	garirahekā thie
tVP	gā̃sirahekî thi.ī
tVP	garā.unu parcha
tVP	heriraheko thiyo
tVP	herirahekā rahechan
tVP	herirahekā thie
tVP	khuwā.irahekī thi.in
tVP	laijānu-parthyo
tVP	lāgekī rahichan
tVP	pakāunu pardā
tVP	pakāunuhūdo ho
tVP	sahekī chu
tVP	sodhisamma dināle
tVP	sunne-bittikai
tVP	ṭhageko cha

6. *Nāso:* Lexicon in order of occurrence

1.1
ghara- cn `home'
mā lc cs.mkr `at, in, on'
cañcalāshrī cn `Goddess of wealth'
bha.ikana iv1 abs.prt <hunu ` having been'
pani advl `also, even'
devīramaṇa- pn ` Deviraman'
kā gn cs.mkr `of'
santāna cn `children'
thienan iv1 pst <hunu+neg ` they were not'

1.2
santāna cn `child'
hos iv1 imp <hunu `may he be'
bhannā- tv1 inf <bhannu `to say'
kā gn cs.mkr `of'
nimitta pp `for'
haraeka adjl `every'
upāya cn `means'
gare tv1 pst <garnu `he did'
cautāro cn `platform under a tree'
cine tv1 pst <cinnu `he built'
bāṭo cn `path'
khane tv1 pst <knannu `he dug (built)'
pashupati- pn `Pashupati'
mā lc cs.mkr `at, in, on'
mahādīpa cmpdcn `great-lamp'
bāle tv1 pst <bālnu `he lit'
gae[ko] prf.prt <jānu `gone, past'
sāla cn `year'
harivaṃsha pn `Harivamsha'
purāṇa cn `Purana (legends)'
lagāe tv1 pst <lagā.unu `he organized'
taipani cc `however'
subhadrā- pn `ṣubhadra'
ko gn cs.mkr `of'
kokha cn `womb'
saphala adjl `fruitful'
huna ev1 inf <hunu `to be'
sakena aux pst <saknu+neg `he could not'
1.3
jorīpārī- cn `neighbors'
saṃga pp `with'
ṭhokābājī cn `competition'
pardā iv1 conj.prt <parnu `while happening'
dhana cn `wealth'
bala cn `strength'
buddhi cn `intelligence'
sabai prol.adj `all'
kurā- cn `things'
mā lc cs.mkr `at, in, on'
devīramaṇa- pn `Deviraman'
ko gn cs.mkr `of'
jita cn `victory'
hunthyo iv1 pst <hunu `he used to be'
tara cc `but'
apūto adj `childless'
bhaneko tv1 prf.prt <bhannu `being said'
sunne- tv1 impf.prt <sunnu `hearing'
bittikai advl `as soon as'
una- pro.pers <unī `he'
ko gn cs.mkr `of'
abhimāna cn `pride'
dhūlo cn `dust'
hunthyo ev1 pst <hunu `used to be'
ātmaglāni- cn `humiliation'
le in cs.mkr `by, with'
pānī cn `water'
hunthe ev1 pst <hunu `he would be'

1.4
purānā adj `old'
vicāra- cn `thought'
kā gn cs.mkr `of'
mānisa cn `man'
thie ev1 pst <hunu `he was'
santāna- cn `child'
vinā pp `without'
āphno prol.adj `his own'
vaibhava- cn `wealth'
lā.ī ac cs.mkr
tuccha adj `trivial, worthless'
samjhanthe tv3 pst <samjhanu `he regarded'

1.5
bicarī adj `poor'
subhadrā pn `ṣubhadra'
pani advl `also'
khinna adjl `sad'
thi.in ev1 pst <hunu `she was'

1.6
chimeka- cn `neighbor'
kā gn cs.mkr `of'
ā.imā.ī cn `woman'
le ag sb.mkr
chorā-chorī cmpdcn `sons and daughters'
khelāeko tv1 prf.prt <khelāunu `play'
dekhera tv1 abs.prt <dekhnu `having seen'
una- pro.pers <unī `she'
lā.i dt cs-mkr `to'
rahara cn `desire'
lāgthyo iv2 pst <lāgnu `used to strike'
santāna- cn `children'
kā gn cs.mkr `of'
āshā- cn `hope'
le in cs.mkr `by, with'
sarala adjl `simple'
nārī-svabhāva- cmpdcn `woman's nature'
vaśa advlzr `because of'
dhāmī-jhā̃krī- cmpdcn `shamans '
ko gn cs.mkr `of'
būṭī-jantara cmpdcn `herbs and amulet'
bā̃dhin tv1 pst <bā̃dhunu `she tied'
devī-devatā- cmpdcn `gods and goddesses'
ko gn cs.mkr `of'
bhākala cn `pledges (to gods)'
garin tv1 pst <garnu `she did'
tīrtha cn `pilgrimage, pilgrimage site'
vrata cn `vow'
pūjā cn `worship'
pāṭha cn `recitation of sacred texts'
pani advl `also'
garin tv1 pst <garnu `she did'

1.7
tara cc `but'
daiva- cn `Fate'
le ag sb.mkr
nasunidie- cmpdtv1 cond <na+sunnu-dinu `if not listen'
pachi pp `after'
kasa pro.interrog <ko `who'
ko gn cs.mkr `of'
ke pro.interrog `what'
lāgdo iv1 conj.prt <lāgnu `striking'
rahecha aux pres <rahanu `is (found)'
raqw

1.8
jyotiṣi- cn `astrologer'
haru nm.plzr
devīramaṇa- pn `Deviraman'
lā.i dt cs.mkr `to'
arko prol.adj `another'
vivāha cn `marriage'
garna tv1 inf <garnu `to do'
sallāha cn `advice'
dinthe tv2 pst <dinu `they used to give'

1.9
parantu cc `but'
subhadrā- pn `ṣubhadra'
ko gn cs.mkr `of'
ādesha cn `order'
vinā pp `without'
unī pro.pers `he'
arko prol.adj `another'
vivāha cn `marriage'
garna tv1 inf <garnu `to do'
saktainathe aux pst <saknu+neg `he could not'

1.10
subhadrā pn `ṣubhadra'
bahuta advl `very'
patiparāyaṇā adj `loyal to husband'
ramaṇī cn `lady'
thi.in ev1 pst <hunu `she was'

1.11
āja- advl `today'

samma pp `until'
kahilyai advl `ever'
una- pro.pers <unī `she'
le ag sb.mkr
devīramaṇa- pn `Deviraman'
ko gn cs.mkr
citta cn `mind'
dukhā.inan tv1 pst <dukhā.unu `she did not hurt'
mana- cn `mind'
ko gn cs.mkr `of'
kurā cn `thought'
jānera tv1 abs.prt <jānnu `having understood'
sevā cn `service'
garthin tv1 pst <garnu `she used to do'

1.12
subhadrā pn `ṣubhadra'
dulahī cn `bride'
bhaera ev1 abs.prt <hunu `having been'
ā.ũdā- iv1 conj.prt <ā._nu `while coming'
ko gn cs.mkr `of'
bakhata- cn `time
ko gn cs-mkr `of'
bhayangkara adjl `dreadful'
duḥkha cn `hardship'
ahile advl `now'
samma pp `until'
pani advl `also'
devīramaṇa- pn `Deviraman'
kā gn cs.mkr `of'
ā̃khā- cn `eye'
kā gn cs.mkr `of'
sāmu pp `in front'
nāciraheko iv1 prf.cont.prt <nāchnu `dancing'
thiyo aux pst <hunu `he was'

1.13
u prol.adj `that'
avasthā cn `condition'
samjhadā tv1 conj.prt <samjhanu `while remembering'
gaha- cn `eye'
bharī pp `fully in'
ā̃su cn `tears'
hunthyo iv1 pst <hunu `used to be'

1.14
sukha-duḥkha- cmpdcn `happiness and sorrow'
kī gn cs.mkr `of'
sāthī cn `friend'
bhaera ev1 abs.prt <hunu `having been'
kanggāla adjl `penniless'
devīramaṇa- pn `Deviraman'
lā.i ac cs.mkr
subhadrā- pn `ṣubhadra'
le ag sb.mkr
dhanavāna adjl `wealthy'
banā.in tv3 pst <banāunu `she made'

1.15
ahile advl `now'
santāna- cn `child'
kā gn cs.mkr `of'
nimti pp `for'
sautā cn `co-wife'
hālidiera cmpdtv1 abs.prt <hālnu-dinu `having imposed'
kasarī adv `how'
kṛtaghna adjl `ungrateful'
banūn ev1 imp <bannu `may he be'

2.1
phāguna pn `Nepali month (Feb-March)'
mahīnā- cn `month'
ko gn cs.mkr `of'
bihāna- cn `morning'
pakha- pp `toward (morning and evening)'
ko gn cs.mkr `of'
sireṭo cn `cold wind'
muṭu cn `heart'
cheḍlā tv1 fut <cheḍnu `he will pierce'

bhane (bhaneko) tv1 prf.prt <bhannu `said'
jasto adj `like'
garthyo tv1 pst <garnu `he used to do'

2.2
devīramaṇa pn `Deviraman'
maṇḍapa- cn `pavillion'
mā lc cs.mkr `at, in, on'
basekā iv3 prf.prt <basnu `seated'
thie aux pst <hunu `he was'

2.3
nayā̃ adjl `new'
dulahī cn `bride'
pani advl `also'
ekai adjl `one and the same'
āsana- cn `seat'
mā lc cs.mkr `at, in, on'
basekī iv3 prf.prt <basnu `seated'
thi.in aux pst <hunu `she was'

2.4
brāhmaṇa- pn `Brahman (a Hindu caste)'
haru nm.plzr
ṛcā cn `Vedic hymns'
paḍhera tv1 abs.per <paḍhnu `having read'
agni- cn `fire'
mā lc cs.mkr `at, in, on'
āhuti cn `sacrificial offerings'
di.irahekā tv1 prf.cont.prt <dinu `giving'
thie aux pst <hunu `they had'

2.5
prārabdha- cn `ḍestiny'
le ag sb.mkr
yo prol.adj `this'
umera- cn `age'
mā lc cs-mkr `at, in, on'
una- pro.pers <unī `he'
lā.ī ac cs.mkr
pheri advl `again'
dulāhā cn `bridegroom'
banāyo tv3 pst <banā.unu `he made'

2.6
eka num `one'
dina cn `day'
yastai adjl `such'
rīta cn `manner'
saṃga pp `with'
una- pro.pers <unī `he'
le ag sb.mkr
subhadrā- pn `ṣubhadra'
ko gn cs.mkr `of'
pāṇigrahaṇa cn `wedding'
garethe cmpdtv1 pst <garnu+hunu
`had done' (garekā thie)

2.7
subhadrā- pn `ṣubhadra'
ko gn cs.mkr `of'
ādesha cn `order'
pā.ī tv1 abs.prt <pā.unu `having received'
ho iv1 pres <hunu `is'
vā cc `or'
napā.ī tv1 abs.prt <na+pā.unu `not having
received'
ho iv1 pres <hunu `is'
āja advl `today'
una- pro.pers <unī `he'
le ag sb.mkr
aghikai adjl `the very previous (emph)'
kṛtya- cn `act'
lā.ī ac cs.mkr
pheri advl `again'
dohoryāe tv1 pst <dohoryāunu `he repeated'

2.8
yasa- pro.dem <yo `this'
bāṭa ab cs.mkr `from'
una- pro.pers <unī `he'
ko gn cs.mkr `of'
bhalo-kubhalo cmpdcn `good or bad'
ke pro.interrog `what'
hune iv1 impf.prt <hunu `being'
ho iv1 pres <hunu `is'
yasa prol.adj <yo `this'
kurā- cn `thing, matter'

ko gn cs.mkr `of'
unai- pro.pers <unī `he' (emph)
lā.ī dt cs.mkr `to'
pani advl `also'
kehī adjl `any, some'
jñāna cn `knowledge'
thiena iv2 pst <hunu+neg `was not'

2.9
bāhra num `twelve'
barṣa- cn `year'
kī gn cs.mkr `of'
abodha adjl `innocent'
bālikā- cn `girl'
lā.ī ac cs.mkr
lyāera tv1 abs.prt <lyā.unu `bringing (in marriage)'
unī pro.pers `he'
shūnya adjl `empty'
ākāsha- cn `sky'
mā lc cs.mkr `at, in, on'
kalpanātīta adjl `highly imaginary'
manomandira cn `fictitious castle'
nirmāṇa cn `construction'
garna tv1 inf <garnu `to do'
khojdathe aux pst <khojnu `he would want'

2.10
shāyada advl `probably'
brahmavādī- cn `the Vedanta philosophers'
haru nm.plzr
tyasai- pro.dem `that (emph)'
lā.ī ac cs.mkr
āshā-pāsha cmpdcn `snare of hope'
yā cc `or'
mṛgatṛṣṇā cmpdcn `mirage'
bhanchan tv1 pres <bhannu `they call'
kyāre nu `probaly, I guess'

2.11
astu advl `anyway'
kara- cn `compulsion'
le in cs.mkr `by, with'
hos iv1 imp <hunu `may (he) be'
vā cc `or'
āntarika advl `internal'
preraṇā- cn `inspiration'
le in cs.mkr `by, with'
hos iv1 imp <hunu `may (he) be'
una- pro.pers <unī `he'
le ag sb.mkr
vivāha-vidhi cmpdcn `ritual of marriage'
samāpta adjl `complete'
gare tv1 pst <garnu `he did'

2.12
dulahī cn `bride'
anmā.une tv1 impf.prt <anmā.unu `sending out (a bride)'
velā- cn `time'
mā lc cs.mkr `at, in, on'
kanyā-pakṣa- cmpdcn `bride's side'
kā gn cs.mkr `of'
mānisa cn `men'
le ag sb.mkr
rūdai iv1 conj.prt <runu `while crying'
dulahī- cn `bride'
lā.ī ac cs.mkr
ḍolī- cn `litter'
mā lc cs.mkr `at, in, on'
hālidie cmpdtv4 pst <hālnu-dinu `they put in'

2.13
dulahī cn `bride'
pani advl `also'
ḍolī cn `litter'
bhitra pp `inside'
runa iv inf <runu `to cry'
lāgin tv1 pst <lāgnu `she began'

2.14
tyasa prol.adj <tyo `that'
bakhata cn `time'
devīramaṇa- pn `Deviraman'
lā.ī dt cs.mkr `to'

sāhrai advl `very'
naramā.ilo adj `unpleasnt'
lāgyo ev2 pst <lāgnu `seemed'

2.15
bāṭā- cn <bāṭo `way'
mā lc cs.mkr `at, in, on'
bariyāta- cn `people in marriage procession'
haru nm.plzr
paraspara advl `mutually'
grāmīṇa adjl `rustic'
ṭhaṭṭā cn `jokes'
garera tv1 abs.prt <garnu `having done'
khitkā cn `titter'
choḍī tv1 abs.prt <choḍnu `having released'
hā̃sthe iv1 pst <hā̃snu `they used to laugh'
parantu cc `but'
devīramaṇa- pn `Deviraman'
kā gn cs.mkr `of'
kapāla- cn `mind, hair, head'
mā lc cs.mkr `at, in, on'
arkai prol.adj `another (emph)'
vicāra- cn `thought'
ko gn cs.mkr `of'
dvanda cn `conflict'
huna iv1 inf <hunu `to be'
lāgeko tv1 prf.prt <lāgnu `begun'
thiyo aux pst <hunu `he had'

2.16
manamana- cn `mind-mind'
le in cs.mkr `by, with'
bhane tv1 pst <bhannu `he said'
ke qw
subhadrā- pn `ṣubhadra'
le ag sb.mkr
sā̃co adj `truthful, honest'
mana- cn `mind'
le in cs.mkr `by, with'
sallāha cn `advice'
dieko tv1 prf.prt <dinu `given'
ho iv1 pres <hunu `is'

2.17
sammati cn `consent'
diṃdā tv2 conj.prt <dinu `while giving'
kina advl `why'
arko- pro.nonpers `other (side)'
paṭṭi pp `toward'
pharkera iv1 abs.prt <pharkanu `having t
urned'
huncha intj `yes (okay)'
bhanekī tv1 prf.prt <bhannu `(she) had said'
ta nu

2.18
mero pro.pers `my'
jyādā adjl `excessive'
āgraha cn `isistance'
dekhera tv1 abs.prt <dekhnu `having seen'
huncha intj `yes (okay)'
bhanekī tv1 prf.prt <bhannu `(she) had said'
ta nu
hoina iv1 pres <hunu+neg `is not'

2.19
aho intj `Oh!'
mānisa- cn `man'
haru nm.plzr
āphno prol.adj `one's own'
tībra adjl `extreme'
icchā- cn `desire'
mā lc cs.mkr `at, in, on'
aru- pro.pers `others'
ko gn cs.mkr `of'
sammati- cn `consent'
lā.i ac cs.mkr
kasarī adv `how'
jabarajastī advl `forcibly'
tānchan tv1 pres <tānnu `they pull'

2.20
chih intj `Fie!, shame!'

2.21
subhadrā- pn `ṣubhadra'

ko gn cs.mkr `ko'
ājīvana adjl `life-long'
sevā- cn `service'
ko gn cs.mkr `of'
puraskāra cn `reward'
yahī pro.dem `this (emph)'
ho ev1 pres <hunu `is'

2.22
ma pro.pers `I'
ke pro.interrog `what'
garū tv1 imp <garnu `may I do'
ma- pro.pers `I'
lā.ī dt cs.mkr `to'
ke prol.adj `what'
doṣa cn `blame'

2.23
santāna cn `child
vinā pp `without'
svarga- cn `heaven'
ko gn cs.mkr `of'
bāṭo cn `path'
chekincha tv1p pres <chekinu `is blocked'
bhanne tv1 impf.prt <bhannu `saying'
hindū pn `Hindu'
dharma cn `religion'
jānos tv1 imp <jānnu `may he know'

2.24
bhoga- cn `enjoyment'
ko gn cs.mkr `of'
lālasā- cn `desire'
le in cs.mkr `by, with'
hoina iv pres <hunu+neg `is not'
dharma- cn `religion'
kā gn cs.mkr `of'
ajñā- cn `precept'
le in cs.mkr `by, with'
vivāha cn `marriage'
gareko tv1 prf.prt <garnu `done'
hū aux pres <hunu `I have'

2.25
bariyāta cn `marriage procession'
devīramaṇa- cn `Deviraman'
kā gn cs.mkr `of'
ghara- cn `house'
nera pp `near'
pugyo iv3 pst <pugnu `he arrived'

2.26
gāuṃle adjl `rural'
chimekī- cn `neighbors'
haru nm.plzr
cautārā- cn `platform under a tree'
mā lc cs.mkr `at, in, on'
ramitā cn `fun'
heriraheka tv1 prf.cont.prt <hernu `watching'
rahechan aux pres <rahanu `they were (found to be)'

2.27
devīramaṇa- pn
le ag sb.mkr
eka- num `one'
eka- num `one'
garī advlzr
niyālera iv1 abs.prt <niyālnu `having peered'
here iv1 pst <hernu `he looked'
tyo prol.adj `that'
hula- cn `crowd'
mā lc cs.mkr `at, in, on'
subhadrā- pn `ṣubhadra'
lā.i ac cs.mkr
dekhenan tv1 pst <dekhnu+neg `he did not see'

2.28
balla advl `finally (with great difficulty)'
una- pro.pers <unī `he'
ko gn cs.mkr `of'
chātī- cn `chest, heart'
bāṭa ab cs.mkr `from'
ḍhunggo cn `rock'
panchiyo iv1p pst <panchinu `moved away'

2.29
āja advl `today'
devīramaṇa- pn `Deviraman'
ko gn cs.mkr `of'
gati cn `condition'
tyasa prol.adj <tyo `that'
bālaka cn `boy'
chātra- cn `student'
ko gn cs.mkr `of'
jasto adj `like'
thiyo evl pst <hunu `he was'
jo pro.rel `who'
pahilo adj `first'
dina- cn `day'
ko gn cs.mkr `of'
pāṭha cn `lesson'
birsera tvl abs.prt <birsanu `having forgotten'
abelā advl `late'
guru- cn `teacher'
kahā̃ pp `at'
pugdacha iv3 pres <pugnu `arrives'
athavā cc `or'
tyasa prol.adj <tyo `that'
aparādhī- cn `criminal'
ko gn cs.mkr `of'
jasto adj `like'
thiyo evl pst <hunu `he was'
jo pro.rel `who'
paricita adjl `acquainted'
mānisa- cn `man'
lā.i ac cs.mkr
dekhera tvl abs.prt <dekhnu `having seen'
lukna ivl inf <luknu `to hide'
khojdacha aux pres <khojnu `wants'

2.30
chimekī- cn `neighbor'
saṃga pp `with'
kurā cn `talk'
garnā- tvl inf <garnu `to do'
ko gn cs.mkr `of'
bahānā- cn `excuse'
le in cs.mkr `by, with'
unī pro.pers `he'
kehī advl `somewhat'
pachī advl `behind'
bhae ivl pst <hunu `he became (honorific)'
jā̃dā ivl conj.prt <jānu `while arriving'
dulahī cn `bride'
bhitryā.isakī cmpdtvl abs.prt <bhitryāisaknu `having already entered'
subhadrā pn `ṣubhadra'
damā.ī-ḍole cmpdcn `band and litter-carriers'
haru nm.plzr
lā.i dt cs.mkr `to'
jyālā cn `wages'
bā̃ḍna tv2 inf <bā̃ḍnu `to distribute, give away'
lāgekī tvl prf.prt <lāgnu `begun'
rahichan aux pst <rahanu `she was

2.31
devīramaṇa- pn `Deviraman'
ko gn cs.mkr `of'
hṛdaya cn `heart'
gadgad adjl `very happy'
bhayo evl pst <hunu `became'
manamana- cn `mind-mind'
le in cs.mkr `by, with'
bhane tvl pst <bhannu `he said'
subhadrā pn `ṣubhadra'
svarga- cn `heaven'
kī gn cs.mkr `of'
devī cn `goddess'
ho evl pres <hunu `is'
vyarthai advl `unnecessarily'
kina advl `why'
shaṃkā cn `suspicion'
garū̃ tvl pst <garnu `I did'

2.32
mānisa- cn `man'
haru nm.plzr
āphno prol.adj `one's own'
kāma- cn `act'
le in cs.mkr `by, with'

kasarī adv `how'
āphai pro.reflx `oneself, themself'
tarsanchan iv1 pres <tarsanu `are scared'

2.33
pāhunā-pāsā- cmpdcn `guests and invited ones
saṃga pp `with'
kurākānī cn `coversation'
garera tv1 abs.prt <garnu `having done'
devīramaṇa pn `Deviraman'
abelā advl `late'
koṭhā- cn `room'
mā lc cs.mkr `at, in, on'
sutna iv1 inf <sutnu `to sleep'
gae iv1 pst <jānu `he went'

2.34
pānasa- cn `lamp-stand'
mā lc cs.mkr `at, in, on'
kaḍuwā cn `mustard'
tela- cn `oil'
ko gn cs.mkr `ko'
battī cn `lamp'
baliraheko iv1 prf.cont.prt <balnu `burning'
thiyo aux pst <hunu `he was'

2.35
nayā̃ adj `new'
dulahī cn `bride'
khāṭa- cn `cot'
mani pp `under'
ochyāna- cn `bed'
mā lc cs.mkr `at, in, on'
sutekī iv1 prf.prt <sutnu `slept'
thi.in aux pst <hunu `she had'

2.36
devīramaṇa pn `Deviraman'
khāṭa- cn `cot'
mā lc cs.mkr `at, in, on'
palṭe iv1 pst <palṭanu `he lay'

usa prol.adj `that'
ṭhā.ū- cn `place'
mā lc cs.mkr `at, in, on'
subhadrā- pn `ṣubhadra'
ko gn cs.mkr `of'
ochyāna cn `bed'
dekhenan tv1 pst <dekhnu+neg `he did not see'

2.37
aghi advl `before'
subhadrā- pn `ṣubhadra'
ko gn cs.mkr `of'
ochyāna cn `bed'
devīramaṇa- pn `Deviraman'
kā gn cs.mkr `of'
khāṭa- cn `cot'
mani pp `under'
hunthyo iv1 pst <hunu `used to be'

2.38
āja advl `today'
usa prol.adj <u `that'
ṭhā.ū- cn `place'
mā lc cs.mkr `at, in, on'
nadekhdā tv1 conj.prt <na+dekhnu `while not seeing'
bīsauṃ num `twentieth, twenties (?)'
barṣa- cn `years'
dekhi pp `since'
sutiraheko tv1 prf.cont.prt <sutnu `having been slept'
koṭhā cn `room'
pani advl `also'
devīramaṇa- pn `Deviraman'
lā.i dt cs.mkr `to'
naulo adj `strange'
jasto adj `like'
lāgyo ev2 pst <lāgnu `seemed'

2.39
eka num `one'
china- cn `momemt'
pachi pp `after'

gṛhakṛtya cn `household chores'
samāpta adjl `complete'
garera tv3 abs.prt <garnu `having done'
subhadrā pn `ṣubhadra'
koṭhā- cn `room'
mā lc cs.mkr `at, in, on'
pasin iv3 pst <pasnu `she entered'
devīramaṇa pn `Deviraman'
ko gn cs.mkr `of'
goḍā cn `foot'
micna tv1 inf <micnu `to press, rub, massage'
lāgin tv1 pst <lāgnu `she began'

2.40
yo pro.dem `this'
una- pro.pers <unī `she'
ko gn cs.mkr `of'
dainika adjl `daily'
kāma cn `job'
thiyo ev1 pst <hunu `he was'

2.41
subhadrā pn `ṣubhadra'
yasa- pro.dem <yo `this'
mā lc cs.mkr `at, in, on'
kahilyai advl `ever'
truṭi cn `mistake'
huna iv1 inf <hunu `to be'
dinnathin tv1 pst <dinu `she would not allow'

2.42
devīramaṇa- pn `Deviraman'
le ag sb.mkr
bhane tv1 pst <bhannu `he said'
sānu pn `ṣanu (nick-name for ṣubhadra)'
timro pro.pers `your'
ochyāna cn `bed'
kho.ī advl* `where is?'
ni nu

2.43
pallo adj `next'
koṭhā- cn `room'
mā lc cs.mkr `at, in, on'
cha iv3 pres <hunu `is'

2.44
kina advl `why'
pallo adj `next'
koṭhā- cn `room'
mā lc cs.mkr `at, in, on'
sāreko iv1 prf.prt <sārnu `moved'

2.45
bholi advl `tomorrow'
ekādashī pn `Ekādashī (eleventh day in lunar calender)'
ho ev1 pres <hunu `is'
saberai advl `early'
gaṇḍakī pn `Gandaki (name of a river)'
nuhāuna iv1 inf <nuhā.unu `to bath'
jānchu iv1 pres <jānu `I (will) go'

2.46
ma pro.pers `I'
pani advl `also'
uhī advl `there (emph)'
sutchu iv1 pres <sutnu `I sleep'

2.47
us intj `Oh no!'
yahā̃ advl `here (emph)'
sutnubhae iv1 cond <sutnu `if sleep'
pani advl `also'
huncha iv1 pres <hunu `(It) is (good)'

2.48
thākera iv1 abs.prt <thāknu `having been tired)
āekā iv1 prf.prt <ā.unu `come'
devīramaṇa- pn `Deviraman'
lā.i dt cs.mkr `to'
cā̃ḍai advl `quickly'
nidrā cn `sleep'
paryo iv2 pst <parnu `fell, happened'

2.49
āphno prol.adj `one's own'
dolā.ī cn `quilt'
sautā- cn `co-wife'
lā.ī ac cs.mkr
khāpera tv1 abs.prt <khāpnu `having overlaid'
subhadrā pn `ṣubhadra'
pallo adj `next'
koṭhā- cn `room
mā lc cs.mkr `at, in, on'
ga.in iv1 pst <jānu `she went'

2.50
madhuro adj `faint'
battī- cn `light'
ko gn cs.mkr `of'
dhamilo adj `dim'
ujyālo- cn `light'
mā lc cs.mkr `at, in, on'
naulī pn `ṇauli'
ghartinī cn `a woman of Gharti cast, once slaves in Nepal'
pāta cn `leaf'
gā̃sirahekī tv1 prf.cont.prt <gā̃snu `joining'
thi.ī aux pst <hunu `she was'

2.51
naulī pn `ṇauli'
devīramaṇa- pn `Deviraman'
ko gn cs.mkr `of'
purāno adj `old'
cākarnī cn `female slave'
ho ev1 pres <hunu `is'

2.52
naulī- pn `ṇauli'
ko gn cs.mkr `of'
umera cn `age'
jhaṇḍai advl `almost'
jhaṇḍai advl `almost'
subhadrā- pn `Deviraman'
saṃga pp `with'
milthyo iv1 pst <milnu `agreed, matched'

2.53
bayāsī num `eighty-two'
sāla- cn `year'
mā lc cs.mkr `at, in, on'
svargavāsī adjl `late (dead)'
mahārāja cn `king'
candrashamashera pn `Chandrashamsher'
janggabahādura- pn `Jangabahadur'
kā gn cs.mkr `of'
karuṇā- cn `compassion'
le in cs.mkr `by, with'
dāsa-jīvana- cmpdcn `slave-life'
bāṭa ab cs.mkr `from'
mukta adj `free'
bhaekī ev1 prf.prt <hunu `been'
thi.ī aux pst <hunu `she had'

2.54
ghara- cn `house'
kī gn cs.mkr `of'
purānī adj `old'
cākarnī cn `slave'
hunā- ev1 inf <hunu `to be'
le in cs.mkr `by, with, because'
devīramaṇa- pn `Deviraman'
le ag sb.mkr
naulī- pn `ṇauli'
ko gn cs.mkr `of'
mola cn `price'
lienan tv1 pst <linu+neg `he did not take'
āphukhushī advl `voluntarily'
bhae iv1 cond <hunu `if be'
pani advl `even'
naulī- pn `ṇauli'
le ag sb.mkr
ghara cn `house'
choḍina tv1 pst <choḍnu+neg `she did not quit'

2.55
naulī pn `ṇauli'
subhadrā- pn `ṣubhadra'
ko gn cs.mkr `of'
bālaka-kāla- cmpdcn `childhood'

dekhiko pp `since'
sukha-duḥkha cmpdcn `happiness and sorrow'
kī gn cs.mkr `of'
sāthī cn `friend'
thi.ī ev1 pst <hunu `she was'

2.56
vidhātā- cn `God (Creator)'
le ag sb.mkr
subhadrā- pn `ṣubhadra'
ko gn cs.mkr `of'
nimitta pp `for'
naulīrūpī cmpdadjl `(in) the form of ṇauli'
euṭā num.specif `one'
duḥkha cn `sorrow'
pokhne tv1 impf.prt <pokhnu `pouring, spilling'
bhhā̃ḍo cn `pot'
diekā tv1 prf.prt <dinu `given'
thie aux pst <hunu `he had'

2.57
dubai pro `both'
mā lc cs.mkr `at, in, on'
ghaniṣṭha adjl `intimate'
prema cn `love, affection'
thiyo iv1 pst <hunu `he was'

2.58
naulī- pn `ṇauli'
le ag sb.mkr
pāta cn `leaf/leaves'
gā̃sdai tv1 conj.prt <gā̃snu `while joining'
bhanī tv1 pst <bhannu `she said'
bajai cn `madam'
āja advl `today'
tā nu `rather'
sāhrai advl `very'
naramā.ilo adj `unpleasant'
lāgyo ev2 pst <lāgnu `seemed'
holā aux fut <hunu `must (probably)'

2.59
kina advl `why'
naulī pn `ṇauli'
kina advl `why'
tyaso advl `so'
bhanis iv1 pst <bhannu `you said'

2.60
naramā.ilo adj `unpleasant'
lāgnu iv1 inf <lagnu `to strike'
parne aux impf.prt <parnu `must'
kurā cn `matter'
ke pro.interrog `what'
cha ev1 pres <hunu `is'
ra qw

2.61
taipani cc `even then'
sautā cn `co-wife'
bhaneko tv1 prf.prt <bhannu `called'
muṭu- cn `heart'
ko gn cs.mkr `of'
baha cn `pain'
ho ev1 pres <hunu `is'
ājai advl `today (emph)'
ochyāna cn `bed'
choḍnu tv1 inf <choḍnu `to leave'
paryo aux pst <parnu `had to'

2.62
bholi advl `tomorrow'
gharai cn `home (emph)'
chāḍnu tv1 inf <choḍnu `to leave'
parcha aux pres <parnu `must'
ki qw
ke pro.interrog `what'
jānisaknu cmpdtv1 inf <jānnu-saknu
`can know'
cha aux pres <hunu `is'
2.63
choḍnu tv1 inf <choḍnu `leave'
pare aux cond <parnu `if must'
choḍidiũlā cmpdtv1 fut <choḍnu-dinu
`I will leave'
kuna prol.adj `which'

daulatha- cn `wealth'
ko gn cs.mkr `of'
caina cn `enjoyment'
garekī tv1 prf.prt <garnu `done'
chu aux pres <hunu `I have'
raqw
eka num `one'
peṭa cn `stomach'
khasro-masinu cmpdcn `rough or fine'
khāera tv1 abs.prt <khānu `having eaten'
dina-rāta cmpdcn `day and night'
buhārtana cn `hardship of a daughter-in-law's life'
sahekī tv1 prf.prt <sahanu `tolerated'
chu aux pres <hunu `I have'

2.64
juṭho-cūlho cmpdcn `dirty-kitchen'
garidie cmpdtv1 cond <garnu+dinu `if do'
jasa- pro.nonpers <jo `anyone'
le ag sb.mkr
pani advl `also'
eka num `one'
gā̃sa cn `mouthful'
khāna tv1 inf <khānu `to eat'
dincha tv1 pres <dinu `he gives'

2.65
tara cc `but'
sojhī adj `simple'
jastī adj `like'
cha ev1 pres <hunu `is'
pasne- iv1 impf.prt <pasnu `entering'
bittikai advl `as soon as'
ḍhogidi.ī cmpdiv1 pst <ḍhogi-dinu `she greeted'

2.66
sikāeko tv2 prf.prt <sikā.unu `taught'
hū̃doho aux prob.pst <hunu `would have been'
bajai cn `madam'
kunai adjl `some'
dina cn `day'
naulī- pn `ṇauli'

le ag sb.mkr
bhanithī tv1 prf.prt <bhannu+hunu `had said'
bhannuholā tv1 fut <bhannu `you will say'

2.67
sojho adj `simple'
bānggina iv1p inf <bāngginu `to be crooked'
bera cn `time'
lāgdaina iv1 pres <lāgnu+neg `does not take'
ali adjl `some'
dina- cn `days'
pachi pp `after'
bāje- cn `sir'
ko gn cs.mkr `of'
ṭupī cn `pig-tail'
samā.unechin tv1 fut <samā.unu `she will catch'

2.68
jesukai pro.nonpers `whatsoever'
hos iv1 imp <hunu `may (he) be'
īshvara- cn `god'
le ag sb.mkr
vīsāsaya adjl `very long (lit. twenty hundred)'
āyu cn `life'
garidiun cmpdtv1 imp <garnu-dinu `may he make'
phalc-phuleko cmpdadj `prosperous'
dekhna tv1 inf <dekhnu `to see'
pā.iyos tv1p imp <pā.unu `may we get'
santāna cn `child'
bhae iv1 cond <hunu `if be'
kara- cn `compulsion'
le in cs.mkr `by, with'
pani advl `even'
eka num `one'
aṃulī cn `cup made by joining two hands'
pānī cn `water'
delā tv1 fut <dinu `he will give'
yina- pro.pers <yī `these'
kā gn cs.mkr `of'
hāta-kākha- cmpdcn `hand and lap'
mā lc cs.mkr 'at, in, on'
sāsa cn `breath (life)'
jāos iv1 imp <jānu `may he go'

saba pro.nonpers `all, everything'
bhandā advl `than'
ṭhūlo adj `great'
santoṣa cn `satisfaction'
yahī̃ pro.dem `this (emph)'
ho ev1 pres <hunu `is'
naulī̃ pn `ṇauli'

3.1
tina num `three'
cāra num `four'
barṣa cn `year'
pachiko pp `after'
kurā cn `matter'
ho iv1 pres <hunu `ho'

3.2
eka num `one'
dina cn `day'
ghāma- cn `sunlight'
mā lc cs.mkr `at, in, on'
basera iv1 abs.prt <basnu `being seated'
subhadrā pn `ṣubhadra'
chorā- cn `son'
lā.i dt cs.mkr `to'
bhāta pn `rice'
khuwā.irahekī̃ tv2 prf.cont.prt <khuwā.unu `feeding'
thi.in aux pst <hunu `she had'

3.3
sushī̃la pn `ṣushil'
cāhī̃ postf `for someone's part'
ā̃gana- cn `courtyard'
mā lc cs.mkr `at, in, on'
carirahekā iv1 prf.cont.prt <charnu `feeding'
parevā- cn `pigeon'
lā.i ac cs.mkr
pakrane tv1 impf.prt <pakranu `catching'
koshisha- cn `effort'
mā lc cs.mkr `at, in, on'
thiyo iv3 pst <hunu `he was'
subhadrā pn `ṣubhadra'
hāta- cn `hand'
mā lc cs.mkr `at, in, on'
bhāta- cn `rice'
ko gn cs.mkr `of'
gā̃sa cn `a measure of mouthful food'
liera tv1 abs.prt <linu `having taken'
ko pro.interrog `who'
khā.i iv1 impf.prt <khānu `eating'
ko pro.interrog `who'
khā.i iv1 impf.prt <khānu `eating'
bhanthin tv1 <bhannu `she used to say'

3.4
sushī̃la pn `ṣushil'
mukha cn `mouth'
bāa.ũdai tv1 conj.prt <bā.unu `while opening'
dauḍera iv1 abs.prt <dauḍanu `having run'
ā.ũthyo iv1 pst <ā.unu `he used to come'
subhadrā pn `ṣubhadra'
gā̃sa cn `a measure of mouthful food'
mukha- cn `mouth'
mā lc cs.mkr `at, in, on'
hālidinthin cmpdtv4 pst <hālnu-dinu `she would put'
bālaka cn `child'
pheri advl `again'
dauḍera iv1 abs.prt <dauḍanu `having run'
parevā- cn `pigeon'
tira pp `toward'
jānthyo iv1 pst <jānu `he would go'

3.5
tī̃ prol.adj `those'
mūka adjl `mute'
pakṣī̃- cn `bird'
haru nm.plzr
pani advl `also'
bālaka- cn `child'
saṃga pp `with'
ānanda- cn `happiness'
pūrvaka advlzr `with'
khelirahekā iv1 prf.cont.prt <khelnu `been playing'
thie aux pst <hunu `they had'

3.6
sushīla pn `ṣushil'
ga.ī iv1 abs.prt <jānu `having gone'
samā.una iv1 inf <samā.unu `to catch'
khojthyo aux pst <khojnu `he would want'

3.7
parevā cn `pigeons'
ali advl `a little'
para advl 'further'
ga.ī iv1 abs.prt <jānu `having gone'
basthe iv1 pst <basnu `used to sit'
sushīla pn `ṣushil'
pheri advl `again'
uhā̃ advl `there (emph)
pugthyo iv1 pst <pugnu `he used to arrive'
parevā cn `pigeons'
uḍera iv1 abs.prt <uḍnu `having flown'
ali advl `a little'
para advl `further'
ga.ī iv1 abs.prt <jānu `having gone'
carna iv1 inf <carnu `to feed'
lāgthe iv1 pst <lāgnu `they would begin'

3.8
subhadrā- pn `ḍubhadra'
ko gn cs.mkr `of'
ko pro.interrog `who'
khā.i- tv1 impf.prt <kānu `eating'
ko gn cs.mkr `of'
āvāja cn `voice'
sunera tv1 abs.prt <sunnu `having heard'
sushīla pn `ṣushil'
bīca-bīca- cn `intervals'
mā lc cs.mkr `at, in, on'
eka num `one'
duī num `two'
gā̃sa cn `a measure of mouthful food'
bhāta cn `rice'
pani advl `also'
khāera tv1 abs.prt <khānu `having eaten'
jānthyo iv1 pst <jānu `he would go'

3.9
devīramaṇa pn `Deviraman'
phalaīcā- cn `bench'
mā lc cs.mkr `at, in, on'
basera iv1 abs.prt <basnu `being seated'
yo prol.adj `this'
anupama adjl `matchless'
ānandaprada advl `pleasant'
bāla-krīḍā cmpdcn `child-play'
heriraheká tv1 prf.cont.prt <hernu
`watching'
thie aux pst <hunu `they had'

3.10
una- pro.pers <unī `he'
lā.i dt cs.mkr `to'
svarga- cn `heaven'
kā gn cs.mkr `of'
ḍīla- cn `edge'
bāṭa ab cs.mkr `from'
pitṛ - cn `ancestor'
haru nm.plzr
pani advl `also'
yasa prol.adj <yo `this'
kulāvalamba- cmpdcn `anchor of the family'
ko gn cs.mkr `of'
bālalīlā cmpdcn `child-play'
heriraheká tv1 prf.cont.prt <hernu 'watching'
holān aux fut <hunu `they must'
bhanne sc `that'
bhāna cn `appearance'
hunthyo iv2 pst <hunu `used to be'

3.11
unī pro.pers `he'
yo prol.adj `this'
shishu-santāna- cmpdcn `child offspring'
kā gn cs.mkr `of'
āḍa- cn `support'
mā lc cs.mkr `at, in, on'
eka num `one'
mahān adjl `great'
baliṣṭha adjl `very strong'

shakti cn `power'
lukiraheko iv1 prf.cont.prt <luknu 'hidden'
dekhdathe tv1 pst <dekhnu `he used to see'

3.12
santānecchuka adjl `desirous of child'
devīramaṇa- pn `Deviraman'
le ag sb.mkr
āja advl `today'
yo prol.adj `this'
dina cn `day'
dekhna tv1 inf <dekhnu `to see'
pāe tv1 pst <pā.unu `he got'

3.13
parivartanashīla adjl `changing'
saṃsāra- cn `world'
ko gn cs.mkr `of'
gati cn `way'
vicitra adjl `strange'
cha ev1 pres <hunu `is'

3.14
parameshvara cn `god'
hā̃sne- impf.prt <hā̃snu `laughing ones)'
lā.i ac cs.mkr
ruwā.ũchan tv1 <ruwā.unu `he causes to cry'
rune- impf.prt <runu `weepers '
lā.i ac cs.mkr
hasā.ũchan tv1 pres <haasā.unu `he causes to laugh'

3.15
eka num `one'
dina cn `day'
sushīla pn `ṣushil'
tulasī- pn `ṭulasi plant'
kā gn cs.mkr `of'
maṭha- cn `mound'
nera pp `near'
kheliraheko iv1 prf.cont.prt <khelnu `playing'
thiyo aux pst <hunu `he had'

3.16
piṃḍī- cn `porch'
bāṭa ab cs.mkr `from'
eka- num `one'
tira pp `on'
lakṣmī pn `Laksmi'
eka num `one'
tira pp `on'
subhadrā- pn `ṣubhadra'
le ag sb.mkr
hāta cn `hand'
thāpera tv1 abs.prt <thāpnu `profferring'
nānī cn `little child'
katā advl `whither'
katā advl `whither'
katā advl `whither'
bhane tv1 pst <bhannu `they said'

3.17
sushīla pn `ṣushil'
eka num `one'
kṣaṇa- cn `moment'
pachi pp `after'
dagurdai iv1 conj.prt <dagurnu `running'
gai iv1 abs.prt <jānu `having gone'
subhadrā- pn `ṣubhadra'
ko gn cs.mkr `of'
chātī- cn `chest'
mā lc cs.mkr `at, in, on'
ṭā̃siyo iv1p pst <ṭā̃sinu `he was stuck'
subhadrā- pn `ṣubhadra'
ko gn cs.mkr `of'
hṛdaya cn `heart'
pavitra adjl `pure'
putra-vātsalya- cmpdcn `love for son'
le in cs.mkr `by, with'
paripūrṇa adjl `filled'
bhayo ev1 pst <hunu `became'
mero pro.pers `my'
rājā cn `king'
bhanera tv1 abs.prt <bhannu `having said'
mwā.ī cn `kiss'
khā.in tv1 pst <khānu `she ate'

3.18
sushīla- pn `ṣushil'
lā.ī dt cs.mkr `to'
lakṣmī- pn `Laksmi'
le ag sb.mkr
janma cn `birth, life'
mātra advl `only'
di.in tv2 pst `she gave'
kevala advl `only'
subhadrā- pn `ṣubhdra'
le ag sb.mkr
hurkā.in tv1 pst <hurkā.unu `she raised'

3.19
subhadrā- pn `ṣubhadra'
lā.ī ac cs.mkr
eka num `one'
china cn `moment'
choḍdainathyo tv1 pst <choḍnu+neg
`he would not leave'

3.20
subhadrā- pn `ṣubhadra'
lā.ī ac cs.mkr
āmā cn `mother'
bhanthyo tv3 pst <bhannu `he used to call'
āphnī prol.adj `one'own'
āmā- cn `mother'
lā.i ac cs.mkr
dulahī cn `bride'
bhanthyo tv3 pst <bhannu `he used to call'
kinaki cc `because'
lakṣmī- pn `Laksmi'
lā.ī ac cs.mkr
ghara- cn `home'
mā lc cs.mkr `at, in, on'
savai prol.adj `all'
janā specif `human individuals'
dulahī cn `bride'
bajyai cn `madam'
bhanthe tv3 pst <bhannu `they used to call'

4.1
māgha pn `ṃagh (Januaray-February)'
mahīnā cn `month'
thiyo iv1 pst <hunu `he was'

4.2
kisāna- cn `farmer'
haru nm.plzr
bālīnālī cn `crops'
thankyā.ī tv1 abs.prt <thankyāunu `having stored'
tīrtha cn `pilgrimage, pilgrimage site'
jāne iv1 impf.prt <jānu `going'
phikrī- cn `concern'
mā lc cs.mkr `at, in, on'
thie iv3 pst <hunu `they were'

4.3
devīramaṇa- pn `Deviraman'
lā.i dt cs.mkr `to'
pani advl `also'
tīrtha cn `pilgrimage, pilgrimage site'
garne tv1 impf.prt <garnu `erforming'
icchā cn `wish'
bhayo iv2 pst <hunu `became'
manamana- cn `mind-mind'
le in cs.mkr `by, with'
bhane tv1 pst <bhannu `he said'
paga cn `feet'
caldai iv1 conj.prt <calnu `while moving'
tīrtha-varta cmpdcn `pilgrimage and vow'
nagare tv1 cond <na+garnu `if not do'
kahile advl `when'
garūlā tv1 fut <garnu `I shall do'

4.4
mānisa- cn `man'
haru nm.plzr
sampatti cn `wealth'
pāera tv1 abs.prt <pā.unu `having gained'
andhā adj `blind'
banchan ev1 pres <bannu `they become'
viveka cn `conscience'

buddhi- cn `intelligence'
lā.ī ac cs.mkr
khopā- cn `hole'
mā lc cs.mkr `at, in, on'
rākhera tv1 abs.prt <rākhnu `having put'
dina-rāta cmpdcn `day and night'
paisā- cn `money'
kā gn cs.mkr `of'
nimitta pp `for'
hāhākāra cn `commotion'
maccā.irahanchan tv1 pres.cont <macca.unu `they keep making (commotion)'

4.5
tī prol.adj `those'
goṭhālā- cn `shepherds (fools)'
haru- nm.plzr
ko gn cs.mkr `of'
sampatti cn `wealth'
eka num `one'
dina cn `day'
agni cn `fire'
yā cc `or'
cora- cn `thief'
kā gn cs.mkr `of'
nimitta pp `for'
huncha iv1 pres <hunu `becomes'

4.6
aghi advl `before'
gareko iv1 prf.prt <garnu `done'
hũdohũ aux prob.pst <hunu `I would have'
ahile advl `now'
eka num `one'
mānā- cn `a measure of food'
ko gn cs.mkr `of'
santoṣa cn `satisfaction'
cha iv1 pres <hunu `is'

4.7
ahile advl `now'
pheri advl `again'
garna iv1 inf <garnu `to do'
sake aux cond <saknu `if can'
santāna- cn `descendents'
kā gn cs.mkr `of'
jarā- `root'
mā lc cs.mkr `at, in, on'
mala cn `firtilizer'
parlā iv3 fut `will fall'
paratra cn `next life'
banlā iv1 fut <bannu `will be (good)'

4.8
ityādi adjl `such'
vicāra cn `thought'
garera tv1 abs.prt <garnu `having done'
devīramaṇa pn
tīrtha cn `pilgrimage, pilgrimage site'
jāna iv1 inf <jānu `to go'
tayāra adjl
bhae ev1 pst <hunu `he became (hon.)'

4.9
una- pro.pers <unī `he'
ko gn cs.mkr `of'
eklai advl `alone'
jāne iv1 inf.prt <jānu `going'
vicāra cn `thought'
thiyo iv1 pst <hunu `he was'
parantu cc `but'
gāũ- cn `village'
kā gn cs.mkr `of'
kaiyana adjl `several'
būḍhā-būḍhī cmpdcn `old men and women'
vidhavā cn `widow'
svāsnīmānisa- cn `woman'
haru plzr
pani advl `also'
tayāra adjl `ready'
bhae ev1 pst <hunu `they became'

4.10
dekhdā- tv1 conj.prt <dekhnu `seeing'
dekhdai tv1 conj.prt <dekhnu `eeing'
devīramaṇa- pn `Deviraman'

ko gn cs.mkr `of'
ā̃gana cn `courtyard'
tīrtha-yātrā- cmpdcn `pilgrimage'
kā gn cs.mkr `of'
kumle adjl `carrying baggages'
phauja- cn `army'
le in cs.mkr `by with'
bhariyo iv1p pst <bhrinu `was filled'

4.11
gāū- cn `village'
kā gn cs.mkr `of'
dherai adjl `many'
ā.imā.ī- cn `woman'
haru nm.plzr
jāna iv1 inf <jānu `to go'
lāgeko tv1 prf.prt <lāgnu `begun'
dekhī tv1 abs.prt <dekhnu `having seen'
lakṣmī pn `Laksmi'
pani advl `also'
jānchu iv1 pres <jānu `I (will) go'
bhanera tv1 abs.prt <bhannu `having said'
jiddī cn `insistence'
garna tv1 inf <garnu `to do'
lāgin tv1 pst <lāgnu `she began'

4.12
sushīla- pn `ṣushil'
cāhiṃ postf `for someome's part'
devīramaṇa- pn `Deviraman'
ko gn cs.mkr `of'
daurā cn `a typical ṇepalese shirt'
samātera tv1 abs.prt <samātnu `having held'
runa iv1 inf <runu `to cry'
lāgyo tv1 pst <lāgnu `he began'

4.13
yo prol.adj `this'
baliṣṭha adjl `very strong'
bāla-haṭha- cmpdcn `child's persistence'
lā.ī dt cs.mkr `to'
devīramaṇa- pn `Deviraman'
le ag sb.mkr
upekṣā cn `disregard'
garna tv3 inf <garnu `to do'
sakenan aux pst <saknu+neg `he could not'

4.14
ākhira advl `finally'
lakṣmī pn `Laksmi'
ra cc `and'
sushīla- pn `ṣushil'
lā.ī ac cs.mkr
pani advl `also
sātha- cn `company
mā lc cs.mkr `at, in, on'
lie tv1 pst <linu `he took'

4.15
eka num `one'
kṣaṇa- cn `moment'
pachi pp `after'
tyo prol.adj `that'
tīrtha-yātrī- cmpdcn `pilgrim'
ko gn cs.mkr `of'
samūha cn `group'
rānu- cn `queen bee'
ko gn cs.mkr `of'
pachi pp `after'
māhurī pp `bees'
jhaī pp `like'
devīramaṇa- pn `Deviraman'
ko gn.cs.mkr `ko'
pachi pp `after'
lāgyo iv1 pst <lāgnu `he moved'

4.16
kintu cc `but'
subhadrā- pn `ṣubhadra'
lā.ī ac cs.mkr
jānchyau iv1 pres <jānu `will you go'
kiqw
bhanera tv1 abs.prt <bhannu `having said'
kasai- pro.pers `anyone'
le ag sb.mkr
eka num `one'

vacana cn `words'
samma advl `only, even'
pani advl `even'
sodhena tv1 pst <sodhnu `did not ask'

4.17
subhadrā- pn `ṣubhadra'
le ag sb.mkr
manamana cn `mind-mind'
le in cs.mkr `by, with'
bhanin tv1 pst <bhannu `she said'
tīrtha-varta cmpdcn `pilgrimage and vow'
garna tv1 inf <garnu `to do'
tā nu
ma pro.pers `I'
lā.i ac cs.mkr
po nu `rather'
laijānu- tv1 inf <laijānu `to take'
parthyo aux pst <parnu `had (pst of must)'

4.18
mero pro.pers `my'
ko pro.interrog `who'
cha iv1 pres <hunu `is'
ra qw
chorā cn `sons'
na cc `nor'
chorī cn `daughter'

4.19
usa- pro.pers <u `she, he'
ko gn cs.mkr `of'
umera cn `age'
thiyo iv1 pst <hunu `he was'
jā̃dai iv1 conj.prt <jānu `going'
gardīho tv1 prob.pst <garnu `she would do'

4.20
u pro.pers `she, he'
choro cn `son'
pāekī tv1 prf.prt <pā.unu `begotten'
svāsnī cn `wife'
bha.ī iv1 pst <hunu `she was'

vacana cn `word'
hārna tv1 inf <hārnu `to lose'
saknubhaena aux pst <saknu+neg `he could not'

4.21
ma pro.pers `I'
ṭekne- iv3 impf.prt <ṭeknu `stepping'
samāune tv1 impf.prt <samā.unu `holding'
kehī pro.nonpers `anything'
nabhaekī iv1 prf.prt <na+hunu `not having'
anātha adj `helpless'
mero pro.pers `my'
keko prol.adj `what'
khojī cn `question, search'
thiyo iv1 pst <hunu `he was'

4.22
mānisa cn `men'
balekai iv1 prf.prt <balnu `burning'
āgo cn `fire'
tāpchan tv1 pres <tāpnu `take the heat of'

4.23
jasa pro.rel <jo `who'
lā.i ac cs.mkr
parameśvara- cn `god'
le ag sb.mkr
ṭhageko tv1 prf.prt <ṭhagnu `cheated'
cha aux pres <hunu `has'
usa- pro.pers <u `she, he'
lā.i ac cs.mkr
mānisa cn `man'
pani advl `also'
helā cn `disregard'
garchan tv1 pres <garnu `they do'

4.24
aho intj `Oh'
saṃsāra cn `world'
kati advl `how much'
matalabī adjl `selfish'
cha ev1 pres <hunu `is'

4.25
yastai adjl `such'
tarka cn `thought'
gardai tv1 conj.prt <garnu `while doing'
subhadrā pn `ṣubhadra'
dherai adjl `much, long'
bera- cn `time'
samma pp `until'
eklai advl `alone'
roirahin iv1 pst <runu `she kept crying'

4.26
subhadrā- pn `ṣubhadra'
le ag sb.mkr
bāhra num `twelve'
varṣa- cn `year'
ko gn cs.mkr `of'
umera- cn `age'
dekhi pp `since'
devīramaṇa- pn `Deviraman'
ko gn cs.mkr `of'
dailo cn `door'
potna tv1 inf <potnu `to paint, clean'
lāgithin comptv1 pst <lāgnu+hunu `had begun'

4.27
yo prol.adj `this'
ghara cn `house'
subhadrā- pn `ṣubhadra'
lā.i dt cs.mkr `to'
saṃsāra- cn `world'
mā lc cs.mkr `at, in, on'
sabai pro.nonpers `all, everything'
bhandā pp `than'
pyāro adj `dear'
vastu cn `thing'
thiyo ev1 pst <hunu `he was'

4.28
yī prol.adj `these'
vastubhāu cn `cattle'
yinai- pro.pers `this (emph)'
ko gn cs.mkr `of'
lālana-pālana- cmpdcn `love and
nourishment'
mā lc cs.mkr `at, in, on'
baḍhera iv1 abs.prt <baḍhnu `having grown'
taruṇa adj `young'
bhaekā ev1 prf.prt <hunu `become'
thie aux pst <hunu `they had'

4.29
yo prol.adj `this'
ghara cn `house'
yī prol.adj `these'
bastubhāu cn `cattle'
yī prol.adj `these'
rukha-vr↑kṣa cmpdcn `trees and arbors'
sabai pro.nonpers `all, everything'
yinai prol.adj `this very'
santānahīnā adj `childless'
ramaṇī- cn `lady'
kā gn cs.mkr `of'
sāthī cn `friends'
thie ev1 pst <hunu `they were'

4.30
yinī- pro.pers `this'
haru nm.plzr
saṃgako pp `with'
viyoga cn `separation'
subhadrā pn `ṣubhadra'
eka num `one'
china cn `moment'
pani advl `also, even'
sahana tv1 inf <sahanu `to tolerate'
saktinathin aux pst <saknu+neg `she could
not'

4.31
jāna iv1 inf <jānu `to go'
tā nu
subhadrā pn `ṣubhadra'
jānthin iv1 pst <jānu `she would go'
ki cc `or'
jā̃dainathin iv1 pst <jānu+neg `she would

not go'
eka num `one'
vacana cn `word'
sodheko tv1 prf.prt <sodhnu `asked'
samma advl `only'
bhae aux cond <hunu `if be'
una- pro.pers <unī `she'
ko gn cs.mkr `of'
ā̃su cn `tears'
puchine tv1p impf.prf <puchinu `be wiped'
thiyo aux pst <hunu `he was'

4.32
eka num `one'
vacana cn `word'
sodhi- cmpdtv1 <sodhnu+ `ask'
samma advl `only'
dinā- cmpdtv1 inf <dinu `to let'
le in cs.mkr `by, because, with'
bakhata- cn `time'
mā lc cs.mkr `at, in, on'
katro adjl `how big'
kāma cn `work'
huncha iv1 pres <hunu `happens'
tyo prol.adj `that'
kurā cn `thing'
manovijñāna cn `psychology'
najānekā tv1 prf.prt <na+jānnu `not knowing'
devīramaṇa- pn `Deviraman'
lā.i dt cs.mkr `to'
thāhā cn `knowledge'
bhaena ev2 pst <hunu+neg `was not'

4.33
mano-mālinya- cmpdcn `animosity'
ko gn cs.mkr `of'
euṭā num.specif `one'
sāno adj `small'
bīja cn `seed'
cāhincha iv1p pres <cāhinu `is needed'
jo pro.rel `which'
samaya- cn `time'
mā lc cs.mkr `at, in, on'
baḍhera iv1 abs.prt <baḍhnu `having grown'
āphaseāpha advl `on its own'
bhayangkara adjl `dreadful'
rūpa cn `form'
dhāraṇa cn `assumption'
gardacha tv1 pres <garnu `does'

4.34
tyasatai advl `likewise'
lakṣmī pn `Laksmi'
tathā cc `and'
subhadrā- pn `ṣubhadra'
kā gn cs.mkr `of'
jīvana- cn `life'
mā lc cs.mkr `at, in, on'
pani advl `also'
yo prol.adj `this'
tīrtha-yātrā cmpdcn `pilgrimage'
mano-mālinya- cmpdcn `animosity'
ko gn cs.mkr `of'
euṭā num.specif `one'
bīja cn `seed'
hunagayo cmpdev1 pst <hunu+jānu `happened to be'

4.35
tīrtha- cn `pilgrimage, pilgrimage site'
bāṭa ab cs.mkr `from'
pharke- iv1 cond <pharkanu `if return'
dekhi pp `after'
dubai- pro `both'
mā lc cs.mkr `at, in, on'
bahudhā advl `often'
jhagaḍā cn `quarrel'
huna ev1 inf <hunu `to be'
lāgyo tv1 pst <lāgnu `he began'

4.36
subhadrā- pn `ṣubhadra'
le ag sb.mkr
kunai adjl `some'
prashna cn `question'
gardā tv1 conj.prt <garnu `while doing'

lakṣmī pn `Laksmi'
cheḍa cn `taunt'
hānera tv1 abs.prt <hānnu `having hit'
uttara cn `answer'
dinthin tv1 pst <dinu `she used to give'

4.37
basa nu `well (?)'
kuraikurā- cn `talks'
kā gn cs.mkr `of'
hānathāpa- cn `competition'
bāṭa ab cs.mkr `from'
ṭhulo adj `big'
kalaha cn `quarrel'
khaḍā adjl `present, standing'
hunthyo ev1 pst <hunu `used to be'

4.38
devīramaṇa pn `Deviraman'
cūpacāpa advl `silently'
bhaera ev1 abs.prt <hunu `having been'
sunirahanthe iv1 pst <sunnu `he kept istening'

4.39
lakṣmī- pn `Laksmi'
lā.i dt cs.mkr `to'
tāḍanā cn `scolding'
garūn tv1 imp <garnu `may he do'
bhane sc `if'
putravatī adj `woman with a son'
patnī cn `wife'
subhadrā- pn `ṣubhadra'
lā.i dt cs.mkr `to'
tāḍanā cn `scolding'
garūn tv1 imp <garnu `may he do'
bhane sc `if'
dharma cn `righteousness'
tathā cc and
viveka- cn `wisdom'
ko gn cs.mkr `of'
hatyā cn `murder'

4.40
ke pro.interrog `what'
garūn iv1 imp <garnu `may he do'
sāṃsārika adjl `worldly'
sukha-lipsā- cmpdcn `desire for pleasure'
ko gn cs.mkr `of'
ṭarro adj `bitter'
ānanda- cn `pleasure'
ko gn cs.mkr `of'
anubhava cn `experience'
gariraheka tv1 prf.cont.prt <garnu `been doing'
thie aux pst <hunu `they had'

4.41
tyasa prol.adj <tyo `that'
bakhata- cn `time'
mā lc cs.mkr `at, in, on'
una- pro.pers <unī `he'
ko gn cs.mkr `of'
tyo prol.adj `that'
prabala adjl `strong'
vāk-shakti cmpdcn `power of speech'
hāvā cn `wind'
hunthyo ev1 pst <hunu `used to be'

4.42
mānisa- cn `man'
ko gn cs.mkr `of'
pāṇḍitya cn `wisdom'
aru- pro.pers `others'
lā.i dt cs.mkr `to'
upadesha cn `advice'
garna- tv1 inf <garnu `to do'
mā lc cs.mkr `at, in, on'
kāma cn `work, use'
lāgdacha ev1p pres <lāgnu `is applied'
naki cc `not'
āphū pro.reflx `oneself'
lā.i dt cs.mkr `to'
pariā.ūdā cmpdiv1 conj.prt <parnu-āunu `while happening'

4.43
yo prol.adj `this'
pratidina- advl `everyday, day after day'
ko gn cs.mkr `of'
gṛhakalaha- cn `family feud'
le in cs.mkr `by, because, with'
subhadrā- pn `ṣubhadra'
ko gn cs.mkr `of'
komala adjl `tender'
hṛdaya-kusuma cmpdcn `flower of heart'
ekadama advl `completely'
oilāyo iv1 pst <oilā.unu `he withered'

4.44
unī pro.pers `she'
kārāgāra- cn `prison'
kī gn cs.mkr `of'
duḥkhī adj `unhappy'
bandī cn `prisoner'
jhaĩ pp `like'
bhāgne iv1 imp.prt <bhāgnu `running away'
maukā cn `opportunity'
khojna tv1 inf <khijnu `to look for'
lāgin tv1 pst <lāgnu `she began'

5.1
kālo adj `black'
andhakāra- cn `darkness'
māthi pp `over'
parkhī iv1 abs.prt <parkhanu `having haulted, waited'
parkhī iv1 abs.prt <parkhanu `having haulted, waited'
karā.une iv1 impf.prt `hooting'
hucīla pn `owl'
pakṣī- cn `bird'
ko gn cs.mkr `of'
virasilo adj `melancholic'
hukahuka onommat `hooting sound'
shabda cn `sound'
thapiṃdā conj.prt iv1p `while being added'
rātrī cn `night'
jhan advl `furthermore'
bhayangkara adjl `dreadful'
pratīta adjl `one that seems'
hunthyo ev1 pst <hunu `would be'

5.2
pallo adj `next'
gā.ũ- cn `village'
mā lc cs.mkr `at, in, on'
kukura cn `dog'
bhukiraheko iv1 prf.prt <bhuknu `been barking'
thiyo aux pst <hunu `he had'

5.3
pṛthvī- cn `earth'
mā lc cs.mkr `at, in, on'
mānava-jāti- cmpdcn `human race'
ko gn cs.mkr `of'
duḥkhamaya adjl `full of misery'
avasthā cn `condition'
dekhera tv1 abs.prt <dekhnu `having seen'
ananta adjl `endless'
ākāsha- cn `sky'
mā lc cs.mkr `at, in, on'
tārā-gaṇa cn `stars'
pilapila advl `atwinkle'
roiraheka iv1 prf.cont.prt <runu `crying'
thie aux pst <hunu `they had'

5.4
subhadrā- pn `ṣubhadra'
le ag sb.mkr
ā̃gana- cn `courtyard'
mā lc cs.mkr `at, in, on'
āera iv1 abs.prt <āunu `having come'
herin iv1 pst <hernu `she looked at'
eka num `one'
china- cn `moment'
pachi pp `after'
tyo prol.adj `that'
vishāla adjl `vast'
nabha-sthala- cmpdcn `firmament'
bāṭa ab cs.mkr `from'
euṭā num.specif `one'

lāmo adj `long'
jyoti cn `light'
salla onomat
bagera iv1 abs.prt <bagnu `having flown'
talatira- advl `downward'
khasyo iv1 pst <khasnu `he dropped'

5.5
kintu cc `but'
yo prol.adj `this'
kālo adj `black'
pr↑thvī- cn `earth'
mā lc cs.mkr `at, in, on'
jharna iv1 inf <jharna `to drop'
napā.ũdai tv1 conj.prt <pā.unu `not getting'
bīcai- cn `middle (emph)'
mā lc cs.mkr `at, in, on'
lupta adjl `lost'
bhayo ev1 pst <hunu `became'

5.6
aghi advl `before'
shaishava-kāla- cmpdcn `childhood'
mā lc cs.mkr `at, in, on'
yastai adjl `such'
dṛśya cn `sight'
dekhekī tv1 prf.prt <dekhnu `seen'
thi.in aux pst <hunu `she had'

5.7
usa prol.adj <u `that'
bakhata cn `time'
āmā- cn `mother'
saṃga pp `with'
sodhdā iv1 conj.prt <sodhnu `while asking'
ākāsha- cn `sky'
kā gn cs.mkr `of'
deva-gaṇa cmpdcn `gods'
hun ev1 pres <hunu `they are'
puṇya cn `religious merit'
siddhinā- iv1p inf <siddhinu `be exhuasted'
le in cs.mkr `because, by, with'
svarga- cn `heaven'
bāṭa ab cs.mkr `from'
patana cn `fall'
bhaekā ev1 prf.prt <hunu `have been'
bhanne sc `that'
javāpha cn `answer'
milethyo tv1 pst <milnu `had been obtained'

5.8
āja advl `today'
uhī prol.adj `same'
kurā cn `thing'
samjhin tv1 pst <samjhanu `remembered'
manamana- cn `mimd-mind'
le in cs.mkr `by, with'
bhanin tv1 pst <bhannu `she said'
ho intj `Oh, yes'
yo prol.adj `this'
ākāsha- cn `sky'
mā lc cs.mkr `at, in, on'
basera iv1 abs.prt <basnu `having stayed'
kehi adjl `some'
dina cn `days'
puṇya-bhoga cmpdcn `enjoyment of religious merit'
garne tv1 impf.prt <garnu `doing'
devatā- cn `gods'
kā gn cs.mkr `of'
jha_pp `like'
ma pro.pers `I'
pani advl `also'
āja advl `today'
salla onomat
bagẽ iv1 pst <bagnu `I slipped'

5.9
yinī- pro.pers `this'
haru nm.plzr
puṇya cn `religious merit'
samāpta adjl `exhausted'
bhae- ev1 cond <hunu `being'
pachi pp `after'
svarga- cn `heaven'
bāṭa ab cs.mkr `from'

ciplera iv1 abs.prt <ciplanu 'having slipped'
khaschan iv1 pres <khasnu `they drop'
hāmī pro.pers `we'
bhokā adj `hungry'
pyāsa cn `thirst'
duḥkha-pīra- cmpdcn `suffering and pain'
le in cs.mkr `by, because with''
nisteja adjl `pale'
tatha cc `and'
ḍhalamala adjl `weak'
bhaera ev1 abs.prt <hunu `having been'
pṛthvī- cn `earth'
ko gn cs.mkr `of'
pṛthvī- cn `earth'
mai lc cs.mkr `at, in, on (emph)'
khaschaũ iv1 pres <khasnu `we drop'

5.10
hāmī pro.pers `we'
khasisake- cmpdiv1 cond <khasi-saknu `if drop'
pachiko `after'
bībhatsa adjl `horrible'
rūpa cn `form'
aru pro `other'
seṣa adjl `remaning'
bhokā adj `hungry'
pyāsā adj `thirsty'
duḥkhī- cn `miserable'
haru- nm.plzr
le ag sb.mkr
dekhchan tv1 pres <dekhnu `they see'

5.11
devatā- cn `god'
haru nm.plzr
cāhiṃ postf `for someome's part'
puṇyabhogī adjl `enjoyer of religious merit'
hunā- ev1 inf <hunu `to be'
le in cs.mkr `because, by, with'
yo prol.adj `this'
pāpapūrṇa adjl `full of sins'
jagata- cn `world'
mā lc cs.mkr `at, in, on'
khasnu iv1 inf <khasnu `to drop'
parlā aux fut <parnu `will have'
bhanera tv1 abs.prt <bhannu `having said, thought (that)'
bīcai- cn `middle (emph)'
mā lc cs.mkr `at, in, on'
alapa adjl `lost'
hunchan ev1 pres <hunu `they become'
mānisa- cn `man'
haru- nm.plzr
mā lc cs.mkr `at, in, on'
ra cc `and'
devatā- cn `god'
mā lc cs.mkr `at, in, on'
kevala advl `only'
yatti adjl `this much'
antara cn `difference'
na nu `simply (?)'
cha iv1 pres <hunu `is'

5.12
subhadrā- pn `ṣubhadra'
le ag sb.mkr
kākhī- cn `human body part under the arm'
mani pp `under'
euṭā num.specif `one'
poko cn `bundle'
cyāpekī tv1 prf.prt <cyāpnu `held'
thi.in aux pst <hunu `she had'

5.13
yasto adjl `such'
andhakāra adjl `dark'
rātrī- cn `night'
mā lc cs.mkr `at, in, on'
pani advl `even'
kasai- pro.pers <ko `anyone (emph)'
le ag sb.mkr
dekhcha iv1 pres <dekhnu `he sees'
kiqw
bhanera tv1 abs.prt <bhannu `having said, thought (that)'

oḍhne- cn `shawl'
le in cs.mkr `by, with'
chopekī ivl prf.prt <chopnu `covered'
thi.in aux pst <hunu `she had'

5.14
yasa prol.adj <yo `this'
bakhata cn `time'
una- pro.pers <unī `she'
ko gn cs.mkr `of'
jīvanādhāra cmpdcn `support of life'
tyahī prol.adj `that (very) (emph)'
sāno adj `small'
poko cn `bundle'
huna.āyo cmpdevl pst <hunu+ā.unu `came to be'

5.15
aho intj `Oh'
kunai adjl `some'
bakhata cn `time'
yo prol.adj `this'
vishāla adj `vast'
āshā-latā cmpdcn `grandoise hope'
kasarī adv `how'
euṭā num.specif `one'
sāno adj `small'
ṭhāū- cn `place'
mā lc cs.mkr `at, in, on'
sīmita adjl `limited'
bhaera evl abs.prt <hunu `having been'
bastacha ivl pres <basnu `ramains'

5.16
parameshvara cn `god'
manuṣya- cn `man'
lā.ī ac cs.mkr
kina advl `why'
āshā- cn `hope'
mā lc cs.mkr `at, in, on'
jhuṇḍyāyau ivl pst <jhuṇḍyā.unu `you hung'

5.17
prabhu cn `Lord'
āshā- cn `hope'
ko gn cs.mkr `of'
badalā advl `instead'
santoṣa cn `satisfaction'
dieko tvl prf.prt <dinu `given'
bhae aux cond <hunu `if be'
yī prol.adj `these'
anātha adj `helpless'
prāṇī- cn `creature'
haru nm.plzr
sukha- cn `happiness'
kā nm.plzr `of'
kati advl `how much'
najīkai advl `near'
pugisakthe cmpdiv pst <pugnu-saknu `would have already reached'

5.18
kehī adjl `some'
bera- cn `time'
pachi pp `after'
ashrupūrṇa adjl `tearful'
nayana- cn `eye'
le in cs.mkr `by, with'
pyāro adj `dear'
gṛha- cn `house'
lā.ī ac cs.mkr
sadaiva- advl `always, ever'
kā gn cs.mkr `of'
nimitta pp `for'
namaskāra cn `greeting, good bye'
garera tvl abs.prt <garnu `having done'
anāthinī adj `helpless'
subhadrā pn `ṣubhadra'
tyo prol.adj `that'
kālo adj `black'
andhakāra- cn `darkness'
mā lc cs.mkr `at, in, on'
vilīna adj `lost'
bha.in evl pst <hunu `she became'

5.19
yo prol.adj `this'
karuṇājanaka adjl `pathetic'
dṛśya cn `scene'
sadhaiṃ advl `always'
jāgā adjl `vigilant'
bhairahane impf.cont.prt ev1 <hunu `being'
vishva- cn `world'
ko gn cs.mkr `of'
catura adjl `wise'
caukīdāra cn `guardian'
bāheka pp `except'
aru prol.adj `another'
kasai- pro.pers <ko `anyone (emph)'
le ag sb.mkr
dekhena tv1 pst <dekhnu `he did not see'

6.1
pashupatinātha- pn `Pashupatinath'
kā gn cs.mkr `of'
mandira- cn `temple'
waripari pp `around'
tila cn `sesame seed'
rākhne impf.prt <rākhnu `putting'
ṭhāũ cn `place, room'
thiena iv1 pst <hunu+na `was not'

6.2
sadbīu cn `a combination of one hundred t
ypes of foodgrains'
charne impf.prt <charnu `scattering'
jātrū- cn `pilgrim'
haru- nm.plzr
ko gn cs.mkr `of'
chicolīnasaknu adjl `impassable'
ghuĩco cn `crowd'
thiyo iv1 pst <hunu `he was'

6.3
yastai- adjl `like this (time, situation)'
mā lc cs.mkr `at, in, on'
pashcima cn `west'
ḍhokā- cn `gate'
nera pp `near'
akasmāt advl `suddenly'
subhadrā- pn `ṣubhadra'
lā.ī ac cs.mkr
dekhera tv1 abs.prt <dekhnu `having seen'
naulī- pn `ṇauli'
le ag cs.mkr
gaha- cn `eye'
bharī pp `in full'
ā̃su cn `tears'
pārera tv1 abs.prt <pārnu `having made'
bhanī tv1 pst <bhannu `she said'
oho intj `Oh'
bajai cn `madam'
hera iv1 imp. <hernu `look'
kati advl `how much'
dublī adj `thin'
cinnai tv1 inf <cinnu `to recognize (emph)'
nasak[i]ne auxp impf.prt <na+sakinu `(one
that) cannot be'
hunubhae[ko] ev1 prf.prt <hunu `become'
cha aux pres <hunu `have'

6.4
ali adjl `a little'
bera- cn `while'
samma pp `for'
ta nu `rather (?)'
ṭhamyā.unai iv1 inf <ṭhamyā.unu
`determine (emph)'
sakina aux pst <saknu+neg `I could not'

6.5
kahā̃ advl `where'
basnubhaeko iv3 prf.prt <basnu `stayed'
cha aux <hunu `have'
hā̃ qw
6.6
yahiṃ advl `here (emph)'
gaurīghāṭa pn `Gaurīhgāṭ (a place name)'
phupū- cn `aunt'
kahā̃ pp `at'
basekī iv3 prf.prt <basnu `stayed'

chu aux pres <hunu `I have'

6.7
kharca-barca cn `things to eat'
nali.ikana tv1 abs.prt <na+linu `not having taken'
ādhā adj1 `half'
rāta- cn `night'
mā lc cs.mkr `at, in, on'
hĩḍnubhaecha pst iv1 `you left'

6.8
thāhā cn `knowlege'
pani adv1 `also'
pā.ina tv1 pst <pā.unu+neg `I did not get'

6.9
yatikā adj1 `so many'
dina- cn `days'
samma pp `for'
ke pro.interrog `what'
khāera tv1 abs.prt <khānu `having eaten'
gujarāna cn `sustenance'
garnubhayo tv1 pst <garnu `did (polite)'

6.10
phupū cn `aunt'
lā.ī dt cs.mkr `to'
sarakāra- cn `government, king'
bāṭa ag sb.mkr
euṭā num.specif `one'
haṇḍī cn `a religious pension'
bakseko tv1 prf.prt <baksanu `given'
rahecha aux pres <rahanu `was (found to)'
tyasa- pro.dem <tyo `that'
bāṭa ab cs.mkr `from'
duī num `two'
janā- specif `human individuals'
le ag sb.mkr
gujārā cn `sustenannce'
calāekā tv1 prf.prt <calā.unu `run, maintained'
chaũ aux pres <hunu `we have'

6.11
ghara- cn `home'
ko gn cs.mkr `of'
hāla cn `news'
kasto adj `how'
cha ev1 pres <hunu `is'
naulī pn `ṇauli'

6.12
bajai cn `madam'
ghara- cn `home'
ko gn cs.mkr `of'
hāla cn `news'
ke pro.interrog `what'
bhanũ tv1 imp <bhannu `may I say'
samjhãdā tv1 conj.prt <samjhanu `while remembering'
pani adv1 `also, even'
ãsu cn `tears'
āũcha iv1 pres <ā.unu `comes'

6.13
cha num `six'
mahīnā cn `month'
bho (bhayo) iv1 pst <hunu `was'
dulahī cn `bride'
bajai cn `madam'
berāmī adj1 `sick'
hunuhuncha ev1 pres <hunu `she is'

6.14
ke pro.interrog `what'
huncha iv1 pres <hunu `happens'
subhadrā- pn `ṣubhadra'
le ag sb.mkr
sāhrai adv1 `very'
utsukatā- cn `curiousity'
sātha advlzr `with'
sodhin tv1 pst <sodhnu `she asked'

6.15
tapanī adj1 `mild'
jaro cn `fever'

cha ivl pres <hunu `is (she has)'
chātī cn `chest'
dukhcha ivl pres <dukhnu `hurts'
bhannuhuncha tvl <bhannu `she says'

6.16
rāta- cn `night'
bhara pp `throughout'
khokirahanuhuncha ivl pres <khoknu `she keeps coughing'

6.17
gorakhā pn `Gorkha'
mula- cn `origin'
kā gn cs.mkr `of'
ḍāgḍara cn `doctor'
subidāra- cn `a post in ṇepalese military'
lā.ī ac cs.mkr
dekhā.ūdā tvl conj.prt <dekhā.unu `while showing'
thāisī cn `phthisis'
bhane tvl pst <bhannu `he said'
ki cc `or'
khāksī cn `phthisis'
bhane tvl pst <bhannu `he said'
ahile advl `now'
samjhana tvl inf <samjhanu `to remember'
sakina aux pst <saknu `I could not'
sāhrai advl `very'
narāmro adj `bad'
roga cn `disease'
ho ivl pres <hunu `is'
are nu (used to report speech)

6.18
sukera ivl abs.prt <suknu `having lost weight'
hāḍa-chālā cmpdcn `bone and skin'
mātra advl `only'
cha ivl pres <hunu `is (she has)'

6.19
bokera tvl abs.prt <boknu `having carried'
bāhira advl `outside'
bhitra advl `inside'
garā.unu tvl inf <garnu (caus.) `cause to do'
parcha aux pres <parnu `must'

6.20
sāno adj `small, little'
bābu cn `boy'
kasto adj `how'
cha evl pres <hunu `he is'
ni nu

6.21
kastā adj `how'
hunthe evl pst <hunu `he would be'
jīu- cn `body'
bharī pp `all over'
khaṭirā cn `boils'
chan ivl pres <hunu `they are'
tela cn `oil'
lā.una tvl inf <lā.unu `to rub, apply'
hūdaina aux pres <hunu+neg `must not'
āmā cn `mother'
kahile advl `when'
ā.unuhuncha ivl <ā.unu `she comes'
bhanera tvl abs.prt <bhannu `having said'
barābara advl `frequently'
tapāī - pro.pers `you'
lā.ī ac cs.mkr
samjhirahanchan tvl pres.cont <samjhanu `he keeps remembering'

6.22
bhāta cn `rice (food)'
ko pro.interrog `who'
pakā.ūcha tvl pres <pakā.unu `cooks'
ni nu
6.23
kahile advl `sometimes'
bāje cn `sir'
āphai pro.reflx `oneself'
pakā.unuhuncha tvl pres <pakā.unu `he cooks'

kahile advl `sometimes'
camenā cn `snack'
khāera tv1 abs.prt <knānu `having taken'
sutnuhuncha iv1 pst <sutnu `he sleeps'

6.24
eka num `one'
dina cn `day'
bārdalī̃- cn `balcony'
mā lc cs.mkr `at, in, on'
basera iv3 abs.prt <basnu `being seated'
eklai advl `alone'
roī̃rahanubhaeko iv1 prf.cont.prt <runu `have been crying'
rahecha aux pres <rahanu `was (found to)'

6.25
āphū- pro.reflx `onself'
le ag sb.mkr
cineko tv1 prf.prt <cinnu `built'
cautāro cn `platform built under a tree'
pāpinī̃- adj `sinner'
le ag sb.mkr
āphai pro.reflx `onself'
bhatkāera tv1 abs.prt <bhatkā.unu `having destroyed'
ga.ī̃ iv1 pst <jānu `she went'
bhannuhunthyo tv1 pst <bhannu `he used to say'

6.26
ke pro.interrog `what'
ke pro.interrog `what'
bhanū̃ tv1 imp <bhannu `may I say'
bajai cn `madam'
bastubhāu- cn `cattle'
kā gn cs.mkr `of'
hāḍachālā cmpdcn `bones and skin'
mātra advl `only'
chan iv1 pres <hunu `they are'

6.27
kheta-bārī̃ cmpdcn `crop fields'
adhiyā̃- cn `half-share'
mā lc cs.mkr `at, in, on'
dieko tv1 prf.prt <dinu `been let out'
cha aux pres <hunu `has'

6.28
asāmī̃pāta cmpdcn `loans and debts'
eka num `one'
paisā pn `smallest unit of Nepalese currency'
uṭhdaina iv1 pres <uṭhnu+neg `does not rise (return)'
nokara-cākara cmpdcn `servants and serfs'
cāra num `four'
dina cn `days'
ṭikdainan iv1 pres <ṭiknu+neg `they do not stay'
sabai pro.nonpers `all, everything'
bhatābhungga adjl `disarrayed'
cha iv1 pres <hunu `is'

6.29
naulī̃- pn `ṇauli'
kā gn cs.mkr `of'
kurā cn `talks'
sunera tv1 abs.prt <sunnu `having heard'
subhadrā- pn `ṣubhadra'
ko gn cs.mkr `of'
hṛdaya cn `heart'
kāṭiyo iv1p pst <kāṭinu `was cut (grieved)'

6.30
manamanai cn `mind-mind (emph)'
bhanin tv1 pst <bhannu `she said'
chiḥ intj `Fie! shame!'

6.31
sautā- cn `co-wife'
ko gn cs.mkr `of'
rī̃sa- cn `jealosy'
le in cs.mkr `by, with'
poi- cn `husband'
ko gn cs.mkr `of'
nāka cn `nose'

kāṭnu tv1 inf <kāṭnu `to cut'
bhaneko tv1 prf.prt <bhannu `said'
yahī pro.dem `this (emph)'
ho ev1 pres <hunu `is'

6.32
umeradāra adjl `young'
thi.ī ev1 pst <hunu `she was'
ke pro.interrog `what'
khā.ū tv1 imp <khānu `may I eat'
ke pro.interrog `what'
lā.ū tv1 imp <lā.unu `may I wear'
bhanne tv1 impf.prt <bhannu `saying'
belā cn `time'
thiyo iv1 pst <hunu `he was'

6.33
mīṭho adj `good (food)'
khā.ī tv1 pst <khānu `she ate'
rāmro adj `good (clothes)'
lā.ī tv1 pst <lā.unu `she wore'
bhanera tv1 abs.prt <bhannu `having said'
mai- pro.pers <ma `I'
le ag sb.mkr
citta cn `mind'
dukhā.una tv1 inf <dukhā.unu `hurt'
nahune aux inf.prt <na+hunu `must not have'

6.34
usa pro.pers <u `she, he'
lā.ī ac cs.mkr
liera tv1 abs.prt <linu `having taken'
tīrtha cn `pilgrimage, pilgrimage site'
jānubhayo iv1 pst <jānu `he went'
ta advl `then'
tyasa- pro.dem <tyo `that'
le in cs.mkr `because, by, with'
ke pro.interrog `what'
bhayo iv1 pst <hunu `happened'
raqw
6.35
pharkanubhae- iv1 cond <pharkanu `if return'
pachi pp `after'
arko prol.adj `another'
sāthī cn `friend'
liera tv1 abs.prt <linu `having taken'
ma pro.pers `I'
jā̃dīhū iv1 prob.pst <jānu `I would go'

6.36
kahilekāhīṃ advl `sometimes'
ali advl `a little'
jharkera iv1 abs.prt <jharkanu `being angry'
boldathī iv1 pst <bolnu `she used to speak'
lau nu
ali advl `a little'
jhaḍangge adjl `ill-tempered'
svabhāva cn `nature'
kī gn cs.mkr `of'
thi.ī ev1 pst <hunu `she was'
svabhāvai cn `nature (emph)'
tyasto adj `like that'
eka num `one'
ṭhāū- cn `place'
mā lc cs.mkr `at, in, on'
base- iv3 cond <basnu `if stay'
pachi pp `after'
kahilekāhiṃ advl `sometimes'
āmā-chorī- cmpdcn `mother and daughter'
mā lc cs.mkr `at, in, on'
pani advl `also'
ta nu
ṭhāka-ṭhuka cn `verbal skirmishes'
huncha iv1 pres <hunu `happens'

6.37
ekai num `one (emph)'
ghara- cn `house, home'
mā lc cs.mkr `at, in, on'
basna iv3 inf <basnu `to stay'
nasake aux cond <na+saknu `if cannot'
kaṭero cn `hut'
bārera tv1 abs.prt <bārnu `having built'
bastīhū iv3 prob.pst <basnu `I would have lived'

6.38
mai- pro.pers <ma `I'
le ag sb.mkr
sāhrai advl `very'
bebujha- cn `fool'
ko gn cs.mkr `of'
kāma cn `act'
garẽ tv1 pst <garnu `I did'

6.39
joṛīpāṛī- cn `neighbors'
le ag sb.mkr
ke pro.interrog `what'
bhandāhun tv1 prob.pst <bhannu `ṭhey would say'
āphno pro.reflx `one's own'
tyatro adj `that big'
daulatha cn `wealth'
choḍera tv1 abs.prt <choḍnu `having left'
yahā̃ advl `here'
eka num `one'
chāka cn `meal'
khāera tv1 abs.prt <khānu `having eaten'
basekī iv3 prf.prt <basnu `stayed'
chu aux pres <hunu `I have'
tyasa- pro.dem <tyo `he, she, that'
kā gn cs.mkr `of'
jīu- cn `body'
mā lc cs.mkr `at, in, on'
kehī pro.nonpers `something'
bhaidiyo cmpdiv1 pst <hunu+dinu `happened'
bhane sc `if'
tyo prol.adj `that'
cicilo adj `infant'
bālakha- cn `child'
ko gn cs.mkr `of'
ke adj.interrog `what'
gati cn `condition'
holā iv1 fut <hunu `will be'
pitṛ - cn `ancestor'
le ag sb.mkr
ke pro.interrog `what'
bhanlān tv1 fut <bhannu `will say'

6.40
chitta cn `mind'
dukhāe tv1 cond <dukhā.unu `if hurt'
pani advl `also, even'
āmā- cn `mother'
le ag sb.mkr
dukhā.ī tv1 pst <dukhā.unu `she hurt'
tyo prol.adj `that'
bālaka- cn `child'
le ag sb.mkr
ke pro.interrog `what'
birāyo tv1 pst <birā.unu `he did wrong'

6.41
aghi advl `before'
eka num `one'
duī num `two'
chāka cn `meal'
bhāta cn `rice'
pakā.unu tv1 inf <pakā.unu `cook'
pardā aux conj.prt <parnu `when having to'
dikka cn `worry, trouble, vexation'
mānnuhunthyo iv1 pst <mānnu `he used to feel'

6.42
ājakāla advl `these days'
dinahũ advl `always, everyday'
kasarī adv `how'
pakā.unu tv1 inf <pakā.unu `cook'
hũdoho aux prob.pst <hunu `he would'
ityādi adjl `such'
manovedanā- cnpdcn `mental pain'
le in cs.mkr `because, by, with'
subhadrā- pn `ṣubhadra'
ko gn cs.mkr `of'
hṛdaya cn `heart'
chiyāchiyā adjl `broken (into pieces)
bhayo ev1 pst <hunu `became'
ā̃su cn `tears'
jhārdai tv1 conj.prt <jhārnu `dropping'

bhanin tv1 pst <bhannu `she said'
naulī pn `ṇauli'
tyastā adj `like that'
belā- cn `time'
mā lc cs.mkr `at, in, on'
taiṃ- pro.pers <t_ `you'
le ag sb.mkr
pani advl `even, also'
choḍera tv1 abs.prt <choḍnu `having left'
ā.iches iv1 pst <ā.unu `you have come'

6.43
bajai cn `madam'
janma- cn `life'
bhara pp `throughout'
arkā- pro.pers `others'
kī gn cs.mkr `of'
dāsī cn slave'
bhaera ev1 abs.prt <hunu `having been'
basnu iv1 inf <basnu `to remain'
paryo aux pst <parnu `had'
cāroṭā num.specif `four ones'
akṣatā cn `sacred rice grains'
bhaepani advl `although, even if'
charera tv1 abs.prt <charnu `having scattered'
ā.ũ iv1 imp <ā.unu `may I come'
bhanera tv1 abs.prt <bhannu `having said, thought (that)'
bāje- cn `sir'
sãga pp `with'
bīsai num `twenty (emph)'
dina- cn `day'
ko gn cs.mkr `of'
bidā cn `leave'
māgera tv1 abs.prt <māgnu `having asked for'
āekī iv1 prf.prt <ā.unu `come (f.)'

6.44
ko- pro.interrog `who'
sãga pp `with'
ā.īs iv1 pst <ā.unu `you came'

6.45
rātamāṭe adj `of Ratamāṭa'
bhãḍārī- pn `Bh_ḍārī'
kā gn cs.mkr `of'
jahāna- cn `family'
sãga pp `with'

6.46
kaile advl `when'
jānches iv1 pres <jānu `you will go'

6.47
bholi advl `tomorrow'
bihānai cn `morning (emph)'
bajai cn `madam'
bintī cn `earnest request'
cha iv1 pres <hunu `is'
ghara cn `home'
jā.auṃ iv1 imp <jānu `let us go'

6.48
tapā.ī pro.pers `you'
nabhae iv1 cond <na+hunu `if not be'
bāje- cn `sir'
ko gn cs.mkr `of'
jahājai cn `ship (emph)'
ḍubcha iv1 pres <ḍubnu `sinks'

7.1
mailo adj `dirty'
bichyā.unā- cn `bed'
mā lc cs.mkr `at, in, on'
sutekī iv1 prf.prt <sutnu `slept'
lakṣmī pn `Laksmi'
jīvana- cn `life'
ko gn cs.mkr `of'
seṣa adjl `remaining'
ghaḍī cn `hour'
ganīrahekī tv1 prf.cont.prt <gannu 'counting'
thi.in aux pst <hunu `she had'

7.2

devīramaṇa pn `Deviraman'
rogī- cn `patient'
kā gn cs.mkr `of'
sirāna- cn `pillow'
mā lc cs.mkr `at, in, on'
basera iv3 abs.prt <basnu `being seated'
bakhata-bakhata- cn time-to-time'
mā lc cs.mkr `at, in, on'
camcā- cn `spoon'
le in cs.mkr `because, by, with'
pānī cn `water'
khwā.uṃthe tv1 pst <khwa.unu `he used to feed'

7.3
bālaka cn `child'
putra cn `son'
sushīla pn `ṣushil'
āmā- cn `mother'
nera pp `near'
basera iv3 abs.prt <basnu `having been seated'
yo adj.dem `this'
cira adjl `long'
mātr↑viyoga cmpdcn `separation from mother'
heriraheko tv1 prf.cont.prt <hernu `been watching'
thiyo aux pst <hunu `he had'

7.4
lakṣmī pn `Laksmi'
kahilekāhiṃ advl `sometimes'
sushīla- pn `ṣushil'
ko gn cs.mkr `of'
mukha- cn `face'
paṭṭi pp `toward'
herera iv1 abs.prt <hernu `having looked'
barara onomat
ãsu cn `tears'
jhārthin tv1 pst <jhārnu `she used to drop'

7.5
malino adj `faint'
battī cn `lamp'
ko gn cs.mkr `of'
dhamilo adj `dim'
prakāsha- cn `light'
mā lc cs.mkr `at, in, on'
rogī- cn patient
ko gn cs.mkr `of'
koṭhā cn `room'
shmashāna cn `cremation ground'
jasto pp `like'
dekhinthyo iv1p pst <dekhinu `used to seem (seemed)'

7.6
tyastai- adjl `like that (time, situation)'
mā lc cs.mkr `at, in, on'
dailo cn `door'
ughārera tv1 abs.prt <ughārnu `having opened'
naulī- pn `ṇauli'
le ag sb.mkr
devīramaṇa- pn `Deviraman'
lā.i ac cs.mkr
ḍhogidi.ī cmpdtv1 pst <ḍhogi dinu `she greeted'

7.7
naulīl- pn `ṇauli'
lā.ī ac cs.mkr
dekhera tv1 abs.prt <dekhnu `having seen'
devīramaṇa- pn `Deviraman'
kā gn cs.mkr `of'
duḥkha- cn `sorrow'
ko gn cs.mkr `of'
laharī cn `wave'
kehī advl `somewhat'
shānta adjl `quiet'
bhayo ev1 pst <hunu `bacame'
bhane tv1 pst <bhannu `he said'
nepāla- pn `ṇepal'
bāṭa ab cs.mkr `from'
kahile advl `when'
ā.īpugis cmpdiv1 pst <ā.unu-pugnu `you arrived'

naulī pn `ṇauli'

7.8
bāje cn `sir'
ā.ũdai iv1 impf.prt <āunu `coming'
chu aux pres <hunu `I am'
dulahī cn `bride'
bajai- cn `madam'
lā.ī dt cs.mkr `to'
kasto adj `how'
cha iv1 pres <hunu `is'

7.9
tela cn `oil'
ta nu
aghi advl `before'
nai nu `(emphatic)'
siddhisakeko cmpdiv1 prf.prt <siddhinu+ saknu `already exhausted'
thiyo aux pst <hunu `was'
aba advl `now'
battī cn `lamp'
nibhna iv1 inf <nibhnu `to die out'
bā̃kī adjl `remaning'
cha iv1 pres <hunu `is'

7.10
bāje cn `sir'
yasa prol.adj <yo `this'
bakhata- cn `time'
mā lc cs.mkr `at, in, on'
ṭhulī adj `big'
bajai cn `madam'
bhae iv3 cond <hunu `if be'
sabai prol.adj `all'
kurā- cn `things'
ko gn cs.mkr `of'
sambhāra cn `care, protection'
hune iv1 impf.prt <hunu `being'
thiyo aux pst <hunu `he was'
ke pro.interrog `what'
garũ tv1 imp <garnu `may I do'
jā.auṃ iv1 imp <jānu `let us go'

bhaneko tv1 prf.prt <bhannu `said'
mānnubhaena iv1 pst <mānnu+neg `did not agree to'

7.11
ke qw
taiṃ- pro.pers <t_ `you'
le ag sb.mkr
bheṭis iv1 pst <bheṭnu `you met
ra qw

7.12
pashupatinātha- pn `Pashupatinath'
ko gn cs.mkr `of'
mandira- cn `temple'
nera pp `near'
bheṭethem compdiv1 prf+pst <bheṭekī thiem <bheṭnu+hunu `I had met'

7.13
kastī adj `how'
thi.ī ev1 pst <hunu `she was'

7.14
ekadama advl `very'
dublī adj `thin'
mailā adj `dirty'
lugā cn `clothes'
lagāekī prf.prt <lagā.unu `wearing'
māyālāgdī adj `pitiable'

7.15
kahā̃ advl `where'
basekī iv3 prf.prt <basnu `stayed'
ra̍icha aux pres <rahanu `she had'

7.16
gaurīghāṭa pn `Gaurīghāṭ (a place)'
phupū- cn `aunt'
kahā̃ pp `at'
basekī iv3 prf.prt <basnu `stayed'
chu aux pres <hunu `I have'
phupū cn `aunt'
lā.ī dt cs.mkr `to'
sarakāra- cs `government, king'

bāṭa ag sb.mkr
eka num `one'
haṇḍī cn `a religious pension'
bakseko tv1 prf.prt <baksanu `given'
cha aux pres <hunu `has'
tyasai- pro.dem `that (emph)'
bāṭa ab cs.kr `from'
duī num `two'
janā- specif `human individuals'
le ag sb.mkr
gujārā cn `maintenance'
calāekā tv1 prf.prt <calāunu `maintained'
chauṃ aux pres <hunu `we have'
bhannuhunthyo tv1 pst <bhannu `she used to say'

7.18
devīramaṇa- pn `Deviraman'
kā gn cs.mkr `of'
dubai prol.adj `both'
ā̃khā- cn `eye'
bāṭa ab cs.mkr `from'
ā̃su- cn `tears'
kā gn cs.mkr `of'
dhārā cn `flow(s)'
bage iv1 pst <bagnu `they flowed'

7.19
manamana cn `mind-mind'
le in cs.mkr `because, by, with'
bhane tv1 pst <bhannu `he said'
yatro adj `so big'
sampatti- cn `wealth'
kī gn cs.mkr `of'
māliknī cn `female owner' mistress'
bha.ikana ev1 abs.prt <hunu `having been'
subhadrā pn `ṣubhadra'
eka num `one'
chāka cn `meal'
khāera tv1 abs.prt <knānu `having eaten'
basekī iv1 prf.prt <basnu `remained'
cha aux pres <hunu `she has'

7.20
usa- pro.dem <u `that'
mā lc cs.mkr `at, in, on'
pani advl `even'
dublī adj `thin'
mailā adj `dirty'
lugā cn `clothes'
lagāekī tv1 prf.prt <lagā.unu `wearing'
māyālāgdī adj `pitiable'

7.21
hare intj `Oh !'
parameshvara cn `Lord'
ma pro.pers `I'
pāpī adj `sinner'
hū̃ ev1 pres <hunu `I am'
mero pro.pers `my'
jīvana- cn `life'
lā.ī dt cs.mkr `to'
hajāravāra num `thousand times'
dhikkāra cn `curse'
cha iv2 pres <hunu `is'

7.22
subhadrā pn `ṣubhadra'
merī pro.pers `my'
gṛhalakṣmī cmpdcn `Goddess of house'
ho ev1 pres <hunu `is'
u pro.pers `she, he'
gae- iv1 cond <jānu `if go'
dekhi pp `since'
vipatti- cn `trouble'
ko gn cs.mkr `of'
bādala- cn `clouds'
le ag cs.mkr
gherirahe[ko]- iv1 prf.cont.prt <ghernu `been surrounding'
cha aux <rahanu `has'

7.23
hāmī- pro.pers `we'
lā.ī ac cs.mkr
nabhae sc `if not'

pani advl `also, even'
yo prol.adj `this'
bālaka cn `infant'
santāna- cn `child'
lā.ī ac cs.mkr
samjhanu tv1 inf <samjhanu `rememeber'
parne aux impf.prt <parnu `must'
sabai pro.nonpers `all, everyone'
lā.ī ac cs.mkr
caṭakka advl `completely'
birsī tv1 pst <birsanu `she forgot'
ityādi adjl `such'
duḥkhamanāu cn `sorrowful complains'
garera tv1 abs.prt <garnu `having done'
ā̃su cn `tears'
jhārdai tv1 conj.prt <jhārnu `dropīng'
bhane tv1 pst <bhannu `he said'
naulī pn `ṇauli'
tā̃ pro.pers `you'
ā.iches iv1 pres <ā.unu `you have come'
ghara- cn `house, home'
ko gn cs.mkr `of'
sambhāra cn `care, protection'
rākhes tv1 imp <rākhnu `may you keep'
ma pro.pers `I'
bholi advl `tomorrow'
bihānai cn `morning (emph)'
nepāla pn `Nepal'
jānchu iv1 pres <jānu `I (will) go'

7.24
tyastai- adjl `like that (time, situation)'
mā lc cs.mkr `at, in, on'
subhadrā pn `ṣubhadra'
ghara- cn `house, home'
bhitra pp `inside'
pasin iv3 pst <pasnu `she entered'

7.25
atyanta advl `extremely'
dublī adj `thin'
nidā.urī adj `sad'
malina adj `faint, dirty'
jhutrā adj `ragged'
lugā cn `clothes'
lāekī tv1 prf.prt <lā.unu `wearing'
mukhamaṇḍala- cmpdcn `face'
mā lc cs.mkr `at, in, on'
asīma adjl `boundless'
karuṇā cn `compassion'
tathā cc `and'
saṃyama cn `self-restraint'
jhalkiraheko iv1p prf.cont.prt <jhalkinu
`appearing'
thiyo aux pst <hunu `he had'

7.26
subhadrā- pn `ṣubhadra'
ko gn cs.mkr `of'
shārīrika adjl `physical'
avasthā cn `condition'
dekhera tv1 abs.prt <dekhnu `having seen'
devīramaṇa- pn `Deviraman'
ko gn cs.mkr `of'
hṛdaya cn `heart'
ṭukrā-ṭukrā cn `broken (into pieces)'
bhayo ev1 pst <hunu `became'

7.27
dubai prol.adj `both'
hāta- cn `hand'
le in cs.mkr `by, with'
mukha cn `face'
chopera tv1 abs.prt <chopnu
`having covered'
runa iv1 inf <runu `to cry'
lāge tv1 pst <lāgnu `he began'

7.28
pati- cn `husband'
lā.ī dt cs.mkr `to'
daṇḍavat cn `greeting'
garera tv1 abs.prt <garnu `having done'
subhadrā pn `ṣubhadra'
lakṣmī- pn `Laksmi'
ko gn cs.mkr `of'

sirāna- cn `pillow'
mā lc cs.mkr `at, in, on'
basin iv3 pst <basnu `she sat'

7.29
naulī- pn `ṇauli'
le ag sb.mkr
bhanī tv1 pst <bhannu `she said'
oho intj `Oh!'
bajai cn `madam'
ā.īpugnubho cmpdiv1 pst <ā.unu-pugnu
`you arrived (honorific)'

7.30
naulī- cn `ṇauli'
ko gn cs.mkr `of'
svara cn `voice'
sunera tv1 abs.prt <sunnu `having heard'
lakṣmī- pn `Laksmi'
le ag sb.mkr
ā̃khā cn `eyes'
ughārin tv1 pst <ughārnu `she opened'

7.31
subhadrā- pn `ṣubhadra'
lā.ī ac cs.mkr
āphnā prol.adj `one's own'
sirāna- cn `pillow'
mā lc cs.mkr `at, in, on'
baseko iv3 prf.prt <basnu `seated'
dekhera tv1 abs.prt <dekhnu `having seen'
sustarī adv `slowly'
larbarieko iv1 prf.prt <larbarinu `faultering'
svara- cn `voice'
le in cs.mkr `by, with'
bhanin tv1 pst <bhannu `she said'
didī cn `sister'
tapā.ī- pro.pers `you'
ko gn cs.mkr `of'
darshana- cn `auspicious meeting'
lā.ī dt cs.mkr `to'
eka num `one'
muṭhī cn `handful'
sāsa cn `breath'
muskila adjl `hard'
le in cs.mkr `by, with'
jhuṇḍiraheko iv1 prf.prt <jhuṇḍinu `been
hanging'
cha aux pres <hunu `has'

7.32
lakṣmī- pn `Laksmi'
ko gn cs.mkr `of'
vacana cn `words'
sunera tv1 abs.prt <sunnu `having heard'
subhadrā- pn `ṣubhadra'
ko gn cs.mkr `of'
hṛdaya- cn `heart'
ko gn cs.mkr `of'
mailo cn `dirt'
ekadama advl `completely'
sāpha adjl `clean'
bhayo ev1 pst <hunu `became'

7.33
bhanin tv1 pst <bhannu `she said'
bābu cn `baby'
mai- pro.pers <ma `I'
le ag sb.mkr
āphno prol.adj `one's own'
kartavya cn `duty'
birsichu cmpdtv1 prf.pres <birsinu+hunu
`I have forgotten'

7.34
lakṣmī- pn `Laksmi'
le ag sb.mkr
subhadrā- pn `ṣubhadra'
ko gn cs.mkr `of'
chāti- cn `heart'
tira pp `toward'
dekhāera iv1 abs.prt <dekhaunu
`having pointed'
bhanin tv1 pst <bhannu `she said'
tyahā̃ advl `there'
sāhrai advl `very'

kaḍā adjl `severe, hard'
coṭa cn `wound'
lāgeko iv1 prf.prt <lāgnu `struck'
cha aux pres <hunu `has'

7.35
subhadrā- pn `ṣubhadra'
le ag sb.mkr
ā̃su cn `tears'
jhārdai tv1 conj.prt <jhārnu `dropping'
bhanin tv1 pst <bhannu `she said'
niko adjl `healed'
bho ev1 pst <hunu `became'
bā intj (used in expressing entreatment)
asti advl `day before yesterady, long before'
nai nu `(emphatic)'
niko adj `healed'
bha.isakyo cmpdev1 pst <hunu-saknu
`already became'
sāno adj `small'
tila- cn `sesame'
ko gn cs.mkr `of'
dānā cn `grain'
jati advl `as much as'
pani advl `also, also'
chaina iv1 pres <hunu+neg `is not'

7.36
tyasa- pro.dem <tyo `that'
pachi pp `after'
didī cn `sister'
tapā.ī- pro.pers `you'
ko gn cs.mkr `of'
nāso cn `property temporarily entrusted
to someone else by its owner'
bhanera tv1 abs.prt <bhannu `having said'
lakṣmī- pn `Laksmi'
le ag cs.mkr
sushīla- pn `ṣushil'
ko gn cs.mkr `of'
hāta cn `hand'
subhadrā- pn `ṣubhadra'
kā gn cs.mkr `of'

kākha- cn `lap'
mā lc cs.mkr `at, in, on'
rākhidi.in cmpdtv4 pst <rākhnu-dinu
`she put'

7.37
chorā- cn `son'
lā.ī ac cs.mkr
kākha- cn `lap'
mā lc cs.mkr `at, in, on'
liera tv1 abs.prt <linu `having taken'
subhadrā pn `ṣubhadra'
runa iv1 inf <runu `to cry'
lāgin tv1 pst <lāgnu `she began'

7.38
yī prol.adj `these'
sabai pro.nonpers `all, everything'
subhadrā- pn `ṣubhadra'
kā gn cs.mkr `of'
nimitta pp `for'
jindagī- cn `life'
bhara pp `throughout'
samjhã̄dai tv1 conj.prt <samjhanu `while
remembering'
rūdai iv1 conj.prt `crying'
garne tv1 impf.prt <garnu `doing'
khuḍkā- cn `sore points'
haru nm.plzr
thie ev1 pst <hunu `they were'

7.39
nibhne iv1 impf.prt <nibhnu
`going out (light)'
belā- cn `time'
ko gn cs.mkr `of'
battī cn `lamp'
jhaī̃ pp `like'
lakṣmī- pn `Laksmi'
ko gn cs.mkr `of'
mukha cn `face'
eka num `one'
kṣaṇa- cn `moment'

kā gn cs.mkr `of'
nimitta pp `for'
tejomaya adjl `brilliant'
bhayo ev1 pst <hunu `became'

7.40
ani advl `and then'
pachi advl `afterwards'
andhakāra cn `darkness'

7.41
lakṣmī pn `Laksmi'
yo prol.adj `this'
duḥkhamaya adjl `miserable'
asāra adjl `meaningless'
saṃsāra- cn `world'
lā.ī ac cs.mkr
choḍera tv1 abs.prt <choḍnu `having left'
ananta- cn `infinite'
mā lc cs.mkr `at, in, on'
pugin iv3 pst <pugnu `she arrived'

7.42
devīramaṇa pn `Deviraman'
naulī- pn `ṇauli'
haru nm.plzr
pani advl `also'
runa iv1 inf <runu `to cry'
lāge tv1 pst <lāgnu `they began'

7. *Nāso:* Lexicon in alphabetical order

Note: Following is a computer sorted lexicon of *Nāso* ‘Ward’. Note that the computer places vowel symbols with special diacritical marks after the last consonant symbol in alphabetical order, i. e., ā̃ with a diacritical mark is listed after all the consonant symbols. For instance, *ā̃gan* ‘courtyard’ is listed after *avasthā* ‘condition’; *kā* ‘of’ is listed after *kyāre* ‘I guess’; *cāhī̃* ‘for someone’s part’ is listed after *cyāpekī̃* ‘she had held’.

(The computer reads a diacritical mark as a letter coming after z.)

aba advl \`now'
abelā advl \`late'
abhimāna cn \`pride'
abodha adjl \`innocent'
adhiyā̃- cn \`half-share'
aghi advl \`before'
aghikai adjl \`the very previous (emph)'
agni- cn \`fire'
ahile advl \`now'
aho intj \`Oh'
ajñā- cn \`precept'
akasmāt advl \`suddenly'
akṣatā cn \`sacred rice grains'
alapa adjl \`lost'
ali adjl \`a little'
ali adjl \`some'
ali advl \`a little'
ananta adjl \`endless'
ananta- cn \`infinite'
andhakāra adjl \`dark'
andhakāra- cn \`darkness'
andhā adj \`blind'
ani advl \`and then'
anmā.une tv1 impf.prt <anmā.unu \`sending out (a bride)'
antara cn \`difference'
anubhava cn \`experience'
anupama adjl \`matchless'
anātha adj \`helpless'
anāthinī adj \`helpless'
aparādhī- cn \`criminal'
apūto adj \`childless'
are nu (used to report speech)
arkai prol.adj \`another (emph)'
arko prol.adj \`another'
arko- pro.nonpers \`other (side)'
arkā- pro.pers \`others'
aru pro \`other'
aru prol.adj \`another'
aru- pro.pers \`others'
asīma adjl \`boundless'
ashrupūrṇa adjl \`tearful'
asti advl \`day before yesterady, long before'
astu advl \`anyway'
asāmīpāta cmpdcn \`loans and debts'
asāra adjl \`meaningless'
athavā cc \`or'
atyanta advl \`extremely'
avasthā cn \`condition'
ā̃gana cn \`courtyard'
ā̃gana- cn \`courtyard'
ā̃khā cn \`eyes'
ā̃khā- cn \`eye'
ā̃su cn \`tears'
ā̃su- cn \`tears'
ā.īpugis cmpdiv1 pst <ā.unu-pugnu \`you arrived'
ā.īpugnubho cmpdiv1 pst <ā.unu-pugnu \`you arrived (honorific)'
ā.īs iv1 pst <ā.unu \`you came'
ā.ũdai iv1 impf.prt <āunu \`coming'
ā.ũdā- iv1 conj.prt <ā._nu \`while coming'

ā.iches iv1 pres <ā.unu `you have come'
ā.iches iv1 pst <ā.unu `you have come'
ā.imā.ī cn `women'
ā.imā.ī- cn `woman'
ā.unuhuncha iv1 <ā.unu `she comes'
ā.ū iv1 imp <ā.unu `may I come'
ā.ūthyo iv1 pst <ā.unu `he used to come'
āūcha iv1 pres <ā.unu `comes'
ādesha cn `order'
ādhā adjl `half'
āekī iv1 prf.prt <ā.unu `come (f.)'
āekā iv1 prf.prt <ā.unu `come'
āera iv1 abs.prt <āunu `having come'
āgo cn `fire'
āgraha cn `isistance'
āhuti cn `sacrificial offerings'
ājīvana adjl `life-long'
āja advl `today'
āja- advl `today'
ājai advl `today (emph)'
ājakāla advl `these days'
ākhira advl `finally'
ākāsha- cn `sky'
āmā cn `mother'
āmā- cn `mother'
āmā-chorī- cmpdcn `mother and daughter'
ānanda- cn `happiness'
ānanda- cn `pleasure'
ānandaprada advl `pleasant'
ānandapūrvaka adv. 'happily'
āntarika advl `internal'
āphai pro.reflx `oneself, themself'
āphaseāpha advl `on its own' (loan from Hindi)
āphnī prol.adj `one'own'
āphno pro.reflx `one's own'
āphno prol.adj `one's own'
āphukhushī advl `voluntarily'
āphū pro.reflx `oneself'
āphū- pro.reflx `oneself'
āsana- cn `seat'
āshā- cn `hope'
āshā-latā cmpdcn `grandiose hope'
āshā-pāsha cmpdcn `snare of hope'
ātmaglāni- cn `humiliation'
āvāja cn `voice'
āyu cn `life'
āḍa- cn `support'
badalā advl `instead'
bagẽ iv1 pst <bagnu `I slipped'
bage iv1 pst <bagnu `they flowed'
bagera iv1 abs.prt <bagnu `having flown'
baha cn `pain'
bahudhā advl `often'
bahuta advl `very'
bahānā- cn `excuse'
bajai cn `madam'
bajai- cn `madam'
bajyai cn `madam'
bakhata cn `time'
bakhata- cn `time'
bakhata-bakhata- cn time-to-time'
bakseko tv1 prf.prt <baksanu `given'
bala cn `strength'
balekai iv1 prf.prt <balnu `burning'
baliraheko iv1 prf.cont.prt <balnu `burning'
baliṣṭha adjl `very strong'
balla advl `finally (with great difficulty)'
banchan ev1 pres <bannu `they become'
bandī cn `prisoner'
banlā iv1 fut <bannu `will be (good)'
banā.in tv3 pst <banāunu `she made'
banāyo tv3 pst <banā.unu `he made'
banũn ev1 imp <bannu `may he be'
barara onomat
bariyāta cn `marriage procession'
bariyāta- cn `people in marriage procession'
barābara advl `frequently'

barṣa- cn 'year'
barṣa- cn 'years'
basa nu 'well (?)'
base- iv3 cond <basnu 'if stay'
basekī iv1 prf.prt <basnu 'remained'
basekī iv3 prf.prt <basnu 'seated'
basekī iv3 prf.prt <basnu 'stayed'
baseko iv3 prf.prt <basnu 'seated'
basekā iv3 prf.prt <basnu 'seated'
basera iv1 abs.prt <basnu 'being seated'
basera iv1 abs.prt <basnu 'having stayed'
basera iv3 abs.prt <basnu 'being seated'
basera iv3 abs.prt <basnu 'having been seated'
basin iv3 pst <basnu 'she sat'
basna iv3 inf <basnu 'to stay'
basnu iv1 inf <basnu 'to remain'
basnubhaeko iv3 prf.prt <basnu 'stayed'
bastĩhũ iv3 prob.pst <basnu 'I would have lived'
bastacha iv1 pres <basnu 'ramains'
basthe iv1 pst <basnu 'used to sit'
bastubhāu- cn 'cattle'
battī cn 'lamp'
battī- cn 'light'
bayāsī num 'eighty-two'
baḍhera iv1 abs.prt <baḍhnu 'having grown'
bebujha- cn 'fool'
belā- cn 'time'
bera- cn 'time'
bera- cn 'while'
berāmī adjl 'sick'
bhãḍārī- pn 'Bhanḍārī'
bha.ī iv1 pst <hunu 'she was'
bha.ikana iv1 abs.prt <hunu ' having been'
bha.in ev1 pst <hunu 'she became'
bha.isakyo cmpdev1 pst <hunu-saknu 'already became'
bhae aux cond <hunu 'if be'
bhae ev1 pst <hunu 'he became (hon.)'
bhae ev1 pst <hunu 'they became'
bhae iv1 cond <hunu 'if be'
bhae iv1 pst <hunu 'he became (honorific)'
bhae iv3 cond <hunu 'if be'
bhae- ev1 cond <hunu 'being'
bhaekī ev1 prf.prt <hunu 'been'
bhaekā ev1 prf.prt <hunu 'become'
bhaekā ev1 prf.prt <hunu 'have been'
bhaena ev2 pst <hunu+neg 'was not'
bhaepani advl 'although, even if'
bhaera ev1 abs.prt <hunu 'having been'
bhaidiyo cmpdiv1 pst <hunu+dinu 'happened'
bhairahane impf.cont.prt ev1 <hunu 'being'
bhalo-kubhalo cmpdcn 'good or bad'
bhanī tv1 pst <bhannu 'she said'
bhanchan tv1 pres <bhannu 'they call'
bhandā advl 'than'
bhandā pp 'than'
bhandāhun tv1 prob.pst <bhannu 'they would say'
bhane (bhaneko) tv1 prf.prt <bhannu 'said'
bhane sc 'if'
bhane tv1 pst <bhannu 'he said'
bhane tv1 pst <bhannu 'they said'
bhanekī tv1 prf.prt <bhannu '(she) had said'
bhaneko tv1 prf.prt <bhannu 'being said'
bhaneko tv1 prf.prt <bhannu 'called'
bhaneko tv1 prf.prt <bhannu 'said'
bhanera tv1 abs.prt <bhannu 'having said, thought (that)'
bhanera tv1 abs.prt <bhannu 'having said, thought (that)'

bhanin tv1 pst <bhannu `she said'
bhanis iv1 pst <bhannu `you said'
bhanithī tv1 prf.prt <bhannu+hunu `had said'
bhanlān tv1 fut <bhannu `will say'
bhanne sc `that'
bhanne tv1 impf.prt <bhannu `saying'
bhannuholā tv1 fut <bhannu `you will say'
bhannuhuncha tv1 <bhannu `she says'
bhannuhunthyo tv1 pst <bhannu `she used to say'
bhannā- tv1 inf <bhannu `to say'
bhanthe tv3 pst <bhannu `they used to call'
bhanthin tv1 <bhannu `she used to say'
bhanthyo tv3 pst <bhannu `he used to call'
bhanū tv1 imp <bhannu `may I say'
bharī pp `all over'
bharī pp `fully in'
bharī pp `in full'
bhara pp `throughout'
bhariyo iv1p pst <bhrinu `was filled'
bhatkāera tv1 abs.prt <bhatkā.unu `having destroyed'
bhatābhungga adjl `disarrayed'
bhayangkara adjl `dreadful'
bhayo ev1 pst <hunu `became'
bhayo iv1 pst <hunu `happened'
bhayo iv2 pst <hunu `became'
bheṭetheṃ compdiv1 prf+pst <bheṭekī thieṃ <bheṭnu+hunu `I had met'
bheṭis iv1 pst <bheṭnu `you met
bhā̃ḍo cn `pot'
bhitra advl `inside'
bhitra pp `inside'
bhitryā.isakī cmpdtv1 abs.prt <bhitryā.unu-saknu `having already entered'
bho (bhayo) iv1 pst <hunu `was'
bho ev1 pst <hunu `became'
bhoga- cn `enjoyment'
bhokā adj `hungry'
bholi advl `tomorrow'
bhukiraheko iv1 prf.prt <bhuknu `been barking'
bhāgne iv1 imp.prt <bhāgnu `running away'
bhākala cn `pledges (to gods)'
bhāna cn `appearance'
bhāta cn `rice (food)'
bhāta pn `rice'
bicarī adj `poor'
bichyā.unā- cn `bed'
bidā cn `leave'
bihāna- cn `morning'
bihānai cn `morning (emph)'
bintī cn `earnest request'
birsī tv1 pst <birsanu `she forgot'
birsera tv1 abs.prt <birsanu `having forgotten'
birsichu cmpdtv1 prf.pres <birsinu+hunu `I have forgotten'
birāyo tv1 pst <birā.unu `he did wrong'
bittikai advl `as soon as'
bībhatsa adjl `horrible'
bīca-bīca- cn `intervals'
bīcai- cn `middle (emph)'
bīja cn `seed'
bīsai num `twenty (emph)'
bīsauṃ num `twentieth, twenties (?)'
bokera tv1 abs.prt <boknu `having carried'
boldathī iv1 pst <bolnu `she used to speak'
brahmavādī- cn `philosopher of the Vedanta school'
brāhmaṇa- pn `Brahman (name of a Hindu caste)'
buddhi cn `intelligence'
buddhi- cn `intelligence'
buhārtana cn `hardship of a daughter-in-law's life'
bā intj (used in expressing entreatment)

bāa.ũdai tv1 conj.prt <bā.unu `while opening'
bābu cn `baby'
bābu cn `boy'
bādala- cn `clouds'
bāheka pp `except'
bāhira advl `outside'
bāhra num `twelve'
bāje cn `sir'
bāje- cn `sir'
bālīnālī cn `crops'
bāla-haṭha- cmpdcn `child's persistence'
bāla-krīḍā cmpdcn `child-play'
bālaka cn `boy'
bālaka cn `infant'
bālaka- cn `child'
bālaka-kāla- cmpdcn `childhood'
bālakha- cn `child'
bālalīlā cmpdcn `child-play'
bāle tv1 pst <bālnu `he lit'
bālikā- cn `girl'
bāṅggina iv1p inf <bāṅgginu `to be crooked'
bārdalī- cn `balcony'
bārera tv1 abs.prt <bārnu `having built'
bāṭa ab cs.kr `from'
bāṭa ab cs.mkr `from'
bāṭa ag sb.mkr
bāṭo cn `path'
bāṭā- cn <bāṭo `way'
būṭī-jantara cmpdcn `herbs and amulet'
būḍhā-būḍhī cmpdcn `old men and old women'
bā̃dhin tv1 pst <bā̃dhunu `she tied'
bā̃kī adjl `remaning'
bā̃ḍna tv2 inf <bā̃ḍnu `to distribute, give away'
caina cn `enjoyment'
caldai iv1 conj.prt <calnu `while moving'
calāekā tv1 prf.prt <calāunu `run, maintained'
camcā- cn `spoon'
camenā cn `snack'
candrashamashera pn `Chandrashamsher'
cariraheka iv1 prf.cont.prt <charnu `been feeding'
carna iv1 inf <carnu `to feed'
catura adjl `wise'
caukīdāra cn `guardian'
cautāro cn `platform built under a tree'
cañcalāshrī cn `Goddess of wealth'
caṭakka advl `completely'
cha aux <hunu `have'
cha aux <rahanu `has'
cha aux pres <hunu `has'
cha aux pres <hunu `have'
cha aux pres <hunu `is'
cha aux pres <hunu `she has'
cha ev1 pres <hunu `he is'
cha ev1 pres <hunu `is'
cha iv1 pres <hunu `is (she has)'
cha iv1 pres <hunu `is'
cha iv2 pres <hunu `is'
cha iv3 pres <hunu `is'
cha num `six'
chaina iv1 pres <hunu+neg `is not'
chan iv1 pres <hunu `they are'
chan iv1 pres <hunu `they are'
charera tv1 abs.prt <charnu `having scattered'
charne impf.prt <charnu `scattering'
chauṃ aux pres <hunu `we have'
chaũ aux pres <hunu `we have'
chekincha tv1p pres <chekinu `is blocked'
cheḍa cn `taunt'
cheḍlā tv1 fut <cheḍnu `he will pierce'
chicolīnasaknu adjl `impassable'
chih intj `Fie!, shame!'
chimekī- cn `neighbors'
chimeka- cn `neighbor'
china cn `moment'
china- cn `momemt'

chiyāchiyā adjl `broken (into pieces)'
chiḥ intj `Fie! shame!'
chopekī iv1 prf.prt <chopnu `covered'
chopera tv1 abs.prt <chopnu `having covered'
chorī cn `daughter'
choro cn `son'
chorā cn `sons'
chorā- cn `son'
chorā-chorī cmpdcn `sons and daughters'
choḍī tv1 abs.prt <choḍnu `having released'
choḍdainathyo tv1 pst <choḍnu+neg `he would not leave'
choḍera tv1 abs.prt <choḍnu `having left'
choḍidiūlā cmpdtv1 fut <choḍnu-dinu `I will leave'
choḍina tv1 pst <choḍnu+neg `she did not quit'
choḍnu tv1 inf <choḍnu `leave'
choḍnu tv1 inf <choḍnu `to leave'
chu aux pres <hunu `I am'
chu aux pres <hunu `I have'
chāka cn `meal'
chātī- cn `chest, heart'
chātra- cn `student'
chāḍnu tv1 inf <choḍnu `to leave'
cicilo adj `infant'
cine tv1 pst <cinnu `he built'
cineko tv1 prf.prt <cinnu `built'
cinnai tv1 inf <cinnu `to recognize (emph)'
ciplera iv1 abs.prt <ciplanu `having slipped'
cira adjl `long'
citta cn `mind'
cora- cn `thief'
coṭa cn `wound'
cyāpekī tv1 prf.prt <cyāpnu `held'
cāhī postf `for someone's part'
cāhincha iv1p pres <cāhinu `is needed'
cāhiṃ postf `for someome's part'
cākarnī cn `female slave'
cākarnī cn `slave'
cāra num `four'
cāroṭā num.specif `four ones'
cūpacāpa advl `silently'
cā̃ḍai advl `quickly'
ḍīla- cn `edge'
ḍhalamala adjl `weak'
ḍhogidi.ī cmpdiv1 pst <ḍhognu-dinu `she greeted'
ḍhogidi.ī cmpdtv1 pst <ḍhognu-dinu `she greeted'
ḍhokā- cn `gate'
ḍhunggo cn `rock'
ḍolī cn `litter'
ḍolī- cn `litter'
ḍubcha iv1 pres <ḍubnu `sinks'
ḍāgḍara cn `doctor'
dagurdai iv1 conj.prt <dagurnu `while running'
dailo cn `door'
dainika adjl `daily'
daiva- cn `Fate'
damā.ī-ḍole cmpdcn `band and litter-carriers'
darshana- cn `auspicious meeting'
daulatha cn `wealth'
daulatha- cn `wealth'
daurā cn `a typical ṇepalese shirt'
dauḍera iv1 abs.prt <dauḍanu `having run'
daṇḍavat cn `greeting'
dekhī tv1 abs.prt <dekhnu `having seen'
dekhcha iv1 pres <dekhnu `he sees'
dekhchan tv1 pres <dekhnu `they see'
dekhdai tv1 conj.prt <dekhnu `while seeing'
dekhdathe tv1 pst <dekhnu `he used to see'
dekhdā- tv1 conj.prt <dekhnu `while seeing'

dekhekī tv1 prf.prt <dekhnu `seen'
dekhena tv1 pst <dekhnu `he did not see'
dekhenan tv1 pst <dekhnu+neg `he did not see'
dekhera tv1 abs.prt <dekhnu `having seen'
dekhi pp `after'
dekhi pp `since'
dekhiko pp `since'
dekhinthyo iv1p pst <dekhinu `used to seem (seemed)'
dekhna tv1 inf <dekhnu `to see'
dekhā.ūdā tv1 conj.prt <dekhā.unu `while showing'
dekhāera iv1 abs.prt <dekhaunu `having pointed'
delā tv1 fut <dinu `he will give'
devī cn `goddess'
devī-devatā- cmpdcn `gods and goddesses'
devīramaṇa pn `Deviraman'
devīramaṇa- cn `Deviraman'
devīramaṇa- pn `Deviraman'
deva-gaṇa cmpdcn `gods'
devatā- cn `gods'
dhamilo adj `dim'
dhana cn `wealth'
dhanavāna adjl `wealthy'
dharma cn `religion'
dharma cn `righteousness'
dherai adjl `many'
dherai adjl `much, long'
dhikkāra cn `curse'
dhāmī-jhā̃krī- cmpdcn `shamans and medicine men'
dhāraṇa cn `assumption'
dhārā cn `flow(s)'
dhūlo cn `dust'
di.in tv2 pst `she gave'
di.irahekā tv1 prf.cont.prt <dinu `been giving'
didī cn `sister'
didī cn `sister'
dieko tv1 prf.prt <dinu `been let out'
diekā tv1 prf.prt <dinu `given'
dikka cn `worry, trouble, vexation'
dina cn `day'
dina cn `days'
dina-rāta cmpdcn `day and night'
dinahū advl `always, everyday'
dincha tv1 pres <dinu `he gives'
dinnathin tv1 pst <dinu `she would not allow'
dinthe tv2 pst <dinu `they used to give'
dinthin tv1 pst <dinu `she used to give'
dinā- cmpdtv1 inf <dinu `to let'
diṃdā tv2 conj.prt <dinu `while giving'
dohoryāe tv1 pst <dohoryā.unu `he repeated'
dolā.ī cn `quilt'
doṣa cn `blame'
dṛśya cn `scene'
dṛśya cn `sight'
duī num `two'
dubai pro `both'
dubai prol.adj `both'
dubai- pro `both'
dublī adj `thin'
dukhcha iv1 pres <dukhnu `hurts'
dukhā.ī tv1 pst <dukhā.unu `she hurt'
dukhā.inan tv1 pst <dukhā.unu `she did not hurt'
dukhā.una tv1 inf <dukhā.unu `hurt'
dukhāe tv1 cond <dukhā.unu `if hurt'
dulahī cn `bride'
dulahī- cn `bride'
dulāhā cn `bridegroom'
duḥkhī adj `unhappy'
duḥkhī- cn `miserable'
duḥkha cn `hardship'
duḥkha cn `sorrow'
duḥkha- cn `sorrow'
duḥkha-pīra- cmpdcn `suffering and pain'

duḥkhamanāu cn `sorrowful complains'
duḥkhamaya adjl `full of misery'
duḥkhamaya adjl `miserable'
dvanda cn `conflict'
dānā cn `grain'
dāsī cn slave'
dāsa-jīvana- cmpdcn `slave-life'
eka num `one'
eka- num `one'
ekadama advl `completely'
ekadama advl `very'
ekai adjl `one and the same'
ekai num `one (emph)'
eklai advl `alone'
ekādashī pn `Ekādashī (eleventh day in lunar calender)'
euṭā num.specif `one'
ga.ī iv1 abs.prt <jānu `having gone'
ga.in iv1 pst <jānu `she went'
gadgad adjl `very happy'
gae iv1 pst <jānu `he went'
gae- iv1 cond <jānu `if go'
gae[ko] prf.prt <jānu `gone, past'
gaha- cn `eye'
gai iv1 abs.prt <jānu `having gone'
ganīraheki tv1 prf.cont.prt <gannu `been counting'
garī advlzr
garchan tv1 pres <garnu `they do'
gardīho tv1 prob.pst <garnu `she would do'
gardacha tv1 pres <garnu `does'
gardai tv1 conj.prt <garnu `while doing'
gardā tv1 conj.prt <garnu `while doing'
gare tv1 pst <garnu `he did'
garekī tv1 prf.prt <garnu `done'
gareko iv1 prf.prt <garnu `done'
gareko tv1 prf.prt <garnu `done'
garera tv1 abs.prt <garnu `having done'
garera tv3 abs.prt <garnu `having done'
garethe cmpdtv1 pst <garnu+hunu `had done' (garekā thie)*
garidie cmpdtv1 cond <garnu+dinu `if do'
garidiun cmpdtv1 imp <garnu-dinu `may he make'
garin tv1 pst <garnu `she did'
gariraheka tv1 prf.cont.prt <garnu `been doing'
garna tv1 inf <garnu `to do'
garna tv3 inf <garnu `to do'
garna- tv1 inf <garnu `to do'
garne tv1 impf.prt <garnu `doing, performing'
garnubhayo tv1 pst <garnu `did (polite)'
garnā- tv1 inf <garnu `to do'
garthin tv1 pst <garnu `she used to do'
garthyo tv1 pst <garnu `he used to do'
garā.unu tv1 inf <garnu (caus.) `cause to do'
garū tv1 imp <garnu `may I do'
garū tv1 pst <garnu `I did'
garūlā tv1 fut <garnu `I shall do'
garūn iv1 imp <garnu `may he do'
garūn tv1 imp <garnu `may he do'
gati cn `condition'
gati cn `way'
gaurīghāṭa pn `Gaurīhgāṭ (name of a sacred place)'
gaṇḍakī pn `Gandaki (name of a river)'
ghaniṣṭha adjl `intimate'
ghara cn `home'
ghara- cn `house, home'
gharai cn `home (emph)'
ghartinī cn `a woman of Gharti cast, once slaves in ṇepal'
ghaḍī cn `hour'
gherirahe[ko]- iv1 prf.cont.prt <ghernu `been surrounding'
ghu_co cn `crowd'

ghāma- cn `sunlight'
gorakhā pn `Gorkha'
goṭhālā- cn `shepherds (fools)'
goḍā cn `foot'
grāmiṇa adjl `rustic'
gṛha- cn `house'
gṛhakalaha- cn `family feud'
gṛhakṛtya cn `household chores'
gṛhalakṣmī cmpdcn `Wealth of house'
gujarāna cn `sustenance'
gujārā cn `maintenance'
gujārā cn `sustenannce'
guru- cn `teacher'
gā.ũ- cn `village'
gāuṃle adjl `rural'
gāũ- cn `village'
gāũ- cn `village'
gā̃sa cn `a measure of mouthful food'
gā̃sa cn `mouthful'
gā̃sdai tv1 conj.prt <gā̃snu `while joining'
gā̃siraheki tv1 prf.cont.prt <gā̃snu `joining'
hā̃ qw
hā̃sā.ũchan tv1 pres <h_asā.unu `he causes to laugh'
hajāravāra num `thousand times'
haraeka adjl `every'
hare intj `Oh !'
harivaṃsha pn `Harivamsha'
haru nm.plzr
hatyā cn `murder'
haṇḍī cn `a religious social security pension'
helā cn `disregard'
hera iv1 imp. <hernu `look'
here iv1 pst <hernu `he looked'
herera iv1 abs.prt <hernu `having looked'
herin iv1 pst <hernu `she looked at'
heriraheka tv1 prf.cont.prt <hernu `been watching'
hĩḍnubhaecha pst iv1 `you left'
hindū pn `Hindu'
ho ev1 pres <hunu `is'
ho intj `Oh, yes'
ho iv1 pres <hunu `ho'
ho iv1 pres <hunu `is'
hoina iv pres <hunu+neg `is not'
hoina iv1 pres <hunu+neg `is not'
holā aux fut <hunu `must (probably)'
holā iv1 fut <hunu `will be'
holān aux fut <hunu `they must'
hos iv1 imp <hunu `may (he) be'
hṛdaya cn `heart'
hṛdaya- cn `heart'
hṛdaya-kusuma cmpdcn `flower of heart'
hucīla pn `owl'
hukahuka onommat `hooting sound'
hula- cn `crowd'
hun ev1 pres <hunu `they are'
huna iv1 inf <hunu `to be'
huna.āyo cmpdev1 pst <hunu+ā.unu `came to be'
hunagayo cmpdev1 pst <hunu+jānu `happened to be'
huncha intj `yes (okay)'
huncha intj `yes (okay)'
huncha iv1 pres <hunu `(It) is (good)'
huncha iv1 pres <hunu `becomes'
huncha iv1 pres <hunu `happens'
hunchan ev1 pres <hunu `they become'
hune iv1 impf.prt <hunu `being'
hune iv1 impf.prt <hunu `being'
hunthe ev1 pst <hunu `he would be'
hunthe ev1 pst <hunu `he would be'
hunthyo ev1 pst <hunu `would be'
hunthyo iv1 pst <hunu `he used to be'
hunthyo iv1 pst <hunu `used to be'
hunthyo iv1 pst <hunu `used to be'
hunthyo iv2 pst <hunu `used to be'
hunubhae[ko] ev1 prf.prt <hunu `become'
hunuhuncha ev1 pres <hunu `she is'
hunā- ev1 inf <hunu `to be'

hunā- ev1 inf <hunu `to be'
hurkā.in tv1 pst <hurkā.unu `she raised'
hāhākāra cn `commotion'
hāla cn `news'
hāla cn `news'
hālidie cmpdtv4 pst <hālnu-dinu `they put in'
hālidiera cmpdtv1 abs.prt <hālnu-dinu `having imposed'
hālidinthin cmpdtv4 pst <hālnu-dinu `she would put'
hāmī pro.pers `we'
hāmī pro.pers `we'
hāmī- pro.pers `we'
hānathāpa- cn `competition'
hānera tv1 abs.prt <hānnu `having hit'
hārna tv1 inf <hārnu `to lose'
hāta cn `hand'
hāta cn `hand'
hāta- cn `hand'
hāta- cn `hand'
hāta-kākha- cmpdcn `hand and lap'
hāvā cn `wind'
hāḍa-chālā cmpdcn `bone and skin'
hāḍachālā cmpdcn `bones and skin'
hũ aux pres <hunu `I have'
hũ ev1 pres <hunu `I am'
hũdaina aux pres <hunu+neg `must not'
hũdoho aux prob.pst <hunu `he would'
hũdoho aux prob.pst <hunu `would have been'
hũdohũ aux prob.pst <hunu `I would have'
hā̃sne- impf.prt <hā̃snu `laughers (laughing ones)'
hā̃sthe iv1 pst <hā̃snu `they used to laugh'
icchā cn `wish'
icchā- cn `desire'
ityādi adjl `such'
ityādi adjl `such'
ityādi adjl `such'
jīu- cn `body'
jīu- cn `body'
jīvana- cn `life'
jīvana- cn `life'
jīvana- cn `life'
jīvanādhāra cmpdcn `support of life'
jabarajastī advl `forcibly'
jagata- cn `world'
jahājai cn `ship (emph)'
jahāna- cn `family'
janggabahādura- pn `Jangabahadur'
janma cn `birth, life'
janma- cn `life'
janā specif `human individuals'
janā- specif `human individuals'
janā- specif `human individuals'
jaro cn `fever'
jarā- `root'
jasa pro.rel <jo `who'
jasa- pro.nonpers <jo `anyone'
jastī adj `like'
jasto adj `like'
jasto pp `like'
jati advl `as much as'
javāpha cn `answer'
jesukai pro.nonpers `whatsoever'
jhaī pp `like'
jhagaḍā cn `quarrel'
jhalkiraheko iv1p prf.cont.prt <jhalkinu `been appearing'
jhan advl `furthermore'
jharkera iv1 abs.prt <jharkanu `being angry'
jharna iv1 inf <jharna `to drop'
jhaḍangge adjl `ill-tempered'
jhaṇḍai advl `almost'
jhaṇḍai advl `almost'
jhutrā adj `ragged'
jhuṇḍiraheko iv1 prf.prt <jhuṇḍinu `been hanging'
jhuṇḍyāyau iv1 pst <jhuṇḍyā.unu `you hung'

jhārdai tv1 conj.prt <jhārnu `dropīng'
jhārdai tv1 conj.prt <jhārnu `dropping'
jhārdai tv1 conj.prt <jhārnu `dropping'
jhārthin tv1 pst <jhārnu `she used to drop'
jiddī cn `insistence'
jindagī- cn `life'
jita cn `victory'
jo pro.rel `which'
jo pro.rel `who'
jo pro.rel `who'
jorīpārī- cn `neighbors'
jorīpārī- cn `neighbors'
juṭho-cūlho cmpdcn `dirty-kitchen'
jyoti cn `light'
jyotiṣi- cn `astrologer'
jyādā adjl `excessive'
jyālā cn `wages'
jñāna cn `knowledge'
jā.auṃ iv1 imp <jānu `let us go'
jā.auṃ iv1 imp <jānu `let us go'
jāgā adjl `vigilant'
jāna iv1 inf <jānu `to go'
jāna iv1 inf <jānu `to go'
jāna iv1 inf <jānu `to go'
jānches iv1 pres <jānu `you will go'
jānchu iv1 pres <jānu `I (will) go'
jānchu iv1 pres <jānu `I (will) go'
jānchu iv1 pres <jānu `I (will) go'
jānchyau iv1 pres <jānu `will you go'
jāne iv1 impf.prt <jānu `going'
jāne iv1 inf.prt <jānu `going'
jānera tv1 abs.prt <jānnu `having understood'
jānisaknu cmpdtv1 inf <jānnu-saknu `can know'
jānos tv1 imp <jānnu `may he know'
jānthin iv1 pst <jānu `she would go'
jānthyo iv1 pst <jānu `he would go'
jānthyo iv1 pst <jānu `he would go'
jānubhayo iv1 pst <jānu `he went (honorific)'
jāos iv1 imp <jānu `may he go'
jātrū- cn `pilgrim'
jā̃dīhũ iv1 prob.pst <jānu `I would go'
jā̃dai iv1 conj.prt <jānu `going'
jā̃dainathin iv1 pst <jānu+neg `she would not go'
jā̃dā iv1 conj.prt <jānu `while arriving'
kī gn cs.mkr `of'
kahile advl `sometimes'
kahile advl `when'
kahilekāhīṃ advl `sometimes'
kahilyai advl `ever'
kahilyai advl `ever'
kahā̃ advl `where'
kahā̃ pp `at'
kaile advl `when'
kaiyana adjl `several'
kalaha cn `quarrel'
kalpanātīta adjl `highly imaginary'
kanggāla adjl `penniless'
kanyā-pakṣa- cmpdcn `bride's side'
kapāla- cn `mind, hair, head'
kara- cn `compulsion'
kartavya cn `duty'
karuṇā cn `compassion'
karuṇā- cn `compassion'
karuṇājanaka adjl `pathetic'
karā.une iv1 impf.prt `shouting, howling, hooting'
kasa pro.interrog <ko `who'
kasai- pro.pers `anyone'
kasai- pro.pers <ko `anyone (emph)'
kasai- pro.pers <ko `anyone (emph)'
kasarī adv `how'
kastī adj `how'
kasto adj `how'
kati advl `how much'
katro adjl `how big'
katā advl `whither'
kaṭero cn `hut'
kaḍuwā cn `mustard'
kaḍā adjl `severe, hard'
ke pro.interrog `what'
ke prol.adj `what'

ke qw
kehĩ adjl `any, some'
kehĩ adjl `some'
kehĩ advl `somewhat'
kehĩ advl `somewhat'
kehĩ pro.nonpers `anything'
kehĩ pro.nonpers `something'
kehi adjl `some'
keko prol.adj `what'
kevala advl `only'
khane tv1 pst <knannu `he dug (built)'
kharca-barca cn `things to eat'
khaschaũ iv1 pres <khasnu `we drop'
khaschan iv1 pres <khasnu `they drop'
khasisake- cmpdiv1 cond <khasi-saknu `if drop'
khasnu iv1 inf <khasnu `to drop'
khasro-masinu cmpdcn `rough or fine'
khasyo iv1 pst <khasnu `he dropped'
khaṭirā cn `boils'
khaḍā adjl `present, standing'
kheliraheko iv1 prf.cont.prt <khelnu `been playing'
kheliraheka iv1 prf.cont.prt <khelnu `been playing'
khelāeko tv1 prf.prt <khelāunu `play'
kheta-bārī cmpdcn `crop fields'
khinna adjl `sad'
khitkā cn `titter'
kho.ĩ intj `where is?'
khojī cn `question, search'
khojdacha aux pres <khojnu `wants'
khojdathe aux pst <khojnu `he would want'
khojna tv1 inf <khijnu `to look for'
khojthyo aux pst <khojnu `he would want'
khokirahanuhuncha iv1 pres <khoknu `she keeps coughing'
khopā- cn `hole'
khuwā.irahekī tv2 prf.cont.prt <khuwā.unu `been feeding'
khuḍkā- cn `sore points'
khwā.uṃthe tv1 pst <khwa.unu `he used to feed'
khā.ĩ tv1 pst <khānu `she ate'
khā.i iv1 impf.prt <khānu `eating'
khā.i iv1 impf.prt <khānu `eating'
khā.i- tv1 impf.prt <kānu `eating'
khā.in tv1 pst <khānu `she ate'
khā.ũ tv1 imp <khānu `may I eat'
khāera tv1 abs.prt <knānu `having taken'
khāksī cn `phthisis'
khāna tv1 inf <khānu `to eat'
khāpera tv1 abs.prt <khāpnu `having overlaid'
khāṭa- cn `cot'
ki cc `or'
ki qw
kina advl `why'
kinaki cc `because'
kintu cc `but'
kisāna- cn `farmer'
ko gn cs.mkr `of'
ko pro.interrog `who'
ko- pro.interrog `who'
kokha cn `womb'
komala adjl `tender'
koshisha- cn `effort'
koṭhā cn `room'
koṭhā- cn `room
kṛtaghna adjl `ungrateful'
kṛtya- cn `act'
kukura cn `dog'
kulāvalamba- cmpdcn `anchor of the family'
kumle adjl `carrying baggages'
kuna prol.adj `which'
kunai adjl `some'
kuraikurā- cn `talks'
kurā cn `matter'
kurā cn `talk'
kurā cn `talks'
kurā cn `thing'
kurā cn `thought'

kurā- cn `thing, matter'

kurā- cn `things'

kurākānī cn `coversation'

kyāre nu `probaly, I guess'

kā gn cs.mkr `of'

kā nm.plzr `of'

kākhī- cn `human body part under the arm'

kākha- cn `lap'

kālo adj `black'

kāma cn `act'

kāma cn `job'

kāma cn `work'

kāma cn `work, use'

kāma- cn `act'

kārāgāra- cn `prison'

kāṭiyo iv1p pst <kāṭinu `was cut (grieved)'

kāṭnu tv1 inf <kāṭnu `to cut'

kṣaṇa- cn `moment'

lagāe tv1 pst <lagā.unu `he organized'

lagāekī prf.prt <lagā.unu `wearing'

lagāekī tv1 prf.prt <lagā.unu `wearing'

laharī cn `wave'

laijānu- tv1 inf <laijānu `to take'

lakṣmī pn `Laksmi'

lakṣmī- pn `Laksmi'

larbarieko iv1 prf.prt <larbarinu `faultering'

lau nu

le ag cs.mkr

le in cs.mkr `because, by, with'

le in cs.mkr `by with'

le in cs.mkr `by, because, with'

lie tv1 pst <linu `he took'

lienan tv1 pst <linu+neg `he did not take'

liera tv1 abs.prt <linu `having taken'

lugā cn `clothes'

lukiraheko iv1 prf.cont.prt <luknu `being hidden'

lukna iv1 inf <luknu `to hide'

lupta adjl `lost'

lyāera tv1 abs.prt <lyā.unu `having brought (in marriage)'

lā.ī ac cs.mkr

lā.ī dt cs.mkr `to'

lā.ī tv1 pst <lā.unu `she wore'

lā.i ac cs.mkr

lā.i dt cs-mkr `to'

lā.una tv1 inf <lā.unu `to rub, apply'

lā.ū tv1 imp <lā.unu `may I wear'

lāekī tv1 prf.prt <lā.unu `wearing'

lāgdacha ev1p pres <lāgnu `is applied'

lāgdaina iv1 pres <lāgnu+neg `does not take'

lāgdo iv1 conj.prt <lāgnu `striking'

lāge tv1 pst <lāgnu `he began'

lāge tv1 pst <lāgnu `they began'

lāgekī tv1 prf.prt <lāgnu `begun'

lāgeko iv1 prf.prt <lāgnu `struck'

lāgeko tv1 prf.prt <lāgnu `begun'

lāgeko tv1 prf.prt <lāgnu `begun'

lāgin tv1 pst <lāgnu `she began'

lāgithin comptv1 pst <lāgnu+hunu `had begun'

lāgnu iv1 inf <lagnu `to strike'

lāgthe iv1 pst <lāgnu `they would begin'

lāgthyo iv2 pst <lāgnu `used to strike'

lāgyo ev2 pst <lāgnu `seemed'

lāgyo iv1 pst <lāgnu `he moved'

lāgyo tv1 pst <lāgnu `he began'

lālana-pālana- cmpdcn `love and nourishment'

lālasā- cn `desire'

lāmo adj `long'

mīṭho adj `good (food)'

ma pro.pers `I'

ma- pro.pers `I'

maccā.irahanchan tv1 pres.cont <macca.unu `they keep making (commotion)'

madhuro adj `faint'

mahīnā- cn `month'

mahādīpa cmpdcn `great-lamp'

mahān adjl `great'
mahārāja cn `king'
mai lc cs.mkr `at, in, on (emph)'
mai- pro.pers <ma `I'
mailo adj `dirty'
mailo cn `dirt'
mailā adj `dirty'
mala cn `firtilizer'
malina adj `faint, dirty'
malino adj `faint'
mana- cn `mind'
manamana cn `mind-mind'
manamana- cn `mind-mind'
manamanai cn `mind-mind (emph)'
mandira- cn `temple'
mani pp `under'
mano-mālinya- cmpdcn `animosity'
manomandira cn `fictitious castle'
manovedanā- cnpdcn `mental pain'
manovijñāna cn `psychology'
manuṣya- cn `man'
matalabī adjl `selfish'
maukā cn `opportunity'
maṭha- cn `mound'
maṇḍapa- cn `pavillion'
merī pro.pers `my'
mero pro.pers `my'
micna tv1 inf <micnu `to press, rub, massage'
milethyo tv1 pst <milnu `had been obtained'
milthyo iv1 pst <milnu `agreed, matched'
mola cn `price'
mṛgatṛṣṇā cmpdcn `mirage'
mukha cn `face'
mukha cn `mouth'
mukha- cn `face'
mukha- cn `mouth'
mukhamaṇḍala- cmpdcn `face'
mukta adj `free'
mula- cn `origin'
muskila adjl `hard'
muṭhī cn `handful'
muṭu cn `heart'
muṭu- cn `heart'
mwā.ī cn `kiss'
mā lc cs-mkr `at, in, on'
mā lc cs.mkr `at, in, on'
māgera tv1 abs.prt <māgnu `having asked for'
māgha pn `ṃagh (Januaray-February)'
māhurī pp `bees'
māliknī cn `female owner' mistress'
mānava-jāti- cmpdcn `human race'
mānisa cn `men'
mānisa- cn `man'
mānnubhaena iv1 pst <mānnu+neg `did not agree to'
mānnuhunthyo iv1 pst <mānnu `he used to feel'
mānā- cn `a measure of food'
māthi pp `over'
mātra advl `only'
mātṛviyoga cmpdcn `separation from mother'
māyālāgdī adj `pitiable'
mūka adjl `mute'
na cc `nor'
na nu `simply (?)'
nabha-sthala- cmpdcn `firmament'
nabhae iv1 cond <na+hunu `if not be'
nabhae sc `if not'
nabhaekī iv1 prf.prt <na+hunu `not having'
nadekhdā tv1 conj.prt <na+dekhnu `while not seeing'
nagare tv1 cond <na+garnu `if not do'
nahune aux inf.prt <na+hunu `must not have'
nai nu `(emphatic)'
najīkai advl `near'
najānekā tv1 prf.prt <na+jānnu `not knowing'
naki cc `not'

nali.ikana tv1 abs.prt <na+linu `not having taken'
namaskāra cn `greeting, good bye'
napā.ī tv1 abs.prt <na+pā.unu `not having received'
napā.ũdai tv1 conj.prt <pā.unu `while not getting'
naramā.ilo adj `unpleasant'
narāmro adj `bad'
nasak[i]ne auxp impf.prt <na+sakinu `(one that) cannot be'
nasake aux cond <na+saknu `if cannot'
nasunidie- cmpdtv1 cond <na+sunnu-dinu `if not listen'
naulī pn `ṇauli'
naulīl- pn `ṇauli'
naulīrūpī cmpdadjl `(in) the form of ṇauli'
naulo adj `strange'
nayana- cn `eye'
nayā̃ adj `new'
nayā̃ adjl `new'
nepāla pn `Nepal'
nera pp `near'
ni nuance word
nibhna iv1 inf <nibhnu `to die out'
nibhne iv1 impf.prt <nibhnu `going out (light)'
nidrā cn `sleep'
nidā.urī adj `sad'
niko adj `healed'
niko adjl `healed'
nimitta pp `for'
nimti pp `for'
nirmāṇa cn `construction'
nisteja adjl `pale'
niyālera iv1 abs.prt <niyālnu `having peered'
nokara-cākara cmpdcn `servants and serfs'
nuhāuna iv1 inf <nuhā.unu `to bath'
nāciraheko iv1 prf.cont.prt <nāchnu `been dancing'
nāka cn `nose'
nānī cn `little child'
nārī-svabhāva- cmpdcn `woman's nature'
nāso cn `property temporarily entrusted to someone else by its owner'
ochyāna cn `bed'
ochyāna- cn `bed'
oho intj `Oh!'
oilāyo iv1 pst <oilā.unu `he withered'
oḍhne- cn `shawl'
pachī advl `behind'
pachi advl `afterwards'
pachi pp `after'
pachiko `after'
pachiko pp `after'
paga cn `feet'
pahilo adj `first'
paisā pn `smallest unit of ṇepalese currency'
paisā- cn `money'
pakha- pp `toward (morning and evening)'
pakrane tv1 impf.prt <pakranu `catching'
pakā.unu tv1 inf <pakā.unu `cook'
pakā.unuhuncha tv1 pres <pakā.unu `he cooks'
pakā.ũcha tv1 pres <pakā.unu `cooks'
pakṣī- cn `bird'
pallo adj `next'
palṭe iv1 pst <palṭanu `he lay'
panchiyo iv1p pst <panchinu `moved away'
pani advl `also, even'
pani advl `also, even'
para advl `further'
parameshvara cn `Lord'
parameshvara cn `god'
parameshvara- cn `god'
parantu cc `but'
paraspara advl `mutually'

paratra cn `next life'
parcha aux pres <parnu `must'
pardā aux conj.prt <parnu `when having to'
pardā iv1 conj.prt <parnu `while happening'
pare aux cond <parnu `if must'
parevā cn `pigeons'
parevā- cn `pigeon'
paricita adjl `acquainted'
paripūrṇa adjl `filled'
parivartanashīla adjl `changing'
pariā.ūdā cmpdiv1 conj.prt <parnu-āunu `while happening'
parkhī iv1 abs.prt <parkhanu `having haulted, waited'
parlā aux fut <parnu `will have'
parlā iv3 fut `will fall'
parne aux impf.prt <parnu `must'
parthyo aux pst <parnu `had (pst of must)'
paryo aux pst <parnu `had'
paryo aux pst <parnu `had to'
paryo iv2 pst <parnu `fell, happened'
paścima cn `west'
paśupati- pn `Pashupati'
pashupatinātha- pn `Pashupatinath'
pasin iv3 pst <pasnu `she entered'
pasne- iv1 impf.prt <pasnu `entering'
patana cn `fall'
pati- cn `husband'
patiparāyaṇā adj `loyal to husband'
patnī cn `wife'
pavitra adjl `pure'
paṭṭi pp `toward'
paḍhera tv1 abs.per <paḍhnu `having read'
peṭa cn `stomach'
phalaĩcā- cn `bench'
phale-phuleko cmpdadj `prosperous'
pharkanubhae- iv1 cond <pharkanu `if return'
pharke- iv1 cond <pharkanu `if return'
pharkera iv1 abs.prt <pharkanu `having turned'
phauja- cn `army'
pheri advl `again'
phikrī- cn `concern'
phupū cn `aunt'
phupū- cn `aunt'
phāguna pn `name of a ṇepali month Phagun (February-ṃarch)'
pilapila advl `atwinkle'
pitṛ - cn `ancestor'
piṃḍī- cn `porch'
po nu `rather'
poi- cn `husband'
pokhne tv1 impf.prt <pokhnu `pouring, spilling'
poko cn `bundle'
potna tv1 inf <potnu `to paint, clean'
prabala adjl `strong'
prabhu cn `Lord'
prakāsha- cn `light'
prashna cn `question'
pratīta adjl `one that seems'
pratidina- advl `everyday, day after day'
prema cn `love, affection'
preraṇā- cn `inspiration'
prārabdha- cn `ḍestiny'
prāṇī- cn `creature'
pṛthvī- cn `earth'
puchine tv1p impf.prf <puchinu `(to) be wiped'
pugdacha iv3 pres <pugnu `arrives'
pugin iv3 pst <pugnu `she arrived'
pugisakthe cmpdiv pst <pugnu-saknu `would have already reached'
pugthyo iv1 pst <pugnu `he used to arrive'
pugyo iv3 pst <pugnu `he arrived'
puraskāra cn `reward'
purānī adj (f) `old'
purāno adj (m) `old'
purānā adj (pl) `old'

purāṇa cn `Purana (legends)'
putra cn `son'
putra-vātsalya- cmpdcn `love for son'
putravatī adj `woman with a son'
puṇya cn `religious merit'
puṇya cn `religious merit'
puṇya-bhoga cmpdcn `enjoyment of religious merit'
puṇyabhogī adjl `enjoyer of religious merit'
pyāro adj `dear'
pyāsa cn `thirst'
pyāsā adj `thirsty'
pā.ī tv1 abs.prt <pā.unu `having received'
pā.ina tv1 pst <pā.unu+neg `I did not get'
pā.iyos tv1p imp <pā.unu `may we get'
pāe tv1 pst <pā.unu `he got'
pāekī tv1 prf.prt <pā.unu `begotten'
pāera tv1 abs.prt <pā.unu `having gained'
pāhunā-pāsā- cmpdcn `guests and invitees'
pānī cn `water'
pānasa- cn `lamp-stand'
pāpī adj `sinner'
pāpapūrṇa adjl `full of sins'
pāpinī- adj `sinner'
pārera tv1 abs.prt <pārnu `having made'
pāta cn `leaf'
pāta cn `leaf/leaves'
pāṭha cn `lesson'
pāṭha cn `recitation of sacred texts'
pāṇigrahaṇa cn `wedding'
pāṇḍitya cn `wisdom'
pūjā cn `worship'
pūrvaka advlzr `with'
rīsa- cn `jealosy'
rīta cn `manner'
rūdai iv1 conj.prt <runu `while crying'
ra cc `and'
ra nuance word
rahara cn `desire'
rahecha aux pres <rahanu `is (found)'
rahecha aux pres <rahanu `was (found to)'
rahechan aux pres <rahanu `they were (found to have)'
rahichan aux pst <rahanu `she was (found to have)'
raicha aux pres <rahanu `she had'
ramaṇī cn `lady'
ramaṇī- cn `lady'
ramitā cn `fun'
roīrahanubhaeko iv1 prf.cont.prt <runu `have been crying'
rogī- cn `patient'
roga cn `disease'
roirahekā iv1 prf.cont.prt <runu `been crying'
roirahin iv1 pst <runu `she kept crying'
rukha-vr̥kṣa cmpdcn `trees and arbors'
runa iv inf <runu `to cry'
runa iv1 inf <runu `to cry'
rune- impf.prt <runu `weepers (weeping ones)'
ruwā.ūchan tv1 <ruwā.unu `he causes to cry'
rājā cn `king'
rākhera tv1 abs.prt <rākhnu `having put'
rākhes tv1 imp <rākhnu `may you keep'
rākhidi.in cmpdtv4 pst <rākhnu-dinu `she put'
rākhne impf.prt <rākhnu `putting'
rāmro adj `good (clothes)'
rānu- cn `queen bee'
rāta- cn `night'
rātamāṭe adj `of Ratamāṭa'
rātrī cn `night'
rātrī- cn `night'
r̥cā cn `Vedic hymns'

rū̃dai iv1 conj.prt `crying'
rūpa cn `form'
sī̃mita adjl `limited'
sãga pp `with'
sãgako pp `with'
sabai pro.nonpers `all, everything'
sabai prol.adj `all'
saberai advl `early'
sadaiva- advl `always, ever'
sadbī̃u cn `a combination of one hundred types of foodgrains'
sadhaiṃ advl `always'
sahana tv1 inf <sahanu `to tolerate'
sahekī̃ tv1 prf.prt <sahanu `tolerated'
sake aux cond <saknu `if can'
sakena aux pst <saknu+neg `he could not'
sakenan aux pst <saknu+neg `he could not'
sakina aux pst <saknu `I could not'
sakina aux pst <saknu+neg `I could not'
saknubhaena aux pst <saknu+neg `he could not'
saktinathin aux pst <saknu+neg `she could not'
salla onomat
sallāha cn `advice'
samaya- cn `time'
sambhāra cn `care, protection'
samjhā̃dai tv1 conj.prt <samjhanu `while remembering'
samjhā̃dā tv1 conj.prt <samjhanu `while remembering'
samjhana tv1 inf <samjhanu `to remember'
samjhanthe tv3 pst <samjhanu `he regarded'
samjhanu tv1 inf <samjhanu `rememeber'
samjhin tv1 pst <samjhanu `she remembered'
samjhirahanchan tv1 pres.cont <samjhanu `he keeps remembering'
samma advl `only'
samma advl `only, even'
samma pp `for'
samma pp `until'
sammati cn `consent'
sammati- cn `consent'
sampatti cn `wealth'
sampatti- cn `wealth'
samā.una iv1 inf <samā.unu `to catch'
samā.unechin tv1 fut <samā.unu `she will catch'
samāpta adjl `complete'
samāpta adjl `complete'
samāpta adjl `exhausted'
samātera tv1 abs.prt <samātnu `having held'
samāune tv1 impf.prt <samā.unu `holding'
samūha cn `group'
santoṣa cn `satisfaction'
santāna cn `child'
santāna cn `children'
santāna- cn `child'
santāna- cn `descendents'
santānahī̃nā adj `childless'
santānecchuka adjl `desirous of child'
saphala adjl `fruitful'
sarakāra- cs `government, king'
sarala adjl `simple'
sautā cn `co-wife'
sautā- cn `co-wife'
savai prol.adj `all'
saṃga pp `with'
saṃsāra cn `world'
saṃsāra- cn `world'
saṃyama cn `self-restraint'
sevā cn `service'
sevā- cn `service'
seṣa adjl `remaining'
seṣa adjl `remaning'

shabda cn `sound'
shaishava-kāla- cmpdcn `childhood'
shakti cn `power'
shaṃkā cn `suspicion'
shishu-santāna- cmpdcn `child offspring'
shmashāna cn `cremation ground'
shānta adjl `quiet'
shārīrika adjl `physical'
shāyada advl `probably'
shūnya adjl `empty'
siddhinā- iv1p inf <siddhinu `to be exhuasted'
siddhisakeko cmpdiv1 prf.prt <siddhinu+saknu `already exhausted'
sikāeko tv2 prf.prt <sikā.unu `taught'
sireṭo cn `cold wind'
sirāna- cn `pillow'
sodhdā iv1 conj.prt <sodhnu `while asking'
sodheko tv1 prf.prt <sodhnu `asked'
sodhena tv1 pst <sodhnu `did not ask'
sodhi- cmpdtv1 <sodhnu+ `ask'
sodhin tv1 pst <sodhnu `she asked'
sojhī adj `simple'
sojho adj `simple'
subhadrā pn `ṣubhadra'
subhadrā- pn `ṣubhadra'
subidāra- cn `a post in ṇepalese military'
sukera iv1 abs.prt <suknu `having lost weight'
sukha- cn `happiness'
sukha-duḥkha- cmpdcn `happiness and sorrow'
sukha-lipsā- cmpdcn `desire for pleasure'
sunera tv1 abs.prt <sunnu `having heard'
sunirahanthe iv1 pst <sunnu `he kept listening'
sunne- tv1 impf.prt <sunnu `hearing'
sushīla- pn `Sushil'
sustarī adv `slowly'
sutchu iv1 pres <sutnu `I sleep'
sutekī iv1 prf.prt <sutnu `slept'
sutiraheko tv1 prf.cont.prt <sutnu `having been slept'
sutna iv1 inf <sutnu `to sleep'
sutnubhae iv1 cond <sutnu `if sleep'
sutnuhuncha iv1 pst <sutnu `he sleeps'
svabhāva cn `nature'
svabhāvai cn `nature (emph)'
svara cn `voice'
svara- cn `voice'
svarga- cn `heaven'
svargavāsī adjl `late (dead)'
svāsnī cn `wife'
svāsnīmānisa- cn `woman'
sāhrai advl `very'
sāla cn `year'
sāla- cn `year'
sāmu pp `in front'
sāno adj `small, little'
sānu pn `ṣanu (nick-name for ṣubhadra)'
sāpha adjl `clean'
sāreko iv1 prf.prt <sārnu `moved'
sāsa cn `breath (life)'
sāsa cn `breath'
sāthī cn `friend'
sātha advlzr `with'
sātha- cn `company
sāṃsārika adjl `worldly'
sā̃co adj `truthful, honest'
ṭarro adj `bitter'
ṭekne- iv3 impf.prt <ṭeknu `stepping'
ṭhageko tv1 prf.prt <ṭhagnu `cheated'
ṭhamyā.unai iv1 inf <ṭhamyā.unu `determine (emph)'
ṭhaṭṭā cn `jokes'
ṭhokābājī cn `competition'
ṭhulī adj `big'
ṭhulo adj `big'
ṭhā.ũ- cn `place'

ṭhā.ũ- cn `place'
ṭhāka-ṭhuka cn `verbal skirmishes'
ṭhāũ cn `place, room'
ṭhāũ- cn `place'
ṭhūlo adj `great'
ṭikdainan iv1 pres <ṭiknu+neg `they do not stay'
ṭukrā-ṭukrā cn `broken (into pieces)'
ṭupī cn `pig-tail'
ṭā̃siyo iv1p pst <ṭā̃sinu `he was stuck'
tī prol.adj `those'
tībra adjl `extreme'
tīrtha cn `pilgrimage, pilgrimage site'
tīrtha- cn `pilgrimage, pilgrimage site'
tīrtha-varta cmpdcn `pilgrimage and vow'
tīrtha-yātrī- cmpdcn `pilgrim'
tīrtha-yātrā cmpdcn `pilgrimage'
tīrtha-yātrā- cmpdcn `pilgrimage'
tã pro.pers `you'
ta advl `then'
ta nu `rather'
taipani cc `even then'
taipani cc `however'
taiṃ- pro.pers <tã `you'
talatira- advl `downward'
tapanī adjl `mild'
tapā.ī (honorific) pro.pers `you'
tara cc `but'
tarka cn `thought'
tarsanchan iv1 pres <tarsanu `are scared'
taruṇa adj `young'
tatha cc `and'
tathā cc `and'
tayāra adjl `ready'
tejomaya adjl `brilliant'
tela cn `oil'
tela- cn `oil'
thankyā.ī tv1 abs.prt <thankyāunu `having stored'
thapiṃdā conj.prt iv1p `while being added'
thi.ī ev1 pst <hunu `she was'
thi.in aux pst <hunu `she had'
thi.in aux pst <hunu `she was'
thie aux pst <hunu `he had'
thie aux pst <hunu `he was'
thie aux pst <hunu `they had'
thie ev1 pst <hunu `he was'
thie ev1 pst <hunu `they were'
thie iv3 pst <hunu `they were'
thiena iv1 pst <hunu+na `was not'
thiena iv2 pst <hunu+neg `was not'
thienan iv1 pst <hunu+neg ` they were not'
thiyo aux pst <hunu `he had'
thiyo aux pst <hunu `he was'
thiyo aux pst <hunu `was'
thiyo ev1 pst <hunu `he was'
thiyo iv3 pst <hunu `he was'
thāhā cn `knowledge'
thāisī cn `phthisis'
thākera iv1 abs.prt <thāknu `having been tired)
thāpera tv1 abs.prt <thāpnu `having proffered'
tila cn `sesame seed'
tila- cn `sesame'
timro pro.pers `your'
tina num `three'
tira pp `on'
tira pp `toward'
truṭi cn `mistake'
tuccha adj `trivial, worthless'
tulasī- pn `ṭulasi plant'
tyahī prol.adj `that (very) (emph)'
tyahā̃ advl `there'
tyasa prol.adj <tyo `that'
tyasa prol.adj <tyo `that'
tyasa- pro.dem <tyo `he, she, that'
tyasa- pro.dem <tyo `that'
tyasai- pro.dem `that (emph)'
tyasatai advl `likewise'
tyaso advl `so'
tyastai- adjl `like that (time, situation)'

tyastā adj `like that'
tyatro adj `that big'
tyo prol.adj `that'
tā nu `rather'
tānchan tv1 pres <tānnu `they pull'
tāpchan tv1 pres <tāpnu `take the heat of'
tārā-gaṇa cn `stars'
tāḍanā cn `scolding'
u pro.pers `she, he'
u prol.adj `that'
ughārera tv1 abs.prt <ughārnu `having opened'
ughārin tv1 pst <ughārnu `she opened'
uhī prol.adj `same'
uhā̃ advl 'there'
uhī advl `there (emph)'
ujyālo- cn `light'
umera cn `age'
umera- cn `age'
umeradāra adjl `young'
unī pro.pers `he'
unī pro.pers `she'
una- pro.pers <unī `he'
una- pro.pers <unī `she'
unai- pro.pers <unī `he' (emph)
upadesha cn `advice'
upekṣā cn `disregard'
upāya cn `means'
us intj `Oh no!'
usa pro.pers <u `she, he'
usa prol.adj `that'
usa prol.adj <u `that'
usa- pro.dem <u `that'
usa- pro.pers <u `she, he'
utsukatā- cn `curiousity'
uttara cn `answer'
uṭhdaina iv1 pres <uṭhnu+neg `does not rise (return)'
uḍera iv1 abs.prt <uḍnu `having flown'
vīsāsaya adjl `very long (lit. twenty hundred)'
vacana cn `words'
vaibhava- cn `wealth'
varṣa- cn `year'
vasha advlzr `because of'
vastu cn `thing'
vastubhāu cn `cattle'
velā- cn `time'
vicitra adjl `strange'
vicāra cn `thought'
vicāra- cn `thought'
vidhavā cn `widow'
vidhātā- cn `God (Creator)'
vilīna adj `lost'
vinā pp `without'
vipatti- cn `trouble'
virasilo adj `melancholic'
vishva- cn `world'
vishāla adj `vast'
viveka cn `conscience'
viveka- cn `wisdom'
vivāha cn `marriage'
vivāha-vidhi cmpdcn `ritual of marriage'
viyoga cn `separation'
vrata cn `vow'
vyarthai advl `unnecessarily'
vā cc `or'
vāk-shakti cmpdcn `power of speech'
waripari pp `around'
yī prol.adj `these'
yahī pro.dem `this (emph)'
yahā̃ advl `here '
yahī advl `here (emph)'
yahā̃ advl `here'
yasa prol.adj <yo `this'
yasa- pro.dem <yo `this'
yastai adjl `such'
yastai- adjl `like this (time, situation)'
yasto adjl `such'
yatikā adjl `so many'
yatro adj `so big'
yatti adjl `this much'
yinī- pro.pers `this'
yina- pro.pers <yī `these'

yinai prol.adj `this very'
yinai- pro.pers `this (emph)'
yo adj.dem `this'
yo prol.adj `this'
yā cc `or'

www.ingramcontent.com/pod-product-compliance
Lightning Source LLC
Chambersburg PA
CBHW022007300426
44117CB00005B/74